Perspectives in Social Gerontology

ROBERT B. ENRIGHT, JR., *Editor*

University of Wisconsin-Stevens Point

Allyn and Bacon

Boston   London   Toronto   Sydney   Tokyo   Singapore

To Joan and Michael

Editor-in-Chief, Social Sciences: Susan Badger
Senior Editor: Karen Hanson
Editorial Assistant: Sarah L. Dunbar
Production Administrator: Deborah Brown
Editorial-Production Service: P. M. Gordon Associates
Composition Buyer: Linda Cox
Manufacturing Buyer: Megan Cochran
Cover Administrator: Suzanne Harbison

Copyright © 1994 by Allyn and Bacon
A Division of Simon & Schuster, Inc.
160 Gould Street
Needham Heights, Massachusetts 02194

Library of Congress Cataloging-in-Publication Data

Perspectives in social gerontology / [compiled by] Robert B. Enright, Jr.
   p. cm.
  Includes bibliographical references.
  ISBN 0-205-15433-6
  1. Gerontology. 2. Aged—United States. I. Enright, Robert B., 1950– .
  HQ1061.P35 1994
  305.26'0973—dc20   93-28829
                                               CIP

Printed in the United States of America
10 9 8 7 6 5 4 3 2 1   98 97 96 95 94 93

CONTENTS

CHAPTER SEVEN
Living Arrangements   163

CHAPTER EIGHT
Work and Retirement   182

CHAPTER NINE
Activities, Roles, and Leisure   199

CHAPTER THIRTEEN
Health Care and Health-Care Policy   299

CHAPTER FOURTEEN
Aging and Social Policy   341

PREFACE

While developing reading lists for my undergraduate sociology courses in aging, I was drawn to original source materials as a way to introduce students to the wealth and diversity of ideas in social gerontology. I realized that many articles published in professional journals could be brought within the reach of my students if they were carefully selected, placed in a meaningful context, and organized in an integrated text. This volume is an effort to bring such original-source readings into the grasp of undergraduate and early graduate students.

Unlike textbooks that provide a distillation of ideas from many sources, this book introduces the reader to a set of concepts as presented by their original authors. This method gives the reader not only an appreciation for the richness of ideas and diversity of approaches involved in the study of aging, but also a genuine understanding of the way ideas are developed. The material presented here is not intended as a collection of theories to be memorized or arguments to be accepted, but as a set of individual contributions, each with its own strengths and weaknesses.

No single theoretical perspective is put forth in this collection. Instead, the articles are intended to demonstrate the diversity of viewpoints in the field. They were drawn from a variety of journals and were originally intended for readers from various fields, including sociology, psychology, political science, economics, policy studies, and nursing.

For the most part, the articles were published recently, and all of them are presented in their original form, except for minor editing in a few instances. They were selected not only because they should be easily understood by undergraduate and early graduate students, but also because they address issues of central importance to the field of gerontology. Readers will find them conceptually rich and provocative, without being methodologically or empirically complex.

From the perspective of social gerontology, human aging, including its biological and psychological aspects, takes place in social milieux. Moreover, it is not just individuals who age. Societies age as well, and an aging society affects the lives of both old and young. The articles included in this volume emphasize the social context, meaning, and impact of aging on all of us.

Two themes run through this collection. The first is the challenges of aging in contemporary American society. The aging of our nation's population has had and will continue to have a dramatic impact on our lives. Many issues face us as individuals and as members of society, including moral and ethical questions regarding the use of life-sustaining medical technology, access to health care, and the way we construct social policy to address our changing needs as we grow older.

The second theme is the diversity of ways that people experience old age. Gerontologists have shown that different people age at different rates, and that even within any single person all features do not age at the same pace. Many of the articles included here take this notion a step further to demonstrate how social factors contribute to the diversity of ways people age.

This book is designed for use either as a text to accompany a comprehensive set of lectures or as a supplement to a standard text in social gerontology. It is divided into fifteen chapters that cover the essential topic areas in the field. Each chapter is self-contained and thus can be used in any order to fit the design of any course in social gerontology.

Each chapter begins with an essay that introduces the subject area, identifies major issues and questions, and describes how the articles fit into this context. Each chapter concludes with a series of discussion questions designed for use in class discussions or individual study. The questions are not designed for tests but to stimulate thought and dialogue on the readings.

Reading ideas as originally presented often generates a recognition that many questions remain unanswered. This encourages the reader to regard the questions in the field as issues to be grappled with rather than as problems to be left to the "experts." So observe the strength of these ideas, but do not overlook their flaws. Take this opportunity to read what others have written, but think for yourself. Challenge the thoughts presented here as well as your own. The final answers have not yet been found.

I am grateful to Karen Hanson of Allyn and Bacon for her support and faith in this project. I would like to thank the University Personnel Development Committee of the University of Wisconsin-Stevens Point for supporting this work with a grant and sabbatical leave and Professor Leslie McClain-Ruelle for helpful suggestions on my proposal. Professors Edward J. Miller and Lawrence Weiser provided helpful comments on the introductory essays. Carole Van Horn led me on searches through library data bases, and Christine Neidlein and the staff of the Interlibrary Loan Department obtained numerous articles for me to review. Jim Rasmussen of the Portage County, Wisconsin, Department on Aging provided timely help with technical aspects of government policy.

I would also like to thank Jodi Hewitt for assistance with the initial literature searches, Carol Chase for pursuing copyright permissions and organizing mounds of paper, and Amy Cattanach, Chris Ballweg, Deb Chapman, Lori Kresal, Sarah Wandke, and Jennie Zick for proofreading, library research, and skilled clerical work. Special thanks go to Lou Fossen, who kept the whole enterprise intact, for contributions above and beyond the call of duty; to my wife Joan for patient listening, careful proofreading, and valuable insights; and to our son, Michael Job, for joy and inspiration.

Robert B. Enright, Jr.

CHAPTER ONE

Introduction: Real and Imagined Effects of Aging

Negative stereotypes of older people have existed for quite some time. In the past, old people were often characterized as poor, in failing health, sexless, and grouchy. While these depictions have not completely disappeared, most people realize that all older people do not conform to such descriptions. In the recent past, newer images of older people have developed that often portray them as vibrant, healthy, and capable of enjoying retirement. Sometimes these portrayals even go so far as to depict older people as wealthy and selfish. The new stereotype of the "greedy geezer" has come to replace the image of the poor, old grandparent sitting on the front porch in the rocking chair. Though less demeaning than earlier portrayals, the more recent stereotypes of older people as wealthy and greedy can be no less damaging.

Socially defined images of the elderly, or of any other group for that matter, can shape the way they regard themselves and how they are treated by others. Ultimately, the social perceptions of older people affect government policy. The "new ageism," driven by envy or resentment of the improved economic condition of the elderly in the United States, has led to the blaming of older people for the difficulties endured by others even when the genuine cause lies elsewhere (Sheppard 1990).

This introductory chapter includes articles from two authors concerned with damaging stereotypes about older people. Robert N. Butler coined the term "ageism" in 1968 to refer to bigotry against the old. In "Dispelling Ageism: The Cross-Cutting Intervention," Butler describes current manifestations of the "disease" of ageism, including the "greedy geezer" stereotype mentioned above. Nevertheless, Butler claims that these are not the views of people at large, and that most people favor keeping and even expanding entitlements for older people. Butler prescribes knowledge as the chief antidote for ageism. He calls for support for older people's sense of "mastery" and emphasizes the need to recognize their potential as contributors to society.

Gerontologists have put a great deal of effort into debunking commonly held myths about growing old. As inaccurate negative images of growing old become discredited, optimistic perceptions of growing old are developing, emphasizing the belief that getting older is not as unpleasant as many expect (Dychtwald and Zitter, 1988).

Although conditions for the elderly have generally improved in the last several decades, illness and disability are conditions still faced by many older people. How are the less fortunate treated in a society where older people are perceived as doing well? In the second selection, "Aging and Disability: Behind and Beyond the Stereotypes," Meredith Minkler argues that the emphasis on a positive outlook toward the aged can create an "elderly mystique" in which prejudice is directed not against all old people, but against those who are disabled.

In attempting to reach beyond stereotypical images of older people, researchers attempt to understand the true effects of growing old. As Kovach and Knapp explain in "Age, Cohort, and Time-Period Confounds in Aging Research," this often is not as simple as comparing older people with younger people at one point in time as is done in cross-sectional studies. The reason is that older people differ from younger people not only in age, but also in cohort membership (*i.e.*, the year they were born), and in the time-period they have reached old age. How does one know whether the differences between older and younger people are due to the effects of age, cohort, or time-period? Kovach and Knapp discuss the ways in which these effects can be confounded and the research approaches that can be used to distinguish between them.

REFERENCES

Dychtwald, Ken, & Zitter, Mark. (1988). Looking beyond the myths of aging America. *Healthcare Financial Management, 42,* 62–66.

Sheppard, Harold. (1990). Damaging stereotypes about aging are taking hold: How to counter them? *Perspectives on Aging, 19,* 4–8.

Dispelling Ageism:
The Cross-Cutting Intervention

ROBERT N. BUTLER

It is increasingly within our power to intervene directly in processes of aging, with prevention, treatment, and rehabilitation. It is also within our power to intervene in social, cultural, economic, and personal environments, influencing individual lives as well as those of older persons en masse. If, however, we fail to alter present negative imagery, stereotypes, myths, and distortions concerning aging and the aged in society, our ability to exercise these new possibilities will remain sharply curtailed. Fortunately, we can treat the disease I call "ageism"—those negative attitudes and practices that lead to discrimination against the aged.

THE DISEASE

I originally coined the term "ageism" in 1968. As chairman of the District of Columbia Advisory Committee on Aging, I had been actively involved in the acquisition of public housing for older people. Stormy opposition arose against the purchasing of a high rise in northwest Washington. The causes for neighbors' negativism were intermixed, for not only were many of the future tenants black, they were also old and poor. In the course of a *Washington Post* interview, I was asked if this negativism was a function of racism; in this instance, I thought it more a function of ageism.[1]

As I originally defined it,

Ageism can be seen as a systematic stereotyping of and discrimination against people because they are old, just as racism and sexism accomplish this with skin color and gender. Old people are categorized as senile, rigid in thought and manner, old-fashioned in morality and skills. . . . Ageism allows the younger generation to see older people as different from themselves; thus they subtly cease to identify with their elders as human-beings.[2]

Not incidentally, in my original formula I was just as concerned with older people's negativism toward young people as I was with young people's negativism toward old people.

I saw ageism manifested in a wide range of phenomena, on both individual and institutional levels—stereotypes and myths, outright disdain and dislike, simple subtle avoidance of contact, and discriminatory practices in housing, employment, and services of all kinds.

Source: Annals of the American Academy of Political and Social Science, 503, 138–147. Reprinted with permission from Sage Publications, Inc., Newbury Park, CA 91320. Copyright 1989.

Lately, we have seen a rising chorus of voices further criticizing the aged, suggesting that they have had too many advantages. These views come from powerful quarters: politicians, scientists, and philosophers. Interestingly enough, however, these rumblings of intergenerational conflict are not the views of the people at large. National polls and surveys reveal just the opposite, that persons of all ages wish to see older persons keep their entitlements or even have them expanded. An excellent case in point is the recent spectacular rise of the long-term-care issue on the nation's agenda in both the halls of Congress and the recent presidential race.

In light of these surveys, which do not support intergenerational conflict but, rather, reaffirm the needs of older persons, how can we justify the continuation of the practice of ageism? On the one hand, I do believe that the last decade has witnessed a steady improvement in the attitudes toward the aged, in part a consequence of general public education, increased media attention, the expansion of education in the community, colleges, and universities, and the continuing growth of gerontology. On the other hand, the success is uneven, of course. Residual pockets of negativism toward the aged still exist, most occurring subtly, covertly, and even unconsciously. Like racism and sexism, ageism remains recalcitrant, even if below the surface. But it can be—and has been—churned up from its latent position.

To ensure a reasonable place for older persons in society, we need to review some of these contemporary myths, stereotypes, and distorted facts, which must be dispelled or reduced.

CURRENT MANIFESTATIONS

Unfortunately, even the medical profession is not immune to ageism. Medical ageism is contracted in medical school. In fact, it was

there that I first became conscious of prejudice toward age, there when I first heard the term "crock"—originally applied to patients with no organic basis for disease thought to be hypochondriacal—applied to middle-aged women and older people. Other terms abounded as well: "gomer" ("get out of my emergency room"); "vegetable"; and "gork" ("God only really knows" the basis of this person's many symptoms).

Medical schools do everything to enhance this virus. The first older person that medical students encounter is a cadaver. Fresh out of college, young people are confronted with death and their own personal anxieties about death, yet they are not provided with group or individual counseling. Not long after, they are exhausted with sleeplessness and hostility for not learning everything fast enough; by the time they are in their third or fourth year of medical school, they are ripe for cynicism. Then comes the internship, and they are working in excess of eighty hours per week, up in the middle of the night—and there is still one of those "gorks" to see.

Few medical school graduates enter the field of geriatrics. In fact, on the whole, physicians do not invest the same amount of time in dealing with elderly patients as they do in their younger counterparts. Doctors question why they should even bother treating certain problems of the aged; after all, the patients are old. Is it worth treating them? Their problems are irreversible, unexciting, and unprofitable.

Then, too, the disease manifests itself in the hospitals themselves. A New York geriatrics professor, currently working at a hospital that, like others, is financially hemorrhaging, fears that his hospital will begin to view the elderly as quite unattractive once administrators see a recent report compiled by accountants tabulating the costs of each diagnosis-related group. Their report gave two tabulations—one for those over 70 and one for those under 70. They correctly concluded that the over-70 group costs the hospital more.

The severe cutback of services following the $750 billion tax cut inaugurated by the Reagan administration has brought steady criticism that Social Security and Medicare provide entitlements for older people yet deny them for the young. Newspapers report that the elderly's median income has risen significantly more than that of any other age group, basically due to Social Security benefits. From such distorted figures has emerged what one author has termed the "New Ageism,"[3] a dangerous viewpoint that envies the elderly for their economic progress and, at the same time, resents the poor elderly for being tax burdens and the non-poor elderly for making Social Security so costly.

Capitalizing on such distorted figures, many are prepared to churn up these worst views of old people. Not long ago, a cover article of the *New Republic* criticized our society for pampering our "affluent" elderly population, the "greedy geezers." The article began:

> Thirty percent of the annual federal budget now goes to expenditures on people over the age of 65. Forty years from now, if the present array of programs and benefits is maintained, almost two-thirds of the budget will go to supporting and cosseting the old. Something is wrong with a society that is willing to drain itself to foster such an unproductive section of its population, one that does not even promise (as children do) one day to be productive.[4]

Groups such as the Americans for Generational Equity promote displacement of Social Security. Wall-Streeter Peter Peterson, former U.S. secretary of commerce, vehemently opposes Social Security; media commentators, seeing the aged as an affluent group, urge Social Security "bashing" and call for privatization of one's retirement planning, which would benefit business and, hence, Wall Street.

Daniel Callahan, expounding the old-age-based rationing of health care originally suggested by former Colorado Governor Richard Lamm in 1983, sees older people as "a new social threat . . . that could ultimately (and perhaps already) do great harm."[5] Programs that benefit the elderly, says Callahan, consume an ever increasing percentage of our taxes; health care expenditures, especially, are becoming extremely disproportionate and costly as the number of our elderly grows. We should use our money to help a sick child live rather than waste it on the old, who have already lived full lives.

It is noteworthy that this sense of renewed threat or concern about the number and proportion of older persons comes in a century of extraordinary increase in average life expectancy. Indeed, in the United States alone there has been a gain of 28 years of life expectancy since the year 1900, nearly equal to what had been attained over the preceding 5000 years of human history. Eighty percent of this gain derives from marked reductions in maternal, childhood, and infant mortality rates. The remainder comes from reductions in death from heart disease and stroke. Although there is considerable chronic disease and disability at later ages, the expanding average life expectancy has yielded large numbers of increasingly vigorous, healthy, and productive older people.

Ageism may bear a relationship to the proportion of older persons in a society. A threshold that might be regarded as an achievement has, instead, become regarded as a burden. Ironically, the long-sought-for gain in life has been met by anxiety. What should have been a celebration has become a sense of threat. What should have been a message of hope has become a matter of despair.

Indeed, my impression, gained from wide travels in varied societies, cultures, and political systems—the Soviet Union, the People's Republic of China, Sweden, France, Argentina, Canada, Mexico, Israel—is that these concerns are universal, in response to the increasing numbers and proportions of older persons. Societies are afraid this increasing older population will become unaffordable, lead to stagnation of the society's productive and economic growth, and generate intergenerational conflict.

TREATMENT

Georges Bernanos wrote, "The worst, the most corrupting lies are problems poorly stated." Let us then state these problems as they really are, putting various myths and distortions into their proper perspectives. In order to treat this disease, we first need to realize what is really true about persons. One antidote to ageism is knowledge.

Knowledge, the Primary Intervention

The belief that neither societies nor individuals will be able to deal with the avalanche of age is reminiscent of the ancient Greek saying, When the Gods are angry with you, they give you what you want. Presumably, human beings wanted an extended life. But the truth is, there has been no extension of the natural inherent life span from the beginning of time, as far as is known. What has happened is an increased survivorship. More and more persons have been able to live out a full life.

Another myth is that all old people are senile and debilitated. But senility is not inevitable with age; rather, it is a function of a variety of brain diseases, most notably Alzheimer's disease and multi-infarct dementia. Nor are the great majority of older people so afflicted. Unfortunately, there may always be some residual gerontophobia and ageism resulting from discomfort and distaste for age and its disabilities. Some profound and pervasive disorders of old age—mobility problems, dementia, and incontinence—are unattractive and provoke disgust and fear.

Then there is the myth that all old people are affluent. Although the elderly are about as likely to be poor as younger populations, income and assets are distributed more unevenly among the elderly, concentrated highly among the rich old. In our rich nation, only 5.6 percent of older people have incomes in excess of $50,000 a year.

Simply stated, the old are, on the whole, the poorest of adults. Of our 28.0 million Americans aged 65 and over, 2.6 million fall below the parsimonious government-recognized poverty line. Two-thirds of them live alone on incomes of less than $104 a week; the other third are couples sharing $131 a week. Additionally, 4.5 million elderly are near-poor. Half of these live alone, existing on between $104 and $156 a week; the other half—elderly couples—live on between $131 and $195 a week.[6] Those in the oldest category—85 years and older—have the lowest income and the greatest percentage of chronic illness. They are more likely to require medical services but less able to afford the care they need.

Widows are the primary victims of elderly poverty and thus bear the brunt of ageism's assault. Their luck in living longer than men has, paradoxically, compounded their problems. Of elderly women, 41 percent are near-poor, contrasted with 17 percent of elderly men. The fact that 75 percent of the poor elderly are women reflects their lower wage levels during their working years, inadequate and inequitable Social Security coverage, and the increased risk of financial devastation from widowhood. Their poverty rate increases with age, from 15 percent for those 65–74 years old to 26 percent for those 85 and older. Of those over 85, 8 percent—50,000 widows—are forced to live on less than $76 per week. Two-thirds of the noninstitutionalized elderly who live alone are widows; over half of them became poor after their husbands died, probably due to consuming medical and funeral expenses and lost pension income.[7] Thus it is really women that New Ageists are referring to when they talk about denying health care to the elderly. Like sexism, racism, too, is interrelated with ageism. Incomes of the minority elderly are significantly below those of their white counterparts. Black men between 65 and 69 have median incomes 47 percent lower and Hispanic men 40 percent lower than white men. Black and Hispanic women also have lower median incomes than white women, 35 percent and 29 percent lower, respectively. Poverty rates are also much higher among the minority elderly: 31.5 percent for blacks and 23.9 percent for Hispanics as compared to 11.0 percent for whites.[8] In addition, it is primarily minority women and children who suffer most from poverty.

The increases in the elderly population, together with the already large number of poverty-ridden elderly in need of health care, have led to the fear that our older population is unaffordable. After all, our country already has a huge deficit. But Canada is able to provide total health care access to all its people and does so at 2 percent less of its yearly gross national product than the United States. Sweden, East and West Germany, and others already have a higher percentage of older people than does the United States, and they are surviving quite well. In comparison with the rest of the world, Sweden has the highest proportion of people over 65—17.0 percent—and people over 80—3.5 percent. Yet, during the recent Swedish elections, the Conservatives as well as the Social Democrats came out for stronger financial support of older people. All parties are in agreement and Sweden is not falling apart; in fact, its economic situation is quite favorable. The People's Republic of China already has 80 million people over 60, and this situation will become even more dramatic, for China will have 240 million over 60 about the year 2045. Yes, China is a very poor country, but its economic position is not due to its elderly population. Thus the concept that nations will become bankrupt

by their growing older populations is not accurate.

How about the myth that our Social Security system is bankrupt, that when young people reach the criterion age, they will not receive Social Security benefits? Social Security is not bankrupt. Rather, trust funds are becoming enormous; they will be in the trillion-dollar range at the turn of the century and will have $12 trillion when all of the baby-boomers are 65 years of age and over.

The dependency ratio is misunderstood. Not everything is given to the elderly. It is true that there is an increasing number of retirees compared to nonretirees. But if one looks at the total dependency ratio, that is, including both people under 18 and people 64 and above, there has been a steady decline in the total dependency-support ratio since the year 1900, and this decline will continue to the year 2050. The reason is the low birthrate—just below zero population growth.

Income transfers do not simply go from young to old through the public means of Social Security, Medicare, and related entitlements. Medicare *in toto* is not an entitlement. Only Part A is an entitlement. Part B is voluntary, not universal, and partially paid for by a premium. By law, 25 percent of the expenditures under Part B are derived from premiums. That is, older people themselves pay for it. Moreover, in 1988 the annual Part B premium increased by 38 percent, from $212 to $298. Two-thirds of poor elderly people receive no coverage under Medicaid, which is, in fact, 50 programs—one in each state—with differing eligibility requirements and benefits. Those elderly living just above the poverty line are often forced into poverty by out-of-pocket medical costs and premiums for private health insurance coverage.[9]

Examination of all income transfers, private and public exchanges, shows that most income, as well as assets and services, go from old to young. In any case, public insurance is an intergenerational compact. Social Security itself is a multigenerational lifelong protection system. Benefits are not limited to retirees; in fact, 3 million children receive Social Security benefits.

If one asks more sophisticated questions related to the actual cost of old versus young, one must take care to look at all sources. When one looks only at federal expenditures, the old certainly receive more than the young. But in our system of government, we desire protection from the authority of the centralized state. Education, the great expenditure for the young, is not supported by the federal sector but rather on a community basis through property taxes. For example, in 1986, $140 billion of state and local moneys alone were spent on elementary and secondary public education in the United States. If the New Ageists would look at all the sources, they would see the huge amount of money that goes to children—and should. A policy analysis of the cost of raising a child compared with the cost of caring for an older person still remains to be done.

Data do show conclusively that the condition of children as a group has deteriorated markedly, while that of older people, on the average, has improved. In fact, both children and the old living alone suffer from 20 percent poverty rate. But the older people have not caused this deteriorating condition. That a society as rich as ours tolerates this suffering is abominable. It is important that the New Ageists realize and emphasize society's failure to deal constructively with the poverty of our children—but correction cannot be at the expense of the older people. We will not improve the welfare of children by tearing down what the elderly have impressively achieved. We need to support intergenerational programs, ones that build a coalition between advocates for the children and advocates for the elderly. One answer to the exploitation of intergenerational conflict has come with the founding of Generations United, which now includes the National Council on the Aging, the Child Welfare

League of America, and all those marvelous mainstream organizations that have been advocacy groups for children. We must realize that we really are a group of generations and we must work together, recognizing that today's older persons are yesterday's children and that today's children are tomorrow's elders. We must recognize that there is a continuity and a unity to human life.

Then, too, the high costs associated with old age are not "disproportionate," as so many New Ageists say, but are, in fact, proportionate to age. In 1830, only 1 in 3 babies born in the United States lived to his or her sixties; today, 8 of 10 do. Death has become the harvest of old age. Medical advances have led to people living longer lives; disease and disability, once affecting the younger population, have been pushed forward and now occur more frequently in old age. This increased longevity has caused high health costs, once associated with maternity, infancy, and childhood, to be shifted to the elderly.

The myth of the high cost of dying needs to be dispelled. Studies show that the aged do not really contribute to rising health costs as much as technology does. And technology, such as that involved in heart transplants, is rarely if ever used in older people. Only 6 percent of U.S. Medicare beneficiaries in their last illness utilize an excess of $15,000 in expenses. Our government needs to create an expanded national center of health services technology to evaluate, monitor, and disseminate information on medical technological innovations.

A Variety of Interventions

Another ageism intervention is the recognition that older people themselves are a market. Japan has the most rapidly growing population of older people in the world, as well as the highest life expectancy. When its Ministry of International Trade and Industry became excited by the "silver community concept"—establishing communities for their older citizens in other countries—there was considerable negative reaction in Japan. When Spain heard this plan, however, it pricked up its ears, for it saw this as a source of jobs. But if "silver communities" are economically valuable for Spain, then they are economically valuable for Japan itself—and for the United States. There is a lot of "gold in geriatrics," as the *Wall Street Journal* once wrote, when one considers capitalism as a connection between producers and consumers. Thus this so-called high cost of health and social services produces jobs and consumption. We speak about the rising costs of health care, but, looking at it another way, the health care enterprise is the second largest producer of jobs. We cannot forget that it does contribute to the gross national product. This is true with Social Security as well. Pension funds, the largest source of capital formation in our country, own half of American stocks. The fact that in 1776 the average life expectancy was 35 and today it is 75—a 40-year difference, more than doubling in 200 years—means bigger markets.

Older persons themselves need to be productive and develop a philosophy on aging if we are to fight ageism. Survival is closely associated with individuals' views of themselves, as well as their sense of continued usefulness. In 1963, our multidisciplinary study of community-residing aged men found that people's experience of aging and their adaptation to it are influenced not only by disease, social adversity, economic deprivation, personal losses, and cultural devaluation, but also by their personalities and their previous life experiences.[10]

In a land where self-help books are plentiful, we need self-help books on aging. Contemporary older persons are rather like pioneers. They do not have a wisdom book to turn to. We need life reviews, reminiscences by the elderly that will help teach others the kinds of lives our older citizens have lived. There are few landmarks, few signposts on the highway, to describe the meaning and character of the new longevity.

Mastery is another important intervention. The simple ability of older people to have some control over their own lives will consequently become evidence to younger populations that the older population is not unproductive, depressed, disengaged, inflexible, or senile—myths that need to be dissipated in the attack on ageism. In fact, in the National Institute of Mental Health Human Aging Studies (1955–66), we found that older persons with life goals and some organization in their daily lives survive; those who do not have such goals and organization do not survive.[11] People need autonomy; in fact, studies show that the relation between health and a sense of control may grow stronger as one ages.[12] When older people's control of their activities is restricted, there are detrimental effects on their health; on the other hand, interventions that enhance their opportunities for control over their activities, circumstances, or health promote health.

Heavy investment in biomedical, behavioral, and social research is the ultimate cost containment, the ultimate disease prevention, and the ultimate service. When we eliminate Alzheimer's disease, the polio of geriatrics, we will empty half of our country's nursing home beds. Spending a few dollars now will dramatically affect the image of senility and debility as inevitable in old age. Through research we can gain freedom from senility and further improvement in the strengthening of the social network that helps sustain people in grief. A better understanding of what accounts for the difference in life expectancy between men and women and the development of a means to assist men to catch up with women by living longer will do much to overcome many of the problems of age, as well as ageism.

CONCLUSION

In conclusion, the war against ageism, even the New Ageism, is largely showing signs of success. The remaining issues are more of social class and race. This does not mean, however, that there must not be continuing vigilance against the possibilities of rationing and denial of care and income. Ageism is a primitive disease, and, unfortunately, our fears about aging are so deep that ageism will probably never totally disappear. But there are interventions we can make now to treat its painful assault.

From the social perspective, certainly, the treatment is to tap those sources responsible for maintaining a dignified and healthy old age. These include the individual, who should remain productive for as long as possible and be attentive to his or her health; the family, which, in fact, in the United States remains the most important caretaker of older persons; and the community, which is rich with strong informal networks of friendly visitors and volunteers and businesses. Union pressures in the 1930s, and particularly during World War II, also played their role in developing fringe benefits that include pensions and health care.

Finally, government needs to be involved at all levels. Legislation such as the Age Discrimination in Employment Act and various other protections, including entitlements and long-term care, are antidotes for ageism. Deciding how to balance all these sources of responsibility is one of the challenges of these next decades.

NOTES

1. Carl Bernstein, "Age and Race Fears Seen in Housing Opposition," *Washington Post*, 7 Mar. 1969.
2. Robert N. Butler, "The Effects of Medical and Health Progress on the Social and Economic Aspects of the Life Cycle" (Paper delivered at the National Institute of Industrial Gerontology, Washington, DC, 13 Mar. 1969), pp. 1–9; idem, "Ageism: Another Form of Bigotry," *Gerontologist*, 9:243–46 (1969).
3. Harold Sheppard, "The New Ageism and the 'Intergenerational Tension' Issue" (Manuscript, International Exchange Center on Gerontology, University of South Florida, 1988).
4. Henry Fairlie, "Greedy Geezers," *New Republic*, 28 Mar. 1988, p. 19.
5. Daniel Callahan, *Setting Limits: Medical Goals in an Aging Society* (New York: Simon & Schuster, 1987).
6. "Aging Alone: Profiles and Projections" (Report, Commonwealth Fund Commission on Elderly People Living Alone, 1988).
7. Ibid.
8. Ibid.
9. "Medicare's Poor: Filling the Gaps in Medical Coverage for Low-Income Elderly Americans" (Report, Commonwealth Fund Commission on Elderly People Living Alone, 20 Nov. 1987).
10. Robert N. Butler, "The Facade of Chronological Age: An Interpretive Summary of the Multidisciplinary Studies of the Aged Conducted at the National Institute of Mental Health," *American Journal of Psychiatry*, 119:721–28 (Feb. 1963), reprinted in *Middle Age and Aging: A Reader in Social Psychology*, ed. Bernice L. Neugarten (Chicago: University of Chicago Press, 1968).
11. Robert N. Butler, "Aspects of Survival and Adaptation in Human Aging," *American Journal of Psychiatry*, 123(10):1233–43 (Apr. 1967); Robert D. Patterson, Leo C. Freeman, and Robert N. Butler, "Psychiatric Aspects of Adaptation, Survival, and Death," in *Human Aging II: An Eleven Year Biomedical and Behavioral Study*, ed. S. Granick and R. D. Patterson, U.S. Public Health Service monograph no. (HSM) 71-9037, 1971, reprinted 1976.
12. Judith Rodin, "Aging and Health: Effects of the Sense of Control," *Science*, 233:1271–76 (19 Sept. 1986).

2

Aging and Disability: Behind and Beyond the Stereotypes

MEREDITH MINKLER

Gerontology has been defined as the science of drawing downwardly sloping lines, and in many respects, that tongue-in-cheek description has been disconcertingly accurate. Geriatrics and biology of aging textbooks are replete with diagrams showing a nearly linear decline in such physiological measures as vital capacity, blood sugar and cardiac index from age 30 to 80 (see Shock 1977; Kenney 1982). Until recently, the inevitability of similar cognitive declines with aging was also widely accepted (Field et al. 1988; Rowe and Kahn 1987).

Early social theories of gerontology also reinforced a "decline and loss" paradigm of normal aging. Both disengagement theory (positing a natural and mutual withdrawal of society and its elderly members) (Cumming and Henry 1961) and activity theory (stressing the importance of new, albeit often proxy roles to replace those lost in the process of aging) (Havinghurst 1968) thus accepted as "givens" many social losses which are in fact more societal artifacts than objective age-related phenomena.

The increasing popularity of what Estes and Binney (1989) have termed the "biomedicalization of aging" also has served to reinforce the "downwardly sloping lines"

approach to gerontology and geriatrics by stressing the individual as the unit of analysis and the clinical/biomedical basis of both the "problem" of aging and its amelioration. As Estes and Binney have demonstrated, the biomedical paradigm has dramatically influenced not only our approach to the care and treatment of elderly patients, but also funding and research priorities in aging, the nature and content of academic geriatrics and gerontology, public policy decisions, and public perceptions of and attitudes toward the aging process.

Alongside the biomedicalization of aging, however, we also have witnessed in recent years some encouraging attempts to counteract the decline and loss paradigm in geriatrics and gerontology.

In "Beyond Ageism: Postponing the Onset of Disability," Riley and Bond (1983) thus forcefully argued that to equate aging with functional impairment is to be guilty of a particularly damaging form of age prejudice which ignores the very real differences between normal aging and disease processes. In a similar way, longitudinal studies by Field et al. (1988) and others have demonstrated that, contrary to myth, no significant decline in intellectual functioning occurs

Source: Journal of Aging Studies 4(3), 246–260. Reprinted with permission from JAI Press, Inc., Greenwich, CT. Copyright 1990.

Note for case study (handwritten)

with aging for the majority of older people, with the exception of the "terminal drop" in cognitive ability that frequently occurs just prior to death (Riegel and Riegel 1972; Jarvik and Bank 1983). Finally, physiologists and geriatricians increasingly have stressed that though declines are observed in many physiological functions often beginning in young adulthood, many of these losses have little functional consequence. The 50% drop in maximum breathing capacity between age 30 and age 80 for example, while interfering with the average elderly person's ability to engage in strenuous prolonged exercise, may have little or no noticeable effect on his or her day-to-day functioning (Bortz 1982).

Furthermore, while "downwardly sloping lines" may accurately be drawn for aggregate population groups on such dimensions as vital capacity, there is in fact considerably *less* clustering around the mean for older people than there is for their younger counterparts. Timiras thus has noted that "one of the characteristics of the aging human population is its substantive heterogeneity" (1988, p. 17). Many healthy and physically active elders, for example, will continue to exhibit the vital capacity, cardiac index, and so on, of far younger people, while 30 year olds will be considerably more uniform in their measurements on these and other physiological indicators. Indeed, some experts now suggest that fully half of the functional decline observed between age 30 and 70 is not related to age per se at all, but to lack of exercise (Gorman and Posner 1988).

Partially on the basis of this kind of evidence, Rowe and Kahn (1987) have suggested that within the category of "normal" aging, a further distinction must be drawn between "usual" or typical aging in which health behavior and psychosocial factors exacerbate the effects of aging, and "successful" aging, in which such extrinsic factors play "a neutral or positive role" (p. 143).

The growing appreciation of an alternative and more diversified vision of aging in short stands as an important contrast to the earlier decline and loss paradigm. Further, it provides an important "reality check" at a time when research and funding priorities in aging are, as noted earlier, increasingly directing attention away from broader, social and biological aspects of aging and toward more narrow biomedical approaches.

Yet the well-intentional attempts to differentiate between normal aging and disease processes or disabilities also have an important downside. First, the new emphasis on healthy or "successful" aging *versus* aging with a disability may reinforce what Cohen (1988) has labelled the "elderly mystique," or the prejudice against disabled elders which often is shared by older people themselves.

Second, and relatedly, such popular concepts as Fries' (1980) "compression of morbidity theses" (projecting a dramatic decline in the relative proportion of late life disability for future cohorts) may lead to a "victim blaming" mentality where disabled or impaired elders are concerned. Increasing appreciation of the role of diet, exercise and other potentially modifiable "lifestyle factors" in influencing the aging process thus may result in a belief that elders with preventable chronic conditions have somehow "brought it on themselves." As will be noted later, such perceptions, coupled with unrealistic expectations concerning the role of early and middle life behavior change in preventing late life disability (Colvez and Blanchet 1981) further may divert attention from needed health and social planning in the face of a rapidly aging society.

This article will begin with a look at several alternative visions of aging and disability and their implications for policy, with particular attention to the popular "compression of morbidity" thesis. Second, it will examine in the social construction of aging and disability, and particularly some of the ramifications of Cohen's notion of the "elderly mystique" as a new and insidious form of age prejudice. Finally, and drawing on the lessons of social and cultural historians, it will consider the need for a rethinking of our philosophy of aging and of what it means to grow old if indeed both "healthy old age" and disability are to be accepted as having a meaningful place in the life of our society.

AGING WITH DISABILITIES: HISTORICAL ABERRATION OR PORTENT OF THINGS TO COME?

The decade of the 1980's saw a heated controversy concerning the extent to which disability could—or should—be considered a natural concomitant of growing older. And the question is far from settled.

On one side of the debate are researchers and disability rights advocates (LaPlante 1989; McBride 1989; Rice and Feldman 1983; Verbrugge 1984) who point to the current high rates of chronic illness and disability among the elderly and combine these with demographic projections to suggest a huge increase in the number and proportion of elders with significant disabilities in the years ahead.

Variously termed the "pandemic theory of chronic illness" (Kramer 1980) and the "failure of success" model (Gruenberg 1977), this scenario turns for support to the facts that 23% of the elderly, and close to 50% of the "oldest old" (age 85+) have difficulty in carrying out one or more activities of daily living (ADL's) such as eating or dressing (NCHS 1987). According to recent projections, moreover, the number of elderly persons with such disabilities will more than double from 6.2 million to 13.8 million from 1990–2030 (McBride 1989).

Proponents of the pandemic theory of chronic illness further point out that the population of disabled persons with major assistance needs is not only growing in size, but also becoming increasingly older over the next several decades. In 1980, for example, 40% of all persons with ADL assistance needs were under 65, but by 2040, only 25% will be non elderly, primarily as a function of population aging (LaPlante 1989). By the year 2000, 45% of those aged 65 and above will be 75 and over (Soldo and Agree 1988), and hence particularly vulnerable to functional impairments (eg. hip fracture) and to those devastating illnesses (eg. Alzheimer's Disease) which occur with greatest frequency late in life. Estimates suggest, for example, that over 15% of persons 80 and over may suffer from Alzheimer's or a related disorder (Hagnell et al. 1981). With the death rate of those 85 and over dropping faster than that of any other age group (Schneider and Brody 1983), the potential impact of this major debilitating condition alone cannot be overstressed.

The pandemic theory of disability and chronic illness in short, suggests that morbidity rates will become greater as life expectancy increases. Consequently, we will see a concomitant increase in the demand for services over the next several decades.

An alternative, and far more optimistic vision is presented by Fries (1980; 1984), whose "compression of morbidity" thesis suggests that we will experience a rectangularization of the survival curve with many more people living out the "normal" human life span (85 years) yet without the significant burden of chronic illness and impairment that accompanies advanced old age today. Briefly, Fries argues that the current, often lengthy period of disability before death is an historical aberration. At the turn of the last century, when life expectancy was less than fifty, the majority of Americans died of acute, rather than chronic illnesses, and prolonged disability at the end of life was therefore relatively rare. By the dawn of the next century, partly because of better diets, more exercise and overall "healthier lifestyles," late life disability similarly will be compressed. Fries indeed is fond of drawing as an analogy Oliver Wendell Holmes' (1881) "one hoss shay" which faithfully pulled its carriage for a century, and then, all at once, broke down and died.

In addition to positing a decrease in the period of disability and chronic illness in late life, Fries' hypothesis rests on the assumption that the number of very old people (those above age 85) will not increase significantly.

As evidence for the compression of morbidity thesis, Fries turns to early actuarial predictions suggesting that mortality rates were reaching a plateau, and to public health data indicating often dramatic secular trends toward reductions in smoking, increases in aerobic exercise, and so on. In the latter regard, Fries (1984) points to a per capita decline of over one-third in both tobacco consumption and intake of saturated fats between the 1960s and the 1980s, and to a similarly dramatic decline in age specific cardiovascular deaths over this period. He then argues that with the implementation of more systematic educational programs and societal changes (eg. mandatory seat belt laws), a further acceleration of these trends might be achieved.

While the Fries hypothesis is a provocative one, it has been criticized on several grounds. First some of the most basic assumption in Fries' model (eg. that the average human life span will remain at approximately 85) are open to question. Schneider and Brody (1983) thus have demonstrated that while mortality rates did reach a plateau in the early 1960s, they subsequently resumed their decline in the early 1970s. Moreover, the mortality rate of those 85+ has continued to drop more rapidly than that of other older age groups (eg. 65–75 or 75–85), with the absolute number of people in this "oldest old" group growing at an unprecedented rate. In the short period between 1985 and 2000, for example, the population aged 85 and above will have doubled, growing from $2^{1}/_{2}$ million to 5 million, and even more dramatic growth lies ahead. Recent estimates by Guralnik et al. (1988)

suggest that women in the United States may have a life expectancy of 91.5 and men of 85.5 by the year 2040. By failing to take into account the possibility that average life expectancy may climb to well beyond 85, the compression of morbidity thesis thus may greatly underestimate the likelihood of longer, rather than shorter, periods of disability and chronic illness in the future.

A second major criticism of the compression of morbidity thesis is that while trends in smoking behavior and several other personal health habits are encouraging, there is little or no hard evidence to date of declining morbidity and disability in any age group, and especially in the large numbers of older middle aged persons (45–64) who will reach advanced old age in record numbers (Colvez & Blanchet, 1981). Moreover, as Soldo and Agree (1988) have pointed out, "even if longevity-inducing habits were adopted en masse tomorrow, it probably would take a half century for the accumulated effects of risk behavior, such as smoking to be removed from the population" (p. 22).

The compression of morbidity thesis thirdly may be called into question for assuming that the onset of disease is followed by a set period of disability, which is then followed by death. This neat but simplistic trajectory fails to take into account the fact that some conditions, eg. arthritis and urinary incontinence, may lead to an extended period of disability, without elevating the risk of mortality (Satariano 1989).

Similarly, the Fries scenario fails to consider the disability impact of concurrent or comorbid conditions. The increasing prevalence of comorbidity (defined as the co-existence of two or more chronic conditions or symptoms [Seeman et al. 1989]) with age is widely appreciated (Ouslander and Beck 1982; Rowe 1985; Seeman et al. 1989). At the same time, however, the prevalence of comorbidity in representative population samples, and many more specific epidemiological questions are in need of systematic study (Satariano et al. 1989; Seeman et al.

1989). More research is needed, for example, on the types of concurrent conditions most commonly found among older cancer patients, the extrinsic factors which elevate the risk of comorbidity for this population, and the impact of such multiple conditions on functional health status and survival (Satariano et al. 1989). Without such knowledge, the efficacy of interventions designed to reduce risk, and hence our ability to achieve significant "compression of morbidity," may be severely compromised.

On still another level, the compression of morbidity thesis may be criticized because the very framing of this hypothesis within a biomedical "healthy lifestyle" paradigm leads to a focusing of attention on aging as a problem of infirmities to be conquered rather than socially constructed realities to be transformed (Estes and Binney 1989). From this perspective, while serious efforts to upgrade prevention and health promotion must be underscored, the primary "problems" of the elderly should not be framed as biomedical or as narrowly defined "lifestyle" problems in nature, when social inequities and other social, economic, and cultural factors are more important determinants of how aging is shaped and experienced than biological forces or personal health habits. When it is recognized, for example, that poverty is still the major risk factor for illness and that its impact remains profound even when smoking, diet, exercise and other lifestyle factors are controlled for (Syme and Berkman 1976; Kaplan et al. 1987), the inadequacy of a narrow lifestyle approach is underscored. When it further is recalled that vast differences in the economic and social circumstances of the elderly exist by race, gender and social class (USDHHS 1986), simplistic analyses and solutions which ignore these more fundamental inequities appear to fall considerably short of the mark.

A final criticism of the compression of morbidity thesis lies in the earlier noted concern that by stressing the preventable nature of many chronic illnesses and disabilities in the old, Fries' approach runs the risk of blaming the disabled elderly for their infirmities. Becker (1986) has noted that the strong emphasis placed in Western ideology on the individual and particularly on "personal responsibility for one's successes or failures" is reflected in the U.S. health promotion movement's tendency to "locate responsibility for the cause and cure of problems in the individual" (p. 19). The recent emphasis on the preventable nature of many chronic illnesses, while in part adding needed momentum to disease prevention efforts, has in fact been a double-edged sword. The accent on "individual responsibility for health" thus frequently has not been accompanied by attention to individual or community "response-ability," or the capacity for responding to personal needs or the challenges posed by the environment (Minkler 1983). Yet when the "response-ability" of the individual is compromised by such factors as low social support, inadequate income, a high stress environment, or poor access to transportation or to affordable, nutritious foods, his or her likelihood of successfully changing deleterious personal health behaviors is limited at best.

Approaches like the compression of morbidity thesis take the individual out of the context of his or her environment, and assume that continued dramatic reductions in smoking, and the modification of other "lifestyle behaviors," is in fact highly likely, since individuals need only a heavy dose of education and related interventions in order to change. Within this simplistic paradigm, those elders who failed to respond to such inputs earlier in life (eg. who continued smoking, overeating, etc.) may be implicitly or explicitly "blamed" or held accountable for the preventable chronic respiratory, cardiac and other conditions over which they "should" have had control.

The compression of morbidity thesis, in sum, has been criticized on scientific grounds, but also on political economic and on moral and ethical grounds. It remains, however, a popular perspective, particularly within the U.S. health promotion movement, and hence has important implications for attitudes, policy and practice, especially where the future elderly are concerned.

Occupying something of a middle ground between the pandemic theory of chronic illness and the compression of morbidity thesis is what Manton (1982) has labelled the "dynamic equilibrium" theory. Briefly, he argues that as improvements in life expectancy occur, we also will see improvements or delays in disability onset. Along with a lowered risk of death at older ages, the theory projects a related slowing of the severity and rate of progression of disease or disability. Consequently, although people will be living longer and spending more time in a diseased or disabled state, the rate of progression of given diseases also will be slowing down.

Unfortunately, as Soldo and Agree (1988) have noted, the United States has a poor national data collection system for looking at morbidity and mortality, since it focuses a disproportionate amount of attention on mortality alone. With the possible exception of studies like the National Health and Nutrition Surveys (USDHHS 1981), consequently, the best U.S. data sets for testing theories like dynamic equilibrium are often large longitudinal community surveys, eg. the Human Population Laboratory's 25 year old Alameda County Study in California (Kaplan et al. 1983) and the four decade old Framingham Study (Branch 1980) in Massachusetts. Such surveys have examined in depth both morbidity and mortality trends in large population cohorts, and their findings have generally been supportive of the dynamic equilibrium theory.

On a larger, national level, Canadian data have demonstrated that while Canadians experienced a 6 year increase in life expectancy between 1951 and 1978, only 20% of this was disease or disability-free (Wilkins and Adams 1983). In the later case, the imperfect correlation between increased life ex-

pectancy on the one hand and the slowing of morbidity on the other hand may be seen to have resulted in some increase in disability time, though considerably less than the pandemic theory of chronic illness would suggest.

While a conclusive answer to the controversy surrounding future chronic illness and disability trends must of course await the test of time, such an answer will undoubtedly prove to be not "either/or" but "both/and". That is, we can likely anticipate *both* more healthy elders in the years ahead, living out the life span with a minimum of functional impairment, *and at the same time* more disabled and chronically ill elders. Such a reality in turn will require policies and programs respectful of and responsive to the heterogeneity of a growing elderly population.

Beyond enacting provisions for a true continuum of health and social services, however, and one stressing in particular personal assistance services and other autonomy promoting options, the increasing diversity of the elderly with respect to health and functioning will require broad changes in our attitudes toward health, aging and disability. Cohen's (1988) "elderly mystique" provides a useful starting point for examining some of the conceptual and attitudinal changes necessary if both non-disabled and disabled elders are to enjoy a meaningful place in American society.

The "Elderly Mystique" Revisited

As noted earlier, Cohen's concept of the new "elderly mystique" is a useful one in describing the transference of prejudice which earlier was directed against elders in general to a more specific prejudice today which combines ageism and handicapism. In Cohen's words:

> American ageism is focused upon the elderly with disabilities, as opposed to the well elderly . . . further. . . . the elderly them-

selves have concluded that when disability arrives, hope about continued growth, self-realization and full participation in family and society must be abandoned so that all energy can be directed toward the ultimate defeat which is not death but institutionalization . . . (p. 25).

While there has been, in recent decades, a growing appreciation of the potential for reaching goals of autonomy, growth, participation and high life satisfaction on the part of the non-disabled elderly, these goals are recalibrated dramatically downward for those elders who become disabled. Whereas "access" and "full participation" have been key by-words for the younger disabled population, the sights of families and professionals for the disabled elderly (and hence often the latter's sights for themselves) tend to be far more circumscribed. We have in this way traded our earlier, limited view of aging for an even more limited vision of what it means to be old and disabled.

That the non-disabled elderly themselves often share this prejudice is apparent. Non-disabled patrons of senior centers and residents of senior housing complexes, for example, frequently harbor strong feelings against having their units "integrated" so that the latter can accommodate the severely disabled elderly as well. In opposing the integration of such centers and facilities, these non-disabled elders are demonstrating in part a desire to avoid reminders that they too may one day suffer such disabilities (Heumann 1989).

In some ways, of course, fear of disability, like fear of death, may be regarded as a near universal human phenomenon. Anthropologists thus have demonstrated pervasive fears among the old in culture after culture over losing one's physical or mental capacities and "becoming a burden" to family or community (Butler 1975; Foner 1985). In advanced industrial societies, however, and particularly in a country like the United States which places an especially high premium on self-reliance and individual auton-

omy, such fears may take on added significance.

The "handicapism" held by many elderly Americans, moreover, not only mirrors broader societal attitudes but further may be reinforced by some of the aged's own best advocates. *Modern Maturity* magazine, for example, the monthly publication of the 31 million member American Association of Retired Persons (AARP), has for years had an unwritten policy of not accepting advertisements for wheelchairs or other products that might connote disability and therefore be "depressing" for their readership (Dychtwald 1988). Through this policy of avoidance, the magazine thus unwittingly may reinforce the fears and denial that already appear prevalent among the non-disabled elderly.

Fears of disability also sometimes are accepted as legitimate grounds for discrimination in services provision. As Heumann (1989) has noted, for example, a senior center director who would never publically state that "his" or "her" white seniors do not want black elderly persons using the center, may nevertheless be quite comfortable in stating that non-disabled elderly patrons "understandably" do not want to share the facility with disabled seniors. While discrimination based on disability is, of course, illegal in the U.S., attitudinal change concerning its acceptability has been slow in many arenas.

Prejudice against the impaired elderly may be intensified by the fact that the elderly frequently do not fit neatly within the category of the "clean" disabled. Looking specifically at the "blindness system" within the United States, Shön (1970) thus pointed out early on the differential treatment of this group of disabled persons depending upon such factors as their socioeconomic status, whether they had single or multiple disabilities, and whether they fell within the ranks of the "deserving" or the undeserving poor. As individuals who frequently suffer multiple disabilities and chronic illnesses, who are often low income and who are old as well as functionally impaired, the disabled elderly frequently fall outside the "clean disabled" category. As such, the prejudice and discrimination they suffer may be considerably more pronounced than that felt by the blind-from-birth younger woman or the middle class "poster-boy" with muscular dystrophy.

Realistic approaches to the problem of prejudice against the disabled elderly must of course include a heavy accent on educating young and old alike—but particularly the elderly and their advocates—as to the true nature of disability. In Cohen's (1987) words:

> The first step forward reformulation of goals and rights is the articulation of what the real potentials are for the elderly with disabilities, particularly in light of the monopoly of services and benefits which are in place, but which get mobilized too frequently in pursuit of goals that fall far short of the right to flourish, to grow and to become (p. 30).

In part, such an articulation may come from sharing some of the lessons of the Independent Living Movement and of various disability rights organizations concerning the abilities and capabilities of the disabled. The Aging and Disability Project of the California-based World Institute on Disability (WID) is an example of one such innovative attempt, working as it does to create dialogue and mutual understanding between the aging and disabled communities and forging in the process a "unified agenda" (Mahoney et al. 1986). Through regional and local workshops, peer support groups and policy research, the project thus has engaged elderly persons and younger people with disabilities in a process of mutual goal setting, resource sharing and program and policy work, toward the end of furthering their collective needs and interests.

Through projects such as this one and related educational, outreach and advocacy efforts, policy makers, family members, practitioners and the elderly themselves further may be helped to see beyond the narrow

goal of avoiding institutionalization where disability is concerned. While such an objective would require attitudinal changes, it also would necessitate a real commitment to the provision of improved paratransit and other services that can help the disabled elderly participate more fully in their own life and the life of their community.

On a more fundamental level, however, research is needed to further explore the nature of prejudice against the disabled elderly and the best means for combatting that prejudice. Some important insights in this regard have been provided by Cole (1988a, 1988b) and others (Achenbaum 1978a, 1978b; Cole and Gadow 1986; Graebner 1980; Kondratowitz 1985) in their examination of the historical roots of Western culture's attitudes toward and treatment of the aged. It is to this and related work that we now turn.

Lessons from History

Historian Thomas Cole (1988b) has argued that recent attacks on ageism, however well intentioned, may themselves be "part of an historical pattern based on splitting or dichotomizing the 'negative' from the 'positive' aspects of aging and old age" (p. 18).

While the early Puritans had "constructed a dialectical view of old age—emphasizing *both* the inevitable losses and decline of aging and hope for life and redemption" (p. 18), that perspective had changed considerably by the early 19th century. In Cole's words,

> The primary virtues of Victorian morality—independence, health, success—required constant control over one's body and physical energies. The decay of the body in old age, a constant reminder of the limits of self control, came to signify precisely what bourgeois culture hoped to avoid: dependence, disease, failure and sin. (p. 18)

The Victorian era's tendency to split old age into "sin, decay and dependence on the one hand [and] virtue, self reliance and health" on the other (p. 18), fit well with the equally pronounced tendency of writers, artists and others to view life as a series of intimately connected stages. A "virtuous youth" was seen as necessary to bring forth successful manhood, just as a moral and benevolent adulthood was a critical precondition to a "respectable and tranquil old age." By contrast, in the words of one late 17th century writer, "if youth be trifled away without improvement, manhood will be contemptible and old age miserable" (Schoemaker 1797 in Achenbaum 1978a).

The view of a dichotomized old age, and of the virtuous and benevolent execution of one life stage as heavily influencing one's happiness in the next, was further reinforced in the spheres of health and medicine. Since many prescriptions for a moral life were also the maxims for good health, physicians of the early 1800's often stressed a life of righteousness as a means of achieving a good and healthy old age. Indeed, those who attained the latter were often by virtue of that achievement viewed as "custodians of virtue," though exceptions were noted. Achenbaum (1978b) has cited as an example of the latter Jeremy Belknap's observation in his *History of New Hampshire* (1813) that:

> There are indeed, some veteran sots, native of this as well as other countries who render themselves burdensome to society and contemptible in their advanced age. The purity of our air, and plenty of food, are doubtless the cause of their surviving such frequent draughts of liquid poison (p. 10).

While the dichotomized view of aging fit well within the overall world view of the early and mid 1800s, it became increasingly problematic in the latter part of the century and the early part of the 1900s when a business recession and related societal changes made it advantageous to redefine aging within a more unitary decline and loss paradigm. Graebner (1980) has explored in detail the many ways in which "scientific management," medicine, and other fields worked

during this period to reconstruct our images of aging, stressing its degenerative aspects as a means of legitimizing forced retirement and related changes that were in the interests of capital.

Within medicine, for example, the notion of "neurasthenia" became popular in the 1870s in reference to an amorphous disease condition, both hereditary and cumulative in nature, which appeared to justify hiring younger workers and retiring the old. Anxiety, fatigue and other symptoms of neurasthenia appeared when prolonged contact with new technology, coupled with an inadequate supply of "nervous force," led to depletion of the latter, at the expense of the (usually older) worker's health. Younger people, who by virtue of their age had limited contact with machines and a more abundant supply of nervous force were considered a better employment risk since they had a longer "work life" ahead (Graebner 1980).

Medical research and writings in England, France, Germany and the U.S. contributed to the devaluation and medicalization of old age from the late 18th to the early 20th century (cf. Haber 1983; Graebner 1980; Kondratowitz 1985; Cole 1988a, 1988b). As Cole (1988a) has noted, "In England and America, the word 'senile' itself was transformed in the 19th century from a general term signifying old age to a medical term signifying the inevitably debilitated condition of the aged." (p. 55) Indeed, the American orientation of geriatrics and gerontology (building in part on European roots) has been described by this historian as the "scientific management of aging." In his words:

> Just as the new corporate managers in industry were learning to break down production into its smallest component parts, analyze and reorganize them for maximum efficiency, so the new scientists of senescence aimed to analyze the economy of the aging body and regulate its vital functioning. By authorizing maximum physical functioning

as the ideal of normality, by denying that maximum functioning was a cultural as well as a biological norm, and by demonstrating that aging involved an inevitable falling away from this ideal, scientific medicine helped create the image of old age as pathological (p. 10).

By the early 1900s, social reformers were also playing a key role in shaping and reinforcing negative stereotypes of the old. By equating old age with disability, for example, reformers in many European countries provided additional momentum in the movement for enacting old age pension schemes. While their motives were often laudable, however, the *effect* of this "compassionate ageism" (Binstock 1983) was much the same as its earlier, less compassionate version: The elderly were systematically devalued and aging became increasingly synonymous with disease, disability and decline.

As noted earlier, more recent attempts to combat this "compassionate ageism" while positive in many respects, have also had some troubling side effects. New and misleading stereotypes of the "healthy and wealthy" elderly thus threaten to decrease support for needed health and social programs for the old, fueling at the same time erroneous charges of "generational inequity" or unjust allocations of scarce public resources that favor the old to the detriment of the young (Minkler 1986). Additionally, the re-emergence of a Victorian era-like notion that healthy old age is a just reward for a life of self control and "right living" opens the door to victim blaming for those elders who dare to become chronically ill or disabled. In Levin's (1987) words, "good health has become a new ritual of patriotism, a market place for the public display of secular faith in the power of will." Within such a vision, where is there a place for the 85 year old man with a disabling chronic respiratory ailment or the post hip fracture widow confined to a wheelchair?

Without a more dialectal vision of aging, one that truly respects its diversity and its place as part of a natural and unified lifetime (Cole 1988b), we are in danger of continuing to limit our understanding of aging to at best a physiological continuum and at worst a pole at either end of that continuum. The current preoccupation with "successful" (healthy) aging, in part because of its concomitant reinforcement of the elderly mystique, must be viewed with caution as another variant of the ageism that has served well neither the aged nor the larger society.

CONCLUSION

The new emphasis on healthy or "successful" aging represents in some respects a refreshing contrast to the earlier "decline and loss" paradigm which has characterized much of geriatrics and gerontology, as well as broader societal perceptions of aging and the elderly. Yet the newer paradigm, like the compression of morbidity thesis which it reflects, is problematic as well. Such a perspective reinforces the "elderly mystique," or the prejudice against disabled elders which often is shared by the elderly themselves. Further, the new emphasis on healthy aging and personal control over health in old age is disconcerting in its tendency to ignore the influence of factors like race, gender and social class on health and disability status in the elderly.

Finally, as Cole (1988b) has argued, the new (or renewed) emphasis on healthy or successful aging is part of an historical pattern based on dichotomizing old age into positive and negative poles and emphasizing one of these poles rather than appreciating the essential unity and dialect which aging ultimately represents.

Reshaping our nation so that it is a welcome and comfortable home to disabled and non-disabled elders alike may constitute what Blum (1982) refers to as a case "where going forward involves, in some respects, going carefully backward"—back to a more unifying, dialectical vision of old age and away from the current, dichotomized view. While working for the prevention of chronic illness and disability in old age to the maximum extent possible, we must nevertheless accept the fact that for many elders, and for disabled young people as they grow old, chronic illness and disability will be a continuing reality.

A dialectical vision of old age that respects elders of all functional abilities and health conditions will enable us to better meet the needs of our increasingly diverse elderly population, and hence of society as a whole.

NOTES

1. The term "elderly mystique" was coined by Rosenfelt in 1965 in reference to a more general negative view of aging and the elderly held by young and old alike. While Cohen resurrected and used the same term more than 20 years later, he has defined it more specifically as prejudice against the disabled elderly. It is the latter conceptualization that is employed in the current discussion.

REFERENCES

Achenbaum, W. Andrew. 1978a. *Old Age in the New Land.* Baltimore: Johns Hopkins University Press.

Achenbaum, W. Andrew. 1978b. *Images of Old Age in America, 1790 to the Present.* Michigan: Institute of Gerontology, University of Michigan, Wayne State University.

Becker, Marshall. 1986. "The Tyranny of Health Promotion." *Public Health Review* 14:15–25.

Belknap, Jeremy. 1813. *History of New Hampshire* Vol. 3. Boston: Bradford and Read. Cited in W. Andrew Achenbaum, 1978, *Images of Old Age in America 1790 to the Present.* Michigan: Institute of Gerontology, University of Michigan, Wayne State University.

Binstock, Robert H. 1983. "The Oldest Old: A Fresh Perspective or Compassionate Ageism Revisited?" *Milbank Memorial Fund Quarterly* 63: 420–541.

Blum, Stephen R. 1982. Personal communication.

Bortz, Walter. 1982. "Disuse and Aging." *Journal of the American Medical Association* 248:1203–1208.

Branch, Laurence G. 1980. "Functional Abilities of the Elderly: An Update on the Massachusetts Health Care Panel Study." In *Second Conference on the Epidemiology of Aging,* edited by Suzanne G. Haynes and Manning Feinleib. Washington, D.C.: United States Department of Health and Human Services, NIH Pub. No. 80-969, pp. 237–267.

Butler, Robert N. 1975. *Why Survive? Being Old in America.* New York: Harper and Row Publishers.

Cohen, Elias S. 1988. "The Elderly Mystique: Constraints on the Autonomy of the Elderly with Disabilities." *Gerontologist* 28:24–31.

Cole, Thomas. 1988a. "Aging, History and Health: Progress and Paradox." In *Health and Aging,* edited by Johannes, J. F. Schroots and James E. Birren. New York: Springer Publishers, pp. 45–63.

Cole, Thomas. 1988b. "The Specter of Old Age: History, Politics and Culture in an Aging America." *Tikkun* 3:14–18 and 93–95.

Cole, Thomas. (in press) *The Journey of Life: A Cultural History of Aging.*

Cole, Thomas and Sally Gadow (eds.). 1986. *What Does it Mean to Grow Old?* Durham, North Carolina: Duke University Press.

Colvez, A. and M. Blanchet. 1981. "Disability Trends in the U.S. Population 1966–1976: Analysis of Reported Causes." *American Journal of Public Health* 71:464–471.

Cumming, Elaine and W. E. Henry. 1961. *Growing Old: The Process of Disengagement.* New York: Basic Books.

Dychtwald, Kenneth. 1988. Personal communication.

Estes, Carroll L. and Lisa Binney. (1989) "The Biomedicalization of Aging: Dangers and Dilemmas." *The Gerontologist* 29:587–596.

Field, Dorothy, Schaie, K. Warner and E. Victor Leino. 1988. "Continuity in Intellectual Functioning: The Role of Self-Reported Health." *Psychology and Aging* 3:385–392.

Foner, Nancy. 1985. "Old and Frail and Everywhere Unequal." *Hastings Center Report.* New York: Hastings on the Hudson.

Fries, James F. 1980. "Aging, Natural Death and the Compression of Morbidity." *New England Journal of Medicine* 303:130–135.

Fries, James F. 1984. "The Compression of Morbidity: Miscellaneous Comments About a Theme." *The Gerontologist* 24:354–359.

Gorman, Kevin M. and Joel D. Posner. 1988. "Benefits of Exercise in Old Age." *Clinics in Geriatric Medicine* 4:181–192.

Graebner, William. 1980. *A History of Retirement.* New Haven, Connecticut: Yale University Press.

Gruenberg, Ernest M. 1977. "The Failure of Success." *Milbank Memorial Fund Quarterly* 55:2–24.

Guralnik, Jack M., Yanagishita, Machiko and Edward L. Schneider. 1988. "Projecting the Older Population of the United States: Lessons from the Past and Prospects for the Future." *Milbank Memorial Fund Quarterly* 66:283–308.

Haber, Carole. 1983. *Beyond Sixty-Five.* New York: Cambridge University Press.

Hagnell, O., Lanke, J., Rorsman, B. and L. Ojesjo. 1981. "Does the Incidence of Age Psychosis Decrease?: A Prospective Longitudinal Study of a Complete Population Investigated During the 25 Year Period 1947–1972: The Lundby Study." *Neuropsychobiology* 7:201–211.

Havinghurst, Robert J. 1968. "Personality and Patterns of Aging." *Gerontologist* 8:20–33.

Heumann, Judy. March 19, 1989. "Are We Creating Segregationist, Dependency Producing Programs for Seniors?" Presentation at the Annual Meeting of the American Society on Aging.

Holmes, Oliver Wendell. 1881. *The Deacon's Masterpiece on the Wonderful 'One Hoss Shay.'* Cambridge, MA: Houghton Mifflin.

Jarvik, Lissy F. and Lew Bank. 1983. "Aging Twins: Longitudinal Psychometric Data."

Pp. 40–63 in *Longitudinal Studies of Adult Psychological Development,* edited by K. Warner Schaie. New York: Guilford.

Kaplan, George A. and Terry Camacho. 1983. "Perceived Health and Mortality: A Nine Year Follow Up of the Human Population Laboratory Cohort." *American Journal of Epidemiology* 117:293–304.

Kaplan, George A., Haan, Mary and S. Leonard Syme. 1987. "Socioeconomic Status and Health." *American Journal of Epidemiology* 125:989–998.

Kenney, R. A. 1982. *Physiology of Aging: A Synopsis.* Chicago, Illinois: Year Book Medical Publishers.

Kondratowitz, H. J. von. 1985. "Die Medikalisierung des Höheren Lebensalters." Paper presented to the conference, "Medizin und Sozialer Wandel."

Kramer, M. 1980. "The Rising Pandemic of Mental Disorders and Associated Chronic Diseases and Disabilities." *Acta Psychiatrica Scandinavica* 62:382–397.

LaPlante, Mitchell. 1989. "Disability in Basic Life Activities Across the Life Span." *Disability Statistics Report,* No. 1. San Francisco: Institute for Health and Aging. University of California, San Francisco.

Levin, David. 1987. *Pathologies of the Modern Self.* New York: New York University Press.

Mahoney, Constance W., Estes, Carroll L. and Judith E. Heumann (eds.). 1986. *Toward a Unified Agenda: Proceedings of a National Conference on Disability and Aging.* San Francisco: Institute for Health and Aging. University of California, San Francisco.

Manton, Kenneth G. 1982. "Changing Concepts of Morbidity and Mortality in the Elderly Population." *Health and Society* 60:183–244.

McBride, Timothy D. 1989. *Measuring the Disability of the Elderly: Empirical Analysis and Projections into the 21st Century.* Washington, D.C.: The Urban Institute.

Minkler, Meridith. 1983. "Health Promotion and Elders: A Critique." *Generations* 7:13–15 and 67.

Minkler, Meredith. 1986. " 'Generational Equity' and the New Victim Blaming: An Emerging Public Policy Issue." *International Journal of Health Services* 16:539–551.

National Center for Health Statistics. 1987. "Aging in the Eighties: Functional Limitations of

Individuals 65 Years and Older." *Advancedata* No. 133. Washington, DC: Government Printing Office.

Ouslander, Joseph G. and John C. Beck. 1982. "Defining the Health Problems of the Elderly." *Annual Review of Public Health* 3:55–83.

Rice, Dorothy P. and J. J. Feldman. 1983. "Living Longer in the United States: Demographic Changes and Health Needs of the Elderly." *Milbank Memorial Fund Quarterly* 61:363–396.

Riegel, Klaus F. and Ruth M. Riegel. 1972. "Development, Drop and Death." *Developmental Psychology* 6:306–319.

Riley, Matilda White and Kathleen Bond. 1983. "Beyond Ageism: Postponing the Onset of Disability." In *Aging in Society: Selected Reviews of Recent Research,* edited by Matilda White Riley, B. B. Hess and Kathleen Bond. Hillsdale, New Jersey: Lawrence Erlbaum Associates.

Rosenfelt, Rosalie. 1965. "The Elderly Mystique." *Journal of Social Issues* 21:37–43.

Rowe, John W. 1985. "Health Care of the Elderly." *New England Journal of Medicine* 312:827–835.

Rowe, John W. and Robert L. Kahn. 1987. "Human Aging: Usual and Successful." *Science* 237:143–149.

Satariano, William A. 1989. Personal communication.

Satariano, William A., Nawal, E. Ragheb, and Mary A. Dupuis. (1989) "Comorbidity in Older Women with Breast Cancer: An Epidemiological Approach." In *Cancer in the Elderly: Approaches to Early Detection and Treatment,* edited by Rosemary Yancik and Jerome Yates. New York: Springer Publishers.

Schneider, Edward L. and Jacoby A. Brody. 1983. "Aging, Natural Death and the Compression of Morbidity: Another View." *New England Journal of Medicine* 309:854–856.

Schön, Donald. 1970. "The Blindness System." *The Public Interest* 18:25–38.

Seeman, Teresa, Guralnik, Jack M., Kaplan, George A., Knudsen, Lisa and Richard Cohen. 1989. "The Health Consequences of Multiple Morbidity in the Elderly." *Journal of Aging and Health* 1:50–66.

Shock, Nathan. 1977. "Systems Integration." Pp. 639–665 in *Handbook of the Biology of Aging,* edited by Caleb Finch and Lenord Hayflick. New York: Van Nostrand Reinhold.

Shoemaker, Abraham. 1797. *U.S. Almanak.* (Elizabeth Town, New Jersey). Quoted in W. Andrew Achenbaum, 1978 (a). *Old Age in the New Land.* Baltimore: Johns Hopkins University Press.

Soldo, Beth J. and Emily M. Agree. 1988. "America's Elderly." *Population Bulletin* 43:5–52.

Syme, S. Leonard and Lisa Berkman. 1976. "Social Class—Susceptibility and Sickness." *American Journal of Epidemiology* 104:1–8.

Timiras, Paola. 1988. *Physiological Basis of Aging and Geriatrics.* New York: Macmillan Publishing Company.

United States Department of Health and Human Services. Public Health Service. 1981. *Plan and Operation of the 2nd National Health and Nutrition Survey, 1976–1980: Programs and Collection Procedures.* Vital and Health Statistics Series #1, No. 15. Washington, D.C.: Department of Health and Human Services, PHS 81-1317.

United States Department of Health and Human Services, Public Health Service. 1986. *Health: United States.* Washington, D.C.: U.S. Government Printing Office.

Verbrugge, Lois M. 1984. "Living Longer but Worsening Health? Trends in Health and Mortality of Middle Aged and Older Persons." *Milbank Memorial Fund Quarterly* 62:475–519.

Wilkins, Russell and Owen B. Adams. 1983. *Healthfulness of Life.* Montreal: Institute for Research on Public Policy.

Age, Cohort, and Time-Period Confounds in Aging Research

CHRISTINE R. KOVACH
THOMAS R. KNAPP

A recent study has concluded that older adult females demonstrated a significantly less positive perception of their body images, as measured by the Draw-A-Person projective technique, in comparison to younger adult females.[1] What inferences can be made from these results? Do these results indicate that, as women age, their body image decreases? Or do they indicate that depression era women have less positive body images than baby boom era women?

This article will explore these questions through a discussion of the age, cohort, and time confounds prevalent in quantitative developmental research. Those interested in developmental issues must understand these confounds so that they can interpret research results in light of these confounds, and not be misled by research results which do not control for age, cohort, and time-period effects.

DEFINITIONS OF TERMS

In almost all studies, age is operationally defined by years since birth. The advantage of this is that everyone clearly knows what age means. The disadvantage is that years since birth does not really tell us much about age or what similarities are possessed by people who are that age. It is a vague definition in one sense, and a clear unarguable definition in another.

Cohort is most often defined as year of birth. Cohorts are people about the same age who, in a given period, have similar experiences that may affect them in the same way. The concept of cohort assumes that common experience may result in common distinctive effects.

Rosow[2] has defined cohort as: "1) consisting of people who share a given life experience; 2) this experience is socially or historically structured; 3) it occurs in a common generational framework; 4) its effects distinguish one generation from another; and 5) these effects are relatively stable over the life course."

This definition seems more adequate than year of birth as a definition of cohort. However, the difficulty in operationalizing this conceptualization has limited its easy application and most studies have neglected the full meaning of cohort in their operationalization.

Source: Journal of Gerontological Nursing 15(3), 11–15. Reprinted with permission from Slack Inc., Thorofare, NJ 08086. Copyright 1989.

Time-period refers to the time at which the measurement was taken. The time-period can be broad, such as the year of measurement. In certain studies, such as neonatal or biorhythmic research, the time-period may be hour of the day or even as restricted as minute or second of measurement.

Confounding refers to research situations in which it cannot be determined if it was variable A or another variable which caused the effect on the dependent variable. This is a common problem in research. It is often difficult, even in experimental designs, to achieve sufficient control to eliminate all confounding influences.

THE CONFOUNDS

Consider the following hypothetical situation: In pursuing developmental research, an investigator interviews women and discovers that older women attempt to teach the investigator many facets of farming: how to preserve fresh cabbage and apples for the winter, how to milk cows the fastest, and how to smoke hams. When she speaks with younger women in the community they do not have farming knowledge. She concludes that as women grow older they improve in their ability to learn farming skills.

This example seems to reflect cohort differences rather than age-related differences. The conclusion made by this researcher is therefore suspect. Imagine the following example where the confound is not as clear: A nurse is interested in memory.

She studies the ability to memorize the side effects of five common cardiac drugs in young and old adults. Since the elderly subjects do not memorize the side effects as well, she concludes that as people age, their ability to learn declines.

These examples represent the confound which exists between age and cohort. In the memory example it seems more appropriate to infer age-related differences rather than cohort-differences as responsible for vari-

ation in ability to memorize side effects of drugs.

But it may, in fact, be a wrong inference. Differences in ability to memorize side effects may relate to age changes, generational influences, or some combination of the two.

It is impossible to sort out the confound of age and cohort in any study based on observations of different age or developmental groups at a single point in time. These studies are called cross-sectional studies because they only look at one cross section of time. In some instances the reader can logically infer a separation of age and cohort in cross-sectional studies, but this is dangerous because erroneous conclusions can be made.

Much research is largely cross-sectional for several reasons. Cross-sectional studies are easy to manage, economical, and take less time to conduct. In cross-sectional studies involving age-related changes, there are usually several rival hypotheses for any observed differences. That is to say, there are a number of alternative explanations in the form of several generational life experiences which could also account for the observed differences.

Anyone reading cross-sectional developmental research should question inferences which have been made, and seek alternative explanations for any observed differences present in research. Too often, researchers become so committed to their area of interest that they cannot "see the forest for the trees." Great caution must be exerted in making inferences about age-related changes in cross-sectional studies.

Research projects designed to collect data over more than one point in time are called longitudinal studies. Some researchers have begun using longitudinal designs in the hope that the age and cohort problem could be resolved. Consider the following example:

In 1970, a nurse studied the attitudes of people to public health policy. These attitudes were quite liberal. In 1985, she studied these same people and found their attitudes toward public health policy were much more conservative. Do these changes indicate that as people age they become more conservative in these attitudes, or do they reflect changes in attitudes due to the influence of time-period effects?

The influence of time-period effects is the confound which is a problem in longitudinal design. As people are studied over time, the observed changes may be true age-related changes but they may also be changes due to time-period effects.

Time-period effects have also been called time effects, or time-of-measurement effects. They are most often thought of as being due to environmental influences but may also relate to changes in subjects over time.

Schaie[3] wrote that time effects "denote that state of the environment within which a given set of data were obtained . . . changes in the state of the environment may contribute to the effects noted in an aging study." It is often difficult to distinguish between cohort and time-period effects. Time-period effects are presumed to only exert an influence during the measurement period. Cohort effects, on the other hand, often begin at birth and are most often thought to have a lifelong impact.[5]

DISENTANGLING THE CONFOUNDS

Due to recognition by researchers of the prevalence of studies plagued with age, co-hort, and time confounds, many complex designs and interpretive decision rules have been developed in an attempt to disentangle these confounds. Since these designs are being used increasingly in developmental studies, several will be presented.

Schaie[3] proposed three sequential strategies designed to permit inferences regarding the relative contribution of age, cohort, and time-period variables to developmental trends. Each of these strategies requires that several analyses of variance be conducted on data classified in terms of age, cohort, and/or time-period.

In the cross-sectional-sequential design, two or more different age cohorts are studied longitudinally so that both changes over time and cohort differences can be detected. From such a design it is possible to detect the contributions of age/cohort and age/time to the observed differences in the study. This design involves a series of simultaneous cross-sectional and longitudinal analyses.

Table 1 shows a cross-sectional sequential design in which three hypothetical cohorts might be studied. Nine different samples would be needed for this study and data could be collected over a four-year period in 1988, 1990, and 1992. Note that in this design, observations are not repeated on the same members of a cohort from one time to the next, but on a different random sample from the same cohort.

Cross-sectional-sequential designs have the advantage of not requiring the same subjects from one observation to the next. This is

TABLE 1   A Cross-Sectional-Sequential Design

COHORT					
1924			1988	1990	1992
1926		1988	1990	1992	
1928	1988	1990	1992		
AGE	60	62	64	66	68

Figures in the table are the years in which data would be collected for each cohort listed.

important because it is often very difficult or impossible to preserve a sample over time and can lead to serious attrition biases in a study. Also, because different samples are used, the effects of being studied and initial selection biases for expected availability over an extended period do not threaten the validity of this design. Cross-sectional-sequential designs are not, however, able to identify changes in individuals over time.

The equivalence of successive samples from a cohort may be difficult to obtain and would threaten the validity of the study.[4] The cross-sectional-sequential design involves both the age/cohort cross-sectional confound and the longitudinal age/time confound.

When different groups of subjects are tested at more than one point in time it is a time-lag comparison. The groups studied are of different cohorts, but are studied when they are the same age. An example of a time-lag study would involve a sample of 60-year-old men studied for reminiscent behavior in 1975, and in 1990 a new sample of 60-year-old men would be studied for reminiscent behavior. This type of longitudinal study confounds time and cohort.

Time-lag-sequential designs involve a comparison of different time-lag groups with cross-sectional comparisons. In the example of this design in Table 2, three samples from each of three cohorts are compared on three occasions. This study could reveal the behavior of subjects aged 60, 62, and 64 from three different cohorts. Notice in this exam-

TABLE 2   A Time-Lag-Sequential Design

COHORT			
1932	1992	1994	1996
1930	1990	1992	1994
1928	1988	1990	1992
AGE	60	62	64

Figures in the table are the years in which data would be collected for each cohort listed.

ple that it has taken eight years to study an age span of four years using this design.

In the time-lag-sequential design, different aged cohorts are compared over the same longitudinal period. This design involves cross-sectional comparisons of cohorts, comparisons of the longitudinal course of development in each cohort over the course of the study, and comparisons between the effect of time of observation and the effect of age at which behavior is studied.[4] This design does not have the attrition, testing, and selection threats which longitudinal designs have because different samples are studied at each testing period. Equivalence of successive cohort samples may also be difficult to ensure in this design. The confounds in this design are cohort/time and age/cohort.

A complex design called the longitudinal-sequential design involves a series of simultaneous cross-sectional and longitudinal comparisons. In the hypothetical example, the same subjects from each cohort would be studied on three occasions from 1988 to 1992 (see Table 3).

TABLE 3   A Longitudinal-Sequential Design

COHORT					
1920	1988	1990	1992		
1918		1988	1990	1992	
1916			1988	1990	1992
AGE	60	62	64	66	68

Figures in the table are the years in which data would be collected for each cohort listed.

Longitudinal-sequential designs make it possible to obtain longitudinal data of development in less time than it takes development to occur. In Table 3 eight years of development could be studied in a four-year period.

The longitudinal-sequential design allows cross-sectional comparisons of cohorts at any point during the study, comparisons of the longitudinal course of development in each cohort, and time-lag comparisons among cohorts as they reach a particular age in successive years.

This design is intended to determine whether changes in behavior are attributable to age, cohort, or the interaction between the two.[4] In this design each cohort is measured at a different time and each age-group is measured at a different time so that it involves the confounds of age/time and cohort/time.

DECISION RULES

In order to interpret the results of these complex studies several authors have developed decision rules or inference schemes to guide the interpretation of results.[5-8] These guides should be referred to by the researcher using one of these designs.

Several warning flags must be raised at this point. First, inference schemes are based on the following assumptions: 1) one and only one of the confounds is important in the data; 2) the effects are linear; and 3) in cross-sectional-sequential and time-lag-sequential analyses, the effects do not interact (i.e. no one age/cohort group changes over time more or less than does another age/cohort group).[5] Unfortunately, in most studies these assumptions are not met. The confounded effects may be multiplicative rather than additive. The data may be curvilinear. And when one age-group changes differently from the others, the inference of age or co-

hort is not as meaningful as the interaction. It is imperative to remember that the scheme and inferences based upon it are only useful if the assumptions are met.

Sample size must also be considered in these studies since sample size plays an important part in determining statistical significance. If the sample size of a study is too small a Type II error can be easily made by wrongly accepting a false null hypothesis. Conversely, statistical significance can be "bought" through a large sample size which serves to increase the power of a study or the probability of rejecting the null hypothesis.[9]

The final warning flag regarding inference schemes is that they are not without error and there are logical limits to any such set of rules. Current researchers working with these designs and strategies have demonstrated and discussed the falsity of the notion that sequential strategies unequivocally permit the separation of age, cohort, and time effects.[5-8] These researchers have concluded that it is not possible to establish firm decision rules regarding the interpretation of developmental studies.

It is important to use one's logical thinking in interpreting the data from these complex designs. At times a researcher's knowledge of the subject matter and logical deduction can come in direct conflict with the interpretation suggested by the inference scheme. Each researcher must decide how to resolve this conflict and include it in the research study discussion.

Another topic to consider in developmental aging research is the intracohort differences which exist in the aged population. The aged are a diverse group and there can be relatively large intracohort differences which can play an important role in the study of intercohort differences. If a study yields a large within cohort variability it is unlikely to obtain between cohort differences from the statistical analysis.[10]

CONCLUSION

This article has attempted to point out some difficulties and hazards inherent in doing research aimed at discovering age-related changes. For those individuals interested in developmental issues, an understanding of these problems is essential so that interpretations of developmental research are done with insight into these confounds.

Much research is cross-sectional. In interpreting cross-sectional data it is not possible to infer whether age or cohort is responsible for the obtained results. There are times when this confound is of little importance and there are times when it is of great importance. If a researcher is interested in adults' attitudes toward nurse practitioners it may matter little to the researcher if the differences in younger and older persons' attitudes are due to age or cohort. This information's descriptive value may still be important even though the differences observed today may not be the same 40 years from today, because cohort may be responsible for the differences rather than age.

When a researcher is interested in cause-effect explanations the cross-sectional approach can lead to erroneous conclusions and the separation of age and cohort becomes necessary. If a researcher is interested in studying the effect of age on ability to self-administer insulin in patients with diabetes mellitus, it may be very important to be able to interpret if differences in ability to self-administer insulin can be attributed to age or cohort effects. Also, nursing research which attempts to examine differences in abilities or psychological traits with age (e.g. learning, compliance, anxiety, self-esteem) should attempt to sort out the confounds of age, cohort, and time.

Longitudinal studies do allow for examination of changes over time and the temporal sequencing of phenomena. Longitudinal designs, however, must deal with threats such as age/time confounds, selection biases, mortality, and the effects of testing. Time effects are often indistinguishable from cohort effects because both involve environmental influences. Longitudinal studies are also time consuming and expensive.

Several complex designs have been presented which allow for some sorting of the age, time, and cohort confounds. These designs involve a considerable investment of time, effort, and money. Only under certain conditions and under certain assumptions is it possible to separate and estimate the age, time-period, and cohort effects. These designs can be useful particularly if the nurse is interested in cause-effect developmental changes.

Anyone who reads and interprets research results must remember that the results obtained are not written in stone. The careful reader of research studies will search her mind for alternate hypotheses which may explain the obtained results in a study. Cross-sectional and longitudinal studies possess many threats to validity and possibilities for erroneous conclusions. The more complex designs presented in this article allow for more comparisons but must also be interpreted with caution and logical rigor.

REFERENCES

1. Janelli LM: The realities of body image. *J Gerontol Nurs* 1986; 12(10):23–27.
2. Rosow I: What is a cohort and why? *Human Dev* 1978; 21:65–75.
3. Schaie KW: A general model for the study of developmental problems. *Psych Bull* 1965; 64:92–107.

4. Achenbach TM: *Research in Developmental Psychology: Concepts, Strategies, and Methods.* New York, Free Press, 1978.

5. Botwinick J: *Aging and Behavior.* New York, Springer Publishing, 1984.

6. Costa PT & McCrae RR: An approach to the attribution of aging, period, and cohort effects. *Psych Bull* 1982; 92:238–250.

7. Palmore E: When can age, period, and cohort be separated? *Social Forces* 1978; 57:282–295.

8. Adam J: Sequential strategies and the separation of age, cohort, and time-of-measurement contributions to developmental data. *Psych Bull* 1978; 85:1309–1316.

9. Cohen J & Cohen P: *Applied Multiple Regression/Correlation Analysis for the Behavioral Sciences.* Hillsdale, NJ: Lawrence Erlbaum Associates, 1983.

10. Dannefer D: Aging as intracohort differentiation: Accentuation, the Matthew effect, and the life course. *Social Forum* 1987; 2:211–235.

Discussion Questions for Chapter One

1. In "Dispelling Ageism: The Cross-Cutting Intervention," Butler challenges "generational equity" advocates, claiming that generations must work together. To what extent are generations really in conflict with one another, and to what extent do they cooperate? Can you think of ways in which different generations and those who advocate for them can be brought closer in order to build support programs for people of all ages?

2. Given the diversity among older people in health, disability, income, and socioeconomic status, how can effective public programs be designed to meet the needs of such a variety of people? Is *age* a justifiable basis for eligibility for entitlement programs such as Social Security and Medicare? If eligibility for such programs were determined on the basis of need rather than age, would public support for these programs increase or decrease?

3. Imagine that you were born 50 years before your actual birthdate. How would your life be different as you age? Describe how aging, cohort, and time-period effects might affect your life as you grow older.

CHAPTER TWO

The Demography of Aging

The American population is growing older. In 1900 slightly over 3 million Americans were 65 or older, representing 4.1% of the population. In 1990, an estimated 31.5 million Americans, or 12.6%, were over 65. Middle-range projections indicate that by 2030, 65.6 million Americans, or 21.8% of the population, will be elderly (Spencer, 1989).

Why is America growing older? The most obvious reason is that mortality rates have declined. However, an even more important reason is that today's older people are members of large cohorts born earlier in this century. The dramatic increase in the older population expected in the next century will be a result of the aging of the large baby boom cohorts that will reach old age between 2010 and 2030.

The rapid expansion of the older population expected in the future has raised concern on the part of policy makers who wish to plan for what is ahead. The social consequences of an aging population, however, cannot be understood by looking only at the number or percentage of older people expected in the future. This is because the elderly population is diverse, and its social characteristics, including gender, race, and socioeconomic status, are as important as its numbers for assessing its social impact. This point is amply demonstrated by William Serow and his colleagues in "Structural Change Within the Older Population: Economic Implications."

Although most gerontologists classify people 65 and over as elderly, it is widely understood that this is a somewhat arbitrary decision. While it is true that most people have retired by age 65, many are vibrant and in good health. Some gerontologists are particularly concerned about the fastest growing group of elderly, those 85 and over. In the next 40 years, this age category is expected to grow by 150% compared with a 20% increase expected in the general population (calculated from Spencer, 1989). At these advanced ages, the need for health care, particularly long-term care, increases significantly, and the incidence of widowhood and poverty reaches its peak. Since the 85-and-over population is predominantly female, overall descriptions of people in this age category fit women better than men. In "A Population Profile of Very Old Men and Women in the United States," Charles F. Longino, Jr., describes the population aged 85 years and over, paying particular attention to the differences between men and women.

When most people think about migration among older people, the image of retirees moving from the north to the sunbelt comes to mind. The popular perception, however, describes only a small portion of older people. First of all, most older adults do not move frequently. Secondly, the migration from the north to the sunbelt is only one type of move made by those who are geographically mobile. In "Migration Patterns Among the Elderly: A Developmental Perspective," Litwak and Longino present a model of migration among older people that links their movement to life course events. Just as many young adults (who are the most geographically mobile) move shortly after completion of college to establish their careers, so too older people move for reasons related to their stage in the life cycle. The sunbelt-bound migrants described above correspond to the first stage of elderly migration, immediately following retirement. They tend to be younger, living independently, not widowed or disabled, and in search of leisure. This group is the most likely to move to a different state and to move from metropolitan areas to less densely settled areas.

Somewhat older migrants, who are more likely to be widowed or disabled, tend to move in the opposite direction, from nonmetropolitan to metropolitan areas and from the sunbelt to the north, in order to return to their states of birth and to be near family members who can care for them.

The third-stage migrants are those moving to institutional settings when family members can no longer provide directly for their care. They too tend to move from Sunbelt states to the north.

The migration patterns of older people have significance for the communities of origin and destination. In the past, a "gray peril" of older people entering popular retirement areas was feared by those concerned about the heavy demand they would place on the local services. This fear has given way to optimism, as older people migrating into communities are now often viewed as an economic asset to those communities. Their pension and social security checks are seen as a boost to the local economy.

REFERENCE

Spencer, Gregory. (1989). Projections of the population of the United States, by age, sex, and race: 1988 to 2080. *Current Population Reports, Population Estimates and Projections* Series P–25, No. 1018. U.S. Department of Commerce, Bureau of the Census.

Structural Change Within the Older Population: Economic Implications

WILLIAM J. SEROW
DAVID F. SLY
MICHAEL MICKLIN

INTRODUCTION

The aging of the United States population is beginning to attract considerable attention among scholars concerned with the future of the U.S. economy. From a simple demographic perspective, it is well established that due to declines in fertility and adult mortality, this nation's population has embarked on a seemingly inexorable course of aging. Our purpose here is to suggest not only that the numbers of the older population will likely increase both relatively and absolutely, but also that the demographic and socioeconomic structure of this population will undergo significant changes. Consequently, we argue that the simple extrapolation of demand for health care and other services, based solely on projected increases in population size, is an incorrect means of ascertaining the economic impact of the aging of the U.S. population. The fallacy of the "collective aged" suggested by Schulz (1985, pp. 20–27) is a major barrier to understanding the social and economic diversity within the elderly population and to developing an array of policies and pro-grams to meet the range of needs exhibited by its members. Significant age differences exist within the age 65 years or over population in terms of sex composition, living arrangements, family structure, employment experiences, sources and amount of income, and related psychological dispositions such as social expectations and life satisfaction. Moreover, period and cohort influences are additional sources of heterogeneity among the elderly. In short, research on the socio-economic consequences of population aging must become more age specific. In this paper, we emphasize structural changes in the most rapidly growing segment of the population, one about which perhaps we know the least—the so-called "oldest old," or those persons age 85 years or over.

DEMOGRAPHIC ASSUMPTIONS

In general terms, one can assume that demographic processes affect the structure and dynamics of the older population in ways strictly analogous to the population in general. Persons are "born" into the older popu-

Source: Contemporary Policy Issues 5, 72–83. Reprinted with permission from the Western Economic Association International, Huntington Beach, CA, and the authors. Copyright 1987.

lation by virtue of reaching that age which defines the lower limit of the older population. The "birth rate" for the older population is therefore determined by fertility levels 55, 60, or 65 years ago, by the age-specific mortality levels that have prevailed during the 55- to 65-year period, and perhaps by the volume and structure of net immigration. Persons exit from the older population by death, and mortality rates at ages 55+, 60+, or 65+ determine the rate at which exits from the older population occur. Thus, it is assumed that previous fertility levels and previous and present mortality levels interact to determine the present size and age composition of the older population, and that previous, present, and future fertility and mortality levels will interact to determine the future size and age composition of the older population (see, for example, Keyfitz, 1968; Coale, 1972).

In addition to these demographic processes, economic, social, and political events can occur and affect the economic and social characteristics of different cohorts as they pass through their respective life cycles. Differences in experiences will lead to different economic and demographic behaviors. Thus successive cohorts entering the older population will bring with them differences in such variables as labor force experience, education, fertility, and family structure, which will have a pronounced impact on their relative demands for health care, income support, community care, and so on.

This paper examines those demographic and socioeconomic changes that will characterize the older population of the U.S. until the year 2020. From the differences that emerge when these changes are contrasted with the present patterns, we seek to add to the store of knowledge regarding the older population and to point out some changes in the structure of the older population that will influence formulating social and economic policy.

DEMOGRAPHIC CHANGES

The most frequently used projections of the U.S. population are the series 14 (middle fertility/middle mortality) produced by the U.S. Bureau of the Census (Spencer, 1984). These projections assume a continuation of fertility rates at about the current level and diminutions in mortality such that life expectancy at birth increases from the current levels of 71 and 78 years to 74 and 82 years for males and females, respectively, by the year 2020. Net international migration is assumed constant at 450,000 persons per year, with an age-race-sex distribution similar to that observed currently. The size and structure of the elderly population stemming from these projections are shown in Table 1.

These data indicate that the total U.S. population will increase by some 56 million persons, from 240 to 296 million, between the present and the year 2020. The proportion of persons age 55 or over will not change appreciably from the current level (21 percent) through the turn of the century, although the absolute number will increase from 51 to 59 million. Over the first two decades of the 21st century, though, the number and proportion of persons in the 55+ age group will rise dramatically. By the year 2020, the 92 million Americans who will be at least 55 years old will constitute nearly one-third of the nation's population.

The population age 65 or over will follow a similar trajectory in the sense that absolute numbers will grow rapidly. But this group's share of total population will increase more moderately, as it necessarily lags 10 years behind increases in the 55+ population. Nonetheless, the 65+ population should increase from the current level of 29 million to 39 million by the year 2010, and a striking increase to 51 million will be reached only 10 years later.

The most telling relative increases are those to be observed among the oldest old,

TABLE 1 U.S. Bureau of the Census Mid-Range Projections of Total Population and Elderly, by Age: 1985–2020 (thousands of persons)

Age (years)	1985	1990	2000	2010	2020
Total	238,631	249,657	267,955	283,238	296,597
55–59	11,245	10,433	13,280	18,825	20,507
60–64	10,943	10,618	10,487	16,023	19,791
65–69	9,214	9,996	9,096	11,703	16,620
70–74	7,641	8,039	8,581	8,615	13,235
75–79	5,556	6,260	7,295	6,782	8,824
80–84	3,501	4,089	5,023	5,544	5,662
85+	2,697	3,313	4,926	6,551	7,081
55+	50,797	52,748	58,688	74,043	91,720
65+	28,609	31,697	34,921	39,195	51,422
% 55+	0.2129	0.2113	0.2190	0.2614	0.3103
% 65+	0.1199	0.1270	0.1303	0.1384	0.1740
% 85+	0.0113	0.0133	0.0184	0.0231	0.0240
85+ as % of					
55+	0.0531	0.0628	0.0839	0.0885	0.0772
65+	0.0943	0.1045	0.1411	0.1671	0.1377

Source: Spencer (1984).

that is, those age 85 or over. The temporal growth pattern of the oldest old differs markedly from that of the older population in general. During the first 15 years of the period (until the year 2000), the population ages 55–84 will grow at slightly less than 10 percent per decade, while the population age 85+ will grow at nearly 50 percent per decade. During the second half of the period, the population ages 55–84 will increase by more than one-fourth during each of the decades as the first elements of the baby boom enter this age group. Meanwhile, growth of the 85+ population will decline to 33 percent from the year 2000 to 2010 and still further, to 8 percent, from 2010 to 2020. However, this latter phenomenon is strictly a transitory one, because it reflects the entrance into the 85+ category by persons born during the Depression decade of the 1930s. Overall, the 85+ population, which accounted for 1.1 percent of the population in 1985, will account for 2.4 percent of the population in 2020 as

the group size increases from 2.7 to 7.1 million persons.

These projections may be the most commonly employed set, but no assurance exists that they will prove to be the most accurate reflection of future events. In fact, it is important to realize that the principal shortcoming of previous mid-range projection series has been underestimating mortality reduction. In the two sets of projections prior to those employed here, mortality error accounted for nearly half of aggregate projection error. And this overprojection of deaths has been particularly evident regarding the oldest segment of the population. Because of this consistent pattern of error, it is useful to consider the effects of an alternative mortality projection—the Census Bureau's low-mortality scenario. This assumes increments in life expectancy at birth of more than two years above those in the mid-range projections shown in Table 1. Table 2 shows the numbers of persons who would be added to the population if the low- rather than the mid-range mortality assumption proves to be closer to reality. The number of persons added to the population under this scenario increases from 359,000 in 1990 to 5.7 million in 2020. In all instances, more than 80 percent of the increment to population would be more than 55 years old and, after the year 2000, more than one-third would be at least 85 years old. In absolute numbers, this amounts to nearly 2 million additional persons among the oldest old. Under this scenario, the proportion of the U.S. population accounted for by the oldest old would stand

TABLE 2 Increments to Projected Population, Low-versus Middle-Mortality Assumptions: 1990–2020

Age (years)	Thousands of Persons	Percentage of Total	Percentage of Middle-Mortality Projection
1990			
Total	359	100.0	0.1
55–64	44	12.3	0.2
65–74	64	17.8	0.4
75–84	87	24.2	0.8
85–89	48	13.4	2.2
90+	45	12.5	3.9
[85+]	[93]	[25.9]	2.8
2000			
Total	1,621	100.0	0.6
55–64	184	11.4	0.8
65–74	251	15.5	1.4
75–84	369	22.8	3.0
85–89	222	13.7	7.3
90+	281	17.3	14.8
[85+]	[503]	[31.0]	10.2
2010			
Total	3,483	100.0	1.2
55–64	475	13.6	1.4
65–74	522	15.0	2.6
75–84	677	19.4	5.5
85–89	459	13.2	12.2
90+	758	21.8	27.1
[85+]	[1,217]	[35.0]	18.6
2020			
Total	5,658	100.0	1.9
55–64	706	12.5	1.8
65–74	1,027	18.2	3.4
75–84	1,026	18.2	7.1
85–89	564	10.0	15.7
90+	1,333	23.6	38.2
[85+]	[1,897]	[33.6]	26.8

Source: Spencer (1984).

at 3 percent in 2020, and their total number– nearly 9 million–would be quadruple that in 1980.

ECONOMIC CHANGES AND POLICY IMPLICATIONS

Regardless of their numbers, the cohorts that will be aging into the oldest-old years during the coming decades will differ appreciably from those currently age 85 years or over. Table 3 shows comparative data for those age 85+ years in 1980 and for those cohorts that will comprise the new oldest old during successive decades until the year 2020. To illustrate some of the principal dimensions over which the oldest old of the future will differ from those of today, we have chosen the proportion foreign born (which illustrates changes in ethnicity and the potential problem of integration into U.S. society), level of educational attainment, labor force participation of women in the cohort when they were 45 years old, income level of men in the cohort when they were 45 years old

relative to overall income in that year (the last three variables will indicate the probable economic status of these cohorts when they become 85 years old), and number of children ever born per 1,000 women in the cohort (to provide a crude measure of the availability of family support).

The proportion of the oldest old which will have been born outside the U.S. is likely to diminish sharply through the year 2010, with a modest increase likely thereafter. Nearly one-fifth of the current generation of oldest old are foreign born, reflecting the relative free-entry policy of immigration to the U.S. characteristic of the period prior to the early 1920s. Given the highly restrictive immigration policy that prevailed during the following 40 years, it is hardly surprising that the proportion foreign born among current cohorts ages 45–84 is much lower. However, with some easing of restrictions based on country of origin in recent years, immigration again has begun to increase the number of foreign born. Of the 1.7 million persons ages 45–54 who are foreign born, more than one-fifth came to the U.S. after

TABLE 3   Social and Economic Characteristics of Present and Future Oldest-Old Cohorts: 1980–2020

	Oldest Old in 1980	Cohort Ages 85–94 Years in 1990	Cohort Ages 85–94 Years in 2000	Cohort Ages 85–94 Years in 2010	Cohort Ages 85–94 Years in 2020
Median Years of School Completed	8.3	8.9	10.7	12.2	12.5
Female Labor Force Participation Rate at Age 45 Years (%)	23.2	34.8	47.4	53.0	61.5
Relative Male Income at Age 45 Years	na	1.24	1.25	1.41	1.58
Children Ever Born per 1000 Women	ca. 3,000	ca. 2,550	ca. 2,300	ca. 2,700	ca. 3,100
Foreign Born (%)	18.6	15.1	9.0	6.3	7.3

Source: 1940, 1950, 1960, 1970, and 1980 U.S. Censuses of Population.

1970, as did one-seventh of the 1.4 million foreign born ages 55–64 in 1980. If the current immigration policy continues, the foreign born among the oldest old will likely be a greater proportion than that suggested by the current data, although they almost certainly will comprise a lesser share than that found among the 1980 oldest old.

The three variables suggestive of prospective economic status are quite consistent in their direction. New cohorts entering the oldest old will likely bring with them appreciably more education, more labor force participation of women during prime working years, and higher income (relative to others in the workforce) during their peak earning years. As a result, income levels among the oldest old should rise in both a relative and an absolute sense over time. This rise will occur because more women will have pension and social security income based on their own earnings in addition to income from survivors' benefits, and because higher relative earnings over the course of the working life will likely have resulted in greater accumulation of assets—leading to more asset income from which to draw during retirement years. It remains an open question whether these greater assets will offset greater lifetime income needs consistent with the increased longevity discussed earlier.

Finally, the number of children able to provide support for their oldest-old parents will follow an irregular course. In the short-term future (until the year 2000), this number will diminish, on average, as those who were parents of the small cohorts of the 1930s and 1940s reach age 85. These cohorts are succeeded by the parents of the baby boom generations of the 1950s and 1960s. Therefore, by the year 2020, there should be more surviving children per oldest-old person than in 1980 or in any subsequent year. However, parents of the baby boom generation probably are the final cohort that will be entering the oldest-old years for whom this can be said. Since the 1950s and 1960s baby boom, U.S. fertility levels have fallen to, and have been sustained at, levels below those of the Depression years.

Persons who, by the year 2020, will not have reached age 85 or over will bring with them quite different experiences over their life cycles relative to those of the oldest old. We have noted that these cohorts, particularly those born after World War II, will be characterized by substantially lower fertility. These cohorts, in particular their female members, will also be characterized by substantially greater labor force experience. These increases in female labor force participation suggest that these future cohorts of older women will reach the retirement years with their own pensions and social security entitlements; given existing and probable future patterns of sex differences in mortality and age at marriage, the incidence of widowhood among older women will not likely change appreciably for future members of the elderly population. Thus, the economic lot of older widows, which has been and remains particularly adverse, will likely improve in the future. Partially offsetting this change, though, will be the relatively low earnings of younger members of the baby boom cohorts (say, those born from the mid-1950s through the mid-1960s) due to limitations in promotion possibilities caused by the sheer sizes of these cohorts and of those that immediately preceded them into the labor market (Easterlin, 1978; Bouvier, 1980). Additionally, one must note that coupled with increased female labor force participation in these cohorts is reduced lifetime fertility. On average, then, older persons will have fewer surviving children to provide financial and emotional support. With fewer familial resources available, responsibility for this support—especially in the area of long-term care—will likely shift away from the family and toward society as a whole. Consequently, we can expect increased demand for nursing homes and similar long-term care arrangements, the bulk of which are publicly funded through Medicaid.

This mention of a health-care issue brings us to one of the most crucial policy issues in the aging of the U.S., namely, the demand for health care and the costs associated with this demand (Davis, 1985). In coming years, income levels of the older population will likely rise, relative to those of the entire population, due to the labor force participation trend and to increased social security and private pension coverage. Income levels among the older population, regardless of age, tend to interact with various measures of health status and health-care utilization in more-or-less predictable ways. As Table 4 illustrates, for each broad age group within the older population (55–64, 65–74, and 75+ years), as the income level increases, generally (a) the fewer the number of chronic conditions limiting activity, (b) the lower the percentage assessing health as being "fair" or "poor," and (c) the fewer the

average number of days spent per year in short-stay hospitals.

Within income groups, the numbers of limiting conditions and of average days in a hospital often increase with age, but this is not the case for self-assessed health status where such a relationship with age holds in only the highest income categories. In fact, with family income levels below $10,000, fair or poor health is reported less frequently among persons age 75+ than among persons ages 55–74. Perhaps persons in the oldest age group survive to that age precisely because they are comparatively healthy. The average number of physician visits per year bears little relationship with income, but generally shows a pattern of increasing frequency of physician use as a function of age.

In brief, the data shown in Table 4, when considered in conjunction with the demographic trends discussed above, suggest two counterbalancing tendencies: (a) increased income (especially among cohorts entering

TABLE 4   Selected Indicators of Health Status, by Age and Income, 1979–1980

Age (years)	Total	$2,999	$3,000–$4,999	$5,000–$6,999	$7,000–$9,999	$10,000–$14,999	$15,000–$24,999	$25,000
Activity Limitations per Person								
55–64	3.0	6.0	5.7	4.5	3.8	3.1	2.3	1.8
65–74	4.1	5.9	5.3	4.7	4.4	3.7	3.2	2.9
75+	5.3	6.0	5.4	5.1	5.4	5.1	5.3	5.5
Percentage in Fair or Poor Health								
55–64	25	57	50	44	37	29	18	13
65–74	32	48	43	38	33	25	21	18
75+	31	35	33	32	31	30	27	27
Physicians Visits per Person								
55–64	5.5	6.2	8.7	5.9	5.5	5.6	5.1	5.4
65–74	6.3	6.9	6.6	6.4	6.2	6.3	6.1	6.6
75+	6.6	6.2	6.1	5.9	6.1	7.2	8.3	7.2
Short-Stay Hospital Days per Person								
55–64	1.8	3.3	2.4	3.1	2.6	2.0	1.4	1.1
65–74	2.4	3.1	3.2	2.7	2.2	2.2	1.9	2.2
75+	3.6	4.0	3.1	3.5	3.1	4.3	3.7	4.0

Source: National Center for Health Statistics (1984).

the ranks of the older population from the present until the year 2020), which has been associated with lower levels of chronic activity-limiting conditions, lower levels of self-assessed poor health, and fewer days of per capita hospital usage; and (b) continued aging of the older population, which has been associated with greater incidence of chronic conditions and greater utilization of healthcare facilities and providers. The critical question in assessing the economic impact of aging of the U.S. population is the extent to which interaction of these tendencies will influence the demand for publicly provided services, especially in the areas of health and long-term care.

Other important issues also emerge regarding consequences of the aging of the U.S.'s older population. It is unlikely that any significant changes will occur in labor force participation of the younger elderly (say, those under age 72) barring a change in the social security means test, which limits earnings within this age group by reducing social security retirement benefits. Yet, with increased eligibility for benefits and higher benefit levels consistent with increased labor force participation among women who will be entering the ranks of the older population, pressures on social security funding will likely exceed those already forecast (Hogan, 1974). This tendency will be further exacerbated if the lower-level mortality projections described previously portray the demographic future accurately. Not only will benefit levels likely be higher, but individuals will likely draw benefits for a greater number of years. Essentially identical statements can be made for the largely publicly funded Medicare program.

Thus, a set of changes in the structure of the older population will emerge over the next 35 years. In general, these changes point to increased demand for publicly provided services and income transfer programs. The ability of policymakers to develop means of providing these services in a manner not ca-lamitous for the U.S. economic growth prospects is critical.

EMERGING RESEARCH ISSUES

This paper has demonstrated that the elderly population of the U.S. exhibits significant internal variation in growth potential, age distribution, and selected social, economic, and demographic characteristics. Our point is that the elderly cannot be analyzed usefully as a single, homogeneous age category. Researchers should recognize the importance of additional sources of variation within the older population which show varying degrees of association with age.

We illustrate this point by considering four variables: sex, race, marital status, and residential location. Sex and race differences in longevity are well established—females and whites are overrepresented in the older age groups. In future years, the number of single, widowed, separated, and divorced elderly will increase both relatively and absolutely (Masnick and Bane, 1980). Although the rural-urban mortality differential has declined, urban residence remains more conducive to longer life due partly to greater access to health care. Moreover, economic differences among these elderly subgroups are substantial, favoring men, whites, married persons with spouses present, and urbanites (Serow, 1982).

Studies are needed to examine the relationship between age and economic status within precisely defined population subgroups. For example, we can expect that elderly unmarried black females living in rural areas will be among the most economically disadvantaged subgroups in the U.S. population. But what about other combinations of these variables? And what if the differentials are further differentiated by age category, e.g., the youngest old versus the oldest old? Further disaggregation of research on the elderly can lead to a better understanding of the social and economic consequences of population aging. More importantly, it can provide the bases for more responsive and more effective policies and programs to meet the needs of this growing segment of the U.S. population, and for determining how the U.S. economy may be affected by the effort to meet these needs.

REFERENCES

Bouvier, F., "America's Baby Boom Generation: The Fateful Bulge," *Population Bulletin*, April 1980, 1–35.

Coale, J., *The Growth and Structure of Human Populations: A Mathematical Investigation.* Princeton University Press. Princeton, NJ, 1972.

Davis, K., "Health Care Policies and the Aged: Observations from the United States," in R. Binstock and E. Shanas, eds., *Handbook of Aging and the Social Sciences*, 2nd ed., pp. 727–744, Van Nostrand Reinhold, New York, 1985.

Easterlin, A., "What Will 1984 Be Like? Socioeconomic Implications of Recent Twists in Age Structure," *Demography*, November 1978, 397–432.

Hogan, T. D., "The Implications of Population Stationarity for the Social Security System," *Social Science Quarterly*, June 1974, 151–158.

Keyfitz, N., "Changing Vital Rates and Age Distribution," *Population Studies*, July 1968, 235–251.

Masnick, G., and M. Bane, *The Nation's Families: 1960–1990*, Harvard University Press, Cambridge, Mass., 1980.

National Center for Health Statistics, *Health Characteristics According to Family and Personal Income*, Vital and Health Statistics, Series 10, No. 147, National Center for Health Statistics, Hyattsville, Md., 1984.

Schulz, J. H., *The Economics of Aging*, 3rd ed., Wadsworth, Belmont, Calif., 1985.

Serow, W. J., "Changes in the Composition of the Elderly Poor: 1969–1978," *Journal of Applied Social Sciences*, Fall/Winter 1982–1983, 57–67.

Spencer, G., *Projections of the Population of the United States by Age, Sex and Race: 1983 to 2080*, Current Population Reports, Series P-25, No. 952, U.S. Government Printing Office, Washington, D.C., 1984.

A Population Profile of Very Old Men and Women in the United States

CHARLES F. LONGINO, JR.

Men make up only 31% of the population 85 years of age or older. Because they are a minority among the very old, they have been invisible in our image of this age group. This article gives us a first look at them in aggregate as they differ from women, who dominate the very old population numerically. This article, an exercise in population decomposition, will show the social and economic differences between men and women age 85 and older in the United States in 1980 so that each can be seen more clearly.

THE DATA

The data reported here were derived from the AARP-Andrus Foundation's recently completed "Oldest Americans Project" (Longino 1986a). In 1960 the U.S. Bureau of the Census made a small sample of individual census records (on computer tape) available to users outside the bureau for the first time. By 1980 the sample had grown from 1% to 5%. The analysis that follows uses Sample A, the 5% sample, of the 1980 census microdata files (Longino 1982; Longino and Teicher 1982). The records of all individuals who were 85 years of age or older on April 1, 1980 were abstracted from the national file, organized in rectangular format so that the individual would be the unit of analysis, and used as the data for the gender profiles presented here.

Four clusters of variables were selected for profiling: demographic, socioeconomic, relational, and environmental. These variables were selected because they allow the researcher to examine the interaction between gender and marital status as it affected economic well-being, living arrangements, and residential mobility (Longino 1986a).

Until this descriptive analysis was conducted, no baseline existed against which researchers could compare their samples of men and women in advanced old age to determine how well they represented the sampling universe (Suzman and Riley 1985). It was impossible to learn how very old men differed from very old women, who made up most of this population. Such data are not available through the census.

FINDINGS

Over 1.5 million women were 85 years of age and over in 1980, but only about 676,000

Source: The Sociological Quarterly 29(4), 559–564. Reprinted with permission from JAI Press, Inc., Greenwich, CT 06836. Copyright 1988.

men; almost 70% of this age group were women.

Women live longer than men largely because men have a higher death rate from heart disease and tend to adopt certain high-risk behaviors. Genetics and hormones also make a major contribution to the difference in longevity between the sexes. The demo-

graphic differences between very old men and women are presented in Table 1. The demographic characteristics of the two groups differed greatly, but consistently higher proportions of men over women belonged to racial and cultural minorities. Further, fully one-fifth of the very old men were naturalized citizens, having been born in an-

TABLE 1 Comparison of the 1980 Demographic and Socioeconomic Characteristics of Men and Women Age 85+ in the United States

	U.S. Residents			
	Men		Women	
Population Characteristics	Percent	Total	Percent	Total
Number of persons age 85+	30.8	676,000	69.2	1,521,120
Demographic Characteristics				
White	90.2		92.0	
Black	7.8		6.7	
Indian	.4		.2	
Asian	.9		.6	
Spanish	2.6		1.8	
Naturalized citizens	20.4		14.0	
Cannot speak English	4.4		4.6	
Socioeconomic Characteristics				
Mean years of school		8.2		8.8
High school graduates	24.3		30.1	
1+ years of college	12.5		13.0	
Employment, full or part-time	4.2		1.4	
Sources of Income	**Percent**	**Dollars**[a]	**Percent**	**Dollars**[a]
Wages and salary	6.1	12,525	2.6	8,420
Nonfarm self-employment	1.8	12,461	.3	7,098
Farm self-employment	2.2	8,050	1.0	6,684
Interest/dividends/rent	40.2	7,171	31.8	5,822
Social Security	79.2	4,873	72.7	3,831
Public assistance[b]	9.1	2,795	14.1	2,552
All other sources[c]	30.6	5,616	15.6	4,634
Total mean person income		10,529		6,931
Total mean household income		20,985		19,737

Source: Prepared by Charles F. Longino, Jr., Ph.D., Center for Social Research in Aging, University of Miami, Coral Gables, FL. Funded by the AARP-Andrus Foundation, Washington, DC.

Notes: [a]Mean income during 1979 (in 1985 constant dollars).
[b]Includes SSI.
[c]Includes pension and annuities.

other country, whereas only 14% of the very old women had immigrated to this country and become U.S. citizens.

Table 1 also shows the socioeconomic differences between very old men and women. Women had a slight edge in education, but men had more income of all kinds, except for public assistance income. Because educational opportunities improved as this century progressed, the very old are collectively less well educated than are younger cohorts of adults. In the 1980s they averaged between eight and nine years of formal schooling. Of the women in this age group, 30% graduated from high school; fewer than 25% of the men had that much education. College graduates were rare among the very old; only 12.5% of the men and 13% of the women attended college for even one year. Education levels for this age group, however, will rise with each passing decade.

Men were more likely than women to work outside the home at all ages, even in this birth cohort. At the time of the 1980 census, over 4% of the men were still working full or part-time. Over 6% had drawn income from wages at some time during the previous year. Proportionately fewer women worked in any capacity; the few women who did work also earned less money than the men in the previous year. (The dollar amounts are given in 1985 constant dollars.) A handful of very old people also earned income from their own businesses in 1979. Again, men were proportionately more likely to do so than women, and they tended to earn more from this source.

Three-quarters of the U.S. population in this age category received income from Social Security in 1979 (Longino 1986a). Nearly 80% of the men reported income from this source as compared to fewer than 75% of the women. The difference probably was due to the men's higher labor-force participation. The closeness of the two proportions can be attributed to the large number of women who had never worked outside the home

and who received survivor's rather than retirement benefits. Because women's incomes were lower on average than men's, retirement benefits for women also were lower. Survivor's benefits tend to be lower than retirement benefits; thus the women who received Social Security income received less than did the men. A higher proportion of women than men received public assistance and supplemental social security income, but the average amount they received was not as large as the men's income even from this source. The "feminization of poverty" seems to be evident even among the oldest Americans (Minkler and Stone 1985).

In summary, very old men had a 20% higher personal income from all sources than did very old women. In 1985 constant dollars, men received about $10,500 and women nearly $7,000 during the year before the census. The gap was almost closed, however, when total household income was considered: women had mean household incomes of about $20,000. To understand why the women approached parity, it is necessary to examine a series of relational items in the census (See Table 2).

Nearly 50% of the men and fewer than 10% of the women over age 84 were married. Some of the reasons for this difference are straightforward. Men's remarriage rate after widowhood far exceeds that of women; in addition women are more likely than men to become widowed, partly because men tend to be older than their wives. Regardless of the reasons, however, most women are widowed and most men are not. Between 5% and 10% of the men and the women in this age cohort have never been married.

Because the popular image portrays the very old as residentially dependent, it was surprising to find that nearly one-half of the women and over two-thirds of the men age 85 and older lived in their own homes. Women were more likely than men to live alone (33% versus 22%) because fewer women were married. In nearly every cate-

TABLE 2   Comparison of the 1980 Socioeconomic Characteristics of Men and Women Age 85+ in the United States

Population Characteristics	U.S. Residents			
	Men		Women	
	Percent	*Total*	*Percent*	*Total*
Number of persons age 85+	30.8	676,000	69.2	1,521,120
Relational Characteristics				
Marital Status:				
Married	48.2		8.5	
Widowed	44.0		81.6	
Never married	5.7		7.9	
Living Arrangements:				
Householder	68.0		48.3	
Parent of householder	11.1		18.7	
Sibling of householder	.9		1.8	
Other relation of householder	1.6		2.3	
Not related to householder	1.5		1.1	
In group quarters	16.9		27.7	
Other Related Information:				
3+ person in household	19.8		19.5	
Mean persons in household		1.9		1.7
In home for the aged[a]	15.1		25.4	
Living alone[b]	21.6		33.3	
Disabled and living alone[b]	5.3		11.2	
Disabled[c]	38.0		52.1	
Environmental Characteristics				
Residence 5 Years Before:				
Same residence	73.7		68.7	
Local move, same county	16.4		20.0	
Migrant from within state	5.7		6.4	
Migrant from another state	3.8		4.7	
Migrant from abroad	.3		.2	

Source: Prepared by Charles F. Longino, Jr., Ph.D., Center for Social Research in Aging, University of Miami, Coral Gables, FL. Funded by the AARP-Andrus Foundation, Washington, DC.

Notes: [a]These are primarily nursing homes.
[b]Not in institutions.
[c]Physical disability for 6+ months that would prevent using public transportation.

gory of residential dependency, however, the proportion of women was half again that of men. Women lived much more often than men in institutions, particularly homes for the aged. Men may not have gone to live in nursing homes as often as women because more of them were nursed at home by a spouse. The average sizes of men's and women's households in this age group do not differ widely—just under two persons per household. About 20% of each sex lived in larger households with three or more members.

The relatively higher rate of residential dependency among very old women may have been due to the costs of greater longevity; a much higher proportion of women than men were disabled. (The 1990 census will include a more accurate measure of disability.) A rather weak measure used in the 1980 census showed that over 50% of the women had had a health problem for six months or longer that prevented them from using public transportation as compared with 38% of the men. As a measure of severe need (or of extreme independence), 11% of the women but only 5% of the men were living alone while disabled. Thus, mortality is higher among men in their advanced years, but morbidity is higher among women.

Because so few very old women are married, their household income was nearly equal to that of very old men, even though their personal income was considerably lower. A higher proportion of women than of men was living in the homes of others: children, siblings, and other relatives. In these households contributions to their income often came from more than one person, including at least one person in the labor force (Longino 1983, 1986b). Because in their later years, women moved into the homes of

others more often than men, residential mobility should have been higher for women than for men in this age category. The data in Table 2 refute this assumption, although the sex differences were not large. In proportion to their numbers the very old were more—not less—mobile than younger people over age 60; within this category, women were more mobile than men. In view of women's higher morbidity rates, much of this mobility was health-related (Patrick 1980).

CONCLUSION

What can be said in summary about the differences between very old men and very old women? First, there are not very many old men. In 1980 nearly 70% of those age 85 and over were women. Second, men were better off than women in both socioeconomic and relational characteristics in that they had higher personal incomes from nearly all sources and were far more likely to be married and living independently. They also were better off in another way: they were cared for in their own homes, often by a younger spouse. Consequently they did not live in nursing homes in as great a proportion as very old women. In a sense, then, the generalizations about the very old have a female bias; the hidden minority of men fits the stereotype of the very old less closely than do women.

REFERENCES

Holden, C. 1987 "Why Do Women Live Longer than Men?" *Science* 238:158–160.

Litwak, E., and C. F. Longino, Jr. 1987 "The Migratory Patterns of the Elderly: A Developmental Perspective." *The Gerontologist* 25:226–272.

Longino, C. F., Jr. 1982. "Applied Gerontology and the 1980 Census." *Journal of Applied Gerontology* 1:19–25.

———. 1983. *A Statistical Profile of Older Floridians*. Coral Gables, FL: University of Miami, Center for Social Research in Aging.

———. 1986a. *The Oldest Americans: State Profiles for Data Based Planning*. Coral Gables, FL: University of Miami, Center for Social Research in Aging.

———. 1986b. "A State by State Look at the Oldest Americans." *American Demographics* 8:38–42.

———. 1988. "Who Are the Oldest Americans?" *The Gerontologist* 28:515–523.

Longino, C. F., Jr., and M. I. Teicher. 1982. "An Introduction to the 1980 Census." Pp. 75–84 in *Data Based Planning in the Field of Aging,* edited by C. C. Osterbind, W. Mangum, and M. E. Teicher. Gainesville, FL: University Presses of Florida.

Minkler, M., and R. Stone. 1985. "The Feminization of Poverty and Older Women." *The Gerontologist* 25:351–357.

Patrick, C. H. 1980. "Health and Migration of the Elderly." *Research on Aging* 2:233–241.

Suzman, R., and M. W. Riley. 1985. "Introducing the 'Oldest-Old.'" *Milbank Memorial Fund Quarterly* 63: 177–186.

Migration Patterns Among the Elderly: A Developmental Perspective

EUGENE LITWAK
CHARLES F. LONGINO, JR.

Demographers are fond of pointing out that the migratory behavior of human beings is closely associated with developmental tasks in their life course (Weeks, 1986). Indeed, America's major migration theorist, Everett Lee, considered the heightened propensity to migrate at certain stages of life as one of the enduring generalizations that can be made about migration (Lee, 1966). The life course patterning of migration seems to be nearly universal, holding for other countries as well as the United States (Castro & Rogers, 1983; Long & Boertlein, 1976; Rogers & Castro, 1981; Rogers & Willekens, 1986).

The age profile of migration in the U.S. has been consistent in shape for decades, changing only gradually over time. The younger children are, the more likely they are to migrate. The migration rate for children bottoms out at about age 10 and does not increase rapidly until the late teens. More than one-third of Americans in their young adult years, age 20–24, had moved at least once between 1982 and 1983, the peak migration years during their life course. Unsurprisingly, this age corresponds with college graduation and marriage for many. The increasing age of children in the home, particu-

larly once they begin their formal schooling, dampens the attractiveness of migration for their parents. The age-specific migration rate declines, slowly at first, then more steeply until age 35, after which it slowly declines throughout the middle years to a life course low point just before the retirement years in the early sixties. Careers are established and mature along with children during these years, often in one community.

At this point the standard demography text ends its discussion of age and migration. Demographers routinely use a human development and life course model for explaining migration patterns. Their strong fixation on nuclear family development and career mobility, however, has blinded them in the past to life course factors in the migration of retired persons. Only in the past decade has the gerontology literature that uses census data on the migration of older persons begun to accumulate (Biggar, 1980, 1984; Flynn et al., 1985; Longino, 1979; Longino & Jackson, 1980; Longino et all., 1984; Serow, 1978). It was stimulated by and, in return, increases interest in the subject among demographers (Barsby & Cox, 1975; Biggar, 1979, 1984; Soldo, 1980, 1981). By now it is abundantly

Source: The Gerontologist 27(3), 266–272. Reprinted with permission from The Gerontological Society of America, Washington, DC 20005. Copyright 1987.

clear that migration after age 60 is not an undifferentiated residual category, but that it, too, is strongly influenced by life course events.

In this paper a developmental context is presented, based on Litwak's (1985) formulations, for the patterns of elderly migration presented in Longino's (1984, 1985) work. Litwak has suggested that the nature of modern technology puts the kinship structures of older people under institutional pressures to make three basic types of moves: one when they retire, a second when they experience moderate forms of disability, and a third when they have major forms of chronic disability. The pressure may be slight for the first type of move, but it may increase for the second type and again for the third. These predicted mobility patterns are supported by census data. Environmental exceptions are also considered.

PRESSURES FOR THREE KINDS OF MOVES AMONG RETIREES IN A MODERN SOCIETY: A DEVELOPMENTAL PERSPECTIVE

Modern industrial development requires a very mobile labor force which will shift geographically as new states of technology develop. The vast movement westward, from rural to urban places, and more recently from the old industry to new industry states in the Sunbelt and New England, has historically dominated American migration patterns. The pressure for labor mobility is evident in each.

The need for such mobility is one major factor in the development of the "modified extended family" (Litwak, 1965; Sussman, 1977), which has a kinship structure and norms that permit parents and children to live at some distance while still maintaining close bonds. Litwak argued that such a structure was possible because modern technology allows communication over great distances. Other structures also arose (neigh-

bors and friends) which managed some tasks that kin could no longer handle (Litwak & Szelenyi, 1969). These early formulations, however, assumed that people were well or suffered only from acute, not chronic illness or disability. More recently Litwak (1985) pointed out that where chronic illness or disability prevents an individual from carrying out ordinary household tasks, neither friends, neighbors nor formal institutions could adequately substitute. The only group which could systematically do so was children. When the burden becomes too great for them, a conjoint effort of children and institution is often attempted. Social pressure for three basic moves derives from the ability of older people in the first stage of their retirement to live at some distance from their children and their need at the second and third stages for their children or a combination of children and institution to help them.

Literalism should be avoided. No assertion is made to the effect that most persons, after their retirement, will make three moves. Many will make none. Some will make only one. Rather, the argument is that there are events in the lives of long-lived persons during their post-retirement lives that might prompt three major categories of residential adjustments and that there are social and geographical environmental changes that might accompany these adjustments. It must be added, however, that residential mobility in the older population is increasing (Longino et al., 1984) and the mean number of moves, for those who move at all, is also likely to increase in the future.

The first move. —When retirees have intact marriages, are relatively healthy, and have enough retirement income, there are social pressures for some of them to relocate. In any 5-year period, about 5% of the population over age 60 makes a long distance move. The majority of these fit the profile of the first movers. Some retirees have planned their move for years and have vacationed at and visited their new location many times in anticipation of the move. The reasons for relocation are complex and have to do with the attraction of amenities, friendship network maintenance (Wiseman, 1980; Wiseman & Roseman, 1979), and the ability to make a psychic move identity from one place to another (Cuba, 1984). At this stage of retirement, kinship functions can be managed over considerable distances. It would be wrong to assume that no recent retirees move closer to their children or other relatives. Many do (Gober & Zonn, 1983; Sullivan, 1985). It could be assumed that when their health declines, the nearness of their children may preclude the necessity of a second move. The argument is, rather, that the support needs of the migrant at the time of the post-retirement amenity move do not *require* the nearness of kin. Typical of kinship tasks related to such support needs are providing emotional support by weekly talks, economic support in cash-flow crises, and recuperative care after acute illnesses. These can be managed through the use of telephones, cars, and air travel. Typical of migrants at this first stage would be those moving to retirement communities in the Sunbelt region or to nonmetropolitan small town settings. Such migrants will tend to be younger, healthier, wealthier, and more often to have intact marriages than migrants in the counter streams. The poorer retiree often cannot afford to make such a move for the sake of amenities and life style considerations.

The second move. —The pressure for the second move occurs when older people develop chronic disabilities that make it difficult to carry out everyday household tasks, such as shopping, cooking, cleaning, emergency first aid, and protecting themselves against crime. The presence of a spouse provides help and motivation for performing these tasks. This second phase, therefore, is typically compounded when deficits from

widowhood and disability are combined. At this phase, if older people live at a distance from their child's home, they must move if they are to get the services they need.

There are usually two questions which are raised when this assertion is made: (1) Why can't they live at a distance and manage with modern technology, and (2) why can't formal institutions, friends, neighbors, or other kin substitute?

A century ago, the only transportation was walking or horse-drawn vehicles. In such circumstances a helper would have had to live within the larger neighborhood in order to provide emotional support by talking to a lonely widow once or twice weekly. The helper would have had to live within the city or its immediate environs to supply daily meals and housekeeping for someone who was bedridden for a week or two. For a parent who was chronically ill the helper would have to live in the same home or next door. The invention of the telephone freed the first tasks from the constraints of geography; people can live at considerable distances and make weekly calls to cheer up lonely widows. The invention of the car and the airplane means people can live at great distances and fly in to provide household help for a week or two and then fly back home. No technological invention, however, as yet permits individuals to live at even moderate distances and provide everyday household services on a continuous basis, as would be needed by those who are chronically disabled. The more household activities and the more intensive services required, the closer the helper must live (Litwak, 1985).

Formal organizations cannot substitute well for informal caregivers when it comes to doing household tasks for people who are only moderately disabled. Institutions either must routinize the task, which leads to a loss of individual choice, or they run the risk of staff laxity and abuse in managing tasks which cannot be easily observed. Formal institutions, however, are essential for those older people who are severely disabled, or who do not have children they can count on, or whose children are overburdened. This notion is developed later when considering the third basic move.

Before doing so, however, the second question must be addressed. Why can't neighbors or friends provide household services to older people and thereby negate the need for a second stage move due to disability? What characterizes household services for the chronically ill is that it takes much time and effort to deliver such services and therefore the helper must be physically strong. If help is not based on economic remuneration, there must be a long history or future potential of exchange between the older person and the helper to build norms of duty or love, or both, necessary to motivate helpers. What typifies friends of older people, especially those with whom they have had a long-term relationship, is that the friends are from the same age cohort and are therefore likely to be equally frail. For this reason there is a low probability of them doing the physically demanding household service (Litwak, 1985; Siegel, 1985). What characterizes neighborhood ties in a modern society is their relatively short time span (Fellin & Litwak, 1963; Litwak, 1985). Neighbors do not have the internalized commitment to take on the burden of continuous household services. In other words, children as a group have the highest probability of being both younger and having a long history of past exchanges which produces the internalized commitments necessary for providing household services. The bulk of the empirical evidence does suggest that this is, indeed, the case (Cantor, 1979; Litwak, 1985; Siegel, 1985).

Many can think of exceptions to these generalizations. Comparative strangers have undertaken household services for older people for prolonged periods of time, or older people have had younger friends who have taken care of them, or older people

have had long-time ties with their neighbors. The argument is that the major industrial forces shaping society lead to low probabilities for such exceptions (Litwak, 1985). They are not, therefore, the basis for developing large scale social programs.

These, then, are the pressures for older people to first move to retirement communities when they are healthy and married and then to move toward children when they become disabled and widowed. With that in mind, it can be argued that older persons moving to retirement destinations like Florida should typify the first basic move, whereas those moving from Florida to Northern urban areas like New York should typify the second and third basic moves.

This is made clear in Table 1, in which people 60 years of age and older who moved to Florida from New York, New Jersey, Pennsylvania and Ohio are compared with those who moved from Florida to these Northern states. First, it can be noted that those moving from each of the states in the North to Florida tended to be younger. The most dramatic evidence of this is the percentage over 75 years of age. On the average, only 15.5% of those moving to Florida are over 75 whereas 40.6% of those moving North from Florida are over 75 (a little over two-and-a-half times as many). In addition, 75.9% of those moving to Florida are married whereas 41.6% of those moving to the North from Florida are married. Put somewhat differently, 47.8% of those moving North are widowed, but only 17% of those moving to Florida are widowed. Of those moving North from Florida, three times as many live with their children (16%) as do those who move to Florida (4.8%). This is only a limited test of the hypothesis that people in the second stage move closer to their children. And it is the case that those moving to the North from Florida are disabled two-and-a-half times as often. Those moving North are also more likely to be institutionalized, which is consistent with the view that they are more

TABLE 1   Characteristics of Migrants Age 60+ in Florida Streams From and To New York, New Jersey, Pennsylvania and Ohio, 1975–80

Migrant Characteristics	New York		New Jersey		Pennsylvania		Ohio	
	To FL	From FL	To FL	From FL	To FL	From FL	To FL	From FL
Total migrants	127,600	9,000	38,440	4,640	31,600	4,480	37,720	5,120
Mean age	69.2	73.2	68.2	72.4	68.3	73.3	68.0	73.1
% Age 75+	15.0	42.2	16.8	34.5	17.2	45.5	14.5	38.3
% Male	46.9	33.8	50.6	32.8	46.8	36.6	49.3	33.6
% Married	75.7	38.2	75.4	46.6	74.6	44.6	78.4	40.6
% Widowed	17.1	49.3	16.9	43.1	18.4	44.6	15.6	50.0
% With a disability	8.0	20.4	8.7	18.1	7.6	17.9	7.9	21.1
% Living independently	90.3	62.7	88.8	66.4	89.0	67.9	90.5	67.2
% Living with a child	4.5	20.0	5.3	17.2	5.3	12.5	5.0	10.9
% In institution	0.9	12.0	1.4	4.3	2.0	13.4	1.3	13.3
% Below poverty	6.8	11.6	7.6	15.5	3.8	6.3	5.4	8.6

likely to be disabled. Approximately 11% of those moving from Florida to the North are institutionalized whereas this is true of only 1.2% of those moving to Florida. Those moving from the North to Florida match the characteristics of the first stage movers whereas those moving from Florida to the North, on average, seem to represent the second and third stage movers.

The third move. —The question still remains as to what the pressures are for the third stage move, the move from more or less exclusive care by the kin to institutional care. How can this move be justified if, as was pointed out, institutions cannot substitute for the family when it comes to providing household services? The second stage move, it must be remembered, is in the context of only moderate forms of disability, in which the assumption could be made that well-functioning child support groups had a high probability of providing sufficient help. That no longer holds true, however, when the older person is suffering from more severe forms of chronic disability or does not have children. In such instances, institutional care is crucial. To understand why, it is necessary

to acknowledge the obvious fact that the typical marital household unit in an industrial society consists of only two adults. That means that the helper of the older parent has very limited resources. The more help the child provides to the older person, the less she (or he) has for her own household unit. When the older person's need for household services increases dramatically, the helper quickly becomes overwhelmed. Hence the recent discussion of "helper burden" (Cantor, 1983; Horowitz, 1985; Johnson, 1983).

It is very important to understand the limits of children's help because individuals who see that kin provide most of the help for older people (Shanas, 1979) might draw the conclusion that formal institutions are not necessary. For instance, some have argued for laws on filial responsibility without understanding the limits of modern kinship systems to provide help. Anderson (1977) pointed out that when such laws were in effect in England, they led to many parents fleeing from children in order to avoid imposing a burden on them that would reduce their child's or grandchild's life chances. Alternatively, many children fled from their older parents for the same reason. Even if more moderate laws on filial responsibility were accepted, the devastating impact on the family's social life, the physical exhaustion that 24-hour continuous care involves, and the mental stress would have equally drastic social consequences (Horowitz, 1985; Litwak, 1985). Perhaps this explains why existing laws on filial responsibility have seldom been enforced in a modern society (Schorr, 1960).

Limited kin resources is the motive for the third basic move. When the older person becomes severely ill, he or she must move away from the immediate neighborhood of the child-helper to an institutional setting. It must be, however, an institutional setting where the child can maintain regular contact and provide meaningful services to the older person. The reason for this lies in the fact that institutions can only provide routinized service or else price themselves out of the market. The child, however, may provide complimentary services (Dobrof, 1976; Litwak, 1985). In a nursing home setting, the child can take the parent out for dinner or occasionally bring food the parent especially likes. They can provide the parent with pictures and special bedspreads to give their rooms the more personal feeling of a home and they can talk to the parent on a weekly basis to provide emotional support. More important, they can be an advocate for the older person, to guard against staff stealing personal objects or even staff neglect of those services that cannot be standardized.

This move may not occur for some. Some continue to be cared for by their children until they suddenly die. Most third-stage moves are local rather than long-distance moves. For that reason, they do not show up very much in studies of long-distance migration. Even so, they are reflected in Table 1 in the row indicating an institution as residence in the state of destination. Of those moving from Florida to Northern states, 11.2% are institutionalized whereas that is true of only

1.2% of those moving to Florida from the North.

BASIC MOVES FOR OLDER PEOPLE IN THE U.S. WHO ARE CHANGING ENVIRONMENT TYPES

There are two groups who do not follow the same migration pattern despite facing similar social pressures to make the three basic moves. The first group is the migrants who are making major shifts in the urbanization or deurbanization of their environment, moving between metropolitan and nonmetropolitan places; and the second is a special variant of environmental changers, migrants from abroad.

Metropolitan-nonmetropolitan movers. — The major expansion of job opportunities since the turn of the century has occurred within the metropolitan areas whereas the greatest decline has occurred in the rural areas and small towns. As a result, when the young enter the job market they are pushed out of the nonmetropolitan areas and attracted to the metropolitan ones by higher standards of living and greater economic opportunities.

Their parents, by contrast, have fewer incentives to leave the rural areas and small towns because their seniority means they hold whatever jobs are available. That, in turn, means that when these older people become disabled and need household help, they must move to their children in the city. This is, typically, mobility of the second kind.

Rowles (1983) describes this process in West Virginia as moving through a sequence of stages. First the children relocate. This is followed by a number of accommodation strategies so that loss of support from children is compensated for by shifts in support within the house and from the surrounding community. The third stage features seasonal migration when the parents visit their children's homes. In Rowles's sequence, a crisis requires the parents to relocate in the fourth stage, generally with or near to a child. After the crisis situation is stabilized, the fifth stage finds the parent holding on to his home and returning for visits to maintain it and to keep up network ties in the community. The sixth stage is severance, when the parent no longer returns. Older persons who have no children or no younger relatives who live nearby may turn earlier to institutional help and some of them may move to a metropolitan area where resources are superior.

As shown in Table 2, more of the older people moving from metropolitan to nonmetropolitan locations may be making their first post-retirement move because they are younger than migrants moving in the other direction. Those moving to the country have more retirement income than migrants moving to the big cities. Data reported elsewhere by Longino et al. (1984) indicated, however, that the highest incomes are found among long-distance movers from one metropolitan area to another. For those exchanging a metropolitan for a nonmetropolitan environ-

ment, the move to a nonmetropolitan area means a less expensive, less harried environment and to many a return to familiar childhood roots. The characteristics of the migrants would seem to suggest that many of those moving to nonmetropolitan areas are first stage migrants whereas many of those moving to metropolitan areas are second stage migrants. Those moving away from big cities are younger and more often married and living independently whereas migrants to big cities are older, less often married, and more often living in various dependent living arrangements, such as with children or in institutions.

Migrants from abroad. —Another group of migrants who are changing environments in an even greater way, those who come from abroad, should be considered. Like the native born environmental exchangers, they are likely to take their second and third moves at a much earlier stage in health decline and are likely to skip the first move to retirement settings entirely. There are, however, some differences. A significant percent of the migrant, 24.5%, are Hispanic, come

TABLE 2   Characteristics of Migrants Age 60+ To and From Metropolitan and Nonmetropolitan Locations, 1975–80

Migrant Characteristics	Interstate Migrants		Intrastate Migrants	
	Metro to nonmetro	*Nonmetro to metro*	*Metro to nonmetro*	*Nonmetro to metro*
Total migrants	266,200	201,480	70,910	49,220
Mean age	68.5	70.7	68.9	71.1
% Age 75+	18.5	29.8	20.4	34.6
% Male	46.2	39.8	45.8	37.8
% Married	65.8	52.6	64.1	46.5
% Widowed	24.1	36.0	23.9	40.1
% With a disability	12.5	19.1	16.6	26.6
% Living independently	84.1	70.3	80.4	65.4
% Living with a child	6.6	16.4	5.8	13.1
% In institution	4.3	6.6	9.4	16.3
% Below poverty	10.9	10.3	10.4	13.9

from developing countries where they do not have easy access to advanced technologies such as personal telephones and where the less skilled nature of jobs permits family members to work closely together. As a result, they often come with kinship norms which stress the importance of kin living close together. For such people, migration to a new country without their parents is viewed as a temporary bow to economic necessity. The intention is to either bring their kin to the new country or to go back to them when they have accumulated enough money. Litwak (1985) found that the ethnic groups with the highest percentage who were foreign born in the New York City area and in Florida were from Latin America and the Caribbean. Ninety-eight percent of them are foreign-born, as contrasted with the next highest group, the East Europeans, of whom 56% were born abroad. Furthermore, the Latins and Caribbeans were also most likely to express traditional kin values, 27% as contrasted with the assimilated Americans, 5%.

As a result, more than any other group the immigrants from developing countries could be expected to place a far greater emphasis on living with their children. They should also be far less likely to use formal institutions as a place of residence due to physical disability. Some of these trends can be seen by comparing migrants from abroad with those from within the U.S. For instance, as shown in Table 3, older immigrants are slightly younger than those who migrate between states. They are more likely to be Hispanics. And they are slightly more likely to be widowed, although in New York and New Jersey they are less likely to be widowed. They are less likely to be disabled. They are, however, substantially more likely to be living with their children, despite their comparative youth and health. Finally, they tend to be poorer, with 18.3% on welfare as contrasted with 6.2% among other migrants.

SUMMARY AND DISCUSSION

It was hypothesized that there are three types of moves that a person might make after retirement: 1) an immediate post-retirement move, primarily for amenity reasons; 2) a move to be near a primary caretaker when the person becomes moderately disabled and can no longer manage without

TABLE 3   Characteristics of Migrants Age 60+ Moving from Other States and from Abroad, 1975–80

	United States		New York		New Jersey	
Migrant Characteristics	*Interstate*	*Abroad*	*Other States*	*Abroad*	*Other States*	*Abroad*
Total migrants	1,662,520	179,520	34,920	27,640	49,400	7,800
Mean age	69.6	68.3	72.2	69.0	70.7	60.9
% Age 75+	23.7	18.3	38.0	22.4	30.7	21.5
% Male	42.9	40.8	35.4	35.9	38.6	38.5
% Hispanic	2.1	24.5	3.6	27.1	3.3	35.9
% Married	59.3	55.0	37.7	47.9	50.2	54.8
% Widowed	28.9	32.9	46.3	36.8	36.1	35.4
% With a disability	15.1	11.8	21.7	17.2	18.0	11.8
% Living independently	77.9	47.8	58.9	44.4	68.7	42.0
% Living with a child	10.6	40.4	20.5	43.7	16.9	47.1
% In institution	5.6	3.0	10.8	3.3	5.6	2.0
% Below poverty	9.7	19.7	11.9	23.6	8.5	21.9

help; and 3) a final move to an institutional setting when the caretaker can no longer handle the burden. It was further argued that persons making the first kind of move tend to predominate in interstate migration streams from the North to the Sunbelt retirement region and from metropolitan to nonmetropolitan areas. It was also hypothesized that persons, making the second move tend to be more frequent among environmental changers moving from nonmetropolitan to metropolitan locations and from abroad. Finally, it was hypothesized that persons making the second and third move predominate in the streams of migrants from Sunbelt retirement states to the North.

The profiles of migrants in the five migration stream types do reflect the characteristics and living arrangements that were expected to be associated with the three types of moves. Migrants in the stream from New York to Florida and from metropolitan to nonmetropolitan areas were collectively less often widowed and disabled and by far most often living independently and least often living with their children. These streams, along with the one from abroad, also contained the fewest migrants who were very old.

The stream expected to contain the most persons making second and third stage moves, the one from the Sunbelt to the North, had the highest proportion of migrants who were very old, widowed, disabled, living in institutions, and having returned to their state of birth. This stream also contained the lowest proportion who were living independently, with one anomalous exception. Migrants from abroad tend to live with their children more and live independently less frequently than any of the migration comparison groups. This anomaly was anticipated in referencing ethnic kinship norms favoring shared residence by choice rather than by necessity. The proportion receiving welfare income is lowest in the

stream characterized as containing primarily migrants making their first move, as expected; it is similar in the other streams, except for the one containing migrants from abroad. The migrants in this stream are again anomalous, having the highest proportion of persons receiving welfare income of the five types of migration streams.

By taking a developmental perspective and separating basic post-retirement moves into three types, it is possible to order migrants in terms of the stage of mobility they represent and to account for their differential age, widowhood, and disability; or whether they live independently, with a child, or in an institution; or the extent to which they depend on welfare or whether they have returned to their state of birth.

Thus far in the analysis, the assumption has been made that older people have children. The overwhelming majority of older people in the U.S. do have children. For those who do not, however, the question arises, how does the lack of children affect migration? The evidence seems to be that those older people who are missing strong components of informal support groups, such as children, tend to die at an earlier age (Berkman & Breslow, 1983; Blazer, 1982; Schoenbach et al., 1983) or enter institutions at a much earlier stage of health decline (Litwak, 1985; Townsend, 1965). The former event need not cause any migration but the latter might. Thus people living in nonmetropolitan areas might find that they would have to move to metropolitan places to locate sheltered or assisted housing that contains the services that would allow them to continue living independently. No doubt many of the disabled elderly would prefer not to relocate if there were enhanced living environments available to them. In states such as Florida the market may not have caught up with the demand for such planned environments for the moderately disabled and this factor alone would encourage such persons to migrate elsewhere, perhaps to their state of birth and surely toward family caretakers, such as children.

Very broad generalizations have been made in this paper to explain the types of migration that are compared. All of these types of streams included some persons making first, second, and third moves. There are some persons in the stream from New York to Florida who are very old, widowed, disabled, living with children or in institutions, the very characteristics associated with second and third moves. Many of these persons may be following children to Florida after a decade or more of retirement in the state of New York. And there are persons in the streams from nonmetropolitan to metropolitan locations who have good retirement incomes and who in their youthful retirement years, like Chekov's three sisters, long for the excitement of city life. The characteristics of these first movers would perhaps resemble many in the New York to Florida stream. It is important to point this out because in the attempt to build a developmental context for migration in the later years, there was no conscious implication that the persons in the streams fit perfectly the pure form that was described. It was only argued that they collectively tend toward it.

Demographers have tended to use a model of migration that takes into account life course issues in explaining migration patterns. Migration is selective. Not all persons are equally likely to migrate. The ones who do migrate tend to be making decisions related to family or work that are most common at certain times in their lives. At the same time (at least in the past) demographers have tended to devalue migration of

the elderly and those who were interested in retirement migration seemed to be attracted to it only as an exotic topic. This is not difficult to understand since demographic research on migration has been focused almost entirely on labor force redistribution. The few researchers in the 1970s who considered the migration of the elderly important found themselves trying to adapt labor force concepts to a population that was, for the most part, outside the labor force (Barsby & Cox, 1975). The conceptual framework for migration needed expanding if it was to consider the mobility of persons beyond the age of full-time employment. Their frustration discouraged others from pursuing the subject until recently (Biggar, 1979, 1984; Soldo, 1981). Now gerontologists are moving forward in exploring the dimensions of migration among the elderly. It is argued in this paper that one important perspective to take in making sense out of the mobility patterns of the elderly is the same developmental perspective that has been implicit in demographic analysis. Among the elderly, however, the labor force is less important than retirement lifestyle, family ties, and health in motivating movement over long distances. There has been an earnest attempt to offer some explanation of why this is so.

A developmental model can predict, to a certain extent, migration patterns and differentials among the elderly. The collection of additional data not currently available, however, is necessary before the verification of this formulation is possible. Results are presented here to fellow researchers as a series of hypotheses with the hope they will collect new data to test them.

REFERENCES

Anderson, M. (1977). The impact on the family relationships of the elderly of changes since Victorian times in governmental income-maintenance provision. In E. Shanas & M. B. Sussman (Eds.). *Family, bureaucracy and the elderly.* Durham, NC: Duke University Press.

Barsby, S. I., & Cox, D. R. (1975). *Interstate migration of the elderly.* Lexington, MA: D. C. Heath.

Berkman, L. F., & Breslow, L. (1983). *Health and ways of living: The Alameda County studies.* New York: Oxford Press.

Biggar, J. C. (1979). *The sunning of America: Migration to the Sunbelt.* Population Bulletin, Vol. 34. Washington, DC: Population Reference Bureau.

Biggar, J. C. (1980). Who moved among the elderly, 1965–1970: A comparison of types of older movers. *Research on Aging, 2,* 73–91.

Biggar, J. C. (1984). *The graying of the Sunbelt.* Washington, DC, Population Reference Bureau, Fall, 1984.

Blazer, D. G. (1982). Social support and mortality in an elderly community population. *American Journal of Epidemiology, 11,* 684–694.

Cantor, M. H. (1979). Neighbors and friends: An overlooked resource in the informal support system. *Research on Aging, 1,* 434–463.

Cantor, M. H. (1983). Strain among caregivers: A study of experience in the United States. *The Gerontologist, 23,* 597–604.

Castro, L. J., & Rogers, A. (1983). What the age composition of migrants can tell us. *Population Bulletin of the United Nations, 1983,* No. 15.

Cuba, L. J. (1984). Reorientations of self: Residential identification in Anchorage, Alaska. In N. K. Denzin (Ed.), *Studies in symbolic interaction, Vol 5.* Greenwich: JAI Press.

Dobroff, R. (1976). *The case of the aged: A shared function.* Unpublished doctoral dissertation, Columbia University, New York.

Fellin, P., & Litwak, E. (1963). Neighborhood cohesion under conditions of mobility. *American Sociological Review, 28,* 364–376.

Flynn, C. B., Longino, C. F., Jr., Wiseman, R. F., & Biggar, J. C. (1985). The redistribution of America's older population: Major national migration patterns for three census decades. *The Gerontologist, 25,* 292–296.

Gober, P., & Zonn, L. E. (1983). Kin and elderly amenity migration. *The Gerontologist, 23,* 288–294.

Horowitz, A. (1985). Sons and daughters as caregivers to older parents: Differences in role performances and consequences. *The Gerontologist, 25,* 612–617.

Johnson, C. L. (1983). Dyadic family relations and social support. *The Gerontologist, 23,* 377–383.

Lee, E. (1966). A theory of migration. *Demography, 3,* 47–57.

Litwak, E. (1965). Extended kin relations in an industrial society. In E. Shanas & G. Streib (Eds.), *Social structure and the family generational relations.* Englewood Cliffs, NJ: Prentice Hall.

Litwak, E. (1985). *Helping the elderly: The complementary roles of informal networks and formal systems.* New York: The Guilford Press.

Litwak, E., & Szelenyi, I. (1969). Primary group structures and their functions: Kin, neighbors, and friends. *American Sociological Review, 34,* 465–481.

Long, L., & Bortlein, C. (1976). The geographic mobility of Americans: An international comparison. *Current Population Reports,* Special Studies, Series P-23, No. 64.

Longino, C. F., Jr. (1979). Going home: Aged return migration in the United States, 1965–1970. *Journal of Gerontology, 34,* 736–745.

Longino, C. F., Jr.(1984). Migration winners and losers. *American Demographics, 6,* 27–29, 45.

Longino, C. F., Jr.(1985, March). Returning from the Sunbelt: Myths and realities of migratory patterns among the elderly. *Returning from the Sunbelt: Proceedings of a symposium.* Brookdale Institute on Aging and Adult Human Development, Columbia University, New York.

Longino, C. F., Jr., Biggar, J. C., Flynn, C. B., & Wiseman, R. F. (1984). *The retirement migration project: A final report to the National Institute on Aging.* University of Miami, Coral Gables, Florida: Center for Social Research in Aging.

Longino, C. F., Jr., & Jackson, J. J. (1980). Migration and the aged: Special issue. *Research on Aging, 2,* 131–280.

Rogers, A., & Castro, L. J. (1981). Age patterns of migration: Cause-specific profiles. *IIASA Reports, 4,* 125–160.

Rogers, A., & Willekens, F. (Eds.). *Migration and settlement: A multiregional comparative study.* Dordrecht, Netherlands: Reidel.

Rowles, G. D. (1983). Between worlds: A relocation dilemma for the Appalachian elderly. *International Journal of Aging and Human Development, 17,* 301–314.

Schoenback, V. J., Kaplan, B. H., Kleinbaum, D. G., & Fredman, L. (1983, March). *Social ties and mortality.* Paper presented at the Annual Meeting of the American Public Health Association, Dallas, TX.

Schorr, A. (1960). *Filial responsibility in the modern American family.* (Social Security Administration), Washington, DC: U.S. Government Printing Office.

Serow, W. J. (1978). Return migration of the elderly in the U.S.A: 1955–1960 and 1965–1970. *Journal of Gerontology, 33,* 29–35.

Shanas, E. (1979). The family as a support system in old age. *The Gerontologist, 19,* 169–174.

Siegel, D. L. (1985). Homogeneous versus heterogeneous areas for the elderly. *Social Service Review, 59,* 217–238.

Soldo, B. J. (1980). *America's elderly in the 1980s.* Vol. 35. Washington, DC: Population Reference Bureau.

Soldo, B. J. (1981). The living arrangements of the elderly in the near future. In S. B. Kiesler et al. (Eds.), *Aging: Social change.* New York: Academic Press.

Sullivan, D. A. (1985). The ties that bind: Differentials between seasonal and permanent migrants to retirement communities. *Research on Aging, 7,* 235–249.

Sussman, M. B. (1977). Family, bureaucracy, and the elderly individual: An organizational linkage perspective. In E. Shanas & M.B. Sussman (Eds.), *Family, bureaucracy and the elderly.* Durham, NC: Duke University Press.

Townsend, P. (1965). The effects of family structure on the likelihood of admission in old age: The application of a general theory. In E. Shanas & G. Streib (Eds.), *Social structure and the family: Generational relations.* Englewood Cliffs, NJ: Prentice Hall.

Weeks, J. R. (1986). *Population,* Belmont, CA: Wadsworth Pub. Co.

Wiseman, R. F. (1980). Why older people move: Theoretical issues. *Research on Aging, 2,* 141–154.

Wiseman, R. F., & Roseman, C. C. (1979). A typology of elderly migration based on the decision-making process. *Economic Geography, 55,* 324–337.

Discussion Questions for Chapter Two

1. Given the population projections and the diversity within the older population expected in the future, what kinds of plans should we as a society and as individuals make for the future?

2. To what extent are the differences between old men and women due to aging and to what extent are they due to time-period or cohort effects? Do you think that the differences between old men and women will increase or decrease in the future?

3. Assess the impact on the communities of origin and destination of elderly migrants. In what ways does their impact depend on their developmental stage?

CHAPTER THREE

Historical and Cross-Cultural Perspectives

What are the implications of growing old in modern society? Modernization theory proposes that industrialization and urbanization have negative effects on the status of older people. In agrarian societies, the status of older people is high. Older people are the source of knowledge that is passed from generation to generation. Elders own land, which is the primary basis of wealth in an agricultural economy. Those of advanced age are also in important positions in two important institutions in pre-modern society: the church and the family.

According to modernization theory, the status of older people declines with modernization and industrialization in the following way (Cowgill, 1974). In the modern world, health technology has improved survivorship, and life expectancies have become longer than at any time in history. Birth rates also have reached historically low levels. These changes in vital rates (known as demographic transition) result in an increase in the proportion of the population that is old. Younger workers find themselves in competition for jobs with larger numbers of older workers. Competition is intensified by developments in economic technology, which increase productivity and consequently reduce the demand for workers. Moreover, modern societies are dynamic and constantly creating new ideas. Since education is focused on the young, youthful workers have an edge in the acquisition of knowledge and therefore gain an advantage in the competition for employment in newly created occupations. Retirement solves the problem of job allocation by removing older people from the workforce. Retirement, however, reduces older peoples' incomes and thus lowers their social status.

Modern societies also reward those who are geographically mobile for the purpose of employment. Since job opportunities are more plentiful in urban areas, young people are drawn to cities, leaving the old behind in small towns and rural areas. The old therefore become socially isolated from the mainstream of society. In the post-World War II era of the United States, development of the suburbs drew young families out of the central cities, again isolating elders and further deteriorating their social standing.

Despite its widespread appeal, a number of criticisms have been made of modernization theory. Critics have charged that the social status of the old actually declined before industrialization became widespread (Fischer, 1978; Achenbaum, 1978). Defenders respond that this does not really discredit modernization theory because modernization is more than just an increase in industrialization, urbanization, and bureaucratization. It is also an alteration in ways of thinking, and the same new ideas at the foundation of the social changes that take place in modernization also lead to the decline in social status of the old (Atchley, 1991).

Others dispute the claim that the social status of the old is greatly diminished with modernization (Laslett, 1976). Still others question the assertion that the old are isolated from children and other relatives (Shanas, 1979). Golant (1990), for example, has revealed that the older population is nearly as metropolitan and suburban as the general population.

This chapter presents three articles on the social status of the elderly in modern society. In "Roles for Aged Individuals in Post-Industrial Societies," Harold Cox uses the framework of modernization theory to speculate on the status of older people in post-industrial society. Cox believes that in the post-industrial period, the social status of older people will rise. Older people, he argues, will have expanded opportunities to participate in a wide variety of roles during retirement, and this will enhance their status in ways not possible in the industrial period.

As described above, the main causal agents in modernization theory are economic and technological development. The importance of cultural factors in affecting the social status of the old in modern society is examined in two selections included in this chapter. In "Aging, Meaning, and Well-Being: Musings of a Cultural Historian," Thomas R. Cole argues that the underlying cause of the elderly's low social status is the absence of meaning attached to old age in modern American society. In the past, meaning was attached to old age through the belief that old age was a spiritual journey. Rare but privileged survivors to old age were to be humble, thankful for a long life, and accepting of old age. Having renounced youth, they could serve their families, communities, and God through "praise, retirement, and devotion." Although older people faced the challenges of growing old, their lives held spiritual meaning.

Modernization eroded this traditional belief system but did not replace it with any alternative ideal of old age. Science and technology focus on solving the problems of aging, but they do not answer the fundamental question of its meaning. Without a viable ideal of old age, the elderly are left in an existential void.

Despite industrialization and modernization, it is widely believed that the Japanese have reserved a special status for the old. This has been traced to their cultural beliefs, particularly Confucianism and the emphasis it places on filial piety (respect for one's parents and ancestors). More recently, scholars have begun to re-examine this belief. Some researchers, such as Anne O. Freed ("How Japanese Families Cope with Fragile Elderly"), believe that the status, power, and respect for the old has declined in Japan. From this perspective, the high status attributed to the elderly in Japanese society may be largely a product of Americans' idealized image of the way old people are treated in Japan.

REFERENCES

Achenbaum, W. Andrew. (1978). *Old age in the new land.* Baltimore, MD: Johns Hopkins University Press.

Atchley, Robert C. (1991). *Social forces and aging* (6th ed.). Belmont, CA: Wadsworth Publishing Company.

Cowgill, Donald O. (1974). *Aging and modernization: A revision on theory.* In Jaber F. Gubrium (Ed.), *Late Life Communities and Environmental Policy.* Springfield, IL: Thomas.

Fischer, David H. (1978). *Growing old in America* (expanded ed.). New York: Oxford University Press.

Golant, Stephen M. (1990). The metropolitanization and suburbanization of the U.S. elderly population: 1970–1988. *The Gerontologist 30,* 80–85.

Laslett, Peter. (1976). "Societal development and aging." In Robert H. Binstock and Ethel Shanas (Eds.), *Handbook of aging and the social sciences.* New York: Van Nostrand Reinhold.

Shanas, Ethel. (1979). The family as a social support system in old age. *The Gerontologist 19,* 169–74.

Roles for Aged Individuals in Post-Industrial Societies

HAROLD G. COX

Historically we find a wide variety of patterns of treatment of the aged in different societies. Fischer traced the statements of Herodotus which indicated that at one extreme were the Issedones who gilded the heads of their aged parents and offered sacrifices before them [1]. They seemed to worship their oldest tribal members. At the opposite extreme were the Bactria who disposed of their old folk by feeding them to dogs. Similarly, the Sardinians hurled their elders from a high cliff and shouted with laughter when they fell on the rocks. In traditional China the old men were granted a privileged position. In politics and in family the aged men occupied the top positions of power in a hierarchical society that lasted for thousands of years. This was a value of the prevalent Confucian ideology. Thus we can find diverse patterns of how the aged were treated in different societies and in different historical eras.

An attempt will be made in this article to trace the changing status of aged individuals in different historical periods and to make some educated guesses about what roles aged persons will occupy in post-industrial society.

CRITICAL VARIABLES DETERMINING THE STATUS OF THE AGED

There are a number of variables, often interrelated, which either separately or in combination seem to relate to the status accorded older persons in various cultures. These include: family form, religion, knowledge base of the culture, harshness of the environment, the means of production, and the speed of social changes.

In the consideration of cultural type and status of the aged person, the general rule has been that in the nonindustrial, settled, agricultural societies aged individuals exercise considerable power and are granted a high status. In industrial societies, on the other hand, aged individuals exercise relatively little power and are granted less status. Cowgill and Holmes, in their work on aging and modernization, found an inverse relationship between the degree of modernization and the status accorded older persons [2]. In other words, the more industrialized the system became, the lower the status of the older person. While this is generally the case, a closer look reveals differential treatment of the elders even in the

Source: International Journal of Aging and Human Development 30(1), 55–62. Reprinted with permission from Baywood Publishing Company, Inc., Amityville, NY 11701, and the author. Copyright 1990

traditional societies. Sheehan, in a study of forty-seven traditional societies, found three different patterns of treatment of aged individuals [3]. Approximately one-fifth of the traditional societies were geographically unstable, as semipermanent bands of people periodically relocating their villages or, in some cases, perpetually mobile. The lowest esteem for seniors was often found in these small and nomadic societies. They have the fewest material resources for seniors to accumulate, thereby gaining respect in the eyes of the younger persons; they are usually located in harsh environments which favor youth and vigor. Food is often in short supply and individual existence is precarious. Elderly individuals may have to be sacrificed to insure the survival of the entire group. Among the societies studied, a plurality were comprised of various forms of tribes which were basically permanently settled, inhabiting fairly large villages, and governed according to a belief in their common ancestry or kinship. Another group of the traditional societies was comprised of small peasant communities whose economic base centered around agriculture or animal husbandry. The most highly developed social organizations were the ones with large landed peasantries; there, the highest esteem was enjoyed by older persons.

It appears that once traditional societies became located in a permanent place with stated residence and property rights, the old began to exercise considerable power over the young by the ownership of the property and the ability to pass it on to their children. Fisher pointed out that [1, p. 6]:

> Nearly to our time, the story goes, western society remained nonliterate in its culture, agrarian in its economy, extended in its family structure, and rural in its residence. The old were few in number, but their authority was very great. Within the extended family the aged monopolized power: within our agrarian economy they controlled the land. A traditional culture surrounded them with

an almost magical mystique of knowledge and authority.

Where property is the only means of production, by controlling property aged individuals are able to control younger generations. The future occupations and chances for success of the younger generation are tied to seeking the favor of their elders, who control all the resources. While one's parents are alive they are of critical importance because they provide employment and means of survival in the form of resources. After they die, the heirs inherit shares of their lands and control of these resources for themselves and their children. Therefore, in traditional societies that are permanently located, the individual is directly dependent upon his own senior generation for the acquisition of the means of production. The anticipated transfer of the property at the death of the parent provides the children with an incentive that encourages respect for their older family members. It is easy to see why the young defer to their elders and attempt to seek their special favor. Similarly, it is easy to understand how the old, by the development of stable institutions and the control of property, are able to maintain their power and privilege in the social system. This may also explain the higher value placed on the family in rural America where the transmission of land to the next generation may secure that generation a livelihood and a secure position in the social structure.

Thus, rather than Cowgill and Holmes's prediction of an inverse relationship between the degree of modernization and the status accorded older persons [2], we find a curvilinear one in which the old are accorded a low status in simple nomadic societies, a high status in settled agricultural communities, and a low status in modern industrial nations.

Sheehan equates what happens to older persons in the nomadic tribes to what happens to them in modern industrial societies [3]. Sheehan believes that with the development of modern technology, social and geographic mobility become goals and individual autonomy reemerges as a primary value. The young forfeit the security of the village or family to work in factories and offices. They attain financial and social separation from many traditional restraints. Lifestyles turn away from extended family ties. There is no special reason for younger family members to secure the favor of their parents and grandparents. The older family members lose their status, decision-making power, and the security they once had in earlier cultural settings. The result is that the old are considered much less valuable in modern contemporary states. In both the simple nomadic and modern industrial societies the old quickly become dependent on the young for their well-being and survival.

The form of the family is often related to the kind of culture and structural relations among institutions in a particular society. In traditional societies that are primarily agricultural in nature, the extended form of the family (most often comprised of mother, father, their sons and their wives and children) is the prevalent one. The extended family is most often patriarchical, which means that power and lineage are traced through the males of the family. The wife, upon marriage, moves in with the husband's family. When their children are old enough to marry, the parents arrange for their marriages; expect the wives of their sons to move into their household and their daughters to move into the households of their husbands. This family arrangement is one in which the oldest male member of the family exercises the greatest power, privilege, and authority. Individualism is discouraged. The individual is always subserviant to the demands of the group. The concept of romantic love (strong, intense emotional attachment between members of the opposite sex) is non-

existent. The criterion for the success of the marriage is the amount of family disruption caused by the entrance of the new bride. If she gets along well with her in-laws and does not cause difficulty it is considered a good marriage. The son's happiness is secondary to the good of the group. The extended family works best in stable cultures which are primarily agriculturally based. This culture is one in which the older members exercise the greatest power and maintain the highest status.

Industrialization leads to the breakup of the extended family. One no longer depends upon land as the principle means of production. New jobs, careers, resources, and opportunities become available. Modern industry requires mobile labor which can be moved from place to place as needed. Extended family ties are broken in order to move the labor force where it is most needed; if not, the industrial system itself would break down. The nuclear family—husband, wife, and children—is dominant. The influence of the father and mother over adult children is weakened. The size of the family declines as children become units of consumption rather than production and thereby become less desirable.

The difference between extended and nuclear families for the status of the aged persons can best be seen in Israel. Weihl observed that the older people among the migrants from the Orient are given a relatively high status in comparison to the relatively low status accorded older immigrants from the Western countries [4]. The migrants from the Orient evidence considerable commitment to the extended family concept in contrast with the commitment to nuclear family evidenced by migrants from the West.

The religions of the Far East have generally supported the extended family and higher status of elder members by the moral and ethical codes that they espouse. The Confucian concept is one in which the aged are to be given tender loving care. They are to be exempt from certain responsibilities when they reach old age. Pre-World War II families in China and Japan were ones in which children cared for their elders, and older family members exercised the most authority. This meant also that the elders were the most respected members of the family.

While Christianity clearly admonishes the individual to honor his father and mother, this religious principle has probably had less impact in the Western world than one might expect. The pressure of industrialization results in the educational functions being gradually removed from the family socialization process to formal training outside the home. The nature of wealth changes from land to tangible property. The emphasis shifts to productivity. The young are always seen as more productive and the old as less productive. Degradation generally occurs for the older, and supposedly slower, workers.

Another aspect of modern industrial society is the location of knowledge. In traditional agricultural societies, the old are the reservoirs of knowledge—of past problems and their solutions, of old customs and the appropriate religious rituals. In industrial societies, books, libraries, universities, and current research enterprises are a base for the generation and transmittal of knowledge. The freshly trained college student is often more valuable in the business and industrial world than the older and more experienced employee whose knowledge and expertise may have become obsolete. The inability to maintain control of critical knowledge in modern society has been another factor that has contributed to the general loss of status of older persons.

American society has a well-developed and sophisticated educational system which prepares young people to enter an occupation, but it is ill equipped to retrain older workers when new technologies require additional schooling.

The harshness of the environment in which the culture is found and the amount of physical labor required for survival are also factors that can reduce the usefulness and thereby the status of the older members of a culture.

Holmberg noted that among the Sirono of the Bolivian rain forest, it is the general belief that [5, pp. 224–225]:

> Actually the aged are quite a burden; they eat but are unable to hunt, fish or collect food; they sometimes hoard a young spouse, but are unable to beget children; they move at a snail's pace and hinder the mobility of the group. When a person becomes too ill or infirm to follow the fortunes of the band, he is abandoned to shift for himself.

Cowgill and Holmes noted that there is some difficulty in adjusting to reduced activity in old age when a society is so strongly dedicated to hard physical labor [2]. Kibbutz society in Israel is one example; there, older persons may arrive at an ambiguous status because of their inability to physically keep up with younger counterparts.

Related to the changing knowledge base in modern society is the speed with which social change occurs within the system. Cowgill and Holmes believe that rapid social change in modern societies tends to undermine the status of older persons [2]. Change renders many of the skills of older Americans obsolete. Not only can they no longer ply their trade, there is also no reason for them to teach it to others. In a rapidly changing society younger people are nearly always better educated and possess more knowledge of recent technology than their elders; thus, the latter lose their utility and the basis of their authority.

Referring to both the speed of social change in modern society and the location of the knowledge base in the system, Watson and Maxwell hypothesized that societies can be arranged along a continuum whose basis is the amount of useful information controlled by the aged individuals [6]. They believe the greater the elders are in control of critical information, the greater is their participation in community affairs. Their participation is, in turn, directly related to the degree of esteem in which they are held by other members of the community. Watson and Maxwell believe this control of information and consequent social participation declines with industrialization and its rapid sociocultural change [6, pp. 26–29].

Watson and Maxwell argued that one of the most fruitful models developed for the investigation of human societies has relied heavily on the information storage and exchange model and is described as systems theory [6]. Goffman has demonstrated that groups which share secret information will tend to be more integrated and unified than those which do not [7]. All stored information, according to Goffman, involve a stated arrangement of elements in the sense that they are a record of past events [7, p. 70].

In traditional societies, one of the main functions of old people is to remember legends, myths, ethical principles, and the appropriate relations that should be arranged with the supernatural, and they are frequently asked about these matters.

Elliott described this pattern among the Aleuts in northern Russia [8, pp. 170–171]:

> Before the advent of Russian priests, every village had one or two old men at least, who considered it their special business to educate the children, thereupon, in the morning or evening when all were home these aged teachers would seat themselves in the center of one of the largest village courts or oolagumuh; the young folks surrounded them and listened attentively to what they said.

Watson and Maxwell believe that the printing press was to end this kind of arrangement in the social system [6, p. 20]. In industrialized societies the information that is important is written down, printed, and sold in bookstores.

Some historians have argued that economically, politically, and socially older people are more conservative than younger people and tend to have a stabilizing effect on any social system. The young, being much more changeable in their view, offer adaptability and in some ways may increase the chances for survival in the social system.

One final factor which may in some way explain the declining status of aged individuals in modern industrial countries is the relative proportion of the entire population that they comprise. In most of the ancient and traditional societies they comprised less than 3 percent of the total population. It is easy to reserve a special status for a group of people that comprise a very small percent of the total. In modern society the old have come to comprise between 8 to 15 percent of the total population. Cox observed that it may become increasingly difficult to preserve privileged status for a group that comprises such a large percentage of a total population [9]. Cowgill's book, *Aging Around the World* indicates how rapidly the older age populations are now expanding in even the underdeveloped countries [10]. This is a phenomenon that neither the anthropologists nor the gerontologists had earlier anticipated.

ROLES FOR THE ELDERLY IN POST-INDUSTRIAL SOCIETY

While historically we find a curvilinear relationship with the old being accorded a low status in nomadic tribes, a high status in settled agricultural communities and a low status in modern industrial societies one wonders what roles and status older persons will be granted in post-industrial society. An educated guess would be that there will be a wider variety of roles to choose from and a slight upturn in the status of older persons in post-industrial society. Thus the pattern would be one of an S curve in which the status of the older adults improves following the low that was experienced by them during the industrial period.

Everett Hughes, Daniel Bell, and other social scientists have speculated on what life will be like in post-industrial society [11, 12]. The consensus of the social scientists seems to be that the post-industrial period will see a shift away from expansion in manufacturing and industry to the expansion of social services, entertainment, athletics, recreation and leisure enterprises. The basic argument of the scientists is that as the industrial development of a nation peaks and as an ever efficient manufacturing technology emerges, less of the population will be required to produce the nation's goods. This will make a surplus of manpower available which will ultimately be employed by the expanding service occupations, the entertainment industry, and industries catering to recreation and leisure activities. The post-industrial period will also bring reduced working hours, the advent of a four-day work week which will result in larger amounts of free time for the average citizen. For both the younger and the older members of the society this will mean greater opportunity for entertainment, athletic events, recreation, and leisure pursuits as well as opportunity for education and cultural enrichment. The Protestant ethic which admonished the person to be totally committed to the work role and view recreation and leisure roles as at best a waste of one's time and at worst as sinful will un-

doubtedly be altered. Recreation, leisure, education and a variety of other emerging roles will be seen as legitimate means of enriching the quality of one's life. They should do two things for the older members of society; first, it will provide a wide range of nonwork roles in which they may choose to participate; and second, these roles will be more highly valued and provide them with a higher status and more respected position in society.

Older persons upon retirement will be deciding whether or not to invest greater time and energy in family roles, recreation and leisure roles, volunteer roles, educational roles, political roles, or perhaps a second career. Post-industrial society will undoubtedly offer a wider range of roles for the elderly to choose whether they will or will not participate.

In all probability they will not have had this much freedom to choose among the different roles they wish to enter at any other time in their lives. Moreover, changing values in post-industrial society will include less emphasis on the importance of productivity and greater emphasis on the quality of life. Volunteer and leisure roles will be more highly valued, giving older persons who occupy them greater respect. In short it would seem that older persons will have a wide variety of roles to choose from in their retirement years and that these roles will bring them greater status than retirees have been accorded in the past.

REFERENCES

1. D. H. Fischer, *Growing Old in America,* Oxford University Press, New York, 1978.
2. D. O. Cowgill and L. D. Holmes, *Aging and Modernization,* Appleton Century Crofts, New York, 1972.
3. T. Sheehan, Senior Esteem as a Factor of Socioeconomic Complexity, *The Gerontologist, 16:5,* pp. 433–444, 1976.

4. H. Weihl, Aging in Israel, in *Aging in Contemporary Society,* E. Shanas (ed.), Sage Publications, Inc., Beverly Hills, California, pp. 107–117, 1970.
5. A. R. Holmberg, *Nomads of the Long Bow,* Natural History Press, Garden City, New York, pp. 224–225, 1969.
6. W. H. Watson and R. T. Maxwell, *Human Aging and Dying: A Study in Sociocultural Ger-*

ontology, St. Martin's Press, New York, pp. 2–32, 1977.

7. E. Goffman, *The Presentation of Self in Everyday Life*, Doubleday, Garden City, New York, 1959.

8. H. W. Elliott, *Our Arctic Province: Alaska and the Sea Islands*, Scribner's New York, pp. 170–171, 1887.

9. H. Cox, *Later Life: The Realities of Aging*, Prentice-Hall, Inc., Englewood Cliffs, New Jersey, 1988.

10. D. O. Cowgill, *Aging Around the World*, Wadsworth Publishing Company, Belmont, California, 1986.

11. E. Hughes, *Men and Their Work*, Free Press, New York, 1964.

12. D. Bell, *The Coming of Post Industrial Society*, Basic Books, New York, 1973.

Aging, Meaning, and Well-Being: Musings of a Cultural Historian

THOMAS R. COLE

In 1924, the American anthropologist Edward Sapir warned against the illusion "that because the technique brought by science is more perfect than anything the world has yet known, it necessarily follows that we are . . . attaining . . . a profounder harmony of life . . . a deeper and more satisfying culture." [1] Indeed, the scientific and technological progress permitting spectacular gains in longevity has been accompanied by widespread spiritual malaise [2, 3] and confusion over the meaning and purpose of human life [4]—particularly in old age.

But how does a culture meet the existential needs of its old people? Essentially, by drawing from its core values and beliefs. The importance of culture to mental health in later life has been emphasized by the psychologist David Gutmann. Drawing on cross-cultural research, Gutmann argues that traditional folk societies integrate the aged into their sacred belief systems. Graduating from control over production to control over ritual, the aged in many preliterate societies serve as "bridgeheads to the sacred." [5]

Although no guarantee in itself, this linkage of older people to the spiritual resources of a society is an important ingredient of psychological well-being. "As a coherent system of idealized rules," writes Gutmann, "culture provides the socialized individual with potent reasons for transforming personal egocentricity . . . in favor of extra-personal social bonds, collective ideals, and . . . purposes. But when culture is weakened . . . then the de-cultured individual loses the rationale for transforming egocentricity and narcissism into the idealizations that sustain the community, the social order, and ultimately, the self." Gutmann, then, essentially interprets much psychopathology among today's aged as an emblem of our culture's failure to provide vigorous meaning. "In a real sense," he writes, "psychosis in later life represents a hectic attempt to find the bases of self-esteem that are normally supplied to elders by a 'transformative' culture." [5]

Gutmann's work together with recent anthropological research [6–9], has clarified the ways that various cultures infuse aging with meaning. Historians, who have only begun to study aging, can make important contributions in this area. To date, we have focused attention on status and treatment of attitudes towards, and ideas about aging and old age. Old people in this recent historiogra-

Source: International Journal of Aging and Human Development 19(4), 329–336. Reprinted with permission from Baywood Publishing Company, Inc., Amityville, NY 11701, and the author. Copyright 1984.

phy, emerge essentially as recipients of society's benevolence, objects of its contempt, or as products of the historical forces of demography, social structure, and political economy. We are just beginning to recapture aging as lived experience, to "listen to" the stories of older people in past times, to discover patterns of meaning and action.

My own research attempts to reconstruct the meaning of growing old among the Northern middle class in America, prior to the social and symbolic crisis of aging that developed in the late nineteenth century [10–13]. By reconstructing American traditions which esteemed the end of life and by tracing the erosion of those traditions and the rise of a value system unable to provide redemption or reintegration in old age, I hope to shed historical light on the contemporary problem of aging and meaning.

Based on a systematic reading of roughly 1,000 Protestant sermons delivered by twenty representative ministers between 1800 and 1900, I have attempted to recapture Northern Protestantism's contribution to the meaning of old age. Nineteenth-century Protestantism's approach to aging and old age grew out of its view of life as a spiritual journey from this world to the next. The controlling metaphor of a pilgrimage, together with the belief in life after death, encouraged individuals of all ages to locate themselves along the route to eternity, and preserved a strong incentive to live with the flow of time rather than against it. The voyage of life did not end when an individual ceased to be socially or economically useful; instead, his or her remaining time on earth became increasingly important, allowing final preparation for the judgment of God [14, 15].

Within this framework of a spiritual voyage, Northern Protestant culture generated two paradigms of old age during the nineteenth century; I have called them the "late Calvinist" and the "civilized" models. Until the 1840's, northern ministers retained much of their Puritan heritage, which had surrounded the journey of the aged pilgrim with social conventions, rituals, beliefs, and symbols cherishing the end of life. The "late Calvinist" model required that each individual recognize and accept his own old age; it instructed believers to look to the Word of God for the duties and comforts appropriate to the last stage of life [16, 17]. Ministers stressed the biblically sanctioned responsibilities of old age: the aged were to spend "the residue of their days in praise, retirement, and devotion." Having fulfilled these responsibilities—and shown themselves to be appropriately grave, sober, vigilant, patient, and resigned (Titus 2:1–5)—the aged could look forward to death and enjoy (in ways twentieth-century Americans can scarcely comprehend) the knowledge that they were serving their families, their communities, and their God.

This model provided an integrated vision of aging and old age. While stressing the physical infirmities and social losses of old age, ministers promised redemption and social reintegration in compensation for renunciation. They preserved an older system of goals, norms, and sanctions for easing people out of powerful positions and socializing them to a culturally viable old age. By 1850, this system was unraveling. An expanding society, committed to ever greater quantities of health and wealth, found it increasingly difficult to acknowledge and redeem the inevitable losses of aging.

Whereas the Puritans had seen life as God's mysterious gift—granted and taken away at His absolute discretion—many nineteenth-century evangelicals came to view life as man's inalienable property, to be rationally invested and indefinitely perpetuated. This transition, together with the gradual decline of infant and childhood mortality, had important consequences for the meaning of aging and old age. Puritanism had always insisted that expectation of long life was unwise. Since survival to old age indicated that God spared a person from the common fate of early mortality, the "late Calvinist" considered old age a "monument of sovereign grace," and argued that gratitude, humility, and hope were the appropriate attitudes for old Christians completing their earthly pilgrimage. In contrast, once the middle-class ideal of self-willed longevity achieved widespread cultural sanction, gratitude, and humility became less appropriate; the sense of being fortunate gave way to the desire to remove the misfortunes and infirmities of age.

Within the Victorian culture that flourished in middle-class America roughly from 1850 to the 1920's, the model of "civilized" old age took shape. I have traced this model both in sermons and in the steadily increasing volume of aging manuals that appeared in the literary marketplace after 1850 [18–21]. Calvinists had warned their parishioners against flattering themselves with hopes of long life and urged them to prepare for death at every age of life. The Victorian ministers urged the reverse: to avoid thinking too much about death and prepare for a ripe old age [22]. Instructions for achieving a "civilized" old age fell into two basic categories:

1. the maintenance of health, character, usefulness, and activity as long as possible; and
2. the development of an inner spiritual and religious life to compensate for the physical and social depreciations of aging.

Writers generally preferred that older people follow the example of "Grandfather's Clock," which kept on ticking perfectly until "the old man died" at ninety. The enormous popularity of this song, which sold 800,000 copies when first published in 1876, testifies to this dimension of "civilized" old age.

With the growth of science and industry, pressures mounted to "master" old age rather than accept it, to eliminate rather than explore the final stage of life. The formula-

tion of intellectual, emotional, spiritual, and religious sources of compensation for the depreciations of aging proved increasingly difficult. Nevertheless, as late as 1920, ministers and writers often counseled people to accept inevitable decline and stressed the higher values of spiritual life, communion with God, and preparation for death. Some proponents of "civilized" old age preached a version of the old Puritan life review, recently resurrected in secular form by the psychiatrist Robert Butler [23].

Toward the end of the nineteenth century, academic writers began clamoring for research on old age—often in the naive view that science would "solve" the problems of aging. The growing cultural dominance of a scientific world-view generally strengthened popular hostility to all forms of decline or decay—especially old age and death. The slow erosion of religious tradition deprived many Americans of a rich source of value, consolation, inspiration in old age. Throughout the seventeenth, eighteenth, and nineteenth centuries, the vision of life as spiritual voyage, with its emphasis on introspection, on receiving experience as well as actively molding it, on reconciling past and future in the present, on yielding one's life up to its maker, had provided an inwardly viable sense of continuity and meaning in old age. During the twentieth century, the accelerating pace of scientific discovery and of capitalist productivity badly weakened this vision—and with it the incentives to grow old at all.

I do not mean to evoke nostalgia for a "golden age" that never existed. We have ample documentation that the lives of older people in the preindustrial West were often filled with economic insecurity, intergenerational family conflict, physical disease and pain, and emotional hardship [24–27]. Nor do I intend to vilify science and simply resurrect religious beliefs that lent meaning to the lives of earlier generations. Rather, I mean to emphasize that the thrust of the modern marketplace and the progress of science and technology, by continually eroding traditional belief systems, make issues of meaning ever more pressing.

In *Insight and Responsibility*, Erik Erikson emphasized that "vigorous meaning" at each stage of the life cycle—emotionally affirmed through sustained, creating intergenerational relationships—is an essential element in human vitality. On this score, the experience of modern American society is not encouraging. In the early nineteenth century, the revolt against patriarchal authority and the pressures of market competition slowly weakened the inner solidarity between generations [13, 26]. Later in the century the ascendancy of science and industrial capitalism began to force older men out of the labor force and eroded cultural traditions that previously esteemed the end of life [10, 11, 29]. "As we come to the last stage," writes Erikson in the same essay, "we become aware of the fact that our civilization does not really harbor a concept of the whole life. . . . As our world-image is a one-way street to never ending progress . . . our lives are to be a one-way street to success—and sudden oblivion." [28, p. 132]

Erikson was not the first modern observer to warn of an impoverishment of social meaning in old age. In 1922, G. Stanley Hall noted that modern progress both lengthened old age and drained it of substance [30, p. 403]. During the 1930's, Carl Jung reported that many persons found little meaning or purpose in the afternoon of life [31]. In 1949, A. L. Vischer wondered whether "there is any sense, any vital meaning in old age, in man's decline." [32, p. 23] Summarizing a large volume of research in 1974, Irving Rosow claimed that American culture provides old people with "no meaningful norms by which to live." [33, p. 148] And more recently, Leopold Rosenmayr has argued that the position of the elderly in

Western society "can only be reoriented and changed if viable ideals, 'existential paradigms,' become visible and receive some social support." [34]

This line of discussion rests on the view that the well-being and social integration of old people depends, among other things, on a culturally viable ideal of old age. Growing out of widely shared images and social values, an ideal old age (or an "existential paradigm" of aging) legitimizes norms and roles appropriate to the last stage of life, providing sanctions and incentives for growing old. Lacking such a cultural ideal, today's older people, once they have relinquished (or been forced to relinquish) central roles in the family and work force, confront an existential void. While many do live through their old age with personal vigor and integrity, many more suffer from segregation, desolation, and loss of self in a culture that does not value the end of life.

Today's "enlightened" view of aging [35], which encourages older people to remain healthy, active, independent, etc., has yet to confront this crucial issue and therefore harbors potentially pernicious effects. As Erikson has argued, human vitality requires a vision of the whole of life, in which each stage is infused with socially valued characteristics. The contemporary attack on negative stereotypes of old age does not achieve this. Aimed at liberating older people from images of passivity and debility, this attack frees (or subtly coerces) old people to retain the ideals of the middle-aged middle class. But what of the frail and poor aged who cannot or will not do so? Unless the attack on agism is amplified to address the existential challenges and tasks of physical decline [36] and the end of life, we will perpetuate a profound failure of meaning.

Our society must answer Robert Butler's question, *Why Survive?*, with more existential integrity and shared commitments than we have yet achieved [23]. "Sooner or later," wrote Edward Sapir in search of what he called a "genuine" culture, "we shall have to get down to the humble task of exploring the depths of our consciousness and dragging to light what sincere bits of reflected experience we can find. These bits will not always be beautiful, they will not always be pleasant, but they will be genuine. And then we can build." [1] Humanists assert that the meaning of life escapes the power of calculation and prediction; we must enrich public perspectives on aging by reaching into philosophy, art, religion, history. By recapturing older traditions and by rethinking contemporary values, perhaps we can help recreate and reaffirm old age as simultaneously the end and the fulfillment of life.

REFERENCES

1. E. Sapir, Culture, Genuine and Spurious, *The American Journal of Sociology, 29,* p. 412, 1924.
2. J. Lears, *No Place of Grace,* Pantheon, New York, 1981.
3. P. Rieff, *The Triumph of the Therapeutic,* Harper and Row, New York, 1966.
4. E. D. Klemke (ed.), *The Meaning of Life,* Oxford University Press, New York, 1981.
5. D. Gutmann, Observations on Culture and Mental Health in Later Life, in *Handbook of Mental Health and Aging,* J. E. Birren and R. B. Sloane (eds.), Prentice-Hall, Inc., Englewood Cliffs, New Jersey, pp. 429–447, 1981.
6. P. Amoss and S. Harrel (eds.), *Other Ways of Growing Old,* Stanford University Press, Stanford, California, 1981.
7. M. Clark and B. Anderson, *Culture and Aging,* Charles C. Thomas, Springfield, Illinois, 1967.
8. D. Holmes, *Other Cultures, Elder Years,* Burgess Publishing Co., Minneapolis, Minnesota, 1983.
9. J. Keith, *Old People as People,* Little, Brown, Boston, Massachusetts, 1982.
10. W. A. Achenbaum, *Old Age in the New Land,* Johns Hopkins University Press, Baltimore, Maryland, 1978.
11. W. Graebner, *A History of Retirement,* Yale University Press, New Haven, Connecticut, 1980.
12. C. Haber, *Beyond Sixty-Five,* Cambridge University Press, New York, 1983.
13. T. R. Cole, G. Stanley and the Prophecy of Senescence, *The Gerontologist,* (forthcoming, 1984).
14. A. Barnes, Life at Three-Score: A Sermon, Philadelphia, Pennsylvania, 1859.
15. A. Barnes, Life at Three-Score and Ten, Philadelphia, Pennsylvania, 1869.
16. N. Emmons, *Works,* J. Ide (ed.), Crocker and Brewster, Boston, Massachusetts, 1842.
17. J. Stanford, *The Aged Christians' Companion,* Stanford and Sword's, New York, 1855.
18. L. M. Child, *Looking Toward Sunset,* Ticknor and Fields, Boston, Massachusetts, 1866.
19. W. H. DePuy, *Three-Score Years and Beyond; or, Experiences of the Aged,* Carlton and Lanahan, New York, 1872.
20. J. S. Holme, *Light at Evening Tide,* Harper and Bros., New York, 1871.
21. L. Sigourney, *Past Meridian,* J. P. Jewett and Co., New York, 1854.
22. H. W. Beecher, Strength According to Days, *Forty-Eight Sermons, I,* R. D. Dickinson, London, pp. 15–16, 1870.
23. R. N. Butler, The Life Review: An Interpretation of Reminiscence in the Aged, Psychiatry, 26, pp. 65–76, 1983.
24. P. N. Stearns, *Old Age in European Society,* Holmes and Meir, New York, 1977.
25. P. N. Stearns (ed.), *Old Age in Pre-Industrial Society,* Holmes and Meier, New York, 1983.
26. D. H. Fischer, *Growing Old in America,* Oxford University Press, New York, pp. 232–269, expanded edition, 1978.
27. D. S. Smith, Old Age and the "Great Transformation": A New England Case Study, in *Aging and the Elderly,* S. F. Spicker, K. M. Woodward, and D. D. Van Tassel (eds.), Humanities Press, Atlantic Highlands, New Jersey, 1978.
28. E. Erikson, Human Strength and the Cycle of Generations, in *Insight and Responsibility,* Norton, New York, 1964.
29. G. J. Gruman, Cultural Origins of Present-Day "Age-ism": The Modernization of the Life Cycle, in *Aging and the Elderly,* S. F. Spicker, K. M. Woodward, and D. D. Van Tassel (eds.), Humanities Press, Atlantic Highlands, New Jersey, 1978.

30. G. S. Hall, *Senescence*, D. Appleton, New York, 1922.

31. C. G. Jung, The Stages of Life, in *Modern Man in Search of a Soul*, Harcourt, New York, 1933.

32. A. L. Vischer, *On Growing Old*, G. Onn (trans.), Houghton Mifflin Co., Boston, Massachusetts, 1967.

33. I. Rosow, *Socialization in Old Age*, University of California, Berkeley, California, 1974.

34. L. Rosenmayr, Achievements, Doubts, and Prospects of the Sociology of Aging, *Human Development*, 23, p. 60, 1980.

35. T. R. Cole, The "Enlightened" View of Aging: Victorian Morality in a New Key, *Hastings Center Report, 13*, pp. 34–40, 1983.

36. S. Gadow, Frailty and Strength: The Dialectic in Aging, *The Gerontologist, 23*, pp. 144–147, 1983.

BIBLIOGRAPHY

Barrett, W., *The Illusion of Technique*, Anchor Press, Garden City, New York, 1978.

Bianchi, E. C., *Aging as a Spiritual Journey*, Crossroads Press, New York, 1982.

Fries, J. F. and L. M. Crapo, *Vitality and Aging*, W. H. Freeman and Co., San Francisco, California, 1981.

Manton, K. G., Changing Concepts of Morbidity and Mortality in the Elderly Population, *Milbank Memorial Quarterly, 60*, pp. 183–244, 1982.

Nouwen, H. J. M. and W. J. Gaffney, *Aging*, Doubleday, New York, 1974.

Schneider, E. L. and J. A. Brody, Aging, Natural Death, and the Compression of Morbidity: Another View, *New England Journal of Medicine, 309*, pp. 854–855, 1983.

Spicker, S. F., K. M. Woodward, and D. D. Van Tassel (eds.), *Aging and the Elderly*, Humanities Press, Atlantic Highlands, New Jersey, 1978.

How Japanese Families Cope with Fragile Elderly

ANNE O. FREED

In Japan, tradition still dictates that elderly parents should be cared for by their oldest son and, more precisely, by the oldest son's wife, the daughter-in-law. Despite the facade of modernization, tradition gives way to change very slowly, even though the post World War II constitution eliminated the correlative right of the oldest son to inherit all the parent's wealth.

However, new patterns are appearing because of changes in society. Today, if the elderly parents cannot live with their oldest son, other children are expected to care for them. Interestingly, fewer elders are sharing the same residence with their children than in pre-War days. Now, only 69% are living with their children (Aging in Japan, 1984), a decrease of 17.5% between 1960 and 1980 (Shimizu, Hotori, Maeda, 1983). That trend is considered by many Japanese gerontologists to be an ominous signal of the need for more institutions and housing for elderly because in the past only never-married elders were likely to be living alone. More elderly couples are remaining in their own homes until widowhood or until they become so fragile or incapacitated that they have to move in with their adult child's family. A recent trend, for those who can afford it, is to live in a separate apartment in the same house or adjacent to the responsible child.

This study is concerned with fragile elders who are living either with or next door to their children. How caretakers are coping with failing elders was explored through interviews with them. Having experienced living as nuclear families and generally in very small homes, how do these caretakers and their families manage when a failing parent lives with them? Also, the fact that more married women are working than in the past produces added difficulties and complications. How are they managing with the fragile elder? What are the attitudes of the families and caretakers? These are the types of questions that have become pertinent.

TRENDS IN JAPAN

The Japanese are confronting Western family dilemmas very slowly while still tied to Eastern, Confucian mandates. Although the oldest son remains the family member expected by relatives and society to take responsibility for his parents, several trends indicate that a shift is slowly taking place. Daughters are being turned to more than past tradition demanded (11.8%), but even in these cases

Source: Journal of Gerontological Social Work 15(1/2), 39–54. Reprinted with permission from the Haworth Press, Binghamton, NY 13904. Copyright 1990.

there is generally a good reason why the oldest son and his wife do not assume responsibility.[1] Perhaps there is no natural son and the parents adopted the daughter's husband, or the parent has had a falling out with the son, or the daughter-in-law refuses adamantly to care for her parents-in-law. The oldest son might have moved to another area to which the parent does not want to move. In a few instances, the oldest son might have to care for his wife's parents, or someone in his family might be disabled. Further, housing in the large cities is so inadequate that, if a family caring for an elderly needs a bed instead of a futon (mat), extreme congestion results. The government reports that 900,000 women aged 65 and over live alone, "Many of them scraping by on meager pensions, doing menial work, dreaming of getting into shabby government nursing homes" (John Burgess, 1986). Times are changing in Japan.

Traditionally, the Japanese frown on nursing home care, regardless of how debilitated or ill the aged person is. Therefore, only 1.6% are in nursing homes, homes for aged, or moderate fee housing (Shimizu et al., 1983, p. 61). However, more of these facilities are desperately needed (Maeda, 1980) considering the fact at least 5% are estimated to be senile (Hasegawa, 1986). Elders in hospitals, as they often are because of the numerous ailments of old age, tend to stay longer than necessary, with family encouragement. Unlike in the United States, there are many ways to extend the duration of hospital stays and there are no caps on stays. Ironically, despite the higher costs of hospitalization, it is considered shameful to place a parent in a nursing home. Relatives become critical and society rejects it. Consequently, a caretaker suffers considerable guilt when placing an elder in a nursing home. It is considered a family obligation to care for the elder at home regardless of physical or mental deterioration or burdens, except when the elder is in the hospital. Therefore, the families encourage long hospitalizations.

Needless to say, the emotional cost of home care is high. This is always true for the caretaker. Moreover, the others in the family also suffer when an elderly parent at home becomes seriously ill, demented, incontinent, and bedridden for a long period. The family equilibrium is disturbed.

LITERATURE REVIEW

Recently, considerable research has appeared in American professional literature about the problems of families caring for fragile elderly parents and their coping patterns (Archibold, 1982; Brody and Lang, 1982; Zarit et al., 1980; Pratt et al., 1986; Brody, 1981; Cantor, 1983; Cicirelli, 1983; Crossman et al., 1981; Fengler and Goodrich, 1979; Reece et al., 1983; Shanas, 1979; Silverstone and Hyman, 1976; Brody, 1985; Campbell and Brody, 1985; Knight and Walker, 1987; Schmidt and Keyes, 1985). These and innumerable other studies stress the factors of isolation, heavy physical labor, financial drain, family disruptions, crises, intergenerational conflicts, caretaker burnout, families' search for resources and emotional assistance, respite needs, support groups, and the determination of many families to carry out the caring tasks. Some indicate that institutions can be a solution; home care is preferable but not the only answer. The literature suggests that the families and caretakers who cope best with these trying jobs show skill in problem solving, use reframing as a strategy, accept their responsibilities passively, seek spiritual support, have extended family and community supports, and reach out to groups of people with similar problems. Reframing means restating a stressful task to make it more acceptable, and passivity is interpreted as avoiding one's feelings about problems (Clara Pratt et al., 1986). Further, the literature emphasizes the changes in the homeostasis of the family when a sick elderly parent is in the home, the potential interpersonal conflicts, and the fact that the woman in the family bears the burden and feels the isolation most strongly. Resentment, guilt, and doubt, along with the determination to find solutions, are expressed by family members, particularly the caretaker.

Considerable Japanese literature is beginning to appear on the subject of care of fragile aged (Sodei, November 1987; Campbell and Brody, 1985; Furuse, 1987; Hasegawa, 1986; Maeda, 1983; Sodei, 1985/1986; Sodei, 1987; Utsumi et al., 1985; Maeda and Shimizu, 1984; Shimizu and Honma, 1978). Their findings were generally similar to those of the Americans, but also stressed the need to develop more community resources. The *Japan Times*, a widely-read English newspaper in Japan, ran articles in 1987 headlined, "Japanese Have Longest Average Life Expectancy" (July 10), "Aging Society Straining Welfare System" (August 10), "Cases of Senile Dementia Expected to Rise" (June 3), and "Senile Dementia, a Growing Problem" (August 27). The last article stated:

> Most people suffering from senile dementia are being looked after at home by relatives and the people caring for them are mostly women, especially wives, daughters-in-law, and daughters, the (government) panel found. Highlighting the urgent need to ease the burden of care of such women, the panel called for the construction of special wards to provide intensive treatment not available in mental hospitals.

The problems are before the general public and not just in professional literature and government surveys.

Professional literature findings indicate that the rise of the nuclear family has introduced the new attitude that the obligation to one's children takes precedence over responsibility to aging parents, which was stressed under the old family (i.e.) system. Women are working in larger numbers, many to help pay for their children's education rather than to support parents. That is characteristic of a

society of rising expectations. The patrilineal family is slowly dying. "People came to prefer self-realization to self-sacrifice" (Sodei, November 1987, p. 8). Attitudes toward living arrangements are changing; filial piety concepts are slowly evaporating; the increasing number of highly educated women resent the traditional expectations; and some women are refusing to stop working despite pressures from relatives or neighbors. Younger and more educated women are looking to social services outside the home to assist the family, and there is a growing rejection of the sex-role differentiation that has prevailed for centuries (Sodei, November 1987). Research, through government surveys, the Tokyo Metropolitan Institute on Gerontology, and private groups (Utsumi et al., 1985), is focusing on the families of demented elderly. There is agreement that "The statement of the care providers' feeling of burden seems to be the negative expression of subjective as well as objective situations in providing care" (Utsumi et al., p. 185). There appears to be agreement that many legislative and institutional changes must be made in the next decade to prepare for the fact that by 2020 one-fourth of the population will be aged and social services and institutional care must be expanded to satisfy the expected needs. Tradition alone will not care for the aged who cannot care for themselves.

While studies on coping are not related only to the aged, their observations and definitions are helpful in studying how families cope with the crisis of caring for a fragile elderly parent. Among the many studies are those by Coelho, Hamburg, and Adams (1974), and Busse and Pfeiffer (1969). Ego psychologists observed in their research that, because the activity of living presents change, stress, and crises during the life cycle, each person develops patterns in the process of growth to handle these trying periods. Lois Murphy (1962) defines coping as an attempt at mastery of a new situation that may threaten, frustrate, challenge, or gratify an individual. Personality, life experiences, ego strengths and weaknesses, upbringing, role expectations, culture, and the particular set of circumstances, all contribute to the kind of coping mechanisms individuals and families muster in crises. Caring for a frail, dependent, ill, possibly senile, likely bedridden elderly parent is a crisis! These circumstances introduce a radical change from the prior situation, a source of tension, and an emotional challenge that force the family, especially the caretaker, to alter their lives and find new ways to adapt and cope.

Coping must be viewed in an emotional context, particularly as we are considering the enormous tasks confronting caretakers, because it is a response to stress, frustration, and disequilibrium. Defense mechanisms become especially important because, if they are healthy and therefore adaptive, they keep anxiety under control and permit mobilization for action. Too much repression, too much denial, too much control, oversensitization, or over-reaction render the defenses maladaptive. That leads to absence of intellectualization, constriction of the ego, unreflectiveness, insufficient capacity for rationalization, and inadequate problem-solving efforts. Coping implies an active effort to reduce the feelings of anxiety and to seek solutions and mastery effectively (Coelho et al., 1974).

STUDY OF JAPANESE FAMILIES COPING WITH A FRAGILE ELDERLY PARENT

This writer spent four and a half months in Japan in late 1986 learning about Japanese customs and attitudes concerning the care of fragile elderly. Twenty families were interviewed, many on videotape, to learn their histories, their coping capacities, their defenses, and their attitudes toward the failing elder. Most of the families were located by the Tokyo Metropolitan Institute on Gerontology with a view to ensure a representative

group of families in Tokyo. They contacted ward welfare offices, day care centers, and senior centers that in turn introduced the writer to the families. A few of the families were contacted directly by the writer. The twenty families reported on the care of twenty-four family members. Of these, nineteen were or had been severely ill, depressed, bedridden, incontinent, or demented. In a few cases, the elderly person had died during the recent past. Some of the demented were ambulatory and required 24-hour surveillance because of wandering or self-destructive behavior. In only two cases did men take major responsibility, one a husband and the other an oldest son who shared the care of his dying mother with his wife. In two cases, a spouse assumed the caring role; in one case, the sick elderly woman employed a full-time housekeeper to care for her after the death of her husband. In the fifteen other cases, the daughter or daughter-in-law had the full burden of care.

The twenty families were from all socioeconomic groups. They lived in either their own homes or rented apartments. Most quarters were modest and small. Several of the apartments were minuscule, called "rabbit hutches" by the Japanese, and the bedridden parent's bed took up much of the preciously little available space. Three families lived in small quarters over a shop. However, several elders lived alone, but close to family members. None complained of poverty, and only one discussed financial problems. Eight of the twenty families took advantage of such community resources as home health aides, homemakers, visiting nurses, day care centers, community diaper services, bathing services, and "short stay" services, i.e., leaving the parent periodically for one week in a nursing home for a brief respite from providing care.[2] The government subsidizes "short stays."[3] In only one instance did the elderly person actually become a resident in a nursing home, and that was at her own request.

An interpreter accompanied the writer in all cases except four in which the family member spoke English. The Japanese interpreter was a gerontologic psychologist who spoke English well and, most importantly, understood the interviewing methods, goals and processes. She and the writer formed an excellent team acting as a single unit. She was not only sensitive to the family reactions, but also interpreted cultural phenomena to the writer. In most cases, the writer and the interpreter interviewed the family member in the home and saw the fragile elder. The elder participated in three cases. In several instances, the caretakers were interviewed in the welfare office because it was close to their work. In one case, the husband of the caretaker took time off from his business to participate and support her.

The interviews were unstructured. Interviewees were told the purpose of the research and were encouraged to discuss their situation in any way they wished. Needless to say, questions were asked to fill in gaps and encourage expression of attitudes and feelings. No questionnaire was administered. Those interviewed had agreed in advance to discuss their family circumstances and, therefore, were not withholding. They expressed negative as well as positive thoughts and feelings and offered spontaneous comments that indicated that they were speaking freely. Those who were visited in their homes were very hospitable; a few insisted upon serving luncheon.

FINDINGS

The words "duty, obligation, and responsibility" were uttered by every caretaker. All insisted that providing care to their elderly parent or in-law was part of the Japanese tradition. While they considered themselves bound by Confucian teachings, at the same time they described their struggles, concerns, and ambivalence in fulfilling their role as caretaker. A number expressed love and empathy for the elder being helped. A few felt sadness watching the deterioration of a once well-functioning person. Some felt trapped by their obligations. Several wept because of their guilt in refusing to give up a job to stay home to care for the elderly in-law in the face of criticism by relatives or neighbors. A number lamented the many years of sacrifice in giving care. Others were concerned about what lay ahead as the elder's condition would worsen. A few acknowledged that the elder had never been pleasant and that providing care was especially trying.

A number of the caretakers presented themselves as martyrs and were disappointed that they did not receive the hoped-for praise from relatives. Most were resigned and passive. Anger was admitted openly by some and frustration, by most. All recounted their great exertions and countless duties in performing unpleasant, demanding tasks, such as bathing or changing diapers. A few complained that "thank you" from the elder or relatives was rarely, if ever, heard. They felt that their efforts were taken for granted, if not by the elder then by the relatives. They saw their role as forced upon them in many instances, although several expressed satisfaction that they could be helpful. On the whole, the interviewees confirmed Plath's conclusion that, "Aging in Japan, as elsewhere, is a matter of deep human ambivalence" (1972). One woman commented that in Japan when a young woman receives a marriage proposal, she should ask about the suitor's earning potential, determine if he is good looking, and inquire if he is the oldest son. If he is the oldest, she should think twice before consenting to the marriage because she might end up being the caretaker of his parents. Most of those interviewed were the wives of the oldest son.

Clearly, the interviews revealed that, in the Tokyo area where they took place, many families were coping with very difficult, sometimes intolerable situations, generally a bedridden or demented parent, and had to seek ways to manage. The individualized examinations dramatized the impersonal findings in the literature. The price they were paying was high as they described their anguish. Those caretakers who appeared to have ailments that they were ignoring probably will have to be cared for after the demise of the elder. Several women admitted that their children avoided the sick elder. However, the writer was impressed with how sensitively one of the grandchildren, a young man of twenty, treated his demented grandmother. Complaints were voiced about critical, unsupportive relatives, feelings of isolation, spouses who were insufficiently helpful and available, physical exhaustion, nervousness, family quarrels, and societal pressures and criticisms. In contrast, a few expressed a determination to care for the impaired elder, as they voiced appreciation for the help and sympathy from a spouse, children, or sibling. In three cases, their martyr-like attitudes bordered on fanaticism. Finally, in one instance the daughter-in-law who could not help her mother-in-law care for her sickly father-in-law by having them move into her home expressed considerable guilt and anxiety. Because all the families interviewed were assisting the frail elder, there was no occasion to discuss guilt because of placement in an institution. Those who did consider nursing homes took no action, fearing relative's criticism. One daughter-in-law threatened her husband and his siblings that, if the mother-in-law's condition deteriorated, she would institutionalize her. She dislikes the older woman intensely. However, it is doubtful that she will carry out this threat because she does not take advantage of help that is offered at the present time. Many described prolonged hospital care to which they resorted to cope with the elder's ailments. Given their small quarters and their need for respite, this was not surprising. One daughter-in-law reported guilt because she and her husband

refused to return to her in-laws' home in another part of the country when the in-laws refused to move to Tokyo. Before World War II, it was expected that if the parents needed the oldest son, he readily would move back to their home.

Needless to say, the coping patterns among the families interviewed varied greatly, but most felt burdened by Japanese traditional demands. The most common coping mechanisms used were religion, martyrdom, passivity, reframing, community supports, a supportive husband, avoidance, a creative pursuit, and flight. The most commonly expressed feelings were frustration, guilt, anger, isolation, loneliness, depression, and being burdened, resignation, duty, obligation, and responsibility. Occasionally, love was manifested.

CASE STUDIES OF FAMILY COPING PATTERNS

Obligation and Anger

Mrs. M. never liked her mother-in-law, who rejected her because her husband selected her on his own. However, when mother-in-law could not care for herself, Mr. M., as the oldest son, was told by his siblings that it was his duty to take in his mother. Mrs. M. is in constant rage because she is expected to wait upon the older woman, who, when she is alone with her son, insists on waiting on him. "My wife has announced to my brothers and sister that, if my mother becomes bedridden, she will send her to a nursing home." Mr. M. feels helpless, angry, annoyed at his siblings, guilty, and ambivalent toward his wife.

Mr. U. was desperate:

My wife refuses outside help in caring for my old father. He is losing his mind, he has no bodily controls, and it is awful caring for him. But she says that my brothers and sisters will criticize her if she gets help. I want him in a nursing home. My children avoid him because he smells. My wife has become a nag.

Mr. U. reacts by coming home late every night, engaging in many activities outside the home, and avoiding his wife. His family life is disintegrating.

Mrs. H. wept as she expressed guilt because she did not stay home to care for her father-in-law. Both in-laws lived with her from the beginning of her marriage until the recent death of father-in-law. She has always worked because her widowed mother brought up five young children in poverty. She resolved never to be caught in such a position. Her husband was supportive and sympathetic. When her father-in-law became ill, withdrawn, and anorexic, he refused hospitalization, a homemaker, and the food she left him. Neighbors criticized her for not stopping work. Now, she feels guilty and responsible for his death.

Martyrdom

Mrs. N., age 60, cares for her dying husband at home. He is tube-fed and cannot speak or move himself. She is physically exhausted, but refuses help even from her adult children. "It is my duty," she declares. The hospital is willing to take him and the visiting nurse observes that she is certain that Mrs. N. will collapse when her husband dies.

Mr. P. proudly shows off his devotion to his bedridden mother, who has had multiple strokes. She is in a bed in the crowded living room. Once a week, a nurse visits and occasionally bath services are provided by the ward. He showed pictures of his mother's past bedsores and described how he boasts to his siblings about the care he gives their mother. He stressed that he is a wonderful, sacrificing son.

Religion

Mrs. W. found religion when confronted by the need to care for her bedridden, 89-year-old mother-in-law who was rejected by her eight children whom she antagonized when she lived with several of them successively upon widowhood. The hospital was pressing the family to take her home at the time Mrs. W. joined a new religion to get help with a hearing problem, which cleared up miraculously. Because the religion stressed care of parents, she insisted upon taking in her mother-in-law even though her husband, the oldest son, was unenthusiastic. Mrs. W. uses her religious meetings as a support and rationale for caring for the unappreciative old woman. She stated sadly, "If only my mother-in-law would once say 'thank you' to me."

Passivity

Mrs. K. despairingly described caring for a demented father-in-law, and upon his death, seeing her mother-in-law developing the same symptoms. She has been burdened for seven years. "I will never have a daughter-in-law care for me. I have three sons, but I will not burden them or their wives." While her husband and sons do help her with small tasks, she feels harassed and discouraged. She turns to friends for support and tries to plan short term relief. Although she sends mother-in-law to a day care center once a week, she refuses a second day because, being unrealistic, she sees no improvement. Thus, she does not take advantage of assistance even when offered it.

Community Supports

Mrs. M. feels burdened and overwhelmed caring for her 89-year-old severely depressed and seemingly senile father, a former physician. Once a week, she can go out when a volunteer provided by the welfare department comes to help. She and her very supportive husband take advantage frequently of the "short stay" provided by the nursing home. Sunday church services satisfy their need for reward for carrying out their duty. They do worry because father is a wanderer and threatens suicide. Mrs. M. wistfully states, "If only my five brothers and sisters would thank me for my sacrifices." Although she is the youngest child, she was expected to assume this responsibility because the others had equally serious obligations.

Mrs. N., the youngest daughter, cares for her mother suffering from Alzheimer's Disease. The family meeting designated her because she and her family could move into her mother's home. Instead, she built a house next door and took mother in with her family. She now sleeps in her mother's room to prevent her from wandering at night. The children and husband are particularly understanding and support her sending grandmother to a day care center three days a week and obtaining a homemaker one day a week.

Creative-Activity and Reframing

Mrs. A.'s parents always lived with her. As the only child, her parents adopted her husband, a common practice in Japan. Her father helped when her mother became seriously ill. When her father fell ill after the mother's death, Mrs. A. was completely tied to her home for several years. An active person, she could not bear only caring for an incontinent, senile, depressed, dying father. Therefore, she decided to learn very complex embroidery. She obtained a home helper one-half day a week, when she would rush to her teacher and then rush back home. Indeed, she mastered an art she is now using in a kimono business with her husband.

Mrs. K., in contrast, realized long before her mother-in-law became ill, that she could not stay home with her. Because her mother-in-law had a mean temper, upon marriage she and her husband agreed that they would start their own business and leave his mother at home. This worked well even after her mother-in-law's illness because Mrs. K. continued in the business and found home helpers.

> I could cope with this unpleasant woman because I kept my distance and ignored her temper. She was even jealous when my husband and I went to a movie without her. This went on for 32 years. I don't feel bitter. During her last year, she even showed me some appreciation.

Three wealthy sickly elders living alone called upon their children or relatives frequently, but insisted upon their independence. Mr. P., a successful lawyer, kept his three daughters on the alert as he pursued various interests in spite of a poor heart. The police checked on him every night. Mrs. N. wanted her independence after having had a domineering husband. "He never let me think for myself and I don't want my children to tell me what to do. Also, I don't like my daughters-in-law." She lives next door to a daughter. Her five children take her places and attend to her numerous ailments. She gets more attention this way. Finally, Mrs. T., a childless widow with several sisters living nearby, employs a full-time housekeeper.

> I worked all my married life with my husband. He drank too much. I'm lonely now, but I do what I want to do. My sisters and nephew help me. I have osteoporosis and can't move about easily. I listen to music, take samisen lessons, entertain my family, and go to my summer home.

All three leaned heavily on family members even when boasting of their independence.

DISCUSSION

The stories of only twenty families cannot present a complete picture of the problems of families caring for frail elders in Japan. But they do show that filial bonds are still strong. The majority are living with their families, and the caretakers are coping remarkably well considering the crowded housing and the deteriorated conditions of the elder. They are quick to express their unhappiness and frustrations. Fewer children want their elderly parents or in-laws to live with them. Some older people are reluctant to impose upon their children. Others fear that their children will not want this responsibility. More families are building adjacent quarters if they can afford to. Tobin (1987), in his study reported:

> Elderly Japanese worry about the present, while younger Japanese wonder when they grow old if their children will respect and care for them and if their society will be able and willing to provide them with adequate medical and social services. (p. 57)

He disagrees with Palmore's and Maeda's (1985) optimism that elders are highly respected, and sees Plath's (1972 and 1980) pessimistic view as more realistic when he points to changes in modern, industrial Japan that have reduced the status, power, and respect of the aged. This writer agrees with Tobin, Sodei, and Plath, but, nevertheless, finds that at the present time, families are helping their dependent elderly. However, the motives of the caretakers are not veneration of the elders, but instead necessity and cultural determinism. The trend in the future is likely to reflect further reduction of cultural dictates and increased government and community responsibility. The capacities of the families to meet the needs of an ever increasing aged population are already being sorely tried. This has happened especially in the rural areas, which many younger people have left, and is in process in urban areas.

> Starting from a traditionally very high culturally patterned status and respect for the elderly, under the pressure of modernization Japan gradually, but steadily, has become or is becoming more like the industrialized West in the way the elderly are viewed and treated. (Tobin, 1987, p. 55)

Furthermore, there is evidence that, even before World War II, the frail, the senile, and the incapacitated may not have received "unconditional support when they ceased to be an asset to the community and family" (Plath, 1978).

The interviews confirm these observations as demonstrated by the attitudes of caregivers toward their elderly parents, the more open admission of obeying traditional mandates reluctantly, the defenses upon rejection of obligations, and the doubts that they should burden their own children in the way they feel burdened themselves. Nevertheless, while apparently more aged are feeling abandoned (Burgess, 1986), the care of most is still seen as a family responsibility, and the women caretakers are meeting the challenge. Interestingly, in the United States, Brody (1985) insists that this is also the case, even though the parents and children are not necessarily living together and resort to institutional care in the most difficult circumstances. In Japan, more institutions are being built and planned for in the future. Unless they solve their extreme housing problems and the growing resistance of women to remain at home to care for a fragile elder, the Japanese will likely move closer to the American model, which combines home care, extensive community supports, day care, and institutional care, as they cope with old age in their country in the 21st century.

NOTES

1. Figures from the International Conference on Social Welfare, Keio Plaza Hotel, August 27 to September 5, 1986, Tokyo.

2. The ward offices in Tokyo have social service departments offering these services. They charge modest sliding-scale fees. Referrals to day centers

and nursing homes are made through the ward social workers.

3. Short stay charges are 1,000 yen ($7 at the 1986 exchange rate) per day, but even that fee may be reduced if the family cannot pay it.

BIBLIOGRAPHY

Aging in Japan, (1984), Policy Office for the Aged, Prime Minister's Secretariat, Japanese Government.

Archibald, P., (Winter 1982), "All-Consuming Activity: The Family as Caregivers," *Generations*, Vol. 7.

Brody, E., (January 1985), "Parent Care as a Normative Family Stress," *Gerontologist*, Vol 25.

Brody, E. and Lang, A., (Winter 1982), "They Can't Do It All: Aging Daughters with Aged Mothers," *Generations*, Vol. 7.

Burgess, J., (October 12, 1986), "Japan Faces 'Graying' Population," *Washington Post*, p. A21.

Busse, E. and Pfeiffer, E., (1989), *Behavior and Adaptation in Late Life*, Boston: Little Brown and Company.

Campbell, R. and Brody, E., (June 1985), "Women's Changing Role and Help to the Elderly: Attitudes of Women in the U.S. and Japan," *Gerontologist*, Vol. 25.

Cantor, M., (December 1983), "Strain Among Caregivers: A Study of Experience in the United States," *Gerontologist*, Vol. 23.

Cicirelli, V., (February 1983), "A Comparison of Helping Behavior to Elderly Parents of Adult Children with Intact and Disrupted Marriages," *Gerontologist*, Vol. 23.

Coelho, G., Hamburg, D., and Adams, J., (1974), *Coping and Adaptation*, New York: Basic Books.

Crossman, L., London, C., and Barry, C., (October 1981), "Older Women Caring for Disabled Spouses: A Model for Supportive Services," *Gerontologist*, Vol. 23.

Fenger, F. and Goodrich, N., (April 1979), "Wives of Elderly Disabled Men: The Hidden Patients," *Gerontologist*, Vol. 19.

Fueuse, T., (November 1987), "Elderly Policy in Japan," *U.S.-Japan Conference on Social Welfare*, Washington University, St. Louis, Unpublished Paper.

Hasegawa, K., (September 15–17, 1986), "Alzheimer's Disease and Related Disorders," *Report to the Fourth Japan-U.S. Conference on Aging*, Tokyo.

Japan Times. (June 3, July 10, August 10, and August 27, 1987), Articles on aging.

Knight, B. and Walker, D., (April 1985), "Toward a Definition of Alternatives to Institutionalization of the Frail Elderly," *Gerontologist*, Vol. 25.

Maeda, D., (1980), "Japan," in Palmore, E. (ed.), *International Handbook on Aging*, Westport, Conn.: Greenwood Press.

Maeda, D., (June 1983), "Family Care in Japan," *Gerontologist*, Vol. 23.

Maeda, D. and Shimizu, Y., (1984), "Factors Related to the Subjective Difficulties of Families Caring for the Impaired Elderly," *Social Gerontology*, No. 19.

Murphy, L., (1962), *The Widening World of Childhood: Paths Toward Mastery*, New York: Basic Books.

Palmore, E. and Maeda, D., (1985), *Honorable Elders Revisited*, Durham, N.C.: Duke University Press.

Philips, L., (1968), *Human Adaptation and Its Failures*, New York: Academic Press.

Plath, D., (1972), "Japan: The After Years," in Cowgill, D. and Holmes, L., (eds.), *Aging and Modernization*, New York. Appleton-Century-Croft Co.

Plath, D., (1980), *Long Engagements: Maturity in Modern Japan*, Palo Alto, Cal.: Stanford University Press.

Plath, D., (1978), "Old Age and Retirement," in *Encyclopedia of Japan*, Tokyo and New York: Kodansha Press.

Pratt, C., Schmall, V., and Wright, S., (February 1986), "Family Caregivers and Dementia," *Social Casework*, Vol. 67.

Reece, D., Waltz, T., and Hageboeck, H., (Spring 1983), "Integenerational Care Providers of Non-Institutional Frail Elderly: Characteristics and Consequences," *Journal of Gerontological Social Work*, Vol. 5.

Schmidt, G. and Keyes, B., (April 1985), "Group Psychotherapy with Family Caregivers of Demented Patients," *Gerontologist*, Vol. 25.

Shanas, E., (April 1974), "The Family as a Social Support System in Old Age," *Gerontologist*, Vol. 19.

Shimizu, Y. and Honma, M., (1978), "Problems in the Familial Domestic Care of the Impaired Elderly and Their Relationship to Family Type," *Social Gerontology*, No. 8.

Shimizu, Y., Hotori, W., Horikawa, K., and Maeda D., (1983), "Residential Care for Elderly in Japan," in McDerment, L. and Greengross, S., (eds.), *Social Care for Elderly People: An International Perspective*, Tokyo: S.C.A. Publication.

Siverstone, B. and Hyman, H., (1982), *You and your Aging Parent*, New York: Pantheon Books.

Sodei, T., (January 10, 1986), "Older Women in Japan," Paper Delivered in a Meeting on Woman in Midlife and Beyond: Perspectives from Abroad, Hosted by Women's Initiative of the American Association of Retired Persons, Washington, D.C.

Sodei, T., (Winter 1985/1986), "Japanese Women Feel Burden of Caring for Relatives with Dementia," *Network News*, Vol. 1.

Sodei, T., (1987), "The Effect of Industrialization on Filial Responsibility Toward Aging Parents: A Comparative Study Based on the Survey in Tokyo, Seoul, and Taipei," Unpublished Paper.

Sodei, T., (November 1987), "Family Care for Frail Elders in Japan," *U.S.-Japanese Conference on Social Welfare*, Washington University, St. Louis, Unpublished Paper.

Tobin, J., (February 1987), "The American Idealization of Old Age in Japan," *Gerontologist*, Vol. 27.

Utsumi, K., Nakajima, K., Nagata, K., and Miyake, Y., (1985), "On Home Care Problems of the Families with the Demented Elderly," Reprint, Publication Unknown.

Zarit, S., (December 1980), "Relatives of the Impaired Elderly: Correlates of Feelings of Burden," *Gerontologist*, Vol 20.

Discussion Questions for Chapter Three

1. Evaluate the evidence supporting Cox's statements about the status of the elderly in post-modern society. Given the slow increases in productivity of the American workforce in the recent past, how likely is it that American society will be able to afford reduced working hours, increased free time, and large numbers of people participating in a variety of roles that are not compensated monetarily?

2. Cole maintains that industrialization and modernization have eroded the traditional belief system that gave meaning to old age. Is it possible for a new sense of meaning to be attached to old age? What are some avenues to bring this about?

3. Freed agrees with the more pessimistic view that the status, power, and respect of the aged have declined in modern Japan. However, the respondents in her study were caregivers for the very fragile elderly. How generalizable are Freed's findings of ambivalence toward caring for the very fragile elderly to the question of the social status of the old? Is it possible that such heavy caregiving responsibilities are too demanding to be performed in the family setting regardless of the family's values and beliefs?

CHAPTER FOUR

Physical Aging in Social Context

Aging is often thought of as a process of inevitable decline. Some have even viewed aging as a disease in itself. This is apparent in expressions such as "a person died from old age." Gerontologists have discovered that a great many misperceptions exist in this respect. Although it is true that aging brings with it an increased vulnerability to disease, a slowing in many physical functions, and a decrease in sensory perceptions, researchers have revealed that a tremendous amount of variation exists in the rate of physical decline from one individual to another and that all physiological systems and physical capabilities, even within a single individual, do not decline at the same rate. Moreover, even at the most advanced ages, "ill-health is not a universal feature of later life" (Victor, 1989). In "An Overview of Physical Ability with Age: The Potential for Health in Later Life," which is included in this chapter, Janna Herman describes the expectations for health and physical activity in the third quarter of life (age 50 to 75). Herman then draws out the implications of research findings on this subject for the feasibility of establishing a senior scholars' institute.

Although the people of the United States and other modern nations are living longer lives than in the past, it does not necessarily follow that they are living healthier lives as well. Morbidity refers to the presence of disease or ill health, whereas mortality refers to death. The notion of the compression of morbidity holds that due to advances in modern medicine and health consciousness, individuals will experience shorter periods of time in poor health before death. Morbidity is thus compressed. As shown by Meredith Minkler in "Aging and Disability: Behind and Beyond the Stereotypes" (see Chapter 1), the compression of morbidity hypothesis has been challenged by those contending that although Americans are living longer lives, there is little evidence of large improvements in health. Many of the years added to our lives have brought with them disability and illness. This point is made in the article, "Older Americans' Health," by Metropolitan Life. Based largely on a report by the National Center for Health Statistics, this article provides a profile of the health conditions of older people in the United States. It also reveals variation in health according to race. The existence of such variation reinforces the notion that declining health is not simply a biological inevitability or even a necessary part of being old, but is related to social conditions (Victor, 1989).

Karen A. Lyman takes the importance of social environment to health a step farther. In "Bringing the Social Back in: A Critique of the Biomedicalization of Dementia," Lyman argues that the biomedical model of senile dementia ignores social factors. Alzheimer's disease is one of the most dreaded illnesses of the late 20th century. It robs its victims of memory, intellectual functioning, and even their personalities until death. It is increasingly recognized that "senility" is not an inevitable part of aging, but it is also known that the risk of Alzheimer's (the most common dementing disease) increases with age. Alzheimer's, however, can only be diagnosed with certainty after death. Since the behavioral patterns manifested by Alzheimer's patients are similar to those found in other afflictions such as depression, there is the possibility of misdiagnosis and the creation of a self-fulfilling prophesy. Persons who think they are demented, for example, may become depressed and consequently more forgetful, inattentive, and anxious. Moreover, as Lyman points out, the same kinds of deformities in the brain that are believed to cause Alzheimer's have been found, through autopsies, in the brains of people who did not manifest the behavioral symptoms of the disease. These findings suggest that other factors, in addition to the biological, play a role in the diagnosis and course of the disease. Since most people, including researchers, accept the biomedical model, Lyman calls for increased attention to social factors in the diagnosis and treatment of dementia.

REFERENCE

Victor, Christina R. (1989). Inequalities in health in later life. *Age and Ageing 18*, 387–391.

An Overview of Physical Ability with Age: The Potential for Health in Later Life

JANNA B. HERMAN

An aging population seems to be a global tendency. In 1975, there were approximately 350 million people over the age of 60 in the world. By 2050, there will be 1.121 billion elderly in the world (Hsun, 1986). Due to technological and other medical advances, one of the implications of an aging society is that one's available productive years will also increase.

The aging of society has an impact not only on the population at large, but also on the age of faculty in institutions of higher education. In the United States, the median age of faculty in institutions of higher education was 38 years in 1968–69 and 45 in 1978–79 (George & Winfield-Laird, 1984) and it is expected to continue to rise through the year 2000. In 1990, 35% of faculty are estimated to be over 55 years of age, and by the end of this century, half will be over age 55 (Claxton & Murrell, 1984).

The question remains whether health would be a deterrent in establishing an institute for senior scholars. The purpose of this article is to examine the expectations for health and physical activity in the third quarter of life (i.e., age 50 to 75 years). This enterprise will have two major foci. First, the author will review the health status of the elderly. The second major focus of the paper will be the topic of exercise and aging.

HEALTH

Health is measured in a number of different ways. These include: mortality-based indicators (i.e., life tables), incidences of disease (acute or chronic conditions), restrictions of activities, limitations of activities of daily living, respondent-assessed health status, and number of physician contacts.

Infant mortality rates, life expectancy, and death rates have historically been used as an indirect means to assess the health of the population. The United Nations defines an aging population as one in which (1) 10% of the population are 60 years or older, or (2) 7% of the population are 65 years or older (Shan, 1987). The countries with aging populations are the more developed ones. In 1984, 44 of the 49 countries considered to have aging populations were economically developed countries (Wen-jo, 1985).

In the United States, the aging of the baby boom generation significantly affects

Source: Gerontology & Geriatrics Education 1(1/2), 11–25. Reprinted with permission from Haworth Press, Binghamton, NY 13904. Copyright 1990.

the age structure of the population. Considerable increases in the older population will begin in 20 years, reflecting the baby boom that began in 1946 and lasted through the early 1960s. There are approximately 48.9 million people 55 years and older (20% of the population) in the United States today. By the year 2010, 74.1 million people will be over age 55 (estimated to be 25% of the population), and by 2050, 104.3 million people will be in this older age group (33%) (McConnell, 1984).

Incidence of disease is the most common direct measure of health. Often, acute diseases are reported separately from chronic diseases. An acute condition is defined as a type of illness or injury that ordinarily lasts less than 3 months and is (1) serious enough to contact a physician regarding the illness or injury and (2) serious enough to cause the person to restrict normal activity for at least half a day. Chronic conditions are defined as lasting three months or longer or belonging to a certain set of medical conditions (i.e., heart disease, diabetes, etc.). Older people, age 65 years and over, are more susceptible to illness, acute or chronic, as compared to middle-aged persons, 45 to 64 years. In fact, chronic conditions represent the number one health care problem of the older population. Older people who do become ill are likely to have a mixture of both acute and chronic illnesses and disabilities, in contrast to younger adults, who usually have only single acute illnesses (National Center for Health Statistics [NCHS], 1988).

The three most prevalent chronic conditions in people over the age of 65 years are: arthritis (48%), hearing impairments (30%), and hypertension (13%) (NCHS, 1988). Women tend to have higher rates of arthritis and hypertension, and lower rates of hearing disorders as compared to men in this age group. The prevalence of heart conditions is similar in both sexes (NCHS, 1985).

Disability refers to the restriction of a person's activity because of impairment or illness (i.e., days lost from work, days spent in bed, and days in which a person cuts down on the things he or she usually does). In 1976, the NCHS found that chronic conditions (including heart disease, cancer, stroke, diabetes, arthritis, and emphysema) in persons age 65 years or older accounted for 81% of their days of restricted activity (White House Conference on Aging, 1981).

Disability can be categorized as either short-term or long-term. Short-term disability is often measured by the number of days during which a person's usual activity is restricted because of injury or illness. Thus, short-term disabilities are interruptions in a person's day-to-day life. Long-term disabilities involve permanent alterations in a person's day-to-day life. For all persons over age 65, 74% reported some chronic limitation of activity (NCHS, 1988), although this did not necessarily result in serious dysfunction.

Indicators measuring activities of daily living (such as independence in eating, dressing, or bathing) or functional capacity (such as ability to stand for long periods of time, or ability to lift 10 pounds) have been developed to provide a more objective, stable reference for evaluating long-term disability. In 1984, the NCHS reported that 23% (6 million) of noninstitutionalized Americans 65 years and over were functionally limited in performing personal care activities (bathing, dressing, eating, transferring, walking, getting outside, and using the toilet) (NCHS, 1986). The elderly were likely to have the most difficulty with walking as compared with any other personal care activity (19%). Ten percent of persons age 65 or older reported difficulty with bathing and difficulty getting outside, 2.5 million persons, or 10% of all noninstitutionalized Americans 65 years or older, are functionally limited to the degree that they receive help with a personal care activity. Those over the age of 85 years have the greatest difficulty with activities of daily living. It would appear then that age and health are intimately linked at 85 years of age.

Functional limitations may be measured by the proportion of persons who experience any difficulty in performing home management activities (e.g., preparing meals, shopping, managing money, using the telephone, doing heavy housework, doing light housework). About 27% (7 million) of noninstitutionalized Americans 65 years and over were functionally limited in that they had difficulty with at least one home management activity (NCHS, 1986). About 24% of those age 65 years or older reported difficulty performing heavy housework. About 11% reported difficulty with shopping. The proportion of those who had difficulty doing heavy housework was more than twice that of anyone having difficulty with any of the other home management activities. The overall prevalence of functional limitation would have been significantly reduced if difficulty with heavy housework had been eliminated as a functional activity. Approximately 22% (5.9 million persons) received help with a home management activity. Regardless of which functional limitation was experienced, its prevalence increased with age.

In 1984, the NCHS provided information on 10 work-related activities in people ages 55 to 74 who had worked at some time since they were age 45 (Kovar & LaCroix, 1987). The work-related activity which caused the most difficulty was stooping, crouching, or kneeling. The next work-related activities in descending order of difficulty were: lifting or carrying 25 pounds (23%), standing on their feet for 2 hours (22%), walking one-quarter of a mile (18%), and walking up 10 steps without resting (15%).

The proportion of people with any difficulty and the proportion unable to perform several of the activities assessed increased with age in the group of people who had worked since they were 45. Difficulty with five of the tasks were found to have almost doubled in the older group when comparing the groups of people ages 55 to 59 and 70 to 74. These five activities were: walking one-quarter of a mile; walking up 10 steps; standing on feet for two hours; stooping, crouching, or kneeling; and lifting or carrying 10 or 25 pounds. For example, 15% of the people 55 to 59 years of age had difficulty standing on their feet for two hours, compared with 30% of those ages 70 to 74 years.

Most (58%) of the people ages 55 to 74 years who had worked during some time since their 45th birthday had no difficulty with any of the 10 work-related activities. Eighty-six percent of those who retired because of health reasons had difficulty, followed by 40% who had retired for reasons other than health, and only 27% of those who were still working. Therefore, the majority of those who were retired for reasons other than health were not impaired. Very few of these potential workers wanted to be employed, although they said that they could work if a job were available. The majority of those who had retired because of their health had at least one limitation and said that they could not work. Public Law 99-592 was approved by the U.S. Congress in October 1986 and it effectively extinguished forced retirement at age 70. However, whether the recent changes in retirement laws will actually change the age at which people retire remains to be seen. According to the Teachers Insurance Annuity Association, the average age at which faculty members begin collecting their pensions (a possible indicator of retirement date) has been declining over the past 10 years.

Respondent-assessed health status results from simply asking respondents to assess their own health as excellent, very good, good, fair, or poor. In 1987, most people assessed their health as being "excellent" (39.3%) or "very good" (27.9%) (NCHS, 1988).

Utilization of medical care is another measurement area included in most comprehensive discussions of health status. Despite the increased prevalence of chronic conditions and restricted activity, the elderly do not make heavy demands for physicians' services. On average they make only one more physician visit a year than do other segments of the population. Use of hospitals goes up with age, but dental care actually decreases (White House Conference on Aging, 1981).

PHYSIOLOGY OF AGING AND EXERCISE

Gerontologists have difficulty in distinguishing between pathological changes due to the cumulative effects of trauma from the environment as one ages and true biological aging processes which are characterized by structural and functional changes. Human aging as a total process begins at conception, accelerates and becomes most noticeable in late middle age when the outward signs of aging are apparent such as graying hair, wrinkling skin, and diminishing muscle strength (McDonald, 1988).

As one ages there are decrements in physiological function. There are two principles to keep in mind when speaking of aging in the human body: (1) in any one person, all organs do not age at the same rate, and (2) any one organ does not necessarily age at the same rate in different people. All systems involved in the physiological functioning of the body appear to be affected to some extent by the aging process. These systems include the sensory, cardiopulmonary, musculoskeletal, metabolic, and neurologic systems.

Sensory Systems

There is a decrease in efficient function in all the senses with age. Hearing and vision diminish with age. The threshold for hearing declines with age, with 8% of the elderly reporting use of a hearing aid (Havlik, 1986). The ability to hear high-pitched-sounds and to understand speech may also decrease (Kimmel, 1974). Visual accommodation (ability of the eye lens to focus on objects close by), adaptation to darkness, and visual acuity (ability to see clearly at a distance) all diminish with age. About 95% of persons 65 and over wear eyeglasses to adjust for failing eyesight (Havlik, 1986). Sense of pain, smell, and taste all diminish with age as well, but they do not have a significant effect on capacities (Riley & Foner, 1968; Schiffman, Moss, & Erikson, 1976; Thornbury & Mistretta, 1981).

Cardiopulmonary System

Many aspects of the cardiopulmonary system's functioning decline with age. A substantial change occurs in the circulation system. With age, the heart and blood vessels become less elastic. There is a significant reduction in the ability of the veins to expand during periods of increased blood flow or volume. The elderly suffer increased risk of hypertension and stroke with the loss of elasticity in the veins and arteries (Kohn, 1977). Systolic and diastolic blood pressure rise with age, thereby putting a greater strain on the heart and circulatory system (Siconolfi, Lasater, McKinlay, Boggia, & Carleton, 1985). Maximal oxygen consumption (VO_{2max}) is the best single indicator of physical working capacity. VO_2 is defined by the Fick formula as: $VO_2 = (HR \times SV = \dot{Q}) \times (a - \bar{v})0_2$, where HR is heart rate, SV is stroke volume, $\dot{Q}$ is cardiac output and $(a - \bar{v})O_2$ is the arterial oxygen content minus the mixed venous oxygen content (Astrand & Rodahl, 1977). Cross-sectional studies indicate that VO_{2max} declines at a rate of 1% per year after the mid-twenties (Heath, Hagberg, Ehsani, & Holloszy, 1981). Longitudinal studies indicate that VO_{2max} declines at an even greater rate (Dehn & Bruce, 1972). There is little alteration in the resting heart rate with age (Shephard, 1978), but the maximal attainable heart rate with exertion declines with age (Sidney & Shephard, 1977). Resting stroke volume falls about 30% from ages 25 to 85 (Brandfonbrener, Landowne, & Shock, 1955). After the age of 50, cardiac output declines by 1% each year (Anderson, 1978). Relatively little is known about the maximum $(a - v)O_2$ difference in the elderly, but there is some evidence that it decreases with age (Grimby, Nilsson, & Saltin, 1966). Therefore, from the above statements it is evident that the decline in maximal oxygen consumption is due to a decline in central adjustments, i.e., maximal heart rate, stroke volume, and cardiac output, as well as a decline in peripheral adjustments, i.e., arteriovenous oxygen difference.

Some characteristics of pulmonary function decline in the elderly. Vital capacity declines with age, and the residual volume increases (Milne & Williamson, 1972). Lung compliance may increase with age, thereby increasing the energy required to sustain any given level of ventilation (deVries & Adams, 1972).

The older person is not able to reach the same maximal ventilation rate as the younger individual due to the stiffening of the thorax and decreased strength of the respiratory muscles (Rizzato & Marazzini, 1970). This is particularly detrimental to the physical work capacity of older adults when they are placed under conditions of increasing workloads (deVries & Adams, 1972).

There is substantial evidence that regular aerobic exercise can bring about positive changes in many aspects of cardiovascular and circulatory function in the older adult. Changes of cardiorespiratory function include an increase in total blood volume and total hemoglobin (Suominen, Heikkinen, Liesen, Michel, & Hollmann, 1977). There are reports of significant decrements in resting systolic blood pressure after physical training (Stamford, 1972).

Regular vigorous exercise can retard the approximate 9% per decade decline in VO_{2max} to only a 5% decrease per decade (Heath et al., 1981). Seals, Hagberg, Hurley, Ehsani, and Holloszy (1984b) studied the effects of six months of low-intensity exercise followed by six months of high-intensity exercise in 11 men and women (63 ± 2 years). They found no change in maximal heart rate, an increase in stroke volume, and an increase in VO_{2max}. After six months of low intensity training there was no change in the $(a - \bar{v})O_2$ difference, but there was a significant increase after six months of high intensity training.

There are conflicting reports on the effects of physical activity on the respiratory system. Some researchers report no change in vital capacity and lung compliance with training (Niinimaa & Shephard, 1978), whereas others do report significant gains in vital capacity (deVries & Adams, 1972). Training has been reported to increase maximal ventilation during exercise (Seals et al., 1984b).

Musculoskeletal System

One universal characteristic of aging is the gradual loss in vigor and speed of muscular movement. Underlying these changes in motor ability are well-documented changes in the musculoskeletal system which includes the muscles, the joints, and the bones. Musculoskeletal function can be examined by measuring muscular strength and endurance, flexibility, and bone density. Muscular strength may be measured isometrically or dynamically. The handgrip dynamometer may be used to measure isometric strength, whereas dynamic strength may be measured by the maximum amount of weight lifted in one repetition. With advanced age there is a gradual loss of both isometric and dynamic strength (Aniansson, Grimby, Hedberg, Rungren, & Sperling, 1978). Functionally, muscular strength is decreased approximately 20% from 20 to 60 years of age (Petrofsky & Lind, 1975).

Muscular endurance is measured both isometrically and dynamically. Isometric endurance, or the ability to hold an isometric contraction at a given percentage of maximal contraction strength may not decrease with age (Larsson & Karlsson, 1978). The capacity of the muscle to perform continuous submaximal contractions parallels the loss in VO_{2max} with age (Makrides, Heigenhauser, McCartney, & Jones, 1985). These losses in muscular strength and endurance are due to decrements in muscle mass, both in muscle fiber size and number (Tomonaga, 1977).

Flexibility refers to the range of motion around a particular joint. Decreased flexibility has been reported with aging (Adrian, 1981). The effects of age on flexibility are more difficult to evaluate and quantify than muscular changes because it is not clear whether the decrease is a result of biologic aging or of degenerative disease. Decreased flexibility with age is probably the result of combined histological and morphological changes in the components of the joint, including cartilage, ligaments, and tendons.

Bone loss with aging is a common event. Men begin to lose bone mass at about age 55, losing 10 to 15% of bone mass by age 70. Women begin to experience bone mineral loss at a rate of 0.75 to 1.0% per year after the age of 35. Higher bone mass loss (2 to 3%) may occur with menopause (Smith, 1982).

Exercise-induced improvements in the musculoskeletal system include increases in maximal strength, muscular endurance, joint flexibility, and retardation of osteoporosis. Older subjects can increase strength with resistance training (Moritani & deVries, 1981). The greatest increase in muscular endurance is found when aerobic training programs are used. An increase in mitochondria, muscle glycogen concentration and aerobic enzyme activity, with a possible increase in anaerobic enzyme activity has been found with physical activity (Suominen et al., 1977). Frekany and Leslie (1975) reported increases in flexibility after a nonstrenuous exercise program. Several investigators report that moderate physical activity may increase bone mineral content in the elderly (Smith, Reddan, & Smith, 1981).

Metabolism

Several metabolic changes occur with aging. Aging is often associated with increases in the percentage of body fat and body weight with concomitant decreases in lean body mass (Brozek, 1952). The decrease in lean body mass may be why basal metabolic rate gradually decreases with age (Shock, 1961). Total cholesterol and low-density lipoprotein cholesterol levels increase with age (Shephard, 1978). As one ages, glucose tolerance is reduced (Fitzgerald, Malins, O'Sullivan, & Wall, 1961).

These metabolic changes may be affected by exercise. Physical conditioning can increase lean body mass and decrease body fat (Sidney, Shephard, & Harrison, 1977). Exercise also can deter age-related glucose intolerance and insulin insensitivity (Seals, Hagberg, Allen, Hurley, Dalsky, Ehsani, & Holloszy, 1984a).

Nervous System

Important changes in the central nervous system also occur with age. Reaction times are slower and nerve conduction velocity decreases 10 to 15% (Shock, 1961).

Physical training has little effect on the deterioration of neural function. Investigators could find no difference in neurobiological factors between extremely fit elderly endurance athletes and sedentary men (Suominen, Heikkinen, Parkatti, Forsberg, & Kiiskinen, 1980).

IMPLICATIONS FOR THE SENIOR SCHOLAR

More research is needed on the health and effects of physical activity on the senior scholar. However, there is sufficient evidence that the health of the senior scholar is better than that of the general population. For example, academicians have a greater life expectancy than the general population.

According to the life tables prepared by the Metropolitan Life Insurance Company, in 1987 life expectancy at birth for boys was 71.4 years and for girls was 78.4 years (Metropolitan Life Insurance Co., 1988). However, the Teachers Insurance Annuity Association (TIAA) adds 1½ years onto the life expectancy tables for its policyholders. This finding may indicate that faculty of institutions of higher education are in better health than the rest of the population.

It appears from available research that age and physical health are not intimately linked until 85 years of age. There also seems to be little support for the notion that faculty productivity declines linearly with age. Research indicates that faculty productivity tends to be bimodal, peaking 10 years after the receipt of the doctoral degree and again just before retirement (Reskin, 1985). Recent studies of adult cognition have shown that intellectual decline occurs later and at a slower pace than previously thought (Willis, 1985). Verbal skills are the last to decline, but the decline is not as noticeable in older faculty since these are the skills most often used, and thereby practice effects accrue.

The effects of regular physical activity on physiological functioning in the older, healthy adult are well documented. One measurement of good health is the absence of risk factors for heart disease. Lack of exercise puts one at risk for developing heart disease. According to the National Center for Health Statistics (NCHS), college graduates are about twice as likely to be physically active as are persons with less than 12 years of education among people 45 years of age and over (NCHS, 1988). This also has positive implications for senior scholars.

CONCLUSIONS

The purpose of this paper was to present information about the health of older persons and to raise issues about the applicability of physical activity on retarding the effects of age. This analysis was based on a review of literature and a synthesis of data on health, exercise, and aging.

There are at least three areas of health which support the feasibility of establishing an institute for senior scholars. First, a stimulating intellectual environment enables faculty, as well as all older persons, to maintain their abilities. Second, health does not seem to be an issue in consideration of productivity of senior scholars, particularly for those under the age of 85 years. In addition, differential morbidity data indicate scholars are in better health than society at large. Third, a physically active lifestyle promotes longevity. Older faculty in higher institutions of learning are twice as active as those people the same age with less than 12 years of education.

In conclusion, it would appear that senior scholars only need the will to continue to learn in order to remain current in their fields and to enhance their productivity.

REFERENCES

Adrian, M. J. (1981). Flexibility in the aging adult. In E. L. Smith & R. C. Cerfass (Eds.), *Exercise and Aging*. Hillside, NJ: Enslow.

Anderson, A. (1978). Old is not a four-letter word. *Across the Board, 15* (5), 20–27.

Aniansson, A., Grimby, G., Hedberg, M., Rungren, A. & Sperling, L. (1978). Muscle function in old age. *Scandinavian Journal of Rehabilitation and Medicine, 6 (suppl.),* 43–49.

Astrand, P. O. & Rodahl, K. (1977). Circulation. *Textbook of Work Physiology, Chapter 6,* 141–205.

Brandfonbrener, M., Landowne, M. & Shock, N. W. (1955). Changes in cardiac output with age. *Circulation, 12,* 557–566.

Brozek, J. (1952). Changes of body composition in man during maturity and their nutritional implications. *Federal Proceedings, 11,* 784–793.

Claxton, C. S. & Murrell, P. H. (1984). Developmental theory as a guide for maintaining the vitality of college faculty. In C. M. N. Mehrota (Ed.), *Teaching and aging. New directions for teaching and learning. No. 19.* San Francisco: Jossey-Bass.

Dehn, M. M. & Bruce, R. A. (1972). Longitudinal variations in maximal oxygen intake with age and activity. *Journal of Applied Physiology, 33,* 805–807.

deVries, H. A. & Adams, G. M. (1972). Comparison of exercise responses in old and young men: II. Ventilatory mechanics. *Journal of Gerontology, 27,* 349–352.

Fitzgerald, M. G., Malins, J. M., O'Sullivan, D. J. & Wall, M. (1961). The effect of sex and parity on the incidence of diabetes mellitus. *Quarterly Journal of Medicine, 15,* 57–70.

Frekany, G. A. & Leslie, D. K. (1975). Effects of an exercise program on selected flexibility measurements of senior citizens. *Gerontologist, 15,* 182–183.

George, L. K. & Winfield-Laird, I. (1984). Implications of an aging faculty for the quality of higher education and academic careers. In C. M. N. Mehrota (Ed.), *Teaching and aging. New directions for teaching and learning, No. 19.* San Francisco: Jossey-Bass.

Grimby, G., Nilsson, N. J. & Saltin, B. (1966). Cardiac output during submaximal and maximal exercise in active middle-aged athletes. *Journal of Applied Physiology, 21,* 1150–1156.

Havlik, R. J. (1986). National center for health statistics. Aging in the eighties, impaired senses for sound and light in persons age 65 years and over, preliminary data from the supplement on aging to the NHIS, United States, 1984. *Advance Data from Vital and Health Statistics No. 125* (DHSS Publication No. (PHS) 86-1250). Hyattsville, Md: Public Health Service.

Heath, G. W., Hagberg, J. M., Ehsani, A. A. & Holloszy, J. O. (1981). A physiological comparison of young and older endurance athletes. *Journal of Applied Physiology, 51,* 634–640.

Hsun, T. (1986). Population aging in the world. *Economic Daily,* 2.

Kimmel, Douglas C. (1974). *Adulthood and aging: An interdisciplinary, developmental view.* New York: Wiley.

Kohn, R. R. (1977). Heart and cardiovascular system. In C. E. Finch & L. Hayflick (Eds.), *Handbook of the Biology of Aging.* New York: Van Nostrand Reinhold.

Kovar, M. G. & LaCroix, A. Z. (1987). National center for health statistics: Aging in the eighties, ability to perform work-related activities. Supplement on aging to the national health interview survey, United States, 1984. *Advance Data from Vital and Health Statistics* (DHSS Publication No. (PHS) 87-1250). Hyattsville, MD: Public Health Service.

Larsson, L. & Karlsson, J. (1978). Isometric and dynamic endurance as a function of age and skeletal muscle characteristics. *Acta Physiologica Scandinavica, 104,* 129–136.

Makrides, L., Heigenhauser, G. J., McCartney, N. & Jones, N. L. (1985). Maximal short-term exercise capacity in healthy subjects aged 15–70 years. *Clinical Science, 69,* 197–205.

McConnell, S. R. (1984). Assessing the health and job performance of older workers. *Business and Health, 1*(7), 18–22.

McDonald, R. B. (1988). The Physiological Aspects of Aging. In H. Dennis (Ed.), *Fourteen Steps in Managing an Aging Workforce.* Lexington, MA: Lexington.

Metropolitan Life Insurance Company. (1988). New longevity record in the United States. *Statistical Bulletin, 69*(3), 10–15.

Milne, J. S. & Williamson, J. (1972). Respiratory function tests in older people. *Clinical Science, 42,* 371–381.

Moritani, T. & deVries, H. A. (1981). Neural factors versus hypertrophy in the time course of muscle strength gain in young and old men. *Journal of Gerontology, 36,* 294–297.

National Center for Health Statistics. (1985). *Utilization of short-stay hospitals: United States, 1983* (DHSS Publication No. (PHS) 85-1744). Hyattsville, Md: U.S. Department of Health and Human Services.

National Center for Health Statistics. (1986). *Current estimates from the national health interview survey: United States, 1984* (DHPA Publication No. (PHS) 86-1584). Washington, DC: U.S. Govt. Printing Office.

National Center for Health Statistics. (February 1988). *Health promotion and disease prevention: United States, 1985.* (DHSS Publication No.

(PHS) 88-1591). Hyattsville, Md: U.S. Department of Health and Human Services.

National Center for Health Statistics. (September 1988). *Current estimates from the national health interview survey, 1987* (DHSS Publication No. 88-1594). Hyattsville, Md: U.S. Department of Health and Human Services.

Niinimaa, V. & Shephard, R. J. (1978). Training and oxygen conductance in the elderly. I: The respiratory system. II. The cardiovascular system. *Journal of Gerontology, 33,* 362–367.

Petrofsky, J. S. & Lind, A. R. (1975). Aging, isometric strength and endurance and cardiovascular responses to static effort. *Journal of Applied Physiology, 38,* 91–95.

Reskin, B. F. (1985). Aging and productivity: Careers and results. In S. M. Clark and D. R. Lewis (Eds.), *Faculty vitality and institutional productivity.* New York: Teachers College, Columbia University.

Riley, M. & Foner, A. (1968). *Aging and Society, Vol. 1.* New York: Trinity.

Rizzato, G. & Marazzini, L. (1970). Thoracoabdominal mechanics in elderly men. *Journal of Applied Physiology, 28,* 457–460.

Schiffman, S. S., Moss, J. & Erickson, R. P. (1976). Thresholds of food odors in the elderly. *Experimental Aging Research, 2,* 389.

Seals, D. R., Hagberg, J. M., Allen, W. K., Hurley, B. F., Dalsky, G. P., Ehsani, A. A. & Holloszy, J. O. (1984a). Glucose tolerance in young and older athletes and sedentary men. *Journal of Applied Physiology: Respiratory, Environmental, and Exercise Physiology, 56*(6), 1521–1525.

Seals, D. R., Hagberg, J. M., Hurley, B. F., Ehsani, A. A. & Holloszy, J. O. (1984b). Endurance training in older men and women, I. Cardiovascular responses to exercise. *Journal of Applied Physiology: Respiratory, Environmental, and Exercise Physiology, 57*(4), 1024–29.

Shan, F. (1987). Aging Population: An Impending Problem on the Chinese Mainland. *Issues and Studies, 23*(7), 56–67.

Shephard, R. J. (1978). *Physical Activity and Aging.* London: Croom Helm.

Shock, N. W. (1961). Physiological aspects of aging in man. *Annual Review in Physiology, 23,* 97–122.

Siconolfi, S. F., Lasater, T. M., McKinlay, S., Boggia, P. & Carleton, R. A. (1985). Physical fitness and blood pressure: The role of age.

American Journal of Epidemiology, 122, 452–457.

Sidney, K. H. & Shephard, R. J. (1977). Maximum and submaximum exercise tests in men and women in seventh, eighth, and ninth decades of life. *Journal of Applied Physiology, 43,* 280–287.

Sidney, K., Shephard, R. J. & Harrison, J. E. (1977). Endurance training and body composition of the elderly. *American Journal of Clinical Nutrition, 30,* 326–333.

Smith, E. L. (1982). Exercise for prevention of osteoporosis: A review. *Physician and Sports Medicine, 10*(3), 72–80.

Smith, E. L., Reddan, W. G. & Smith, P. E. (1981). Physical activity and calcium modalities for bone mineral increase in aged women. *Medicine and Science in Sports and Exercise, 13*(1), 60–64.

Stamford, B. A. (1972). Physiological effects of training upon institutionalized geriatric men. *Journal of Gerontology, 27,* 451–455.

Suominen, H. E., Heikkinen, H., Liesen, H., Michel, D. & Hollmann, W. (1977). Effects of 8 weeks' endurance training on skeletal muscle metabolism in 56–70 year old sedentary men. *European Journal of Applied Physiology, 37,* 173–180.

Suominen, H., Heikkinen, E., Parkatti, T., Forsberg, S. & Kiiskinen, A. (1980). Effects of lifelong physical training on functional aging in men. *Scandinavian Journal of Social Medicine, 14*(Suppl.), 225–240.

Thornbury, J. M. & Mistretta, C. M. (1981). Tactile sensitivity as a function of age. *Journal of Gerontology, 36,* 34.

Tomonaga, M. (1977). Histochemical and ultrastructural changes in senile human skeletal muscle. *Journal of the American Geriatrics Society, 25,* 125–131.

Wen-jo, H. (1985). Population aging and economic development in developed countries. *World Economy, 7,* 16.

White House Conference on Aging. (1981). *Report of Technical Committee on Employment.* Washington, DC: U.S. Govt. Printing Office.

Willis, S. L. (1985). Towards an educational psychology of the older adult learner: Intellectual and cognitive bases. In J. E. Birren and K. W. Schaie (Eds.), *Handbook of the Psychology of Aging.* New York: Van Nostrand Reinhold.

Older Americans' Health

METROPOLITAN LIFE INSURANCE

The United States is increasingly challenged by the rising number of elderly and their medical care needs. To date, the country lacks the necessary systematic programs to deal with this present and projected worsening problem. More and more, the private sector is being asked to respond.

In the past few years, Metropolitan Life Insurance Company demographers have published articles in the *Statistical Bulletin* detailing demographic characteristics of persons 65 and over, and presented projections of their impending explosive increase.[1] In this analysis, we will call attention to another aspect pertaining to our senior citizens—their health—and more specifically how they assess their own well-being. The article draws heavily on a report prepared by the National Center for Health Statistics in which data from various information systems were brought together in an attempt to address the need for health statistics on older Americans.[2]

SELF HEALTH ASSESSMENT

It is encouraging to observe that more than one-third of the population aged 65 or over, residing in their communities, reported that their health was excellent or very good. Moreover, the proportion did not change with advance in age—from ages 65–74 through ages 85 and over. These findings (shown in Table 1) were determined from the National Health Interview Survey (NHIS) conducted in 1983–84. The survey is national in scope and is based on household interviews of the noninstitutional population. Thus, by definition, the study excludes persons in hospitals or nursing homes—the segment of the population in poorest health—and as a result underestimates the true health status of older persons. Another cautionary note is in order. Since the prevalence of chronic conditions increases with age—thus placing a larger proportion of persons aged 85 and over in long-term institutionalized settings (22 percent in 1985)[3]—comparisons with younger groupings must be tempered.

RACIAL DIFFERENCES

Although a sizable percentage of all our elders assess their health to be excellent or very good, substantial disparities arise when race is taken into consideration. For example, over one-third of white men and women re-

TABLE 1 Respondent-assessed Health Status and Degree of Activity Limitation Due to Chronic Conditions Persons Aged 65 and Over, by Race, Sex and Age: United States, 1983–84

	Percentage Distribution						
	Respondent-assessed* health status			Degree of activity limitation			
Race, sex and age	Excellent or very good	Good	Fair or poor	No activity limitation	Limited but not in major activity	Limited in amount or kind of major activity	Unable to carry on major activity
Total†							
65 years and over	35.9	31.0	32.6	60.4	14.6	14.4	10.6
65–74 years	36.2	31.7	31.7	62.7	13.5	12.9	10.9
75–84 years	35.2	30.5	33.6	60.5	17.2	14.4	7.9
85 years and over	35.5	27.8	36.2	40.4	12.4	27.3	19.9
White Men							
65 years and over	36.7	30.6	32.3	61.3	15.6	10.3	12.8
65–74 years	37.3	30.5	31.8	62.1	13.2	9.7	15.0
75–84 years	35.2	31.4	32.7	62.8	20.5	9.7	7.0
85 years and over	36.8	28.3	34.8	44.2	18.5	20.7	16.7
Black Men							
65 years and over	26.6	25.1	47.7	53.5	14.9	13.1	18.5
65–74 years	26.2	26.0	47.4	53.9	12.6	11.3	22.4
75–84 years	27.7	23.1	48.1	55.0	19.6	15.0	10.0
85 years and over	24.3‡	24.3‡	48.6‡	40.5‡	16.2‡	27.0‡	18.9‡
White Women							
65 years and over	36.8	32.5	30.1	61.2	14.0	16.4	8.3
65–74 years	37.2	33.9	28.4	64.8	13.6	14.7	6.9
75–84 years	36.5	31.1	31.9	60.4	15.9	16.1	7.6
85 years and over	36.3	27.8	35.2	39.4	9.7	29.9	21.0
Black Women							
65 years and over	24.1	21.2	53.0	47.4	14.5	24.1	13.9
65–74 years	23.8	20.6	54.5	49.7	16.3	22.0	12.0
75–84 years	25.4	21.6	50.8	47.2	11.8	26.1	14.8
85 years and over	21.8‡	25.5	50.0	31.8	10.0‡	32.7	24.5

Source: Division of Health Interview Statistics, National Center for Health Statistics. Data from the National Health Interview Survey.

*Excludes unknown respondent-assessed health status.

†Includes races other than white and black.

‡The numerator of the estimate has a relative standard error of more than 30 percent.

plied that their physical well-being was at least very good, whereas the proportion of black men and women who felt this way was only one-fourth. Moreover, around half of all blacks residing in a noninstitutionalized setting said their health was only fair or even poor—the corresponding percentage for whites was less than one-third

ACTIVITY LIMITATION ANALYSIS

Not surprisingly, the comparatively unfavorable self health assessment of black older Americans is reflected in their reported degree of activity limitation. A visual representation of the sex and race differences in the degree of self-reported activity limitation is shown in Figure 1. An analysis of the data by age group reveals that at ages 65–84 roughly one-half of black men and women said they experienced no limitation in their

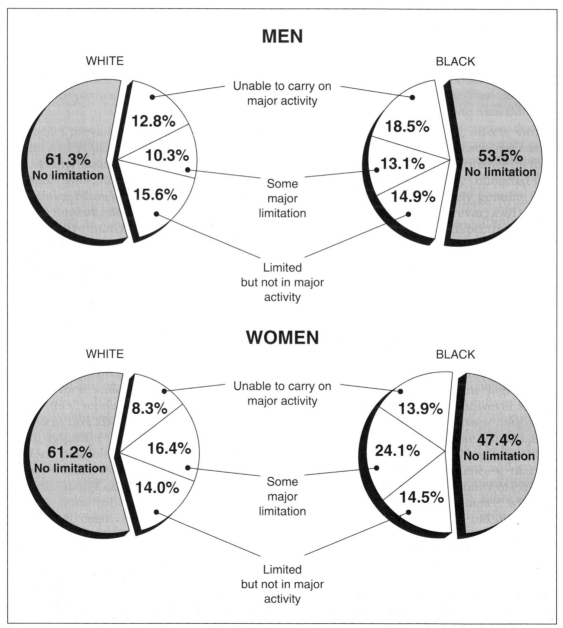

Source: Table 1.

FIGURE 1   Degree of Activity Limitation Among Persons 65 and Over United States, 1983–84

activities. By contrast, over three-fifths of all whites reported the same status. On the other end of the activity spectrum, 15 percent of white men aged 65–74 and only 7 percent of those aged 75–84, as well as white women aged 65–84, stated they were unable to carry on major activities. The proportion of black men in this category was about 50 percent larger than the reported value of white men. Among black women the percentage was three-fourths higher at ages 65–74 and was nearly double at ages 75–84.

COMMON IMPAIRMENTS

The frequency of visual and hearing impairments among the elderly increases rapidly with increasing age. Visual impairment comprises blindness in one or both eyes as well as other problems with sight. As may be observed from Table 2, white males have comparatively more difficulty with vision and hearing than white women. On the other hand, the prevalence of cataracts was higher among women. Overall, the incidence rate of cataracts among white women aged 65 and over—185.6 per 1,000—was three-fourths higher than the rate for white men, but the disparity steadily diminished with increased age.

Hearing problems were much more prevalent than vision difficulties. As a group, more than three out of 10 senior citizens said they had problems hearing. Moreover, this problem was present in half of those aged 85 and over. It is noteworthy that with regard to deformities and orthopedic impairments, the frequency increases sharply at ages 85 and over, especially in women.

Respiratory infections were the most frequently reported acute conditions among the aged. In general, the incidence rates were slightly higher among white women than white men. At the extreme ages, injuries were reported more often than respiratory problems. The big jump in prevalence rates may be distorted because multiple injuries to the same person were included in the data. For the purpose of this study, the most common injuries were contusions, sprains and strains, and open wounds and lacerations.[4]

CHRONIC DIFFICULTIES

The reported incidence of many common longstanding illnesses did not exhibit significant variability by age. The lower tier of Table 2 presents the 1982–84 prevalence rates of selected chronic conditions. Nearly half of all persons aged 65 and over living in the community said they had arthritis. Among women, the incidence of this disability was about one-third higher than among men. This was true for both whites and blacks. Additionally, the level of arthritis in black men and women was much greater than in whites. The second most frequently reported condition was hypertension. This problem was almost as often reported as arthritis and also showed similar incidence patterns. Black women reported a hypertension rate of 643 per 1,000 compared with 429 per 1,000 for white women. At the same time, the prevalence rate among men was 371 per 1,000 for blacks and 317 per 1,000 for whites.

Not as frequently reported, but no less important, were problems associated with ischemic heart disease. In this condition, the prevalence rate was significantly higher in whites—especially among men. A related problem—cerebrovascular disease—was reported much less frequently. However, this condition increased with age, and among white women aged 85 and over was reported nearly as commonly as ischemic heart disease. Prevalence rates for three other conditions—emphysema, chronic bronchitis and diabetes—are also shown in the table. For diabetes, the reported incidence rates among white persons aged 65–74 were higher among women than among men, but the opposite was true for ages 75 and over. Black women reported a diabetes prevalence rate 150 percent higher than white women, while

TABLE 2 Reported Impairments for Persons 65 Years of Age and Over by Type of Impairment, Race, Sex and Age United States, 1982–84 (per 1,000)

Race, sex and age	Selected Impairment				Acute Impairment			
	Visual impairment	Cataract	Hearing impairment	Deformity or orthopedic impairment	Respiratory	Digestive	Injuries	Other
All Persons								
65 years and over	98.0	149.3	308.7	167.6	38.7	6.2	21.0	31.4
65–74 years	73.2	94.4	260.7	165.2	42.4	5.8	18.1	32.9
75–84 years	119.7	217.8	361.3	162.1	32.6	6.3	22.3	28.5
85 years and over	218.6	327.4	495.7	211.1	32.7	8.9*	40.5	30.6
White Men								
65 years and over	105.6	105.0	368.1	143.5	37.6	4.7	15.8	23.2
65–74 years	83.8	64.2	329.4	145.9	40.6	5.2	14.3	23.9
75–84 years	127.8	163.8	429.7	132.9	32.7	3.2*	16.1	20.0
85 years and over	246.8	283.4	508.2	168.2	27.4*	7.3*	31.1*	30.2*
Black Men								
65 years and over	147.9	79.8*	261.7	171.4	16.8*	10.1*	6.9	44.2
White Women								
65 years and over	88.6	185.6	275.6	179.7	40.5	7.5	26.4	36.1
65–74 years	61.7	121.0	219.8	175.4	45.5	6.8	22.3	38.2
75–84 years	108.7	258.6	320.4	176.1	31.7	7.8	27.8	33.3
85 years and over	198.3	355.4	492.7	224.0	39.5	10.8*	48.8	31.8
Black Women								
65 years and over	112.9	136.1	261.4	208.0	41.1	1.6*	16.4*	33.2

Race, sex and age	Chronic Condition						
	Ischemic heart disease	Hypertension	Cerebro-vascular disease	Emphysema	Chronic bronchitis	Diabetes	Arthritis
All Persons							
65 years and over	135.5	394.9	58.0	40.5	57.8	90.5	485.6
65–74 years	137.1	393.6	41.8	43.2	62.9	93.6	475.7
75–84 years	135.4	398.1	80.9	40.8	51.1	86.5	497.7
85 years and over	122.2	392.8	99.7	16.6*	42.9*	80.9	519.8
White Men							
65 years and over	178.4	316.7	62.9	75.0	52.6	79.9	392.2
65–74 years	192.2	334.9	52.9	73.8	52.3	73.8	390.7
75–84 years	148.0	289.0	79.5	84.7	57.4	92.0	386.2
85 years and over	168.2	245.0	95.1*	40.2*	32.9*	85.9*	438.8
Black Men							
65 years and over	61.0*	370.9	108.0	41.1*	16.4*	120.9	468.3
White Women							
65 years and over	118.6	428.8	50.4	20.3	66.5	85.2	540.4
65–74 years	109.6	414.2	29.8	24.2	75.0	90.4	527.2
75–84 years	137.5	446.2	74.9	17.5*	54.6	79.6	560.0
85 years and over	108.2	464.4	99.6	3.4*	53.2*	70.4*	556.2
Black Women							
65 years and over	76.6	642.7	75.8	11.6*	36.3*	211.1	639.6

Source: Division of Health Interview Statistics, National Center for Health Statistics. Data from the National Health Interview Survey.

*The numerator of the estimate has a relative standard error of more than 30 percent.

among men, the frequency was about 50 percent greater for blacks.

FUTURE CONCERNS

As the population of the United States slowly grows older, it is becoming extremely important to ascertain the health status of the aged. This group is acknowledged to utilize a disproportionate share of the nation's health resources. Most medical attention and costs are expended during the last years of life; this implies that during the 20th century, resources have been shifted from children and young adults to the care of people well over the age of 65.[5] Studies of self-health perceptions are providing a useful way of gauging the magnitude of the impending national burden. These analyses give public health officials a means of determining the success of rehabilitation programs, and related questions about the quality of life.

It is known that Americans are living longer, but are the added years of life years of vigor and independence or years of frailty and [excessive] dependence?[6] Unfortunately, trend data show no dramatic gains in the health status of the aged. Instead, it appears that while life expectancy slowly moves up, Americans are rapidly increasing the number of years that they live with significant disabilities. While progress has been made in preventing and alleviating the discomfort of many chronic illnesses, more improvements will be forthcoming. However, our health care system could gradually be inundated by the volume of the aged requiring services for nonfatal conditions. Now appears to be the time for the private sector to join in national efforts to formulate long-term health care management policy, to provide additional resources, and to give it the high priority it requires.

REFERENCES

1. *Statistical Bulletin.* Jan–Mar and Apr–Jun 1984, Apr–Jun 1986 and Jan–Mar 1987.
2. National Center for Health Statistics. "Health statistics on older persons, United States, 1986." Series 3, No. 25, DHHS Pub. No. (PHS) 87-1409. June 1987.
3. Ibid p. 73.
4. National Center for Health Statistics, "Types of injuries and impairments due to injuries, U.S." Series 10, No. 159, DHHS Pub. No. (PHS) 87 1587, November 1986.
5. Brody, Jacob A., Brock, Dwight B., Williams, T Franklin. "Trends in the health of the elderly population." *Annual Review of Public Health,* 8:211–34, 1987.
6. Branch, Laurence G. & Meyers, Allan R. "Assessing physical function in the elderly." *Clinics in Geriatric Medicine* 3(1):29–51, February 1987.

3

Bringing the Social Back in: A Critique of the Biomedicalization of Dementia

KAREN A. LYMAN

Alzheimer's disease emerged as an illness category and policy issue in the 1980s, more than 70 years after Alois Alzheimer documented the first case. Dementing illnesses only recently have received attention from researchers and policymakers because "senility" previously was viewed as an inevitable part of normal aging (Ruscio & Cavarocchi, 1984).

Today, Alzheimer's disease is identified as the most common of the dementing illnesses, progressive brain disorders characterized by gradual deterioration of memory, language, other intellectual abilities, and general competence over a 7- to 15-year period until death. There is as yet no cure. A clinical diagnosis results only in a prescription for basic custodial care, perhaps assisted by drugs for symptomatic relief of "agitation."

The clinical manifestations of dementia are associated with many other conditions that may be reversible or treatable. Differential diagnosis, however, is unequivocal only postmortem. Neuropathological analysis often reveals a misdiagnosis of Alzheimer's disease, and autopsies of healthy adults who functioned without symptoms of dementia reveal that approximately 10% show the classic Alzheimer's neuropathology (Bergmann, 1985; Brody, 1982; Lauter, 1985; McKhann et al., 1984; Mortimer & Hutton, 1985; Mortimer & Schuman, 1981; U.S. Government Office of Technology Assessment, 1987; Zarit, Orr, & Zarit, 1985).

Alzheimer's disease and related disorders arouse a sense of urgency with policymakers and federal research funding agencies because of the prospect of staggering health care costs for a large population of severely impaired older people (Shanas & Maddox, 1985; Terry & Katzman, 1983). Although dementing illnesses affect less than 5% of people over 65, approximately 20% of people 80 and older are affected. Therefore, the rapid population increase among the oldest old represents escalating numbers of those most at risk for dementia (Brody, 1982; Gilhooly, Zarit, & Birren, 1986, pp. 2–4; Lauter, 1985; Mortimer & Schuman, 1981).

Many other more prevalent and treatable conditions of old age have not received as much attention, largely because Alzheimer's is now viewed as an epidemic, an emerging problem of increasing magnitude. The "discovery" of Alzheimer's disease has involved a political process more than simply biomedical discovery. Consciousness

Source: The Gerontologist 29(5), 597–605. Reprinted with permission from The Gerontological Society of America, Washington, DC 20005. Copyright 1989.

raising about Alzheimer's disease is addressed later in this paper. This consciousness is reflected in the title of a 1987 Office of Technology Assessment publication, *Losing A Million Minds: Confronting the Tragedy of Alzheimer's Disease* (U.S. Government Office of Technology Assessment, 1987).

The growing public consciousness of Alzheimer's as "the disease of the century" has refuted the myth that senility is an inevitable condition of old age, and has legitimized research and policy interests that offer hope for a cure. Funds for Alzheimer's research through the National Institutes of Health and National Institute of Mental Health have dramatically increased in the 1980s. Fruits of this research include increasingly precise assessment tools that differentiate treatable from nonreversible dementias and the promise of clinical markers that may identify patients by disease stage for inclusion in new treatment trials. Clearly, dementing illnesses involve disease processes for which biomedical research may hold the key to an eventual cure. But while awaiting a cure, care occurs in social settings and relationships that are seldom examined in regard to their contribution to dementia. It is this neglect of the social component of dementing illness that should be of interest to social gerontologists.

The argument presented here is that reliance upon the biomedical model to explain the experience of dementing illness overlooks the social construction of dementia and the impact of treatment contexts and caregiving relationships on disease progression. The neglect of social factors in dementia will be addressed by this analysis: first, a historical perspective on the medicalization of senility; second, a critical analysis of the prevailing biomedical model of dementia; third, an examination of the impact of the biomedical model in research on caregiver strain; and finally, an outline of a model that acknowledges social factors in dementing illness.

THE MEDICALIZATION OF SENILITY

Throughout this paper, the problem of dementia is viewed as an example of the "medicalization of deviance," which refers to explaining and treating personal and social troubles as medical problems (Conrad & Kern, 1986; Conrad & Schneider, 1980; Zola, 1972). Troublesome behavior is explained by pathological conditions of somatic origin subject to treatment by medical authority. In regard to dementia, difficulties in caring for increasing numbers of impaired older people are commonly defined as medical problems, and difficulties in the caregiving relationship are explained by the progression of the disease. Recently the "medicalization of senility" has become the "biomedicalization of senility," with the emergence of biomedicine as a medical specialty (see Estes & Binney in this issue).

Conrad and Schneider's historical overview (1980) of the emergence of concepts of mental illness, the "medicalization of madness," includes definitions of dementia prior to the 1980s. In the Middle Ages, dementia was not distinguished from other forms of madness, which was interpreted within the prevailing theological model that identified various dissidents and deviants, especially older women, as witches. Some physicians argued that witches really were mentally ill persons, including melancholy (depressed) old women, but they were largely ignored until the 17th century. Meanwhile, of the half million people hanged, drowned, or burned at the stake as witches during the Middle Ages, large numbers were old women who today would be identified as suffering from a dementing illness and/or depression.

The first direct reference to *dementia* identified by Conrad and Schneider was an 1801 psychiatry text by Pinel, a director of French asylums. His classification of mental diseases precurses the American Psychiatric Association's Diagnostic and Statistical Manual of Mental Disorders (DSM), in its third—revised—edition in 1987 (DSM-III-R). Pinel's classification comprised only a handful of mental diseases, including *dementia*, *melancholy* (depression), *mania*, and *idiocy*. DSM-III, on the other hand, contains more than 250 labels and symptomatic descriptions of mental disorders (a dramatic increase from 60 psychiatric conditions in the 1952 DSM-I).

The 19th century was a period of humanitarian reform in the asylums. Moral restraints were substituted for chains and other physical restraints. Moral treatment for madness consisted of establishing a constant, stable daily routine, "careful coercion," and work therapy. During this period, there was little scientific evidence to support the claims of doctors that madness was a "mental illness." But, Conrad and Schneider argue that the definition of mental illness supported the expansion of medical turf and professional dominance (Friedson, 1970) to include the "moral treatment" of madness. Doctors became the administrators of asylums. By the end of the 19th century, asylums had become simply custodial institutions, in an era of somatic pessimism in which no cure for mental illness was expected. And although there was yet no scientific evidence of somatic origin or medical treatment for mental illness, it was in this period that psychiatry was established as a medical specialty, essentially a "tinkering trade" (Goffman, 1961) practiced by asylum administrators.

Early in the 20th century, the first evidence of somatic origin for at least one form of mental illness encouraged further development of the medical concept of madness, including dementia. Third-stage syphilis was found to produce neurological breakdown resulting in "general paresis." This discovery renewed interest in the classification of mental illness. During this period, the first specific classification of dementia was made, "dementia praecox," a reference to "early senility" (Conrad & Schneider, 1980). It is important to note that only *premature*

senility was considered an illness earlier in this century. Senility in old age was considered normal. Thus, the very definition of dementia was an instance of medicalized deviance. The violation of age norms was the basis for the medical label.

There are parallels between the emergence of Alzheimer's disease as a diagnostic category in the 1980s and Peter Conrad's account of the "discovery of hyperkinesis" in children (Conrad, 1975). Until recently, hyperactivity in children, like senility in old age, was considered to be within the normal range of behavior. Now there is biomedical ownership of these recently discovered "diseases" of childhood and old age, which are attributed to biological causes and subject to medical treatment. An explanation for this trend may be found within Estes' framework of the "political economy" of the "aging enterprise" and the "biomedicalization of aging" generally (Estes, 1979; Estes et al., 1984; and Estes & Binney in this issue). Also, political scientist Neal Cutler provides an analysis of the politics of Alzheimer's disease (Cutler, 1986), which may be seen as a process of "claimsmaking" in which "facts" are constructed by "moral entrepreneurs" who have an interest in the creation of a new disease category (see Becker, 1973; Conrad & Schneider, 1980; Friedson, 1970; Gusfield, 1967; Spector & Kitsuse, 1977).

The "facts" generally accepted about Alzheimer's disease today have been defined by the American Psychiatric Association, specified further by several national research organizations. In the 1980s, DSM-III has identified the criteria for diagnosing "primary degenerative dementia," and a joint work group of the National Institute of Neurological Communicative Disorders and Stroke (NINCDS) and the Alzheimer's Disease and Related Disorders Association (ADRDA) has specified standards for a probable diagnosis of Alzheimer's disease and related dementing illnesses (Dick, Kean, & Sands, 1988; Mace, 1987). The primary criteria of senile dementia of the Alzheimer's type (SDAT) include global cognitive impairment, more specifically a *decline* in intellectual functioning. The question of decline is crucial, most often answered by the family's or other caregiver's retrospective assessment rather than prospective studies of community samples.

Conrad and Schneider (1980) argue that the medicalization of hyperactivity in children shifts attention from the school and family situation of the child to an individual/physiological deviance designation. The recent conceptualization of dementing illness results in a similar shift, with consequential limitations on the research questions that are asked about dementia and caregiving. In *Oldtimers and Alzheimer's*, Jay Gubrium (1986) presents a critical review of the evidence (or lack thereof) for the "discovery" of Alzheimer's as a disease category. Gubrium's argument is that it is not yet possible to clearly differentiate dementing illness from normal aging, and that the attempt to do so is a social construction to create order from the disorderly aspects of living with dementia (Gubrium, 1987).

Viewing dementia as a biomedical condition helps bring order to dementia care. Like other chronic illnesses, dementia is characterized by an "uncertain trajectory" (Strauss, 1975). Dementia typifications, medical labels, and medical authority (carried out by paraprofessionals and family caregivers, supported by medical diagnosis and, in some cases, prescribed pharmacological restraints) ease the stress of dementia care by increasing the sense of predictability and control for caregivers. Particularly with dementing illness, there is an overriding "therapeutic nihilism" (Cohen, 1988; Mace, 1987) in regard to the inevitability of intellectual decline and self-deterioration. "Losing" people long before they die is one of the most stressful aspects of dementia care. A model of stagelike disease progression can make more tolerable the difficult

role of caring for and deciding future care for a demented loved one. If the illness can be defined as having a beginning and middle, the end may be predicted.

In some respects, the myth of "senility" has been replaced by the myth of "Alzheimer's disease," the ready acceptance by clinicians, service providers, and families of an oversimplified diagnosis and prognosis (Gubrium, 1986; Lynott, 1983). Observations of caregivers in several settings have found that, once the label *Alzheimer's* is applied, even normal behavior is interpreted in terms of disease stages (Gubrium, 1975; Gubrium & Lynott, 1987; Lyman, 1988, 1989; Smithers, 1977). The result may be a self-fulfilling prophecy of impairment. "Excess disabilities" (Brody et al., 1971) and "learned helplessness" (Hofland, 1988) may result because the person is expected to decline, and few opportunities are provided to continue meaningful activity.

THE BIOMEDICAL MODEL OF DEMENTIA

Most of the social and behavioral science research on dementia gives little consideration to social factors affecting disease progression, including the power relationship of caregiving and dependency. Greater attention to this relationship and to the sociophysical context in which care is provided is required to understand caregiver stress and the distress of demented persons.

The major features of the biomedical model of dementia are outlined below, within the framework of the "medicalization of deviance" perspective (Conrad & Kern, 1986; Conrad & Schneider, 1980; Zola, 1972) and Estes and Binney's discussion of the "biomedicalization of aging" (in this issue). Dementia is now in this domain.

Dementia has fallen through the cracks between social gerontology and medical sociology, with neither specialty paying much attention to the social forces that affect the conceptualization and experience of the disease. A *Journal of Health and Social Behavior* associate editor recently explained that research on dementia has not yet been published by the JHSB because dementia is "at the cusp of gerontology and medical sociology" (Radelet, 1987). No articles on dementia have appeared in *Social Science and Medicine* from 1984–88 either. Apparently, the social context surrounding dementia has been of little interest to mainstream medical sociologists.

Social gerontologists have also had little to say about dementia. A review of recent work (1984–88) on dementia in *The Gerontologist*, the *Journal of Gerontology*, *Research on Aging*, and the *Annual Review of Gerontology and Geriatrics* finds little social and behavioral science research on dementing illness, except in *The Gerontologist.* Dementia research in these publications occurs primarily within neuropsychology, contained by the biomedical model. Even the large literature on dementia "caregiver strain" is framed by the biomedical model, focusing primarily on the medicalization of troublesome behavior problems attributed to disease progression.

The biomedical view of the behavior referred to as "senile dementia" includes three features. First, dementia is pathological and individual, an abnormal condition of cognitive impairment, dysfunction, and mental disorder. Second, chronic dementia is somatic or organic in etiology, caused by progressive deterioration of brain regions that control memory, language, and other intellectual functioning, resulting in stages of increasingly severe impairment. And third, although there is currently no cure, dementia is to be diagnosed by biomedical assessments of brain disease and clinical functioning, and treated and managed according to medical authority, including the possible prescription of chemical and/or physical restraints.

The widespread acceptance of the biomedical model of dementia has countered the longstanding ageist assumption that se-

nility is an inevitable condition of old age, has legitimized research and policy interests that offer hope for a cure, and has offered caregivers some degree of order and control in the difficult work of dementia care. However, the biomedical view of dementia is narrow, limited, and sometimes distorted in its ignorance of social forces that affect the definition, production, and progression of dementia. Employing only the biomedical model to explain dementia often results in the paradigmatic dilemma Kuhn described as "a strenuous and devoted attempt to force nature into conceptual boxes. . . ." (Kuhn, 1962, p. 5). In reality, the psychosocial experience of a dementing illness often cannot be contained within biomedical concepts of brain disease.

This critique addresses all three parts of the biomedical model of dementia: the definition of pathology; disease stage attributions; and the legitimation of medical control over persons with dementing illnesses.

Pathology Versus Normalcy

First, if senile dementia is a pathological condition, what is normal? How might we distinguish dysfunction from the degree of memory loss associated with normal aging? In the epidemiologic literature, "mild" dementia is only vaguely defined and prevalence rates range from 5 to 50%. It is very difficult to distinguish mild dementia from the stable condition of normal aging known as "benign senescent forgetfulness" (Kral, 1978) or "everyday memory problems" (Cutler & Grams, 1988). Also, in community studies in the United States and Scandinavia, mild dementia has been found not to be predictive of progressive dementia (Bergmann, 1985; Lauter, 1985).

Second, how might we distinguish mental disorder from behavioral quirks and eccentricities developed over a lifetime that are found within the normal range of heterogeneity in aging? (This question is developed in more detail by Gubrium, 1986; and Shomaker, 1987.) Aberrant behavior, continuous over a lifetime, including memory problems that are normal for a given person, may be erroneously attributed to a dementing illness. And, behavior that would not be considered abnormal if displayed by others is often attributed to dementia if exhibited by someone "known" to be impaired, someone with a clinical diagnosis of dementia (Gubrium, 1986; Lyman, 1988; Shomaker, 1987).

For example, consider behavior known as "wandering," one of the most frequently identified "behavioral problems" associated with dementia (Mace, 1987). Wandering has been defined as "frequent and/or unpredictable pacing, with no discernible goal" (Dawson & Reid, 1987). The relativity of this definition becomes clear if it is applied to a young man pacing the halls of a maternity ward. The definition of wandering and many other behavioral problems associated with dementia indicate social deviance or misbehaving more than pathological dysfunction.

Two recent articles make it apparent that wanderers are viewed as deviant because they behave *more* normally than other impaired elderly persons. In one study, wanderers are distinguished from nonwanderers in a long-term care facility primarily by something called "hyperactivity," which included these traits: "not withdrawn, hearing normal, good gait, perpetual motion, socially skilled" (Dawson & Reid, 1987). Another recent study found that these "problem" patients are "often mistaken for visitors" because they are "quite physically able and appeared mentally alert" (Rader, 1987). Both studies reveal that wanderers are difficult to distinguish from normal people, leading the staff in one facility to mark these residents with a red dot on their clothing between the shoulder blades (Rader, 1987). Clearly, the

conceptualization of wandering and other misbehavior involves social definitions of deviance not explained by the biomedical model.

Even the neuropathological changes associated with Alzheimer's disease do not neatly distinguish normal from pathological. Alzheimer's-type brain lesions are found at autopsy in many intellectually preserved normally functioning elderly (Mortimer & Hutton, 1985; McKhann et al., 1984). Additionally, the pathologic criteria used by neurologists to identify an "Alzheimer's brain" vary by age. With increasing age, a microscopic examination of tissue samples within the neocortex finds an increasing number of neuritic plaques and neurofibrillary tangles. The increasing number of plaques and tangles may be within a "normal" range, not associated with disease or dysfunction. For a patient over 65, an Alzheimer's brain is identified by twice the number of plaques and tangles than for a patient under 50. However, the standard number may be revised downward if the older patient is "known" to be demented, with a clinical diagnosis of a dementing illness (Henderson, 1988). If even the diagnosis and neuropathology of dementia is subject to such negotiation and interpretation, pathology must be framed within a sociocultural as well as a biomedical definition.

The biomedical definition of abnormality begins a process Goffman has called the "moral career" of people who are officially labeled abnormal (Goffman, 1961, pp. 127–130). The effect of being identified and treated as if one were demented must be seen as distinct from the effect of traits stemming from a pathological condition. Whether by misdiagnosis or in the medicalization of deviance, medical labels designating irreversible chronic impairment result in limited social opportunities.

Charmaz (1983) and Strauss (1975) have identified the severe blows to self-esteem that accompany chronic illness, largely as a result of social isolation and negative expectations of others. Particularly for persons with a dementing illness, the self-deterioration accompanying the disease is exacerbated by negative experiences in social relationships. For example, in one day care center, persons suffering from dementing illnesses were identified as "the dementias," very little was expected of them compared with other nonimpaired day care clients, and staff frequently took over activities they could have managed by themselves (Lyman, 1989). For persons labeled demented, the outcome may be "excess disabilities" (Brody et al., 1971), "learned helplessness" (Hofland, 1988), or other forms of social impairment.

Those labeled demented often are aware of and embarrassed by their stigmatic condition and its social consequences. Illustrations are provided from field notes in an ongoing study of dementia day care.

> The director at Metropolitan Day Care told me about the family situation of several clients. One man was neglected, given no new clothes, and was infrequently bathed. "It's as if he already were dead."

> The wife of another man strips his dignity; she pulls his pants down in front of others to give him shots.

> A woman told me her husband would not buy her new clothes because he said, "No one wants to look at you anyway."

> Another man told me how he felt in his relationship with caregivers at home and at day care. Searching for memory of his own age, he said, "I'm . . . 80 or 90 something . . . and I'm like a ten-year-old. . . . I don't want to do much because . . . people about 40 something. . . ." He didn't complete the sentence, but it was clear he was referring to his powerlessness relative to younger caregivers.

These examples indicate an awareness of loss, as a result not only of dementing illness but also of being identified and treated as a demented person.

Disease Stage Attributions

Sociological questions also may be addressed to the causal analysis of the biomedical model: that stages of progressive brain deterioration result in corresponding clinical stages of impairment. The epidemiologic and medical knowledge about the causes of chronic dementia is still very limited (Bergmann, 1985; Freed, 1987; Mortimer & Hutton, 1985; Secretary's Task Force, 1984). Also, there is considerable evidence contradicting the assumption of universal stages of progressive impairment, mainly from longitudinal community surveys in the United States, Great Britain and Scandinavia (Bergmann, 1985; Brody, 1982; Lauter, 1985). Nonetheless, even in writings that acknowledge flaws in the stage theory of dementia, progressive staging is the framework for the discussion. (For a recent example of this contradiction, see Mace [1987], who identifies three stages in the "progression of dementia," just after stating that there is considerable variability among people with dementia, and nonconformity to stagelike progression.) Perhaps more important, caregivers and service providers who interact daily with persons identified as demented often characterize dementia in terms of typical stages of decline, and attribute most of the demented person's behavior to the presumed clinical condition (Gubrium, 1986; Lyman, 1988). The person's disease progression often is reconstructed retrospectively to fit the rational stage model (Lynott, 1983).

Even persons identified as demented adopt the biomedical perspective in attributing behavior to disease. In field notes from one day care center, this conversation was recorded between two clients:

> One client asks (about another who rubs her hands): "Why does she do that?"

The second responds: "Just nervousness, I say."

The first persists: "No, I think it's a disease, maybe a brain disease. . . . "

The attribution of behavior to disease progression sets the stage for limited opportunities based on expectations of increasing incompetence. A kind of social death accompanies the diagnosis of Alzheimer's disease, a sense of hopelessness given visual expression by an Alzheimer's Disease and Related Disorders Association poster showing the demented person gradually fading away, in successive frames (or stages) of the picture. According to the assumption of typical disease progression, no new learning takes place in "later stages" of dementia, and the person is expected to become increasingly incompetent. However, even those who employ the biomedical model recognize that "there is significant variability" and "there are no noticeable hallmarks that mark a person's passage from one stage to the next" (Mace, 1987). And so, it is never entirely clear who is in which stage, or what kind of treatment is appropriate for people presumed to be in the same stage.

Research with institutionalized elderly has found that "iatrogenic treatment" and other environmental factors result in increased dependency (Hofland, 1988). Further research is needed to examine the impact of situational conditions on the demented elderly, in families as well as institutional settings. For example, clinical depression is common in old age and is difficult to differentiate from senile dementia (Thompson et al., 1987). The hopelessness associated with clinical depression impairs intellectual performance; an Alzheimer's diagnosis may lead to depression because the disease seems hopeless.

Even the assessment procedures used to determine degree of impairment may depress the demented person. On several occasions during an ongoing field study in dementia day care centers, I have overheard clients who were concerned about "failing" the "tests" (such as the Mini Mental State Exam) used by day care providers to report client characteristics to the California Department of Aging. Also, if caregivers have low or negative expectations of persons diagnosed with dementia, depression and further intellectual decline may occur. Therefore, an erroneous Alzheimer's diagnosis, distressing assessment procedures, or negative expectations by caregivers may produce depression, resulting in behavior that may be attributed to dementia. A staff member in one dementia day care center observed, "People think 'agitation' is inevitable, but it's because they're depressed about how they're being treated!" The biomedical model, focusing only on disease stage progression, precludes the possibility that diagnostic error or iatrogenic treatment in the caregiving relationship contribute to dementia.

The widespread acceptance of the notion of disease stages is understandable for caregivers and service providers, who seek structure, order, and control in their attempts to "do something" for the demented person and the family (Gubrium, 1987). Making plans for the future is not possible unless the disease course is somewhat predictable. Researchers also find the conceptual boxes of the biomedical model attractive. Staging of the disease would allow researchers to compare different individuals at similar stages of the illness, and would allow measurement of the effects of experimental interventions in postponing the next stage (Mace, 1987). However, this narrow biomedical view neglects social factors in disease progression.

Medical Control

The assumption that dementia is to be treated according to medical authority raises a number of sociological questions. Medical authority and control are exercised over the demented person by medical practitioners, paraprofessionals, and family caregivers as well. This power relationship in which "caregiving" takes place should be of primary interest to social gerontologists. For example, physical and chemical restraints still are commonly used to control wanderers and other "troublesome" demented elderly in long-term "care" facilities in the United States (Dawson & Reid, 1987; Rader, 1987).

Generally, dependency is encouraged and acts of independence are either ignored or punished in long-term care facilities (Hofland, 1988), and perhaps in the family as well. When caregivers are under stress, they may increase their control over demented persons, restricting care receivers' self-determination and increasing their dependency. In contrast, if caregivers encourage self-determination, the functioning of demented persons may improve. A field experiment with nursing home residents in which choice and personal responsibility were encouraged for the experimental group found significant improvement in alertness, active participation, and general well-being as a result of increased self-determination (Langer & Rodin, 1976). Whereas this group became more responsive, the control group became more debilitated.

A recent review of similar intervention studies and related research on autonomy in long-term care settings concludes that self-determination for impaired elderly is a primary characteristic of quality care (Hofland, 1988). However, the emotional exhaustion associated with caregiver stress often results in increased control over demented persons, as illustrated by this example from field notes in one dementia day care center:

> The design of the facility at Inland Day Care created problems in supervising "wanderers." There were many exits, and a highly visible locked gate was the main entrance. Some clients persisted in requesting that the gate be unlocked, and the staff grew weary of answering these requests. The program often was short staffed, so that workers could not accompany clients on walks outside the gate. On one particularly difficult day, after another round of repeated requests by a persistent client to go for a walk outside the gate, an exasperated staff member responded, "I'm going to give her a pill. I'm going to give her *five* pills! I'm getting a headache!" Pharmacological control over the clients seemed to be the only recourse, rather than changing the design of the facility.

Medicalization, through medical labels, disease typifications, and medical authority, justifies control as appropriate treatment for the good of the patient.

The biomedical model does not consider ways in which the caregiving relationship and conditions in the caregiving context affect stress for the dementia caregiver as well as the impaired person. If dementia is viewed only as a biomedical condition, the behavior of the demented person is individualized and power relationships involving the elderly and their caregivers are depoliticized. Thus, the impact of power relationships on illness production and disease is not examined.

CAREGIVER STRAIN: THE IMPACT OF THE BIOMEDICAL MODEL

In the new field of dementia caregiving, families are a major component of the long-term care delivery system (George & Gwyther, 1986). Families provide free services to the rapidly increasing number of impaired older adults. It is understandable, then, that their burnout or strain is a concern to policymakers concerned with curtailing health care costs. If family caregiver strain can be minimized, demented persons may be maintained in the community longer than they are now.

Caring for persons with dementing illnesses is difficult work, in institutional settings as well as in families. Much of the strain is associated with what Strauss has called the "uncertain trajectory" associated with some chronic illnesses (Strauss, 1975), the fact that disease progression most often does not conform to predictable patterns.

To cope with the uncertainty surrounding dementing illness, both family and paid caregivers readily adopt the biomedical model of dementia. The biomedical model predicts stagelike disease progression and inevitable deterioration, and rationalizes certain treatment strategies by caregivers. For families, the possibility of institutionalization as a last resort is deemed appropriate in the "later stages." Institutionalization may seem to be the only alternative, as families become drained by the financial and emotional burden of dementia care. Families may find some comfort in making the institutionalization decision if "disease progression" is the reason for this difficult choice.

Strauss has described similar "abandonment rationales" for other "stigmatic . . . or terribly demanding" diseases (Strauss, 1975, pp. 56–57). For families and service providers, the expectation of regression to a childlike state of dependency rationalizes the management of "behavior problems" presumed to be caused by the dementing illness. And so, for either paid or family caregivers, the biomedical model offers a "knowledge" base to face some of the uncertainty associated with caring for the demented.

There is greater certainty in facing the future tasks of caregiving within the biomedical framework. The result may be a reduction in stress for caregivers. However, the biomedical model includes disease typifications that limit the self-identity of demented persons, overgeneralizations Strauss has referred to as "identity spread" in describing other chronic illnesses (Strauss, 1975). Research in family caregiver support groups by Gubrium and Lynott (1987) finds a similar pattern of overgeneralization about

dementia: once the family member has been diagnosed, people see "impairment everywhere."

The literature on family caregivers presents a one-sided view of the caregiving relationship and illustrates the "medicalization of deviance." Caregiver strain is explained by the deterioration of the demented care recipient. The source of trouble in caregiving is located in the misbehavior of the demented person, which is explained by the progression of the dementing illness.

The large gerontological literature on the health and mental health of family caregivers portrays families as the "second victims" of Alzheimer's disease, the "hidden victims" of dementing illnesses (for the most comprehensive work on this question, see: Brody, 1981, 1985; Cantor, 1983; George & Gwyther, 1986; Ory et al., 1985; Zarit, Orr, & Zarit, 1985; Zarit, Reever, & Bach-Peterson, 1980). Most of the articles on dementia in *The Gerontologist* in recent years have focused on the "burden" and "strain" of providing care for persons with dementing illnesses. Also, of the three articles on dementia that have appeared in *Research on Aging* from 1984–88, two concerned caregiver burden. The first was a review of current knowledge about Alzheimer's disease and family caregiving (Ory et al., 1985). This is one of the few articles to consider the social and behavioral aspects of age-related chronic diseases and disabilities, including the impact of the family on demented persons. The second article was more typical, discussing caregiver strain and lack of social support as primary factors in the desire to institutionalize demented family members (Morycz, 1985).

Certainly, families suffer as their loved one slowly deteriorates and requires increasingly demanding care. However, in much of the recent literature, family troubles become medical problems, reflecting what Michel Foucault has called "the medicalisation of the family" and of the caregiving relationship (Foucault, 1976, pp. 166–176). While "the first wave of this offensive bears on the care of children" in the 18th century (ibid., p. 173), the last wave in the medicalization of family relations is the care of the old, especially those with dementing illnesses.

Much of the recent gerontological literature on caregivers as "victims" of dementia perpetuates the medicalization of the family, and neglects important questions about the social dynamics of families in which one member has a dementing illness. George and Gwyther (1986) review current research on caregiving and find weaknesses in sample selection and research design. There is little awareness of heterogeneity among caregivers and no longitudinal research on the dynamics of caregiver burden. George and Gwyther propose a multidimensional model of caregiving, since they have found that caregiver strain and institutional placement are better predicted by characteristics of the caregivers and the caregiving context than by the impairment and behaviors of demented patients.

There are problems in much of the caregiver burden literature in regard to the conceptualization and measurement of burden and strain (Ory et al., 1985). Much of this research equates impairment with burden, and predicts a decision to institutionalize at higher levels of impairment. Gubrium and Lynott (1987) are critical of these assumptions, finding there is no uniformity of impairment, and no equivalence to burden in the institutionalization decision. All are part of a "care equation." Caregiver burden is the product of the ongoing dyadic relationship between caregiver and care recipient (Johnson & Catalano, 1983; Montgomery, Stull, & Borgatta, 1985). However, this reciprocal relationship most often is not examined in the caregiver strain literature.

Ironically, the interest in the "victims" of Alzheimer's disease generally does not include an interest in the perspective of the person with dementia (Rakowski & Clark, 1985). Changes in the caregiving relationship are traced to disease progression, rather than examining disease progression as a consequence of changes in the caregiving relationship. The demented person is viewed as burdensome but not burdened by the illness or by changes in relationships. The demented one is viewed as a stressor, not as one who is experiencing stress. As a result, people with dementia are largely invisible in most of this literature; they are merely disease entities, independent variables. (Two recent exceptions are Cohen and Eisdorfer, 1986, and Shomaker, 1987, which take the perspectives of both the person with a dementing illness and the caregiver.) From a review of this research, it becomes clear that it is those suffering from the impairment, not their caregivers, who are still "hidden victims" of dementia.

In the caregiver strain literature, one consistent finding is that it is not cognitive decline that is most burdensome, resulting in a decision to institutionalize the demented family member; it is troublesome behavior (Diemling & Bass, 1986; Mace, 1987; Morycz, 1985). A poignant irony is that many of the "behavior problems" associated with dementia may be traced to problems in the caregiving relationship, which are overlooked if the behavior is attributed to disease. The medicalization of senility shifts attention from problems in the social situation of caregiving to locate problems in the pathology and misbehavior of the demented person. This focus overlooks the impact of the treatment context and caregiving relationship on the experience of dementing illness.

SOCIAL FACTORS IN DEMENTIA

Eliot Friedson (1970) has charged that sociologists should study the development of social conceptions of illness, as well as social causes of illness behavior. Among social scientists who study dementia, few have examined either the cultural definitions of brain disease or the experience of a dementing illness within caregiving relationships. There are some exceptions in the recent social gerontological literature on dementia, research that pays some attention to individual variation, autonomy, and negotiation, and to the effects of power relationships and other socioenvironmental factors in disease progression (see Cohen & Eisdorfer, 1986; Diamond, 1983; Gilhooly, Zarit, & Birren, 1986; Gilliland & Brunton, 1984; Hanson, 1985; Lawton, 1980; Ory et al., 1985; Rader, 1987; Shomaker, 1987; Winogrand et al., 1987). For example, a recent supplement of *The Gerontologist* is devoted entirely to articles on "autonomy and long-term care." Three of the articles specifically address questions of autonomy for mentally impaired elderly (Cohen, 1988; Hegeman & Tobin, 1988; Stanley et al., 1988)

Within sociology, Jay Gubrium and Robert Lynott are exceptional for their critical contributions concerning the social construction of dementia by family caregivers and service providers (Gubrium, 1986, 1987; Gubrium & Lynott, 1987; Lynott, 1983). However, social gerontologists generally have had little to say about dementia, except that it is a dysfunctional disease with profoundly negative consequences for caregivers and the larger society.

What is missing from most of the current social and behavioral science research on dementia and caregiver strain is an analysis of the impact of cultural definitions, care settings, and the caregiving relationship on the experience of dementing illness. These social factors in dementia may be identified within the "sociogenic" model proposed by Dannefer (1984) to replace the predominant "ontogenetic" normative/developmental "stage theory" of aging. The sociogenic model counters the view of "medicalized devi-

ance," in which the impaired elderly become mere disease entities, deviants who cause social and interpersonal problems.

This sociogenic perspective recognizes that all human experience involves intentional social action and interaction, in socially structured environments, in the context of taken-for-granted socially constructed knowledge about aging, development, and disease. Employing the sociogenic model in research would view demented persons as social actors who live with impairment and interact with others in caregiving relationships, within a variety of socially structured environments such as long-term care facilities, day care centers, and in families. Within this framework, shared "knowledge" of dementia is a collective definition, part of the sociocultural world of the demented and their caregivers, not a fixed biomedical reality. For example, in dementia day care facilities, I have heard caregivers assert that they "know" there is only a "decline" in functioning, "no new learning," which results in these caregivers expecting very little from demented persons. If demented people withdraw from interaction to save face, their nonresponsiveness is taken as confirmation of the negative dementia expectations, a classic example of the self-fulfilling prophecy.

Schmidt (1981) identified a similar pattern in other care settings for the aged, from an exchange theory perspective. The sociogenic model suggests that when caregiving is stressful, for either caregivers or recipients, explanation may be found within the sociocultural care context and caregiving relationship, rather than located only within the condition of impairment.

The biomedical paradigm offers a nearsighted view of dementing illness, focusing only on those aspects that can be explained as brain disease. The predominance of this view in social and behavioral science research on dementing illness neglects much of the daily experience of chronic illness and intellectual impairment, both for demented persons and their caregivers. Social gerontology should offer a broader vision of the social forces involved in dementia: cultural definitions of illness, the socioenvironmental context in which impaired people receive care and the dynamics of the caregiving relationship.

REFERENCES

Becker, H. S. (1973). *Outsiders: Studies in the sociology of deviance.* New York: Free Press.

Bergmann, K. (1985). Epidemiological aspects of dementia and considerations in planning services. *Danish Medical Bulletin, 32,* 84.

Brody, E. M. (1981). Women in the middle and family help to older people. *The Gerontologist, 21,* 471–480.

Brody, E. M. (1985). Parent care as a normative family stress. *The Gerontologist, 25,* 19–29.

Brody, E. M., et al. (1971). Excess disabilities of mentally impaired aged: Impact of individualized treatment. *The Gerontologist, 11,* 124–133.

Brody, J. A. (1982). An epidemiologist views senile dementia: Facts and fragments. *American Journal of Epidemiology, 115,* 155–162.

Cantor, M. (1983). Strain among caregivers: A study of experience in the United States. *The Gerontologist, 23,* 597–604.

Charmaz, K. (1983). Loss of self: A fundamental form of suffering for the chronically ill. *Sociology of Health and Illness, 5,* 168–195.

Cohen, D., & Eisdorfer, C. (1986). *The loss of self: A family resource for the care of Alzheimer's disease and related disorders.* New York: W. W. Norton.

Cohen, E. S. (1988). The elderly mystique: Constraints on the autonomy of elderly adults with disabilities. *The Gerontologist, 28* (supplement), 24–31.

Conrad, P. (1975). The discovery of hyperkinesis: Notes on the medicalization of deviant behavior. *Social Problems, 23,* 12–21.

Conrad, P., & Kern, R. (1986). *The sociology of health and illness: Critical perspectives,* 2nd ed. New York: St. Martin's.

Conrad, P., & Schneider, J. W. (1980). *Deviance and medicalization: From badness to sickness.* St. Louis: C. V. Mosby.

Cutler, N. (1986). Public response: The national politics of Alzheimer's disease. In M. L. M. Gilhooly, S. M. Zarit, & J. E. Birren (Eds.), *The dementias: Policy and management.* Englewood Cliffs, NJ: Prentice-Hall.

Cutler, S. J., & Grams, A. E. (1988). Correlates of self-reported everyday memory problems. *Journal of Gerontology, 43,* S82–90.

Dannefer, D. (1984). Adult development and social theory: A paradigmatic reappraisal. *American Sociological Review, 49,* 100–116.

Dawson, P., & Reid, D. W. (1987). Behavioral dimensions of patients at risk of wandering. *The Gerontologist, 24,* 104–107.

Diamond, T. (1983). Nursing homes as trouble. *Urban Life, 12,* 269–286.

Dick, M. B., Kean, M., & Sands, D. (1988). The pre-selection effect on the recall facilitation of motor movements in Alzheimer-type dementia. *Journal of Gerontology, 43,* P127–135.

Diemling, G. T., & Bass, D. M. (1986). Symptoms of mental impairment among elderly adults and their effects on family caregivers. *Journal of Gerontology, 41,* 778–784.

Estes, C. L. (1 979). *The aging enterprise.* San Francisco: Jossey-Bass.

Estes, C. L., Gerard, L., Zones, J. S., & Swan, J. H. (1984). *Political economy, health and aging.* Boston: Little-Brown.

Estes, C. L., & Binney, E. A. (1989). The biomedicalization of aging: Dangers and dilemmas. *The Gerontologist* (this issue).

Foucault, M. (1976). The politics of health in the 18th century. In C. Gordon (Ed.), 1980, *Power/knowledge: Selected interviews and other writings 1922–77 by Michel Foucault.* New York: Pantheon.

Freed, D. (1987). Long-term occupational exposure in the diagnosis of Alzheimer's disease. Lecture to the Andrus Gerontology Center Director's Series, University of Southern California, Los Angeles.

Friedson, E. (1970). *Profession of medicine.* New York: Dodd, Mead and Company.

George, L. K., & Gwyther, L. P. (1986). Caregiver well-being: A multidimensional examination of family caregivers of demented adults. *The Gerontologist, 26,* 253–259,

Gilhooly, M. L. M., Zarit, S. M., & Birren, J. E. (Eds.). (1986). *The dementias: Policy and management.* Englewood Cliffs, NJ: Prentice-Hall,

Gilliland, N., & Brunton, A. (1984). Nurse's typifications of nursing home patients. *Ageing and Society, 4,* 45–67.

Goffman, E. (1961). *Asylums.* Garden City, NY: Doubleday.

Gubrium, J. F. (1986). *Oldtimers and Alzheimer's: The descriptive organization of senility.* Greenwich, CT: JAI Press.

Gubrium, J. F. (1987). Structuring and destructuring the course of illness: The Alzheimer's disease experience. *Sociology of Health and Illness, 9,* 1–24.

Gubrium, J. F., & Lynott, R. J. (1987). Measurement and the interpretation of burden in the Alzheimer's disease experience. *Journal of Aging Studies, 1,* 265–285.

Gusfield, J. R. (1967). Moral passage: The symbolic process in the public designations of deviance. *Social Problems, 15,* 175–188.

Hanson, B. G. (1985). Negotiation of self and setting to advantage: An interactionist consideration of nursing home data. *Sociology of Health and Illness, 7,* 21–35.

Hegeman, C., & Tobin, S. (1988). Enhancing the autonomy of mentally impaired nursing home residents. *The Gerontologist, 28* (supplement), 71–75.

Henderson, V. (1988). Neocortical symptoms of Alzheimer's disease. Lecture to the Andrus Gerontology Center Director's Series, University of Southern California, Los Angeles.

Hofland, B. F. (1988). Autonomy in long term care: Background issues and a programmatic response. *The Gerontologist, 28* (Supplement), 3–9.

Johnson, C. L., & Catalano, D. J. (1983). A longitudinal study of family supports to impaired elderly. *The Gerontologist, 23,* 612–618.

Kral, V. A. (1978). Benign senescent forgetfulness. In R. Katzman, R. D. Terry, & K. L. Bick (Eds.), *Alzheimer's disease: Senile dementia and related disorders (Aging, v. 7).* New York: Raven Press.

Kuhn, T. S. (1962). *The structure of scientific revolutions.* Chicago: University of Chicago Press.

Langer, E., & Rodin, J. (1976). The effect of choice and enhanced personal responsibility for the aged: A field experiment in an institutional setting. *Journal of Personality and Social Psychology, 34,* 191–198.

Lauter, H. (1985). What do we know about Alzheimer's disease today? *Danish Medical Bulletin, 32,* 1–21.

Lawton, M. P. (1980). Psychosocial and environmental approaches to the care of senile dementia patients. In J. O. Cole & J. E. Barrett (Eds.), *Psychopathology in the aged.* New York: Q. V. Raven Press.

Lyman, K. A. (1988). Infantilization of elders: Day care for Alzheimer's disease victims. In Dorothy Wertz (Ed.), *Research in the sociology of health care, v. 7.* Greenwich, CT: JAI Press.

Lyman, K. A. (1989). Day care for persons with dementia: The impact of the physical environment on staff stress and quality of care. *The Gerontologist, 29,* 557–560,

Lynott, R. J. (1983). Alzheimer's disease and institutionalization: ongoing construction of a decision. *Journal of Family Issues, 4,* 559–574.

Mace, N. L. (1987). Characteristics of persons with dementia. In U.S. Congress, Office of Technology Assessment, *Losing a million minds: Confronting the tragedy of Alzheimer's disease and other dementias.* OTA-BA-323. Washington, DC: U.S. Government Printing Office.

McKhann, G., Drachman, D., Folstein, M., Katzman, R., Price, D., & Stadlan, E. M. (1984). Clinical diagnosis of Alzheimer's disease: Report of the NINCDS-ADRDA work group. *Neurology, 34,* 939–944.

Montgomery, R. J. V., Stull, D. E., & Borgatta, E. F. (1985). Measurement and the analysis of burden. *Research on Aging, 7,* 137–151.

Mortimer, J. A., & Hutton, J. T. (1985). *Senile dementia of the Alzheimer's type,* pages 177–196. New York: Alan R. Liss.

Mortimer, J. A., & Schuman, L. M. (1981). *The epidemiology of dementia.* New York: Oxford.

Morycz, R. K. (1985). Caregiving strain and the desire to institutionalize family members with Alzheimer's disease: Possible predictors and model development. *Research on Aging, 7,* 329–361.

Ory, M. G., Williams, T. F., Emr, M., Lebowitz, B., Rabins P., Salloway, J., Sluss-Radbaugh, T., Wolff, E., & Zarit, S. (1985). Families, informal supports, and Alzheimer's disease: Current research and future agendas. *Research on Aging, 7,* 623–644.

Radelet, M. L. (1987). Response to questions in roundtable session 80, Review criteria for the Journal of Health and Social Behavior. American Sociological Association annual meeting, Chicago, IL.

Rader, J. (1987). A comprehensive staff approach to wandering. *The Gerontologist, 27,* 756–760.

Rakowski, W., & Clark, N. M. (1985). Future outlook, caregiving and care receiving in the family context. *The Gerontologist, 25,* 618–623.

Ruscio, D., & Cavarocchi, N. (1984). Getting on the political agenda: How an organization of Alzheimer families won increased federal attention and funding. *Generations, 9,* 12–15.

Schmidt, M. G. (1981). Exchange and power in special settings for the aged. *International Journal of Aging and Human Development, 14,* 157–166.

Secretary's Task Force on Alzheimer's Disease, U.S. Department of Health and Human Services. (1984). *Alzheimer's Disease.* Washington, DC: U.S. Government Printing Office. DHHS Pub. No. (ADM) 84–1323.

Shanas, E., & Maddox, G. M, (1985). Health, health resources and the utilization of care. In R. H. Binstock & E. Shanas (Eds.), *Handbook of aging and the social sciences,* 2nd ed. New York: Van Nostrand Reinhold.

Shomaker, D. (1987). Problematic behavior and the Alzheimer patient: Retrospection as a method of understanding and counseling. *The Gerontologist, 27,* 370–375.

Smithers, J. A. (1977). Institutional dimensions of senility. *Urban Life, 6,* 251–276.

Spector, M., & Kitsuse, J. (1977). *Constructing social problems.* New York: Benjamin Cummings.

Stanley, B., Stanley, M., Guido, J., & Garvin, L. (1988). The functional competency of elderly at risk. *The Gerontologist, 28* (Supplement), 53–58.

Strauss, A. (1975). *Chronic illness and the quality of life.* St. Louis: C. V. Mosby.

Terry, R. D., & Katzman, R. (1983). Senile dementia of the Alzheimer's type. *Annals of Neurology, 42,* 50–54.

Thompson, L. W., Gong, V., Haskins, E., & Gallagher, D. (1987). Assessment of depression and dementia during the later years. *Annual Review of Gerontology and Geriatrics,* pp. 295–324. New York: Springer.

U.S. Government, Office of Technology Assessment. (1987). *Losing a million minds: Confronting the tragedy of Alzheimer's disease and other dementias.* OTA-BA-323. Washington, DC: U.S. Government Printing Office.

Winogrond, I. R., Fisk, A. A., Kirsling, R. A., & Keyes, B. (1987). The relationship of caregiver burden and morale to Alzheimer's disease patient function in a therapeutic setting. *The Gerontologist, 27,* 336–339.

Zarit, S. H., Orr, N. K., & Zarit, J. M. (1985). *The hidden victims of Alzheimer's disease: Families under stress.* New York: NYU Press.

Zarit, S. H., Reever, K. E., & Bach-Peterson, J. (1980). Relatives of the impaired elderly: Correlates of feelings of burden. *The Gerontologist, 20,* 649–654.

Zola, I. (1972). Medicine as an institution of social control. *Sociological Review, 20,* 487–504.

Discussion Questions for Chapter Four

1. Janna Herman describes a number of ways in which health can be measured, including mortality-based indicators and morbidity indicators. How appropriate is the use of mortality-based indicators of health in light of Meredith Minkler's discussion of the compression of morbidity in Chapter 1?

2. The article "Older Americans' Health" points out some significant differences in health indicators between whites and blacks and between men and women. What factors are most likely to account for these differences across race and gender?

3. What are the implications of Karen Lyman's thesis regarding the importance of social factors in dementia for the way dementia patients ought to be cared for on a daily basis?

CHAPTER FIVE

Psychological Aspects
of Aging

How do personalities (or social selves) change and develop as people age? This question has been approached in a number of ways, but no single theory has offered a complete explanation. It is widely agreed that human personalities are formed through a combination of internal psychological processes and interaction with the social environment. The importance attached to each factor is the main point where theorists differ. Nevertheless, the strong connection between psychological and social factors implies that personality development can be understood as *psychosocial* development. Developmental life span theorists see psychological development as taking place in a series of stages. The individual faces a new set of challenges and opportunities for growth in each stage of life. Much of the attention in human development has focused on the early stages of life. Freud's work on human development, for example, did not even include adulthood, but other theorists, such as Erikson (1980) and Levinson (1978), have placed much more emphasis on development in adulthood.

Individuals do not develop in social isolation. People interact with others in a wide array of social groups and institutions. From a sociological perspective, it is in these encounters that the processes of identity development take place. These processes are also intimately connected with the roles an individual performs. Age norms are social expectations about roles a person ought to perform at any particular stage of life. For example, societies have understandings about when a person ought to go to school, get married, bear and raise children, embark on a career, and retire. In this way, a person learns to conform to the expectations of what a young or an old person ought to do and be. Disengagement theory, activity theory, exchange theory, and continuity theory are all examples of attempts to understand older adult development in social context. In "Psychosocial Theoretical Aspects of Aging: Explanatory Models," Aaron Lipman and Ira F. Ehrlich summarize the major perspectives on changes caused by aging, including developmental lifespan and psychosocial theories.

The lengthening of life we have seen in this century may mean increased potential for human development later in life. Some gerontologists refer to the period beginning at age 60 as the "Third Age." During this time, an individual is freed from many of the role responsibilities of adulthood, including childrearing and employment, and is free to work on the later stages of development such as Erikson's ego integrity, or Maslow's self actualization. Such development may increase older people's potential to make significant contributions to society (Dychtwald and Flower, 1990). Do individuals still have the potential to be creative even at advanced ages? Studies in this area have revealed a high level of continuity in creativity as people age (Atchley, 1991). In "Creativity in the Later Years: Optimistic Prospects for Achievement," Dean Keith Simonton explains why the potential for creativity in the later years remains quite good.

REFERENCES

Atchley, Robert C. (1991). *Social forces and aging* (6th ed.). Belmont, CA: Wadsworth.

Dychtwald, Ken and Flower, Joe. (1990). *Age wave: The challenges and opportunities of an aging America.* New York: Bantam.

Erikson, Erik, H. (1980). *Identity and the life cycle.* New York: W. W. Norton.

Levinson, Daniel J. (1978). *The seasons of a man's life.* New York: Ballantine.

Psychosocial Theoretical Aspects of Aging: Explanatory Models

AARON LIPMAN
IRA F. EHRLICH

Gerontology, the study of aging, is a field in search of a theory. At present there is no single unifying social science theory of aging. This article limits itself to the aspects of changes caused by aging and psychosocial perspectives on aging that include: population identification, developmental life span—adjustment to aging, and psychosocial theory.

POPULATION IDENTIFICATION

Whether the aged constitute a genuine social group (ie, a subculture) or merely a statistical aggregate or social category, has been discussed in the literature on aging, with Rose[1] arguing for a group identity, and Streib[2] taking the opposite view.

The Elderly as a Subculture

According to Rose,[1] a subculture arises within a population category when the members of that category interact with each other more than they do with members of other categories. This tends to happen because of two sets of circumstances: the members have positive attitudes toward each other, based on shared interests, friendship, etc, and often the members are excluded by other groups in the population. At the same time that the elderly share an affinity for each other on the basis of a similar experiential history, the younger population rejects them and grants them a much lower status as diminished persons. As a result, a subculture is formed as the elderly interact more with each other and less with younger people.

At the same time that these subcultural pulls are developing, opposite influences work to keep the elderly person involved in the general culture. These include family contacts, the influence of the mass media in disseminating the general culture to all groups, continued employment through which the elderly person maintains ties to an occupational group and the economic norms of the society, and an attitude of resistance toward aging and participation in any aging subculture.

Rose[1] differentiates between two types of status for the elderly: their status in the general society and that in the aging subcul-

Source: Topics in Geriatric Rehabilitation, 1(2), 46–57. Reprinted with permission from Aspen Publishers, Inc., Gaithersburg, MD 20978, and the authors. Copyright 1986.

ture. Those status factors carried over from the general culture include wealth, occupational prestige, the former holding of power, achievement in earlier life, and educational attainment. He postulates that when an elderly person remains in the same community, his or her sources of status carried over from the general society remain much stronger; conversely, these sources diminish for persons who move out of their home communities. In the elderly subculture, two factors are especially important in conferring status: physical and mental health, and social activity and participation.

Basic to Rose's concept of the aged's group-consciousness (or group-identification) is the phenomenon of the aged's self-conception. While the exact chronologic definition of elderly is difficult to determine, most Americans eventually come to think of themselves as elderly. This shift in self-perception leads persons to view themselves as progressively less capable physically and mentally, with a shift from autonomy to dependence, and from ascent to decline. Because the concept of elderly in the larger society is associated with negative evaluations, the self-conception of the elderly often brings with it feelings of self-hatred, depression, and disengagement. In the eyes of some of the elderly, their peers are being transformed from a social category to a social group. The steps in this evolution begin with persons' joining an expressive association populated exclusively by people their age, with feelings of group pride developing next. The recognition and discussion of common problems constitutes the next phase, followed by plans for social action to correct these shared problems; in this manner the elderly evolve as a political pressure group. All the manifestations of group consciousness among the aging as postulated by Rose are the signs of group identification that previous sociologists had found to characterize ethnic minority groups.

The Elderly as a Social Category

Streib's[2] position is diametrically opposed to the above viewpoint. He writes that the elderly constitute a social category or statistical aggregate, rather than a true social group, and certainly not a minority group in the ociologic sense. He specifies six general criteria that define a true minority group, and measures the elderly against each of these standards.

The first criterion is that the members of the social group possess identifying characteristics that adhere throughout their entire life cycle, and that carry with them status and role expectations that also last through out the life cycle. The elderly obviously do not conform to this criterion.

Second in Streib's list of minority characteristics is the prevailing feeling that group members demonstrating this identifying characteristic are held less worthy of esteem by the majority. Stereotypes and cliches regarding their work performance and appropriate activities would demonstrate these derogatory sentiments.

The third criterion, that of group identity, requires that there be a consciousness-of-kind within the group, as well as an intergroup identity. In the first context, Streib cites four surveys of populations over age 60, where the majority of the people consider themselves "middle aged"; only after age 65 is there any tendency to identify themselves as "elderly" or "old."

The fourth criterion is readiness to organize as a political pressure group. While Rose[1] has postulated that this is beginning to happen among the elderly, Streib[2] believes that the weak sense of identity among the elderly inhibits this type of political expression. For a true minority, readiness to organize as a political pressure group is linked, he postulates, to the belief that possession of their group characteristic denies them their civil rights or their access to power and privilege (Streib's fifth criterion). The elderly have neither been denied their civil rights, nor have they been denied access to power and privilege; in fact, there is evidence that they receive some special benefits not accorded to younger groups.

Streib's sixth criterion for a minority group concerns deprivation; possession of that status characteristic may lead to economic hardship, unequal access to work, residential segregation, and social isolation. Streib agrees that many elderly are underprivileged, but disapproves of classifying them as a minority group on this basis. While some workers are denied jobs because they have gotten older, Streib considers this more a problem for the middle-aged than the elderly. Nor do the elderly suffer from either residential segregation or social isolation in the same manner as do true minorities.

Streib concludes that the elderly do not share a separate and distinct culture, nor is membership in the group exclusive or permanent; everyone will eventually become a member of the aged category merely by virtue of living long enough. Since the aged do not satisfy the criteria of true minority groups defined by Streib, he rejects the concept of the aged as a minority group, claiming that it obscures rather than clarifies understanding of the elderly. The aged, he concludes, are to be studied as a sociologic aggregate, rather than a social group.

DEVELOPMENTAL LIFE SPAN— ADJUSTMENT TO AGING

In addition to examining the aged population as a group, in their attempt to derive valid generalizations concerning that period of an adult's life, theoreticians are also looking at aging from the vantage of the person's developmental life span.

In the past, attention focused only on segments of the life span, usually childhood and adolescence. Today this developmental view encompasses all ages; it divides the life cycle into recognizable phases or states through which all persons pass in their journey from the cradle to the grave. The stages are hierarchical, with each one depending on the successful completion of preceding ones for its success. The tasks and accomplishments of each phase of the life cycle have been variously delineated in the past by social scientists, beginning with Freud's description of the psychosexual stages of childhood development. While Freud's analysis did not continue through adulthood and old age, those of Jung, Erikson, Havighurst, and Levinson addressed the entire life cycle, with theoretic implications for both the psychologic and social development of the total person. Peck[3] and Büehler[4] addressed middle age and old age building on Erikson's work. The significance of this life-span approach for theories of aging is that, by postulating a continuity of developmental stages, it links each elder to his or her past. This developmental approach attempts to explain how persons of the same age cohort (including the elderly) are similar by virtue of their shared life stage, yet different as a result of the unique ways in which they developed through their earlier life stages.

Each of these theorists perceived aging as a natural process of change, not as a pathologic system nor just a response to one's environment. All recognized that few persons attain the ideal state.

Jung

Carl Jung[5] was one of the first to designate adult stages on the basis of his own clinical theory and practice. He described the youth period as lasting between puberty and middle age. During this stage the person is concerned with sexual instincts, broadening horizons, and conquering feelings of inferiority. In the next important adult stage, ages 35 to 40, the person tries to transport the youthful self into the middle years. According to Jung, at this stage of development, the person's convictions strengthen until they become somewhat rigid and intolerant at age 50. In later years activities decrease, men become more expressive and nurturant, and women become more instrumental.[5,6]

Erikson

Erik Erikson's[7] eight stages of ego development are probably the best known of the psychologic models of life cycle continuity. He has been referred to as the first of the psychoanalytic theorists to go beyond the stage of genital maturity. In Erikson's schema, each of the eight stages presents the person with an ego-threatening crisis that must be surmounted and resolved satisfactorily before he or she can proceed to the next stage of personality development. Rogers[8] says, "Crisis in this sense is not some catastrophic event but is instead a critical period of increased vulnerability and potential."[8(p34)] As a result of this crisis, the person's life is restructured, for better or for worse, depending on how the crisis was met and resolved.

The final stage of Erikson's portrayal, old age, comprises the most years (40) of all the stages. In old age the individual must achieve wisdom and integrity—the sense that his or her life has been meaningful and appropriate, as opposed to a feeling of despair or self-disgust. Such ego-integration allows for both participation by followership and acceptance of the responsibility of leadership. Erikson's contribution to stages of human development beyond childhood and young adulthood is considered a breakthrough.

Havighurst and Levinson

While Erikson's focus had been on ego and personality development, Havighurst[9] and Levinson[10] were concerned with the social tasks and roles that must be managed at each developmental stage of the person's life course. According to Havighurst, if these tasks are successfully mastered at one stage of the life cycle, the person achieves happiness during that phase and becomes better prepared to deal successfully with the tasks of his or her next developmental stage; the converse would also hold true.

Havighurst's model[9] divides adulthood into three periods: early adulthood, from age 18 to age 30; middle age, from 30 to 55; and old age, after 55. Some of the tasks for each stage include the following: in early adulthood, each person must commence his or her occupational role, find a congenial social group, and find a marriage partner and learn to live amicably with that partner. This is the stage where the tasks also include managing the home, raising children, and accepting civic responsibilities. In middle age, to achieve happiness the person must successfully perform the tasks of establishing and keeping a standard of living appropriate for his or her status, help adolescent children develop their potential, relate well to his or her spouse as an individual, take a responsible role in social and civic affairs, adjust to elderly parents, and accept and adapt to the physiologic changes of middle age. After age 55, the person must adjust to retirement and its reduced income, to establishing relationships with others of the same age cohort, to the death of a spouse, to fulfilling social and civic responsibilities, and to the deficits of declining health and strength.

Levinson[10] also approaches the stages or "seasons" of the adulthood (of men) as a developmental process, involving such components as " . . . his occupation, his love relationships, his marriage and family, his relation to himself, his use of solitude, his roles in various social contexts—all of the relationships with individuals, groups, and institutions that have significance for him."[10(p41)] According to Levinson, these components, especially family and occupation, make up the underlying structure or pattern of a person's life. He refers to this pattern as the person's "life structure"; the two basic types of developmental periods involved in determining life structure are structure building and structure changing.

The "novice" phase of adult development consists of three seasons: early adult transition, a structure-changing season; entering the adult world, which is structure building; and age 30 transition, during which structure changing again takes place. Levinson has designated the most important developmental tasks of the early adult season as entering an occupation, developing a mentor relationship, and forming a love or marriage relationship.

During the age 30 transition season, a reappraisal of the first life structure is the primary task. This reexamination of the life choices made in the early adult stage is a phase that researchers have found leads to changes in the lives of most men in the age 30 category. The magnitude of these changes and the amount of stress they entail varies with the person. The transition may be relatively tranquil or forcefully dramatic, but it is characteristic of persons at this developmental stage of their lives that they either make new life choices or reaffirm old ones. These choices have both significant impact on the life structure of that period, as well as ramifications for the next one.

The next phase of adult development is that of settling down, and its major tasks include establishing a person's niche in society (this includes family, occupation, and community, and has implications for sense of self), and working toward advancement.

The mid-life transition, the next phase, is a structure-changing one that is both past and future oriented. The first of the three major tasks of this phase is the reappraisal of the settling down period, followed by steps to initiate the period of middle adulthood. The third task consists of dealing with and resolving the polarities of the person's rela-

tionship to him- or herself and to the world. Levinson designates these polarities as young/old, destructive/creative, masculine/feminine, and attachment/separateness. Levinson sees the resolution of these polarities as constituting the main task of individuation during the mid-life transition, especially for the young/old category. During this period the person must come to terms with real or impending biologic decline, accompanied by the recognition of his or her own mortality, as well as the societal attitudes (often internalized as well) that denigrate or devalue the status of middle age in favor of youth.

The next phase is once again a structure-building period, entering middle adulthood. Having faced the polarities of the mid-life transition, the person makes new choices or reaffirms old ones concerning his or her life situation, and works to make these choices meaningful in order to negotiate the middle years successfully.

While Levinson's respondents in his longitudinal study have not yet reached old age, he postulates the existence of a structure-changing age 50 transition, followed by a late adult transition and late adulthood.

Peck

Peck[3] acknowledging his debt to Erikson, divides Erikson's final crisis (integrity versus despair) into several different kinds of psychologic learnings and adjustments in later life. He first divides the last half of life into two broad chronologic periods: (1) middle age, the 40s and 50s and (2) old age, from 60 on. Each of these stages revolves around a central physical or social issue at which point persons can (at variable ages) adjust their value systems so as to move in a positive direction.

For middle age there are (1) valuing wisdom versus physical powers; (2) socializing versus sexualizing in human relationships; (3) cathectic flexibility versus cathectic impoverishment (when a person's love objects disappear, parents die or children leave home it is desirable to reinvest emotions in other people or activities); and (4) mental flexibility versus mental rigidity (using one's life experience to arrive at new ways of doing things). Peck's stages and sequence in old age are even clearer and have an unusual quality. Old age, beginning in the 60s, poses the following three developmental tasks or crises: ego differentiation versus work role preoccupation (one redefines one's worth as separate from a prior role, such as work, and shifts to new accepting roles of intra- as well as interpersonal relationships); body transcendence versus body preoccupation (one handles the decline in physical power, lowered resistance to illness, and lowered recuperative powers by defining well-being in terms of satisfying relationships and activities); and ego transcendence versus body preoccupation (one adapts positively to the inevitable prospect of death and devotes one's energy to helping others so they may be happy now and after one's own death). This approach not only ensures others' well-being but develops a satisfying and preferable alternative to denial of mortality.

Peck's tasks are useful in that they not only take a positive approach to what are usually considered unwelcome aspects of old age, but they also support personality change as possible in later years.

Büehler

Büehler,[4] dissatisfied with both Freud's and Erikson's ego psychology model, adopts a biophysical model of a living open system where both maintenance and change of the organism are equally important. She conceives of two forms of maintenance: that directed to satisfying need and that directed to maintaining internal order. Two types of change are adaptation and creativity. According to Büehler, maturity is the age of fulfillment when the following four basic

life tendencies are met to a person's satisfaction: needs satisfaction (maintenance), adaptive self-limitation (change), creative expansion (change), upholding internal order (maintenance).

Successful passage through each of these stages requires integrating and balancing conflicting and competing trends from earlier stages to a new stage. This integration becomes particularly crucial in moving from middle age to old age. In middle age self-assessment evolves, and whatever order existed previously is questioned. This critical self-assessment succeeds when self-actualization is at a high level (eg, acceptance of self and others for what they are; having a fresh appreciation of people and the world; and being autonomous and serene within oneself). This serious consideration of last moments for change determines to a large extent how one faces old age.

PSYCHOSOCIAL THEORETICAL ATTEMPTS

Disengagement, conflict, exchange, activity, and continuity are examples of theoretical attempts in the field of gerontology. Some of these theoretical orientations deal with the adjustment of the person to his or her own aging; some deal with the relationship between the social system and the older person; some deal with both; some overlap and are evaluated as more descriptive than scientific. It can be stated, however, that these attempts provide a basis for further research toward a theory of aging.

Disengagement theory

Disengagement uses the sociologic perspective of functionalism. Functionalism assumes that society has certain needs that must be fulfilled if stability and equilibrium are to be maintained. A structure is said to have a function if it contributes to the fulfillment of one or more of the social needs of the system.[11]

First proposed in 1961 by Cumming and Henry,[12] the disengagement theory depicts aging as a process of gradual physical, psychologic, and social withdrawal. Disengagement is considered as functional during the aging process, purportedly preparing the person and society to face the inevitability of death. Changes in the personality of the individual are viewed as either the cause or the effect of decreased involvement with others; the authors claim that once this process starts it is irreversible and that morale may remain high or improve as part of the process of disengagement. Disengagement is perceived as mutually advantageous to both the older person's personality system and the larger social system. As the elderly shift their attention and progressively withdraw from adult roles, such as working, society relinquishes the elderly from those social roles, and a mutual withdrawal process occurs.

Within this process Cumming and Henry have described three types of changes resulting in an older person's becoming less tied to the social system of which he or she is a member. These are changes in the amount of interaction, the purposes of the interaction, and the style of interaction with others. Ehrlich[13] conceptualized an isolated life style as being most consonant with reduced social interactional aspects of disengagement. When this withdrawal from interaction with others was voluntary, life satisfaction was high. In outlining their theory, Cumming and Henry indicate that the process of social and psychologic withdrawal is modal for the aging, that this process is both intrinsic and inevitable, and that the process is not only a correlate of successful aging but may also be a condition of it, since those who accept this inevitable reduction in social and personal interactions in old age are usually satisfied with their lives.

As one of the first explanatory models attempting to explicate the process of suc-

cessful aging, disengagement evoked a great deal of positive attention when it was advanced. Today, however, it has been largely discredited. Lipman and Smith[14] while agreeing that a person's death may be dysfunctional for the social system if it is not prepared for, found that those who reduce their activities as they age tend to suffer a reduction in overall life satisfaction. They warn that in functional analysis it is essential to distinguish the consequences for different systems or subsystems.

Criticisms of disengagement theory range from questioning the total concept of disengagement to a lack of support for tested points of the theory. The areas in question include the universality and inevitability of disengagement, the modal loss of adult roles, the separation of illness from aging, the fact that the theory is based only on the later stage of the life cycle, and the need for sharper definition of the concepts. The inherent weaknesses of the theory make the observer wonder why it received so much acclaim when it was first proposed. Blau[15] suggests that this was because the theory can be best understood in the context of the conservative and regressive *weltanschauung* characterized by the 1950s and early 1960s, when a Republican general occupied the presidency.

Functionalism-versus-Conflict Theory

In the 1960s, the challenge to functionalism came from several sources because functionalism was believed to be too consensus oriented, it has a built-in conservative bias, and it treats both change and conflict in society negatively. Whereas the functionalists emphasize order, stability, and equilibrium, and thus can devise an orientation that assumes that the person and the society mutually acquiesce to the withdrawal from work and other adult roles, the conflict perspective is radically different. Consent and acquiescence (from the conflict perspective) take place through oppression, coercion, domination, and exploitation of one group by another. The conflict perspective stresses that there are always competing interests as groups struggle over claims to scarce resources, including status, power, and social class. While functionalists also assume that stratification is based on scarcity, the problem is often defined by functionalists as how to integrate the different sectors, groups, or classes. Conflict theorists, however, see the solution to this scarcity as occurring through the reduction of structural inequalities. These structural changes, they argue, will occur only in the presence of intense struggle.[16] This perspective is also shared by de Beauvoir,[17] who views aging as a class struggle. Estes, in her analysis of the Older Americans Act, states that her research attempts to "make explicit how certain ways of thinking about the aged as a social problem . . . are rooted in the structure of social and power relations."[18(p2)]

Exchange Theory

Another theoretical orientation that emerged as a reaction to functionalism is exchange theory. Based on the belief that functionalism is too abstract and structural, and cannot explain actual human behavior, exchange theory is firmly rooted in rationalism. That is, human beings tend to choose courses of action on the basis of anticipated outcomes from among a known range of alternatives. Underlying this rational view of human behavior is the principle of hedonism, expressed in the contention that people tend to choose alternatives that will provide the most beneficial outcome. Everyone attempts to optimize gratifications; that is, people continually try to satisfy needs and wants and to attain certain goals, and most of this occurs through interaction with other persons or groups. Persons attempt to maximize rewards, while reducing costs. Voluntary social behavior is motivated by the expectation

of the return or reward this behavior will bring from others. One gives things in hope of getting something in return.[19]

Another proposition essential to exchange theory is the principle of reciprocity. In its simplest form it can be stated that a person should help (and should not hurt) those who have helped him or her. The principle of reciprocity further assumes that a person chooses alternative modes of behaving by comparing the anticipated rewards, the possible costs that may be incurred, and the magnitude of investment required to achieve those rewarding outcomes. Accordingly, rewards in human social interaction should be proportional to investment, and costs should not exceed rewards, or else the person will shun that course of activity. Homans[20] has extended the principle of reciprocity to include this concept, which he calls distributive justice. When rewards are not proportional to investments over the long term, he asserts, persons tend to feel angry with social relations, instability is created, and the propensities for conflict increase.

Persons exchange not only tangible and material objects, but also intangibles such as the expression of love, admiration, respect, power, or influence. Anything that can be given or taken away is a resource that can be exchanged. Persons invest in a relationship with the expectation of being rewarded. During interaction with others, exchange of resources is continual, which contributes to the satisfaction of the person's needs, as well as to the attainment of individual or group goals. If power is defined as the ability to impose one's will upon the other, it is obvious that the person who has more of the valued resources to exchange has more power in the relationship. Homans,[20] in fact, defines power as a person's ability to provide valuable resources believed to be scarce. The problem of the aged, according to Dowd,[21] is that in the social exchange process between the elderly and society, the elderly lose those resources. By losing power, the elderly are increasingly unable to enter into equal exchange relationships with significant others and all that remains for them is the capacity to comply. Just as the conflict theorists focus on inequalities and class struggle, Dowd believes that "to understand the situation of the aged . . . we must examine the relationship of society's stratification system in the aging process."[22(pix)]

Activity Theory

The activity theory, which is related to social role concepts, was advanced as an alternative interpretation to disengagement. It affirms that the continued maintenance of a high degree of involvement in social life is an important basis for deriving and sustaining satisfaction. It claims that those who maintain extensive social contacts, who engage in regular physical activities, and who pursue emotionally and intellectually stimulating activities, similar to their engagement level in midlife, age most successfully. Declines in activity and role loss are thus associated with lower levels of satisfaction.

In 1972, Lemon and colleagues[23] attempted to test the activity theory empirically and distinguished different types of activities. Informal activity was measured by self-reported interaction with close friends, relatives, and neighbors. Formal activities were self-reported participation in voluntary organizations. Solitary activity was solitary leisure and household activities. The authors reported that except for informal activity with friends, which had a low level of significance, none of their hypotheses relating frequency of activity to life satisfaction received consistent support. In repeating this research, Longino and Kart[24] found that while solitary activities had no effect, and while formal activities had a negative effect, again informal activities had a positive effect on life satisfaction.

Continuity Theory

Continuity theory as espoused by Neugarten[25] assumes that in the process of becoming adults, persons develop habits, preferences, etc that become part of their personalities throughout their life experience. These habits and preferences are brought into old age. The continuity theory claims that neither activity nor inactivity assumes happiness. It posits that most older people want to remain engaged with their social environment and that the magnitude of this engagement varies with the person according to life-long established patterns and self-concepts. It further recognizes the interrelationships of biologic and environmental factors with psychologic preferences. Positive aging becomes an adaptive process involving interaction among all elements.

In sum, activity and continuity theories assume the need for continued involvement throughout life; disengagement assumes mutuality in decline of involvement. Exchange theory assumes neither. It posits that the degree of engagement is the outcome of a specific change relationship between the person and society in which the more powerful exchange partner dictates the terms of the relationship.

With relatively inadequate longitudinal studies of men and women as they move through life, researchers have attempted to formulate theories for the social and psychologic processes involved in aging. As can be seen, they have not yet been able to describe a meaningful context for the understanding of these transformations. An accurate and complete theoretic model should have concepts that are clearly understood and can be properly operationalized. These concepts should be linked with propositions that suggest hypotheses, and these hypotheses should be capable of empirical verification. Dissatisfaction has been voiced with theories of aging, since most of them do not follow this theoretic model, and thus have very little predictive power. Despite the enormous complexities and unknowns concerning the social processes of aging, however, researchers remain confident that a comprehensive theory regarding the trajectory of change that takes place in the third age of life will emerge in the foreseeable future.

Positive aging is out of the hands of rehabilitation therapists. However, the more therapists understand stages that men and women are likely to undergo as they age, the more responsive they can be to persons in their care. Developing a meaningful context within which the transformations of aging can be understood will be aided by information offered by all who work with the elderly, especially those involved in their day-to-day rehabilitation.

REFERENCES

1. Rose AM: The subculture of the aging: A topic for sociological research. *Gerontologist* 1962;2:112–127.

2. Streib GF: Are the aged a minority group? in Gouldner AW, Miller SM (eds): *Applied Sociology*. New York, Free Press of Glencoe, 1965.

3. Peck RC: Psychological developments in the second half of life, in Neugarten B (ed): *Middle Age and Aging: A Reader in Social Psychology*. Chicago, University of Chicago Press, 1968.

4. Büehler C: Theoretical observations about life's basic tendencies. *Am J Psychother* 1959; 13:561–581.

5. Jung CG: *The Stages of Life. The Structure and Dynamics of the Psyche*. New York, Pantheon, 1960.

6. Lipman A: Marriage and family roles of the aged, in Wolman BB (ed): *International Encyclopedia of Neurology, Psychiatry, Psychoanalysis and Psychology*, vol 7. New York, Van Nostrand Reinhold, 1977, pp 24–26.

7. Erikson E: *Childhood and Society*, ed 2. New York, Norton, 1950.

8. Rogers R: *Issues in Adult Development*. Belmont, Calif, Wadsworth, 1980.

9. Havighurst RJ: *Developmental Tasks and Education*. New York, David McKay, 1972.

10. Levinson D: *Seasons of a Man's Life*. New York, Knopf, 1978.

11. Lipman A: Latent function analysis in gerontological research. *Gerontologist* 1969;5:256–259.

12. Cumming E, Henry WE: *Growing Old: The Process of Disengagement*. New York, Basic Books, 1961.

13. Ehrlich IF: Life styles among persons 70 years and older in age-segregated housing. *Gerontologist* 1972; 12:27–31.

14. Lipman A, Smith KJ: Functionality of disengagement in old age. *J Gerontol* 1968;23:517–521.

15. Blau ZS: *Aging in a Changing Society*, ed 2. New York, Franklin Watts, 1981.

16. Brodsky DM: The conflict perspective and understanding aging among minorities, in Manuel RC (ed): *Minority Aging*. Westport, Conn, Greenwood Press, 1982.

17. De Beauvoir S: *The Coming of Age*. New York, Putnam Books, 1972.

18. Estes CL: *The Aging Enterprise*. San Francisco, Jossey-Bass, 1979.

19. Lipman A: Minority aging from the exchange and structural-functionalist perspectives, in Manuel RC (ed): *Minority Aging*. Westport, Conn, Greenwood Press, 1982.

20. Homans G: *Social Behavior in Elementary Forms*. New York. Harcourt Brace & World, 1961.

21. Dowd JJ: Aging as exchange: A test of the distributive justice proposition. *Pacific Sociol Rev* 1978; 21:351–375.

22. Dowd JJ: *Stratification Among the Aged*. Monterey, Calif., Brooks Cole, 1980.

23. Lemon BW, Bengtson VL, Peterson JA: An exploration of the activity theory of aging: Activity types and life satisfaction among in-movers to a retirement community. *J Gerontol* 1972;27:511–523.

24. Longino CF Jr, Kart CS: Explicating activity theory: A formal replication. *J Gerontol* 1982;37:713–722.

25. Neugarten BL: Adult personality: A developmental view. *Human Dev* 1966;9:61–73.

Creativity in the Later Years: Optimistic Prospects for Achievement

DEAN KEITH SIMONTON

The belief prevails that creativity is the prerogative of youth, whereas old age is virtually synonymous with a decline in creative powers. This stereotypical expectation is sometimes blamed on a supposed intellectual decrement, and is other times attributed to a putative motivational loss. An expression of the former possibility is found in Shakespeare's words "When the age is in, the wit is out" (*Much Ado About Nothing*, c. 1598/1952, p. 520), whereas the latter was expressed by Lord Byron when he complained that "Years steal/Fire from the mind, as vigor from the limb/And life's enchanted cup but sparkles near the brim" (*Childe Harold*, 1812–16/1905, p. 36). Are beliefs like these valid articles of folk wisdom? Or do they represent mere illustrations of persistent prejudices against the advantages of full maturity?

One possible response is to have individuals of diverse ages take psychometric tests that gauge creativity, divergent thinking, or some other capacity presumably pertinent to creative achievement. This psychometric approach has been pursued most vigorously by Birren and his associates (e.g., Alpaugh & Birren, 1977; Ruth & Birren, 1985). Although this line of attack can teach us much about how aging affects various cognitive changes, this approach also has the built-in limitation that performance on these instruments is only remotely connected with behavioral creativity, namely genuine creative accomplishments (Hocevar, 1981).

Therefore, second perspective is also worth pursuing: that is, to look at the actual careers of artists and scientists to see how the production of notable contributions varies with age. Is it true that we cannot reasonably expect creative products from individuals supposedly "past their prime"? To address issues like these does not require us to scrutinize how creativity changes "from the inside," nor need we inquire into how creativity transforms in some highly idiographic fashion with age—however significant such fine-grained analyses may be in other contexts. Instead, the emphasis is squarely placed on unearthing nomothetic principles, or general tendencies, that describe how the overall probability of exerting a broad and enduring influence within a creative domain changes in old age. These longitudinal trends are best discerned by applying historiometric methods to respectable samples of distinguished creators whose achievements span a diversity of endeavors

Source: The Gerontologist 30(5), 626–631. Reprinted with permission from The Gerontological Society of America, Washington DC 20005. Copyright 1990.

(Simonton, 1990). Thus, if we count the output of recognized creative achievements per age period, is the forecast in the final years bright or dim?

Amazingly, this second research tactic was first implemented over 150 years ago, in what may represent the oldest clear example of quantitative research in life-span developmental psychology! Quetelet (1835/1968), a pioneer in the application of statistics to behavioral data, tabulated how the output of plays by notable French and English dramatists changes from young adulthood to old age. A few decades later, Beard (1874) extended this approach to a far wider range of creative endeavors. This historiometric strategy was continued in the 20th century by Lehman (1953) who summarized his key results in *Age and Achievement* (see also Lehman, 1962). Although Lehman's empirical conclusions provoked some criticisms, these mostly of a methodological sort (e.g., Dennis, 1966), subsequent research, using more sophisticated statistical designs, has only slightly qualified the broad picture that emerged (Simonton, 1988a). Let us turn to the gist of this long and continuing research tradition to learn what it tells us about the prospects for creativity in the later years of life.

One pessimistic finding does seem incontrovertible: If one plots the number of creative contributions produced each age period—such as at yearly, 5-year, or decade intervals—the same general longitudinal curve appears over and over. Beginning somewhere in the 20s, output first increases fairly rapidly until a peak is reached, usually sometime in the 30s or 40s, after which a gradual decline sets in. This age curve holds even after introducing all varieties of statistical controls for potential artifacts and spurious relationships (Simonton, 1988a). Hence, the age decrement in creativity after the midlife optimum seems very real. Indeed, evidence strongly suggests that the longitudinal changes in creative achievement are cross-

culturally and transhistorically invariant (Simonton, 1988a). In addition, the age curves for creative behavior are roughly paralleled by agewise shifts in performance on the psychometric measures (e.g., Bromley, 1956; McCrae, Arenberg, & Costa, 1987). Are we compelled by these findings to infer that the prediction of a noncreative old age is well founded? Not at all! Close scrutiny of recent empirical findings indicate seven distinct reasons why it is possible for creative individuals to anticipate continued activity right until the end of life:

1. *The decrement in achievement is rarely so substantial that creative individuals become devoid of creativity at life's end.*—On the average, the rate of creative output in the seventh decade of life drops to about half the rate witnessed at the career optimum (Simonton, 1988a). Thus, even an octogenarian can expect to produce many notable contributions to any creative activity. Moreover, even though a 50% decrement may seem substantial, the decline does not oblige the last decade of a normal life span to pale in comparison with the first decade of a creative career. On the contrary, creators in their 60s and 70s will most often be generating new ideas at a rate exceeding that of the same creators in their 20s (cf. Dennis, 1966).

Finally, it is essential to point out that toward the end of life the post-peak decline decelerates, meaning that the depressing baseline of zero output is approached only asymptotically (Simonton, 1984a). This is not to say that a "terminal drop" may not occur for those individuals who experience severe disability, but only that so long as a person's health holds out, no theoretical or empirical reason exists to expect the absence of creativity in senior citizens. In fact, it is easy to list monumental achievements that were inspired by minds advanced in years (Lehman 1953, chap. 14). Among artists, Cervantes wrote the second part of *Don Quixote* in his 68th year, Verdi composed his last opera *Fal-*

staff in his 80th year, and Titian painted "Christ Crowned with Thorns" when he was nearing 90 years of age. Among scientists, Laplace completed his *Celestial Mechanics* when he was 79, Humboldt finished his *Cosmos* when he was 89, and the chemist Chevreul took up the study of gerontology in his 90s and published his last scientific paper when 102!

2. *Insofar as extrinsic factors interfere with late-life creativity, these negative effects can often be mitigated.*—In the preceding paragraphs it was acknowledged that circumstances in the later years of life may not always be conducive to the maintenance of output, despite any reservoir of creative potential. Empirical studies suggest that a portion of the age decrement can be blamed on the intrusion of these extraneous influences (see also Lehman, 1953, chap. 20). Certainly a deterioration of physical health and vigor will aggravate the post-peak descent, and the decrease may be prompted even more by increased professional and personal responsibilities (e.g., Simonton, 1977a).

Even so, these detrimental consequences are not necessarily permanent. For one thing, tremendous advances have been made in medicine that can render the latter part of life far more productive than in earlier days, transforming retirement into "golden years." Furthermore, creative individuals can often adapt to the altered conditions so as to maintain productivity in spite of the changes. As an example, research suggests that the rate of information processing may slow down somewhat in late life, a longitudinal trend that could possibly limit the speed at which original ideas can be generated (Birren, Woods, & Williams, 1980). Nonetheless, many creative individuals can manage to adjust to this aging effect by the judicious use of assistants. It was common for Renaissance artists to employ a team of apprentices to perform the more mundane tasks, such as preparing materials and filling in the lesser details of a painting under the

master's watchful eye. Likewise, illustrious scientists nowadays may gather whole research teams to facilitate their creative work, allowing the senior investigator to concentrate on hypothesis generation and theoretical interpretation while assistants and junior collaborators execute the experiments that would otherwise consume the invaluable time of the older researcher.

In fact, I would argue that the self-actualization process that motivates creativity will frequently drive an individual to surmount even the more debilitating infirmities of old age. Far from rare are instances of notable creators refusing to allow newly acquired handicaps from blocking their continued output. Bach and Handel continued to compose despite their late-life blindness; Beethoven composed the masterpieces of his famed Third Period unable to hear their performances, an achievement nearly matched by Smetana as well. Goya spent his last years painting while deaf; Renoir was so disabled by rheumatism that he was forced to have a paint brush tied to his hand, and eventually had sculptures executed by dictating instructions to an assistant; Matisse in his last years was often forced to work from a wheelchair with a crayon attached to a long bamboo pole.

In the sciences, Galileo continued making contributions to science in his 70s despite becoming blind, an affliction that equally failed to stop Euler who, also in his 70s, was obliged to execute complex mathematical calculations totally in his head in order to maintain his prolific output. More remarkable still are the examples set by Stephen Hawking, the theoretical physicist, and Franz Rosenweig, the Jewish religious existentialist, individuals who refused to let almost total paralysis from sclerosis stop them from generating their ideas. In light of these exemplars, we have no reason to doubt the power of the human mind to create notwithstanding the frailties of an aged body.

3. *Neither data nor theory require that the observed age decrements in creative productivity be taken as conclusive proof of psychological impairments in old age.*—One reason why Lehman's (1953) research provoked such hostile critiques is that researchers were too quick to surmise that if creative output diminished with age, that must imply some corresponding loss in intellectual or motivational capacities (Simonton, 1988a, 1990). Yet such an implication is a non sequitur, given how many alternative explanations there are for a declining age function. Besides extrinsic influences like physical illness, it is possible to explain the age curves without making any assumptions whatsoever about some loss in psychological faculties. This possibility does not prove that such age decrements are not contributing factors, but only that we cannot assume a connection without further direct proof. For example, the age curve can be precisely predicted according to an information-processing model of the creative process (Simonton, 1984a, 1988b, 1989a, in press). This mathematical model explicates the key empirical features of the longitudinal changes without having to postulate declines in psychological functioning.

More important, this model maintains that the age curve is really not an age curve at all, but rather a career curve. That is, creative output changes primarily as a function of career (or professional) age, not chronological age, a switch of perspective in line with empirical research (Simonton, 1988a). Because career age explains more variance in longitudinal output rates than does chronological age, one cannot conclude that the age curve is the result of extraneous events associated with the aging process. On the contrary, what this dependence implies is that the age curve is the repercussion of the manner in which a creative career naturally unfolds over time. According to the theoretical model, the career consists of the intrinsic manifestation of the latent possibilities in a person's creative potential, a self-actualiza-

tion process that yields the age curve empirically observed (Simonton, 1984a; see also Simonton, 1980). This causal priority of career over chronological age leads to a significant expectation regarding late-life creativity. Sometimes an individual will be a "late bloomer." If the cause of creative productivity is the endogenous exploitation of creative potential, then an individual who has a late start can anticipate a later peak and a higher rate of output in the last years.

This helps explain why some creative personalities did not attain the acme of their careers until the end of their lives. Thus the classical composer Anton Bruckner did not really discover his true mission as distinctive symphonist until he was in his 40s, his first masterpiece in this form, the Fourth, emerging when he was 50, two of his greatest symphonies, the Seventh and the Eighth, not appearing until a decade later, whereas what some consider his most impressive work, the Ninth, was left with the last movement missing when he died in his 70th year. And the philosopher Immanuel Kant did not find his unique voice until his 50s, producing his famous *Critique of Pure Reason* when 57, and following that with the almost as noteworthy *Critique of Practical Reason* and *Critique of Judgment* in his 64th and 66th years, respectively.

4. *The level of creative productivity in the last years depends on an individual's initial creative potential at the career outset.*—As stated, some creators are late bloomers, yet this assertion must be qualified. Given two persons with the same creative potential, the one who begins the career later will peak later and maintain a high output rate far later too. Yet people are far from identical in creative potential, and any individual differences must be incorporated in an exhaustive treatment of how creativity changes throughout the life span (see, e.g., Over, 1982a, 1982b). A chief deficiency in earlier longitudinal studies was indeed the failure to consider the impact of cross-sectional variation (Simonton, 1988a).

What do I mean by creative potential? Because a complete theoretical discussion requires more space than is available here, may a simple definition suffice: Creative potential signifies the total capacity for generating ideational variations, such that individual differences on this trait correspond to contrasts in the ability to produce new combinations of ideas (Simonton, 1988b). According to the mathematical model, if two individuals in the same creative endeavor initiated their careers at the same time, in the sense of beginning the business of creative rumination, then that individual with the higher initial creative potential will make his or her first major contribution earlier in life, produce at a higher rate throughout that person's career, and, most critically, generate his or her last major contribution much later in life (Simonton, 1984a, in press). In other words, creative potential is associated with creative precocity, output rate, and creative longevity.

Another way of expressing this association is perhaps more provocative. Say that a sample of creative individuals reached their productive peaks at the same chronological age (and consequently can be assumed to have begun their careers at the same age): Those persons in the sample who were the most precocious will tend to exhibit the most impressive creative longevity, a theoretical forecast that has received considerable empirical support (e.g., Albert, 1975; Simonton, 1977b, 1988a, in press). A concrete example is Goethe, who launched his literary career in his early 20s, became world famous with his *Sorrows of Young Werther* in his 25th year, and yet was applying the finishing touches to Part II of *Faust,* his greatest masterpiece, when he was 83 years old. Another example is Bach, who began composing in his early teens, and never stopped, dictating from his death bed in his mid 60s the final chorale that closes the *Art of the Fugue.* The phenomenal initial creative potential of these geniuses was transformed into careers of exceptional

duration. Indeed, it is typical of creative luminaries that their productive careers be stretched out by their precocity at one end and their longevity at the other (Albert, 1975; Simonton, 1977b, in press).

The above remarks clearly gainsay the recurrent claim that truly outstanding creativity is a monopoly of the young. These assertions also look incompatible with the notion that youthful prodigies may burn the candles at both ends, and by doing so die young. Yet these two perceptions can be shown to have real but quite misleading foundations. In the first place, because those who exhibit exceptional creative potential tend to make a splash quite early in life, we often forget how creative they were later on, even when their creative optima appeared at more mature ages. This is especially a problem when an individual receives honors for early works even though later contributions are even more deserving. Thus was Albert Einstein given a Nobel prize for the photoelectric effect paper of his 26th year when his masterwork, the general theory of relativity, came from a mind in its late 30s and early 40s.

With respect to the supposed abbreviated life span of precocious creators, we must take care not to reverse inadvertently cause and effect. The reason why precocious creators may die young is because they *can* die young and still leave enough behind for the appreciation of posterity. Those prodigies who manage to survive to a ripe old age will prove that the world would have lost much of priceless value had their careers been cut short out of season. Goethe could have died in his 30th year, and still have an enviable claim to fame, after the same manner as Keats or Shelley. On the other hand, that Mozart died in his 35th year and Schubert in his 31st cannot be taken as hinting that their productive careers were on the wane anyway. Indeed, both data and theory suggest that had Mozart and Schubert lived as long as Haydn or Brahms, their final years would have been so replete with landmark contributions that they might have eclipsed Beethoven, whose career both composers flank.

5. *The expected age decrement in creativity varies across disciplines in such a conspicuous manner that in some domains we can scarcely speak of a decline at all.*—It is a significant fact that the age curves are not identical no matter what form the creativity takes. The information-processing model handles such interdisciplinary contrasts by postulating different ideational and elaboration rates in the emergence of creative products (Simonton, 1984a, 1988b, in press), yet other substantive interpretations are available as well (Beard, 1874; Simonton, 1988a). Whatever the correct explanation, the ramifications of these differences are far reaching. Although in some creative activities, such as lyric poetry and pure mathematics, the peak may occur relatively early in life, sometimes even in the late 20s and early 30s, with a sudden drop thereafter, in other activities, such as scholarship and geology, the age optimum may appear much later, in the 50s even, with a gradual and almost undetectable decline thereafter (e.g., Dennis, 1966). Stated in more dramatic terms, whereas in some endeavors the late life may see output rates only 10% as high as witnessed at the career maxima, in other endeavors the productivity seen in the final years may come very close to the level of output reached in the supposed productive prime.

Such interdisciplinary contrasts support the notion that the career course is dictated more by the intrinsic needs of the creative process than by generic extrinsic forces, whether physical illness, family commitments, or administrative responsibilities. This inference is strengthened by the fact that the distinctive age curves for various disciplines tend to be replicated in different times and places (Lehman, 1962). For example, the age differences between the youthful peak for poetry and the more mature peak

for literary prose constitute a cross-cultural and transhistorical universal (Simonton, 1975). Furthermore, if creativity in some domains can persist until the final days, then it becomes more patent that we cannot speak of general decrements in the psychological functioning required for productivity (Simonton, 1988a). To be sure, for creators who aspire to contribute to fields that favor early career optima, these empirical and theoretical conclusions may look discouraging. A lyric poet, after all, can be "over the hill" at a rather young age. Even so, there is nothing preventing the person from switching fields in order to preserve creative vitality. By carefully selected mid-career changes, individuals can resuscitate their creative potential. Coleridge, for example, began his career as a lyric poet, but in later life became much more a literary critic and philosopher.

6. *According to the constant-probability-of-success model, creativity (quality) is a probabilistic function of productivity (quantity), meaning that on an item-for-item basis we cannot really speak of an age decrement at all.*—So far I have made no distinction between quantity of output over a career and quality. Perhaps productivity is one thing and creativity quite another. Yet studies on individual differences in total lifetime output have consistently shown that those who produce the most total works also have the strongest tendency to generate the most masterpieces as well (Simonton, 1984b, chap. 5, 1988b, chap. 4). As Auden expressed it, owing to the prolific output of great poets, "The chances are that, in the course of a lifetime, the major poet will write more bad poems than the minor" (quoted in Bennett, 1980, p. 15).

The same principle has been shown to apply to longitudinal changes in creativity as well (e.g., Simonton, 1977a, 1985). Those periods in a career in which the most major contributions are made are also those, on the average, in which the most minor contributions are offered. In different terms, if one calculates the ratio of major products to total products for each age period, that success probability neither increases nor decreases, nor exhibits any curvilinear form, as the creator ages. One interesting implication of this constant-probability-of-success model is that creative individuals are apparently unable to improve their success rates as they grow in maturity. The essential responsibility is merely to generate a profusion of candidates for posterity's consideration; the more possibilities advanced, the better chance that one will earn recognition (Simonton, 1988a).

A second consequence of this model is more profound for our understanding of creativity in the latter part of life: If the probability of a creative hit in any age period is a mere consequence of the number of times the creator takes aim, then in this sense we cannot speak of an age loss at all. Elderly individuals of a creative discipline may be producing fewer notable creations than they did in their prime, yet these individuals are proportionately yielding less "rubbish" as well. Even more significant, if we switch our level of analysis from the age period to the single creative product, age becomes largely irrelevant to the anticipation of creative success. That is, on a product-for-product basis, a work by an octogenarian has about the same odds of having an impact as a work by someone in their 40s or even 20s (see, e.g., Oromaner, 1977; Over, 1988, 1989). One curious qualification on this generalization exists, however, which brings us to the seventh and last argument on behalf of late-life creativity.

7. *Creativity can undergo a resurgence in the later years of life, and especially in life's last years.*—The life-span developmental research on the relation between age and the rate of creative contribution has consistently isolated a post-peak decline, yet one peculiar twist frequently emerges in the longitudinal tabulations: Sometime in the late 60s or 70s a renaissance in output may appear (Simonton, 1988a). This resuscitation is not nearly so pronounced as the midlife optimum, but it is conspicuous enough to suggest that creative potential in the final portion of life may exceed the actual exhibited productivity. Something is evidently occurring in those years to inspire the individuals to dedicate themselves once more to the creative enterprise. Considering that this burst of new activity occurs around the age when a human being must begin to contemplate the prospect of death, this secondary peak may be a manifestation of this contemplation.

This conjecture led me to consider the possible existence of a swan-song phenomenon, or "last-works" effects (Simonton, 1989b). In this inquiry, 1,919 compositions by 172 classical composers were assessed on numerous aesthetic attributes, and then for each work it was determined how many years before the creator's death the piece was composed. In order not to confound the last-works effects with the consequences of chronological age, the latter variable was added to the list of statistical controls. The pattern was clear: As the composers approached their final years, when death was raising a fist to knock on the door, they began to produce compositions that are more brief, that have simpler and more restrained melodic lines, and yet that score high in aesthetic significance according to musicologists and that eventually become popular mainstays of the classical repertoire. It is as if when the composers see the end approaching fast on the horizon, warning that their last artistic testaments dwell among their current works in progress, they put their utmost into every creation, yielding truly noteworthy products. Therein arises, for example, the Four Serious Songs of Brahms and the Four Last Songs of Strauss, prototypical swan songs. Although last-works effects have thus far only been empirically demonstrated on classical composers, last-works effects may eventually be found for other forms of creativity as well (see Simonton, 1990). If so, we would have good cause for anticipating great things from those in their final years.

The foregoing seven points, taken in sum, project a rather optimistic picture of creativity in the final years. Of course, one may argue that these results may hold only for monumental forms of creativity, not for more everyday guises of creative behavior. Yet I see no reason to make this distinction. Many of these conclusions have been replicated on relatively average persons, such as research scientists and college faculty who certainly cannot be counted as world-re-

nowned geniuses; and striking parallels have been found between these results and findings based on the psychometric examination of even more commonplace subject pools (Simonton, 1988a). Furthermore, let us adopt the worse-case scenario and presume that the seven qualifications apply only for the luminaries of art and science. We may still expect that each creative individual, no matter how old, may have a masterpiece waiting to be unveiled to the world. Aging need not silence outstanding creativity in the last years.

REFERENCES

Albert, R. S. (1975). Toward a behavioral definition of genius. *American Psychologist, 30,* 140–151.

Alpaugh, P. K., & Birren, J. E. (1977). Variables affecting creative contributions across the adult life span. *Human Development, 20,* 240–248.

Beard, G. M. (1874). *Legal responsibility in old age.* New York: Russell.

Bennett, W. (1980). Providing for posterity. *Harvard Magazine, 82,* 13–16.

Birren, J. E., Woods, A. M., & Williams, M. V. (1980). Behavioral slowing with age: Causes, organization and consequences. In L. W. Poon (Ed.), *Aging in the 1980s: Psychological issues* (pp. 293–308). Washington, DC: American Psychological Association.

Bromley, D. B. (1956). Some experimental tests of the effect of age on creative intellectual output. *Journal of Gerontology, 11,* 74–82.

Byron, George (1812–16). Childe Harold. In P. E. More (Ed.), *The complete poetical works of Lord Byron* (pp. 1–83). Boston: Houghton Mifflin, 1905.

Dennis, W. (1906). Creative productivity between the ages of 20 and 80 years. *Journal of Gerontology, 21,* 1–8.

Hocevar, D. (1981). Measurement of creativity: Review and critique. *Journal of Personality Assessment, 45,* 450–464.

Lehman, H. C. (1953). *Age and achievement.* Princeton, NJ: Princeton University Press.

Lehman, H. C. (1962). More about age and achievement. *The Gerontologist, 2,* 141–148.

McCrae, R. R., Arenberg, D., & Costa, P. T., Jr. (1987). Declines in divergent thinking with age: Cross-sectional, longitudinal, and cross-sequential analyses. *Psychology and Aging, 2,* 130–137.

Oromaner, M. (1977). Professional age and the reception of sociological publications: A test of the Zuckerman-Merton hypothesis. *Social Studies of Science, 7,* 381–388.

Over, R. (1982a). Does research productivity decline with age? *Higher Education, 11,* 511–520.

Over, R. (1982b). Is age a good predictor of research productivity? *Australian Psychologist, 17,* 129–139.

Over, R. (1988). Does scholarly impact decline with age? *Scientometrics, 13,* 215–224.

Over, R. (1989). Age and scholarly impact. *Psychology and Aging, 4,* 222–225.

Quetelet, A. (1968). *A treatise on man.* New York: Franklin. (Reprint of 1842 Edinburgh translation of original 1835 publication.)

Ruth, J.-E., & Birren, J. E. (1985). Creativity in adulthood and old age: Relations to intelligence, sex and mode of testing. *International Journal of Behavioral Development, 8,* 99–109.

Shakespeare, W. (c. 1598). Much ado about nothing. In R. M. Hutchins (Ed.), *Great books of the western world* (pp. 503–531). Chicago: Encyclopaedia Britannica, 1952.

Simonton, D. K. (1975). Age and literary creativity: A cross-cultural and transhistorical survey. *Journal of Cross-Cultural Psychology, 6,* 259–277.

Simonton, D. K. (1977a). Creative productivity, age, and stress: A biographical time-series analysis of 10 classical composers. *Journal of Personality and Social Psychology, 35,* 791–804.

Simonton, D. K. (1977b). Eminence, creativity, and geographic marginality: A recursive structural equation model. *Journal of Personality and Social Psychology, 35,* 805–816.

Simonton, D. K. (1980). Thematic fame, melodic originality, and musical zeitgeist: A biographical and transhistorical content analysis. *Journal of Personality and Social Psychology, 38,* 972–983.

Simonton, D. K. (1984a). Creative productivity and age: A mathematical model based on a two-step cognitive process. *Developmental Review, 4,* 77–111.

Simonton, D. K. (1984b). *Genius, creativity, and leadership: Historiometric inquiries.* Cambridge, MA: Harvard University Press.

Simonton, D. K. (1985). Quality, quantity, and age: The careers of 10 distinguished psychologists. *International Journal of Aging and Human Development, 21,* 241–254.

Simonton, D. K. (1988a). Age and outstanding achievement: What do we know after a century of research? *Psychological Bulletin, 104,* 251–267.

Simonton, D. K. (1988b). *Scientific genius: A psychology of science.* New York: Cambridge University Press.

Simonton, D. K. (1989a). Age and creative productivity: Nonlinear estimation of an information-processing model. *International Journal of Aging and Human Development, 29,* 23–37.

Simonton, D. K. (1989b). The swan-song phenomenon: Last-works effects for 172 classical composers. *Psychology and Aging, 4,* 42–47.

Simonton, D. K. (1990). Creativity and wisdom in aging. In J. E. Birren & K. W. Schaie (Eds.), *Handbook of the psychology of aging* (3rd ed.), (pp. 321–329). New York: Academic Press.

Simonton, D. K. (in press). Career landmarks in science: Individual differences and interdisciplinary contrasts. *Developmental Psychology.*

Discussion Questions for Chapter Five

1. Considering the theories summarized by Lipman and Ehrlich, what conditions of inner (psychological) life and external (social) life are the most conducive to attaining a sense of satisfaction in old age?

2. Consider the findings reported by Simonton that the decrement in creativity varies across disciplines, so that in some activities there is hardly a decline in creativity in late life, while in other fields the decline might be greater. What significance does this idea hold for those who are considering a career change in mid or late life?

CHAPTER SIX

Aging and the Family

Families play a major role in the care for elderly people. Contrary to the myth that younger people usually send older relatives off to nursing homes, families provide the majority of long-term care in the United States. Rather than being less involved in care for the elderly than in the past, families are more involved because improvements in survivorship have led to increased numbers of people at the most advance years when disability and dependence are most common.

The majority of caregiving for family members is done by women. Elaine Brody (1990), who has done extensive research on caregiving, believes that eldercare responsibilities have become so common among women that they constitute a "normative family stress." Since women have moved into the labor force in large numbers in the recent past, some have been faced with the combined responsibilities of employment and caring for an elderly family member. Brody coined the term, "women in the middle" to describe women who combine paid employment with eldercare, or who are caring for an older family member and children at the same time. In "Family Care of the Frail Elderly: A New Look at 'Women in the Middle,' " Sandra Boyd and Judith Treas examine the extent to which women face the responsibilities of eldercare combined with child care or paid employment.

Marriage is one of the most important factors affecting life satisfaction in the later years. Marriage is also a gateway to social involvement for many people. In "Marriages in Later Life: Strength and Strains," Rosalie Gilford reviews the literature on older marriages in order to describe their strengths, as well as the challenges they face.

American society has traditionally viewed the primary function of marriage as procreation. Sexuality not connected with reproduction is now viewed as a significant part of life, but the importance of sexual and contactual relations among the elderly is just beginning to be recognized. The stereotypes about older peoples' sexuality are not flattering. Most often, older people are portrayed as sexless, but to the extent that they are perceived as sexual, they are most often seen as deviant, as in the "dirty old man" stereotype, or the nymphomaniac old lady in *Playboy* cartoons. In "Older Adults' Sexuality and Remarriage," Shirley S. Travis offers a much more realistic portrayal of aging and sexuality. She also discusses the desires and prospects for remarriage among older people.

REFERENCE

Brody, Elaine M. 1990. *Women in the middle: Their parent-care years.* New York: Springer Publishing Co. Inc.

Family Care of the Frail Elderly: A New Look at "Women in the Middle"

SANDRA L. BOYD
JUDITH TREAS

Unprecedented demographic shifts in this century have profoundly affected the lives of middle-aged and older women. As the population ages, increasing numbers of women provide care to elderly relatives. The elderly population currently is the fastest growing segment of American society. By 1985, average life expectancy at birth was 71.2 years for men and 78.2 years for women.[1] Sixty percent of fifty-five-year-old women could expect to have at least one living parent in 1980, compared to just 6 percent in 1800.[2] It is estimated that 20 percent of a woman's lifetime will be spent with at least one parent over the age of sixty-five.[3]

We now know that offspring do not abandon their elderly parents[4]; family members provide roughly 80 percent of care to the elderly.[5] A vast caregiving literature shows that women in the family—primarily wives, daughters, and daughters-in-law—are most involved in caregiving.

Elaine M. Brody has coined the phrase "women in the middle" to refer to women who "are in their middle years, in the middle of older and younger generations, and in the middle of competing demands."[6] She suggests that long-term parent care has become a "normative" family stress for a growing number of middle-aged women.[7] Other researchers, however, contend that studies based on small, nonrandom samples overstate the prevalence of "women in the middle."[8] Furthermore, the gerontological literature focuses almost exclusively on the negative consequences of caregiving and competing demands; few studies have examined positive aspects.[9]

"WOMEN IN THE MIDDLE": BETWEEN GENERATIONS

Brody's definition embraces two, sometimes overlapping types of "women in the middle": 1) those who are "caught" between older and younger generations and 2) those who combine parental care and paid employment.

Although some women provide both parental care and child care simultaneously, the life cycle provides some insulation against experiencing such dual demands. Table 1 shows that 17 percent of women between the ages of forty and forty-four have children under the age of eighteen at home, and 97 percent have parents over the age of

Source: Women's Studies Quarterly, 1/2, 66–73. Reprinted with permission from the authors. Copyright 1989.

TABLE 1 Women with Parents over Age 65 and Children under Age 18 in Household

Women's ages	Percent with parent over age 65[a]	Percent with children under age 18 in household[b]
40–44	97	17
45–49	92	8
50–54	78	4
55–59	60	2
60–64	35	1
65–74	14	less than 1

[a]Based on estimates applied to a synthetic cohort under 1980 conditions. Susan C. Watkins, Jane A. Menken, and John Bongaarts, "Demographic Foundations of Family Change," *American Sociological Review* 52, no. 3 (1987): 346–58.

[b]Children under eighteen living with one or both parents, all races, 1984. Age of parent was based on the age of the householder, defined as the homeowner or renter. Since homeowners are still more likely to be men than women, and since husbands are somewhat older on average than their wives, these percentages may slightly underestimate the number of children under eighteen living with women. Current Population Reports—Population Characteristics, Series P-20, No. 399, *Marital Status and Living Arrangements*, March 1984.

Source. Women's Studies Quarterly 1989: 1 & 2

sixty-five. But many of these parents can be considered part of the "young-old"; they are under the age of seventy-five, enjoy relatively good health, and are married.[10] Moreover, because money, goods, and services flow down the generational ladder to a greater extent than they flow up,[11] these "young-old" parents are apt to be assets, not liabilities; rather than posing burdens to their children, they provide critical financial help and emotional support.

Sixty percent of fifty-five-year-old women have living parents; unlike the parents of younger women, these often are over the age of seventy-five, many are widowed, and a significant proportion suffer from impairments limiting their daily activities. But only a tiny fraction of women in their mid-to-late fifties still have children at home.

A constellation of factors, including postponed childbearing, "crowded nests", and increased sickness among older persons may mean that child dependency and parentcare overlap more frequently in the future.

Postponed Childbearing and Childlessness

Although some well-educated women are remaining childless altogether, others in recent cohorts have delayed childbearing until their late twenties and thirties.[12] For such women, child rearing may well coincide with parent care. Moreover, responsibilities for grandchildren may impinge on some middle-aged women, especially blacks, as a result of the rise in teenage illegitimacy.[13]

"Crowded Nests"

Declining proportions of adult children over the age of eighteen are married, and increasing proportions either remain in their parental home or return there.[14] Thirty percent of eighteen to thirty-four year olds lived in their parents' households in 1983, compared to 25 percent in 1970. Adult children living at home typically are single and between the ages of eighteen and twenty-two; most are in school rather than in the work force.[15] Adult children aged twenty-three to twenty-nine living in their parents' home typically either are preparing for independent living or have returned temporarily following job loss or failed marriages. The prolonged dependency of adult children may mean that middle-aged women are responsible simultaneously for their children and their parents.

Increasing Sickness of the "Young-Old"

Researchers recently have found a significant increase in the the prevalence of chronic disease among the "young-old," though not among the rest of the elderly population; more people suffering from chronic illness are surviving today than in the past.[16] Some women thus may be compelled to provide parental care when their children are still relatively young.

In summary, although many middle-aged women experience competing demands, most are not "caught between older and younger generations." When middle-aged women still have dependent children, their aging parents typically have not reached an age when they are likely to be impaired and in need of assistance. Middle-aged women who do have frail elderly parents tend not to be responsible for children living at home. If future cohorts of middle-aged women care for sicker parents and have younger children or children who remain at home longer, they may be more likely to be "caught in the middle."

"WOMEN IN THE MIDDLE": BETWEEN CAREGIVING AND PAID EMPLOYMENT

In addition to competing family responsibilities, "women in the middle" confront conflicting demands of care for elderly family members and paid work. Between 1947 and 1986, the number of women in the labor force grew from 29.8 to 54.7 percent[17]; the most notable increases occurred for middle-aged married women and mothers of small children. Over 60 percent of married women aged forty to fifty-four are in the labor force.[18] According to data from the National Long-Term Care Survey, 31 percent of all unpaid caregivers also hold paying jobs, including 10 percent of wives and 44 percent of daughters.[19] Some observers fear that women who simultaneously work for pay and care for parents suffer from "burn out" as a result of role strain.

Women who have competing demands from paid work and caregiving adapt in a number of ways, including leaving the labor force, making changes at work, and making changes at home.

Leaving the Labor Force

Although the three generations of women interviewed by Elaine Brody stated that women should not have to quit their jobs to provide care to elderly parents,[20] daughters are much more likely to actually do so than sons. According to a variety of studies, between 12 and 28 percent of caregiving daughters leave the work force to provide care.[21] These women often lose salary and benefits, retirement pensions, social networks, and work satisfaction. Caregiving responsibilities also may compel some women to remain unemployed.[22]

Brody found that women who quit work are older, provide more help to their mothers, and have lower status jobs than those who remain in the work force.[23] Because their family incomes are low, such women may face financial difficulties. Some of these women, however, may prefer caregiving to unrewarding jobs and thus welcome the opportunity to depart the labor force.

Changes at Work

Women who continue to work often make changes on the job to accommodate caregiving obligations. Robyn Stone et al. (1987) reported that 20 percent of caregivers cut back their hours, 29 percent rearrange their work schedules, and 19 percent take time off without pay. The tendency to make such changes is directly related to the level of impairment of disabled parents.[24]

Patricia Archbold (1983) argues that women in higher status positions are more able to accommodate caregiving in their work lives because they have more flexible work schedules.[25] According to Brody, however, the higher status, career-oriented workers feel more conflicted and report more work interruptions and missed job opportunities.[26]

Changes at Home

Many working caregivers give up free time and leisure activities while maintaining rigid schedules.[27] Some also adjust their caregiving responsibilities to alleviate the strain. Although caregivers in the labor force provide the same levels of help as unpaid workers in terms of housework, financial management, and emotional support, they provide significantly less assistance with personal care and meal preparation.[28] Employed caregivers also tend to supplement their own assistance with help from other family members and paid providers.

ROLE STRAIN FROM COMPETING DEMANDS

Most caregiving literature focuses on the negative consequences of providing care, and most studies report at least moderate stress for many caregivers. Researchers have directed considerable attention to women in the middle of paid work and informal caregiving, assuming that role conflict and overload predispose them to stress. Studies suggest that a quarter of caregivers who remain in the labor force do have conflicted feelings,[29] and many suffer from fatigue and strained personal relationships.[30] But employment does not appear to be the most important determinant of stress. The primary predictor of stress is the quality of the relationship between the caregiver and care recipient.[31] Working women providing care to older family members do not systematically exhibit more stress than their counterparts who do not work outside the home.[32] Moreover, contrary to the assumption that an increase in the number of roles is detrimental to psychological well-being,[33] there is some evidence that the ability to handle diverse roles can promote self-esteem.[34] Multi-ple roles provide women with added sources of satisfaction, not simply increased burdens. Individuals also can compensate for failure in any one sphere by relying on rewards from another. Some caregivers may find that a job provides a respite from the demands, and often failures, of caregiving.

At the same time, caregiving provides a sense of usefulness, compensating for frustrations at work. Although most gerontological literature emphasized the stress of caregivers, many of the findings on caregiving stress come from small samples recruited from service agencies. Families who are most visible to community agencies are those who are experiencing more stress than they can handle and who feel that they need help.[35] As Horowitz notes, "most caregivers can identify at least one positive aspect of caregiving, primarily a feeling of self-satisfaction and increased self-esteem stemming from the knowledge that one is successfully fulfilling a responsibility and coping with a personal challenge."

SUMMARY AND CONCLUSION

Despite warnings about many women being "caught in the middle," the situation is not as grim as many observers would have us believe. The life cycle helps protect women against competing family responsibilities; only a small percentage of women care simultaneously for dependent parents and children. The addition of paid work to caregiving responsibilities may have positive as well as negative consequences. Moreover, many women cope successfully with competing demands. By focusing exclusively on the stress of caregiving, we ignore the tremendous resiliency and adaptive capabilities of many women and send young women a depressing message about their future. Although it is necessary to alert policymakers and employers to the problems of women who do find caregiving overwhelming, we should retain a sense of perspective.

It should be emphasized, however, that those women who are experiencing stress from competing responsibilities do need special assistance. A small but growing number of corporate employers offer "elder care" to assist employees with caregiving obligations. The current wave of corporate interest is encouraging, but more employers could provide programs that help working women deal with family responsibilities, whether child care or elder care. Support groups and counselors can also be a tremendous source of help to caregivers. Women who have been able to balance competing demands successfully may be an important resource to others. Finally, researchers should explore the complexities of different competing demands. Although being a "woman in the middle" may not be a "normative" experience, demographic trends suggest it may become more common in the future.

NOTES

1. National Center for Health Statistics, *Vital Statistics of the United States, 1985* Life Tables, Vol. 11, Sec. 6, Department of Health and Human Services Pub. No. (PHS) 88–1104 (Public Health Service, Washington, D.C.: U.S. Government Printing Office, 1988).

2. Susan C. Watkins, Jane A. Menken, and John Bongaarts, "Demographic Foundations of Family Change," *American Sociological Review* 52, no. 3 (1987): 346–58.

3. Ibid.

4. Ethel Shanas, "The Family as a Social Support System in Old Age," *The Gerontologist* 19 (1979): 169–74.

5. National Center for Health Statistics, *Vital Statistics of the United States, 1973 Life Tables* (Rockville, Md.: U.S. Government Printing Office, 1975).

6. E. M. Brody, " 'Women in the Middle' and Family Help to Older People," *The Gerontologist* 21 (1981): 471–80.

7. E. M. Brody, "Parent Care as a Normative Family Stress," *The Gerontologist* 25, no. 1 (1985): 19–29.

8. Sarah H. Matthews, "The Burdens of Parent Care: A Critical Assessment of the Recent Literature" (Revision of a paper presented at the Gerontological Society of America, New Orleans, 1985); Carolyn J. Rosenthal, Victor W. Marshall, and Sarah H. Matthews, "The Incidence and Prevalence of 'Women in the Middle' " (Revision of a paper presented at the Gerontological Society of America, Chicago, 1986).

9. Emily K. Abel, *Love is Not Enough: Family Care of the Frail Elderly,* APHA Public Health Policy Series. (Washington, D.C.: American Public Health Association, 1987); Amy Horowitz, "Family Caregiving to the Frail Elderly," in *Annual Review of Gerontology and Geriatrics, Volume 5,* ed. C. Eisdorfer (New York: Springer, 1985).

10. Rosenthal et al., "Incidence and Prevalence of 'Women in the Middle.' "

11. Vern L. Bengtson et al., "Generations, Cohorts and Relations between Age Groups," in *Handbook of Aging and the Social Sciences,* 2d ed., ed. Robert H. Binstock and Ethel Shanas (New York: Van Nostrand Reinhold, 1986), pp. 304–38.

12. David E. Bloom and James Trussell, "What Are the Determinants of Delayed Childbearing and Permanent Childlessness in the United States?" *Demography* 21, no. 4 (1984): 591–609.

13. Linda M. Burton and Vern L. Bengtson, "Black Grandmothers: Issues of Timing and Continuity of Roles," in *Grandparenthood,* ed. Vern L. Bengtson and Joan F. Robertson (Beverly Hills, Calif.: Sage Publications, 1985).

14. David M. Heer, Robert W. Hodge, and Marcus Felson, "The Cluttered Nest: Evidence That Young Adults Are More Likely to Live at Home Now Than in the Recent Past," *Sociology and Social Research* 69 (April 1985): 437–41.

15. Jill S. Grigsby and Jill B. McGowan, "Still in the Nest: Adult Children Living with Their Parents," *Sociology and Social Research* 70 (January): 146–48.

16. Eileen M. Crimmins, "Evidence on the Compression of Morbidity," *Gerontologica Perspecta* 1 (1987): 45–49.

17. U.S. Bureau of the Census, *Statistical Abstract of the United States* (Washington, D.C.: Government Printing Office, 1987).

18. U.S. Bureau of Labor Statistics, *Handbook of Labor Statistics,* March 1984 population survey, table #52 (Washington, D.C.: Government Printing Office, 1985), p. 119.

19. Robyn Stone, Gail Cafferata, and Judith Sangl, "Caregivers of the Frail Elderly: A National Profile," *The Gerontologist* 27, no. 5 (1987): 616–26.

20. E. M. Brody et al., "Women's Changing Roles and Help to the Elderly: Attitudes of Three Generations of Women," *Journal of Gerontology* 38 (1983): 597–607.

21. Stone et al., "Caregivers of the Frail Elderly"; E. M. Brody et al. "Work Status and Parent Care: A Comparison of Four Groups of Women," *The Gerontologist* 27, no. 2 (1987): 201–208.

22. Beth J. Soldo and Jaana Myllyluoma, "Caregivers Who Live with Dependent Elderly," *The Gerontologist* 23, no. 6,(1983): 605–11.

23. Brody et al., "Work Status and Parent Care."

24. Robert B. Enright, Jr. and Lynn Friss, *Employed Caregivers of Brain-Impaired Adults: An Assessment of the Dual Role* (San Francisco: Family Survival Project, 1987).

25. Patricia G. Archbold, "Impact of Parent-caring on Women," *Family Relations* 32 (1983): 39–45.

26. Brody et al., "Work Status and Parent Care."

27. A. M. Lang and E. M. Brody, "Characteristics of Middle-aged Daughters and Help to Their Elderly Mothers," *Journal of Marriage and the Family* 45 (1983): 193–202; Brody et al., "Work Status and Parent Care."

28. E. M. Brody and Claire B. Schoonover, "Patterns of Care for the Dependent Elderly when Daughters Work and when They Do Not," *The Gerontologist* 26, no. 4 (1996): 372–81.

29. Stone et al., "Caregivers of the Frail Elderly"; Brody et al., "Work Status and Parent Care."

30. Dorothy A. Miller, "The 'Sandwich' Generation: Adult Children of the Aging," *Social Work* 26 (1981): 419–23; Andrew E. Scharlach, "Role Strain in Mother-Daughter Relationships in Later Life," *The Gerontologist* 27, no. 5 (1987): 627–31

31. Horowitz, "Family Caregiving."

32. Ibid.

33. W. J. Goode, "A Theory of Role Strain," *American Sociological Review* 25 (1960): 488–96.

Marriages in Later Life

ROSALIE GILFORD

It is generally assumed that older married persons, whether survivors in long-lived intact marriages or newlyweds in old age, are among the most fortunate of the older population. Because they still have a life partner, presumably providing emotional support and integration into social networks, and also because they generally have higher incomes and social status, older husbands and wives are thought to be less vulnerable to personal and social breakdown than are their widowed or divorced counterparts. However, despite these advantages, older marriages also encounter unique challenges that may undermine their positive tenor and stability. For example, personal developmental processes may unfold over the life course to lead spouses in opposite directions, causing marital discord and dysfunction (Troll et al., 1979). Further, the socially structured role losses that frequently accompany aging may exert pressures on couples as the marital relationship becomes a primary source of social reinforcement in the face of shrinking social networks (Rosow, 1973). Thus, while marriage may function as a resource to older couples, marriage also sustains particular tensions that may strain the marital bond in later life. Given current longevity projections, it is estimated that spouses in one out of every five marriages will survive to celebrate a 50th wedding anniversary (Glick and Norton, 1977). The growth in the number of older couples in our society calls for systematic study of the dynamics of these long-lived marriage relationships.

This paper reviews selected literature on older marriages for the purpose of identifying their special strengths and strains. The evidence is examined from the perspective of three broad questions:

1. What are the strengths of older marriages? What power has the relationship to enrich and enhance the quality of spouses' later lives?
2. What strains do older marriages endure? How do the personal and social events of later life impinge upon the relationship?
3. What insights can service providers and planners gain from an understanding of long-lived marriages? What opportunities exist for systematic interventions that increase the solidarity of the marital bond?

MARITAL STATUS & QUALITY

Despite rising divorce rates and changing attitudes, marriage continues to occupy a cen-

Source: Generations, 10(4), 16–20. Reprinted with permission from *Generations*, 833 Market St., Suite 512, San Francisco, CA, 94103, and the author. Copyright 1986 by the American Society on Aging.

tral place in the lives of most Americans; the vast majority—95 percent—marry at least once, and most who divorce, particularly at young ages, tend to marry again (Skolnick, 1981). While the ranks of aging marriage cohorts become depleted over the years as the result of death and divorce, more than half of the approximately 26 million Americans over the age of 65 are married and living with a spouse in an independent household. However, this finding is more true of men than women because women outlive men. At ages 55–64, 81 percent of men and only 67 percent of women are married. By age 75 and over, this gender discrepancy in marital status has widened; 70 percent of men and only 22 percent of women still have a spouse (U.S. Senate Special Committee on Aging, 1984). Moreover, the probability of having a spouse in old age differs by race and ethnicity as well as by gender. More older whites than Hispanics and more Hispanics than blacks are married.

Marriages are quite stable and divorce is rare among the elderly. Only about 1 percent of all divorces granted during 1975 involved a husband or a wife age 65 years or over (Uhlenberg and Myers, 1981). However, the number of divorced persons in the older population is projected to increase as a result of the rising divorce rate at earlier ages; more individuals who enter old age will have experienced a divorce at an earlier point in their lives.

While some marriages take place in old age, they are rare and more likely to be remarriages of widowed and divorced persons than first-time marriages. It is estimated that older persons constitute only about 1 percent of all brides and 2 percent of all grooms (Treas and VanHilst, 19–6). Again, older men are favored: they are twice as likely to marry as older women because they have a larger pool of eligible people from which to select a mate, particularly given the tendency among men to marry women younger than themselves (Atchley, 1985). Moreover, the remar-

riage interval is only half as long for men as for women. For blacks, the remarriage probabilities for both sexes are lower and the remarriage interval is longer (Brubaker, 1985). In other words, marriage and remarriage rates in later life favor white men.

Older spouses appear to be quite happy in their marriages. They report higher levels of marital satisfaction than do middle-aged spouses, although not as high as youthful newlyweds (Rollins and Feldman, 1970; Gilford and Bengtson, 1979; Markides and Hoppe, 1985). Many older spouses report their marriages to have improved over time (Skolnick, 1981), with the aging years among the happiest periods of the entire family life cycle (Sporakowski and Hughston, 1978). Again, gender differences are observed; men are frequently more satisfied with marriage and the degree to which their emotional needs are fulfilled than are women (Stinnett et al., 1972; Rhyne, 1981; Gilford, 1984), while older women are less hopeful that the warmth and intimacy they seek will be forthcoming in their marriages (Lowenthal et al., 1975). Despite the greater prominence of the marital role for men after midlife (Tamir, 1982), men's happiness may be less dependent than women's upon events within marriage (Rollins and Feldman, 1970), with the likelihood that marriage is more satisfying to men because they need it less.

These same life-course and gender differences in marital satisfaction are found in Hispanic families as well (Markides and Hoppe, 1985). Less is known about older black couples than about whites; data are rare and do not distinguish between middle-class and lower-class couples (Troll et al., 1979). Black couples who are poorly fortified by income, education, and family solidarity against the stresses of late life (Gibson, 1982) might be less likely to report the close, harmonious marital relations (Parron, 1982) enjoyed by their counterparts with greater resources. Regardless of spouses' race or ethnicity, social and personal hardship might be expected to have a negative influence on marital interaction.

Another indication of the quality of older marriages is the desire of older persons to remarry after experiencing marital disruption, usually death of a spouse. Following a mourning period during which attempts at adaptation to the dramatic role-shifts associated with this transition are made, widows and widowers may seek companionship, social roles, and emotional support in a new marriage. Judging by spouses' evaluations and the low divorce rate, later-life remarriages are likely to be successful, especially for couples who have known each other well over a period of years, whose children and peers approve of the marriage, and who have good health, finances, and living conditions (McKain, 1972; Vinick, 1978).

Thus, marriage is a popular status in old age, and if a "happy marriage" is ranked among the most important aspects of life by adult Americans (Campbell et al., 1976), then older spouses are indeed favored, for, as a group, most older husbands and wives appreciate each other and are satisfied with their marriages. What are the special qualities of the marriage relationship that make it so highly valued?

STRENGTHS

Marriage appears to enhance the quality of life for spouses in important ways; married persons, regardless of age, appear to be happier, healthier, and longer-lived than widowed or divorced persons of the same ages (Gove et al., 1983). Older spouses report greater general happiness (Glenn, 1975) and more satisfaction with finances, family life, and friendships (Uhlenberg and Myers, 1981) than any age category of unmarried persons. Satisfaction with marriage is the strongest predictor of life satisfaction for older women and for men is second only to good health (Lee, 1978). Moreover, marriage is said to minimize the potentially disruptive

impact of such events as retirement, reduced income, and declining physical capacity that characterize later life for many persons.

These positive effects may emanate from three major functions that marriage, according to Atchley (1985), performs for older couples: intimacy, interdependence, and sense of belonging.

Intimacy, including sexual intimacy, involves mutual affection, regard, trust, and loving (Atchley, 1985). Indeed, a close intimate relationship is a goal for a majority of older couples (Atchley and Miller, 1983), and being in love is considered by older spouses to be the most important factor contributing to the success of their marriages (Stinnett et al., 1972; Sporakowski and Hughston, 1978). These spouses value the marriage relationship for the opportunity to freely express respect, honesty, and their true feelings for one another (Stinnett et al., 1972; Parron, 1982). Sexual interest and activity remain an integral part of marriage, although many older husbands and wives tend to report a decline in frequency of coitus, which they generally attribute to the husband's physiological limitations (Newman and Nichols, 1970). Fortunately, sexual expression in old age takes many forms other than sexual intercourse, including cuddling, touching, exchanging fond looks, dating, dining, and being a couple—all of which continue to be an important source of gratification to older couples.

Interdependence involves sharing of housework, income, and other resources (Atchley, 1985). Spouses are important sources of help to each other and they appear to value the postparental period of marriage for the opportunities that it presents for give and take (Sporakowski and Hughston, 1978; Parron, 1982). Older wives tend to give advice, personal and nursing care, and meal preparation, while husbands help with transportation, and both spouses commonly share household tasks (McAuley et al., 1984). Couples who divide responsibility for tasks along nontraditional gender role lines tend to report higher morale and marital satisfaction (Lipman, 1962), but because of women's greater longevity, wives tend to engage in more caregiving than do husbands (Lopata, 1973).

A *sense of belonging* involves identification with couplehood, sharing of values and perspectives, and a routine source of comfortable interaction and socializing (Atchley, 1985). To older spouses, the very meaning of the word marriage denotes a joining of two people as a family (Sporakowski and Hughston, 1978). Such a feeling of unity appears to signal marital success; for long-married couples who value close ties with each other, family, and children tend to enjoy high levels of marital satisfaction (Atchley and Miller, 1983; Gilford, 1984), and couples who have marked the golden wedding milestone claim that a harmonious blending of values and togetherness has continued throughout their marital lives (Parron, 1982).

While the marriage relationship at all stages of its evolving career is far from trouble-free—and long-established marriages are no exception—intimacy, interdependence, and belonging appear to provide meaning and support to partners. Interpersonal support may constitute the special strength that links marital status to the superior well-being of married over unmarried individuals (Gove et al., 1983), and in later life may take on even greater salience as a source of identity and stability of life style. While realization of their greater interdependence in old age draws many couples closer together (Nye and Berardo, 1973), others may find that their marital situation grows worse as they age. What are the conditions that test the strength of the marital bond in later life?

STRAINS

It might seem obvious that older spouses are happy in their long-term marriages; otherwise, it is reasonable to assume, they would have divorced along the way. However, these couples exchanged marriage vows at a time when social pressures ruled out divorce as an alternative to an unhappy marriage. While some unhappy marriages may have been terminated, on the whole the present cohort of "golden-era" couples saw marriage as a lifetime commitment governed by obligation. But commitment is not synonymous with happiness, and obligation may not be the route to marital success.

For example, while older husbands and wives as a group may report moderate to high levels of marital satisfaction (Gilford and Bengtson, 1979), their positive feelings about their marriages do not necessarily persist throughout the remainder of the marital careers. In fact, spouses at the younger and older extremes of old age (ages 55–62 and 70–90) report considerably lower marital satisfaction than do spouses at the mid-state of old age (age 63–69) (Gilford, 1984). Furthermore, over the years of marriage, a decline in spouses' joint participation in activities (Orthner, 1975) and in the amount of love and commitment they express to each other (Swensen et al., 1981; Swensen and Trahaug, 1985) suggest diminished feelings of marital intimacy and belongingness. Declines in marital quality are also indicated in lack of mutual interests, differing values, inability to express true feelings, and frequent disagreements, which a substantial proportion of older spouses freely mention as troublesome aspects of their marriages (Stinnett et al., 1972).

It is also possible that marriage does not play the central integrative role attributed to it. In fact, the widowed, particularly women, who tend to have social skills may be more integrated into informal social networks than are their married counterparts (Kohen, 1983). For older men, a close relationship with a confidant and voluntary participation in an organization contribute more to overall life satisfaction than does marital status (Mouser et al., 1985). And widowed persons who have a confidant frequently have higher morale than married persons without such a close relationship (Lowenthal and Haven, 1968).

Marital conflict may also arise when personal development of husbands and wives follows noncomplementary paths over the life course (Troll et al., 1979; Swensen et al., 1981). The paths are determined by different sets of external demands such as family, work, and community, as well as personalities of the spouses. Developmental trajectories lead men to become more nurturant and women to become more aggressive and assertive (Neugarten, 1968) as they age. These changes in spouses' personal and behavioral orientations may lead to alterations in their expectations and performance of domestic roles. In turn, disagreement over role performance in everyday married life is associated with feelings of inequity and depression in older spouses (Keith and Schafer, 1985) that may impair marital harmony.

Retirement and ill health of one or both spouses are events that most long-lived marriages confront sooner or later. While retirement in and of itself may have no negative effect on the quality of most couples' lives (Atchley and Miller, 1983), the role adjustments that retirement requires can bring out the negative aspects of a marriage, particularly for women. Women appear to benefit less from husbands' retirement than do the retiring husbands, at least in working-class families. The husbands anticipate and enjoy retirement more than their wives do (Kerckhoff, 1964). The wives, particularly those who are older and in poor health, tend to be sorry their husbands retired and to regret it more the longer they are retired (Heyman and Jeffers, 1968). Even with good health and adequate finances, retirement can be problematic. Many wives consider it their responsibility alone to negotiate the couple's transition into retirement. This perception of responsibility may make the wives overly solicitous in planning activities for their husbands, which husbands frequently resent (Keating and Cole, 1980). With the current increase in women's labor force participation, more couples are now called upon to accommodate to the multiple interactive changes in life style associated with retirement of both spouses. Research is needed on the effects of retirement on two-worker marriages.

About 47 percent of all older persons suffer some limitation of activity because of chronic conditions (U.S. Senate Special Committee on Aging, 1984), and their primary source of help is a spouse (Shanas, 1979). Accordingly, care-giving to an ill spouse, usually a husband, is a commonplace role in later life—one which is becoming more prevalent with the dramatic surge occurring in the size of the old-old population. Wives who care for disabled husbands suffer poor health, social and emotional isolation, anger, and frustration (Crossman et al., 1981). The limited data on older husbands who give care indicate that they, too, report strain, though less of it, and use more formal community supports than do wives (Johnson, 1985). Regardless of which spouse gives care, the attendant burdens on both spouses have consequences that severely test the social and emotional resources that maintain the marital bond. Caregiving couples may express satisfaction with their marriages but their responses have a muted quality, with evidence of underlying anger and tension (Johnson, 1985).

In sum, long-lived relationships are a contemporary phenomenon; never in history have the lives of husbands and wives remained interwoven in intact marriages so long as to encounter the constellation of life-changing events that the last stages of the marital career now bring. Earlier socialization and emergent role models do not adequately prepare marital partners to take on the combined stresses, vulnerabilities, and potentials of this new stage of life. Although some couples may have built reserves of intimacy and belongingness on which to draw, other couples may find their interdependency in late life to be inequitably distributed, burdensome, and a source of conflict. These dynamics point to older marriages as a potential focus for the supportive interventions of social-service providers.

IMPLICATIONS FOR PRACTICE

Older spouses have few outlets for deflecting the tensions that arise in their marriages. They generally have fewer kin, friends, and co-workers with whom to discuss personal and marital issues, and they are reluctant to violate the norm of marital confidentiality between the generations by discussing problems with their children. Few older spouses seek professional help for marital problems. When older adults do see social-service providers, the elders more commonly present problems of anxiety, individual adjustment and family relationships, physical illness and medical planning, finances and housing. However, the association of these problems with alterations in the marriage relationship is seldom explored or moderated because professional counseling is available in only a minority of community-service agencies, and when it is available, it is in high demand (Lowy, 1980).

Service providers in the range of community settings are in a position to strengthen the ties that bind spouses in older marriages. In situations where providers customarily gather information from married clients, providers should inquire into the quality of the marital relationship, assess the types of help that client and spouse exchange, and understand the history of the relationship and its perceived strengths and weaknesses. This procedure allows older clients an opportunity to express their concerns and provides the practitioner with information to guide interventions and referrals. The procedure is particularly important for older women on whom the consequences of

their spouses' retirement and illness tend to have a deleterious effect and who may need to express and reconcile their feelings concerning altered patterns of marital interdependence.

Practitioners in social contact settings such as senior centers and congregate meal sites can assist older couples in the development of larger social networks and renewed social skills suitable to this stage of the marital career. Meaningful volunteer, leadership, and recreational opportunities that these programs offer can replace lost work and other instrumental roles as a source of validation of aspects of the self that may be lacking in spouses' interaction. At the same time, these programs can provide the occasion for socialization and enrichment experiences that renew and reaffirm the spouses' sense of belonging to a couple, a dimension of their lives they may have neglected during the earlier family life-cycle stages so heavily invested in work and parental identities. Task-oriented activity groups offer couples instruction in new skills, for example, cooking, sewing, household repairs, car maintenance, and consumerism, that can introduce and support a more flexible balance of interdependence in household responsibilities. Education programs prepare spouses for the common experiences that may be expected in an aging marriage, helping to reduce strain and improve understanding within couples.

Social services, quite appropriately, have traditionally tended to focus on the remedial needs of the frail, dependent, and deteriorated elderly, who comprise from 5 to 20 percent of people over the age of 65. But there is also need for social programs that increase opportunities for adequate functioning and contribution of the well elderly, who constitute the majority of the older population (Hartford, 1985). Social programs have appeared to overlook well, older couples as a consumer population, possibly on the common assumption that their marital status protects them from distress. Yet older husbands and wives may need social and professional support as they undertake to redefine the marital relationship and re-establish the bases of mutuality that bind them. For better or for worse, the marital bond represents the last major primary rela-

tionship in later life. Service providers have the knowledge, skills, values, and capacity to strengthen this relationship with programs that support older spouses in accomplishing the developmental tasks that enable marriages to survive and thrive.

REFERENCES

Atchley, R., 1985. *Social Forces and Aging.* 4th ed., Belmont, Calif.: Wadsworth.

Atchley, R. and Miller, S., 1983. "Types of Elderly Couples." In T. Brubaker, ed., *Family Relationships in Later Life.* Beverly Hills, Calif.: Sage Publications.

Brubaker, T., 1985. *Later Life Families.* Beverly Hills, Calif.: Sage Publications.

Campbell, A., Converse, P. and Rodgers, W., 1976. *The Quality of American Life.* New York: Russell Sage Foundation.

Crossman, L., London, C. and Barry, C., 1981. "Older Women Caring for Disabled Spouses: A Model for Supportive Services." *Gerontologist* 21(5):464–70.

Gibson, R., 1982. "Blacks at Middle and Late Life: Resources and Coping." *The Annals* 464(November):79–90.

Gilford, R., 1984. "Contrasts in Marital Satisfaction Throughout Old Age: An Exchange Theory Analysis." *Journal of Gerontology* 39(3):325–33.

Gilford, R. and Bengston, V., 1979. "Measuring Marital Satisfaction in Three Generations: Positive and Negative Dimensions." *Journal of Marriage and the Family* 41(2):387–98.

Glenn, N., 1975. "The Contribution of Marriage to the Psychological Well-Being of Males and Females." *Journal of Marriage and the Family* 37(3):594–601.

Glick, P. and Norton, A., 1977. "Marrying, Divorcing, and Living Together in the U.S. Today." *Population Bulletin* 32:1–39.

Gove, W., Hughes, M. and Style, C., 1983. "Does Marriage Have Positive Effects on the Psychological Well-Being of the Individual?" *Journal of Health and Social Behavior* 24(June):122–31.

Hartford, M., 1985. "Understanding Normative Growth and Development in Aging: Working with Strengths." *Journal of Gerontological Social Work* 8(3/4):37–54.

Heyman, D. and Jeffers, F., 1968. "Wives and Retirement: A Pilot Study." *Journal of Gerontology* 23(4)488–96.

Johnson, C., 1985. "The Impact of Illness on Late-Life Marriages." *Journal of Marriage and the Family* 47(1):165–72.

Keating, N. and Cole, P., 1980. "What Do I Do With Him 24 Hours a Day? Changes in the Housewife Role After Retirement." *Gerontologist* 20(1):84–89.

Keith, P. and Schafer, R., 1985. "Equity, Role Strains, and Depression Among Middle Aged and Older Men and Women." In W. Peterson and J. Quadagno, eds., *Social Bonds in Later Life.* Beverly Hills, Calif.: Sage Publications.

Kerckhoff, A., 1964. "Husband-Wife Expectations and Reactions to Retirement." *Journal of Gerontology* 19(4):510–16.

Kohen, J., 1983. "Old But Not Alone: Informal Social Supports Among the Elderly by Marital Status and Sex." *Gerontologist* 23(1):57–63.

Lee, G., 1978. "Marriage and Morale in Later Life." *Journal of Marriage and the Family* 40(1):131–39.

Lipman, A., 1962. "Role Conceptions of Couples in Retirement." In C. Tibbitts and W. Donahue, eds., *Social and Psychological Aspects of Aging.* New York: Columbia University Press.

Lopata, H., 1973. *Widowhood in an American City.* Cambridge, Mass.: Schenkman.

Lowenthal, M. and Haven, C., 1968. "Interaction and Adaptation: Intimacy as a Critical Variable." *American Sociological Review* 33(1):20–30.

Lowenthal, M., Thurnher, M. and Chiriboga, D., 1975. *Four Stages of Life.* San Francisco: Jossey-Bass.

Lowy, L., 1980. "Mental Health Services in the Community." In J. Birren and R. Sloane, eds., *Handbook of Mental Health and Aging.* Englewood Cliffs, N.J.: Prentice-Hall, Inc.

Markides, K. and Hoppe, S., 1985. "Marital Satisfaction in Three Generations of Mexican Americans." *Social Science Quarterly* 66 (March):147–54.

McAuley, W., Jacobs, M. and Carr, C., 1984. "Older Couples: Patterns of Assistance and Support." *Journal of Gerontological Social Work* 6(4):35–48.

McKain, W., 1972. "A New Look at Older Marriages." *Family Coordinator* 21(1):61–69.

Mouser, N., Powers, E., Keith, P. and Goudy, W., 1985. "Marital Status and Life Satisfaction: A Study of Older Men." In W. Peterson and J. Quadagno, eds., *Social Bonds in Later Life*. Beverly Hills, Calif.: Sage Publications.

Neugarten, B., 1968. "Toward a Psychology of the Life Cycle." In B. Neugarten, ed., *Middle Age and Aging*. Chicago: University of Chicago Press.

Newman, G. and Nichols, C., 1970. "Sexual Activities and Attitudes in Older Persons." In E. Palmore, ed., *Normal Aging*. Durham, N.C.: Duke University Press.

Nye, I. and Berardo, F., 1973. *The Family: Its Structure and Interaction*. New York: Macmillan.

Orthner, D., 1975. "Leisure Activity Patterns and Marital Career." *Journal of Marriage and the Family* 37(1):91–102.

Parron, E., 1982. "Golden Wedding Couples: Lessons in Marital Longevity." *Generations* 7(2):14, 15, 34.

Rhyne, C., 1981. "Bases of Marital Satisfaction Among Men and Women." *Journal of Marriage and the Family* 43(4):941–55.

Rollins, B. and Feldman, H., 1970. "Marital Satisfaction Over the Family Life Cycle." *Journal of Marriage and the Family* 32(1):20–28.

Rosow, I., 1973. "The Social Context of the Aging Self." *Gerontologist* 13(1):82–87.

Shanas, E., 1979. "The Family as a Social Support System in Old Age." *Gerontologist* 19(2):169–74.

Skolnick, A., 1981. "Married Lives: Longitudinal Perspectives on Marriage." In D. Eichorn, J. Clausen, N. Haan, M. Honzik and P. Mussen, eds., *Present and Past in Middle Life*. New York: Academic Press.

Sporakowski, M. and Hughston, G., 1978. "Prescriptions for Happy Marriage: Adjustments and Satisfactions of Couples Married for 50 or More Years." *Family Coordinator* 27(4)321–27.

Stinnett, N., Carter, L. and Montgomery, J., 1972. "Older Persons' Perceptions of Their Marriages." *Journal of Marriage and the Family* 34(4):665–70.

Swensen, C. and Trahaug, G., 1985. "Commitment and the Long-Term Marriage Relationship." *Journal of Marriage and the Family* 47(4):939–45.

Swensen, C., Eskew, R. and Kohlhepp, K., 1981. "Stage of Family Life Cycle, Ego Development, and the Marriage Relationship." *Journal of Marriage and the Family* 43(4):841–53.

Tamir, L., 1982. "Men at Middle Age: Developmental Transitions." *The Annals* 464(November):47–56.

Treas, J. and VanHilst, A., 1976. "Marriage and Remarriage Rates Among Older Americans." *Gerontologist* 16(2):132–36.

Troll, L., Atchley, R. and Miller, S., 1979. *Families in Later Life*. Belmont, Calif.: Wadsworth.

Uhlenberg, P. and Myers, M., 1981. "Divorce and the Elderly." *Gerontologist* 21(3):276–82.

U.S. Senate Special Committee on Aging/American Association of Retired Persons, 1984. *Aging America: Trends and Projections*, 2nd ed., Washington, D.C.

Vinick, B., 1978. "Remarriage in Old Age." *Family Coordinator* 27(4):359–63.

Older Adults' Sexuality and Remarriage

SHIRLEY S. TRAVIS

In the early part of this century Victorian ideas of human relationships were the underpinnings of the scant literature on sexual activity and sexuality. Even the relatively contemporary thinking of Havelock Ellis in the late 1920s retained the belief that the purpose of sex was for procreation and motherhood was a woman's primary role in life.[1] Since fewer women and men than today lived many years beyond childbearing age, there was little incentive to challenge these beliefs or to give much thought to aging sexuality. It made sense, in terms of "historical relativity" (explaining social behavior within the context of a particular period of historical time[2]), to associate all sexuality with marriage and marriage with procreation functions.

The increase in the number and ages of older adults in our society is well documented. We can now expect a record 32 million older Americans by the year 2000 with current estimated life expectancies for males and females of 70.3 and 77.9 years respectively.[3] These increases in size and longevity of our older population are causing American society to rethink and redefine longstanding cultural biases about aging sexuality and the older adult years. Now, more than ever before, nurses may find themselves the primary information/education source for older, healthier, sexually active married, unmarried, and remarried older adults.

AGING SEXUALITY

In 1948 and 1953 two history-making reports on human male and female sexual behavior were published by an entomologist specializing in gall wasps.[4] Dr. Alfred Kinsey based his reports on the verbal sexual histories of more than 10,000 white males and females. Perhaps the greatest criticism of Kinsey's work is the possible selection bias in his sample of voluntary respondents. Among the most obvious concerns of the representativeness of the Kinsey sample are the exclusion of nonwhite respondents in the published reports, the nonrandom selection procedures, over-representation of individuals in the northeastern United States, and the relatively small portion of the data set reporting on the aging adult. Despite what appear to be major methodological shortcomings, surveys completed in the United States since his published works tend to confirm or very closely agree with the key Kinsey findings.[4]

Source: Journal of Gerontological Nursing, 13(6), 9–14. Reprinted with permission from Slack, Inc., Thorofare, NJ 08086. Copyright 1987.

Kinsey's first volume on human sexual behavior addressed the male.[5] Throughout the volume Kinsey pointed to declining sexual activity as a result of numerous psychological factors such as fatigue, familiar contacts, and old techniques rather than as a solely age-related physiological event. Kinsey also found two physiological effects of aging most prevalent in his sample: decreased speed in reaching full erection and decline in length of time over which erection could be maintained.

Five years after publishing the volume on male sexual behavior Kinsey published a volume on female sexuality.[6] Contrary to popular beliefs about female frigidity, Kinsey reported a strong interest in sexual relations by women which actually increased with age. Many women (65%) reported reaching orgasm in their late 50s. Most of Kinsey's females maintained an interest in sexual relations until their 60s and then experienced a steady decline in frequency of marital coitus. Kinsey concluded that the decline of sexual activity must be related to aging husbands, rather than a decline in the desire for sexual relations, since in American society women usually marry men approximately four years their senior.

Masters and Johnson were the first researchers to publish a reference on the physiology of the human sexual response.[7] In subsequent years of research on aging sexuality, they have been joined by several other sex researchers in providing insight into our aging population's sexual responsiveness.

However, even today, American society does not totally allow aging adults the freedom to openly express their sexuality. Both aging males and females can be shamed into hiding their sexuality or curiosity about normal physiologic changes in sexual expression to the point where they begin to see themselves as perverse or ultimately as sexless individuals.[8,9]

Most of the concerns about sexual inadequacy in the aging female are primarily related to normal vaginal alterations which occur secondary to steroid changes during menopause. Opportunity for regular coital activity in the aging female will usually promote a higher capacity for sexual performance than in females who do not have similar coital opportunity.

Yet, even among regularly sexually active older women, common physical changes after menopause may cause symptoms of painful penetration, vaginal burning, pelvic aching, or irritation in urination lasting up to 36 hours after coitus.[7] Many women who are faced with the situation of an older or infirmed spouse may resort to masturbatory practices to relieve sexual tensions. Masturbation is not, however, an adequate substitution for counteracting the effects of sex-steroid deprivation on the vagina.[10,11]

Unlike the aging female, most males in sound physical and mental health can expect adequate sexual performance beyond 80 years of age. When alterations in male responsive ability do occur, they generally fall within one or more of the following categories:

1. monotony of a repetitious sexual relationship;
2. preoccupation with career or economic pursuits;
3. mental or physical fatigue;
4. overindulgence in food or drink;
5. physical and mental infirmities of either self or spouse; and
6. fear of failure in sexual performance.[7]

At least one study suggested the importance of socioeconomic status on sexuality in older adulthood. In a study of 188 high socioeconomic males, ages 60 through 79 who resided in the Washington-Baltimore metropolitan area, Martin found that, in spite of apparent good health, over one third of 60- to 79-year-old respondents reported no more than six sexual events within the year.[12] Most of the subjects who were less than fully potent regarded their marriages as highly successful and their wives as physically attractive. According to the study findings, these men remained relatively sexually inactive while also feeling free from performance anxiety, and free of feelings of sexual deprivation and loss of self-esteem.

Persons over age 65 in 1980 averaged 1.1 episodes of disability from acute conditions (lasting less than three months and involving medical attention or activity restriction). During this same year, the aging adult averaged 10.6 days of restricted activity because of acute conditions, four days of which were spent in bed. Nearly half of all noninstitutionalized persons aged 65 and over were reported to have a chronic health condition that limited their activity for about $5\frac{1}{2}$ weeks, with about two weeks spent in bed. In addition, one in four persons in this age group spent some time in the hospital and 17 out of 100 sustained an accidental injury during the year.[13] Finally, the National Center for Health Statistics reported the leading chronic conditions in the 1981 population of men and women age 65 and over were arthritis and hypertensive disease.[14] With a large portion of the elderly population receiving antihypertensives, the two most common side effects were depression and impotence which pose a serious problem to aging sexuality. These statistics suggest that almost universally every surviving spouse of an aged marriage has had to live with coital continence for some period of time before or following the death of the spouse.

The widower's syndrome, reported by Masters and Johnson as sexual continence by a man in his late 50s or beyond, frequently follows an extended illness and death of the spouse.[11] The male simply cannot achieve or maintain a functional erection. The widow's syndrome is the female counterpart of the widower's syndrome. Typically, the aging female is contending with voluntary or involuntary sexual continence compounded by postmenopause. As sexual continence is prolonged, the walls of the vagina become

atrophic, the vaginal barrel constricts, the vaginal outlet constricts, and the major and minor labia are thinned.[11] Clearly the aging adult male and female cannot easily recover from prolonged lack of sexual relations.

On any one day 5% of the nation's older adults reside in a nursing home. In reality, however, current estimates of the lifetime risk of some period of institutionalization for our nation's elders actually exceeds 35%.[15]

In 1978, Kaas reported a study dealing with differences between elderly nursing home residents and nursing staff on attitudes toward sexual expression of the elderly.[8] Utilizing 85 residents age 65 years and older from five nursing homes in the Detroit area, several important points were raised by the residents. Although the research of aging sexuality up to this time was generally very positive, the institutionalized residents in the study said they did not feel sexually attractive. In addition, these residents said they would not enjoy sexual activity if they had a willing partner.

Although the residents felt that sex was normal, most residents felt it was needed more for older women than older men, the double standard in reverse! Also, the residents saw lack of privacy in the nursing home as a deterrent to sexual expression.

As the residents in the study reported, if one does not feel sexually attractive, the desire for a sexual relationship is usually absent. As more and more older adults spend some portion of their lives recovering in a nursing home, perhaps posthospitalization, healthcare providers must attend to these perceived losses of sexual attractiveness and self-esteem.

Sexuality is not, of course, entirely equated with coitus. The older adult, like people at any age, has strong emotional needs which may be met by holding, touching, and closeness without intercourse. Touching of two older adults can bring sensual pleasure with no further goal than enjoyment of the physical presence of another human being. In addition to or in the absence of coitus, touching may satisfy the need for sexual expression of aging adults.

As the next section will show, many authors suggest that contactual relationships, more so than sexual relationships, are an important force in bringing aging individuals together in their later years.

REMARRIAGE IN OLDER ADULTHOOD

When an individual has experienced a gratifying relationship in a marriage, there is inevitable pain and grief when one partner dies. Most survivors eventually feel free to start life again and even to contemplate remarriage.[20] As mentioned earlier, when there were only a few persons living to old age, love and marriage in later life weren't given much significance. Today, however, millions of older men and women are in remarriages and are finding that there are no models for these relationships.[16]

Early indicators of the emerging sexuality of older senior singles suggest a sex ethic similar to other adult age groups in America. Young and old adults generally view sex in a liberal, romantic way.[16] The emerging trend is for sexual activity to be viewed as more than a procreative function and for relationships to include companionship as well as coitus.

The desire to share an intimate relationship with a new marriage partner is not, unfortunately, always enough to have the dream of remarriage come true. In 1970, there were more than 6 million widows and 1½ million widowers in the United States. From 1974 to 1985, the number of single females in the United States was expected to rise by 3 million and single men by about 700,000.[17]

Since women who reach age 65 live about seven years longer than men at the same age and since 80% of American women reach age 65 versus only 65% of the males, there are about five times as many eligible widows as widowers.[17] A man who wants to remarry can usually find a willing woman either in his age group or younger. A woman who wants to remarry may not be so successful.

More older people are marrying today because there are greater numbers of older people. However, the propensity of older people to marry has not changed over time. Social norms ordain that men wed brides younger than themselves, a custom which expands the number of potential partners for older men and severely restricts marital choices for older women.[18]

Several consequences of widowhood also can influence a person's desire for another mate. Among these reported by Cleveland and Gianturco[19] are:

1. lack of companionship;
2. less economic security;
3. high morbidity and mortality compared to married counterparts; and
4. poor social adaptation due to isolation and loneliness.

The opportunity to meet and court prospective mates is an important selective factor in remarriage. Data on courtship and remarriage of older adults are scarce. Jacobs and Vinick interviewed 24 couples who had been married between two and six years in which at least one spouse was 65 years or older and in which both spouses had been married previously.[17] In this small sample they found that the length of time between the death of a spouse and the subsequent remarriage varies between men and women. Two years was the shortest time living alone for the women in the study; nearly half lived alone ten years or longer. The men, on the other hand, remarried much sooner. More than half of the men remarried in a year or less. Similar findings have been reported in an earlier study at the University of Connecticut on 100 older couples.[20] In this earlier study, widowers seldom waited more than a year or two before remarrying, while widows frequently waited several years.

It seems obvious that the issue of more eligible widows for every eligible widower is a factor in the length of time men and women remain alone after the death of a spouse. The "numerical disparity" between the sexes is compounded by the fact that most single elders depend on ordinary methods to meet potential mates.

Many couples who marry knew each other for many years during their previous marriages as neighbors or members of the same church, or were introduced by a mutual friend or relative. Meetings at adult functions are also a source of meeting a potential mate but not as often as prior relationships.[17,20] At least one author has suggested broadening one's mating network to include newspaper advertisements, computer dating, and video services.[21] While this may not be attractive to today's elderly singles, elders of the near future may find innovative dating devices very attractive.

Children of the dating couple are sometimes resistant to the idea that their parents would be comfortable in a relationship with someone other than the dead parent. Many times a concern about inheritance, should the parent remarry, causes some concern of the children. Most often, however, children are supportive; perhaps because they feel relieved of the care and companionship requirements of the widowed parent.[22,23]

Men and women ultimately decide to remarry late in life for a variety of reasons. Companionship is by far the major reason given for remarriage.[20] The elderly widowed of today are in better health, have greater financial security, and greater mobility than the previous aging cohorts. When faced with the options of living the remainder of their years alone, living with children. moving into congregate living or remarrying, the choice of remarrying appeals to most elders who are given the opportunity to make such a choice.[20]

Obviously love and companionship are not the objects of all second marriages. Especially for the elderly woman, financial security may be a factor in the decision to remarry. The male's incentive to remarry may be for a housekeeper or a nurse, if his health is declining. In general, widows and widowers who looked for a housekeeper, more income, or a nurse in the remarriage do not have as good a chance for happiness as those who selected a mate based on companionship and love.[20]

Once the aging couple decides to remarry, data indicate that most couples bow to public opinion to the extent of having a simple ceremony.[20] The second ceremony is usually more personal than the first but with less tradition and pomp. The guests are usually close friends and family. Reports conflict over the type of ceremony and choice of honeymoon with McKain[20] citing a preference for a civil ceremony with no honeymoon while Treas and Van Hilst[18] report a preference for a religious remarriage with a honeymoon.

When at least one partner in a remarriage is a widowed person, Bernard reported three major areas of potential difficulty for marital adjustment:

1. the tendency of the widowed spouse to idealize the deceased mate.
2. the knowledge of the new spouse that the partner's first marriage was not terminated voluntarily
3. the feelings of friends and relatives that the new spouse is an intruder.[24]

Despite the areas of potential conflict, most older remarriages report a high success rate. Contrary to popular thinking on marital happiness, older couples put a premium on calmness and holding back angry feelings rather than open, free expression of negative feelings.[17] Older people seem to bring the important ingredient of experience to a successful marriage. In general, success in remarriage has five major variables:[20]

1. widows and widowers who knew each other well usually had a successful marriage;

2. remarriages which had approval of friends and relatives had greater chance for success than those which did not;
3. those who had adjusted to role changes that accompany aging usually had successful remarriages;
4. those who owned a house but did not live in it after remarriage tended to have successful remarriages; and
5. couples with sufficient income were more likely to have a successful remarriage.

CONCLUSION

As the number of older Americans increases into the next century, the amount of remarriages in older adulthood will probably increase even though the proportion of remarriages in the age group is not expected to change from current rates. American society has traditionally equated marriage with procreation and has been reluctant to sanction the union of partners of any age for any other purpose.

Sex researchers in the last 20 years have demonstrated the value of aging sexuality as a desirable component of successful aging. Remarriage in later life can be a positive and feasible alternative to being alone following the death of a spouse in older adulthood.

One issue of aging sexuality that emerged in this literature review was the need for understanding other elements of human sexuality including touch, kissing, and close warm contact. It would seem that greater attention to contactual stimulation needs for aging couples is in order.

So much of today's knowledge of aging sexuality and sexual activity was developed on a very small group of subjects almost two decades ago. This research represents a different aging cohort than we see today. Yet, these data are cited over and over again as though the findings can be generalized to all older adults indefinitely.

There are numerous research questions to be generated from this literature and our daily interactions as healthcare providers with older individuals and couples. For example, what about the issue of diminished sexual attractiveness in institutionalized elders in the Kaas study? How are we addressing the lack of privacy issue in nursing homes?

How can we most effectively counsel or support the sexually continent spouse of a chronically ill, disabled mate? What expectations of older adults' sexuality do we impose on our elderly clients, by our actions or attitudes? Are we as tuned in to the family dynamics of newly wed older adults as we are to more traditional family dynamics in the hospital? In the community? In the nursing home? Each of us in our own clinical setting can probably generate many more questions in need of additional research.

REFERENCES

1. Ellis H: *Man and Woman.* New York, Houghton Mifflin Co. 1929.
2. Hall E: A conversation with Erik Erikson. *Psychology Today* 1983; 17(6):22–30.
3. US Department of Health and Human Services: Annual summary of births, deaths, marriages and divorce: United States, 1981. *Monthly Vital Statistics Report.* December 20, 1982, 30(13).
4. Beecher E: *The Sex Researchers.* San Francisco, Specific Press. 1979.

5. Kinsey A, Pomeroy W, Martin C: *Sexual Behavior in the Human Male.* Philadelphia, WB Saunders Co. 1948.
6. Kinsey A, Pomeroy W, Martin C: *Sexual Behavior in the Human Female.* Philadelphia, WB Saunders Co. 1953.
7. Masters W, Johnson V: *Human Sexual Response.* Boston, Little, Brown and Co. 1966.
8. Kaas M: Sexual expression of the elderly in nursing homes. *The Gerontologist* 1978; 18(4):372–378.

9. Stanford D: All about sex . . . after middle age. *American J Nurs* 1977; 77(4):608–611.

10. Bachmann G, Leiblum S: Sexual expression in menopausal women. *Medical Aspects of Human Sexuality* 1981; 15(10):96B–96H.

11. Masters W, Johnson V: Sex and the aging process. *Medical Aspects of Human Sexuality* 1982; 16(6):40–57.

12. Martin C: Factors affecting sexual functioning in 60–79 year old married males. *Archives of Sexual Behavior* 1981; 10(5):399–420.

13. Metropolitan Life Foundation. Health of the elderly. *Statistical Bulletin* 1982; 63(1):3–5.

14. National Center for Health Statistics. 1981 National Ambulatory Medical Care Survey, unpublished.

15. Liang J, Tu E: Estimating lifetime risk of nursing home residency: A further note. *The Gerontologist* 1986; 26(5):560–563.

16. Peterson J, Payne B: *Love in the Later Years.* New York, Association Press. 1975.

17. Jacobs R, Vinick B: *Re-engagement in Later Life: Re-employment and Remarriage.* Stamford, Conn, Greylock Publishers. 1979.

18. Treas J, VanHilst A: Marriage and remarriage rates among older Americans. *The Gerontologist* 1976; 16(2):132–136.

19. Cleveland W, Gianturco D: Remarriage probability after widowhood: A retrospective method. *J Gerontol* 1976; 31(1):99–103.

20. McKain W: A new look at older marriages. *The Family Coordinator* 1972; 21(1):61–69.

21. Jedlicka D: Formal mate selection networks in the United States. *Family Relations* 1980; 29(2):199–203.

22. Vinick B: Remarriage by the elderly. *Medical Aspects of Human Sexuality* 1983; 17(10):111–116.

23. Pattison EM: When an adult's parent remarries. *Medical Aspects of Human Sexuality* 1983; 17(5):60B–60U.

24. Bernard J: *Remarriage.* New York, Russell and Russell. 1971.

Discussion Questions for Chapter Six

1. Although Boyd and Treas conclude that being a "woman in the middle" may not be normative, it certainly is normative that women assume the majority of responsibility for informal elder care. Why do women take on this role more frequently than men? Has elder care become normative in the sense that it is a common aspect of a woman's life, much like the responsibility for child rearing.

2. Describe what the marriages of future cohorts of older people may be like in light of both Gilford's descriptions of the strengths and strains of older marriages and the fact that younger cohorts have higher rates of divorce, delayed child bearing, and new definitions of gender roles.

3. As Travis explains, by social custom men are more likely to marry a person younger than themselves than are women. Why is this the case? How would the lives of older people be different if this social norm were just the opposite?

CHAPTER SEVEN

Living Arrangements

Living arrangements have major consequences on the quality of older people's lives. Where and with whom one lives can affect one's living standard, frequency and quality of social contact, and level of independence and assistance in daily life.

Most older people live in communities rather than in institutions such as nursing homes, and most are not socially isolated. Two-thirds of those who live in the community live with other family members (AARP and AoA, 1990). Only 30% of noninstitutionalized older people live alone or with nonrelatives.

Living with other people, even if they are family members, can sometimes have negative consequences. As reported by Jill Korbin and her colleagues, elders are most likely to be abused by a person with whom they live. Spousal abuse is more common than abuse by an offspring because older people are more likely to live with their spouses than their children, but the *rate* of elder abuse is slightly higher among older people living with their offspring than among those living with spouses. In "Elder Abuse and Child Abuse: A Consideration of Similarities and Differences in Intergenerational Family Violence," Korbin and her colleagues focus on intergenerational abuse, drawing comparisons between elder abuse and child abuse.

Independent living is not always possible because older people sometimes need assistance with activities of daily living. Only 5% of people over age 65 live in institutions such as nursing homes, but the likelihood of living in an institution increases dramatically with age: 22% of those aged 85 and over live in institutions. Since the 85-and-over age group is the most rapidly expanding among the elderly population, the need for nursing home beds is expected to rise dramatically in the future. In "Long-Term Care Options for the Frail Elderly," Muriel R. Gillick explains why, despite the current trend toward avoiding institutionalization, home care is often not a viable alternative for the severely incapacitated, and why more institutional care will be needed in the future. In order to propose models for the future, Gillick places institutional care for the aged in its historical context. Present day nursing homes, unlike their predecessors (19th-century alms houses and old age homes), are much more oriented toward medical treatment. Since the major needs of the frail elderly are help with activities of daily living (e.g., dressing, bathing, toileting) rather than medical treatment, she proposes that they would be served better by institutions that are demedicalized and "homier."

REFERENCE

American Association of Retired Persons (AARP) and Administration on Aging (AoA). (1990). A profile of older Americans. Washington, DC: AARP.

Elder Abuse and Child Abuse: A Consideration of Similarities and Differences in Intergenerational Family Violence

JILL E. KORBIN
GEORGIA J. ANETZBERGER
J. KEVIN ECKERT

INTRODUCTION

In the United States awareness of and research attention to elder abuse arose after attention to child and spousal abuse. Child abuse in the 1960s and spousal violence in the 1970s emerged as significant research and policy issues. The "Greying of America" intensified concern about a range of issues facing the elderly, and elder abuse was "discovered" in the late 1970s and early 1980s. As elder abuse became the newest form of family violence, attempts were made to fit violence against elder family members into existing frameworks developed for other forms of family violence, in particular child abuse and neglect. Postulated causal explanations of child and elder abuse are similar largely because factors implicated in the child abuse literature have been echoed in the rapidly expanding literature on elder abuse, often with little empirical justification (Block and Sinnot 1979; Legal Research and

Services for the Elderly 1981; Pedrick-Cornell and Gelles 1982). As considerations of elder abuse have moved beyond the initial, and often dramatic accounts, it is time to step back and consider what an understanding of child maltreatment can contribute to knowledge of elder abuse and vice versa.

While historical precedents and the social milieu promote tolerance of physical force directed at a recalcitrant child (Erlanger 1974; Stark and McEvoy 1970; Straus et al. 1980), the same attitude is not in evidence for such behaviors directed against one's parents. Admonishments dating from Biblical times to "honor thy mother and thy father" are in stark contrast to "spare the rod and spoil the child." Many states continue to permit corporal punishment of children in the schools while similar treatment of elders in institutions, when it comes to public attention, arouses ire and condemnation. Acts of physical restraint or force directed at children may fall under the rubric of maintain-

Source: Journal of Elder Abuse & Neglect, 1(4), 1–13. Reprinted with permission from Haworth Press, Inc., Binghamton, NY 13904. Copyright 1989.

ing control and even providing instruction, while the same act directed at an adult could constitute assault, or at least a violation of rights. That both elder and child abuse constitute socially recognized problems in our society provides a critical, but as yet untapped, comparison for research on intrafamilial violence and relations among the generations.

Despite obvious age and status differences, young children and elder parents exhibit similarities that make the linking of child and elder abuse compelling. Young children and oftentimes elder parents, particularly those with impairments, are in powerless positions vis-à-vis their middle generation caretakers. They require substantial time and energy investments for caretaking. They exhibit behaviors that may be perceived as troublesome, willful, and difficult to manage. They may be a source of emotional or financial stress. However, at the same time, differences in the nature of parent-to-child and child-to-parent relationships and in the social and legal status of adulthood versus childhood argue against a too-facile linking of the two problems.

ELDER ABUSE AND OTHER FORMS OF FAMILY VIOLENCE

Elder abuse has been compared with both child and spousal abuse (Finkelhor 1983; Finkelhor and Pillemer 1988; Phillips 1986). While much of the literature draws the primary parallel with child abuse, Pillemer and Finkelhor (1988) found spousal abuse to be more frequent (58%) than abuse by offspring (24%). However, they also found that living circumstances were critical in that the elders were abused by those with whom they resided. Elders living with offspring were slightly more likely to experience violence than those living with spouses. In our preliminary data analysis, 86% of elders abused by their adult offspring also lived with that offspring. Pillemer and Finkelhor argue that dominant living arrangements mean that spousal violence among elders will be more frequent, and they suggest greater attention to spousal abuse among the elderly. While spousal violence among elders has been neglected relative to offspring abuse, the state of current knowledge demands further investigation of both of these types of elder maltreatment. Elder abuse, like other forms of intrafamilial violence, has multiple manifestations.

Neither child abuse nor elder abuse is homogeneous and cannot be studied as such. Elder abuse between spouses may have more commonalities with spousal abuse in younger couples. Elder abuse that involves self abuse or neglect must be considered separately from that involving a perpetrator. Elder abuse by filial caregivers may have important parallels with child abuse by parents. While direct parallels between child and elder abuse are clearly premature, research efforts should be directed at determining what meaningful commonalities and differences exist.

DEFINITIONS AND LIMITATIONS OF OFFICIAL REPORT DATA

Despite the progress that has been made in the twenty-five years since the coining of the term "the battered child" (Kempe et al. 1962), problems of definitional ambiguity and unreliable incidence and prevalence statistics have hampered the formulation of adequate explanations for the occurrence of intrafamilial violence against children. The growing literature on elder abuse, borrowing liberally from experience in child abuse, is plagued by many of the same problems.

Definitional ambiguity exists in both child and elder abuse. The label "the battered child syndrome" was intentionally chosen to grasp public, professional, and legislative attention. It referred specifically to children who had been seriously injured by their caretakers, usually their parents. In twenty-five years, definitions of child abuse and neglect have expanded to include a range of caretaker behaviors and child outcomes. In a sense, "child abuse and neglect" has come to be used as a singular term, encompassing almost everything deemed "bad" for children for which caretakers can be held accountable. Similarly, in the elder abuse literature, definitions cut a wide swath (Callahan 1988; Pedrick-Cornell and Gelles 1982). For example, in our research, of 545 cases reported (but not necessarily substantiated) to Cuyahoga County, Ohio Adult Protective Services over a 12 month period in 1985–86, 60.2% represent a designation of self-abuse. While self-abuse is a serious problem and its inclusion in elder abuse statutes allows adult protective services to provide services to the elderly, including this designation under the rubric of "elder abuse" creates substantial problems for research. The breadth of definitions of elder abuse is a problem in many states, making comparability of incidence and prevalence rates problematic (Salend et al. 1984).

Elder and child abuse share the problem that official report data is too frequently inadequate to assess the scope of the problem. Official reports are thought to underestimate actual incidence and prevalence, both for child and elder abuse. It is estimated that between one-fifth and one-sixth of actual cases of elder abuse are reported (U.S. House of Representatives 1981, 1984). Since official reports do not encompass all cases, speculation can be rampant on the bias involved. The debate continues whether the poor are overrepresented in child abuse reports due to increased stress and thus increased abuse or due to increased scrutiny and bias by public service agencies (e.g., Pelton 1981). Certain types of elder abuse also may be more likely to be reported: filial more than spousal

perpetrators; physical more than psychological; and severe more than mild abuse.

Differences in estimates of incidence and prevalence based on self-reported violent behavior versus official reports that depend on whether there was an injurious or potentially injurious consequence of such behavior represent a long-standing debate in the family violence literature (Straus et al. 1980). Among the limitations of official reporting statistics of both elder and child abuse that make interpretation and comparison problematic, is the heterogeneity of behaviors included (Gelles 1979; Pillemer and Wolf 1986; Rizley and Cicchetti 1981; Salend et al. 1984).

Problems may also arise from differences in the level of violence that individuals report. Parents, backed up by cultural values on discipline of children, may be unselfconscious in reporting spanking their children. However, an adult offspring might be more hesitant to admit to breaking strongly held cultural values and slapping his/her elder parent.

COMMONALITIES AND DIFFERENCES: SOME SUGGESTED DIMENSIONS

The following section considers similarities and differences between elder abuse and child abuse. The discussion will be limited to intergenerational abuse, that is parental abuse of children and adult offspring abuse of their parents. Since the terms elder abuse and child abuse encompass a wide range of behaviors, the discussion will be limited to physical abuse. The purpose of this discussion is to suggest dimensions relevant to a comparison of these two forms of intrafamilial violence. These dimensions are amenable to research efforts, without which comparisons of forms of family violence will remain speculative; and current knowledge will continue to be limited by research and service division according to the victimized group (Finkelhor 1983; Gelles 1979; Straus et al. 1980).[1]

Culturally-Approved Scripts for Modifying Behavior

> Sarah sat sullenly in her chair at the kitchen table, refusing to eat. Margaret prepared Sarah's favorite cereal, hoping to tempt her to eat. After much pleading to get Sarah to eat the cereal, Margaret asked if she would rather have eggs. Sarah looked interested and Margaret set about preparing them. When Margaret set the eggs on the table, however, Sarah flew into a rage and threw all of the food off the table. Milk, cereal, and eggs went flying everywhere. Margaret lost her temper, began to scream and slapped Sarah.

How would one respond to this incident if Sarah were a two-year old versus an eighty-year old? If Sarah were a child, many parents would sigh with recognition, even if not necessarily approving of the use of physical discipline. But what if Sarah were one's eighty-year-old mother? While parents are expected to exert some form of discipline with their children, what are adults expected to do with respect to their elder parents?

Despite the near-continuous debate in American society about proper methods of child rearing, parents have culturally-approved scripts for coping with difficult and disapproved behavior in their children. Advice on child rearing is often conflicted and there are multiple models from which to choose. Margaret Mead once noted, that the only regularity of American child rearing is that one generation is committed to doing things differently than their parents. Parents are expected, by one means or another, to mold and modify the behavior of their immatures through the process of socialization to fit the needs of society. However, there are not similar guidelines for implementing behavior change in one's elder parents. Adult offspring caring for elder parents may have to cope with behaviors that can be difficult, but they have little recourse in demanding better. They can plead, cajole, and negotiate, but the use of force is not within the accepted cultural repertoire.

Profiles of Violence

Profiles of violence directed at children and elders may vary in frequency and severity. Children may receive more frequent, less severe violence, for example, spankings. The threshold may be different for elder parents. While children are subjected to more routine violence, when violence erupts against elder parents, it may be either more severe or perceived as such. Spanking of a child may not be viewed as serious or out of the ordinary while similar striking a parent would be (Straus and Gelles 1986). Physical discipline of children occurs with sufficient frequency in the United States that it cannot be considered unusual (Straus et al. 1980). Further, physical discipline of children is instituted early. One-fourth of those mothers visiting a health care clinic reported spanking infants younger than six months of age, and one-third spanked infants younger than one year (Korsh et al. 1965).

It has been suggested that physical discipline of children is particularly dangerous among individuals that disapprove of it (Parke and Collmer 1975). Parents who use physical discipline as a first resort may administer it before emotions get out of hand. In contrast, if physical force is a matter of last resort, following negotiation, threats, and pleas, by the time it is actually administered emotions are frayed; and anger and frustration may be more likely to exceed acceptable boundaries. Similarly, if physical force is a culturally disapproved measure of last resort against elder parents, it may be more likely to get out of control.

This dimension squarely confronts the definitional issues facing a comparison of child and elder abuse. How is "abuse" to be operationalized? Considering the widespread acceptance of physical discipline of children, would slapping a child be equated with slapping an elder parent?

Dependency

Dependency has been raised as a contributory factor in child and elder abuse. In earlier considerations of elder abuse, it was postulated that dependent elders, like young children, put stress on their caregivers that can lead to abuse. In both child and elder abuse this may be an oversimplification. More current research on elder abuse (e.g., Anetzberger 1987; Pillemer 1986) has indicated that it may be the perpetrator, the abusive offspring, that is the dependent one. Some proportion of abusive adult offspring are in fact dependent on their elder parents, and the frustrations of continued dependency in this direction contribute to elder abuse. Similarly, the nature of childhood leads to an easy, and usually correct, assumption that children are dependent on their parents. However, abusive parents also may be dependent on their young children. This may not be readily apparent because they are not financially or physically dependent on their children for care. Nevertheless, abusive parents may be quite dependent on their young children emotionally. The concept of role-reversal has been implicated in child abusing families, in which parents look to their young children to fulfill their emotional needs (Morris and Gould 1963; Spinetta and Rigler 1972; Steele 1980).

Caretaking Commitment and Social Isolation

Both children and dependent elder parents require a caretaking commitment of time and energy. This is necessarily so for children and becomes more likely with increasing age and the existence of physical or psychological impairment in an elder parent. Whether this is a "burden" depends importantly on the caregiver's perception. Adult offspring are more likely to abuse their elder parents when they perceive a greater burden (Steinmetz 1983). The individual's perception of stress and burden may be more closely related to abuse than seemingly more objective measures (Steinmetz 1988). Negative feelings towards elders are more related to perceived parental dependency than to actual tasks performed (Cicirelli 1983). The investment required to care for an elder parent is often perceived as detrimental to an adult offspring's own health and happiness (e.g., Koopman-Boyden and Wells 1979; O'Malley et al. 1979). Cross-culturally, the greater the mother's sole burden for caretaking and the less likely she is to receive periodic help or relief from her burdens, the more likely she is to be rejecting and harsh with her children (Minturn and Lambert 1964).

Both child and elder abusing families have been characterized as socially isolated (e.g., Garbarino 1977; Garbarino and Sherman 1980; Gelles 1973; Pillemer 1986; Wolf et al. 1984). That both types of families seem to have fewer social resources and diminished abilities to use what is available, provides an important commonality. This becomes particularly important in the face of caretaking tasks.

Role Clarity

Family roles appear to be disrupted and distorted in both child and elder abusing families. Role reversal, in which the parent expects the child to nurture him/her has been implicated in the etiology of child maltreatment (Morris and Gould 1963; Spinetta and Rigler 1972; Steele 1980). A comparable dynamic in families caring for elder parents, generational inversion (Steinmetz and Amsden 1983), or an unresolved filial crisis has been implicated in elder abuse.

Difficult Behaviors

Both children and elder parents may exhibit behaviors that are perceived as stressful and difficult by their caregivers. Children are at increased risk of child abuse during difficult developmental stages, particularly those dealing with issues of oppositionality. Straus et al. (1980) suggest that young children and adolescents are more likely to be abused because of noncompliant behaviors at these ages. This could apply to elders who are not accustomed to accepting the authority of their children or willing to comply with their instructions.

While child behavior is cited as an important contributor to abusive situations (Friedrick and Boriskin 1976; Friedrick and Einbender 1983; Frodi 1981; George and Main 1979; Martin 1976; Milowe and Lourie 1964), data are sparse on the precise child behaviors that precipitate maltreatment (Kadushin and Martin 1981). Child behaviors that are reported by parents as precipitating abusive incidents may be noxious and stressful or may be normal child behaviors such as crying, soiling, or refusing to eat. These "normal" behaviors are stressful in and of themselves but precipitate abuse based on the interpretation of the parent, for example, when toileting accidents are seen as defiance rather than developmentally normal. Similar behaviors are not generally expected of elders and may be stressful when they occur (Anetzberger 1987). While it is accepted that young children sometimes refuse to eat, cry inconsolably, or soil their clothing, such behavior is less anticipated in adulthood and may be equally or more problematic. Anetzberger (1987) found that elder behaviors were more bothersome to their abusive caregivers than the actual tasks of caretaking. In both child and elder abusing families, a single behavior or incident is rarely sufficient to precipitate abuse. Rather, continuing negative interactions escalate into abuse (Anetzberger 1987; Kadushin and Martin 1981).

Expectations of Improvement

Closely related to the above, many disturbing or troublesome behaviors in children are part and parcel of a transitory stage of normal development. In contrast, with the elderly, the same behaviors represent deterioration and decreased capacity rather than immaturity and a stage in development. The expectation is not of an upwards trajectory, but of a downward one. Parents, for example, look forward to completing toilet training and relief from diapers. In contrast, one cannot wait out incontinence in an elder parent with the expectation that the parent will outgrow the condition.

Cycle of Violence

While the inevitability of intergenerational transmission of family violence has been challenged (Kaufman and Sigler 1987; Widom 1989), it is the most commonly reported causal factor in the child abuse literature. That abusive parents were abused as children was reported in the cornerstone article on child abuse and neglect (Kempe et al. 1962) and has been reported as a near-constant in subsequent literature. A previous history of intrafamilial violence also has been suggested in the elder abuse literature: that abusive adult offspring were abused as children by their now abused parents (Pillemer and Suitor 1988). Adult offspring may be retaliating for past or continued physical violence from their parents (Steinmetz 1981). Pillemer cautions that an intergenerational cycle of abuse may involve different dynamics for child abusing versus elder abusing individuals. The child abuser does not aggress against his or her aggressor, but against a child. But for elder abuse, " . . . the cycle becomes more direct: the formerly abused child strikes out at his or her own abuser. This involves a different psychological process—one with elements of retaliation as well as imitation" (1986:243).

Policy Implications

The policy implications involved in child and elder abuse cannot be ignored (Schene and Ward 1988). Adult protective services and related laws have been molded on experience with child abuse, assuming similarities that may or may not exist. The social and legal status of childhood versus adulthood argues against direct parallels in service provision. For example, while controversy continues concerning the degree and nature of permissible state intervention in parental rights, the state nonetheless may assume protective custody of a minor child. The child's permission is not required for protective services and intervention. In contrast, an elder, unless deemed incompetent by clearly defined legal procedures, must be reckoned with in decisions about out of home placement. Elders are competent adults whose custody cannot be dictated without their consent.

CONCLUDING REMARKS

In the past approximately twenty-five years, multiple forms of intrafamilial violence and assault have emerged from dark family secrets to matters of public and professional concern. That both child and elder abuse occur in our society despite differing cultural values demands careful research attention. This paper has suggested several dimensions being studied in a systematic comparison of the dynamics involved in physical violence directed at elder parents by their adult offspring and young children by their parents. It is anticipated that a better understanding of the commonalities and differences in these two populations will further knowledge about the underlying dynamics of family violence and contribute to policy decisions about how to best serve these populations.

NOTE

1. Our recently completed research project has compared and contrasted intergenerational violence towards elders by their adult offspring and towards young children by their parents. The sample consists of adult offspring perpetrators of elder abuse and two comparison samples: (a) child abusing parents and (b) non-elder abusing offspring. Additionally, a small sample of elders who have initiated legal proceedings against their abusive offspring has been included.

REFERENCES

Anetzberger, G. J. (1987). *The etiology of elder abuse by adult offspring.* Springfield, IL: Charles Thomas.

Block, M. R. & Sinnott, J. D. (Eds.) (1979). *The battered elder syndrome: An exploratory study.* College Park, MD: University of Maryland Center on Aging.

Callahan, J. J. (1988). Elder abuse: Some questions for policymakers. *The Gerontologist, 28*(4), 453–458.

Cicirelli, V. (1983). Adult children and their elderly parents. In T. Brubaker (Ed.), *Family relations in later life.* (pp. 31–46). Beverly Hills, CA: Sage Publications.

Erlanger. H. B. (1974). Social class and corporal punishment in childrearing. A reassessment. *American Sociological Review, 39,* 68–85.

Finkelhor, D. (1983). Common features of family abuse. In D. Finkelhor, R. J. Gelles, G. T. Hotaling & M. A. Straus (Eds.). *The dark side of families: Current family violence research.* (pp. 17–28). Beverly Hills, CA: Sage Publications.

Finkelhor, D. & Pillemer, K. (1988). Elder abuse: Its relationship to other forms of domestic violence. In G. Hotaling, D. Finkelhor, J. Kirkpatrick & M. Straus (Eds.), *Family abuse and its consequences: New directions in research* (pp. 244–254). Beverly Hills, CA: Sage Publications.

Friedrich, W. & Boriskin, J. A. (1976). The role of the child in abuse. A review of the literature. *American Journal of Orthopsychiatry, 46*(4), 580–590.

Friedrich, W. & Einbender, A. J. (1983). The abused child. A psychological review. *Journal of Clinical Child Psychology, 12*(3), 244–256.

Frodi, A. M. (1981). Contributions of infant characteristics to child abuse. *American Journal of Mental Deficiency, 85,* 341–349.

Garbatino, J. (1977). The human ecology of child maltreatment: A conceptual model for research. *Journal of Marriage and the Family, 39,* 721–735.

Garbatino, J. & Sherman, D. (1980). High risk neighborhoods and high risk families: The human ecology of child maltreatment. *Child Development, 51,* 188–198.

Gelles, R. J. (1973). Child abuse as psychopathology: A sociological critique and reformulation. *American Journal of Orthopsychiatry, 43*(4), 611–621.

Gelles, R. J. (1979). *Family violence.* Beverly Hills: Sage Publications.

Gelles, R. J. (1982). Toward better research on child abuse and neglect. A response to Besharov. *Child Abuse and Neglect: The International Journal, 6*(4), 495–496.

Kadushin, A. & Martin, J. (1981). *Child abuse: An international event.* New York: Columbia University Press.

Kaufman, J. & Sigler, E. (1987). Do abused children become abusive parents? *American Journal of Orthopsychiatry, 57*(2), 186–192.

Kempe, C. H., Silver, F., Steele, B. F., Droegmueller, W. & Silver, H. (1962). The battered child syndrome. *Journal of the American Medical Association, 181,* 17–24.

Koopman-Boyden, P. G. & Wells, F. (1979). The problems arising from supporting the elderly at home. *New Zealand Medical Journal, 89,* 265–268.

Korsh, B., Christian, J., Gozzi, E. & Carlson, P. (1965). Infant care and punishment: A pilot study. *American Journal of Public Health, 55*(12), 1880–1888.

Legal Research and Services for the Elderly. (1981). *Elder abuse and neglect: A guide for practitioners and policymakers.* Boston.

Milowe, I. & Lourie, R. (1964). The child's role in the battered child syndrome. *Journal of Pediatrics, 65,* 1079–1081.

Mintern, L. & Lambert, W. *Mothers of six cultures: Antecedents of child rearing.* New York: Wiley and Sons.

Morris, M. & Gould, R. (1963). Role reversal: A necessary concept in dealing with "The Battered Child Syndrome." *American Journal of Orthopsychiatry, 33,* 298–299.

O'Malley, H., Segars, H., Perez, R., Mitchell, V. & Kneupfel, G. *Elder abuse in Massachusetts: A survey of professionals and paraprofessionals.* Boston: Legal Research and Services for the Elderly.

Pedrick-Cornell, C. & Gelles, R. J. (1982). Elder abuse: The status of current knowledge. *Family Relations, 3,* 457–465.

Pelton, L. (1981). *The social context of child abuse and neglect.* New York: Human Sciences Press.

Phillips, L. (1986). Theoretical explanations of elder abuse. In K. A. Pillemer & R. S. Wolf (Eds.) *Elder abuse: Conflict in the Family* (pp. 197–217). Dover, MA: Auburn House.

Pillemer, K. A. (1986). Risk factors in elder abuse: Results from a case-control study. In K. A. Pillemer & R. S. Wolf (Eds.) *Elder abuse: Conflict in the family* (pp. 239–263). Dover, MA: Auburn House.

Pillemer, K. A. & Finkelhor, D. (1988). The prevalence of elder abuse: A random sample survey. *The Gerontologist, 28*(1), 51–57.

Pillemer, K. A. & Suitor, J. (1988). Elder abuse. In V. Van Hasselt, R. Morrison, A. Belack & M. Hensen (Eds.) *Handbook of family violence.* New York: Plenum Press.

Pillemer, K. A. & Wolf, R. S. (Eds.) (1986). *Elder abuse: Conflict in the family.* Dover, MA: Auburn House.

Rizley, R. & Cicchetti, D. (Eds.) (1981). *Developmental perspectives on child maltreatment.* San Francisco: Jossey-Bass.

Salend, E., Kane, R. A., Satz, M., & Pynoos, J. (1984). Elder abuse reporting: Limitations of statutes. *The Gerontologist, 24*(1), 61–69.

Schene, P. & Ward, S. (1988). The relevance of the child protection experience. *Public Welfare, 46*(2), 14–21.

Spinetta, J. & Rigler, D. (1972). The child-abusing parent: A psychological review. *Psychological Bulletin, 77*(4), 296–304.

Stark, R. & McEvoy, J. (1970). Middle class violence. *Psychology Today, 4,* 52–65.

Steele, R. F. (1980). Psychodynamic factors in child abuse. In C. H. Kempe & R. E. Helfer (Eds.) *The battered child. Third edition* (pp. 49–85). Chicago: University of Chicago Press.

Steinmetz, S. (1981). Elder abuse. *Aging,* January-February, 6–10.

Steinmetz, S. (1983). Dependency, stress, and violence between middle-aged caregivers and their elderly parents. In J. Kosberg (Ed.), *Abuse and maltreatment of the elderly: Causes and interventions* (pp. 139–149). Boston: Wright PSG.

Steinmetz, S. (1988). *Duty bound: Elder abuse and family care.* Beverly Hills: Sage Publications.

Steinmetz, S. & Amsden, G. Dependent elders, family stress, and abuse. In T. Brubaker (Ed.), *Family relations in later life.* Beverly Hills: Sage Publications.

Straus, M. A. & Gelles, R. A. (1986). Societal change and change in family violence from 1975 to 1985 as revealed by two national surveys. *Journal of Marriage and the Family, 48,* 465–469.

Straus, M. A., Gelles, R. A. & Steinmetz, S. (1980). *Behind closed doors: Violence in the American family.* Garden City, NY: Anchor Books.

U.S. House Select Committee on Aging. (1981). *Elder abuse: An examination of a hidden problem.* Washington, DC: U.S. Government Printing Office.

U.S. House Select Committee on Aging. (1984). *Elder abuse: A national disgrace.* Washington, DC: U.S. Government Printing Office.

Widom, C. S. (1989). The cycle of violence. *Science, 244,* 160–166.

Wolf, R. S., Godkin, M. A. & Pillemer, K. A. *Elder abuse and neglect: Final report from three model projects.* Worcester, MA: University of Massachusetts Medical Center, University Center on Aging.

Long-Term Care Options
for the Frail Elderly

MURIEL R. GILLICK

Current projections forecast that by 2040, there will be close to five million people over the age of 65 living in nursing homes. The majority of these, nearly three million, will be over 85.[1] As of a recent survey, there were 15,000 Medicare- or Medicaid-certified nursing homes in the United States, with approximately 1.5 million beds.[1] The widening gap between needed and available beds, as well as a society-wide trend to avoid institutionalization for a variety of populations, has led to a renewed interest in home care, even for the very frail elderly. As one geriatrics textbook asserts: "We should begin with the premise that elderly people belong at home and want to be cared for at home. Institutional care should be considered only when all efforts to keep the patient at home have failed."[2]

As geriatricians and policymakers plan for the future needs of an aging society, particularly for the old old—the 13 million people who will be over 85 in 2040—we need to consider the full range of options, from home at one extreme to nursing home at the other, with lifecare communities, congregate living, social health maintenance organizations, and other, still to be designed alternatives in between. In planning and in seeking creative new solutions to the dilemma presented by an increasing number of severely disabled elderly, it is imperative that we ascertain in what ways we have failed and in what ways we have succeeded in caring for the elderly. By placing current options in a historical perspective, we may be able to escape from the tendency to regard the structure of existing institutions as inviolate, and leap imaginatively into the future.

WHAT IS BEST FOR THE PATIENT?

What to do with old, debilitated individuals who cannot survive without substantial care from others has been a perennial problem. The solutions to the problem have addressed, in various ways, the fundamental issues of the autonomy and privacy of the individual, the need for community, and the need for physical care. In an attempt to understand what is best for different older people, it is helpful to contrast contemporary home care, contemporary nursing-home care, and care in nineteenth-century old-age homes. Each of these settings has attributes that are worthy of incorporation into future models.

Source: Journal of the American Geriatrics Society 37(12), pp. 1198–1203. Reprinted with permission of the American Geriatrics Society and the author.

THE NINETEENTH-CENTURY OLD-AGE HOME

The nineteenth-century old-age home was typically a small, culturally homogeneous institution that catered to the "worthy poor," housewives married to working-class men or those women who had worked for years but who lacked the support necessary to enjoy a comfortable old age. The Winchester Home for Aged Women in Charlestown, Massachusetts, for instance, admitted 31 women between 1911 and 1914. Of these, occupational data is available for 26: seven were housewives, 11 were or had been housekeepers for others, and the remaining eight had worked at a variety of occupations, including dressmaking and nursing. All had been residents of Charlestown for a number of years, as stipulated by the admissions committee.[3]

The Winchester Home for Aged Women was by no means unique at the turn of the century. In another part of Boston, the Roxbury home for Aged Women served as a home for a similar clientele.[4] It was one of the largest old-age homes in existence—the largest in Boston, with 199 residents in the year 1900. Only its counterpart, the Home for Aged Men, also housed over 100 residents; the remaining seven homes in Boston and five homes in contiguous communities that were devoted exclusively to care of the elderly each had under 60 occupants, with a median population of 29.[5] The women in the Roxbury Home for Aged Women, like those in the Winchester Home, were respectable women, with limited means of support in their old age. The women were not entirely destitute: as of 1904, new residents were charged $500, a considerable sum, although the fee covered room, board, and medical care for life. In 1905 the home began to require that anyone entering the home should sign over all property or money they had at the time of admission, as well as any subsequent inheritance.[4] Though less exclusive than today's life-care communities, the old-age homes of the turn of the century were clearly desirable institutions for many elderly people of modest income. Such private institutions for the elderly underwent explosive growth after the Civil War. Of the 1,200 such facilities in existence in the United States in 1939, nearly two-thirds were founded between 1875 and 1919.[6]

WEAKNESS OF TODAY'S NURSING HOMES

Contemporary nursing homes bear little resemblance to their nineteenth-century predecessors. They tend to be large; 58% house 50 or more patients. They are mandated by law to have a sizable nursing staff; an intermediate care facility boasts an average of 2.4 registered nurses and 6.3 licensed practical nurses per 100 beds.[7] They are structured like hospitals, with corridors of two-, three-, and four-bed rooms, and a central nursing station. Each patient has a medical record, medications are dispensed by nurses, and doctors' orders govern the residents' activities, much as in an acute-care general hospital. The rooms are sparsely furnished in standard institutional fashion, leaving minimal space for personal possessions. Communal activities are few and interaction with the world outside the nursing home minimal.

The lack of autonomy characteristic of nursing-home life has been demonstrated to have adverse effects on psychological and physiological well-being.[8] For the 45% of today's nursing-home residents whose cognitive function is unimpaired,[7] the lack of personal property leads to a loss of individuality and the loss of control leads to debilitating dependence and to "learned helplessness."[9] It is to avoid this sense of being superannuated that home care rather than nursing care is frequently advocated.

HAZARDS OF HOME CARE FOR THE FRAIL ELDERLY

Remaining at home in old age, even if it requires outside support, is deeply gratifying to many older individuals. However, living at home dependent on community agencies to provide assistance with eating, dressing, and bathing, can be lonely, stressful, and hazardous. One representative elderly woman living in New York, whose story has been related by a perceptive reporter, lived in fear that her homemaker would fail to show up or would not speak English or that her home health aide would treat her roughly.[10] Over a five-month period, she had 15 different home attendants assigned to her case. Many of the home-care providers were irresponsible or incapable; the best often left for other jobs with better pay. The instability of the arrangements on which the homebound frail elderly depend creates a profound sense of anxiety, an anxiety that sometimes reaches a level of fear or desperation if they are left alone and unable to obtain food, get to the bathroom, or change their clothes. The elderly individual alone at home who relies on assistance for basic functioning is at the mercy of others for survival. In an institutional setting, though there may be staffing shortages, there are many employees, so that if one worker fails to show up, each resident suffers only a slight diminution in the care he or she needs. In the home situation, if the sole caretaker does not appear, the individual receives none of his or her needed care. In addition, attendants in the home setting work without supervision so that neglect or abuse may go unnoticed; in a nursing home there is the possibility of overseeing the work of all employees and the potential for peer-group pressure to promote adherence to at least minimal standards.

Staying home does not always mean residing in the family home, a home filled with fond memories. Remaining at home often means living in a cramped studio or perhaps a one-bedroom apartment in a housing project for the elderly. Some such buildings are well-maintained with active social programs; many are run-down, with little sense of community. Created to foster a sense of esprit de corps, they perpetuate the social isolation they were designed to help prevent.

It is, of course, not just physicians who seek to keep the elderly at home: it is the elderly themselves, who fear nursing homes. They fear nursing homes because of the scandals that have been associated with them and, more fundamentally, because of the loss of privacy and autonomy they face if they become institutionalized. They fear that in the nursing home they will "live out the last of their days in an enclosed society without privacy, dignity, or pleasure, subsisting on minimally palatable diets, multiple sedatives, and large doses of television."[11] But surely it should be possible to enjoy both privacy and community in an institution, to benefit from the security of guaranteed assistance without forfeiting one's individuality.

THE SUCCESSES OF THE NINETEENTH-CENTURY OLD-AGE HOME

Nineteenth-century old-age homes were successful in domains where today's nursing homes fail. They were successful because of the homogeneity of their population and because they were custodial, not medical facilities. Many institutions were established by religious denominations or ethnic groups to provide for their less fortunate aging members. In the Boston area, the Burnap Free Home for Aged Women was established in 1901 for elderly Protestant women, and initially accommodated 11; the German Ladies Aid Society of Boston was founded in 1893 for "indigent Germans," and the Baptist Home in Cambridge, Massachusetts was established in 1892 to support aged members.[5] These homes were founded on the belief that familiar food, a common language, and shared customs were essential to the older person's comfort.[12] The nonsectarian homes maintained homogeneity by selecting their members from the surrounding community: many residents of the Cambridge Home for Aged People or the Old Ladies Home Association of Chelsea or the Mount Pleasant Home in Dorchester very likely knew each other. If they had not formerly been acquainted, they nonetheless had much in common by virtue of similar backgrounds. The Roxbury Home for Aged Women admitted 58 women between 1881 and 1910.[13] The employment of these women's husbands, a good indicator of socioeconomic class, reveals an assortment of working-class occupations. They were masons, painters, builders, machinists, and mechanics. A prototypical applicant to the Winchester Home for Aged Women was a 74-year-old widow whose husband had been a watchman in the Charlestown navy yard. She had lived in Charlestown for 40 years as a housewife and seamstress. She was a Baptist and had no relatives able to contribute to her support, although she received "widow's coal." Another applicant, also a widow, had lived in Charlestown for 50 years. Her husband had been a salesman in a provisions store, and she had worked as a housekeeper.[3]

Records detailing life in nineteenth-century old-age homes are scanty, but it is clear that the homes were not primarily medical institutions. Most of the residents were fairly healthy—they had to be able to take care of their rooms themselves as a criterion for admission. Their good health at the time of admission is attested to by their durability. The average age at the time of entry to the Roxbury Home for Aged Women was 67.5 years, with an average length of stay of 13.3 years. Most lived in the home until their death, although occasionally a resident became too ill to be cared for in the old-age home. One lady "met with a serious accident" and returned to the Home after some time at Massachusetts General Hospital but, found to be "hopelessly impaired physically and men-

tally," she went to reside with her sister (with board paid by the home).[13] The ladies of the Home for Aged Women were attended by one or two regular home physicians, as well as by a nurse. Medical care was provided intermittently, as needed by the residents, just as it would have been had they lived at home. The residents were supervised by a matron, who set the tone for the institution. Matrons were expected to be solicitous of the needs of the residents. As the supervisory board of the Roxbury Home for Aged Women made clear, "our dear old ladies must receive every attention necessary to their comfort," and if the matron did not adequately minister to their needs, she would be replaced.[4]

Unlike old-age homes of the nineteenth century, only a minority of contemporary nursing homes (more commonly, the 20% of nursing homes that are voluntary, or nonprofit) make any attempt to develop a culturally homogeneous community. Unlike their predecessors in the nineteenth century, they are principally medical facilities. The reason that nursing homes have become low-technology, chronic-disease hospitals is related to the historical development of the modern nursing home.

THE EVOLUTION OF NURSING HOMES

American society has been struggling for a long time with the question of how to care for the frail elderly. The solutions to the problem in the past have had far more to do with the funding sources for care and with institutions' self-image than with the needs of the elderly.

The primary locus of care for the impoverished elderly in America until the first half of the nineteenth century was the almshouse, a government-run institution for the destitute poor.[11] As nonprofit, general hospitals sprang up in the nineteenth century, they often found themselves saddled with "old chronics," patients who developed an acute illness and then could not be discharged to their homes.[14] Many of these lingered on in the hospital, accounting for the average length of stay of 81 days at the Massachusetts General Hospital in 1855.[15] The hospital increasingly defined itself as an acute-care, teaching institution: hence it selected patients with diseases amenable to the "brave new weapons of medical science" such as x-rays, antiseptic surgery, and laboratory tests[12] and aimed for a high turnover of patients in order to provide teaching material. As these changes occurred, length of stay fell, declining to less than four weeks in 1886, and falling down to 17 to 20 days by the turn of the century.[15] At the same time, the prevalent distinction between the worthy and unworthy poor (those who were poor out of misfortune versus those who were poor out of sloth), produced a consensus that the respectable poor older people ought to have a place to go besides the almshouse. Some private hospitals, primarily those serving a defined ethnic group, resolved the dilemma by creating a special chronic ward. The Roman Catholic Carney Hospital, for instance, which opened in 1869 in Boston, established one of its floors for "old people who may not be sick but come here for a home."[16] Other hospitals, such as the Hartford Hospital in Connecticut, sought to build their own old-age homes to provide for their chronic patients.[16] Private ethnic and religious organizations picked up the slack by establishing old-age homes. Before 1860, private old-age homes were virtually unheard of. By the turn of the century, Massachusetts still had 3,480 persons over the age of 65 in state almshouses, but it also had 2,589 older people in old-age homes.[16] Interestingly, the total Massachusetts population over 65 was 143,000,[17] yielding a 4.2% rate of institutionalization among the elderly, not very different from contemporary norms. The move of the elderly from the hospital to the old-age home occurred because of hospitals' new self-definition, not because it was calculated to be in the best interest of the elderly.

After World War I, the locus of care for dependent elderly shifted again, this time to the mental hospital.[18] In 1920 roughly half of the institutionalized elderly lived in almshouses and half in charitable, private old-age homes. By 1930, there were more elderly people in mental hospitals than in private old-age homes and almshouses combined.[11] This shift did not occur out of a belief that mental hospitals were better for the elderly than other institutions, and it surely did not arise from a sudden increase in the incidence of mental illness among the old. The shift from almshouses to mental hospitals arose because of new state legislation mandating state responsibility for all mentally ill persons—laws passed in New York (in 1890), in Massachusetts (in 1900), and elsewhere. These laws encouraged the reclassification of demented elderly as "psychotic due to arteriosclerosis and senility" and gave an incentive to fiscally straitened local communities to transfer their older mental patients from rural and town almshouses to state mental institutions.[18] As a result, the Chicago State Hospital, for example, found 70% of its patients to be "aged or infirm" in the 1930s, "suffering from no psychoses which would be beyond the capacity of the old-fashioned detached city cottage or rural home or of a well-managed county home."[18]

The Old Age Assistance program established under the Social Security Act of 1935 continued the trend away from poorhouses as means of caring for the elderly by prohibiting old-age assistance funds to residents of public institutions. The intent was to abolish poorhouses, which was undoubtedly beneficial to the elderly. The more general goal was to discourage institutional care for the elderly. The bill's effect, however, was to stimulate the growth of proprietary and voluntary nursing homes as it made federal assistance available to individuals residing in such facilities.

In the 1950s, for the first time, government policy evolved to cater to the needs of the elderly themselves. Regulations were drawn up to end the abuses that had been uncovered in old-age homes: fire hazards, safety risks, and inadequate diets. State licensing regulations mandated changes in sanitation, ventilation, and management. They drove out "mom and pop" operations because the means found to correct the problems involved restructuring the facilities and staffing them with nurses, changes that only large institutions could afford.

The passage of the Hill–Burton amendments in 1954, which granted public money for building nursing homes, exacerbated the trend to build nursing homes modeled on hospitals. With public money came federal regulations: the Public Health Service became the agency responsible for formulating staffing and design requirements. Decisions about what constituted good care for the debilitated elderly were not based on an analysis of their actual needs. Instead, Public Health Service officials recreated the only environment with which they were familiar, the general hospital, scaling it down in size and intensity of technology.[11]

The passage of Medicaid legislation in 1965—and to a lesser extent Medicare —has permitted the proprietary nursing home industry to take off. In recent years, the kind of nursing-home care offered to the elderly has been influenced by the conflict between the state and federal governments over who should foot the bill. The federal Medicare program only covers sophisticated "skilled nursing care," whereas the joint state/federal Medicaid program pays for "intermediate care facilities." Patients have been incorrectly classified as needing more intensive medical care in part so that they will qualify for a skilled nursing facility, for which Medicare will pay: a government study reported 40% of skilled nursing facility patients did not require skilled nursing

care.[19] Such decisions, like many that shaped policy before, have more to do with the politics and economics of funding long-term care and little to do with what would be best for the patient.

MODELS FOR THE FUTURE

It would be sheer romanticism to claim that today's nursing home clients could thrive in nineteenth-century style old-age homes. Old people today live longer than their counterparts in the nineteenth century, long enough to develop Alzheimer's disease and other degenerative illnesses. Not only do individuals survive long enough to be afflicted by diseases that were relatively rare in earlier eras, but modern technology has made it possible to keep people alive who previously would have succumbed to complications of their underlying condition. The elderly of today for whom nursing homes are considered often have multiple medical and nursing needs—they are not the relatively robust elderly with mild cognitive impairment who populated the turn of the century old-age home. Only a minority can live in contemporary "rest homes," which are the true descendants of the nineteenth-century homes.

It is equally foolish to expect that home care will be the answer to the long-term needs for the growing numbers of elderly surviving into their 80s and 90s. The "compression of morbidity" that was prophesied[20] has not come to pass: on the contrary, the last years of life are increasingly marred by disability and dependence.[21] Not only is home care often inadequate for the severely incapacitated, but it is also expensive and inefficient. (Only when cost is defined as the cost to third-party payers rather than as the total cost does home care appear to be economical.) Thus, it appears inescapable that more and more institutional care will be necessary for the foreseeable future— where institutional care encompasses all but care at the individual's longstanding residence.

In planning for institutional long-term care, it is important to recall that the needs of the frail elderly, even the sickest nursing home residents, are chiefly related to activities of daily living: they need help with dressing (69%), bathing (80%), and toileting (53%).[7] The majority do not require the knowledge and skills of a registered nurse on a daily basis. Families can administer medications to their older relatives at home without special certification, and surely aides can dispense medicines to institutionalized elderly. Other jobs such as turning patients or putting them on bedpans or even changing dressings, which are now commonly regarded as skilled, do not inherently require extensive training to perform. Such tasks were expected of every housewife in the nineteenth century. A manual of home economics, intended as a primer for the newly married, included sections on prevention and cure of bed sores, bathing the sick patient, giving medications (including suppositories and injections), and use of enemas and bedpans.[22] These skills could be taught to aides and do not necessitate skilled nursing care.

Institutional care could be made homier by demedicalizing nursing homes. Of greater benefit than daily nursing surveillance or physician visits at preprogrammed intervals (as currently mandated by many Medicaid programs) would be the availability of a group of physicians or geriatric nurse practitioners to evaluate individuals who developed acute problems.[23] Of greater benefit than a hospital-style environment would be an atmosphere in which residents were allowed to have their own furniture and other belongings,[24] and were encouraged to remain as independent as possible.

Long-term care outside the home setting would probably be more attractive if it occurred within culturally homogeneous environments. Congregate living arrangements and lifecare communities are of necessity evolving some degree of homogeneity. For people with intact cognition to live together voluntarily and harmoniously, they must form compatible groupings. If religious and ethnic groups made long-term care a priority, devoting significant resources to the development of institutions catering to their members, increased numbers of facilities would feature the special food and holiday observances that are the hallmarks of ethnicity.

Financing appears to be a major obstacle to the development of a new model of nursing home.[25] If Medicare and Medicaid unbundle nursing home payments by paying for the medical component and letting individuals select homes based on their preferences for type of facility and on their ability to pay for room and board, the financial burden of long-term care will not rest exclusively on the medical sector. If religious and ethnic groups take long-term care as a special mission, as suggested above, part of the start-up capital costs of new facilities can be defrayed.

Home care is a marvelous option for the majority of elderly Americans. For others, it is desirable only because of the lack of acceptable alternatives. As we design new long-term care institutions that are in-between nursing homes and home care, we should seek to incorporate the better features of each, keeping the model of the nineteenth-century old-age home firmly in mind.

REFERENCES

1. Institute of Medicine: Improving the Quality of Care in Nursing Homes. Washington, D.C., National Academy Press, 1986

2. Kane R, Ouslander J, Abrass I: Essentials of Clinical Geriatrics. New York, McGraw Hill, 1984

3. Admission applications, Winchester Homes for Aged Women. Archives, Schlesinger Library of Radcliffe College, Cambridge, Mass

4. Minutes of the Executive Board Meetings of the Ladies Unity Club, Inc., 1904–1923. Archives, Schlesinger Library of Radcliffe College, Cambridge, Mass

5. 23rd Annual Report of Charity of Massachusetts. Boston, Wright and Potter Printing Co., 1900

6. Achenbaum WA: Old age in the New Land. Baltimore, Johns Hopkins University Press, 1978

7. United States Department of Health and Human Services: Characteristics of Nursing Home Residents, Health Status and Care Received. National Nursing Home survey. PHS 81-1712. Vital and Health Statistics, Series 13, #51

8. Rowe J, Kahn R: Human aging: usual and successful. Science 237:143–149, 1987

9. Avorn J, Langer E: Induced disability in nursing home patients: a controlled trial. J Am Geriatr Soc 30:397–400, 1982

10. Sheehan S: Kate Quinton's Days. Boston, Houghton Mifflin Co, 1984

11. Vladeck B: Unloving Care: The Nursing Home Tragedy. New York, Basic Books, 1980

12. Rosenberg C: The Care of Strangers. New York, Basic Books, 1987

13. Admission Records, Home for Aged Women. Archives, Schlesinger Library of Radcliffe College, Cambridge, Mass

14. Rosenberg C: And heal the sick: hospital and patients in 19th Century America, in Branca P (ed): The Medicine Show. New York, Science History Publications, pp 121–140, 1977

15. Vogel D: The Invention of the Modern Hospital: Boston, 1870–1930. Chicago, University of Chicago Press, 1980

16. Haber C: Beyond Sixty-Five: The Dilemma of Old Age in America's Past. Cambridge, Cambridge University Press, 1983

17. Commonwealth of Massachusetts: Annual Report on the Vital Statistics of Massachusetts. Boston, Wright and Potter Printing Co., 1919

18. Grob G: Explaining old age history: the need for empiricism, in Van Tassel D, Stearns P (eds): Old Age in a Bureaucratic Society. New York, Greenwood Press, pp 30–45, 1986

19. General Accounting Office, US Comptroller General: Problems in providing guidance to states in establishing rates of payments for nursing home care under Medicaid programs. Report to Congress B-164031 (3). Washington, DC, 1972

20. Fries J: Aging, natural death, and the compression of morbidity. N Engl J Med 313:130–135, 1980

21. Verbrugge L: Longer life but worsening health: trends in health and mortality of middle-aged and older persons. Milbank Mem Fund Q 62:475–519,1984

22. Pope AE: Home Care of the Sick. Chicago, American School of Home Economics, 1907

23. Master R, Feltin M, Jainchill J, et al: A continuum of care for the inner city: assessment of its benefits for Boston's elderly and high-risk population. N Engl J Med 302:1434–1440, 1980

24. Brody E: A million procrustean beds. Gerontologist 13:430–435, 1973

25. Somers A: Insurance for long-term care: some definitions, problems, and guidelines for action. N Engl J Med 317:23–29, 1987

Discussion Questions for Chapter Seven

1. Korbin and her colleagues restrict their investigation to intergenerational, physical abuse. Do any of their findings apply to other types of elderly abuse such as spousal abuse or nonphysical abuse?

2. Gillick suggests that culturally homogeneous environments would probably be more attractive settings for long-term care. Is this idea viable in a culturally diverse society such as the United States? Would members of all cultural and social groups obtain the same quality of care if they were in culturally homogeneous settings?

CHAPTER EIGHT

Work and Retirement

Most of us are aware that women's participation in the labor force has increased dramatically in the last several decades. Less well recognized is that men's involvement in the work force has declined. One reason for men's labor force withdrawal is early retirement. In 1950, 90% of American men aged 55 to 64 were in the labor force (i.e., they were either employed or looking for work). By 1991, the proportion had declined to about two-thirds of this population. In the last twenty years, labor force participation rates among women up to age 59 have increased, but among women aged 60 and over, they have declined (Clark, 1988).

What accounts for early withdrawal from the labor force? Reasons for early retirement can be divided into pull and push factors. Pull factors are the attractive features about retirement that serve as incentives to retire early, such as the desire for more leisure. Push factors include age discrimination, work force reduction programs, physical disability, and poor health. Another push factor is the widespread but mistaken belief that older workers do not perform as well as younger ones. In "Job Performance Among Older Workers," Paul R. Sparrow examines the link between age and job performance and concludes that the evidence does not support the belief that age influences performance.

Is early retirement good or bad for society and the individual? Given the declining ratio of workers to retirees, our nation could benefit from workers remaining in the labor force longer, yet individuals who desire leisure and employers who wish to cut labor costs or to thin their ranks to make room for younger employees may prefer retirement at early ages. In fact, public and private policy with respect to early labor force withdrawal seems to be aimed in opposite directions. Public policy seems headed toward keeping older people in the labor force, while private policy tends to encourage them to leave. Congress has outlawed mandatory retirement for most occupations, and starting in the year 2000, the age for eligibility for full Social Security retirement benefits will gradually rise from 65 to 67. On the other hand, employers are making greater use of early retirement incentive programs which have exactly the opposite effect. In "Employment Policy and Public Policy: Options for Extending Work Life," Marilyn Moon and Judith Hushbeck discuss possible policy changes with respect to retirement and their effect on the economy and individuals.

Significant differences still remain between men's and women's patterns of labor force participation. Moreover, the work histories of today's older people reflect gender differences of earlier times when women's job participation was much more limited and occupations were even more sex-segregated than they are today. The impact of work experience does not end when people leave their jobs. In "Gender & Work at Midlife & Beyond" Laurie Russell Hatch describes how differences in men's and women's work histories affect their economic status in later life.

REFERENCE

Clark, Robert L. (1988). The future of work and retirement. *Research on Aging 10*, 169–193.

Job Performance Among Older Workers

PAUL R. SPARROW

It is clear that to make sense of the many and varied findings about age and work performance we need to do two things. First, be aware of the methodological problems which can render the findings from a study useless (more on that below), and second, think of changes in work performance related to age in two ways. Changes may be due to "biological aging" (changes in sensorimotor performance, muscle strength, brittleness of skeletal structure, vision and reaction time). Changes can also be due to "psychological aging" in which personality, needs, expectations and performance may systematically change with age because of the experience and social roles of older people. For personnel directors of organizations confronted with an aging workforce in which age appears to be linked to performance, it is of fundamental importance whether they can break that link by overcoming physical changes in people, or by more easily changing some of the psychosocial aspects of the job.

More fundamentally, though, do personnel directors even have a problem to worry about? Is age linked to job performance? The answer to those questions, and the solution, appears to depend very much on the type of work.

THE EVIDENCE

Clerical and Sales Work

Most studies of clerical and sales work have shown that age has nothing whatsoever to do with work performance. For example, a study by the U.S. Department of Labor in 1957 found no changes in output per man hour with age for office workers. Performance of federal mail sorters aged over 65 had declined by 8%, but the decline started after age 25, rather young to be considered as biological aging. Nor was any relationship found in a sample of 1,525 insurance salesmen, or in a sample of 6,000 office workers, once service was controlled for. Indeed, job performance in two large department stores was found to improve with age and experience.

Semi-skilled and Skilled Manual Labor

Most studies of age and productivity in semi-skilled and skilled manual work have shown an "inverted-U" relationship—*i.e.*, performance of younger workers starts low, then rises, peaking somewhere between the ages of 30 to 40, and then drops (*Clay*, 1956; *King*, 1956). The decline in performance was attributed to changes in sensorimotor capacity with age, which affect the ability to deal

Source: Ageing International, Autumn/Winter 13: 5–6, 22. Reprinted with permission from International Federation on Ageing, Washington, DC 20049. Copyright 1986.

with new tasks more than the ability to maintain an already established skill. However, it should be noted that the performance of the oldest workers was still far better than that of the youngest. Also, these studies only looked at the effect of age. Other variables, such as experience, are often assumed to counteract the effects of age on performance. A study by Schwab and Heneman (1977) clearly showed this. Positive correlations were initially found between both age and length of service with job performance. However, when both variables were separately considered, the relationship between age and performance fell to almost zero, while that between length of service and performance remained significantly positive. It seems that many relationships between age and work performance may, in fact, be due to the greater experience resulting from increases in the length of time spent at the job.

Managerial Work

There have been few studies on the relationship of age and managerial work, because of the difficulty in measuring performance. Most studies have looked at performance in simulation exercises. For example, a study by *Taylor* (1975) systematically described how age and experience related to the use of different decision strategies in managerial work. The results showed that when it came to arriving at the right answer, no difference in accuracy was found. However, older managers took a longer time to reach a decision. This was not due to the fact that they took longer to process information but because they sought more information before making a decision. They were less confident about their decisions and so more flexible about changing it. Taylor concluded that age does not affect the efficiency of managerial performance in decision-making situations. Rather, older and younger managers just tend to perform differently, rather than better or worse.

Technical and Professional Work

This issue of a link between age and technical or professional performance is very relevant to today's society because the number of "knowledge workers" who apply ideas, concepts and information, rather than manual skill or brawn, will increase. Obsolescence in these jobs is less likely to be caused by a loss in physical or mental skills, but rather by a deterioration in the quality of information used to form a knowledge base. Studies of practitioners in the sciences, medicine, surgery, philosophy, music, art and literature have found that the rate of publications or occurrence of important discoveries tended to peak in the thirties. However, it has also been noted that initially strong publishers remained strong throughout their lifetimes, and only initially poor performers showed a drop in publications. If you are good, you can stay good.

In some jobs, especially technical ones such as air traffic control, the job controls the pace of work rather than the individual, and age here does become a problem. Numerous studies conducted by the *U.S. Civil Aeromedical Institute* have consistently shown that age at time of entry into air traffic control specialist training was negatively related to ranked performance and aptitude test scores, with the chance of being successful dropping from one in two if aged under 33, to one in five when older, because of the increased stress with age.

MAINTAINING JOB PERFORMANCE

How can organizations maintain productivity among older workers? One way as we have seen in management work, is to allow people to perform differently, and not to force the pace. Another way is to design careers so that older workers can remain motivated. Studies of age and technological obsolescence in engineers (*Dalton* and *Price*, 1977) found that performance rose until the mid-thirties, thereafter showing a consistent decline to only 57% of peak performance by the age of 55 to 65. However, career stage accounted for many such differences. All professionals aged over 40 and still in the lowest career stage were poor performers, whilst all engineers aged 40 and over and in the top career level were above average performers. They concluded that a successful transition through career stages reversed the age decline in performance in knowledge occupations.

The extent to which age may be kinder to the initially more able, who are presumably more likely to advance to the higher career stages, perhaps poses some problems of interpretation for this study, but it seems possible, nonetheless, that the challenge, stimulation, and sense of accomplishment through the various career stages may prevent the occurrence of any age-related decline in job performance among professional workers.

Another often neglected aspect of age and work performance is training. *Sparrow* and *Davies* (1985) conducted a multivariate study of speed and quality performance in a sample of 1,308 service engineers, in which the effects of age, length of service, recency of training and task complexity were all controlled. Speed performance was shown to significantly drop with age, but the deterioration was only very slight and the least important amongst the variables. The quality of performance showed an inverted-U relation to age. However, age and training significantly interacted. Training was shown to clearly mediate the effects of age on technical performance, particularly on complex tasks. Training delayed the onset of age declines in performance, and made subsequent drops in performance insignificant.

METHODOLOGICAL ISSUES

Some words about the methodological difficulties associated with studies of job performance among older workers. While there are a number of studies that purport to study this subject, their conclusions are often unreliable. It is difficult to establish if any observed differences are due to the process of aging, or rather to an age-related change. Most studies of performance take a cross-section of the workforce. Older or younger people represent a "cohort", each with their own set of life experiences. Differences in their performance may be due to the attitudes and behaviors arising out of these experiences, and not to age.

Conducting longitudinal studies, following an individual's performance over a long period of time, however, also has its problems. Selective sampling may occur because repeated and prolonged participation in studies can bias participants. Such "volunteers" normally have higher intelligence and a higher socio-economic background. Similarly, "selective survival" can bias results of studies of production records. It is unlikely that a marked drop in productivity goes unnoticed. Poor performers are likely to have left the sample, and if such behavior is linked to age, then those left no longer truly represent their cohort. Studies of jobs with high levels of turnover are subject to this error.

A number of other problems make interpretation of results difficult. Many studies do not fully report on the age characteristics of their sample, or have only a few people in older age bands. Others use a bad measure of performance, such as salaries or ratings, which may not reflect true performance. Most studies only consider the one variable of age, and are based on only a small number of people. Finally, as age increases, so do individual differences. Performance varies far more around the average in older samples than in younger ones. Many older employees show superb performance even if the average for their age group shows a decline.

CONCLUSION

While methodological difficulties associated with the study of age and work performance make firm conclusions difficult to draw, it is apparent from a number of well-designed studies that age often has no real influence on performance. Wide individual differences exist and experience often counteracts any age effects.

Where age differences are found, it appears they may be caused often by psychosocial factors, such as a reduced work commitment because of limited career advancement opportunities. The use of training is also an important factor in ensuring that age differences in technical jobs which require a continually updated knowledge base or set of sensorimotor skills are kept at a minimum. By minimizing such productivity differences, the real benefits of older workers such as lower turnover, increased loyalty and job satisfaction, less frequent (if longer) absenteeism, and greater experience will be given a chance to show their importance.

(For a fuller discussion of this subject, please see Davies, D. R. & Sparrow, P. R., "Age and Work Behaviour," in Charness, N. (Ed.) *Aging and Human Performance,* Chichester: Wiley, 1985.)

BIBLIOGRAPHY

Clay, H. M., "Study of Performance in Relation to Age at Two Printing Works," *Journal of Gerontology, 11* (October, 1956), 417, 424.

Dalton, G. W. & Thompson, P. H., "Accelerating Obsolescence of Older Engineers," *Harvard Business Review, 49* (September/October, 1971), 57–68.

Dalton, G. W., Thompson, P. H. & Price, R. L., "The Four Stages of Professional Careers—A New Look at Performance by Professionals," *Organizational Dynamics, 6* (Summer, 1977), 19–42.

Davies, D. R. & Sparrow, P. R., "Age and Work Behaviour," in Charness, N. (Ed.) *Aging and Human Performance* (Chichester: Wiley, 1985).

King, H. F., "An Attempt to Use Production Data in the Study of Age and Performance," *Journal of Gerontology, 11* (October, 1956), 410–416.

Schwab, D. P. & Heneman, H. G., "Effects of Age and Experience on Productivity," *Industrial Gerontology, 4* (Spring, 1977), 113–117.

Sparrow, P. R. & Davies, D. R., "Age and Performance of Skilled Workers," paper presented at the *13th International Congress of Gerontology,* New York, July, 1985.

Taylor, R. N., "Age and Experience as Determinants of Managerial Information Processing and Decision-Making Performance," *Academy of Management Journal, 18* (March, 1975), 74–81.

Employment Policy & Public Policy: Options for Extending Work Life

MARILYN MOON
JUDITH HUSHBECK

The 1980s [were] characterized by confusing and somewhat inconsistent policies and attitudes toward older workers in the United States. The 1983 Social Security Amendments mandated that the age for full retirement-benefit eligibility be gradually raised from 65 to 67 beginning in the year 2000. Concerns about the federal deficit have led some to argue for reducing Social Security benefits and for accelerating the pace of retirement age increases.

At the same time, private employers have been intensifying their efforts to encourage employees' early retirement by offering enhancements to benefits packages. At least in part in response to such inducements, the average age of retirement has continued its long-run downward trend.

What explains this paradox? More than anything else, perhaps, the answer lies in recognizing that we are in a period of transition, affecting both our attitudes about older workers and their actual importance to society. It is too soon to know how or when policies and attitudes toward older workers will change, but some departures from past practice are probably inevitable, largely because of the demographic shifts in the age structure of the population.

This article explores some potential policy changes for meeting the needs of the economy and of older individuals themselves.

THE BIG PICTURE

Demographic data suggest that society will be better off if workers remain in the labor force later in life, contributing to the nation's production of goods and services and demanding less from retirement programs. But employers and workers may be reluctant partners in attaining such a goal.

The continued lowering of the retirement age no doubt reflects individuals' preferences for more leisure time and their increased affluence. Income from Social Security, private or other public pensions, and savings have largely replaced earnings for millions of older Americans. Many retire with incomes sufficient to maintain their pre-retirement standard of living.

In addition, special early retirement programs can induce people to retire earlier than they had planned. Employers use such

Source: Generations, 13(3), 27–30. Reprinted with permission from *Generations,* 833 Market St., Suite 512, San Francisco, CA 94103 and the authors. Copyright 1989 by the American Society on Aging.

incentives to reduce both payroll size and the average employee age, thus lowering employment costs. A recent survey conducted in Rochester, New York, found that the average age of those who took an early retirement option was 58.7 years, yet only 8 percent of the early retirees indicated that they had planned to retire before the age of 59 (Meier, 1988). Indeed, only 26 percent said they had hoped to retire before age 62. Some older workers feel pressured to leave work when offered the early retirement option, but many view these incentive programs as desirable opportunities. The Rochester survey found that about equal proportions indicated negative and positive reasons for retiring. Thirty-eight percent felt some pressure, while 39 percent welcomed the opportunity.

Another factor that causes the picture to be murky is the diversity of the category we call "older workers." This population includes individuals making midlife career changes, retirees returning to the labor force full- or part-time, so-called "displaced workers" who have been wrenched from their accustomed employment, and those who have had little or no work experience outside the home. Probably no single population category exhibits the heterogeneity of older Americans, and no labor-force category is more complex than that of the older worker.

THE EMPLOYMENT OUTLOOK

The aging of the American population is already beginning to have an impact on the shape of the labor force. The last of the baby boomers are turning 25 years old in 1989, and these young adults have now largely been absorbed into the labor force. The subsequent "baby bust" has resulted in a decline in youthful job-seekers and a growing frequency of help-wanted signs across the country for part-time, low-skilled workers. Shortages of workers in the more skilled professions and trades will probably follow in a

few years. Workers of all ages may find themselves wooed in ways that encourage more years in the labor force and more hours of work per year.

In the meantime, however, shifts in the economy's employment patterns have created a potential problem for older workers. When some industries are contracting significantly while others are growing, job turnover can be expected to be quite high. Employers often view older workers as relatively expensive, less productive, and less flexible. According to Paul Gibson, executive editor of the *Commerce Clearing House*, a national business publication, a recent survey of 600 human-resource managers found two-thirds reporting their older workers as "complacent and lacking in motivation," and 65 percent said their older workers were clogging the promotion pipeline (Kleiman, 1988). Thus, when employers decide they must reduce their staffs, they often turn to early retirement incentives for older workers as the most painless way of cutting back.

Older workers seeking new employment are not as well protected by age discrimination legislation. Data on duration of unemployment indicate that older workers remain out of work longer than younger workers. Furthermore, it is often estimated that older workers make up the great proportion of "discouraged workers," those who have given up the job search and hence are not reported as being available for work. A period characterized by rapid change in the economy's industrial structure may thus create greater barriers for older workers who seek to find work.

In addition, the much publicized shift toward service sector jobs that pay lower wages may make remaining in the labor force an unattractive option. A recently published study for the Joint Economic Committee of the Congress found that in the 1980s, industries with expanding shares of employment paid an average of $10,404 less per year than declining industries (Costrell, 1988). As the economy substitutes lower-paying jobs for higher-paying jobs, workers who are sufficiently well off to be able to choose retirement will be more inclined to do so. Given a choice between employment at McDonald's or receiving Social Security (even at relatively low benefit levels), they may find the retirement option the more attractive.

Yet, some aspects of service jobs might appeal to older workers. In particular, service jobs are more likely to be divisible, making part-time employment easier to find. Similarly, relatively easier requirements for job entry can make it easier for workers to make the transition to new employment.

PUBLIC POLICY OPTIONS

Several goals should be considered in assessing public policy choices for encouraging older workers' employment. First, what makes good public sense must be considered in a broader context, taking into account more than just the impact on the federal budget; what's good for society as a whole is the relevant criterion. Some policies that would be desirable for the overall society may have adverse consequences for the federal budget, at least in the near term. Some policies might impose costs on the Social Security system, but could result in a net gain from society's perspective. For example, raising the Social Security earnings limit might stimulate greater economic activity by older Americans, yielding payroll taxes that could more than offset increased costs. Ultimately, benefits to society, not the more narrow issue of government costs, ought to be the priority in determining government spending decisions.

Both society as a whole and individual workers would benefit from increased employment of older workers, to the extent that such changes were voluntary and reflected workers' preferences. However, changes brought about through coercion, while they would probably improve our ability to produce goods and services and fund new social programs, would be at the expense of the well-being of those whose preference would have been to retire earlier. Thus, a second goal of public policy changes should be to offer individuals choices and positive incentives wherever possible, rather than resorting to more heavy-handed mandates or sanctions. Such an approach is more likely to treat individuals equitably, since not all people can or should work longer than they currently do.

Positive incentives. What policies are likely to encourage workers to remain in the labor force later in life? The most important "policy"—good economic opportunities—must come from the private sector. Good jobs with reasonable working conditions will attract and retain committed workers. Older workers who wish to phase into retirement can be attracted by flexible working conditions and part-time employment opportunities.

Several possible public policy changes could offer positive incentives to reinforce continued work. For example, stricter enforcement of the Age Discrimination in Employment Act would send the message that discrimination against older workers is not acceptable. Particular attention will need to be given to the employment process to ensure that older workers receive consideration for new jobs. Over time, the demonstrated success of older workers can help reduce stereotyping and change employers' attitudes.

Government programs that offer training, job referral or other worker support services should be scrupulous in including older workers as well as the young. In particular, people who have spent many years in one job or one industry may find the job search very difficult; their job-hunting skills are rusty to nonexistent, and they often have no informal network of the kinds of contacts that can be critical to reemployment. Strong public commitment to assisting older workers sends a message to employers and others that these are worthy potential employees.

Should the public sector subsidize the employment of older workers? If postponing retirement would promote economic growth for an aging society, public programs that could actively encourage employment of older workers should be examined. Of course, a careful weighing of benefits and costs would be necessary to ensure that such activities lead to real expansions in employment, rather than merely changing the composition of the labor force or rewarding employment practices that would have occurred anyway.

One positive policy option would be the elimination of the requirement that Medicare be the secondary payer of insurance claims for older workers in firms offering health insurance. Many employers claimed at the time this policy was implemented that it would bias them against hiring older workers because of fears that insurance costs would rise. If the employer rather than Medicare must bear the primary insurance costs, fringe benefit expenses naturally rise for those aged 65 and above. The primary purpose of the policy was to reduce federal Medicare expenditures without having to shift the costs onto beneficiaries (Ruggles and Moon, 1985). However, if this provision discourages employment of older workers, the net effect for society could be negative: the ratio of retirees to active workers would be higher than otherwise, and Medicare costs could rise anyway. But this option needs careful study to assess its impact on employment.

Another policy change that could benefit older workers and encourage them to remain longer in the labor force would be to guarantee that those who delay retirement beyond age 65 would get an actuarially equivalent return from Social Security. They would thus be assured of additional Social Security benefits as compensation for delaying retirement. Policy has moved in that direction, but only modestly: the transition established in the 1983 Social Security Amendments will not be completed until 2008. The transition could be accelerated, although there would be some cost to the Social Security trust funds from this change. Again, it is necessary to weigh the shorter-run costs to Social Security against the longer-term benefits to society.

Both of these possible changes would aid only workers over the age of 65, however. Because so many individuals have retired by that age, some having been retired for quite a few years, it might be more effective to focus on policies that affect workers aged 55 to 64. For people aged 62 to 65, Social Security benefits already actuarially adjust for differences in life expectancy, so that on average there is no benefit to retiring at age 62 versus age 65. It thus becomes difficult to find positive incentives through the retirement system for this age group. Further expansion of the Earned Income Tax Credit, to cover those with somewhat higher incomes and particularly to make workers without children eligible, could make part-time employment more attractive. Incomes to workers would be implicitly raised via this income-tax mechanism.

Another positive incentive might be legislation to facilitate pension portability. If workers could build on credits earned in earlier jobs, employment for a few additional years might be viewed as more desirable. People who change jobs or are laid off in their late 50s or early 60s might be encouraged to remain in the labor force if they could continue to build on a pension. If pension portability were used in this way to expand transitional employment before retirement, coordination with health benefits would probably need to be made more flexible. Employers might be willing to contribute modestly to a pension already in place, but might balk at picking up the full tab for the retiree health benefits that often accompany pension vesting. The federal government might be able to serve as a record-keeping or accounting clearinghouse to facilitate such pension plans.

Negative incentives. One possible way of influencing people's labor-force attachment would be to make retirement less attractive, not by enhancing opportunities but by reducing retirement benefits. For example, reducing the Social Security benefits available at age 62, or increasing the Medicare eligibility age to 66 or 67, would undoubtedly apply pressure on older workers to remain in the labor force. It could also discourage employer offerings of early retirement incentives if pension and health benefits had to cover the interim years. Indeed, some have suggested that the anticipated changes in required reporting of future health benefit liabilities on corporate balance sheets will discourage early retirement offerings by some employers.

In addition to violating the goal of individual choice, such proposals ignore the fact that a substantial number of individuals retire involuntarily each year. For those who cannot find new employment, further restrictions on retirement benefit availability would simply make a bad situation worse. Although liberalization of disability qualifications could compensate for some, that would solve only part of the problem. The violation of individual choice may create adverse incentives and equity problems that offset other benefits from postponing workers' average age of retirement.

CONCLUSION

The United States is poised at a crossroads in choosing its stance toward older workers.

Considerable change has occurred in recent years that may help to extend work lives. The 1993 Social Security Amendments, elimination of mandatory retirement, and changes in pension regulations to allow pension accruals beyond normal retirement age are but a few of these. Other changes in public policy could also help, with the most successful approaches likely to be those relying on positive rather than negative incentives. However, at least in the short run, the positive incentives are more likely to raise government spending at a time of fiscal austerity; the negative incentives impose little immediate cost, but their long-run costs would probably be much greater and would work a hardship on those least able to bear it.

Probably most important in brightening the prospects for older workers will be the private sector's response to imminent demographic changes. It can be anticipated that employers confronting labor shortages will be more likely than heretofore to try to accommodate older workers' preferences, particularly with regard to part-time employment and flexible hours. Public policy should be ready to meet the opportunities presented by such changes, ensuring that employment and retirement programs promote longer work lives while continuing to protect the well-being of those for whom continued work is not feasible.

REFERENCES

Costrell, R. M., 1988. *The Effects of Industry Employment Shifts on Wage Growth: 1948–1987.* A Study Prepared for the Joint Economic Committee of the U.S. Congress. Washington, D.C.: Intercommunications Group, Ltd. Mimeo.

Kleiman, C., 1988. "The Graying of the Workforce: Can Productivity Be Maintained?" *Washington Post*, Sept. 4.

Meier, E., 1988. Survey of Retirees from Early Retirement Incentive Programs. Washington: Public Policy Institute, American Association of Retired Persons. Issue Brief.

Ruggles, P. and Moon, M., 1985. "The Impact of Recent Legislative Changes in Benefit Programs for the Elderly." *Gerontologist* 25 (2):153–60.

Gender & Work at Midlife and Beyond

LAURIE RUSSELL HATCH

Over the course of this century the United States, along with other Western industrialized countries, has shown divergent trends in women's and men's work-force participation (Treiman, 1985; Clark, 1988). Women's labor-force participation has increased substantially, and especially so in the period since 1940. Larger proportions of women at all ages under 65 are in the labor force, with striking increases shown among midlife women. In contrast, work-force participation has declined among middle-aged and older men. There is some controversy over when this trend began among men aged 65-plus, but there is no question of substantial labor-force declines for this age group over the past four decades. Participation among men age 55 to 64 has also declined significantly during this period (Clark, 1988).

More women today are approximating the work patterns typically associated with men. Fewer women are following the so-called "traditional" female pattern of labor-force withdrawal (either permanent or for lengthy periods) after marriage or childbearing. These trends should not be construed as representing convergence in women's and men's paid work experiences, however. Women's work histories are far more diverse (Lopata and Norr, 1980), and older women

do not show the trend toward early retirement observed among men (Clark, 1988). These and other gender differences in work experience (such as continuing sex segregation in occupations) have critical implications for the economic status of older men and women.

It must be noted that existing gender differences in work experience tend to be smaller among African-Americans than they are among whites (Gibson, 1988). Black women have historically had much longer, though not necessarily more continuous, labor-force histories than white women (Andersen, 1988). Blacks of both genders are far more likely than whites to experience "a constancy of sporadic work" throughout life (Gibson, 1988:315) and to be disadvantaged on other work-related dimensions as well. However, older women in all racial and ethnic groups have fewer economic resources compared to their male counterparts (AARP, 1987).

This essay provides an overview of gender differences in work-force experiences and examines how those differences translate into differential economic resources in older age. The primary focus is on work experiences of middle and later life, but these are closely tied to previous work patterns

Source: Generations, 14(3), 48–52. Reprinted with permission from Generations, 833 Market St., Suite 512, San Francisco, CA 94103 and the author. Copyright 1990 by the American Society on Aging.

(Treiman, 1985). Because the labor-force involvements of minorities often differ greatly from those of whites, some racial comparisons will be offered.

DIMENSIONS OF WORK EXPERIENCE

For both women and men, lifetime patterns of labor-force experience lay the foundation for economic resources available in later life (Holden, 1989). History of labor-force participation, type of occupation, and the industrial sector in which that occupation is located are important predictors of retirement income (O'Rand and Henretta, 1982). The following discussion is intended to provide a brief overview of gender differences on each of these dimensions.

Work History

Especially among today's cohorts of older and midlife adults, women's work histories are briefer and less continuous than men's (Andersen, 1988). As noted previously, these differences have historically been much smaller among blacks than whites. Although the work histories of women and minorities are more sporadic than those of white men, this does not automatically mean that the careers of the latter are always continuous. Periods of irregular work become increasingly frequent for men following the age of 45 (Hendricks and Hendricks, 1986). The link between work history and pension income is incontrovertible. Those whose work careers have been interrupted or delayed may be unable to qualify for a private pension, or they may receive reduced benefits. In addition, earnings-related Social Security payments are contingent not only upon earnings but also upon time in the labor force (O'Rand and Henretta, 1982).

Labor-force history has long been recognized as a critical predictor of men's retirement income, but it is also important for the economic status of older women. The vulnerability of many unmarried women to poverty in old age can be attributed in large measure to sporadic work careers. Even among married couples, those in which the woman is eligible for her own work-related benefits usually have higher retirement incomes than couples in which the woman is eligible only for benefits as a spouse (Holden, 1989).

Occupation

Type of occupation also is an important predictor of economic status in later life. Greater pension benefits, whether from private pensions or earnings-related Social Security, accrue to those in higher-paying occupations. Persons with higher-paying occupations may be better able to save money for their retirement, though workers do not always save out of current earnings (Holden, 1989). Those more highly paid are also more likely to have access to preretirement counseling and a benefit package.

Women earn less than men at all ages, with smaller gender gaps among minority groups and among today's younger workers. On average, women earn 69 percent of the income earned by men (Grambs, 1989). Much of this earnings gap can be explained by continuing sex segregation in occupations. Only about 25 percent of all women work at jobs in which at least half of the incumbents are male (Grambs, 1989). The pay attached to such "female" jobs as clerical and social service work and teaching invariably is lower than that for jobs traditionally held by men (Andersen, 1988; O'Rand and Henretta, 1982). The problem of occupational segregation includes race as well as sex differences in jobs. Minorities are disproportionately represented in service and operative occupations, which are typically low-paying, low-status jobs (Hendricks and Hendricks, 1986).

Though occupational segregation by sex and race is observed for all ages, today's midlife and older cohorts are especially likely to work in segregated jobs (Baron and Bielby, 1985; Grambs, 1989). Further, the pattern among many women in these cohorts of returning to work after their children were at least partially grown has often translated into low-paying, low-skill jobs that are vulnerable to layoffs (Treiman, 1985). While these occupational disadvantages obviously affect the economic well-being of most married couples, they are devastating to women who have worked within the home much of their adult lives but who must now support themselves following divorce, separation, or widowhood.

Sex segregation and discontinuous work histories do not provide a complete explanation for women's lower earnings. A recent Department of Labor study showed that women earn significantly less than men even when their work is in the same job category (see Andersen, 1988). Further, women with continuous labor-force histories are no more likely than other women to have higher-paying jobs (England, 1982). Andersen (1988) cites research showing a persisting wage gap even when gender differences in occupational status, work history, and education are taken into consideration. Compared to white men, women and minorities receive lower economic returns on their investments in "human capital," including years of education and years of labor-force participation (Brown et al., 1980; see also Andersen, 1988; and Hendricks and Hendricks, 1986).

Industrial Sector

Lower earnings and lower subsequent retirement incomes also are tied to the industrial sector in which jobs are located. The jobs women and minorities hold tend to be clustered in industries with high job turnover, low wages, and low fringe benefits. The retail trade and the service sectors, where women workers are overrepresented, are examples of such industries. The pension plans these industries offer tend to be inadequate (if any are offered at all), even for those workers with continuous work-force participation (O'Rand and Henretta, 1982).

Together, these dimensions of work experience combine to place many older women at economic risk. Discontinuous work histories, low-paying jobs, and disadvantageous industrial placement translate into inadequate or nonexistent pension benefits. Comparison of older women who delay retirement with those who retire earlier shows the latter to have significantly lower incomes in older age (see Holden, 1989). As Holden explains, it is not retirement per se that explains the relative economic position of these groups of older women. Rather, lifetime patterns of work participation and earnings are keys to understanding why women who retire earlier often have lower incomes in older age. Among current cohorts of older women, those who retire earlier are less likely to have long work histories and less likely to work at jobs from which they expect to derive pension benefits.

WORK & RETIREMENT

Economic variables, along with health status and age, are important predictors for the work and retirement decisions of both genders (O'Rand and Henretta, 1982; Beck, 1983). When workers are married, the available evidence suggests that their retirement decisions are influenced by the relative earnings, age, pension eligibility, and expected retirement income of each partner (Holden, 1989). The retirement decisions of married couples are not necessarily symmetrical, however. Studies indicate that women's decisions are influenced more strongly by their husbands' age and pension eligibility than men's decisions are influenced by their wives' characteristics (see Vinick and Ekerdt, 1989).

Of course, workers are not always able to choose the timing or circumstances of their retirement. It is true that increasing numbers of older men are electing to retire early, but poor health promotes this decision among a significant proportion (see Parnes, 1989). However, workers of both genders face increasing job instability and declining earnings potential as they grow older (Hendricks and Hendricks, 1986; Wanner and McDonald, 1983). Age discrimination in the work place can help to explain in part why the employment rates of older men have been declining (Parnes, 1989). Women's increased labor-force participation at all ages under 65 may obscure a comparable trend toward early retirement (whether voluntary or involuntary) among women (see Kasl, 1980).

Estimates of retirement vary greatly depending upon the measure used. Both objective and subjective measures of retirement have been criticized as inadequately reflecting changes in women's labor-force status. The use of objective measures such as eligibility for pensions or length of time employed, for example, will exclude many women with discontinuous work histories. Subjective measures can be problematic too, since the meaning of retirement may differ for women and men (see Hatch, 1987; Holden, 1989). Gender differences in the subjective meaning of retirement have not been found among African-Americans, however (Gibson, 1987, 1988). Gibson attributes this racial difference to the fact that most black women have worked throughout their lives.

Traditional retirement measures often misidentify the work status of not only women, but also minorities and other workers with sporadic work histories. To illustrate: The "unretired-retired" have been described by Gibson (1987, 1988) as those who are 50 years of age or older who are not working, but who do not identify themselves as retired. Gibson estimates that about 40 percent of all blacks aged 55 and over are represented in this category. For many blacks of both genders, there is often no clear demarcation between work and retirement,

but rather a continuing pattern of irregular work.

The categorization of individuals as either "retired" or "not retired" may be especially problematic for workers with irregular work patterns. However, retirement should not necessarily be considered an either/or phenomenon even for workers with continuous work histories. Gustman and Steinmeier (1984) found partial retirement to be a fairly common pattern among their sample of white men. A return to the labor force following retirement has been reported as an increasingly common pattern among men (Morgan, 1980), although Parnes (1989) argues that this occurs among no more than one-third of all retirees and usually involves part-time work.

CONCLUSIONS

The trend for early retirement has been a continuous pattern among men for over four decades. Although a comparable trend has yet to be observed among women, the evidence suggests that they, too, will retire at earlier ages in the future (see Clark, 1988). Concerns about potential labor shortages have prompted some policy analysts to advocate extending the age of retirement. Since the retirement decisions of both genders are responsive to economic considerations, changes in the monetary incentives offered through retirement programs could quickly alter these trends.

Current patterns indicate that increasing numbers of American women will participate in the labor force until their retirement (Block, 1982; Szinovacz, 1983). More women will have access to Social Security and private pensions resulting from their own labor-force experience. Economic independence is critical given that more older women in the future are expected to be single, primarily because of increases in divorce and women's lower likelihood of remarriage (Keith, 1986; Uhlenberg and Myers, 1981). This does not mean that the economic position of older women will be particularly advantageous, however. The movement of women into nontraditional jobs is exceedingly slow, with most concentrated in "female" jobs typically associated with lower pay and less adequate pension benefits.

Sub par job characteristics, including a pattern of sporadic labor, also continue to typify the work of many minorities. In fact, evidence suggests that lifetime work histories of blacks in the future will be even *less* continuous than those observed among today's older cohorts (Gibson, 1988). Giving examples of drug abuse and out-of-wedlock births, Gibson argues that negative social phenomena that have first become evident in the black community have then moved on to white America. Thus, the discontinuous work patterns seen among blacks may soon extend more pervasively to other groups. Regardless of whether sporadic labor becomes more widespread or remains a greater risk for some groups, social policies must be implemented to help workers guard against the long-term economic effects of layoffs and temporary employment. Requiring the portability of private pensions represents one step in this direction.

Over the past few decades the economic status of older Americans has improved substantially, leading some policymakers and others to argue that social policies are benefiting elderly people at the expense of younger age groups (see Wisensale, 1988). In considering such debate, the heterogeneity of the older population must be stressed. Largely as a result of their lifelong work experiences, women, along with many minorities, are at risk for poverty in older age—now and for the foreseeable future.

REFERENCES

American Association of Retired Persons, 1987. *A Portrait of Older Minorities.* Long Beach, Calif.: AARP Fulfillment.

Andersen, M. L., 1988. *Thinking About Women* (2d ed.). New York: Macmillan.

Baron, J. N. and Bielby, W. T., 1985. "Organizational Barriers to Gender Equality: Sex Segregation of Jobs and Opportunities." In A. S. Rossi, ed., *Gender and the Life Course.* New York: Aldine.

Beck, S. H., 1983. "Position in the Economic Structure and Unexpected Retirement." *Research on Aging* 5(2):197–216.

Block, M. R., 1982. "Professional Women: Work Pattern as a Correlate of Retirement Satisfaction." In M. Szinovacz, ed., *Women's Retirement: Policy Implications for Recent Research.* Beverly Hills, Calif.: Sage.

Brown, R. S., Moon, M. and Zoloth, B. S., 1980. "Occupational Attainment and Segregation by Sex." *Industrial and Labor Relations Review* 33(4):506–17.

Clark, R. L., 1988. "The Future of Work and Retirement." *Research on Aging* 10(2):169–93.

England, P., 1982. "The Failure of Human Capital Theory to Explain Occupational Sex Segregation." *Journal of Human Resources* 17(3):358–70.

Gibson, R., 1987. "Reconceptualizing Retirement for Black Americans." *Gerontologist* 27(6):691–98.

Gibson, R., 1988. "The Work, Retirement, and Disability of Older Black Americans." In J. S. Jackson et al., eds., *The Black American Elderly.* New York: Springer.

Grambs, J. D., 1989. *Women Over Forty: Visions and Realities.* New York: Springer.

Gustman, A. L. and Steinmeier, T. L., 1984. "Partial Retirement and the Analysis of Retirement Behavior." *Industrial and Labor Relations Review* 37(3):403–15.

Hatch, L. R., 1987. "Research on Men's and Women's Retirement Attitudes: Implications for Retirement Policy." In E. F. Borgatta and R. J. V. Montgomery, eds., *Critical Issues in Aging Policy: Linking Research and Values.* Newbury Park, Calif.: Sage.

Hendricks, J. and Hendricks, C. D., 1986. *Aging in Mass Society: Myths and Realities* (3d ed.). Boston: Little, Brown.

Holden, K. C., 1989. "Economic Status of Older Women: A Summary of Selected Research Issues." In A. R. Herzog, K. C. Holden and M. M. Seltzer, eds., *Health & Economic Status of Older Women.* Amityville, N.Y.: Baywood.

Kasl, S. V., 1980. "The Impact of Retirement." In C. I. Cooper and R. Payne, eds., *Current Concerns in Occupational Stress.* New York: John Wiley & Sons.

Keith, P. M., 1986. "The Social Context and Resources of the Unmarried in Old Age." *International Journal of Aging and Human Development* 23(2):81–96.

Lopata, H. Z. and Norr, K. F., 1980. "Changing Commitments of American Women to Work and Family Roles." *Social Security Bulletin* 43(6):3–14.

Morgan, J. N., 1980. "Retirement in Prospect and Retrospect." In G. J. Duncan and J. N. Morgan, eds., *Five Thousand American Families: Patterns of Economic Progress,* Vol. 8. Ann Arbor: Institute for Social Research, University of Michigan.

O'Rand, A. M. and Henretta, J. C., 1982. "Midlife Work History and Retirement." In M. Szinovacz, ed., *Women's Retirement: Policy Implications of Recent Research.* Beverly Hills, Calif.: Sage.

Parnes, H. S., 1989. "Postretirement Employment." *Generations* 13 (Spring):23–26.

Szinovacz, M., 1983. "Beyond the Hearth: Older Women and Retirement." In E. W. Markson, ed., *Older Women: Issues and Prospects.* Lexington, Mass.: Lexington Books.

Treiman, D. J., 1985. "The Work Histories of Women and Men: What We Know and What We Need to Find Out." In A. S. Rossi, ed., *Gender and the Life Course.* New York: Aldine.

Uhlenberg, P. and Myers, M. A. P., 1981. "Divorce and the Elderly." *Gerontologist* 21(3):276–82.

Vinick, B. H. and Ekerdt, D. J., 1989. "Retirement and the Family." *Generations* 13 (Spring):53–56.

Wanner, R. A. and McDonald, L., 1983. "Ageism in the Labor Market: Estimating Earnings Discrimination Against Older Workers." *Journal of Gerontology* 38(6):738–44.

Warlick, J. L., 1985. "Why is Poverty After 65 a Women's Problem?" *Journal of Gerontology* 40(6):751–57.

Wisensale, S. K., 1988. "Generational Equity and Intergenerational Policies." *Gerontologist* 28(6):773–88.

Discussion Questions for Chapter Eight

1. Smaller cohorts of workers are expected to enter the labor force in the next decade, causing the American work force to age. Given the evidence presented by Sparrow on job performance of older workers, what recommendations can you make to employers regarding older workers?

2. What are the advantages and disadvantages of early retirement for individual retirees, employers, and our nation as a whole? Are the costs and benefits the same for all three?

3. How will future cohorts of women differ from present cohorts in their retirement years as a consequence of their work histories?

CHAPTER NINE

Activities, Roles, and Leisure

As shown in the previous chapter, most older people do not have jobs. Only about 12% of Americans over 65 are in the labor force (AARP and AoA, 1990). Retirement brings a shift in the allocation of time to life's activities. When people leave employment, time is sometimes freed for them to participate in other activities. Of course, retirees do not necessarily need to find new activities or roles. They may simply distribute their time and energy among their remaining activities (Atchley, 1991). Three possible areas of nonemployment activity for older people are leisure, volunteerism, and religious participation. This chapter includes selections on each.

For many Americans, work is a central activity of life. In addition to monetary remuneration, work structures time, defines an individual's role, and justifies one's effort in terms of its contribution toward worthy objectives. After retirement, how can leisure activities be justified in a society that values work so highly? In "The Busy Ethic: Moral Continuity Between Work and Retirement," David J. Ekerdt shows how the "busy ethic," leisure's counterpart to the work ethic, justifies the way a retiree spends time. Keeping busy is a means of defining a role for oneself, maintaining a positive self-image, and assuring others that the capacity for activity has not been lost.

Many contributions are made to society without monetary compensation. Older people have gained years of experience in living and working, but these valuable human resources often go untapped. Many Americans, however, continue to make social contributions after they have left the labor force through volunteer work. In "Productive Aging and Senior Volunteerism: Is the U.S. Experience Relevant?", Kerschner and Butler describe the volunteer activities of older Americans and the potential for adapting model volunteer programs developed in the United States to other nations.

It is widely believed that as people age, they become more religious. As one's life is drawing to a close, concerns with the meaning of life and the possibility of an afterlife seem to become more pronounced. Despite the apparent veracity of this idea, there is little factual evidence to support it. Older people do come out higher on some measures of religiousness than younger adults, but it is unclear whether the differences between young and old are due to aging or cohort effects. For example, the reason may be that older people have lived much of their lives during a time when religious involvement was more widely practiced, and so they have been more religious throughout their lives. Nevertheless, there are many unsettled questions about the relationship between religion and aging. In "Religious Factors in Aging, Adjustment, and Health: A Theoretical Overview," Jeffrey S. Levin evaluates the evidence on the linkages among various kinds of religious involvement, aging, and life satisfaction.

REFERENCES

Atchley, Robert C. (1991). *Social Forces and Aging* (6th ed.). Belmont, CA: Wadsworth.

American Association of Retired Persons (AARP) and Administration on Aging (AoA). (1990). A Profile of Older Americans. Washington, DC: AARP.

The Busy Ethic: Moral Continuity Between Work and Retirement

DAVID J. EKERDT

There is a way that people talk about retirement that emphasizes the importance of being busy. Just as there is a work ethic that holds industriousness and self-reliance as virtues so, too, there is a "busy ethic" for retirement that honors an active life. It represents people's attempts to justify retirement in terms of their long-standing beliefs and values.

The modern institution of retirement has required that our society make many provisions for it. Foremost among these are the economic arrangements and mechanisms that support Social Security, private pensions, and other devices for retirement financing. Political understandings have also been reached about the claim of younger workers on employment and the claim of older people on a measure of income security. At the same time, our cultural map of the life course has now been altered to include a separate stage of life called retirement, much as the life course once came to include the new stage of "adolescence" (Keniston, 1974).

Among other provisions, we should also expect that some moral arrangements may have emerged to validate and defend the lifestyle of retirement. After all, a society that traditionally identifies work and productivity as a wellspring of virtue would seem to need some justification for a life of pensioned leisure. How do retirees and observers alike come to feel comfortable with a "retired" life? In this paper I will suggest that retirement is morally managed and legitimated on a day-to-day basis, in part by an ethic that esteems leisure that is earnest, occupied, and filled with activity—a "busy ethic." The ideas in this paper developed out of research on the retirement process at the Normative Aging Study, a prospective study of aging in community-dwelling men (Bosse et al., 1984).

THE WORK ETHIC IN USE

Before discussing how the busy ethic functions, it is important to note a few aspects about its parent work ethic. The work ethic, like any ethic, is a set of beliefs and values that identifies what is good and affirms ideals of conduct. It provides criteria for the evaluation of behavior and action. The work ethic historically has identified work with virtue and has held up for esteem a conflation of such traits and habits as diligence, initiative, temperance, industriousness, com-

Source: The Gerontologist, 26(3), 239–244. Reprinted with permission from The Gerontological Society of America, Washington, DC 20005. Copyright 1986.

petitiveness, self-reliance, and the capacity for deferred gratification. The work ethic, however, has never had a single consistent expression nor has it enjoyed universal assent within Western cultures.

Another important point is that the work ethic historically has torn away from its context, become more abstract and therefore more widely useful (Rodgers, 1978). When the work ethic was Calvinist and held out hope of heavenly rewards, believers toiled for the glory of God. When 19th century moralists shifted the promise toward earthly rewards, the work ethic motivated the middle class to toil because it was useful to oneself and the common weal. The coming of the modern factory system, however, with its painful labor conditions and de-emphasis on the self-sufficient worker, created a moral uncertainty about the essential nobility and instrumentality of work that made individuals want to take refuge in the old phrases and homilies all the more. As work ideals became increasingly abstract, they grew more available. Rodgers (1978) pointed out that workingmen now could invoke the work ethic as a weapon in the battle for status and self-respect, and so defend the dignity of labor and wrap themselves in a rhetoric of pride. Politicians of all persuasions could appeal to the work ethic and cast policy issues as morality plays about industry and laziness. Thus, despite the failed spiritual and instrumental validity of the work ethic, it persisted in powerful abstraction. And it is an abstract work ethic that persists today lacking, as do many other of our moral precepts, those contexts from which their original significance derived (MacIntyre, 1981). While there is constant concern about the health of the work ethic (Lewis, 1982; Yankelovich & Immerwhar, 1984), belief in the goodness of work continues as a piece of civic rhetoric that is important out of all proportion to its behavioral manifestations or utilitarian rewards.

Among persons approaching retirement, surveys show no fall-off in work commitment and subscription to values about work (Hanlon, 1983). Thus, assuming that a positive value orientation toward work is carried up to the threshold of retirement, the question becomes: What do people do with a work ethic when they no longer work?

CONTINUITY OF BELIEFS AND VALUES

The emergence of a busy ethic is no coincidence. It is, rather, a logical part of people's attempts to manage a smooth transition from work to retirement. Theorists of the life course have identified several conditions that ease an individual's transitions from one status to another. For example, transitions are easier to the extent that the new position has a well-defined role, or provides opportunities for attaining valued social goals, or when it entails a formal program of socialization (Burr, 1973; Rosow, 1974). Transitions are also easier when beliefs are continuous between two positions, that is, when action in the new position is built upon or integrated with the existing values of the person. Moral continuity is a benefit for the individual who is in transition, and for the wider social community as well.

In the abstract, retirement ought to entail the unlearning of values and attitudes—in particular, the work ethic—so that these should be no obstacle to adaptation. Upon withdrawal from work, emotional investment in, and commitment to, the work ethic should by rights be extinguished in favor of accepting leisure as a morally desirable lifestyle. Along these lines, there is a common recommendation that older workers, beginning in their 50s, should be "educated for leisure" in preparation for retirement. For example, the 1971 White House Conference on Aging recommended that "Society should adopt a policy of preparation for retirement, leisure, and education for life off the job . . . to prepare persons to understand and benefit from the changes produced by retirement" (p. 53).

But the work ethic is not unlearned in some resocialization process. Rather, it is transformed. There are two devices of this transformation that allow a moral continuity between work and retired life. One—the busy ethic—defends the daily conduct of retired life. The other—an ideology of pensions—legitimates retirees' claim to income without the obligation to work. As to the latter, a special restitutive rhetoric has evolved that characterizes pensions as entitlements for former productivity. Unlike others, such as welfare recipients, who stand outside the productive process, whose idleness incurs moral censure, and who are very grudgingly tendered financial support (Beck, 1967), the inoccupation of retirees is considered to have been *earned* by virtue of having *formerly* been productive. This veteranship status (Nelson, 1982) justifies the receipt of income without work, preserves the self-respect of retirees, and keeps retirement consistent with the dominant societal prestige system, which rewards members primarily to the extent that they are economically productive.

THE BUSY ETHIC: FUNCTIONS AND PARTICIPANTS

Along with an ideology that defends the receipt of income without the obligation to work, there is an ethic that defends life without work. This "busy ethic" is at once a statement of value as well as an expectation of retired people—shared by retirees and nonretirees alike—that their lives should be active and earnest. (Retirees' actual levels of activity are, as shall be explained, another matter altogether; the emphasis here is on shared values about the conduct of life.) The busy ethic is named after the common question put to people of retireable age, "What

will you do (or are you doing) to keep yourself busy?", and their equally common reports that "I have a lot to keep me busy" and "I'm as busy as ever." Expressions of the busy ethic also have their pejorative opposites, for example, "I'd rot if I just sat around." In naming the busy ethic, the connotation of busyness is more one of involvement and engagement than of mere bustle and hubbub.

The busy ethic serves several purposes. It legitimates the leisure of retirement, it defends retired people against judgments of obsolescence, it gives definition to retirement role, and it "domesticates" retirement by adapting retired life to prevailing societal norms. Before discussing these functions of the busy ethic, it is important to emphasize that any normative feature of social life entails endorsement and management by multiple parties. There are three parties to the busy ethic.

First, of course, are the subjects of the busy ethic—older workers and retirees—who are parties to it by virtue of their status. They participate in the busy ethic to the degree that they subscribe to the desirability of an active, engaged lifestyle. When called upon to account for their lives as retirees, subjects of the busy ethic should profess to be "doing things" in retirement or, if still working, be planning to "do things." Retirees can testify to their level of involvement in blanket terms, asserting: I've got plenty to do, I'm busier than when I was working. Or they can maintain in reserve a descriptive, mental list of activities (perhaps exaggerated or even fictitious) that can be offered to illustrate a sufficient level of engagement. These engagements run heavily to maintenance activities (e.g., tasks around the house, shopping) and involvement with children and grandchildren. Obviously, part-time jobs, volunteering, or major life projects ("I've always wanted to learn how to play the piano") can be offered as evidence of an active lifestyle. Less serious leisure pursuits (hobbies, pastimes, socializing) can also contribute to a picture of the busy life as long as such pursuits are characterized as involving and time consuming. In honoring the busy ethic, exactly what one does to keep busy is secondary to the fact that one purportedly *is* busy.

A second group of parties to the busy ethic comprises the other participants—friends, relatives, coworkers—who talk to older workers and retirees about the conduct of retired life. Their role is primarily one of keeping conversation about retirement continually focused on the topic of activity, without necessarily upholding ideals of busyness. Conversation with retirees also serves to assure these others that there is life after work. Indeed, apart from money matters, conversation about retired life *per se* is chiefly conversation about what one does with it, how time is filled. Inquiries about the retiree's lifestyle ("So what are you doing with yourself?") may come from sincere interest or may only be polite conversation. Inquiries, too, can be mean-spirited, condescending, or envious. Whatever the source or course of discussion, it nonetheless frequently comes to assurances that, yes, it is good to keep busy.

The third group can be called institutional conservators of the busy ethic, and their role is more clearly normative. These parties hold up implicit and explicit models of what retired life should be like, models that evince an importance placed on being active and engaged. Prominent institutional conservators of the busy ethic are the marketers of products and services to seniors, the gerontology profession, and the popular media. More shall be said about these later.

Returning to the purposes that the busy ethic serves, its primary function is to legitimate the leisure of retirement. Leisure without the eventual obligation of working is an anomalous feature of adulthood. Excepting the idle rich and those incapable of holding a job, few adults escape the obligation to work. Retirement and pension policies, however, are devised to exclude older adults from the labor force. In addition, age bias operates to foreclose opportunities for their further employment. How can our value system defend this situation—retirement—when it is elsewhere engaged in conferring honor on people who work and work hard? The answer lies in an ethic that endorses leisure that is analogous to work. As noted above, leisure pursuits can range from the serious to the self-indulgent. What legitimates these as an authentic adult lifestyle is their correspondence with the *form* of working life, which is to be occupied by activities that are regarded as serious and engaging. The busy ethic rescues retirement from the stigma of retreat and aimlessness and defines it as a succession to new or renewed foci of engagement. It reconciles for retirees and their social others the adult obligation to work with a life of leisure. This is the nature of continuity in self-respect between the job and retirement (Atchley, 1971).

In an essay that anticipates some of the present argument, Miller (1965) took a stricter view about what justifies retirement leisure. Mere activity is not meaningful enough; it must have the added rationale of being infused with aspects of work that are culturally esteemed. Activity legitimates retirement if it is, for example, economically instrumental (profitable hobbies), or contributes to the general good (community service), or is potentially productive (education or skill development). Whether people in fact recognize a hierarchy of desirable, work-correlative activities at which retirees can be busy remains to be determined. What Miller's essay and the present argument have in common, nonetheless, is the view that what validates retirement, in part, is activity that is analogous to work.

The busy ethic serves a second purpose for its subjects, which is to symbolically defend retirees against aging. Based on the belief that vigor preserves well-being, subscription to the norm of busyness can recast retirement as "middle-age like." Adherence to the busy ethic can be a defense—even to oneself—against possible judgments of obsolescence or senescence. To accentuate the contrast between the vital and senescent elder, there is an entire vocabulary of pejorative references to rocking chairs and sitting and idleness. As an illustration, a recent piece in my local newspaper about a job placement service for seniors quoted one of the program's participants, who said: "I am not working for income. I am working for therapy, to keep busy. There is nothing that will hurt an elderly person as much as just sitting alone all day long, doing nothing, thinking about nothing." It is appropriate to note here that, in scope, the busy ethic does not apply to all retirees. The busy life is more likely to be an expectation on the conduct of the "young-old" retiree, or at least the retiree who has not been made frail by chronic illness.

A third purpose of the busy ethic is that it places a boundary on the retirement role and thus permits some true leisure. Just as working adults cycle between time at work and time off, retirees too can have "time off." Because the busy ethic justifies *some* of one's time, the balance of one's time needs no justification. For example, if the morning was spent running errands or caring for grandchildren, one can feel comfortable with napping or a stretch of TV viewing in the afternoon. The existence of fulfillable expectations allows one to balance being active with taking it easy—one can slip out of the retirement role, one is allowed time offstage. Being busy, like working, "pays" for one's rest and relaxation.

The busy ethic serves a fourth function, and this for the wider society by "domesticating" retirement to mainstream societal values. It could be otherwise. Why not an ethic of hedonism, nonconformity, and carefree self-indulgence as a logical response to

societal policies that define older workers as obsolescent and expendable? Free of adult workaday constraints, retirees could become true dropouts thumbing their noses at convention. Or why not an ethic of repose, with retirees resolutely unembarrassed about slowing down to enjoy leisure in very individual ways? Retirees do often describe retirement as a time for sheer gratification. In response to open-ended questions on Normative Aging Study surveys about the primary advantages of retirement, men overwhelmingly emphasize: freedom to do as I wish, no more schedules, now I can do what I want, just relax, enjoy life. Such sentiments, however, do not tend to serve drop-out or contemplative models of retired life because retirees will go on to indicate that their leisure is nonetheless responsibly busy. The busy ethic tames the potentially unfettered pleasures of retirement to prevailing values about engagement that apply to adulthood. For nonretirees, this renders retirement as something intelligible and consistent with other stages of life. Additionally, the busy ethic, in holding that retirees can and should be participating in the world, probably salves some concern about their having been unfairly put on the shelf.

The active domestication of retirement is the province of the institutional conservators of the busy ethic. The popular media are strenuous conservators. An article in my local newspaper last year bore the headline, "They've retired but still keep busy," which was reprised only a few months later in another headline, "He keeps busy in his retirement." Both articles assured the reader that these seniors were happily compensating for their withdrawal from work. It is common for "senior set" features to depict older people in an upbeat fashion, though in all fairness the genre of newspapers' lifestyle sections generally portrays everybody as occupied by varied and wonderful activities regardless of age. The popular media are also staunch promoters of aged exemplars of activity and achievement—Grandma Moses, Pablo Casals, George Burns, and so on through such lists (Wallechinsky et al., 1977). A current National Public Radio series on aging and creativity bears the preceptive title: "I'm Too Busy to Talk Now: Conversations with American Artists over Seventy."

Marketers, with the golf club as their chief prop, have been instrumental in fostering the busy image. A recent analysis of advertising in magazines designed specifically for older people found that the highest percentage of ads in these magazines concerned travel and more often than not portrayed older people in an active setting such as golfing, bicycling, or swimming (Kvasnicka et al., 1982). Calhoun (1978) credited the ads and brochures of the retirement home industry, in particular, with promoting an energetic image of older Americans. This industry built houses and, more importantly, built a market for those houses, which consisted of the dynamic retiree. While few retirees ever live in retirement communities, the model of such communities has been most influential in the creation of an active, if shallowly commercial, image of the elderly. One writer (Fitzgerald, 1983), visiting Sun City Center in Florida ("The town too busy to retire"), reflected:

> Possibly some people still imagine retirement communities as boarding houses with rocking chairs, but, thanks to Del Webb and a few other pioneer developers, the notion of 'active' retirement has become entirely familiar; indeed, since the sixties it has been the guiding principle of retirement-home builders across the country. Almost all developers now advertise recreational facilities and print glossy brochures with photos of gray-haired people playing golf, tennis, and shuffleboard. (p. 74)

The visitor noted that residents talked a great deal about their schedules and activities. The visitor also noted how their emphasis on activities was an attempt to legitimate retire-

ment and knit it to longstanding beliefs and values:

> Sun Citians' insistence on busyness—and the slightly defensive tone of their town boosterism—came, I began to imagine, from the fact that their philosophies, and, presumably, the [conservative, work ethic] beliefs they had grown up with, did not really support them in this enterprise of retirement. (p. 91)

The gerontological community has been an important conservator of aspects of the busy ethic. Cumming and Henry (1961) early on pointed out the nonscientific presuppositions of mainstream gerontology's "implicit theory" of aging, which include the projection of middle-aged standards of instrumentality, activity, and usefulness into later life. This implicit, so-called "activity theory" of aging entailed the unabashed value judgment that "the older person who ages optimally is the person who stays active and manages to resist the shrinkage of his social world" (Havighurst et al., 1968, p. 161). Gubrium (1973) has noted the Calvinistic aura of this perspective: "Successful aging, as the activity theorists portray it, is a life style that is visibly 'busy' " (p. 7). Continuing this orientation over the last decade, gerontology's campaign against ageism has, according to Cole (1983), promoted an alternative image of older people as healthy, sexually active, engaged, productive, and self-reliant.

Institutional conservators of the busy ethic are by no means monolithic in their efforts to uphold ideals of busyness. Rather, in pursuing their diverse objectives they find it useful to highlight particular images of retirement and later life that coalesce around the desirability of engagement.

SOURCES OF AUTHORITY

The busy ethic is useful, therefore, because it legitimates leisure, it wards off disturbing thoughts about aging, it permits retirees some rest and relaxation, and it adapts retirement to prevailing societal norms. These benefits to the participants of the busy ethic are functional only in an analytic sense. No one in daily life approves of busy retirements because such approval is "functional." It is useful at this point to ask why people ultimately assent to the notion that it is good to be busy.

The busy ethic has moral force because it participates in two great strong value complexes—ethics themselves—that axiomatize it. One, of course, is the work ethic, which holds that it is ennobling to be exerting oneself in the world. The other basis for the busy ethic's authority is the profound importance placed on good health and the stimulating, wholesome manner of living that is believed to ensure its maintenance. The maintenance of health is an ideal with a deep tradition that has long carried moral as well as medical significance. Haley (1978), for example, has pointed out how Victorian thinkers promoted the tonic qualities of a robust and energetic lifestyle. The preservation of health was seen to be a duty because the well-knit body reflected a well-formed mind, and the harmony of mind and body signified spiritual health and the reach for higher human excellence. Ill, unkempt, and indolent conditions, by contrast, indicated probable moral failure. Times change, but current fashions in health maintenance still imply that a fit and strenuous life will have medical benefits and testify as well to the quality of one's will and character. Thus, admonitions to older people that they "keep busy" and "keep going" are authoritative because they advocate an accepted therapy for body and soul.

CORRESPONDENCE WITH BEHAVIOR

One crucial issue is the correspondence between the busy ethic and actual behavior. It is important to mention that not all self-reports about busy retirements are conscious presentations of conformity to a busy ethic.

There are retirees who by any reckoning are very active. But in the more general case, if people believe it is important to keep busy, should they not therefore *be* busy by some standard or another?

This paper's argument in favor of the busy ethic has implied that belief is not necessarily behavior. On one hand, the busy ethic may—as any ethic should—motivate retirees to use their time in constructive or involving pursuits. It may get them out of the unhealthful rocking chair or away from the can-of-beer-in-front-of-the-TV. On the other hand, the busy ethic can motivate people to *interpret* their style of life as conforming to ideals about activity. An individual can take a disparate, even limited, set of activities and spin them together into a representation of a very busy life. It would be difficult to contradict such a manner of thinking on empirical grounds; "engagement" is a subjective quality of time use that simple counts of activities or classifications of their relative seriousness or instrumentality are not likely to measure. Indeed, gerontologists should be wary about the extent to which the busy ethic may shape people's responses on surveys about their leisure, frequency of activities, and experience in retirement.

In posing the question, "How busy do retirees have to be under such a set of values?", the answer is they don't objectively have to be very busy at all. Just as with the work ethic, which has been an abstract set of ideals for some time (Rodgers, 1978), it is not the actual pace of activity but the preoccupation with activity and the affirmation of its desirability that matters. After all, all of us are not always honest, but we would all agree that honesty is the best policy. The busy ethic, like the work ethic and other commonplace values, should be evaluated less for its implied link with actual behavior than for its ability to badger or comfort the conscience. The busy ethic, at bottom, is self-validating: because it is important to be busy, people will say they are busy.

CONCLUSION

The busy ethic is an idea that people have about the appropriate quality of a retired lifestyle. It solves the problem of moral continuity: how to integrate existing beliefs and values about work into a new status that constitutes a withdrawal from work. The postulation of a busy ethic is an attempt to examine sociologically people's judgments of value and obligation regarding the conduct of daily life—their expectations of each other and of themselves.

To be sure, there are other superseding expectations on the conduct of retirees. Writing about the duties of a possible retirement role, Atchley (1976) has noted that a stability of behavior is expected, as well as self-reliance and independence in managing one's affairs. Such normative preferences are fairly vague and open-ended. Rosow (1974) surveyed the prospects for socialization to later life, in which the retirement role is nested, and found that behavioral prescriptions for older people are open and flexible, and norms are limited, weak, and ambiguous. Even admonitions to be active carry virtually no guidance about the preferred content of such activity. Perhaps this is just as well. Streib and Schneider (1971), summarizing findings from the Cornell Study of Occupational Retirement, pointed out that the vagueness of retirees' role expectations may protect retirees from demands that they might be disinclined to fulfill or from standards that diminished health and financial resources might not allow them to meet.

The busy ethic, too, comprises vague expectations on behavior. It is a modest sort of prescription—less a spur to conformity and more a way to comfortably knit a new circumstance to long-held values. Social disapproval is its only sanction. Not all retirees assent to this image of retirement, nor do they need to. Judging by the ubiquity of the idea, however, subscribers to the busy ethic are probably in the majority; one cannot talk to retirees for very long without hearing the rhetoric of busyness. The busy ethic also legitimates the daily conduct of retired life in a lower key than has been claimed by some gerontologists, who propose that work substitutes and instrumental activity are essential to indemnify retirement. While some retirees do need to work at retirement to psychologically recoup the social utility that working supplied (Hooker & Ventis, 1984), for most it is enough to participate in a rather abstract esteem for an active lifestyle and to represent their own retirement as busy in some way.

To conclude, the busy ethic, as an idealization and expectation of retired life, illustrates how retirement is socially managed, not just politically and economically, but also morally—by means of everyday talk and conversation as well as by more formal institutions. Drawing its authority from the work ethic and from a traditional faith in the therapeutic value of activity, the busy ethic counsels a habit of engagement that is continuous with general cultural prescriptions for adulthood. It legitimates the leisure of retirement, it defends retired people against judgments of senescence, and it gives definition to the retirement role. In all, the busy ethic helps individuals adapt to retirement, and it in turn adapts retirement to prevailing societal norms.

REFERENCES

Atchley, R. C. (1971). Retirement and leisure participation: Continuity or crisis? *The Gerontologist, 11,* 13–17.

Atchley, R. C. (1976). *The sociology of retirement.* New York: Halsted Press.

Beck, S. (1967). Welfare as a moral category. *Social Problems, 14,* 258–277.

Bosse, R., Ekerdt, D. J., & Silbert, J. E. (1984). The Veterans Administration Normative Aging Study. In S. A. Mednick, M. Harway, & K. M. Finello

(Eds.), *Handbook of longitudinal research. Vol. 2, Teenage and adult cohorts*. New York: Praeger.

Burr, W. R. (1973). *Theory construction and the sociology of the family*. New York: John Wiley.

Calhoun, R. S. (1978). *In search of the new old: Redefining old age in America, 1945–1970*. New York: Elsevier.

Cole, T. R. (1983). The 'enlightened' view of aging: Victorian morality in a new key. *Hastings Center Report, 13*, 34–40.

Cumming, E., & Henry, W. H. (1961). *Growing old: The process of disengagement*. New York: Basic Books.

Fitzgerald, F. (1983, April 25). Interlude (Sun City Center). *New Yorker*, pp. 54–109.

Gubrium, J. F. (1973). *The myth of the golden years: A socio-environmental theory of aging*. Springfield, IL: Charles C Thomas.

Haley, B. (1978). *The healthy body and Victorian culture*. Cambridge, MA: Harvard University Press.

Hanlon, M. D. (1983). Age and the commitment to work. Flushing, NY: Queens College, City University of New York, Department of Urban Studies (ERIC Document Reproduction Service ED 243 003).

Havighurst, R. J., Neugarten, B. L., & Tobin, S. S. (1968). Disengagement and patterns of aging. In B. L. Neugarten (Ed.), *Middle age and aging: A reader in social psychology*. Chicago: University of Chicago Press.

Hooker, K., & Ventis, D. G. (1984). Work ethic, daily activities, and retirement satisfaction. *Journal of Gerontology, 39*, 478–484.

Keniston, K. (1974). Youth and its ideology. In S. Arieti (Ed.), *American handbook of psychiatry. Vol. 1, The foundations of psychiatry*. 2nd ed. New York: Basic Books.

Kvasnicka, B., Beymer, B., & Perloff, R. M. (1982). Portrayals of the elderly in magazine advertisements. *Journalism Quarterly, 59*, 656–658.

Lewis, L. S. (1982). Working at leisure. *Society, 19* (July/August), 27–32.

MacIntyre, A. (1981). *After virtue: A study in moral theory*. Notre Dame, IN: University of Notre Dame Press.

Miller, S. J. (1965). The social dilemma of the aging leisure participant. In A. M. Rose & W. Peterson (Eds.), *Older people and their social worlds*. Philadelphia: F. A. Davis.

Nelson, D. W. (1982). Alternate images of old age as the bases for policy. In B. L. Neugarten (Ed.), *Age or need? Public policies for older people*. Beverly Hills, CA: Sage.

Rodgers, D. T. (1978). *The work ethic in industrial America: 1850–1920*. Chicago: University of Chicago Press.

Rosow, I. (1974). *Socialization to old age*. Berkeley, CA: University of California Press.

Streib, G. F., & Schneider, C. J. (1971). *Retirement in American society: Impact and process*. Ithaca, NY: Cornell University Press.

Wallechinsky, D., Wallace, I., & Wallace, A. (1977). *The People's Almanac presents the book of lists*. New York: William Morrow.

White House Conference on Aging. (1971). *Toward a national policy on aging: Proceedings of the 1971 White House conference on Aging, Vol. II*. Washington, DC: U.S. Government Printing Office.

Yankelovich D., & Immerwhar, J. (1984). Putting the work ethic to work. *Society, 21* (January/February), 58–76.

Productive Aging and Senior Volunteerism: Is the U.S. Experience Relevant?

HELEN K. KERSCHNER
FRANCES F. BUTLER

INTRODUCTION

In the United States, the phrase "productive aging" is often associated with the participation of older members of the population in the labor force. But "productive aging" also refers to contributions to the community made by the more than 400,000 older Americans directly involved in government-sponsored senior volunteer programs, along with those millions of older Americans who participate in a variety of local and private sector, as well as informal volunteer service activities for friends and neighbors.

For older people, being productively engaged in volunteer activities is important—indeed vital—in that it can increase their sense of involvement and self-esteem; can provide avenues for contributing wisdom and experience to the community; and can have a positive impact on society's views of the role and value of the older population.

From the standpoint of national policy planning and implementation, the ability of society to tap into the human resources of its older population may require changes in attitudes about the potential of the elderly to contribute to their communities, as much as it will require the development of mechanisms for channeling those contributions.

OLDER PEOPLE AS A RESOURCE TO SOCIETY

The importance of respecting the old, of appreciating and utilizing their wisdom and experience, and of acknowledging the importance of the elder in the community is a given in most societies. However, one's view of aging will affect how one translates that respect and appreciation of the elderly into opportunities for their participation in the society. For example, if older people are seen as frail and in need of assistance and support, whatever resources are allocated for them will be allocated to meet those needs. On the other hand, if older people are seen as physically and mentally capable of participating in and contributing to society, efforts will be aimed at facilitating their participation in and contribution to society.

While the actual situation of the aging spans the spectrum of functional capacity,

Source: Ageing International 15, December, 15–18. Reprinted with permission from International Federation on Aging, Washington, DC 20049. Copyright 1988.

for the most part, resource allocation for research, education, and practice is weighted heavily toward the view of the aging as frail and in need. An additional barrier is the traditional role of the elder. The notion of older people providing help or support to others beyond one's family is not a general practice in many countries, particularly in less developed countries. Whatever the reason, in most nations, regardless of the state of industrial development or the numbers of the elderly in the population, few programs have been developed within the public or private sectors which provide opportunities for older people to contribute their time, energy, expertise and experience in a volunteer capacity.

THE EXPANSION OF SENIOR VOLUNTEER ACTIVITIES IN THE U.S.

While volunteering through churches or affinity groups in the United States has been a longstanding tradition among adult Americans, older or senior volunteerism has not. As recently as twenty years ago there was an accepted view by society and by older people themselves that, for the most part, the aged were frail and in need of services and support, and that their productive years were behind them. In short, the aged were seen as a "problem" rather than as a "solution." And yet, today millions of older Americans are providing volunteer services to their communities, their states, their nation and to other countries of the world. What accounts for this change? In part it is due to medical breakthroughs which have enabled people to live longer and to stay healthier longer, as well as the tendency toward early retirement which provides those often referred to as the "young old" with more leisure time. But a major factor has been attitudinal changes which have come about as a result of the growth of a network of senior volunteer programs which have promoted a volunteer role model of "productive aging."

Older American volunteer contributions in the form of informal volunteer services or support to friends and neighbors can never be accurately calculated, though they are known to be substantial. Older Americans' energies are also channelled through church-sponsored volunteer programs and community-based volunteer organizations which, in addition to including older people in their organized volunteer programs, also frequently provide service to the elderly.

Finally, a number of community-based volunteer programs designed specifically to provide volunteer opportunities for older Americans have come into existence in the U.S. in the past two decades. Today more than 400,000 people over the age of 60 are participating in Older American Volunteer Programs supported by the Federal Government. They include the *Retired Senior Volunteer Program (RSVP)*, the *Foster Grandparent Program* and the *Senior Companion Program*, all administered by a Federal volunteer agency known as *ACTION*. Another program under the ACTION umbrella is *VISTA* (Volunteers in Service to America), a program requiring a full year, full time volunteer commitment. Twenty percent of VISTA volunteers (about 600) are seniors. In addition, the *Service Corps of Retired Executives (SCORE)* has been organized to tap the skills of retired executives for the benefit of small, public and private sector organizations. SCORE is supported by the *U.S. Small Business Administration*.

The United States *Peace Corps* has also joined the older American volunteer movement in the U.S. by undertaking a senior volunteer effort which recruits and places older Americans age fifty and over in Peace Corps assignments throughout the world. There has been substantial growth in the number of senior Peace Corps volunteers in the past twenty years; an increase from 1% in the 1960's to 10% in the 1980's. (In 1987 there were approximately 450 senior volunteers.) Senior Peace Corps volunteers are engaged in assignments similar to younger volunteers, and their contributions are praised by the Peace Corps and host countries alike.

In addition, an array of private sector senior volunteer programs are also thriving in the U.S. Among these are the *Family Friends Program*, the many programs offered by the *American Association of Retired Persons (AARP)*, and the *National Executive Service Corps (NESC)*. Family Friends, developed by the *National Council on Aging* in Washington, pairs senior volunteers with families whose members include a child with special needs. NESC is a series of community-based service organizations, supported by private contributions, which pair retired executives with small organizations in the community in need of assistance. And, AARP, whose motto is *"To serve, not to be served,"* utilizes many thousands of its older members in volunteer programs ranging from widowed persons' counseling to legislative advocacy at the state and national levels.

Despite this impressive array of volunteer activities, it has still been suggested by national leaders that by the turn of the century, current activities in senior volunteerism in the U.S. will be viewed as "efforts in their infancy." Certainly, there is considerable room for growth. In spite of the popularity of the federally-sponsored senior volunteer programs, budgetary constraints limit opportunities for participation to less than 2% of the more than twenty-eight million older persons in the U.S. Yet, the numbers of older persons in the U.S. who can be described as "active aging" are increasing. The value and importance of productive aging to older people and to society is gaining acceptance. The avenues for older people to engage in volunteer work are being expanded. These factors, if combined with additional financial support for senior volunteer programs within the public and the private sectors, will assure expansion of senior volunteer efforts in the next century.

MEASURING THE VOLUNTEER CONTRIBUTION

What is the impact of these volunteer programs?

The contribution of senior volunteers is certainly substantial. Today, senior volunteers are assisting emotionally disturbed and retarded children; they work with the handicapped and the frail elderly; they help young mothers assume the responsibilities of parenting; they work in libraries, museums, and civic centers; they lend a helping hand to the poor, the sick, and the homeless; they provide expertise in planning and management; they teach crafts and technical skills; and they share the experiences of their lives with younger generations.

While it is known that 23,000 volunteers participating in the Foster Grandparent and Senior Companion Programs must volunteer 20 hours per week (or 29,920,000 hours per year), it is virtually impossible to accurately calculate the number of hours contributed by all senior volunteers throughout the United States. Why? Many volunteer programs are so informal that they do not calculate volunteer hours. Others do not identify volunteers by age, and many organizations do not provide statistics on volunteer hours. Despite this lack of information, it is worth noting that if every older American (over the age of 65) volunteered only one hour per week through an informal arrangement or a formal program, it would total an annual contribution of almost one and one-half billion volunteered hours. In monetary terms, at the current minimum wage of $3.35 per hour, this volunteer contribution translates into almost five billion dollars per year.

It is also important not to overlook the health-related aspects of volunteering. Researchers are demonstrating that involvement in regular volunteer activity may increase life expectancy; that doing good for others actually increases overall vitality and health; and that altruism promotes a healthier heart and immune system.[1]

THREE MODEL VOLUNTEER PROGRAMS

It is sometimes said that program models cannot be replicated across national and cultural boundaries. However, three government sponsored Older American Volunteer Programs—the *Retired Senior Volunteer Program (RSVP)*, the *Senior Companion Program* and the *Foster Grandparent Program* have been examined by many people in other countries for possible replication or adaptation. Some, in fact, are already successfully operating elsewhere. These three programs are summarized below.

Each of these programs has been refined over time. Additionally, their financial support during the early years was much smaller than it is today. Certainly, public and private sector organizations which are considering transferring and adapting these models should not be concerned about the program's complexity or expense based on the current U.S. situation. Each can be started quite simply and relatively inexpen-

TABLE 1   Selected Federal Senior Volunteer Programs in the U.S.

Program Elements	Retired Senior Volunteer Program	Foster Grandparent Program	Senior Companion Program
1. Program Provides:	Community volunteer opportunities for all persons 60 and over	Opportunities for low-income persons 60 and over	Opportunities for low-income persons 60 and over
2. Focus Client Group:	RSVP volunteers provide community service to people of all ages	Foster Grandparents work with children with special needs	Senior Companions work with adults with special needs, but particularly with the frail, home-bound elderly
3. Volunteer Service Commitment:	RSVP volunteers serve part-time, as little or as much as they choose	Foster Grandparents work 20 hours per week and receive a stipend of $2.20 per hour	Senior Companions work 20 hours per week and receive a stipend of $2.20 per hour
4. Types of Programs:	Programs involve volunteers in courts, schools, hospices, hospitals, nursing homes and other community service centers	Volunteers work with approximately 68,000 children and young people (under age 21) beset by such problems as abuse and neglect, physical and emotional handicaps, drug and alcohol abuse, mental retardation, illiteracy, juvenile delinquency, or teenage pregnancy	Volunteers are assigned to work with acute care hospitals/discharge planning programs, home health agencies, senior centers, nursing homes, hospices, and community mental health agencies
5. Number of Volunteers in U.S.:	In 1987, the 15th year of the program, there were nearly 400,000 RSVP volunteers in the U.S.	In 1987, the 22nd year of the program, there were nearly 17,600 Foster Grandparent volunteers in the U.S.	In 1987, the 12th year of the program, there were nearly 5,400 federally-sponsored Senior Companion volunteers in the U.S.
6. **Number of Projects in U.S.:**	745 projects around the country	250 federally-supported projects across the nation	96 projects nation-wide, serving 21,000 clients
7. Annual Federal Support:	Annual federal support for RSVP is in the $30 million range	Annual federal support for Foster Grandparents is approximately $60 million annually	Federal support for Senior Companions was increased in fiscal year 1988 from $18 million to $23 million. An additional 1,500 volunteers and 20 to 25 new projects will be supported as a result of this new funding

sively as a single program in a single community.

IT CAN BE DONE:
THE BORDER EXPERIENCE

The American Association for International Aging (AAIA)[2] has long supported the sharing of these senior volunteer models with other countries and has provided information and materials, as well as financial support to groups in both more and less developed countries to facilitate the transfer and adaptation of these models.

In addition to preparing a series of manuals which describe program activities as well as organizational arrangements of each of the Older American Volunteer Programs, AAIA has also developed a long-term plan which will enable senior volunteer programs in the U.S. to develop "sister" or twin relationships with groups in other countries. Such arrangements will enable both groups to benefit from the exchange. The first demonstration of this "sister senior volunteer program" is an RSVP initiative which was undertaken between the cities of El Paso in Texas and Juarez in Mexico.

In early 1987, *Winifred Dowling*, the director of the El Paso, Texas RSVP, began considering ways to help counterparts in Juarez, Mexico establish a senior volunteer program modeled after RSVP in the U.S. At the same time, two groups in Juarez, including the Mexican social service agency known as DIF and the "Association of Pensioned and Retired Persons (APRP)", were already working with the elderly and pondering ways to tap into their productive energies. Additionally, AAIA expressed interest in providing information, ideas and financial resources to this collaborative effort. Border agreements between the U.S. and Mexico also proved important mechanisms for facilitating cooperation and exchange between organizations and cities along the U.S./Mexican border.

This local, national and international interest culminated in what the press has described as an attempt "to show that good will has no boundary." At the July 26, 1988 kick-off celebration in Juarez for the first border RSVP program, *Ms. Olivia Espinoza Bermudez*, DIF president and wife of the Mayor of Juarez, described the program as being important to the Juarez community "because of the increasing numbers of older people who are in good health in Juarez and numerous ways which RSVP gives them for supporting each other and other groups in the community."

Several of the ingredients which helped make this particular model from the U.S. a reality in Mexico include:

- imagination and hard work by a senior volunteer program in the U.S. and two organizations in Mexico interested in the aging;
- support of public officials in the two cities, and communication between them across international borders;
- interest and support by regional, state and federal agencies in both the U.S. and Mexico;
- formal mechanisms in the form of border agreements for facilitating exchange across international boundaries;
- financial and moral support from international organizations working in aging and development; and
- a border committee composed of representatives from Mexico and the United States which oversees ongoing program planning and development and identifies new programs for possible collaboration.

Surely, the ingredients which facilitated this border or "sister" effort between El Paso and Juarez can be cultivated and expanded to encourage the development of similar exchanges around productive aging in other national settings.

QUESTIONS TO BE CONSIDERED

In considering action to encourage volunteer participation by older persons, the following questions should be asked:

1. Are additional human resources needed for the country or the community? If so, have older people been identified as one of those resources?

2. Is volunteering service through formal programs a community tradition? If so, what kinds of programs are available which might include the older population?

3. Does society view older people primarily as frail? If so, does that view need to be changed?

4. Does society view older people as a resource? If so, what avenues are available for channeling that resource to the benefit of the community?

5. Do perceptions of the elderly toward their own capability and role in society need to be modified to facilitate their participation in volunteer programs? If so, what might be done to change those perceptions and enhance the self-esteem of the older population?

6. Are there fears that through volunteer activities and contributions older people might replace younger workers? If so, how could those fears be alleviated?

7. Would efforts to foster senior volunteer programs be most appropriately located in the public or private sectors or both sectors working together? Would existing community groups be willing to lend their support to facilitate a senior volunteer effort?

8. Would a series of community-based volunteer efforts or a national initiative be the most appropriate action? Who might take the lead in such action?

9. Would there be a willingness to develop a strong administrative foundation for the program through the training and support of personnel? If so, who would provide training and who would receive it?

10. Could a source of funds for the senior volunteer program(s) be found? What combination of resources could be made available?

CONCLUSION

With the aging of the world's population, policy makers increasingly will be called upon to respond to the challenges of aging societies. And, while the needs of the frail elderly are great, it is critical not to lose sight of the tremendous resources offered by those older persons who remain healthy, alert, and full of potential to be part of the solution to problems associated with progress and change. The models of senior volunteerism highlighted above are proven and replicable. Technical resources have been developed to assist community and national leaders interested in adapting them. Ongoing senior volunteer projects in the U.S. have expressed interest in "sister" efforts like the El Paso/Juarez RSVP Border Project as a means of facilitating the development, implementation and ongoing support of similar programs around the world. AAIA and other organizations in the U.S. are prepared to assist in such exchanges.

For further information, contact:

ACTION
Marianne Link, Director
Older American Volunteer Programs
806 Connecticut Avenue, NW
Washington, D.C. 20525, U.S.A.

American Association for International Aging
Helen K. Kerschner, President
1511 K Street, NW, Suite 443
Washington, D.C. 20005, U.S.A.

RSVP International
Arthur Garson, President
261 Madison Avenue
New York, New York 10016, U.S.A.

NOTES

1. Eileen Rockefeller Growald and Allan Luks, "Beyond Self: The Immunity of Samaritans," *American Health*, March, 1988.

2. The *American Association for International Aging (AAIA)* is a Washington-based organization which promotes cross-national exchange and action in aging. AAIA is the only private voluntary organization in the U.S. which has as its mission collecting and disseminating information, developing materials, and providing technical and financial resources to and for the aging and those who serve them both at home and abroad.

RESOURCES

The Retired Senior Volunteer Program: A Manual for Planning, Implementing and Operating RSVP; produced by the American Association for International Aging in cooperation with the National Association of RSVP Directors, Inc., 1988.

The Senior Companion Program: A Manual for Planning, Implementing, and Operating Senior Companion Programs; produced by the American Association for International Aging in cooperation with the National Association of Senior Companion Program Directors, Inc., 1988.

The Foster Grandparent Program: A Manual for Planning, Implementing, and Operating Foster Grandparent Programs; produced by the American Association for International Aging in cooperation with the National Association of Foster Grandparent Program Directors, Inc., 1988.

Religious Factors in Aging, Adjustment, and Health: A Theoretical Overview

JEFFREY S. LEVIN

INTRODUCTION

For nearly thirty years, gerontologists have explored the relationship over the life cycle between religious participation and measures of health and well-being, such as subjective health and personal adjustment. However, findings are often contradictory, and the evidence linking religious behavior to health and well-being is largely inconclusive.[1] A major explanation for this may lie in the general lack of attention to theoretical issues in many of these studies. While the empirical literature on religion and health in social gerontology is less atheoretical than its counterpart in social epidemiology,[2] sociologists of religion have apparently neglected this field of inquiry.[3] The work of those scholars who have written in this area appears to be founded in several somewhat overlapping theoretical orientations. Implicit in each of these perspectives are expectations regarding the ways in which aging affects both the intensity of religious involvement and the salience of religion to health and well-being.

This paper will identify six theoretical viewpoints which have guided gerontological research on religion and health. Each of these offers different predictions regarding the (changing) nature of the relationship between religion and health as people grow old. These perspectives include activity theory, a "deterioration" perspective, the social decrement or isolation model, disengagement theory, an "eschatological" perspective, and the multidimensional disengagement perspective of Mindel and Vaughan.[4]

Next, empirical findings addressing religion, health, and aging will be critically reviewed. Nearly twenty such studies have appeared in recent years, and their findings will be considered in light of the expectations of the competing perspectives. Finally, some conclusions will be drawn as to which set of predictions appears to most closely account for the data.

ALTERNATIVE THEORETICAL ORIENTATIONS

In attempting to understand how religion and health are associated as people grow old, it is apparent that there are two rather distinct dimensions to this problem. On the one hand, there is the matter of religion's salience

Source: Journal of Religion & Aging, 4(3/4), 133–146. Reprinted with permission from Haworth Press, Inc., Binghamton, NY 13904. Copyright 1988. Permission to publish this material has been granted by the World Health Organization.

to health—that is, the strength of a religion and health relationship. As people age, does this association grow stronger? Does it weaken? Does it remain unchanged? Furthermore, does religion relinquish its "therapeutic significance"[5] at some point in the life cycle? In other words, does religious involvement lose its epidemiologically significant protective value[6] and begin to take on the characteristics of a risk factor?

On the other hand, there is the matter of religious involvement itself. Independent of its (changing) salience to health, evidence suggests that patterns of religious activity change to some extent as people age. However, there are conflicting findings in this area[7] due to the infrequent differentiation of organized religious activity (i.e., activity outside the home, such as religious attendance) from "nonorganizational" types of religious involvement, such as prayer and religious feelings, as well as the other sorts of religious behavior engaged in by shut-ins (e.g., watching the PTL Club in lieu of attending services). Nevertheless, the issue remains that any examination of religion and health, in an aging context, must address religious involvement per se as independent of its salience to health. In other words, when considering the effects on health of either organizational or nonorganizational religious involvement, one must also determine whether such activity increases or decreases with increasing age.

The literature suggests that there are at least six potential ways in which a religion and health relationship may behave as people grow older. These competing perspectives will now be briefly outlined. It should be stressed that these are not discrete theoretical perspectives. Rather, they are alternative sets of expectations governing religious involvement and its relationship to health and well-being as people age.

One perspective takes a decidedly "eschatological" view. Namely, this orientation

suggests that, as people grow old, they face numerous crises (e.g., retirement, loss of wealth, declining health, loss of power, bereavement, etc.)—crises which challenge the very assumptions which may have guided one's life. Some people are then led to take an inventory of their life as they begin to prepare for their inevitable demise. This preparation may involve an increase in religious involvement.[8] Furthermore, religion may take on a much more dominant role in one's life. Religious considerations will become increasingly more salient as one makes adjustments in his or her style of life, and religion may become an increasingly powerful determinant of one's health and well-being. This eschatological perspective is characteristic of work in theology and religion, especially that which looks favorably to the "cure of souls" as a pastoral role of increasing importance as people steer their way through life.[9] In sum, this perspective predicts increased religious involvement, both organizational and nonorganizational, and expects this involvement to be increasingly salient to health and well-being.

Another possible radix of expectations governing the relationship between religion and health as people age is a "deterioration" perspective. This is similar in many respects to the previous orientation, yet diverges slightly. This perspective suggests that, as people grow old, they deteriorate physically and mentally, leading them to seek out religion as a source of comfort or even healing. However, disability and concomitant activity limitation should limit their ability to participate in organized religious activities. Therefore, nonorganizational religious behavior and heightened religiosity should take its place. For these reasons, poorer health should be associated with both decreased religious attendance and increased religiosity, and these associations should grow stronger with age, as people grow less healthy and more devout and attend church less. While this perspective is often not explicitly stated, it is implicit in studies offering conclusions such as, "Apparently, if frail elderly persons overcome their health limitations sufficiently to attend religious services, they experience considerable happiness, excitement, and satisfaction in their lives. But regular attendance makes little difference to the well-being of healthy older people."[10]

In sum, this perspective predicts decreased organizational religious involvement and increased nonorganizational involvement. In addition, the association between health and organizational religion should grow increasingly stronger in a positive direction as religious attendance becomes increasingly a proxy for health status. Furthermore, the association between health and nonorganizational religion should also grow increasingly stronger, but in a negative direction.

A third perspective on religion, health, and aging is provided by activity theory, which suggests that, as folks age, they slough old activities, trading them for new ones such as renewed religious attendance. This increased vigor of religious activity can occur late in life, or may commence at an earlier age with the arrival of marriage and children. In either event, religious attendance then begins a steady rise which persists until the very oldest ages, when disability leads to decline. This view is quite reminiscent of what has been labelled the "traditional model" of the relationship between religious attendance and aging, in contradistinction to other models which predict a general decline in religious attendance with age.[11] However, an activity perspective does not presume that religion, per se, represents any more or less salient determinant of health and well-being as people age. In other words, while religious attendance might increase, the association between religion and health should not necessarily change in intensity. In sum, this perspective predicts that, up until the

very oldest ages, organizational religious involvement will increase, yet be neither more nor less salient to health and well-being.

Another perspective on this issue is provided by disengagement theory. This influential theoretical orientation[12] suggests that, as people get older, they voluntarily disengage from society and social institutions, including organized religion. These institutions play less significant roles in their lives, and one would expect, then, that religion would become less salient a factor to one's health and well-being. This perspective, though, has been criticized on the grounds that it ignores the subjective or affective (attitudinal) dimension of social relationships.[13] In other words, individuals may disengage formally, yet, informally remain highly involved in the social relationship or institutions from which they appear, on the surface, to have disengaged. These comments suggest at least two additional perspectives on the relationship between religion, health, and aging, both spin-offs of disengagement theory.

One such perspective is the social decrement or isolation model, which, like disengagement theory, anticipates a decline in religious attendance as people get older. However, unlike disengagement, this perspective raises the issue of acquiescence to disengagement; meaning, this withdrawal from social relationships and social institutions may not actually be desired. In other words, some older people become socially isolated against their will, and due to any number of reasons—living alone, lack of transportation, institutionalization, few surviving friends in church, the increasing secularization of religious services, etc.—they may be unable to participate actively in organized religious activity. However, this notion that older people may disengage yet not "go quietly" suggests that, in this case, religion may not necessarily decline in its salience to health or to life satisfaction in general. In fact, because religion may still be important, yet formally practiced to a lesser extent, disengagement from religious attendance may transpire only to the detriment of one's general well-being.

For example, much of the early work of Moberg linked church membership and attendance in older people to better personal adjustment.[14] What, then, would be the fate of such folks if they could not attend church? Moberg[15] suggests that when organized religious activity declines it is replaced by heightened religious feelings. However, one study noted that isolated older people do not necessarily rely more upon religion than other older people.[16] Regardless, this social decrement perspective is conceptually differentiable from disengagement theory, and its expectations merit separate presentation. In sum, this perspective predicts decreased organizational religious involvement, which is an increasingly salient determinant of poor health. However, unlike the "deterioration" perspective, this strengthened association is not merely the result of the increasing identity of religious attendance as a proxy for health. Rather, declines in religious attendance are themselves considered detrimental to health.

A sixth and final theoretical orientation, and like the decrement model, a variation of disengagement theory, is the multidimensional disengagement perspective suggested by Mindel and Vaughan.[4] This orientation is founded in the observation that aging is accompanied by a decrease in organizational religious involvement, yet an increase in nonorganizational involvement (e.g., prayer, listening to religious music, reading the Bible, etc.). Therefore, while consistent with disengagement theory and contrary to the social decrement perspective, religious attendance should grow less salient a factor in health, this multidimensional orientation suggests an increase in the strength of the association between health and some types of nonorganizational religious involvement

due to the increased disability of older people. In sum, this perspective predicts increased nonorganizational religious involvement, which is of increasing salience to health.

Nearly twenty published studies in social gerontology have given empirical attention to the relationship of religious factors to health and well-being. Findings bearing on the (changing) relationship between religion, adjustment, and health across the life cycle will now be reviewed in order to determine which of the six competing perspectives best predicts how religion and health covary as people grow old.

REVIEW OF EMPIRICAL FINDINGS

Religious Involvement

Evidence from various settings demonstrates that, contrary to the deterioration, social decrement, and disengagement perspectives, religious involvement does not generally decline as people age except with respect to religious attendance and only among those individuals with a serious disability. Markides and his associates[1] have noted that despite contradictory, ambiguous, and inconclusive results characterizing research in religion and aging, the stability of religious involvement including religious attendance in most older people is one finding which "has been established with some certainty" (p. 67).

In a longitudinal study of older Anglos and Mexican Americans, Markides[17] determined that religious attendance is relatively stable as older people age. Ortega et al.,[18] in a study in Alabama, found the frequency of church-related visits to be fairly consistent during adulthood and old age. In a recent study of older Mennonites, Ainlay and Smith[19] found only a partial disengagement of organizational religious activity, and this was offset by increases in nonorganizational, private religious activities. The authors thus conclude that total religious disengagement does not occur as people grow old, and furthermore, that religion retains its salience in old age. Finally, Heisel and Faulkner,[20] in a study of middle-aged and older Blacks, found that church membership and attendance increase slightly with age while religiosity remains constant. However, these findings are based upon cross-sectional data, suggesting that even the minor increase in religious attendance may reflect a cohort effect.

In sum, it appears that religious attendance is fairly stable throughout life, and may decline only in the very old whose physical activity has been limited by disability. In addition, notwithstanding these declines in organizational religious involvement, personal religious activity remains stable and may even increase somewhat with age.

Religion, Adjustment, and Health

Findings linking religious activity to health and well-being are mixed. However, negative findings (i.e., nonsignificant associations) reported by some studies may be unreliable for a number of reasons. A 30-year-old study[21] reported no significant differences between religious adjustment and both health and total adjustment. However, institutionalized and noninstitutionalized subjects were combined, nearly all of the subjects were females, what was meant by "religious adjustment" is uncertain, and the failure to detect a significant difference may have been a function of insufficient statistical power (there were only 32 noninstitutionalized subjects). In a study completed a quarter century ago,[22] religious activity and a physician-rated functional health index were not significantly associated. However, the religious activity variable did not differentiate between organizational and nonorganizational activity, perhaps obscuring a significant relationship. A more recent study using National Opinion Research Center (NORC) data[23] found nonsignificant zero-order associations between life satisfaction and church attendance. However, life satisfaction was measured by only a single item in contrast to the more conventional use of scales.

Reports of statistically significant associations between religion and health and well-being are of two types. First, three studies have linked religious attendance to general measures of personal adjustment or well-being. In a longitudinal study of older people, Keith[24] found that subjects who had experienced continuity in religious attendance were more likely to have positive attitudes toward life than were those who had experienced a decremental change in attendance. Furthermore, these "positivists" and "activists" were also likelier to have maintained their health. In the Duke Longitudinal Study of Aging, Blazer and Palmore[25] found that religious activities, including church attendance, correlated significantly with personal adjustment, while "religious attitudes" did not. Using NORC data, Steinitz[10] found that religious attendance, but not self-rated religiosity, was consistently associated with well-being. Similar findings were obtained longitudinally by Markides.[17] In sum, among older people organizational religious involvement is positively related to well-being, and this relationship does not appear to decline with age.

Second, there is some evidence that nonorganizational religious involvement may, in fact, be inversely related to well-being in the aged, although findings are mixed. A positive association is suggested by two studies,[26] and by another study[27] in which a negative association with "psychic well-being" reversed after controls were added, though it failed to attain significance. However, one recent study revealed a strong negative association between religiosity and well-being. In their research on older adults, Mindel and Vaughan[4] found that nonorganizational religious involvement was greater among those whose health impairment was greatest. In sum, these findings demonstrate that the relationship between nonorganizational religious involvement and health and well-being in older people may be in a negative direction. However, results are inconclusive, and an inverse association certainly should not be taken as evidence that subjective religiosity leads to poorer health. Rather, declines in health might engender heightened private expressions of religiosity.

A third group of positive findings deals specifically with measures of life satisfaction. In a study of men and women aged 45 and over, Edwards and Klemmack[28] found that the intensity of church-related involvement was significantly related to life satisfaction. Furthermore, these results persisted after controlling for every other variable in their dataset, including perceived health. A recently published report[29] of a bi-racial study of adults aged 60 and over found that church attendance strongly predicts life satisfaction. As in the previous study, the analysis controlled for health, in this case a measure of functional health. In sum, organizational religious involvement is strongly related to life satisfaction in older adults.

Fourth, a couple of recent studies have linked religious attendance directly to health. Markides et al.[1] found a strong, significant, positive association between religious attendance and both subjective health and a health index. The authors note that, as people grow older, religious attendance and subjective religiosity become increasingly differentiated. They suggest that organizational religious involvement may increasingly become a proxy for functional health or the ability to perform the activities of daily living. More recently, Levin and Markides[30] found that the relationship between religious attendance and subjective health is significant only among older people. In sum, among older people, religious attendance is significantly related to health.

SUMMARY

In summarizing all of the above findings, the nature of the relationship between religion, adjustment, and health as people age begins to emerge:

1. Religious attendance is fairly stable over the life cycle, and then may decline slightly among the very old or disabled.

2. Nonorganizational religious involvement and subjective religiosity remain stable as people age, but may increase slightly to offset those eventual declines in organizational religious involvement.

3. Nonorganizational religious involvement may be inversely related to health and well-being in older people, although results are mixed.

4. Among older people, religious attendance is positively related to general measures of personal adjustment and this association does not appear to decline with age.

5. Among older people, religious attendance is positively related to both subjective health and life satisfaction, the latter measured by either single items or scales.

CONCLUSIONS

It is apparent that these findings fit none of the six competing perspectives exactly. However, it is also apparent that Mindel and Vaughan's multidimensional disengagement perspective comes the closest. This theory suggests that, as people grow old, they disengage from organized religious activities such as attending religious services, and make up for this loss by increasing their nonorganizational religious involvement. While such expectations may be a bit overstated, the data do suggest that these predictions may work quite well among the very old, where religious attendance declines somewhat and where self-rated religiosity may increase slightly.

This multidimensional disengagement perspective also anticipates that nonorganizational religious involvement might become more strongly related to health in older people. This is, in fact, just the position the data support, although the relationship is possibly an inverse one (i.e., higher nonorganizational religious involvement may be associated with poorer health). However, the issue of causality remains unresolved. As mentioned earlier, these findings should not necessarily be taken as evidence of an increased, detrimental salience of religiosity to health in old age. Rather, as Mindel and Vaughan[4] themselves note, "Apparently being ill does not draw one away from religion but perhaps draws one to it in a more subjective, personal way" (p. 107). In other words, the increased significant association with age may be due to less healthy people becoming more religious.

Future social gerontological research into religion and health should attempt to clarify these findings. In particular, several tasks present themselves to investigators. These include the need for longitudinal studies, the inclusion of more than one outcome variable, the use of multidimensional measures of religious involvement, and attention to theoretical issues.

First, longitudinal studies are needed to clarify the causal relationship between nonorganizational religious involvement and health and well-being. Results from cross-sectional studies may leave the impression that such religious involvement has adverse effects upon health. In reality, the possibility that sicker people become more subjectively religious may explain such findings, but a longitudinal design would be needed to confirm this. In addition, there is some recent evidence of a significant period effect.[31]

Second, the outcome variables considered here—health status, subjective health, life satisfaction, general measures of personal adjustment—are a rather heterogeneous lot. Although the relationships between these constructs and religious involvement are quite similar, it would be desirable to include measures of each within a single study. Significant paths between religion and health status could then be determined after controlling for subjective health, life satisfaction, and adjustment. A path-analytic approach would permit the calculation of direct and indirect effects.

Third, neither organizational nor nonorganizational religious involvement is a unidimensional construct. There are innumerable measures of each, and investigators should not limit themselves to just religious attendance and subjective religiosity. One might also consider Sunday School attendance, holding a church office, attendance at Wednesday night prayer meetings, Sunday School teaching, frequency of Bible study, watching religious television, private prayer, even missionary work. Then again, one might move beyond religious involvement altogether and broach issues of religious ideology and belief. Of course, a substantial barrier to the inclusion of such variables is that much of the empirical social gerontological work on religion and health has been spun-off from larger studies of health and well-being, where the inclusion of more than a few token religion variables is highly unusual.

Finally, some clarification is needed of the theoretical bases for these findings. The multidimensional disengagement perspective comes the closest to anticipating the way in which religion and health are interrelated as people age. However, it is possible that other variables left unconsidered here might explain away these results. For example, studies of religious attendance and health must avoid basing conclusions solely upon zero-order analyses. According to Levin and Markides,[32] this is an especially serious issue in studies of older people, where religious attendance may represent a proxy for functional health, or disability. A significant, uncontrolled association between religious attendance and health may mean only that older people who are healthy enough to do so. Such tautological conclusions can probably be avoided through higher-order analyses.

Alternatively, the associations between religious involvement and health and well-being might be different within different strata of society. Or, furthermore, findings might vary depending upon the religious affiliation of the subjects. Nearly all of the subjects in the studies reviewed here were either Protestants or Catholics. Until these issues are addressed, the true relationships between religion, aging, adjustment, and health will remain somewhat obscured.

NOTES

1. K. S. Markides and H. W. Martin with E. Gomez, Older Mexican Americans: A Study in an Urban Barrio (Austin: University of Texas Press, 1983).

2. See J. S. Levin and P. L. Schiller, "Is There a Religious Factor in Health?" Journal of Religion and Health, 26 (1987), pp 9–36.

3. E. F. Heenan, "Sociology of Religion and the Aged: The Empirical Lacunae," Journal for the Scientific Study of Religion, 2 (1972), 171–176.

4. C. H. Mindel and C. E. Vaughan, "A Multidimensional Approach to Religiosity and Disengagement," Journal of Gerontology, 33 (1978), 103–108.

5. H. Y. Vanderpool, "Is Religion Therapeutically Significant?" Journal of Religion and Health, 16 (1977), 255–259.

6. K. Vaux, "Religion and Health," Preventive Medicine, 5 (1976), 522–536.

7. K. S. Markides and T. Cole, "Change and Continuity in Mexican American Religious Behavior: A Three-Generation Study," Social Science Quarterly, 65 (1984), 618–625.

8. R. Stark, "Age and Faith: A Changing Outlook or an Old Process?" Sociological Analysis, 29 (1968), 1–10.

9. W. A. Clebsch, "American Religion and the Cure of Souls," 249–265 in Religion in America, W. G. McLoughlin and R. N. Bellah, eds. (Boston: Beacon Press, 1968).

10. L. Y. Steinitz, "Religiosity, Well-Being, and Weltanschauung among the Elderly," Journal for the Scientific Study of Religion, 19 (1980), 62.

11. C. R. Wingrove and J. P. Alston, "Age, Aging, and Church Attendance," The Gerontologist, pt. 1 (1971), 356–358.

12. E. Cumming and W. Henry, Growing Old: The Process of Disengagement (New York: Basic Books, 1961).

13. A. Hochschild, "Disengagement Theory: A Critique and Proposal," American Sociological Review, 40 (1975), 533–569.

14. David O. Moberg made several excellent contributions in this area in the 1950s. These include: "The Christian Religion and Personal Adjustment in Old Age," American Sociological Review, 18 (1953), 87–90; "Church Membership and Personal Adjustment in Old Age," Journal of Gerontology, 8 (1953) 1, 207–211; "Leadership in the Church and Personal Adjustment in Old Age," Sociology and Social Research, 37 (1953), 184–185; "Religious Activities and Old Age," Religious Education, 48 (1953), 184–185; "Religious Activities and Personal Adjustment in Old Age," Journal of Social Psychology, 43 (1956), 261–267; and "Christian Beliefs and Personal Adjustment to Old Age," American Scientific Affiliation Journal, 10 (1958), 8–12.

15. D. O. Moberg, "Religiosity in Old Age," The Gerontologist, 5, 2 (1965), 78–87, 111.

16. C. T. O'Reilly, "Religious Practice and Personal Adjustment of Older People," Sociology and Social Research, 42 (1957), 119–121.

17. K. S. Markides, "Aging, Religiosity, and Adjustment: A Longitudinal Analysis," Journal of Gerontology, 38 (1983), 621–625.

18. S. T. Ortega, R. D. Crutchfield, and W. A. Rushing, "Race Differences in Elderly Personal Well-Being: Friendship, Family, and Church," Research on Aging, 5 (1983), 101–118.

19. S. C. Ainlay and D. R. Smith, "Aging and Religious Participation," Journal of Gerontology, 39 (1984), 357–363.

20. M. A. Heisel and A. O. Faulkner, "Religiosity in an Older Black Population," The Gerontologist, 22 (1982), 354–358.

21. J. R. Lepkowski, "The Attitudes and Adjustments of Institutionalized and Non-Institutionalized Catholic Aged," Journal of Gerontology, 11 (1956), 185–191.

22. F. C. Jeffers and C. R. Nichols, "The Relationship of Activities and Attitudes to Physical Well-Being in Older People," Journal of Gerontology, 16 (1961), 67–70.

23. E. Spreitzer and E. E. Snyder, "Correlates of Life Satisfaction among the Aged," Journal of Gerontology, 29 (1974), 454–458.

24. P. M. Keith, "Life Changes and Perceptions of Life and Death among Older Men and Women," Journal of Gerontology, 34 (1979), 870–878.

25. D. Blazer and E. Palmore, "Religion and Aging in a Longitudinal Panel," The Gerontologist, 16, 12, pt. I (1976), 82–85.

26. L. J. Beckman and B. B. Houser, "The Consequences of Childlessness on the Social-Psychological Well-Being of Older Women," Journal of Gerontology, 37 (1982), 243–250; and, R. W. Bortner and D. F. Hultsch, "A Multivariate Analysis of Correlates of Life Satisfaction in Adulthood," Journal of Gerontology, 25 (1970), 41–47.

27. V. Tellis-Nayak, "The Transcendent Standard: The Religious Ethos of the Rural Elderly," The Gerontologist, 22 (1982), 359–363.

28. J. N. Edwards and D. L. Klemmack, "Correlates of Life Satisfaction: A Re-Examination," Journal of Gerontology, 28 (1973), 497–502.

29. W. M. Usui, T. J. Keil, and K. R. Durig, "Socioeconomic Comparisons and Life Satisfaction of Elderly Adults," Journal of Gerontology, 40 (1985), 110–114.

30. J. S. Levin and K. S. Markides, "Religion and Health in Mexican Americans," Journal of Religion and Health, 24 (1985), 60–69.

31. R. A. Witter, W. A. Stock, M. A. Okun, and M. J. Haring, "Religion and Subjective Well-Being in Adulthood: A Quantitative Synthesis," Review of Religious Research, 26 (1985), 332–342.

32. J. S. Levin and K. S. Markides, "Religious Attendance and Subjective Health," Journal for the Scientific Study of Religion, 25 (1986), 31–40.

Discussion Questions for Chapter Nine

1. Ekerdt contends that the "busy ethic" legitimates leisure in retirement and gives definition to the retirement role. Nevertheless, does our society regard the pursuit of leisure with the same level of respect as so-called productive work?

2. One could argue that much work is left to be done in our society (*e.g.,* improving our educational systems, providing child care, caring for the frail and ill, rebuilding our nation's infrastructure), yet retirement is removing capable people from productive work at younger ages. Can you think of ways to bring the talents of our nation's older citizens together with the needs of our society in ways that could benefit all generations?

3. The multidimensional disengagement perspective described by Levin predicts a decrease in organized religious activities (such as attending religious services) and an increase with age in nonorganizational religious involvement (such as prayer, listening to religious music, or reading the Bible). Given that certain religions attach more importance to the former type of activity while others attach more importance to the latter, what do Levin's findings mean for older people of different faiths?

CHAPTER TEN

Economics of Aging

It is often reported that older people are economically better off than the general population in the United States. Older people, it is said, have more wealth, less poverty, and more discretionary income than those under age 65 (Dychtwald and Flower, 1990). While true, such statements can be misleading by what they do not say. First, poverty rates are lower among the elderly than among those under 65, but they are higher among the elderly than among the *adult* population under age 65 (AARP and AoA, 1990). Children have higher poverty rates than both the elderly and the nonelderly adult population, and this accounts for why elderly poverty rates are lower than those for the general population.

The second shortcoming of overall comparisons between elderly and nonelderly people is that average figures conceal variation within age groups. Among those over age 65, poverty rates vary tremendously. For example, in 1988, the poverty rate for elderly women (nearly 16%) was almost twice as high as it was for elderly men. In the same year, the poverty rate was 46% for Hispanic elders living apart from relatives and over 56% for black women living alone (U.S. Bureau of the Census, 1989). In addition, one-fifth of the very old (those over 85) live below the poverty line (see the Minkler article in this chapter). Moreover, the income level used by the government to indicate poverty status is lower for people over age 65 than for younger people, so that some nonelderly people who are counted below the poverty line would not be if they were over age 65. This is especially disadvantageous to the old because a substantial proportion of elderly people have incomes only slightly above what has been designated as the poverty level.

Nevertheless, economic conditions for older people have advanced in the last three decades in large part because of improvements in private pensions and changes in Social Security retirement benefits which since 1975 have been tied to the Consumer Price Index. While some people seem to resent the elderly because of the reduction in old age poverty, others would declare it a major achievement of social policy.

Michael Hurd ("The Economic Status of the Elderly") describes the economic position of the elderly. Hurd agrees that due to rapid income growth among the elderly in recent decades, they are now, on average, at least as well off as the nonelderly. Nevertheless, Hurd points out the high degree of variation in wealth and income among the older population, showing that wealth is highly concentrated and that a significant proportion of elderly people have almost no private wealth.

The prospects for the elderly population, overall, are good in the near future because large baby-boom cohorts are in the labor force. For the distant future, however, Hurd is less optimistic. Aging baby boomers will mean larger numbers of older people in relation to the size of the workforce, and this may cause a decline in the economic well-being of the elderly.

The new perception of older people as an economically advantaged group has paved the way for their discovery as a viable consumer market. According to Meredith Minkler ("Gold in Gray: Reflections on Business' Discovery of the Elderly Market"), this is a mixed blessing. On the one hand, the discovery of "gold in gray" draws older people into the mainstream, where their needs are valued and producers provide goods and services aimed at them. On the other hand, the portrayal of older people as economically well off draws attention away from the income variation among the elderly and may undercut support for public programs and trivialize the meaning of old age by reducing it to a new form of consumerism.

REFERENCES

American Association of Retired Persons (AARP) and Administration on Aging (AoA). (1990). A profile of older Americans. Washington, D.C.: AARP.

Dychtwald, Ken, & Flower, Joe. (1990). *Age wave.* New York: Bantam.

U.S. Bureau of the Census. (1989). *Money income and poverty status in the United States: 1988.* Washington DC: U.S. Department of Commerce, Current Population Reports, Series P–60, No. 166, U.S. Government Printing Office.

1

The Economic Status of the Elderly

MICHAEL D. HURD

For many years a large fraction of the elderly in the United States were poor. Encouraged by growing national income after the Great Depression, society established programs such as Social Security, Supplementary Security Income, and Medicare and Medicaid, which transferred resources to the elderly and increased their incomes. The elderly are particularly vulnerable to uncertainty. For example, many elderly could not recover from an income loss by working or from a large medical expense by borrowing against future labor earnings. The programs reduced uncertainty by stabilizing a large part of their incomes and by providing medical insurance. No other group has been protected against uncertainty to the same extent.

The elderly population has increased rapidly, and it is expected to continue to grow. The percentage of the U.S. population 65 and older was 4% in 1900, 11% in 1980, and is projected to rise to 23% by 2060. The rate of increase in the old-old (85 and above) should be even greater, from a small fraction of a percent in 1900, to 1% in 1980, to 5% by 2060. Should the economic resources of the elderly prove to be inadequate in the future, the ability of society to respond as it has in the past will be constrained by these demographic changes. It is important, therefore, to assess the economic status of the elderly and

to make an informed estimate of what it will be in the future *(1)*.

INCOME OF THE ELDERLY

Economic status is the measure of the consumption opportunities available to an individual or household *(2)*. Although, as discussed below, the correspondence between income and economic status is far from perfect, income is the most widely used measure of economic status. Therefore, I first present data on the incomes of the elderly (aged 65 and older) with the goal of answering these questions: Have the incomes of the elderly been increasing? Have their incomes been increasing faster than the incomes of the nonelderly? Are their incomes higher than the incomes of the nonelderly?

Real incomes (incomes after the effects of inflation have been removed) of the elderly grew both absolutely and relative to the rest of the population during the last 20 years. For example, in 1970 average income of households headed by an elderly person was $13,907, which was 54% of the average income of all households; in 1987 it was $17,827, 63% of average household income (both dollar figures measured in 1983 prices) *(3, 4)*. Incomes increased even as work effort and earnings dropped. For example, the la-

Source: Science, 244, 659–664. Reprinted with permission from the American Association for the Advancement of Science, Washington, DC 20005, and the author. Copyright 1989 by the AAAS.

bor force participation rate of elderly males fell from 33.1% in 1965 to 16.3% in 1987; the participation rate of elderly females fell from 10.0 to 7.4%. Incomes of the working-age population also increased during the past 20 years, but the gain has come from increased work (mainly from an increase in two-worker households) rather than from an increase in the rate of pay (5): the participation rate of the entire population rose from 58.9 to 65.9% between 1965 and 1987.

This improvement in income has been found by a number of researchers (6–9), but its interpretation as a measure of the trend in economics status is less clear. Because households of the elderly are smaller than other households, it is hard to compare household income levels to arrive at a measure of economic status. No accounting is made of fringe benefits, which are an important part of the earnings of the nonelderly, of income-in-kind, of taxes, and of misreporting of income. Income and relative income after adjusting for these omissions are shown in Tables 1 and 2.

After adjusting for inflation and household size, the incomes of the elderly increased substantially in real terms and increased faster than the incomes of the nonelderly (Table 1) (10). By 1984 the incomes of the elderly were 84% of the incomes of the nonelderly. Among the elderly the incomes of the old-old (>84 years) are the lowest. This is due in part to historical reasons: they had lower lifetime earnings than the 65- to 84-year-old group, and, therefore, lower

TABLE 1 Real incomes of the elderly and nonelderly adjusted for household size (6, p. 14).

Age	Mean income (1982 dollars)			Change (%) 1967–1984
	1967	1979	1984	
< 65	13,322	16,393	16,825	26
≥ 65	9,134	11,813	14,160	55
65–69	11,095	13,703	16,496	49
70–74	9,127	11,727	14,401	58
75–79	7,640	10,847	12,617	65
80–84	6,927	9,752	11,469	66
≥ 85	6,571	9,064	11,825	80

lifetime savings; they contributed less to Social Security, so their Social Security benefits are lower; and few would have had private or government pensions. Their incomes had the largest rate of increase. One would expect this trend to continue as the younger, more wealthy cohorts age.

Income comparisons depend in an important way on the method of adjusting for household size and on other adjustments to income (Table 2). The entries are the ratios of elderly income to nonelderly income. The first line of the table gives ratios of money income, which is the sum of earnings, pensions, Social Security benefits, investment income, business income, and so forth. It is what most people would call their income. The second line, augmented income, accords roughly with what economists would call income. It adds in nonmoney income, which is the value of employee benefits, and income-in-kind such as housing and Medicare,

TABLE 2 Income comparison: ratios of the incomes of the elderly to the nonelderly in 1979 (35).

Income measure	Income				Income			
	House-hold	Poverty scale	Adult equivalents	Per capita	House-hold	Poverty scale	Adult equivalents	Per capita
Money income	0.52	0.64	0.84	0.90	0.66	0.82	1.07	1.16
Augmented income*	0.65	0.80	1.04	1.14	0.79	0.99	1.28	1.40

*That is, money income plus employment benefits and income-in-kind less taxes.

and subtracts taxes. The entries by column show how income ratios vary as the method used to adjust for household size varies. The columns labeled "household" have no adjustment; they are just the ratios of household income. "Per capita" has the ratios of income per person; "poverty scale" uses the size adjustment implicit in the government poverty scale *(10)*; and "adult equivalents" is based on a size adjustment estimated from the consumption patterns of households of different sizes and compositions *(11)*. The main difference between "adjusted income" and "income" is a correction for the underreporting of income.

Did the elderly have higher incomes in 1979 than the nonelderly? The answer depends on the income measure and the adjustment to income. Because augmented income is more inclusive than conventional income, it is a better measure of economic resources. In my view the household entries are too low, and the per capita entries too high; at least conceptually, the adult-equivalent entries are superior to the poverty-scale entries *(12)*. According to augmented income adjusted for adult equivalents but not for underreporting, the average income of the elderly was about 4% higher than the average income of the nonelderly in 1979 (Table 2). A further adjustment for underreporting raises this to 28% *(13)*. My conclusion would be that elderly were at least as well off as the nonelderly in 1979, and possibly better off. It should be recognized, however, that none of the income measures are universally accepted, so other conclusions are certainly possible.

Although this kind of detailed information is not available for later years, we can get an idea of the changes since then by applying the rates of income growth from Table 1. According to Table 1, between 1979 and 1984 income of the nonelderly grew by 3%, and that of the elderly by 20%. If all the incomes that underlie the ratios in Table 2 grew at the same rate, all the ratios could be

updated to 1984 by multiplying the entries by 1.20/1.03 = 1.17. This is probably appropriate for conventional income because the components of conventional income in Table 2 are the same as the components in Table 1. Therefore, one would estimate the adult equivalent income ratios in 1984 to be 0.98 (income) and 1.25 (adjusted income). As far as augmented income is concerned, the updating factor of 1.17 is probably somewhat large because, whereas the nonmoney components of income grew, there is no reason to think they grew differentially in favor of the elderly. If one assumes that the nonmoney components grew for both the elderly and nonelderly at the same rate as average income over all households, one can calculate the updating factor for augmented income to be 1.16 *(14)*. This factor applied to the augmented income, adult equivalent entries in Table 2 produces income ratios of 1.21 for income and 1.48 for adjusted income in 1984. According to these estimates of income ratios, which range from 0.98 to 1.48, one would conclude that by 1984 the elderly were at a minimum as well off as the nonelderly, and possibly substantially better off.

Many people would be surprised by the growth in incomes over the high inflation period of the 1970s and early 1980s because it is generally thought that the elderly live on fixed incomes which are vulnerable to inflation *(15)*. In fact, the elderly do not live on fixed incomes, and, except for the wealthy elderly, they are not particularly vulnerable to inflation because their most important sources of income (fully measured as in augmented income of Table 2) are indexed to inflation *(16)*. The indexed components of income include Social Security benefits, which since 1975 have been indexed to the consumer price index (CPI), imputed income from housing (a larger fraction of the elderly own homes than of the nonelderly), imputed income from Medicare and Medicaid, and earnings. These categories plus miscellaneous indexed earnings account for about 75% of total income. The inflation-sensitive components include interest income, dividend income, and private pensions. Because these components are concentrated among a small fraction of wealthy elderly, the typical elderly person has even more of his income indexed than these averages suggest, and, therefore, is not especially vulnerable to inflation.

Social Security benefits have been an important factor in raising the incomes of the elderly. In part, benefits grew because the Social Security contributions of workers grew: according to the Social Security law an individual's benefits increase with his contributions. But, in addition, between 1969 and 1973 the Social Security benefit schedule (the schedule that relates Social Security contributions to benefits) was increased by Congress by about 30% in real terms; that is, even had Social Security contributions remained constant, benefits would have increased by 30%. The increase in contributions and the increase in the benefit schedule together caused Social Security benefits to increase rather substantially, especially from 1967 to 1979: real average Social Security benefits measured in 1982 dollars were $2,575 in 1967, $4,520 in 1979, and $5,148 in 1984 (6). By 1979 Social Security benefits accounted for 36% of cash income of the elderly and 57% of the cash income of the middle income quintile (elderly households whose incomes fall between the 40th and 60th percentiles of the income distribution). Social Security has an important component of average income; for the elderly whose incomes are below the median it is by far the most important component.

Although average incomes can provide broad generalizations about the economic status of a group, they reveal nothing about the distribution of income. One measure of the distribution is the official government poverty rate, the fraction of a population whose incomes fall below the poverty level.

The level, which is indexed to the CPI, varies with household composition and with the age of the head of the household (17). As shown in Table 3, the poverty rate of the elderly has fallen sharply, and in 1984 was actually lower than the rate of the nonelderly. (It has remained lower through 1987, but it is not shown because the detail by age is not available.) The poverty rate of all the elderly age groups improved, although the rate of the old-old is still high. One would expect the oldest to have the highest poverty rates because they have lived beyond their life expectancies; thus, they have had to spread their lifetime economic resources over more years. Furthermore, because of the long-term rising trend in incomes, the oldest would have had lower lifetime earnings than 65- to 84-year-olds, resulting in their having fewer resources during retirement.

Even though the poverty rate of the elderly has fallen to the rate of the rest of the population, income distribution among the elderly still remains a matter of social concern. First, a substantial fraction of the elderly has incomes only marginally above the poverty level: although this group might not be in poverty as officially measured, they are "near poor." Furthermore, this group is particularly vulnerable to economic misfortune because their money incomes are too high to qualify them for social programs which would protect them; yet their own incomes

TABLE 3 Poverty rates in the United States for three different years (6, p. 19).

Age	Percentage in poverty		
	1967	*1979*	*1984*
< 65	11.8	11.1	14.5
≥ 65	28.1	15.1	12.4
65–69	21.9	12.2	9.4
70–74	25.8	13.4	11.5
75–79	33.8	17.9	13.7
80–84	38.2	19.4	17.7
≥ 85	38.9	22.7	18.5

and assets are not high enough to provide adequate protection (18). Second, elderly widows still have a high poverty rate, 21% in 1986. The rate is partly a consequence of the high mortality rates of men: most of the old-old, who could be expected to have higher poverty rates, are widows. In addition, husbands in poor families die at younger ages than husbands in wealthy families; therefore, among the younger elderly a high fraction of widows will have come from poor families, and will be poor. Finally, when husbands die, part of the family wealth disappears, leaving the widow even less well off (19, 20).

WEALTH OF THE ELDERLY

Income is often used to measure economic status because income statistics are readily available and because for some groups it is an accurate measure. For the elderly, however, income can give a misleading impression of economic status. Consider the retired millionaire who keeps his wealth in cash. His income is zero, yet no one would say that he is poor. He would be expected to spend his cash as he ages, and, if he has no heirs, he would aim to spend all his cash by the time he dies. Therefore, his consumption, which measures his economic welfare, would be high even though his recorded income would be zero. Of course, this is an extreme example, but most elderly would be expected to follow a lifetime plan that would reduce their wealth (21). Their consumption each year would be greater than their incomes (causing wealth to decrease); income would understate their economic welfare.

Consumption is difficult to measure because most people only have the vaguest idea of their expenditures during a year. Wealth is easier to measure than consumption, and, because it measures the consumption opportunities of retired persons, in some circumstances it can be used to compare their economic status. It is of little use,

however, in comparing the economic status of the elderly and nonelderly because most of the wealth of the nonelderly is in their future earning capabilities, which are not observable. Even if we had a complete measure of wealth, comparison of the economic status of individuals of different ages would be difficult. For example, who is better off: a 60-year-old with $150,000 in wealth or a 70-year-old with $100,000? Although the 60-year-old has more wealth, he can expect to live more years, so he should spend his wealth more slowly. That is, he should consume a smaller fraction of his wealth each year. To compare their economic well-being in terms of their annual consumption we need to know how fast each will spend the wealth. However, we do not have widely accepted empirical estimates of these rates of wealth decumulation.

Despite the difficulties in interpreting wealth data, they provide a valuable supplement or alternative to income data. Table 4 shows estimates of average wealth and the composition of wealth from the Retirement History Survey (RHS), a representative sample of the elderly, most of whom were 68 to 74 in 1979. The table is meant to give a rough idea of what total economic resources were shortly after retirement, so it includes the estimated wealth-value of future incomes flows. The estimated wealth-value is called the expected present value; it answers the question, "How much wealth is equivalent to a specified expected future flow of income?" For example, the RHS sample had annual Social Security benefits of $3,590 in 1979. From the Social Security law, and given assumptions about interest rates and mortality rates, one can calculate that the Social Security system will pay over the lifetimes of the households in the RHS about $44,000 (discounted to 1979) on average. This is the average wealth-value of Social Security in the RHS sample.

The most speculative entry in the table is the wealth-value of Medicare and Medicaid.

TABLE 4 Average wealth (in thousands of 1979 dollars) and distribution of wealth of 1979 Retirement History Survey sample. Wealth estimates are based on 6,610 observations from the survey; farm families and farm wealth are excluded (*16*, p. 140).

Wealth category	All		Lowest decile	
	Wealth	Percent	Wealth	Percent
Housing	26.7	19	1.4	4
Business and property	11.6	8	1.1	3
Financial	22.5	16	0.7	2
Pensions	18.0	13	1.6	5
Welfare and transfers	2.3	2	3.6	10
Medicare and Medicaid	17.7	12	11.9	34
Social Security	44.0	31	14.2	41
Total	142.8	100	34.5	100

It is the cost of a medical insurance policy that would pay the part of expected Medicare and Medicaid benefits that is now paid by the government. It is counted as an asset because the government, in essence, is expected to transfer the wealth-value to each elderly person over his or her remaining lifetime (*22*).

Average total wealth was about $142,800 in 1979. Is, say, a 71-year-old with this level of economic resources well off? No definitive answer can be given because we do not know how fast the person will spend the wealth. But to get an idea consider a 71-year-old man who has 15 years to live and can invest at an annual rate of interest (adjusted for inflation) of 5%. Suppose he chooses to consume all of his wealth in equal amounts over 15 years. What would his annual consumption be? It would be $13,532 in 1979 dollars or $20,704 in 1987 dollars. According to Table 1, this is somewhat above the income level of 70- to 74-year-olds in 1979, and substantially above the income levels of 80- to 84-year-olds, but it includes an income flow from housing and from Medicare and

Medicaid and excludes earnings. Of course, equal consumption levels in each of the 15 years are probably not the optimal consumption path for a 71-year-old. (Suppose the individual lives to be 87?) Furthermore, the analysis is more complicated for a couple because they should take into account their joint and separate life expectancies. Nonetheless, the sustainable consumption levels give the same impression as the income levels discussed earlier: a representative group of the elderly seems reasonably well-off.

The composition of wealth shows that financial wealth (stocks and bonds, savings accounts, and cash), which is what most people call savings, is not nearly as important as other kinds of economic resources. Only 16% of wealth is financial wealth. Many would probably find the small amount of financial wealth at retirement rather surprising, but apparently most households do not save much in this form. The sum of the first three rows in Table 4 represents savings at the household level; the other rows represent saving done on behalf of the household by employers, in the case of pensions, and by government. Only 43% of the saving is done at the household level. Just why households save so little is not known, although some economists would say that it is precisely because of the saving done on behalf of the households: households react by reducing their own saving.

Social Security and Medicare and Medicaid account for about 43% of wealth. Considerable credit for the strong financial status of the elderly is due to these programs. The transformation of their economic status is a major success of public policy.

The discussion has been about average wealth, but the distribution of economic resources across households is certainly a matter of public concern. Here the conclusions are less optimistic. The last two columns of Table 4 give wealth and the composition of wealth over the lowest wealth decile (*23*). Average wealth is just $34,500, only about

24% of the average over all deciles. This wealth level would finance annual consumption over 15 years of $3,248. Even this probably overstates economic status because $11,900 of the wealth is from Medicare and Medicaid, but it is highly unlikely that someone so poor would be willing to pay that much for access to the Medicare and Medicaid system (24). The conclusion is that for the RHS population average economic resources seem adequate, but a significant fraction has almost no assets beyond their claims to public programs.

The high end of the wealth distribution is not shown in Table 4 because the RHS is not a good data set for estimating the wealth of the very wealthy. Wealth is highly concentrated, so special surveys that oversample the wealthy are needed. The 1983 Survey of Consumer Finances (SCF) is such a survey, and, although it does not have the fully inclusive wealth measures of the RHS, it can give a better idea of wealth concentration (25).

Among the elderly, 49% had less than $50,000 in wealth in 1983 (26). Because the wealth measure includes housing equity, this figure confirms the findings in the RHS that many elderly retire with little financial assets. Fourteen percent had more than $250,000; 7% more than $500,000, and 3% more than $1 million. Mean wealth was $250,000, yet median wealth was just $52,000. The ratio of median to mean is 0.21, which indicates a high degree of wealth concentration. Among the nonelderly the ratio is 0.23, indicating somewhat less concentration. These results confirm substantial heterogeneity among the elderly.

FUTURE ECONOMIC STATUS OF THE ELDERLY

It is a useful simplification to say that in 20 years the elderly will be composed of two groups: those who have recently retired and those who will retire within 20 years. The first group has economic resources that are,

with some adjustment for the passing of 10 years, approximately given in Table 4. Their major assets are claims on Social Security, Medicare and Medicaid, housing, financial assets including business and properties, and pensions. On average, they have enough assets that, under stable economic conditions, their economic status should remain adequate as they age. The major uncertainties affecting their assets are the stability of the Social Security system and Medicare and Medicaid, the value of housing, the rates of return on financial assets, and the inflation rate. Conditional on an adequate performance of the economy, the ability of the Social Security system to pay benefits according to the current law is practically certain over the next 20 years (and, in fact, much beyond 20 years). In that Social Security benefits are indexed, the part of economic status due to Social Security should remain constant as the recently retired age.

The future of the Medicare and Medicaid system is much less certain. Benefits per person have grown more rapidly than the CPI, and unlike the Social Security retirement program there is no cap on total Medicare and Medicaid costs. Even with adequate economic growth, the capacity and desire of the nonelderly to finance this continuing expansion is doubtful. Cuts in the program will have some adverse effect on economic status, but at least during the next 20 years it is unlikely to be substantial.

The movement of the baby-boom generation into its prime consumption years should keep the prices of housing up for the next 20 years. If the elderly wish to reduce their holdings of housing to finance other types of consumption as they age, the market for their houses should be good. Similarly the value of their financial assets should remain high because the baby-boom generation can be expected to purchase assets to save for their own retirements. Inflation will affect the value of pensions because most pensions are in fixed dollars, which decrease in value with inflation. It is useless to speculate about the future course of inflation, but even if it were to be high, the average holdings of pensions are not large enough to cause a great impact.

It is much more difficult to predict the economic status in 20 years of those who are now, say, 45. Although their claims on Social Security and Medicare and Medicaid will be roughly the same as those of 65-year-olds today (with the uncertainties about Medicare and Medicaid that have been discussed), we do not know what their private assets will be at retirement. The main private assets are homes, financial assets, and pensions. It seems reasonable to assume that this age group will accumulate housing wealth at least as fast as the older generation and reach retirement with as much housing wealth. As far as the other two components are concerned, we do know that today very little saving takes place at the household level (27, 28). Should this low saving rate continue, average financial wealth will not be much greater than the financial wealth of today's 65-year-olds. The one component that may increase substantially during the next 20 years is pensions: coverage and levels are increasing rapidly, and one can expect pensions changing from a small component of post-retirement resources to a major component. For example, one study predicts that when today's 40-year-olds reach age 67 they will have about as much income from pensions as they will have from Social Security benefits (29). Today the 67-year-olds have only about half as much.

Given reasonable economic growth, then, we could expect that in 20 years the retirement-age elderly will have economic resources that are somewhat greater than those of retirement age today, but not substantially greater. After retirement, however, they will face an economic environment that, as viewed today, will not be nearly as stable as that faced by today's 65-year-olds. This is due in part to the uncertainty of forecasting economic growth rates far into the future. But it is also due in part to the age distribution of the population. Because much of the population that will be alive 20 years from now has already been born, and because mortality and fertility rates change rather slowly, one can make a pretty good forecast of the population distribution. Today about 3.3 workers support each Social Security beneficiary; in 2010 about 2.9 workers will support each beneficiary. More importantly for today's 45-year-olds, the ratio is forecast to decline to 1.9 by 2030 (30). With fixed Social Security tax rates, Social Security benefits relative to incomes of the nonelderly will fall. The aim of the 1983 Social Security law changes, however, was to keep Social Security constant in absolute terms, not in relative terms; this can be done for the next 50 years if the economy grows at a reasonable rate. Should economic growth be substantially lower than the official forecasts, however, further adjustments in the system will be required.

The consequences of the change in the age distribution of the population are not limited to the Social Security system. The basic problem is how to allocate the output of the economy between the retired elderly, who are increasing in relative numbers, and workers, who are decreasing in relative numbers. Taxation, which is relied on by Social Security and other public programs, is one solution, but it has limits that arise from the political process. Private pensions also have limits imposed by the need of business to show current profit. Private saving is another solution. It too has limits because to finance their consumption during retirement the elderly need to sell their financial assets to someone. As long as the population is growing, they can sell their assets to an expanding pool of workers who are saving for their own retirements. But the changing age distribution means that the pool of workers who want to buy will be shrinking relative to the pool of the retired who want to sell. To induce each person in the smaller pool to hold larger amounts of assets the prices of those assets will have to fall; that is, the return on the assets will be smaller than anticipated. This argument implies that while the fundamental problem of the age distribution can be alleviated by private saving, it cannot be eliminated.

CONCLUSION

During most of history, to be old was to be poor. This is certainly no longer the case in the United States. On average the elderly appear to be at least as well off as the nonelderly and possibly better off. Their economic status should be adequate in the near term: the average level of resources should rise gradually as the younger and more wealthy elderly replace the older, less wealthy elderly. However, one should not expect the large improvements of the last 20 years to continue. The currently retired receive much more from the Social Security system than they contribute, but each successive retiring cohort will get smaller windfall gains (31, 32). The Medicare and Medicaid system is unlikely to expand. Private saving for retirement at the household level has been weak. Even with some growth in pensions, economic resources at retirement are unlikely to be substantially larger.

Since the establishment of Social Security in 1935, considerable public policy has been aimed at the elderly. Because on average they were not as well off as the nonelderly, the policies transferred resources from the nonelderly to the elderly with limited regard for variation in need among the elderly. Thus, for example, both the wealthy and the non-wealthy elderly have large windfall gains from Social Security and from the Medicare and Medicaid programs (33). Now, however, there is little reason for additional transfers based purely on age. New policy should recognize the great range of economic resources among the elderly. Many are poor and can pay for very

little, yet many are well-to-do and can pay for the programs that benefit them.

Two general classes of distributional problems remain. The first is that, for reasons that are not well understood, many reach retirement age with few economic resources beyond public programs and possibly housing. Some have always been poor, so their poverty at retirement reflects lifetime poverty. In this case a broad social policy is needed to address the fundamental issue of poverty at all ages. Others have had adequate lifetime incomes, but, either deliberately or in response to unforeseen events, they saved little. Public policy such as programs to encourage saving and insurance programs would reduce poverty among this group.

The second problem is that many reach retirement with assets that seem adequate, yet as they age they fall into poverty. In a group as diverse as the elderly, no single cause is responsible; it is hard to suggest public programs that will not require intergenerational transfers, yet will reduce the incidence of poverty. An important exception is the risk of large medical costs. The addition to Medicare this year of catastrophic medical insurance has eliminated some of this risk, but the risk of substantial nursing home costs remains. In 1984, 42% of the out-of-pocket medical costs of the elderly went to nursing-home expenses, yet only 5% of the elderly were in nursing homes, implying that large expenses were concentrated among a few people, especially among the very elderly (34). Because an insurance program to cover nursing-home costs would probably require the universal enrollment of the covered population, even a self-supporting program would have to be government-sponsored, just as the new Medicare insurance program is self-supporting and government-sponsored. A well-designed-program would eliminate the last major source of medical cost risk, leading to an increase in the welfare of the elderly without an increase in intergenerational transfers.

REFERENCES AND NOTES

1. In most of this article, I will discuss "the elderly" as if they were a homogeneous group. In fact they are at least as heterogeneous as the rest of the population. (J. Quinn, *Rev. Income Wealth* **32**, 63 (1987)].

2. Economic status measures economic resources, not what economists call utility (how well off or happy a consumer judges himself to be). Utility depends both on economic status and on the consumer's preferences or needs. Because preferences are not observed, utility comparisons across individuals cannot generally be made. Any utility comparison between the elderly and nonelderly is especially difficult because tastes or needs are probably quite different along some dimensions. Therefore, I will only discuss economic resources, which can be observed.

3. Bureau of the Census, *Money Income of Households, Families and Persons in the United States* (Current Population Reports Series, P-60, Washington, DC, various years).

4. Before incomes can be compared through time, they must be adjusted for inflation. The consumer price index (CPI), which measures the cost of the consumption bundle of a representative consumer, is typically used for the adjustment. Because the elderly consume a different bundle from the representative consumer, spending more on medical needs and housing, and less on transportation and recreation, the CPI might mismeasure the rate of inflation faced by the elderly. Comparisons of a price index based on the actual expenditure patterns of the elderly with the CPI show, however, that the CPI is an accurate price index for the elderly [B. Bridges and M. Packard, *Soc. Secur. Bull.* **44**, 3 (1981); M. Boskin and M. Hurd, *Public Finan. Q.* **13**, 436 (1985)].

5. In 1987 average adjusted hourly nonagricultural earnings were exactly the same as those in 1967. Thus, during this 20-year period there was no gain in the average reward from working.

6. D. Radner, *Soc. Secur. Bull.* **50**, 9 (1987).

7. R. Clark, G. Maddox, R. Schrimper, D. Sumner, *Inflation and the Economic Well-being of the Elderly* (Johns Hopkins Univ. Press, Baltimore, 1984).

8. M. Hurd and J. Shoven, *Am. Econ. Assoc. Pap. Proc.* **72**, 314 (1982); C. Ross, S. Danziger, E. Smolensky, *Contemp. Polic. Issues* **5**, 98 (1987).

9. T. Smeeding, in *Research in Economic Inequality*, D. Slottje and D. Bloom, Eds. (JAI Press, Greenwich, in press), vol. 1.

10. The size adjustment is based on the official government poverty scales. Its aim is to convert households of different sizes to a common unit. In the poverty scaling a two-person household counts as 1.26 of a one-person household, which recognizes that two people need to spend less than twice what one person must spend. The choice of 1.26, rather than, say, 1.5 is arbitrary.

11. It counts an elderly couple as 1.75 of an elderly single female and as 1.5 of an elderly single male (J. van der Gaag and E. Smolensky, *Rep. Income Wealth* **28**, 17 (1982)].

12. In 1980 the households of the elderly had 1.7 persons on average and the households of the non-elderly had about 3 persons. At the same income level individuals in the smaller households could consume more than individuals in the larger households, which implies that for a comparison of economic status household incomes of the elderly should be adjusted upward. The per capita entries are probably too high. Because a child consumes less than an adult, households of the nonelderly have fewer than three adult-equivalent individuals. Therefore, per capita income understates the economic status of the households of the nonelderly.

13. In surveys, the elderly underreport their incomes by much more than other groups (about 37% versus 3%); therefore, the adjustment will increase substantially the incomes of the elderly compared to the nonelderly *(9)*.

14. The calculation is based on 5% income growth *(4, table 5)* applied to 1979 taxes and non-money income *(9, table 3)*, and on 20% and 3% growth in money income of the elderly and nonelderly, respectively.

15. The CPI increased by a factor of 3.11, an annual rate of inflation of 6.7%. This is a high rate by historical standards: during the 17 years before 1967 the CPI increased by a factor of 1.39, an annual rate of just 1.9%.

16. M. Hurd and J. Shoven, in *Horizontal Equity, Uncertainty and Economic Well-Being*, M. David and T. Smeeding, Eds. (Univ. of Chicago Press, Chicago, 1985), pp. 125–172.

17. The poverty level for a single elderly person was $3,479 in 1979, and $4,388 for an elderly two-person household ($5,447 and $6,871 in 1987 dollars). The poverty level is probably far below what most people would think of as poor.

18. T. Smeeding, *J. Policy Anal. Manage.* **5,** 707 (1986).

19. M. Hurd and D. Wise, in *The Economics of Aging,* D. Wise, Ed. (Univ. of Chicago Press, Chicago, 1989), pp. 177–199.

20. R. Burkhauser, K. Holden and D. Feaster, *J. Gerontol.* **443,** S46 (1988).

21. Apparently the elderly do reduce their wealth as they age [M. Hurd, *Am. Econ. Rev.* **77,** 298 (1987)].

22. This method of valuing the transfer at market cost is generally used *(7, 9).* This (or any other) gives measures that are inherently less accurate than measures of financial wealth because the individuals cannot spend the wealth freely. That is, were the individuals given the Medicare and Medicaid wealth shown in Table 4, they might choose not to spend that amount on the medical insurance policy.

23. Average wealth is taken over those households whose wealth is in the bottom 10% of the wealth distribution.

24. A related point is that Medicare and Medicaid wealth is high because medical needs are high. For example, 68% of Medicaid expenditures in 1984 were for nursing home expenses. As discussed above *(2),* one cannot make utility comparisons across individuals, especially if they have different medical needs; but the availability of Medicaid to finance nursing home expenses, should the need arise, make an elderly individual better off than were Medicaid not available.

25. Wealth in the SCF is assets less debts. It includes housing, property, businesses, and financial assets. It does not include Social Security, pension wealth, or Medicare and Medicaid wealth.

26. R. Avery and G. Elliehausen, *Fed. Reserve Bull.* **72,** 857 (1986).

27. Median household net worth of 45- to 49-year-olds, excluding housing equity, was $11,040 in 1984 *(30).*

28. There is some evidence, however, that saving for retirement has been stimulated by IRAs (individual retirement accounts) [S. Venti and D. Wise, in *Pensions in the U.S. Economy,* Z. Bodie, J. Shoven, D. Wise, Eds. (Univ. of Chicago Press, Chicago, 1988), pp. 9–47].

29. E. Andrews and D. Chollet, in *Social Security and Private Pensions,* S. Wachter, Ed. (Heath, Lexington, MA, 1988), pp. 71–95.

30. Congressional Research Service, *Retirement Income for an Aging Population* (U.S. Government Printing Office, Washington, DC, 1987).

31. R. Burkhauser and J. Warlick, *Rev. Income Wealth,* **27,** 401 (1981).

32. M. Hurd and J. Shoven, in *Pensions, Labor, and Individual Choice,* D. Wise, Ed. (Univ. of Chicago Press, Chicago, 1985), pp. 193–216.

33. In the RHS, about two thirds of Social Security benefits are windfall gains. The wealthy have larger windfall gains than the non-wealthy *(31).*

34. U.S. Senate Committee on Aging, *Aging America, Trends and Projections.* (U.S. Department of Health and Human Services, Washington, DC, 1988). Because nursing home expenditures are concentrated among the very elderly, their financing will become an important problem as the population ages.

35. The entries under "income" are taken from Smeeding *(9,* table 5). The entries under "adjusted income, household" are from table **4** *(9).* I calculated the other entries under "adjusted income" by multiplying the corresponding entry under "income" by the ratio of "adjusted income, household" to "income, household." Thus, for example, "adjusted income, poverty scale" is (except for rounding error) 0.64 (0.66/0.52). At the individual level, this procedure is accurate for finding adjusted income for the different household scalings.

36. Support from the National Institute on Aging is gratefully acknowledged.

2

Gold in Gray: Reflections on Business' Discovery of the Elderly Market

MEREDITH MINKLER

Almost a decade ago, Estes (1979) coined the phrase "the aging enterprise" in reference to the vast array of programs, bureaucracies, providers, interest groups, and industries that serve the elderly population but in reality do more to meet the needs of the servicing system of which they are a part. In Estes' words:

> The social needs of the elderly . . . are defined in ways compatible with the organization of the American economy. The effect . . . is to transform these needs into government funded and industry-developed commodities for specific economic markets, commodities that are then consumed by the elderly and their 'servants.' "

In the 10 years since the publication of Estes' landmark book, the concept of an "aging enterprise" appears increasingly to have been prophetic. The elderly population not only is seen as providing serviceable needs to fuel the nation's vast health and social services industries, but indeed is considered the newest exploitable growth market in the private sector.

A sudden plethora of books and newsletters with titles like "Selling to Seniors" and "The Mature Market Report," are doing a brisk business. *Modern Maturity,* the monthly magazine of the 28 million member American Association of Retired Persons (AARP), has been listed by *Adweek* each year since 1983 as one of the nation's 10 "hottest magazines" in terms of advertising growth revenue (Dolliver, 1988). And in Emeryville, California, gerontologist and entrepreneur Ken Dychtwald receives $15,000 per speech for telling businesses how to profit from an aging population (Hartman, 1988).

The private sector's discovery of the gray market represents a decidedly mixed blessing. On the one hand, business and industry's sudden attention to elderly consumers may provide a welcome contrast to an earlier day when the omission of older people from advertisements and other marketing strategies both reflected and helped reify their exclusion from active participation in the cultural and social mainstream (Powell & Williamson, 1985).

At the same time, however, current efforts to develop and capture the aging market may sometimes have the effect of creating needs where none exist, reinforcing age-separatist policies and approaches, and especially diverting attention from the needs of low income elderly people. The creation of

Source: The Gerontologist, 29(1), 17–23. Reprinted with permission from The Gerontological Society of America, Washington, DC 20005. Copyright 1989.

a new image of older Americans as a largely affluent consumer group further may work to support public policies which de-emphasize the provision of needed government programs and services.

This paper begins with a brief review of the financial status of older Americans, and the private sector's changing image of the elderly population from a negligible consumer group to a $500 billion market (Longman, 1987). The concepts of mainstreaming, consumerism, the social industrial complex, and privatization of care and services for elderly people then are used to help understand the growth and nurturing of the aging market as well as the problems which may accompany this phenomenon. Although both the positive and the problematic aspects of the targeting of older Americans as a potent and neglected consumer population are considered, the attempt primarily is to raise questions about the ethical issues involved in exploiting the new gray market in a heavily consumer-oriented society.

IS THERE 'GOLD IN GRAY'?: THE FINANCIAL STATUS OF OLDER AMERICANS

In 1984, President Reagan's Council of Economic Advisers (1985) declared that contrary to myth, elderly Americans were "no longer a disadvantaged group." The poverty rate for the elderly population, they argued, was just 12.4% (compared to 14.4% for younger Americans) and dropped to just 4% if the value of Medicare and other in-kind benefits was taken into account.

In point of fact, the economic situation of the elderly population has improved dramatically over the past 16 years and particularly in relation to younger cohorts. Since 1970, for example, Social Security benefits have increased 46% in real terms whereas inflation adjusted wages for the rest of the population have declined by 7%. Similarly, median adjusted family incomes for families headed by people 65 and above rose 54% over that period whereas young families with heads under age 25 saw their median adjusted family income fall by 15% (Congressional Budget Office, 1988).

The elderly as a group also have impressive financial assets: Some three-quarters of those 65 and over own their own homes (compared to a total U.S. home ownership rate of 65%), and of the total financial assets held by U.S. families, 40% are accounted for by the 12% of the population aged 65 and above (Consumer Research Center, 1985).

Of even greater significance from the point of view of corporate America is the fact that people 55 and over control about one-third of the discretionary income in the U.S. and spend 30% of it in the marketplace, roughly twice that of households headed by persons under 35 (American Society on Aging, 1987). Americans 55 and over purchase close to 80% of all commercial vacation travel (Mature Market Report, 1988) and a disproportionate share of many other nonessential commodities as well.

Yet this optimistic picture obscures several important facts. There is tremendous income variation within the elderly cohort, for example, and deep poverty pockets continue to exist. Minority elders and the oldest old (persons 85 and above) thus constitute two of the fastest growing and poorest segments of the elderly population. According to the 1980 census, close to 40% of aged blacks, 26% of elderly Hispanics, and fully 20% of persons 85 and above lived in poverty (U.S. Bureau of the Census, 1982), and these rates show no sign of abating in the near future.

Analyses stressing the low poverty rates of the elderly population also are misleading in their failure to acknowledge that two different poverty lines are used in the U.S., one for persons 65 and above and the other for all other age groups. The poverty line for a single person under 65 thus was $5,593 in 1985, fully 8.5% higher than the $5,156 poverty line used for single persons 65 and over. For couples, the differential between the two poverty lines was an even more pronounced 11.2% (Pollack, 1987). When the same poverty yardstick is used for all Americans, the percentage of poverty in the elderly population rises to 15.4%, giving the aged a higher poverty rate than any other age group except children (Pollack, 1987).

Other problems in the measurement of poverty in the elderly population are discussed elsewhere (Binstock, 1986; Kingston et al., 1986; Minkler, 1986; Pollack, 1987) and a full analysis of them is beyond the scope of this paper. Suffice it to say, however, that the new stereotype of the affluent elderly population breaks down when this group is disaggregated and when the methods traditionally used to measure income and poverty levels are examined more closely.

This is not to dispute, of course, that many elderly persons do have substantial assets and discretionary income, but rather to suggest that the overall financial picture of older Americans is less rosy than the mature market analysts would have us believe. Indeed, when it is realized that close to 43% of elderly persons live below 200% of the poverty line (for a single person living alone, under $10,000/year) (U.S. Bureau of the Census, 1985), a different and more modest assessment of the economic circumstances of many of the nation's elderly people comes into focus.

FACTORS CONTRIBUTING TO BUSINESS' DISCOVERY OF THE NEW OLD MARKET

Although the financial picture of elderly Americans remains a complex one, with millions doing well while millions of others live at or near poverty, the stereotypic images of the aged tend to ignore these complexities. The decade from the late 1970s to the late 1980s witnessed a major shift in the stereotypes of the elderly population from a weak,

poor, and deserving subgroup to a wealthy and powerful voting block whose costly entitlement programs were busting the federal budget (Binstock, 1983).

In part, of course, this change in image was a function of the earlier-mentioned real and impressive financial gains made by elderly people as a group in the 1970s. A 20% increase in Social Security payments in 1972 and the tying of these benefits to the Consumer Price Index to protect them against high inflation thus had the effect of dramatically decreasing poverty rates among the elderly population. Subsequent governmental proclamations that elderly people were "no longer poor" and indeed were financially better off than other Americans helped cement new images of the economically secure aged, while gingerly raising questions as to whether government entitlements for this privileged group shouldn't perhaps be scaled back.

Other analysts were more outspoken on this topic, among them the new non-profit, non-partisan coalition, Americans for Generational Equity (AGE). Founded in 1985 under the leadership of Republican Senator Dave Durenberger and Democratic Representative Jim Jones, AGE described its mission as that of building a national movement to promote the interests of younger and future generations in the political process (Minkler, 1986). Arguing that young families had become "indentured servants" in part as a consequence of bloated entitlement programs for the aged (Hewitt, 1986), AGE advocated major reforms in Social Security and Medicare and has received impressive corporate backing and media attention for its efforts.

Several leading academic figures also have helped bolster and shape the new image of elderly people as a costly and financially secure population group. Preston (1984), former head of the Population Association of America, received national attention in 1984 for his *Scientific American* article in which he stressed that the nation's comfortable elderly population was in direct competition with youth for scarce resources. Skyrocketing rates of poverty and other problems plaguing America's children, according to Preston, were in part a consequence of the country's skewed priorities in putting elders' needs ahead of youths'.

Concurrent with the attempts of such analysts to argue that the elderly population was no longer disadvantaged economically were other efforts to shape a new image of the elderly as a vigorous and independent new generation which also constituted a new and lucrative consumer market. Age-Wave Inc. in Emeryville, California is perhaps the best known contributor to this new image of the elderly population as an untapped gold mine for business and industry. With a substantial consulting business and products like a $1100 resource book for hospitals on how to capture the aging market, Age-Wave Inc. and its founder, Ken Dychtwald, have received extensive national publicity for their vision of the "tinting of America" and its meaning for society in general and business in particular (Hartman, 1988).

Another contributor to the new image of the elderly population as a dynamic generation and potent consumer market is, of course, the senior lobby itself. For senior membership and advocacy organizations, however, projecting a new image of elderly people to business and the general public often involves a delicate tightrope walk. The AARP, for example, has found itself in the position of aggressively lobbying Congress against a freeze on Social Security Cost of Living Adjustments (COLA's) at the same time that it has been sending to the business community a different image of elderly people as a healthy, vigorous and financially lucrative market. A media kit promoting AARP's magazine, *Modern Maturity*, to potential advertisers thus describes its constituency as "Affluent . . . Aware . . . Active Buyers with over $500 billion to spend" and goes on to proclaim:

50 & Over people are putting into practice the credo of Living for Today. They're spending on self-fulfillment *now* (Hedonism vs. Puritanism) rather than leaving large sums behind. (Longman, 1987)

Critics such as Samuelson (1988) have branded as hypocritical the tendency of groups like AARP to change the image they evoke of elderly people from destitute widow to wealthy and hedonistic consumer depending on whom these organizations are targeting and toward what end. Other analysts, such as gerontologist Torres-Gil (1988), have been more generous, however, in viewing this duality as a logical, if problematic, outcome of a pluralistic society: Interest groups like the senior lobby must continue to put forward images of elderly people as needy and deserving to garner resources, while at the same time working to improve the public's image of elderly people by breaking down negative stereotypes.

A variety of factors, in short, are contributing to business' discovery of the aging market, among them real changes in the overall financial status of the aged, government and other analysts' arguments that elderly people are "no longer poor," entrepreneurs who have recognized the profits to be made from selling businesses on selling to seniors, and a gray lobby which increasingly has projected positive images of the new old age. Yet beneath all these contributing factors may be seen to lie several key values and historical developments that helped make the business community ripe for the discovery of the gray market.

The development of a geriatric "social industrial complex," through programs like Medicare and Medicaid (O'Connor, 1973), introduced the health care industry early on to the profits to be made in aging. Defined by O'Connor as a vast service industry born of the merger of private enterprise and public capital, the social industrial complex ideally brought together the best of both worlds to benefit those in need. In reality, however, the primary beneficiaries of such mergers have tended to be instead the providers (Estes, 1979; O'Connor, 1973), and this frequently is not an unintended outcome. As McKnight (1978) has noted, in times of declining natural resources and overseas markets, a new exploitable commodity often is people and their serviceable needs. The client often is "less a person in need than a person who is needed." His or her function becomes one of meeting the needs of servicers, the servicing system, and the national economy.

Viewed in this context, the proclaimed crisis of the elderly in the 1970s was less a function of the inherent needs of this group and more one of the demands of a service based economy in times of economic recession. As Estes (1979) has suggested, the elderly population and their needs became the raw materials fueling the expansion of one of the few growth sectors in the economy, that is, aging and gerontology.

For the elderly medical care client, this analysis seems particularly apt. Medicare and Medicaid had, for example, helped revitalize small and rural hospitals and indeed enabled the hospital industry overall to emerge as one of the nation's key growth areas. Expenditures on hospital care grew from $14 billion in 1965 to $167 billion in 1985 (Schlesinger et al., 1987). When inflation is corrected for, the rate of growth still represents a three-fold increase over this period, much of it a direct consequence of the Medicare payment system (Schlesinger, 1988).

In pointing out that the hospital industry profited substantially from Medicare, the author does not mean to detract from the importance of this legislation in increasing the elderly population's access to medical care. As Brown (1984) has noted, the non-poor elderly population had substantially more physician visits in the year prior to Medicare's introduction than did their low income counterparts. By 1978, however, that gap had been cut in half, dropping from 22%

to 10%. Utilization differences between elderly blacks and whites also were markedly reduced as a consequence of the legislation and differences in use between poor and non-poor chronically ill elderly people all but disappeared (Brown, 1984). Yet Medicare's other role in bolstering profits in the hospital and medical care sector should not be overlooked.

Bergthold et al. (1987), Estes (1988), Ovrebo (1987), and Schlesinger et al. (1987) have examined in more detail the commodification of care for the elderly population, and particularly the recent role of privatization in making health care for the aged one of the fastest growing businesses in the U.S. Briefly, although the term *privatization* is used in reference to the reduction in state provision of some goods or services, it frequently also is "a euphemism for cuts in the total amount of public expenditures" in health and other areas (Bergthold et al., 1987). As Bergthold et al. have noted:

> . . . because of the introduction of market criteria, distribution of services becomes based in large part on the ability to pay. After privatization, therefore, the distribution of resources is not likely to reflect the same order of social priorities as under a predominantly public system.

Decreased public provision of health services for elderly people, and the private sector's discovery of a fertile new market (with elderly people accounting for one-third of all health care expenditures, and Medicare covering only about 44% of the bill) (Health Care Financing Administration, 1985; U.S. Congress, Special Committee on Aging, 1985), in fact, may be viewed in retrospect as a portent of things to come. By the late 1970s business was discovering that elderly people were good, or potentially good, consumers not only of hospital and nursing home beds and of denture creams, but of a huge array of goods and services in almost every market sector.

Moreover, as early as the mid-1970s, a new strategy of "recapitalizing capitalism" was leading to a renewed emphasis upon both individual consumption and corporate profits (Miller, 1976). Particularly under the Reagan Administration, the dramatic lowering of corporate taxes, stepped up deregulation of business, a lessening of inflation and an accent on individual responsibility helped bolster the ideal of consumerism as the heart of the American economy. The notion that the consumption of goods was "the greatest source of pleasure, the highest measure of human achievement . . . the foundation of human happiness" (Galbraith, 1973) indeed appeared to have received renewed meaning and emphasis in an era that de-emphasized values such as equity, equality, and access and stressed instead individualism, self-reliance, government cost containment, and privatization.

SELLING TO SENIORS: A MIXED BLESSING

As noted earlier, the private sector's discovery of the elderly population market may be seen as having both positive and problematic features. On the plus side, as Beck (Perry, 1987–88) has noted, it represents an overdue realization that older people increasingly represent "a major force in society, not just a shadow population content to sit on the sidelines."

Whereas some goods and services (e.g., Geritol and burial insurance plans) have, of course, long been targeted to elderly people, the very nature of such products may have served, in retrospect, to reinforce the social distance between elderly persons and the rest of society. By contrast, the 1980s have witnessed the increasing appearance of silver-haired models in advertisements for automobiles and other valued social goods. In this way, the private sector's new attention to the elderly population market may provide an important partial corrective for the still pronounced tendency of advertisers to employ predominantly youthful models

and to reinforce, through their marketing strategies, the youth bias prevalent in American society.

The significance of this contribution should not be underestimated. Indeed, the concept of mainstreaming or integration into dominant social institutions may be seen as having relevance to the elderly population in some of the same ways that it earlier was important for the mentally and physically disabled. Although the issue here is not mainstreaming through the public schools but rather through advertising and the mass media, some similar principles may apply. As Powell and Williamson (1985) have noted, "omission implies lack of value [and] exclusion from active participation in the mainstream of American social life." Such omission further suggests that the needs, opinions, and demands of the group in question "are of no real consequence and can therefore safely be ignored." By turning their attention to the long-neglected elderly population market, business and industry may be conferring visibility and value onto this population group which, in turn, should help improve society's images of and attitudes toward its older members.

The private sector's discovery of the elderly consumer also may work to promote tailoring of needed products and services to better meet the requirements of an aging population. As Dychtwald has pointed out, the design of everything from door knobs to automobiles should be rethought as America ages, hopefully in the process developing products which take into account the physical as well as some of the social changes that may accompany old age (Hartman, 1988). Market surveys, which historically have ignored the population 50 and above, similarly must avoid such ageism if they are to help businesses discover what older consumers want and need, and how best to meet those needs.

There is often a fine line, however, between finding out what a given population group may want or need and creating in that group needs and concerns that didn't exist previously. The newly launched *Lear's* magazine for "women over 40" for example, although designed to boost the image of older women, contains ads for "anti-aging supplements" and other products aimed at creating in women a felt need to look younger than their chronological age (Wang, 1988). To the extent that such appeals exploit the "gerontophobia" or cultural dread of aging pervasive in American society (Fisher, 1978), hard questions must be raised concerning the ethics involved in their use to sell products. On a more philosophical level, the extensive use of such appeals may be seen as raising yet again the "embarrassing question" asked by foreign observers since de Tocqueville's day: "Have Americans ever developed an appropriate model of maturity?" (*Christian Science Monitor*, 1987). In Cole's (1988) words,

> We need . . . to criticize liberal capitalist culture's relentless hostility toward physical decline and its tendency to regard health as a form of secular salvation . . .

> The one-sided drive to alter, ameliorate, abolish, retard or somehow control the biological process of aging intensifies the impoverishment of meaning instead of confronting it.

The fine line between meeting older consumers' needs and artificially creating needs to exploit the gray market also is seen in many of the new appeals to business to aggressively target older Americans as a critical new consumer group. In *Midlife and Beyond: The $800 Billion Over-Fifty Market*, the Consumer Research Center (1985) has argued that "What we have, then, is potentially a highly receptive market for a wide range of luxury goods, for frills and services and top of the price line merchandise." Note that no mention is made in this statement of meeting elderly people's needs, but rather of selling them "frills and services," "luxury goods," and the most costly, top line merchandise.

It can be argued, of course, that such marketing only is effective if there is a consumer demand for these products in the first place, because the power of the market system really lies in individuals rather than in the businesses and organizations that cater to them. Yet as Galbraith (1973) has suggested, this perspective may be more myth than reality: a myth promoted by the corporate economy to remove the business sector from accountability ". . . if the goods that it produces or the services that it renders are frivolous" or worse.

In the same way that a fine line exists between meeting elderly peoples' needs and having corporations create and shape their needs for profit, a delicate balance also must be struck between, on the one hand, tailoring goods and services to meet the special needs of the elderly population and, on the other, reinforcing age-separatist approaches.

The rapid growth of resort style life care communities provides a good case in point. Although only about 850 such facilities (with and without nursing homes) were operating in 1986, projections by the Real Estate Research Corporation have suggested that an additional 4,400 are likely to spring up by 1995, creating a $46 billion industry (Lublin, 1986). As such facilities become big business, hard questions need to be raised concerning the relative merits of promoting these approaches vis à vis alternatives that would provide for more age-integrated housing and health care arrangements. In particular, the fact must be confronted that the heavy advertising of life care communities and other age-separatist services may have the opposite effect of the positive mainstreaming role of business mentioned earlier. By buying into the notion of elderly persons as "separate and different" (Estes, 1979) and requiring therefore separate and different housing and basic human services, such business appeals may increase the psychological and social distance between the elderly population and the rest of society.

A final problematic aspect of the sudden emphasis on affluent older Americans as a vibrant new consumer market is that this development, coupled with privatization and other recent trends, may have the effect of obscuring the very real economic problems faced by the millions of elderly people who do not conform to the new stereotype. As noted earlier, more than 15% of elderly people still live in poverty and among women, minorities, and the oldest old these figures are considerably higher.

Marketing appeals which wittingly or unwittingly homogenize elderly people and recast them as a monolithic, $500 billion consumer group (Longman, 1987) present a misleading and incomplete picture of the social and economic situation of older Americans today. And this inaccurate portrait, in turn, is troublesome for two reasons. First, in the proprietary sector, such image creation and reinforcement may render even less audible the demands of low income consumers, a group for whom affordable housing, rather than high-priced condominiums, may represent the most pressing consumer need. Decreased attention to the needs of low income elderly people presents special problems in areas such as health and social services where privatization, along with serious threats to the viability of non-profit agencies, is occurring at a rapid rate. As Estes (1988) has noted, in fields like home health care and home delivered meals, deregulation and the entry of for-profit providers "are challenging the ability of non-profit agencies to continue serving the low income elderly who may need services, but who cannot afford to pay privately for them."

A second, and potentially even more important problem, however, is that business' creation and reinforcement of a misleadingly homogeneous picture of the afflu-

ent older consumer may adversely affect public policy. As low income elderly persons are rendered less visible through such marketing approaches and imaging, for example, governments may find increasing justification for cutbacks in the programs and services that are most needed by those elderly people who fail to fit the new, affluent stereotype. Further, as the private sector aggressively markets goods and services that ideally government should provide, public pressure for such assistance (and hence government incentives to respond) may be reduced.

Long-term care insurance provides an important case in point: When it is realized that 46% of persons 75 and above who are living alone spend down to poverty level within just 13 weeks of institutionalization (U.S. House of Representatives, Select Committee on Aging, 1985), the critical need for government provision of long-term care coverage becomes clear. By appearing to provide a viable alternative to government support, however, long-term care insurance policies (most of which are prohibitively expensive and many of which have loopholes excluding things like coverage for Alzheimer's disease) may, in fact, be acting to retard movement in this important direction. Privatized services seeking lucrative market niches, in short, may be hurting the elderly population and their families by undermining the provision of needed public services.

CONSUMERISM AND THE THIRD AGE: A FINAL NOTE

The last few years have witnessed a dramatic and for the most part welcome new accent on the positive aspects of aging. Developmental psychologists have begun to view old age as a period of continued growth and development, with Erikson (1986) defining the final stage of life as one in which "a sense of integrity," completeness, and personal wholeness help offset the negative psychological effects of inevitable physical decline. Literature and humanistic gerontology similarly have helped further a perception of old age as "a period of unique capacity for wisdom, for understanding the experience of a whole lifetime and (therefore) for service to the young" (Cole, 1988). Yet as Cole has cautioned, "so called 'positive' aspects of aging often turn out to be disguised forms of the effort to restore youth, rather than appreciation of growing or being old as a fundamental dimension of human existence." If the latter, richer view of aging is to be achieved, the "Third Age" must be reconceptualized, that period in life from age 50 to 75 which is largely roleless (Pifer, 1986) and which, in Fahey's (1987) words, "we tend to waste through inertia."

Fisher (1978), Pifer (1986), and others (Butler, 1975; Estes, 1979) have argued that this period of life should be marked by an appreciation of people intrinsically, and not merely in terms of their role as consumers. Yet it must also be a time of opportunity for contributing, whether through new job options made possible by retraining (Pifer, 1986) or by other, non-employment-related activities in a world where paid work is but one of many organizing principles and legitimating ethics (Estes, 1979; Fisher, 1978).

Viewed optimistically, business' new attention to elderly people as consumers can contribute to a meaningful old age by providing those goods and services that foster autonomy and contribute to a sense of competence, without setting the elderly population apart in the process (American Society on Aging, 1987). By helping to mainstream elderly people, giving them greater visibility and legitimacy through the use of older models, the world of advertising similarly can play a key role in improving both society's perceptions of elderly people and older

people's images of themselves (Swayne & Greco, 1987).

Viewed in a less positive light, however, the targeting of elderly people by business and industry may, as noted earlier, lead to distorted images of the actual financial adequacy of older Americans, redirecting attention away from the still sizable proportion of elderly persons who live in or near poverty. It may rob old age of some of its unique meaning by "channeling" the lives of elderly people primarily into "trivialized leisure and the consumption of professional services" (Cole, 1988). In so doing, it may reinforce some of the less desirable aspects of American culture, key among them a valuing of people in terms of their consumption patterns and the exploiting of fears of aging to sell products.

Finally, the growth of privatized goods and services in need of profitable markets may wittingly or unwittingly undermine support for needed public services.

America is a society heavily dominated by consumerism and a "market justice" view of the world in which obligations to the larger society are de-emphasized whereas individual responsibility is assigned a high premium (Beauchamp, 1976). Such a society provides fertile ground for a business orientation stressing profits over need and reinforcing a vision of human worth that values people not "inherently, in terms of their basic humanity, but contingently, in relationship to the market place" (Ovrebo, 1987).

Business and industry are discovering the elderly market and the new age wave which it represents. In making this discovery, they can play an important role in helping to meet the health and social needs of the elderly population. Yet both they and society must grapple with the serious ethical dilemmas posed by the extensive targeting of the new gray market in a heavily consumerist nation.

REFERENCES

American Society on Aging. (1987). *EASE. Education in aging for scientists and engineers.* San Francisco: American Society on Aging.

Beauchamp, D. (1976). Public health as social justice. *Inquiry, 12,* 3–14.

Bergthold, L., Estes, C. L., Alford, R. R., & Villaneuva, T. (1987, August). *Public light and private dark: The privatization of home health services for the elderly.* Paper presented at the American Sociological Association, Chicago, IL.

Binstock, R. H. (1983). The aged as scapegoat. *The Gerontologist, 23,* 136–143.

Binstock, R. H. (1986). Perspectives on measuring hardship: Concepts, dimensions and implications. *The Gerontologist, 26,* 60–62.

Brown, E. R. (1984). Medicare and Medicaid: The process, value and limits of health care reforms. In M. Minkler & C. L. Estes (Eds.), *Readings in the political economy of aging.* New York: Baywood Press.

Butler, R. (1975). *Why survive? Being old in America.* New York: Harper & Row Publishers.

Cole, T. (1988). The spectre of old age: History, politics and culture in an aging America. *Tikkun, 3,* 14–18, 93–95.

Congressional Budget Office. (1988). *Trends in family income: 1970–1986.* Washington, DC: U.S. Government Printing Office.

Consumer Research Center. (1985). *Midlife and beyond. The $800 billion over 50 market.* New York: The Conference Board, Inc.

Dolliver, M. (1988). Personal communication, June 9.

Erikson, E. (1986). *Vital involvement in old age.* New York: W. W. Norton & Company.

Estes, C. L. (1979). *The aging enterprise.* San Francisco: Jossey-Bass Publishers.

Estes, C. L. (1988). Cost containment and the elderly: Conflict or challenge? *Journal of American Geriatric Society, 36,* 68–72.

Fahey, C. (1987, October). *Aging: It has never been this way before.* Presentation to the Annual Meeting of Grantmakers in Aging, Cleveland, Ohio.

Fisher, D. H. (1978). *Growing old in America.* New York: Oxford University Press.

Galbraith, J. K. (1973). *Economics and the public purpose.* New York: Mentor Books.

Hartman, C. (1988). Redesigning America. *Inc.,* (June), 58–74.

Health Care Financing Administration (HCFA). (1985). *Health care financing review: 20 years of Medicare and Medicaid.* (Annual Supplement). Washington, DC: U.S. Government Printing Office.

Hewitt, P. (1986). *A broken promise.* Washington, DC: Americans for Generational Equity.

Kingston, E., Hirshorn, B. A., & Cornman, J. (1986). *Ties that bind: The interdependence of generations in an aging society.* Cabin John, Maryland: Seven Locks Press.

Longman, P. (1987). *Born to pay. The new politics of aging in America.* Boston: Houghton Mifflin.

Lublin, J. (1986, October 22). Costly retirement home market booms, raising concern for the aged. *Wall Street Journal.*

McKnight, J. (1978). Professionalized service and disabling help. In I. Illich, I. K. Zola, J. McKnight, J. Kaplan, & H. Shaiken (Eds.), *Disabling professions.* London: Marion Boyars, Inc.

Miller, S. M. (1976). The political economy of social problems: From the sixties to the seventies. *Social Problems, 24,* 131–141.

Minkler, M. (1986). 'Generational equity' and the new victim blaming: An emerging public policy issue. *International Journal of Health Services, 16,* 539–551.

O'Connor, J. (1973). *The fiscal crisis of the state.* New York: St. Martin's.

Ovrebo, B. (1987). Commodification of care of elders. Paper presented at the Annual Meeting of the American Public Health Association, New Orleans, LA, Oct. 18, 1987.

Perry, M. J. (1987–88). The two hats of corporate America. *Connections* (Dec/Jan), 5–6.

Pifer, A. (1986). The public policy response. In A. Pifer & L. Bronte (Eds.), *Our aging society.* New York: W. W. Norton & Company.

Pollack, R. F. (1987). *On the other side of easy street.* Washington, DC: The Villers Foundation.

Powell, L. A., & Williamson, J. B. (1985). The mass media and the aged. *Social Policy* (Summer), 38–49.

President's Council of Economic Advisers. (1985). *Annual report.* Washington, DC: U.S. Government Printing Office.

Preston, S. (1984). Children and the elderly in the U.S. *Scientific American, 251,* 44–49.

Samuelson, R. J. (1988). The elderly aren't needy. *Newsweek,* March 21, p. 66.

Schlesinger, M. (1988). Personal communication, June 22.

Schlesinger, M., Bentkover, J., Blumenthal, D., Musacchio, R., & Willer, J. (1987). The privatization of health care and physicians' perceptions of access to hospital services. *The Milbank Quarterly, 65,* 25–58.

Swayne, L., & Greco, A. (1987). The portrayal of older Americans in television commercials. *Journal of Advertising, 16,* 47–54.

Tórres-Gil, F. (1988, March). *Interest group politics.* Presentation at the School of Public Health, University of California at Berkeley.

(1988, January). Travelling seniors broaden insurance horizons. *Mature Market Report, 2,* 4.

U.S. Bureau of the Census. (1982). *Current population reports,* Series P-60, No. 134. From *Statistical abstracts of the U.S.: 1982–1983.* Washington, DC: U.S. Government Printing Office.

U.S. Bureau of the Census. (1985). Money income and poverty status of families and persons in the U.S., 1984. *Consumer Income,* Current Population Reports Series, P-60, No. 149 (Aug.), p. 12. Washington, DC: U.S. Government Printing Office.

U.S. Congress, Senate Special Committee on Aging. (1985). *Developments in aging: 1984.* Washington, DC: U.S. Government Printing Office.

U.S. House of Representatives, Select Committee on Aging. (1985). *America's elderly at risk,* (July), p. 20. Washington, DC: U.S. Government Printing Office.

Wang, C. (1988). Lear's magazine 'For the woman who wasn't born yesterday': A critical review. *The Gerontologist, 28,* 600–601.

Discussion Questions for Chapter Ten

1. In his conclusion, Michael Hurd states that in 1935, when Social Security was established, the elderly were not as well off as the nonelderly, but since this is no longer the case, there is little reason for additional intergenerational transfers based purely on age. Others have argued that the social programs that have helped low-income elderly were successful specifically because they were based on age rather than need, thereby acquiring the political support of the middle class necessary to keep them viable. If public programs like Social Security and Medicare were based on need rather than age, would they retain the widespread support they have enjoyed in the past?

2. Meredith Minkler is concerned that the attention given to older consumers by business and industry may lead to distorted images of the financial conditions of older people. Are stereotypical images of older people a necessary part of life in modern society? Is it possible for Americans to attain an appreciation of the diversity among the elderly population in the face of mass market advertising?

CHAPTER ELEVEN

Inequality: Gender and Race

Older people are often described as a single demographic group. Although useful for providing a profile of the elderly, such generalizations overlook the tremendous degree of variation in the older population. The experience of growing old is not the same for everyone. Instead, inequality exists in health, wealth, income, and education. The opportunities to gain these resources and rewards are known as "life chances." Life chances vary according to gender, ethnicity, and social class. Social class differences that existed in youth and middle-age do not disappear when people grow old; in fact, in many instances, they become magnified. The oldest-old (over age 85), females, and nonwhites have the greatest risk of suffering from low incomes, poverty, and inadequate medical care.

Although women's life expectancies are longer than men's, this apparent advantage can sometimes work against them. Outliving their husbands can mean years of loneliness and social isolation for some older women, and because women's financial circumstances are generally less secure than men's, they are often more vulnerable to economic hardship in old age.

Women and men have different work histories. Women's participation in the labor force has been sporadic as they have often left jobs in order to rear children and assume family responsibilities. Women also have worked in less rewarding sectors of the labor force, and this means that they often have had lower paying jobs and have received less adequate retirement pensions (if any at all) and lower Social Security benefits.

In "Gender and Aging: The Demographic Parameters," Beth Hess describes important differences between older men and women in social position and traces these differences to our society's work, family, cultural, and economic systems. Hess argues that these systems are unfavorable to women, and the result is that women are much more likely than men to find themselves in poverty and poor health in old age.

In "Gender, Race, and Class: Beyond the Feminization of Poverty in Later Life," Paula Dressel makes the point that both race and gender must be taken into account in order to reach a complete understanding of inequality in old age. She warns that descriptions of the most disadvantaged people in old age that depend on one single demographic dimension (such as gender) conceal other bases of inequality, particularly race.

Gender and Aging:
The Demographic Parameters

BETH B. HESS

Sociologists have long recognized age and sex as universal bases for the differential distribution of societal resources such as power, prestige, and property. Yet, it is only in the past decade that scholars have asked how the two variables interact to produce a sex/age stratification system (Levy, 1988). But the study of *gender* is more than just including women in the research design—"add women and stir" (Andersen, 1988). Gender is a sociocultural construction rather than an individual trait; it is a property of the social structures within which women and men forge identities and through which they realize their life chances. Gender is less a reflection of immutable natural differences than a means of dividing people into distinct categories (Ferree and Hess, 1987). The gender stratification system is a set of power relationships, at both the macrolevel of social structure and the microlevel of daily interaction and negotiation.

The underlying argument of this essay on gender and aging is that the position of older men and women in the various status hierarchies of our society is a reflection of the importance of gender in past and present systems of work and family and a reflection

of a value system based on an essentially masculine work ethic in which peoples' moral worth is measured by their market value. Thus we find that with the exception of life expectancy, women are relatively disadvantaged along most of the demographic parameters reviewed here. Inequalities between the sexes in old age are not unique to that life stage but are continuous, with patterned inequities throughout the life course. By placing the demographic data already familiar to most of us within the emergent gender/structure paradigm, perhaps we can find fresh insights into the interaction of social systems and the life chances of older Americans.

LIFE EXPECTANCY

The two-and-one-half- to three-year difference between the sexes in life expectancy at birth in 1900 has now grown to almost seven years for whites and slightly over seven for African-Americans (U.S. Bureau of the Census, 1989a) (Table 1). This means that the older population has become overwhelmingly female, although it would have been difficult to tell this from the gerontological

Source: Generations 12 (3), 8–13. Reprinted with permission from *Generations*, 833 Market St., Suite 512, San Francisco CA 94103 and the author. Copyright 1990 by the American Society on Aging.

TABLE 1   Life Expectancy at Birth by Sex & Race 1900–1990, United States (in Years).

	1900		1990	
	Male	*Female*	*Male*	*Female*
White	48.2	51.1	73	78.9
Black	32.5	35.0	68.4	75.6

Sources: National Center for Health Statistics, 1989; U.S. Bureau of the Census, 1989a:153 (middle mortality assumptions).

literature of only a decade ago. Sex ratios, for example, decline from 85 men per 100 women at ages 65 to 69 to under 40 per 100 at age 85-plus. Among centenarians, women outnumber men by over three to one (U.S. Bureau of the Census, 1987).

As noted by Smith (1990), sex differences in mortality are only partially explained by biological risks such as male vulnerability to heart disease and other "killer" conditions. In fact, Verbrugge (1989) estimates that only 10 to 20 percent of sex differences in mortality can be explained by hormonal or genetic factors. Far more important are acquired risks and health habits, in which men and women display very different behaviors, some related to conceptions of masculinity and femininity and others to the locations of men and women in the worlds of work and family.

In general, women benefit from their relatively more healthful lifestyles and their greater exposure to the healthcare system, as well as from declining risks of maternal mortality. To the extent that men adopt better health habits, it is possible that the gender gap in life expectancy will narrow slightly in the next decade (Verbrugge, 1983).

Although life expectancy is often used as an index of "quality of life" when comparing societies as a whole, living long does not necessarily translate into living well. And there is much in the demographic data to suggest that women's longer life exposes them to unfavorable life chances.

FAMILY STATUS & LIVING ARRANGEMENTS

Although most marriage markets are constructed to favor younger brides and older grooms, wives will not necessarily outlive husbands. Throughout the nonindustrialized world, women's life expectancies are lowered by continual childbearing and by customs that reduce access to food and other community resources (Weeks, 1988). It is primarily in developed nations that differential life expectancies yield an excess of women over men at older ages, leading to extended widowhood.

In the United States today, men age 65-plus are almost twice as likely as their female age peers to be married, and women of that age are three-and-a-half times more likely to be widowed (U.S. Bureau of the Census, 1989b) (Table 2). As a consequence, older men are much less likely than older women to live alone or in the home of a relative (U.S. Bureau of the Census, 1989c) (Table 3). But because there are so many more women than men at these ages, the percentages obscure the very wide differences in numbers: 6.5 million women age 65-plus are living alone, compared to fewer than 2 million men (Commonwealth Fund, 1988).

Women living alone are also particularly at risk of being placed in an institution, especially after an illness that makes it impossible for them to maintain an independent household. Disabled men are most likely to be cared for by a spouse (55 percent compared to 18

TABLE 2   Marital Status of Persons 65-Plus Years of Age 1987 (in Percents).

	Men	**Women**
Never married	4.6	5.3
Married, spouse present	75.1	39.8
Married, spouse absent	2.5	1.6
Widowed	13.9	48.7
Divorced	3.9	4.5

Source: U.S. Bureau of the Census, 1989b.

TABLE 3 Living Arrangements of Noninstitutionalized Persons 65-Plus Years of Age, 1987 (in Percents).

	Men		Women	
	Age 65–74	*Age 75+*	*Age 65–74*	*Age 75+*
Family householder	78.3	65.7	10.1	10.1
Nonfamily householder	1.2	0.7	0.7	1.1
Living alone	12.3	21.8	33.5	51.1
Spouse of householder	3.6	2.5	48.3	21.2
With other relative	3.3	7.3	6.4	13.9
With non-relative	1.3	1.2	0.8	1.3
Group quarters	—	0.8	0.2	0.9

Source: U.S. Bureau of the Census, 1989c.

percent for women), and disabled women by an adult child (one-third of caregivers) or other relatives (30 percent). It should not come as a surprise that three out of four nursing home residents are women, three-quarters are over age 80, 84 percent are unmarried, and 93 percent are white (U.S. Senate, 1988). Women of color are the most likely sex/race category to be cared for by a relative.

INCOME

Income adequacy. Older men and women are also located differently on indices of economic well-being (Table 4). When data on income for all Americans 65-plus are lumped together it is easy to see why many younger people might think that the elderly are living quite well. In 1987, median income for a household headed by a person 65-plus was approximately $19,000. Not too bad when compared to the U.S. median of $26,000 for all households, considering that the older householder probably owns the home and has no children to support.

These "overall" numbers, however, mask extremely wide discrepancies between families and unrelated individuals, between male and female householders, and between whites and people of color. While the median for white married couples was $21,000, the comparable figure for a woman living alone was $8,000, slightly higher if she was white, but only $5,000 if African-American (U.S. Bureau of the Census, 1989d). To put it another way, 80 percent of American women age 65-plus today have yearly incomes of under $13,000.

Poverty. Older women and men have both benefited from the dramatic decline in poverty among America's elderly following Social Security Act amendments in the 1960s and 1970s. The poverty rate for those 65 or older has fallen from one in three before 1960 to approximately one in eight today, or slightly under the U.S. total of 13.5 percent. Once more, however, the summary statistic masks striking differences by sex and race. Households headed by older women are almost twice as likely as those headed by older men to have incomes below the poverty threshold of $5,500 for a single person 65-plus and $6,900 for a two-person household (U.S. Bureau of the Census, 1989e).

In 1987, the poverty rate for older white females was 12.5 percent compared to 6.8 percent for white males. For African-Ameri-

TABLE 4 Sources of Income for Persons 65-Plus Years of Age, 1987 (By Percent Reporting Income from Each Source).

	Men	Women
Wages, salary	16.5	9.7
Property, interest	72.7	67.9
Social Security	92.3	94.0
Welfare, public assistance	3.6	7.0
Other pensions	46.0	23.4

Source: Adapted from U.S. Bureau of the Census, 1989d.

cans, the rates were 24.6 percent for men and 40.2 percent for women. For older women living alone as "unrelated individuals," 25 percent of whites and 63 percent of African-Americans fall below the poverty line. Because many of these women are the survivors of poor men, their current status is a continuation of their earlier circumstances; others will be living on Social Security benefits earned many decades earlier when wages were lower (McLanahan et al., 1989). These percentages probably underestimate the true extent of poverty among old women because many will have moved to the residence of an adult child, while some others may have joined the uncounted legions of the homeless.

Sources of income. These differences in income adequacy in old age reflect a number of gender-based conditions present at earlier ages. Because our Social Security system, unlike those of other industrial societies, is uniquely geared to a person's work history, retirement benefits perpetuate earlier work place inequities. Even with the "replacement ratio," or percent of preretirement earnings received as a Social Security benefit, favoring lower earners, income differentials remain vast. Few women or African-Americans of either sex will have had the same number of work years at the same pay level as white men or have held jobs in industries that provide additional pensions.

Although over 90 percent of both older men and women receive Social Security payments, women are twice as likely as men to depend on these as their sole source of income, even though the average monthly benefit for a retired woman worker was roughly 73 percent of a man's ($412 to $567). Men were twice as likely as women to receive a private pension, and only half as likely to receive welfare benefits. Of the 1.5 million recipients of the Supplemental Security Income at the beginning of 1988, 75 percent were women living alone, for whom the

average monthly payment was $182 (U.S. Department of Health and Human Services, 1988).

In terms of a gender stratification model, sex differences in both amount and variety of old-age income can be ascribed to such structural characteristics as the following: (a) the dual economy and split labor markets that explain much of the clustering of male workers in the core sector and female in peripheral firms; (b) wage discrimination within sectors; (c) total dependence of nonemployed married women on husbands' earnings; (d) lack of family allowances, retirement benefit credits, or other public recognition of the economic contribution of homemakers.

HEALTH AND HEALTHCARE

One consequence of the trends already discussed is that the older population, being largely female and increasingly long-lived, will also be characterized by extended chronic illness. This not only places a strain on healthcare facilities designed for the treatment of acute illnesses, but also adds to the spiraling costs of medical treatment. Having left access to healthcare to the whim of the marketplace and having failed to provide adequate financial coverage to either providers or patients, it is no wonder that we now face a "national healthcare crisis."

The "crisis" and its resolutions will have a differential impact by sex. Although men are more likely than women to be able to afford "medigap" insurance, they also spend fewer days in the hospital and have wives who can care for them at home. In comparison, although elderly women are less likely to be hospitalized in any given year, they remain longer in acute-care beds and are more frequently transferred to long-term-care facilities or discharged to the care of an adult child.

In the absence of appropriate and adequate community-based care programs, the independence of older women is more at risk than that of men. It is truly remarkable that so many ill and disabled older persons—over 5 million, mostly women—are able to remain in the community. Community-dwelling women who are ill or disabled are for the most part younger than those in nursing homes and are more likely to have a child upon whom they can rely (U.S. Senate, 1988).

For a family member to care for a severely disabled older relative is time-consuming, emotionally draining, and almost as expensive as professional care. Over 90 percent of this cost is borne by the elderly and their caregivers, over three-quarters of whom are female relatives (Stone et al., 1987). It is all too common that caregivers are themselves approaching old age, and a majority have incomes at or below the national median. While some are full-time labor force participants, others will have to leave paid employment to care for an aged mother. Yet very few public resources are directed to caregivers of the frail elderly, in part because the mystique of "woman as nurturer" allows policymakers to evade responsibility in the name of "traditional family values" (Hess, 1985). Indeed, some political conservatives have suggested that public policy be focused not on providing community-based care or parental leave, but on encouraging higher birth rates lest current low fertility endanger the future supply of caregivers (Wattenberg, 1987). This problem also haunts European nations experiencing a second demographic transition (van de Kaa, 1987). From birth to death, it appears that women's fate is in the hands of lawmakers who bring to their deliberations a perception of reality that is heavily influenced by ingrained notions about gender.

CONCLUSION

Women and men enter old age with vastly different personal and social resources as a result of life course experiences within social structures influenced by gender. This reality is often overlooked by researchers who compare the young-old and old-old without reference to the sex composition of the two populations. Upon closer scrutiny we may likely find the problems of the very old are as much the result of gender as of age. When, as in the 1950s, the elderly poor were male unemployed workers and family heads, a vast extension of old-age benefits was a priority. Today, when the poor elderly are primarily women and people of color, such programs are in danger of further reductions.

Gender issues are also obscured by a well-intentioned use of inclusive language. In their eagerness to avoid sexist terms, authors often refer to a genderless, classless, raceless "older person," thus obscuring the full effects of structured inequality. The life experience of older women is not the same as that of older men, nor is that of persons of color the same as for whites, regardless of gender or age. Because the life course is played out within systems of stratification, sex and race distinctions will remain crucial to understanding the process of aging in any society as long as gender and racial equality remain distant goals.

REFERENCES

Andersen, M., 1988. *Thinking About Women: Sociological Perspectives on Sex and Gender, 2nd Edition*. New York: Macmillan.

Commonwealth Fund Commission on Elderly People Living Alone, 1988. *Aging Alone—Profiles and Projections*. Baltimore, Md.: Commonwealth Fund.

Ferree, M. M. and Hess, B. B., 1987. "Introduction." In B. B. Hess and M. M. Ferree, eds., *Analyzing Gender: A Handbook of Social Science Research*. Newbury Park, Calif: Sage.

Hess, B. B., 1985. "The Withering Away of the Welfare State: Manufactured Crises in Policies for the Aged." Paper presented at the

Annual Meeting of the Eastern Sociological Society, Philadelphia, Pa.

Levy, J. A., 1988. "Intersections of Gender and Aging." *Sociological Quarterly, 29* (4):479–86.

McLanahan, S. S., Sorensen, A. and Watson, D., 1989. "Sex Differences in Poverty, 1950–1980." *Signs 15*(1):102–22.

Smith, David W. E., 1990. The biology of gender and aging. *Generations* Vol. 14 (3):7–11.

Stone, R., Cafferata, G. L. and Stangl, J., 1987. *Caregivers of the Frail Elderly: A National Profile.* Washington, D.C.: U.S. Department of Health and Human Services, National Center for Health Services Research and Health Care Technology Assessment, U.S. Government Printing Office.

U.S. Bureau of the Census, 1987. *America's Gentenarians.* Current Populations Reports, Series P-23, No. 153. Washington, D. C.: U.S. Government Printing Office.

U.S. Bureau of the Census, 1989a. *Projections of the Population by Age, Sex, and Race: 1988–2080.* Current Population Reports, Series P-25, No. 1018. Washington, D.C.: U.S. Government Printing Office.

U.S. Bureau of the Census, 1989b. *Household and Family Characteristics: March 1988.* Current Population Reports, Series P-20, No. 437. Washington, D.C.: U.S. Government Printing Office.

U.S. Bureau of the Census, 1989c. *Marital Status and Living Arrangements: March 1987.* Current Population Reports, Series P-20, No. 433. Washington, D.C.: U.S. Government Printing Office.

U.S. Bureau of the Census, 1989d. *Money Income of Households, Families and Persons in the United States: 1987.* Current Population Reports, Series P-60, No. 162. Washington, D.C.: U.S. Government Printing Office.

U.S. Bureau of the Census, 1989e. *Poverty in the United States: 1987.* Current Population Reports, Series P-60, No. 163. Washington, D.C.: U.S. Government Printing Office.

U.S. Department of Health and Human Services, Social Security Administration, 1988. *Fast Facts and Figures About Social Security.* Washington, D.C.: U.S. Government Printing Office.

U.S. Senate, Special Committee on Aging, 1988. "The Long-Term Care Challenge." *Developments in Aging: 1987.* Vol. 3. Washington, D.C.: U.S. Government Printing Office.

van de Kaa, D. J., 1987. "Europe's Second Demographic Transition." *Population Bulletin* 42(19).

Verbrugge, L. M., 1983. "Women and Men: Mortality and Health of Older People." In M. W. Riley, B. B. Hess and K. Bond, eds., *Aging in Society: Selected Reviews of Recent Research.* Hillsdale, N.J.: Lawrence Erlbaum Associates.

Verbrugge, L. M., 1989. "Pathways of Health and Death." In R. D. Apple, ed., *The History of Women, Health, and Medicine in America.* New York: Garland.

Wattenberg, B., 1987. *The Birth Dearth.* New York: Pharos.

Weeks, J. R., 1988. "The Demography of Islamic Nations," *Population Bulletin* 43(4).

Gender, Race, and Class: Beyond the Feminization of Poverty in Later Life

PAULA L. DRESSEL

Increasing popular and scholarly attention is devoted to the feminization of poverty argument, which is focused both on women in general (Ehrenreich & Piven, 1984; Pearce, 1978) and on older women in particular (Minkler & Stone, 1985; Older Women's League, 1986). Such publications have made important contributions to the understanding of gender inequalities. For example, their discussions of the family wage system, the sexual division of paid and unpaid labor, and the existence of dual labor markets have highlighted structural and ideological bases of different economic opportunities and barriers for men and women. The writings have also provided a wealth of statistics that have documented gender inequalities and described the many social policies that undergird and reproduce different experiences by gender. Political activism by various age-based and feminist advocacy organizations has been fueled by the growing literature on the feminization of poverty across women's lives.

Although acknowledgement is due the contributions made in the literature, a concern is that the feminization of poverty argument in isolation also has the potential for distorting and simplifying the issue of old

age poverty and for being politically divisive. In the subsequent sections, it is maintained that gerontology scholars and activists need to move beyond the feminization of poverty argument to acknowledge how complexly the factors of race and gender are interlocked with the variable of social class in the United States. Emphasis on only one of these factors, gender, seriously misrepresents the phenomenon of poverty in later life, promotes policy and programming decisions whose efficacy is limited, and has the potential to undermine broad-based political coalitions seeking economic equality.

In part, in the arguments which follow, recent criticisms of social science in general and specific criticisms of the feminization of poverty argument in particular (Burnham, 1985) are applied to the topic of the feminization of poverty in later life. Recent general criticisms (Scott, 1982; Zinn et al., 1986) explicated ways in which social science research and theory reflect racism, either by omission (such as through the untested assumption that research findings or theoretical formulations apply similarly across groups) or commission (such as through the use of biased research instruments). Writings on the feminization of poverty in later life revealed

Source: The Gerontologist, 28(2), 177–180. Reprinted with permission from The Gerontological Society of America, Washington, DC 20005. Copyright 1988.

both types of errors: Authors tended to ignore the inextricable link between race and social class in the U.S. and they bolstered their claims through selective utilization and interpretations of statistics.

The purpose herein is not to challenge the argument that patriarchy creates significant burdens for older (as well as younger) women. Nor is it to engage in debate over whether one form of stratification is more oppressive than another or that the experiences of one oppressed group are any more tolerable than those of another. Rather, the point is to argue that racial stratification is also a primary feature of the political economy of the U.S. Once the racialized character of social class is made explicit, it is then possible to show how this feature of the political economy differentiates women with regard to later life experiences and vulnerabilities and renders racial-ethnic men disproportionately vulnerable to poverty in old age. The criticisms and reconceptualizations that follow are offered with the hope that a more complex understanding of poverty in later life will generate more effective efforts to eliminate economic inequalities.

ACKNOWLEDGING RACIAL OPPRESSION

The writings of selected Black political economists (Baron, 1985; Hogan, 1984; Marable, 1983) have detailed the central way in which racial oppression informs the development of the U.S. political economy. Although the forms of oppression have changed historically with transformations of the economic base, shifting from slavery to sharecropping to low-wage labor, racism is nevertheless an ever-present, if increasingly subtle characteristic of U.S. capitalism.

The economic marginality of racial-ethnic groups is built on capital's need for low-wage labor. Ideologies that systematically devalue racial-ethnic groups rationalize their low pay and occupational clustering and legitimate their location at the bottom of the socioeconomic structure. Within a dual labor market racial-ethnic workers are found disproportionately in the peripheral sector, where jobs are characterized by low wages, minimal, if any, fringe benefits, virtually no union protection, and high vulnerability to economic fluctuations (O'Connor, 1973). The limited individual mobility that has occurred for some Black Americans since the 1960s is due largely to government employment and work in Black-owned businesses, both of which are highly vulnerable to economic downturns and to government anti-discrimination initiatives whose level of enforcement varies with political administrations (Collins, 1983).

As a result, racial-ethnic group members, male and female alike, are more susceptible to the experiences of unemployment, underemployment, and unstable low-wage employment than are their white counterparts (U.S. Commission on Civil Rights, 1982). As noted elsewhere (Dressel, 1986), the limited upward mobility that has occurred within the past 2 decades for some members of racial-ethnic groups has not significantly altered inter-group inequalities (Collins, 1983; Oliver & Glick, 1982; U.S. Commission on Civil Rights, 1982). Furthermore, any advances may be short-lived, having most recently been negatively affected by economic decline (Gramlich & Laren, 1984; U.S. Commission on Civil Rights, 1982), judicial action upholding the primacy of seniority over affirmative action (Jacobs & Slawsky, 1984), and budgetary cutbacks for civil rights enforcement by the federal administration (U.S. Commission on Civil Rights, 1981).

In sum, race is a primary stratifier of peoples' lives, as is gender. Recognition of this fact mandates reconceptualization of the bases of poverty in later life. Furthermore, it challenges implicit assumptions of the feminization of poverty argument.

Burnham (1985) cited several problems created by the feminization of poverty argument precisely because it fails to account for the complex interplay of gender, race, and class in the U.S. Among the problems are that it obscures class differences among women, understates racial oppression, and ignores the poverty of Black men. Furthermore, she took issue with what gerontologists have frequently conceptualized as double or triple jeopardy by arguing that oppression is not an additive phenomenon. Rather, because Black women experience the intersection of racism and sexism, their circumstances are qualitatively, not quantitatively, different from those of white women. Although Burnham speaks to the general feminization of poverty argument, her criticisms are applicable to its specialized emphasis on later life as well.

Racial-ethnic women have not been overlooked in most writing on the feminization of poverty in later life. The tendency has been, however, to take the add and stir approach (Anderson, 1983), which leads to race-blind theoretical formulations. That is, what are meant to be general statements about gender and poverty are made, and then, as an afterthought or elaboration, specialized statements about Black (or Hispanic or Native American) women are made. For example, "In 1982, over half of women aged 65 and over with incomes below the poverty level reported fair or poor health. . . . Among poor Black women the proportion approaches two-thirds" (Older Women's League, 1986).

The point here is subtle but critical. In the illustration of the add and stir approach (of which there are many instances in a variety of gerontological publications) it is implied that similar outcomes in women's lives are produced by the one and only factor of patriarchy. Acknowledged but not accounted for are the worse (and sometimes different) conditions faced by racial-ethnic women. Indeed, the differences cannot be accounted for because the model of the feminization of poverty glosses over the

variable of race for heuristic and political purposes. In other words, racial-ethnic women's experiences are forced into the model rather than being utilized to refine or critique the model itself.

The important fact that racial-ethnic men are systematically rendered economically marginal is also ignored in the literature on the feminization of poverty in later life. An insistence on dichotomizing elders by gender alone dismisses fundamental political economic dynamics with respect to race as unimportant for understanding poverty in old age. In other words, the claim that poverty is "feminized" makes patriarchy the primary factor in socioeconomic stratification. A parallel argument could be developed about the "racialization of poverty" in later life (as well as across the life span), thereby claiming white supremacy as the primary motive in socioeconomic stratification. The point, however, is that neither argument integrates the variables of gender, race, and class into a richer appreciation of poverty and economic vulnerability. What is required is movement away from debates in which implicitly, if not explicitly, one form of oppression is posited as more serious, primary, or worthy of attention than another.

RE-EXAMINING STATISTICS

Once race is acknowledged as a central factor in how people fare economically, statistics can be re-examined with race and gender in mind. Upon re-examination, what is frequently found is that white women fare better than Blacks and Hispanics, female or male, and that white family units fare better than other family units.

With gender as a filter for examining statistics it can be argued that elderly women are worse off than their male counterparts. For example, Minkler and Stone (1985) reported that 49% of non-married elder white women compared to 34% of non-married elder white men fell below 125% of the poverty line; similarly, 80% of non-married elder Black women compared to 64% of non-married elder Black men fell below that line. They also found that non-married white women have a median Social Security income of $4490 compared to $5080 for their male counterparts; similarly, non-married Black women receive a median $3050 from Social Security compared to $3710 for their male counterparts. If the analysis stopped here, then the conclusion that ".... elderly women represent ... the single poorest segment of American society ..." (Minkler & Stone, 1985) might be tenable. Now let race be used as a filter for examining the same sets of statistics. What is seen is the non-married Black men are more likely (64%) to fall below 125% of the poverty line than non-married white women (49%); the median income from Social Security for non-married Black men in $3710 compared to $4490 for non-married white women; married white couples receive a median $7670 from Social Security benefits compared to $5920 for their Black counterparts. From this perspective an argument could be made for the racialization of poverty in later life.

But again, the point is not to debate which oppression is worse, gender or race. Rather, it is to argue that the history of the U.S. political economy mandates that analysts take race into account, along with gender, age, and other relevant factors (Palmore & Manton, 1973; Whittington, 1986) when trying to understand economic inequality and impoverishment. Patriarchy and racism are played out similarly in some respects (such as with occupational clustering) but differently in other respects (such as with opportunities for advancement). Consequently, both must be considered for a more complete understanding of economic marginality. Furthermore, because some sources indicated that race-sex patterns of economic marginality characterizing current elders are not substantially different for younger cohorts of workers (U.S. Commission on Civil Rights, 1982), gerontologists cannot assume that each succeeding cohort of elders will have benefitted (or benefitted equally [Palmore & Marton, 1973]) from anti-discrimination legislation, whether directed toward race or gender.

In part the feminization of poverty argument depends in selectively interpreted statistics. Caution must also be employed in terms of what particular statistics are utilized to develop arguments about poverty in later life. For example, if Social Security benefits alone (including SSI) are analyzed, economic differences between Blacks and whites appear considerably smaller than when private pensions and income from assets are also factored in. Schulz (1985) cited data indicating the differential sources of income for Black and white elders, with the latter more likely to be covered by private pensions and to receive income from assets. Although it is true that women's work is also less likely than men's to offer pensions as a fringe benefit, it is also true that white women married to white men have greater access to private pension benefits than Black women married to Black men. Once again, the picture is incomplete unless both race and gender are taken into account.

RETHINKING POLITICAL ACTION

For several reasons the feminization of poverty argument is politically appealing to various age-based and feminist advocacy groups. Most importantly, it directs much-needed attention to the widespread implications of patriarchy for women of all ages. No doubt it has also engendered sympathy for all the poor by being focused on a relatively non-threatening sub-segment, women. Indeed, elderly women may be the least threatening and politically palatable of all possible categories of economically marginal adults. Finally, the feminization of poverty argument underlies attempts to develop links across age, racial-ethnic, and social class strata of women, whose political alliances historically have been problematic (Davis, 1981; Dill, 1983; Hooks, 1981, 1984). To be sure, exposing sexism, generating concern over poverty, and attempting to unite women are all worthy goals. The pursuit of these goals through emphasis on the feminization of poverty, however, has important shortcomings as well.

As suggested earlier, a singular focus on gender and a consequent disregard for the factor of race as another primary stratifier of people has negative latent functions. First, it creates the tendency for fruitless and diversionary debates about which form of oppression is worse. Second, it disregards the fact that some men also are systematically marginalized in the economy, thereby diminishing opportunities for cross-gender coalitions. Third, by failing to paint the full picture of exploitation and discrimination, it impedes a more complex analysis of both welfare state and capitalist contradictions.

Furthermore, whatever concern the feminization of poverty argument generates about the poor will be limited because of the inherent limitations of the analysis. That is, all who are poor will not be embraced by whatever policy and programmatic actions arise from attention to the feminization of poverty. As already noted, racial-ethnic men's systematic marginality is ignored. In addition, there is legitimate concern that only selected groups of impoverished women will become the focus of political interventions, namely downwardly mobile white women who comprise the "nouveau poor" (Ehrenreich & Stallard, 1982). For example, displaced homemaker legislation, in which critical needs of a specific segment of women are addressed, provides politicians with evidence of their concern over the feminization of poverty. It also enables them to sidestep long-entrenched working class and underclass poverty whose alleviation requires far more extensive social change.

Even progressive social democratic groups have purposefully emphasized the female nouveau poor and underplayed race and class issues in efforts to broaden their base of political support (Burnham, 1985). In other words, the feminization of poverty argument has been appropriated to serve limited ends at the expense of other historically dispossessed groups.

Consequently, the feminization of poverty analysis may prove to be a fatal remedy (Sieber, 1981), despite the desire of its proponents to build coalitions among diverse groups of women. That is, they may accomplish just the opposite of their intentions. In the analysis, the failure to acknowledge race as a primary stratifier of peoples' life chances diminishes its utility for Black and other racial-ethnic women; its insistence on the primacy of gender implies the unrealistic expectation that racial-ethnic women separate their political interests from those of racial-ethnic men. Finally, the failure to incorporate class and race into the analysis of women's conditions provides convenient opportunities for politicians to target for intervention those women who are the least fiscally and politically costly. As a result, women may become divided because only some will benefit from the selective targeting of putatively limited resources.

A more complex understanding of old age poverty is needed by gerontology scholars and activists. Single-variable conceptualizations of political economic dynamics (whether based on gender, race, age or any other variable) may serve short-term consciousness-raising functions for select categories of people. But the detail necessary for the formulation of well-targeted social policies cannot be provided (Whittington, 1986). And in the long run, the potential for broadbased political alliances among the heterogeneous people comprising the working poor, the underclass, and other economically vulnerable groups in the U.S. can be undermined. Gerontologists have realized the diversity contained within age groups; likewise they must recognize the diversity within gender groups and move beyond the feminization of poverty argument. To do so does not require abandoning concern over women's disproportionate impoverishment. But it does require abandoning appealing political rhetoric that is built on an incomplete model of the U.S. political economy.

REFERENCES

Anderson, M. L., (1983). *Thinking about women: Sociological and feminist perspectives.* New York: Macmillan.

Baron, H. M. (1985). Racism transformed: The implications of the 1960s. *Review of Radical Political Economics, 17,* 10–33.

Burnham, L. (1985). Has poverty been feminized in Black America? *The Black Scholar, 16,* 14–24.

Collins, S. M. (1983). The making of the Black middle class. *Social Problems, 30,* 369–382.

Davis, A. (1981). *Women, race & class.* New York: Vintage Books.

Dill, B. T. (1983). Race, class, and gender: Prospects for an all-inclusive sisterhood. *Feminist Studies, 9,* 131–150.

Dressel, P. (1986). Civil rights, affirmative action, and the aged of the future: Will life chances be different for Blacks, Hispanics, and women? An overview of the issues. *The Gerontologist, 26,* 128–131.

Ehrenreich, B., & Piven, F. F. (1984). The feminization of poverty. *Dissent, 31,* 162–170.

Ehrenreich, G., & Stallard, K. (1982). The nouveau poor. *Ms. 11,* 217–224.

Gramlick, E. M., & Laren, D. S. (1984). How widespread are income losses in a recession? In D. L. Bawden (Ed.), *The social contract revisited: Aims and outcomes of President Reagan's social welfare policy.* Washington, DC: Urban Institute Press.

Hogan, L. (1984). *Principles of Black political economy.* Boston: Routledge & Kegan Paul.

Hooks, B. (1981). *Ain't I a woman: Black women and feminism.* Boston: South End Press.

Hooks, B. (1984). *Feminist theory from margin to center.* Boston: South End Press.

Jacobs, J., & Slawsky, N. (1984). Seniority vs. minority. *Atlanta Journal and Constitution, 35,* 1D, 7D.

Marable, M. (1983). *How capitalism underdeveloped Black America.* Boston: South End Press.

Minkler, M., & Stone, R. (1985). The feminization of poverty and older women. *The Gerontologist, 25,* 351–357.

O'Connor, J. (1973). *The fiscal crisis of the state.* New York: St. Martin's Press.

Older Women's League (1986). *Report on the status of midlife and older women.* Washington, DC: Older Women's League.

Oliver, M. L., & Glick, M. A. (1982). An analysis of the new orthodoxy on Black mobility. *Social Problems, 29,* 511–523.

Palmore, E. B., & Manton, K. (1973). Ageism compared to racism and sexism. *Journal of Gerontology, 28,* 363–369.

Pearce, D. (1978). The feminization of poverty: Women, work, and welfare. *Urban and Social Change Review, 11,* 28–36.

Schulz, J. H. (1985). *The economics of aging.* Third edition. Belmont, CA: Wadsworth.

Scott, P. B. (1982). Debunking Sapphire: Toward a non-racist and non-sexist social science. In G. T. Hull, P. B. Scott, & B. Smith (Eds.), *But some of us are brave.* Old Westbury, NY: Feminist Press.

Sieber, S. (1981). *Fatal remedies: The ironies of social intervention.* New York: Plenum.

U.S. Commission on Civil Rights (1981). *Civil rights: A national, not a special interest.* Washington, DC: U.S. Commission on Civil Rights.

U.S. Commission on Civil Rights (1982). *Unemployment and under-employment among Blacks, Hispanics, and women.* Clearinghouse Publication 74, Washington, DC: U.S. Commission on Civil Rights.

Whittington, Frank (1986). Personal communication.

Zinn, M. B., Cannon, L. W., Higginbotham, E., & Dill, B. T. (1986). The costs of exclusionary practices in women's studies. *Signs, 11,* 290–303.

Discussion Questions for Chapter Eleven

1. According to Hess, gender is a property of social structure rather than an individual trait. What society-wide changes are necessary in order to reduce or eliminate gender inequality in aging?

2. Hess criticizes research that uses the "add and stir" approach with respect to women. Dressel takes Hess's argument a step further by criticizing researchers of the feminization of poverty for using the add and stir approach with respect to race. Dressel also claims that the experiences of gender, racial-ethnic, and social class groups differ not only quantitatively but qualitatively as well. What are some ways that the experiences of these groups differ? What kinds of studies would be necessary to avoid the pitfalls of the "add and stir" approach in order to reveal subtle bases of inequality among elders?

CHAPTER TWELVE

Death and Dying

In premodern societies, infectious and communicable diseases were widespread. These illnesses most often struck the young. With modernization came improvements in personal hygiene and public sanitation, as well as developments in medical science that have reduced the incidence of death from such causes. The main causes of death are now chronic conditions such as heart disease, cancer, and stroke, which tend to afflict people when they are older. Consequently, life expectancies have increased.

The advances in modern medicine that have contributed to a lengthening of life have also prolonged the process of death. Modern medicine can often keep people alive long past the time they would have otherwise died. Life-sustaining technology has created situations and raised questions that were unthinkable only a few years ago. Sometimes people remain alive while suffering from chronic diseases for which there is no cure. Others can be kept alive knowing of their impending death or with the prospect of deteriorating mental capacities. Still others remain alive but unconscious or in a persistent vegetative state. Our culture has no agreed upon or easy answers to questions involving appropriate use of life-sustaining technology, suicide, euthanasia, and ultimately the meaning of life and death (Robinson, 1990).

Several highly publicized cases have brought the question of appropriate use of life-sustaining technology to the public's attention. A particularly prominent one was the case of Nancy Cruzan, a 32-year-old woman who was involved in an automobile accident. Cruzan lay in a persistent vegetative state for seven years while her parents and physician requested permission to disconnect her nutrition and hydration tube. In June 1990, the United States Supreme Court upheld a Missouri Supreme Court's decision denying the request of Cruzan's family and physician. The court ruled against their request to "pull the plug" because of lack of sufficient evidence that Cruzan had expressed this decision when she was competent. Had she done so using an appropriate legal document, her family or physician would have had a constitutional right to order cessation of life-sustaining medical treatment (Robinson, 1990).

As a result of the Cruzan decision, Congress passed the Federal Patient Self-Determination Act of 1990. This law requires hospitals to ask adult inpatients if they have an "advance directive" for health care. If the patient does not, the hospital must offer the patient the appropriate information. Two main kinds of advanced directives are the Living Will and the Durable Power of Attorney for Health Care. Living Wills allow persons to state in advance their wishes regarding the use of medical treatment should they become unable to express themselves. A Durable Power of Attorney for Health Care allows a person to appoint someone else to make health care decisions in case he or she is incapacitated.

By reaffirming the patient's constitutional right to refuse medical treatment that could save his or her life, the courts have, in effect, confirmed the legality of voluntary, passive euthanasia. Nevertheless, many questions remain about the legitimacy of various ways of ending human life, including suicide and active euthanasia.

In 1991, the Hemlock Society published a best-selling suicide manual by Derek Humphry called *Final Exit.* Aimed at people suffering from terminal illnesses, Humphry's book is an effort to promote the Hemlock Society's goal of "death with dignity." Skeptics complain that the book may legitimize suicide by people who are not terminally ill but who are depressed. They point to studies showing that most older people who commit suicide are physically healthy.

Suicide rates among older Americans are remarkably high. Following a 30 year decline, rates among the older population made a sharp upturn during the 1980s, increasing by 21 percent between 1980 and 1986 (Meehan et al., 1991). Suicide among elderly persons still outpaces the frequently reported and alarmingly high rate among teenagers and young adults. In 1990, for example, the suicide rate among persons aged 75 to 85 was nearly twice as high as it was among 15- to 24-year-old persons.

The ability to commit suicide has always existed, but recently the question of whether it should be legal for a physician to assist a suicide has entered the public debate. In November 1991, Washington state voters defeated a citizen initiative that would have legalized physician-assisted suicide of terminally ill but mentally competent persons. In June 1990, a retired pathologist named Jack Kevorkian helped a 54-year-old woman diagnosed with Alzheimer's disease commit suicide in his specially equipped van parked in a public campground in suburban Detroit. In November 1991, Kevorkian assisted two other women in commiting suicide, but this time a Michigan court ordered Kevorkian to stand trial on two counts of murder. The charges were dropped due to a court ruling that Michigan law did not prohibit helping someone commit suicide. In February 1993, Michigan passed a law making it a felony to assist in a suicide. In May 1993, Kevorkian was arrested under the new law for assisting a 16th suicide.

In "Death-Making in the Human Services" Sandra Meucci criticizes the right-to-die movement, claiming that it reflects the social devaluation of dependent persons. She argues that the notion of death with dignity has its psychological roots in the fear of dependency and that it pressures older people to "die on time." Meucci cites parallels between the right-to-die movement and the Nazi eugenics movement, claiming that both promote the science of improving the "qualities of the human race" and are concerned with the cost of keeping highly dependent people alive.

One of the reasons so much attention is focused on questions about choosing death is that today many more people die in hospitals surrounded by life-sustaining technology than in decades past. Generally, hospitals are much more effective in treating persons with acute, curable diseases than chronic, terminal illnesses. Consequently, leaders of the hospice movement do not believe that hospitals are the appropriate setting for a person dying from an incurable illness. Death is not solely a medical phenomenon, and medical technology is limited in what it can do for the fatally ill patient. While strongly supporting pain control, hospices work neither to terminate the dying process through active euthanasia nor to delay impending death by the use of medical technology. Instead, hospices aim to assist dying persons and their loved ones by having them participate in the process of dying in a comfortable environment, preferably at home. The selection by Judith Levy, "The Hospice in the Context of an Aging Society," describes the social forces of an aging society that have led to the emergence of the American hospice movement. Levy explains both how hospice services meet the needs of an aging population and the potential problems such services are expected to face in the future.

The death of a loved one is a painful experience, and it precipitates a major adjustment in life. Because of longer life expectancies, old people are most likely to experience bereavement intimately through the death of a spouse or a contemporary. Bereavement is associated with psychological depression, morbidity (illness), and mortality. In "Grief in Old Age: A Review of the Literature," Christopher Nigel Fasey reviews the literature on grief and describes the effect grief has on older people.

REFERENCES

Robinson, Barry. (1990). Questions of life and death: No easy answers. *Ageing International, 17,* 27–35.

Meehan, Patrick J., Saltzman, L. E., and Sattin, R. W. (1991). Suicides among older United States residents: Epidemiologic characteristics and trends. *American Journal of Public Health, 81,* 1198–1200.

Death-Making in the Human Services

SANDRA MEUCCI

Euthanasia, the practice of inducing a painless death for reasons assumed to be merciful, is gaining popular support all over the world. A 1986 report by researcher Dr. Samuel Waller states that support for euthanasia has increased during the past 20 years, particularly in Australia, the Netherlands (where support rose from 30 to 70 percent between 1972 and 1984), and in Canada (where support rose from 45 to 65 percent between 1968 and 1984). In Denmark, almost 90 percent of the younger population approves of active euthanasia and, since 1975, approval rates have not been below 70 percent of any of the countries surveyed by Dr. Waller.[1]

In California, a 1983 statewide poll revealed that 95 percent of the population approved of active euthanasia.[2] California is the home of Derek Humphrey, who assisted his wife in suicide (some may call it homicide), published a suicide manual, *Let Me Die Before I Wake*, which sold 70,000 before going into a fourth edition, and founded the Hemlock Society that promotes assisted suicide. Similar organizations are Concern for the Dying, which has 160,000 members, and the Society for the Right to Die, with a membership of 147,000 people.[3] A "World Federation of Societies for the Right to Die" was founded in 1980 and included member groups in 18 countries by 1986.[4] In that year, a committee of the American Medical Association endorsed mercy killings by physicians,[5] and in September of 1987 the American Bar Association, under the guidance of the Hemlock Society, proposed legislation to legalize the practice of euthanasia.[6]

The notion of the benevolence of euthanasia has found its way into an array of supportive literature in recent years. *Euthanasia Review*, the Hemlock Society publication, James Rachel's *The End of Life: Euthanasia and Mortality*, Frohock's *Special Care: Medical Decisions at the Beginning of Life*, and Shelp's *Born to Die* are among the most widely read in the United States, while Dr. Peiter Admiraal's *Justifiable Euthanasia: A Manual for the Medical Profession* is popular in the Netherlands where between 6,000 and 10,000 patients per year are being "euthanized."[7]

Discourse on ethics among medical professionals has focused on distinctions between "real life" and "mere biological life" in an attempt to posit the correct "quality of life" quotient and thereby determine who is fit to live and who to die. To understand the growing popularity of mercy killing, one must examine not only the psychological and sociocultural dimensions of this expanding social trend, but its historical antecedents as well. Only then can we begin to fathom

Source: Social Policy, 18 (Winter), 17–20. Reprinted with permission from Social Policy Corporation, New York, NY. Copyright 1988.

the implications of euthanasia on what is likely to emerge as a new social policy.

FEARS OF DEPENDENCY

The best known example of the case for mercy killing in recent times is that of Karen Ann Quinlan, who lay comatose in the fetal position in a hospital for seven years, unresponsive, yet alive. The media manipulation of her situation, characterized by constant reports of her lack of progress, the mounting costs of her medical care, and the continuing suffering of her parents, capitalized on our fears of being useless and burdensome so powerfully that there were few who didn't silently or actively join in the clamor to "pull the plug."

The media were able to sensationalize the Quinlan case to create public sympathy for and identification with her family, and to catalyze fear of becoming dependent upon artificial means of support. The public's fear of slipping into a similar state engendered by this media coverage, grew in such a way as to be entirely out of proportion with the likelihood of such an event. There are approximately 10,000 people in the United States who are currently in a comatose condition.[8] While it is true that some are attached to life-support systems (intravenous feeding tubes, respirators), many of these people will recover and not degenerate into what can only be called a macabre condition of having no vital life signs but being hooked up to machines nonetheless. We are left to wonder, if it were not for the worship of modern technology would these scenarios even occur?

Our current fixation on the notion of "death with dignity" has psychological roots in the fear of being completely dependent on others. This fear is particularly acute in contemporary American society where adult dependency stands in sharp contrast to the prevailing sociocultural ethos, i.e., unbridled expression of personal choice, individualism over collectivism, the commodification of re-lationships reducing them to "exchange" or "use" value,[9] and the requirement of our capitalist political economy for competitive relationships among people. These social mores, perhaps deriving from the values of our ancestral pioneers with their stoicism and determination, are nonetheless antithetical to the more caring and supportive values upon which society must rely in order to assimilate its weaker and inherently more vulnerable members. Both a moral and psychological measure of society can be made by an examination of the treatment of its weakest members. Emerging is a consensus of opinion that people would rather die than become highly dependent upon others.

This helps explain why more and more people are drawing up what is called living wills, believing that they should have assisted suicides when they can no longer take independent care of themselves. The increasing pressure on older people in America to die on time is demonstrated by the New York Society for the Right to Die newsletter, published in the summer of 1986, in which the promotion of "death with dignity" was suggested by the following facts:

> There are about 3,000,000 Americans over 85 today and the number is rapidly growing. Some 8,000 facilities house 800,000 people whose average age is 84. Most suffer from more than one ailment and require help in activities in daily living. About half of this number are mentally or decision-making impaired to some degree.

Why did the Society for the Right to Die decide to offer its members this information? Might it have been to show how much merciful work there is yet to be done? No matter how well intended, the inevitable effect of such "helpful" information is to increase the dread of dependent people, and to erode the barriers of conscience in society in general, paving the way for the legally unchallenged killing of disabled or helpless old people.

Our fear of dependency and belief that we are entitled to unrestrained freedom in pursuit of individual liberty causes us to want to rid ourselves of those who mirror our own dependency or place high demands upon our capacity for care-giving. This is true even though we may simultaneously feel love for those of whom we wish to be rid. The unpleasant reality of the wish to rid ourselves of dependents, standing in contrast to the higher and more noble ideals consciously professed, is thus apt to be repressed into the unconscious.

AN HISTORICAL PARALLEL

In a recent book, Daniel Callahan of the Hasting Center asserts:

A goal of the extension of life combined with an insatiable desire for improvement in health—a long and simultaneously better life for the elderly—is a recipe for monomania and bottomless spending. By the year 2040, 45% of all health expenditures will be on the elderly. . . . it makes no sense to improve the medical care for the elderly while some 35 million Americans have no health insurance at all.[10]

The Daniel Callahans, the Derek Humphreys, and other gurus of the death-with-dignity persuasion are arguing that some identifiable groups of people do not deserve to live. They are the forerunners of a cost-benefit-to-the-federal-government social policy that is the spectre of the national eugenics program the Nazis adopted to deal with people they called "useless eaters."[11]

Whether or not it is explicitly stated, there is a prevailing notion that no comparisons can be made to the atrocities committed by the SS in Nazi Germany, since to do so would only serve to denigrate the unique significance of the suffering of the Nazi victims. However, the comparison of this cost-benefit thinking in social service fields with the emergence of the eugenics movement in Nazi Germany is profoundly instructive.

Both are eugenics programs, promoting the science of improving the qualities of the human race, and both begin by citing examples of the cost of keeping highly dependent people alive. In 1920 Dr. Alfred Hoche, considered by some to be the architect of the Nazi euthanasia program, stressed the heavy cost involved in operating institutions for the mentally retarded. In a lamentation strikingly similar to modern arguments against improving the level of care for the elderly, Hoche stated:

The average expenditure per idiot person is 1,300 marks. If we add up all the idiots, they number 20,000 to 30,000. If we take an average span of 60 years, we can calculate how much capital in the form of food, clothing, energy, and national resources is deducted for unproductive purposes.[12]

In *The Nazi Doctors: Medical Killings and the Psychology of Genocide*, Robert Lifton cites:

The killing of children which ended in the entire Nazi "euthanasia" program began simply with a petition to allow the "mercy killing" (gnadentod, literally "mercy death") of an infant named Knaur, who was born blind with one leg missing, and apparently an "idiot".[13]

Nat Hentoff, writing in New York's *Village Voice*, speaks about the similarities between the Nazi program and the current perils of the aged and handicapped people in the United States. He points out:

The Germans at least had the good grace to feel queasy at the early stage—in the presence of the killers of the old, unfit, the schizophrenic, the too expensive to keep alive. And people in the towns, said the appellate judge in Frankfurt-am-Main in 1939, were disquieted by the question of whether old folk who had worked hard all their lives and maybe had come into their dotage were also being liquidated. There was talk that homes for the aged were to be cleaned out too.[14]

In 1942, more than 2,450 mentally ill patients were taken by the Nazis from two psychiatric hospitals and shot to death on the outskirts of Riga, Latvia. Nazi communiques of the time said nothing of what happened to the victims. One hospital doctor disclosed that he had been instructed to write on the sick lists simply "evacuated by the SS." By 1945, 300,000 handicapped people had been killed by the Nazis.[15]

POLICY IMPLICATIONS

The analogy of the Nazi eugenics program is pertinent because it is illustrative of the manner by which social service programs serve *institutional* purposes (defining, segregating, depersonalizing, institutionalizing, and objectifying people believed to be inferior or sick) that veer from shared sympathy on the part of individuals to cost-calculating government policy.

There is a distinct similarity between euphemisms used to conceal the Nazi program of annihilation of dependent populations and language now used in human services. The use of basic resuscitation, antibiotics, intravenous feeding as life support of a sick, handicapped, or elderly person is called "heroic measures." The voluntary withholding of food by parents to a newborn with Down Syndrome so it starves to death is called a "courageous decision." This infant should otherwise be expected to lead a relatively normal life, if exposed to a developmentally challenging environment.[16]

There are subconscious resemblances in these inversions of meaning to the "altruistic" propaganda of the Nazis. (The actual killing of physically handicapped and mentally ill patients was coordinated by an organization known as "The Charitable Foundation for Institutional Care.")[17] The "right to die" evolves into a license to kill.

Hand in glove with these institutional attitudes leading toward a social policy of euthanasia are institutional practices to control and minimize the resistance of dependent or helpless people.

- Regular use of "aversive therapies," sometimes called "negative reinforcement": shocks given with implements such as shock wands, buzzer pants, or other devices; use of cattle prods; confinement, isolation, and seclusion for days or weeks, called "time out."
- "Placement" of people into segregated environments to live, work, and recreate, calling this practice "specialized programming."
- Use of restraining "holds," soft or hard ties, confinement into inadequate spaces such as cage-like beds.
- Administration of high dosage levels and combinations of drugs with debilitating effects in the name of "medication."
- Restriction of access to belongings, money, food, significant others, and the outside world by making it necessary to earn one's rights vis-à-vis "token economy."
- Use of surveillance systems called "behavior monitoring" or "behavior charting": cameras connected to video screens in central control units, sound detectors, and body devices to measure "escape," "acting out," or other undesirable behavior.

These practices, which seem to originate in empathetic, well-regulated environments of care for dependent people, are, in fact, disguises for the policy-level establishment of eugenics and genocide practiced by service institutions with the tacit consent of the public. A Syracuse University professor and contemporary theoretician, Wolf Wolfensberger, witnessed the social trends that resulted in the Nazi euthanasia program. He uses the term "death making" to describe our current human services situation. Death-making means any action or pattern of actions that directly or indirectly hastens the death of a person or group, and that covers overt, direct killing as well as concealed or indirect killing—the kind that takes a long time to accomplish and may be difficult to trace. The people devalued by society are much more likely to be the victims of direct forms of death-making than people held in conventional social esteem. Dr. Wolfensberger estimates conservatively that every year 200,000 handicapped and afflicted people in the United States die as a direct result of what is done to them.[18]

This claim is corroborated by numerous independent chronicles of abuse. *Institutions, Etc.,* an investigative human service journal, regularly reports the deaths that occur as a result of neglect and abuse in nursing homes, rehabilitation facilities, and prisons. In 1984, this journal carried the results of a nine-month investigation of the California Community Care System.

The committee inspected 22,000 licensed homes housing 151,000 children and adults who were diagnosed as mentally retarded or disordered, elderly, or otherwise handicapped. These "community care facilities" are licensed by the state, and cost $583 million per year in public funds, with an additional $181 million in private payments. The commission found unspeakable abuse and neglect, daily beatings, sexual abuses, people left lying in their own excrement for days, people denied medical services, cases of malnourishment, and some documented cases of murder. Many victims had contracted gangrene, resulting in the loss of limbs. Some died from the effects of bedsores; still others were cleaned up by being taken outside and hosed down.[19]

This chronicle of death-hastening in California is not an isolated account.[20] In May 1983, the Public Broadcasting Service aired an hour-long program on children's psychiatric institutions. It claimed that at least 500 mental patients die every year under questionable circumstances. Death-making in human services exists in a matrix of consent since human services is reflective of the values of the culture. For example, the

death rate from prescribed psychoactive drugs is now as high as 100,000 per year in the "free" population.[21] Even more chilling is the fact that vulnerable people, virtually incarcerated as human services clients, are now being given much higher doses of mind- and behavior-altering drugs than is a drug user.

Often the drugs given to people considered mentally incompetent have side effects that are irreversible such as tardive dyskinesia.[22] It could be said that the term "side effects" is a euphemism for the real effects of the drugs, including a cause of death. The state of torpor induced by overmedication is, in fact, the real intent of drugging, making the client too weak to resist other coercive treatment and too confused to appear believable when disclosing the truth of his or her condition to outsiders such as evaluators, inspectors, advocates, or family.

There is a history in the United States of the disenfranchisement and disabling of people in the name of client or patient care. In the late 1800s and early 1900s, castration was used as a cure for masturbation with people who were mentally retarded. By 1914, sterilization was used not only for eugenic reasons but for punishment as well. The U.S. courts held that such measures constituted neither cruel nor unusual punishment. In cases of vasectomy, it was believed that the retarded did not require an anesthetic since all that was being done was to cut the vas deferens.[23]

This history of abuse grew directly out of the policies of the major mental health organizations of the day. In 1802, the president of the American Medical Association on Mental Deficiency declared,

> Of all dependent classes, there are none that so entirely drain the social and financial life of the body politic as the imbecile, unless it be its close associate, the epileptic.[24]

This is the social psychological setting in which the dehumanization and the abuse and death-making of dependent populations continue to be carried out today. The origin of the German eugenics movement, the "science" of improving the qualities of the human race, likewise began in the devaluation of dependent people to achieve Aryan supremacy. A sober examination of recent U.S. immigration restrictions, the purported "tax burden" of our elders on the Social Security system, and the social policies of prevention and segregation of mentally retarded people reveals the degree to which people are increasingly socially devalued.

Genocide is apt to be established as policy, no matter its semantic disguises, if there exists sufficient intensity of social devaluation of a victim group and sufficient stresses upon a perpetrator group, according to Dr. Wolfsberger. The outbreak of genocide will be preceded by the death-imaging of potential victims and will be accompanied by permission from moral authorities.[25]

There is evidence that the technology and management skills used in the German death camps were first perfected in institutions for people who were handicapped and described as incurably ill, whose lives were "devoid of value."[26] It is clear that Americans fail to acknowledge the possibility that death-making in this country has reached genocidal proportions.

Only 40 years ago, were scenes such as two grey buses with painted windows picking up residents at an institution in Stetten and transferring them to a crematorium in a castle in Grafeneck. As we grow older and memory fades, our steps grow shorter, and having only our children upon whom to rely, reared as they were in a culture of narcissism and nihilism, will we too be faced with those grey buses with windows painted at our own death's door?

NOTES

1. "Death-Making Again," *Syracuse University Training Institute Publication Series*, vol. 6, no. 6 (April 1987), p. 5.
2. Jenifer Donovan, "The Right to Die," *San Francisco Chronicle* (February 15, 1986), p. 21.
3. Anne Fadiman, "The Liberation of Lolly and Gvonky," *Life* (December 1986), p. 82.
4. "Death Making Again," p. 10.
5. Nat Hentoff, "The Death Doctors," *Village Voice* (September 8, 1987), p. 34.
6. "Evening News," KPFA, Berkeley, Calif. (September 8, 1987).
7. M. Nesirky, "Dutch AIDS Victims Find a Quiet End to Suffering," *Toronto Star* (May 17, 1987), pp. H1, H3.
8. R. Steinbrook, "Man in Coma Is Focus of Right-to-Die Controversy," *Louisville Courier Journal* (February 18, 1987), p. 1.
9. Russell Jacoby, "Narcissism and the Crisis of Capitalism," *Telos* (Summer 1980), pp. 63–64. Jacoby suggests, "All relations are appraised with an eye on the psychic bank account; spendings must balance earnings. Psychic bankruptcy is

avoided by retrenching, cutting off losing investments: the old, sick, and so on."
10. Daniel Callahan, *Setting Limits: Medical Goals in an Aging Society* (New York: Simon and Schuster, 1987).
11. Karl Binding and Alfred Hoche, *The Release of the Destruction of Life Devoid of Value* (Leipzig, Germany: Felix Mainer, 1920), compiled by Robert L. Sassone (Santa Ana: A Quality Life Paperback, 1975).
12. Ibid.
13. Robert J. Lifton, *The Nazi Doctors: Medical Killing and the Psychology of Genocide* (New York: Basic Books, 1986).
14. Hentoff, p. 34. His account is based on Leo Alexander, "Medical Services Under Dictatorship," *New England Journal of Medicine*, vol. 24 (July 14, 1949). Dr. Alexander served with the Office of the Chief Counsel for War Crimes in Nuremberg.
15. Jewish Black Book Committee, *The Black Book: The Nazi Crimes Against the Jewish People* (New York: Duell, Sloan and Pearce, 1946), p. 329.

16. Richard Kearsley, *Iatrogenic Retardation: A Syndrome of Learned Incompetence* (Medford: Tufts Center for Behavioral Pediatrics and Infant Development, New England Medical Center Hospital, 1974). Kearsley postulates that the procedures used to monitor the development of slow infants are inadequate and misleading, yet are generally accepted diagnostic measures used to draw inferences about children's levels of mental abilities; they influence not only the manner in which the child is treated, but also future care. Treatment consisting of parenting practices modified to accommodate a lowered level of expectation of a child's mental abilities likely will engender developmental retardation. The direct result of the manner in which such children are diagnosed by professionals and treated by parents are thus physician-caused, or "iatrogenic." Case studies of such children receiving normal parenting practices in highly developmentally challenging environments suggest that iatrogenic retardation can be reversed and is probably entirely preventable.

17. Alexander, pp. 39–40.

18. Wolf Wolfensberger, *The New Genocide of Handicapped and Afflicted People* (Syracuse: Training Institute for Human Service Planning, Leadership and Change Agentry, 1987), p. 71.

19. Lindsay Hayes et al., "California's Defenseless Citizens," *Institutions, Etc.*, vol. 7, no. 3 (1984), pp. 7–9.

20. In 1985, there was a 12.8 percent death rate among clients of psychiatric centers in New York State; the state itself admitted that 400 of them were under dubious circumstances. In November of 1981, the *Chicago Sun Times* ran an investigation of Illinois mental institutions, where in the previous year period, over 300 residents had died in five mental institutions. Some of these deaths occurred under peculiar circumstances: Some victims were under restraint, some froze to death, some got mangled on nearby railroad tracks, some drowned in rivers, some appear to have been victims of violence, and there were signs suggesting that residents may have been tortured and slain by personnel on the scene. Between 1973 and 1976, there were 1,285 residents of state-run facilities in California who were reported to have died, and questionable administration of drugs was implicated in at least 120 of these (*Institutions, Etc.*, vol. 4, no. 1, 1981, pp. 6–7). Approximately 14 percent of all deaths occurring in special care nurseries in 1982 are associated with withholding treatment and nourishment of impaired newborns. See William Brennan, *The Abortion Holocaust: Today's Final Solution* (St. Louis: Landmark Press, 1983). Based on the U.S. Center for Disease Control figures on the birthrate and the incidence of impairments, it is estimated that 82 children are born in the U.S. each day who are at risk of being killed. Cited in J. Manning and J. C. Blattner, *Death in the Nursery: The Secret Crime of Infanticide* (Ann Arbor: Servant Books, 1984). The New York State Commission on Quality Care for the Mentally Disabled reported that, of the roughly 2,700 deaths of residents in state mental health and mental retardation facilities during a 12-month period in 1984–85, 23 percent were due to "unusual or unnatural circumstances and indicated possible problems in care and treatment." See "Miscellaneous Death-Making News," *Training Institute Publication Series*, vol. 5, no. 6 (April/June 1986), p. 36.

21. Richard Hughes and Robert Brewin, *The Tranquilizing of America* (New York: Harcourt, Brace, Jovanovich, Inc., 1979).

22. Ibid.

23. S. D. Risley, "Is Assexualization Ever Justifiable in the Case of Imbecile Children?" *Journal of Psycho-Aesthetics*, vol. 9 (1905), pp. 92–98.

24. Wolf Wolfensberger, *The Origin and Nature of Our Institutional Models* (Syracuse: Human Policy Press, 1975).

25. Wolfensberger, 1987.

26. Wilhelm Tuefel, *Das Schloss Der Barmherzigkeit* (Stuttgart: Quell-Verlag, 1960).

The Hospice in the Context of an Aging Society

JUDITH A. LEVY

With the declines in mortality and fertility rates of the 20th century, the demographic profile of the United States emerged as that of an "aging society" where most people survive childhood and the middle years to die in old age (Pifer and Bronte 1986). The demands of meeting the needs of an increasingly older population have placed enormous strain on American social institutions and raised serious questions about their ability to adapt (Palmer and Gould 1986). Pressure to reorganize the delivery of medical care and social services to the fatally ill, most of whom are older adults, has become particularly salient because of rising costs (Callahan 1987) and perceived insensitivity to patient and family needs (Greer et al. 1986). Terminal care, therefore, provides a useful focus for studying the context and processes of institutional change in response to a growing aged population.

In following such an agenda, this article examines how the demographic forces of an aging society contributed to the development of the American hospice movement and institutionalization of the hospice concept as a new form of terminal care. Based on a philosophy that developed in England, the term "hospice" denotes both a social move-ment and a coordinated system of home and inpatient services designed to alleviate the physical, emotional, social, and economic stresses of terminal illness and family bereavement. In examining hospice in terms of both forms of collective action, the following analysis is organized around three questions: What are the social forces of an aging society that led to the emergence of the hospice movement in the United States? How do hospice services coincide with the needs of an aging population? What challenges do the pressures of an increasingly aging society pose for the future of the hospice concept? The article draws upon previous research and a comprehensive review of the literature.

SOCIAL FORCES THAT EVOKED THE HOSPICE MOVEMENT

Social movements emerge when people's lives are affected by some form of structural change or transformation in society (Garner 1972). As Mills (1959) observes, a person loses his job, a marriage breaks up, or someone dies, and these circumstances merely reflect the personal troubles of the parties involved. But when unemployment soars,

Source: Journal of Aging Studies, 3(4), 385–399. Reprinted with permission from JAI Press Inc., Greenwich, CT. Copyright 1989.

divorce rates drastically climb, or death takes place through famine or war, we have the makings of a public issue that can fuel collective action. The hospice movement represents one such instance.

The hospice movement draws its momentum from the demographic transition and technological change that followed the close of the nineteenth century (Lofland 1978). In 1900, most deaths occurred from infectious disease with pneumonia, influenza, tuberculosis, and gastroenteritis heading the list (McKinlay and McKinlay 1977). By the last quarter of the twentieth century, however, the epidemiological profile had changed. As a result of public health measures, improved nutrition, institution of occupational health standards, and the pharmacological advances of the twenties and thirties, infectious disease yielded to heart disease, cancer, and other chronic disorders as the major cause of death. This demographic transition created a new set of societal problems affecting the fatally ill, their families, and the network of interlocking institutions that comprise the American health care system. Collective response to the personal and institutional stress of contemporary dying led to the emergence of the hospice movement and pressure to alter existing provisions of terminal care. We can understand this process better by examining the sources of strain in an aging society that led to collective action.

The Modern Terminal Care Consumer

The human life course consists of a series of bio-socially defined stages in which dying represents the final stage (Marshall 1980). Each stage has its own set of expectations, role responsibilities, and normative prescriptions for people to follow. In societies where death occurs primarily through infectious disease or catastrophic events such as famine or war, the period of the life course spent in dying typically is short, entered suddenly, and comes with little warning. Scant biological time may be available to tie up the loose ends of living or bring one's life to anticipated closure. Investments in the social career of dying tend to be low and the content of the role is restricted by the brief time available for role performance and elaboration (Levy 1982a).

Change in patterns of mortality and morbidity during the first quarter of the twentieth century altered the existing temporal phasing of the life course by expanding the period in which the average person dies. In contrast to the swift and often sudden death characteristic of infectious disease, chronic disorders often involve a lingering trajectory that may be further prolonged through medical science (Glaser and Strauss 1965). Early detection programs and improved diagnostic techniques also can lengthen the dying period by informing people of a fatal illness long before the symptoms are subjectively felt. Following the disclosure of a terminal illness, the individual is thrust into a new phase of living based upon an altered biological and social status that may last for months or even years.

Considerable research points to the enormous strains of confronting impending death (see Riley 1983). Like members of all cultures, people in an aging society face the difficult problem of finding meaning in personal finitude and death (Marshall 1980). When compared to death from infectious disease, however, the person dying of a degenerative disorder typically has a longer period to contemplate dying and what it means to be dead.

Because having a foreseeable death is the primary criterion that biosocially locates a person in the final period of the life course, "dying" can become a master status that overrides all other designates through which people are recognized and embedded in their social networks. As a fatal illness progresses, waning strength can force the individual to withdraw from the work force, a primary source of personal identity in industrial societies. Normal family roles may need to be relinquished at the very time when the person is struggling to counter a diminished social self. Meanwhile, family and friends may shun the dying out of discomfort with that person's altered status or to avoid the burden of caregiving (Charmaz 1980). Anticipatory grief over the death can also result in people socially treating the terminally ill as if they already are dead (Sudnow 1967).

Because of the negative properties associated with the social role of dying, the challenge for a person with a terminal illness is to find ways to live out what can be a lengthy period of the life course in a manner that is personally satisfying and which preserves a positive self-image. This need is well illustrated by an anecdote related by a nurse who was caring for a young man dying of cancer (Levy 1982a, p. 47). Thinking that he might be anxious about death, she tried to reassure her patient that palliative methods would be used to make his dying more comfortable and that he would have someone with him when the time came. Rather than feeling comforted, the young man turned angrily to her and said, "Nobody has to help me die, I can do that for myself. Just help me live until I get to die."

These words offer an example of what Mills meant when he wrote of the individualized experience of personal trouble. Beyond receiving medication and comfort, the young man also wanted to remain socially anchored in everyday life. When others in society also have similar feelings or experiences, personal trouble can give way to public concern and action. It was this collective response that helped fuel the hospice movement.

At the cultural level, evidence of a shared search for meaningful dying can be seen in the recent popularity in the United States of films and books that deal with terminal illness. Death has always been a topic

guaranteed to sell newspapers, magazines, and movies. Indeed, the staples of prime time television—murder, war, suicide, and accidental killings—attest to an audience's appetite for stories of violent and impersonal death (Arlen 1978). With the prolonged fatal illnesses of an aging society, however, a new market has emerged for media accounts that deal with the social aspects of *dying* in contrast to *death* (Levy 1982a). Recent films over the last two decades, for example, include the dying of a young woman in both "Love Story" and "Terms of Endearment", an athlete's demise in "Brian's Song", and the gentle death of an adolescent with a disfiguring disease in "Mask". However imperfect or stylized by Hollywood imagery these films may be, they reflect a cultural resource through which the general public learns about and seeks meaning in chronic illness and dying (Kastenbaum 1979).

Perhaps not by happenstance, at least one of the primary roles in each of these media portrayals involves a friend or family member struggling to cope with the impending death. In an aging society, the increased longevity of the human life course has given rise to a dramatic prolongation of the social linkages between family members (Riley 1985). This circumstance has extended both the number and intensity of kinship relations that a person potentially can have (Hagestad 1986). In doing so, it has also increased the number of opportunities in which individuals confront the death of someone with whom they have shared a considerable portion of life.

Hospice emerged out of personal experiences and in partial response to the needs of family members to have their loved ones die more comfortably and to have some relief from the burdens of family care (Abel 1986). As we will see shortly, concerned family members were joined in this effort by health care providers with similar concerns. Such advocacy for change led by people other than the terminally ill was necessary for hospice movement formation, as those who are dying typically lack the biological time or physical strength needed to forge or maintain a movement on their own behalf.

In this regard, what has been described so far is a series of societal stresses, brought about by demographic changes in mortality and morbidity, that led to a generalized perception that "something ought to be done". Studies of social movements suggest that social strain is a necessary element for collective action. Nonetheless, Dahrendorf (1958) also observes that strain is an inherent and ubiquitous problem within any social structure. Thus, social movement theorists have come to recognize that other factors must also be present for a movement to ignite. One of these elements is an emergent world view or ideology that can unite people together in joint purpose and provide a direction for advocates to follow (Garner 1972). Within hospice, the emergence of such a shared vision can be traced to the writings and personal experience of a growing cadre of clinical professionals with an interest in redefining the values and structure of terminal care.

Ideology

Kastenbaum (1979) notes that the first collective awareness of the dysfunctions of modern terminal care began in the 1950s. Epidemiologically, this decade corresponds to the period in which the prevalence of heart disease, cancer, and stroke began its rapid climb (see McKinlay and McKinlay 1977). Although a few health care professionals and other clinicians were aware of their experience with the dying, it wasn't until Feifel published an edited volume, *The Meaning of Death* in 1959, that the professional community began to actively discuss the social circumstances surrounding institutional death and its negative affect on the patient and family.

Death as a social problem gained public awareness approximately ten years later

with the publication in 1968 of *On Death and Dying* by Kubler-Ross. Contained within this volume, and the subsequent writings produced by her and others following the same philosophy, are a set of clinically-based guidelines for patients, families, and providers for managing the problematic and social roles of contemporary death. These prescriptions include methods for maintaining the psychosocial well-being of the dying person and bringing an organized closure to the life that is about to end. The clinical goal, underlying much of this body of literature and research, is to provide a supportive physical and social environment where people can "die with dignity" (Koff 1980).

Such public and professional concern with bringing greater dignity to contemporary death in the United States found its philosophical counterpart in England where Cicely Saunders, a British physician, instituted a new model of palliative care at St. Christopher's Hospice in London. Here, a homelike environment was created within the structure of an institutional setting and patients were kept largely free of pain through new techniques of palliative care (Paradis and Cummings 1986). By reorganizing the mode and setting through which terminal care was delivered, Saunders' methods gave the dying greater control over their daily existence and the opportunity to live more fully before death. Taken together, Kubler-Ross provided the ideology and Saunders provided a set of practical techniques through which a social movement directed toward improving terminal care in the United States could be mobilized (Torrens 1985). This influence was to support the emergence and growth of the American hospice movement in three ways (Levy 1982a).

First, the concept of death with dignity provided in ideological base for the movement by specifying a set of values and objectives around which to build collective action.

Koff (1980, p. 24) summarizes this ideal by noting:

> Enabling a person to die with dignity includes taking whatever measures reduce or eliminate pain and discomfort and always treating the total person not his symptoms. These practices provide security and build trust by focusing on the patient's needs and treating each person as a special and unique being . . . Permitting death with dignity also means enabling the person and those important to him to practice rituals or to behave in ways in keeping with their culture and/or lifestyle.

Second, the death with dignity philosophy also provided leadership and support from occupations and professionals strategically situated within the medical system. Hospice is a reform movement that took place *within* medicine and not from *outside* medicine as is popularly believed. At the start of the movement, it was common in volunteer training sessions and hospice literature to routinely point to organized medicine as an enemy to be changed (Abel 1986). This practice served the important function of promoting solidarity by providing a common antagonist against which hospice advocates could rally (Levy 1982a). Yet, close inspection of movement organizers and supporters show that many of the first hospice programs in the United States were located in hospitals and other medical care institutions (Paradis and Cummings 1986). Moreover, many of its earliest advocates were doctors, nurses, and other professionals in the health care sector (Levy 1982b).

The death with dignity philosophy approach also provided a third advantage to hospice growth by linking the movement to existing extra movement networks and institutions sharing a similar philosophy. By building alliances with groups such as Reach for Recovery or Widows Helping Widows, the movement broadened its organiza-tional base to gain added support (Abel 1986). Such linkages and overlaps provide access to communication and other resources which otherwise might be unattainable (Garner 1972).

Institutional Support

In any social movement, outside interests such as government or special interest groups can facilitate or impede collective actions (Garner 1972). Almost from the start, hospice received support from a number of extra movement constituencies including health insurers and government (Levy 1982a; Paradis and Cummings 1986). Concern had grown over the rapidly rising cost of health care, much of which was being spent on older people in the last year of life (see Callahan 1987). Hospice care was seen as a low-cost substitute for traditional life-extending treatment (Tames 1987). Its concept of a home death also coincided with a growing health care industry (Abel 1986). Moreover, its humane methods attracted financial help from a number of foundations and philanthropies such as the American Cancer Society, the United Way, and the Robert Wood Johnson Foundation. Thus, hospice was perceived by many as one of the vehicles through which the medical system could be transformed (Paradis and Cummings 1986).

In sum, the hospice movement can be seen as a collective response to strain in the personal and institutional arrangements of an aging society resulting from demographic change. Shifts in patterns of disease produced the necessary ingredients for a movement: a constituency, ideology, resources, and tentative support from powerful interests within society. By 1984, over 1500 hospice programs existed in the United States, attesting to the movement's growing popularity and successful mobilization (McCann 1985). That hospice has become a growing component of the American health care system raises a salient question: How does the hospice concept ameliorate the societal strains that led to its emergence?

CONGRUENCE BETWEEN HOSPICE SERVICES AND THE NEEDS OF AN AGING SOCIETY

Congruence between the perceived benefits of the hospice philosophy and the needs of an aging society can be assessed by examining its application to meeting the problems of social institutions. Since exploration of all societal institutions is beyond the scope of a single article, the following discussion is limited to one societal institution—that of the family. The family offers a particularly rich opportunity to gain insight as hospice services target the patient and family as a single unit of care (Koff 1980). Moreover, the plight of patients and families dealing with an impersonal medical system and the crises associated with death and dying was an important force in sparking the movement (Levy 1982b; Greer et al. 1986). The following discourse focuses on congruency between the hospice service functions and the needs of dying people and families. These functions, which are carried out by both nursing staff and volunteers can be summarized as: constructing supportive networks, mediating interaction, providing a structure of meaning, aiding in biographical work, and serving as a "midwife" in the dying process (see Levy 1987).

Constructing Supportive Networks

As noted earlier, the high prevalence of chronic illness in an aging society creates a great burden of care for the person's family and friends. Hospice attempts to ameliorate this stress by providing volunteers to help the patient and family with simple nursing and homemaking chores (Abel 1986). In ad-

dition, hospice programs typically admit only those patients for whom there is a family member or close friend willing to serve as caregiver. If no one is available, the hospice may press a neighbor or acquaintance into service. From a hospice survival standpoint, this requirement lowers organization risk by assuring that someone outside the hospice takes final responsibility for the patient's care and legal status (Levy 1986). It also has the latent function of creating a caregiver where none might otherwise exist. In creating the social role of "hospice caregiver", the hospice specifies and reinforces a set of role relations and responsibilities that bind the provider and recipient of care.

Mediating Interaction

When a family member is dying, the processes and final outcome typically disrupt the interlocking patterns of responsibility and habit that families establish in their daily lives. Death and dying call for a reassignment of family roles and, eventually, adjustment to life without the person who is dead. Hospice volunteers aid in the coping process by babysitting young children and performing routine chores to give family members time together to make these changes before and after the death. Such mediation of relationships also extends to encouraging successful interaction with the many institutions that intersect with a person's death. For example, volunteers may drive the person to see their lawyer or help the family with funeral arrangements (Koff 1980).

Considerable evidence also suggests that many people feel uncomfortable being around someone who is dying, a circumstance than can result in stilted interactions or avoidance (Sudnow 1967). Hospice volunteers help to mediate this discomfort by encouraging frank discussions about death. Host hospice programs stipulate that prospective clients must be told that they are dying as a condition for admission. This rule, which reinforces what Glaser and Strauss (1965) refer to as an "open awareness context," forces the person to confront the reality of impending death and clears the way for further talk.

Providing Structures of Meaning

Hospice also addresses the psychological needs of an aging society by providing patients and families with a supportive context in which to search for and, perhaps, find the meanings of life and death (Ingles 1980). Personal awareness of finitude begins early in life and intensifies as aging brings the specter of death closer (Marshall 1980). Hospice volunteers aid in the search for meaning by encouraging the person and family to face the inevitability of death and find comfort in one another's support. The "death with dignity" philosophy aids in this work by providing volunteers and staff with a structure of meaning around which to organize their work and which they, in turn, pass on to the patient and family.

Biographical Work

When people experience an alteration of personal identity through serious illness, they or their families may engage in what Gubrium and Lynott (1985) refer to as "biographical work" to preserve or construct a satisfying identity despite the stigma associated with dying. Hospice volunteers aid in this process by helping to construct a supportive environment where people can live out the final days of their lives within the context of their former self. For example, volunteers organize birthday parties and other special events so that these experiences remain part of their patients' lives (Koff 1980; Zimmerman 1986). Great emphasis is placed in hospice services on helping people maintain personal contacts and continue activities they enjoyed before their illness.

Serving as Midwives for the Process of Dying

Death and dying as social phenomena are highly visible in traditional societies where death care and burial preparations typically are located within the family or immediate community and where high mortality rates force repeated confrontations with death (Marshall 1980). In those societies, death roles are well known and are learned within the context and flow of daily life. Such socialization for death and death care, however, does not have an equal counterpart in industrial societies. Here, death and care for the dying typically takes place in formal settings, and family, friends and the individual may have little experience with directly managing the realities of death.

To ameliorate this problem, hospice programs provide volunteers with special training that prepares them to work with the dying person and family in managing the common psychological and physiological problems likely to occur with a home death (Levy 1982a). In this, hospice volunteers function much like midwives for the dying by overseeing the physical and social properties of a hospice death. Their role can be as technically important and emotionally supportive to the family as the traditional role of midwives in birthing.

In sum, when the various functions of hospice volunteers in relation to the family are considered, we find considerable congruency between hospice goals and the personal and institutional needs of an aging society. Like all forms of emergent culture, however, hospice undoubtedly embodies certain inherent properties that are socially dysfunctional. Within the social sciences, theoretical rebellion against the structural/functionalist contention that "what exists must work" has taught us to consider the troublesome and problematic elements of emergent culture in addition to its positive contributions. With the exception of the National Hospice Project, few systematic evaluations of hospice have taken place (Greer and Mor 1985). Nonetheless, the challenge of hospice's survival and success as a reform movement rests heavily upon discovering both the concept's weaknesses and considerable strengths. Given the hospice operates within the complex and constantly changing environment of an aging society, what are the challenges to the hospice movement that lie ahead?

CHALLENGES FOR THE FUTURE

In predicting the future of social movements, many researchers have turned to a natural history approach to explain the process through which movements emerge and reach their final form. While no two movements are alike, the life cycle approach provides a valuable framework for predicting the success and future of the movement as well as for understanding its internal organization. Mauss (1975) summarizes the stage model approach by pointing to five phases that make up the natural history of a social movement: (1) incipiency; (2) coalescence; (3) institutionalization; (4) fragmentation; and (5) demise.

Widespread public and private acceptance of the hospice concept marked the successful movement of hospice into the institutional phase. Hospice programs are a common component of many hospitals and other forms of health care facilities. The U.S. government has underwritten the availability of hospice services through Medicare reimbursement (Fraser 1985). Other third-party payers have made similar commitments.

With institutionalization, the stresses on a movement change. Pressures for accountability emerge in the wake of the movement having successfully advanced its claim. For hospice, these challenges can be observed by examining three major areas where prob-

lems occur: ideology, service, and accommodation. Each of these bears closer inspection.

Ideology

Hospice emerged as a service alternative to traditional forms of terminal care that encourage the often futile use of medical measures to prolong life, at considerable pain and loss of dignity (Levy 1982a). In contrast to the medical model's emphasis on heroic intervention, the death with dignity philosophy incorporates the concept of a "natural death" without the use of painful life-sustaining measures (Koff 1980). Consequently, for ideological reasons, most hospices only admit patients for whom further curative therapies appear useless and who make the decision to forego further extraordinary treatment.

Because of the concept's emphasis on natural death, hospice advocates have been sensitive to the importance of dispelling medical and public opinion that hospices represent death houses. Opposition to the hospice concept is often expressed in the fear that widespread acceptance of hospice principles will lead to reduced measures in fighting disease and forestalling death (Gibson 1984). Within hospice itself, both lay and professionals frequently struggle with ethical questions of how to support the decision of the dying to forego further treatment while, at the same time, protecting their rights to obtain a full life. These ideological dilemmas offer some of the knottiest challenges for hospice volunteers and staff (Levy and Gordon 1987).

Part of the ambiguity stems from the difficulties of identifying the appropriate level where the potential for medical cure has been exhausted (Lynn and Osterweis 1985). Spontaneous or therapeutically induced remission, which are common with some forms of cancer, complicate predictions of life expectancy making it difficult to decide when to discontinue treatment (Zimmerman 1986). Too early a decision to discontinue treatment shortens a patient's life needlessly.

One solution to the dilemma requires patients to try all curative options before admission into a hospice program (Lynn 1985). This policy, however, denies potential patients the right to stop treatment at will. Moreover, some patients may prefer death to undergoing successful but highly painful and distressing intervention.

Iatrogenic complications during hospice care pose another set of dilemmas. For example, creating a supportive environment where patients can die with dignity entails the use of analgesics and similar forms of symptom control. Use of these measures raises serious ethical questions of whether or not caregivers are justified in providing palliative treatment (Lynn and Osterweis 1985). Such a quandary can arise when the doses of morphine required to ease a patient's pain makes him or her susceptible to pneumonia or decreased breathing (Gibson 1984).

Similarly, in the course of treatment, a hospice patient may fall and fracture a hip or react adversely to a drug. Such unexpected treatment complications occurred after the decision was made to forego further active treatment. In such instances, certain questions arise (Lynn and Osterweis 1985). Should iatrogenic complications be treated to prolong life, while other physical conditions are not? Or do these iatrogenic complications become part of a natural death and the patient allowed to die? Not only is the patient's well-being at stake, but also the caregivers'. Families have a great need to know that they are doing the right thing, and watching a loved one die of a treatable condition can lead to guilt and remorse (Crane 1975).

Meanwhile, the line that separates palliative methods from curative treatment is frequently blurred. With antitumor treatment, for example, it is often difficult to decide at what point pain controlled through radiation crosses over into extraordinary measures (Zimmerman 1986). In such instances, comfort may dictate using measures considered inappropriate for patients experiencing lesser pain.

In short, the ideological decisions in hospice are complex and require constant vigilance to protect patient rights. Hospice programs are typically sensitive to such problems and much of patient review sessions involve such delicate decision-making (Levy and Gordon 1987). Meanwhile, despite attempts to clarify what hospice entails, many patients and families enter hospice not knowing what is involved (Levy 1982a). Part of the difficulty of communicating this reality stems from the general lack of consensus with which essential terms are defined (Lynn 1985). Terms such as "imminent" or "extraordinary" mean different things to different people. Also, the hospice concept is still new to many people, and a patient's or family's first encounter with the concept may come as part of the death.

Service

Despite the rapid growth of two hospice organizations, hospice programs still serve only a small proportion of the two million people who die in the United States each year (Lynn and Osterweis 1985). Most of those served are cancer patients (Zimmerman 1986). Because of its success in providing emotional support and palliative comfort care, pressure now exists to extend the availability of hospice services to a wider population and to other diseases.

In the United States, hospices are most likely to serve white, middle or working class patients from reasonably intact families where there are sufficient resources for someone to devote considerable time to caregiving (Lynn 1985). Because most hospices require patients to have a full-time caregiver, individuals without families or other resources are unlikely to qualify for care (Greer and Mor 1985). Moreover, individuals who request care are often screened for having those psychosocial characteristics that would make them successful patients. These policies tend to exclude a number of potential populations that are not currently served.

AIDS patients constitute one underserved population, even in geographic areas where transmission of the virus is prevalent (Tames 1987). Because people with AIDS could benefit greatly from emotional support and palliation, they make good candidates for hospice services (Pollatsek 1987). Also, many public health experts perceive that hospice may be a cost-effective mode of treatment—a judgment that may result in pressure on hospice to accept more people with AIDS.

Accepting AIDS patients into a hospice program, however, carries considerable organizational risk (Tames 1987). People with AIDS who are close to death have often run out of insurance benefits. Meeting their medical needs can seriously drain a hospice's resources. Moreover, volunteers find that caring for AIDS patients is difficult because of the social stigma and emotional crises that these patients experience. As an infectious disorder, AIDS also carries risk of contagion. A number of hospices have reported community opposition to admitting AIDS patients into the same program that serves individuals with other diseases. Fear exists that the disease may spread to patients already weakened by their conditions and to family members.

Children represent a second large, underserved population. In an aging society where death is associated with the old, death in childhood takes on special sadness. Historically, many hospices have been reluctant to care for dying children because of the added emotional stress and special problems that caring for babies and young people represents (Lazarus 1985). Yet, families need the respite care that hospice offers and, like

adults, children benefit from the psychological, spiritual, and social aspects of the hospice approach (Corr and Corr 1985).

A third large underserved population is comprised of society's oldest old, those 75 years of age or older, most of whom in an aging society are likely to be women. A large proportion of these women are likely to be living without a spouse who can serve as a caregiver during terminal illness. Moreover, they are less likely to have been gainfully employed to the same extent as men throughout their life course. Consequently, they tend to have lower retirement benefits and fewer resources in old age than do men of similar social class (Longino 1989). The absence of someone to serve as caregiver along with an increase in the number of special problems possibly explain why so few women past their seventies receive hospice care.

Accommodation

Unlike social movements of the past, which were financed solely by contributions from their members, today's successful social movements typically draw upon business, foundations, and the government for their resources (Garner 1972). As a result, most social movement organizations must accommodate to the rules and regulations of those from whom they seek help. The danger with this mode of movement financing is that it easily leads to organizational goal displacement through programs redefining their goals and objectives to meet funding priorities or reimbursement guidelines. Over time, program values become isomorphic with those of the institutions and organizations from which they gain their resources (DiMaggio and Powell 1983).

In this regard, Medicare reimbursement is expected to have a strong impact on the structure and quality of the delivery of future hospice services. Already, signs exist that hospice programs may be "creaming" pools of potential patients from those individuals most likely to fit the Medicare reimbursement profile (Torrens 1985). The best candidates include patients who are unlikely to require extensive resource investments (Tehan 1985). Estimating prognosis is important since programs cannot discharge patients who become costly or outlive their benefits (Pitorak 1985). Meanwhile, Medicare stipulates that the majority of benefits must be delivered in the home, a condition that encourages early hospital discharge despite the need for further hospitalization (Corless 1985).

Medicare and other forms of third-party reimbursement have also had an enormous impact on the organization and philosophy of hospices themselves. Third-party payment requires hospice personnel to supply detailed records, follow complex legal regulations, and be ready to defend the treatment they deliver (Dorang 1982). Qualifying for benefits also requires considerable growth and investment in professional staff, a condition likely to undermine the movement's initial emphasis upon lay participation (Abel 1986). At the same time, programs that deviate from the single, expensive model for licensing and Hospice Certification must forego this form of financial aid (Fraser et al 1986). The result has been a movement toward increased homogeneity and less innovation among programs (Paradis and Cummings 1986). Incentives for programmatic improvement have been reduced by the establishment of minimum standards of operation and restrictions imposed by licensing and certification (Tehan 1985).

Hospice reimbursements recognize the dilemmas and irony that third-party reimbursements pose. Under intense pressure to comply or forego the benefit, many hospices were reluctant to qualify for benefits as they perceived that these changes would have undesirable effects (Fraser 1985). Programs that decline to qualify, however, may find themselves pushed out of the service market by certified hospices carrying the Medicare "stamp of approval" (Fraser et al. 1986).

Such restriction and change in the movement appears inevitable from a social movement perspective. If the hospice movement follows the typical life course of a social movement, the success of the institutional stage will be followed by fragmentation and demise of the movement itself (Mauss 1975). Buoyed by success, members and the general public will lose interest and turn to other pursuits. Conflict may erupt among remaining members and factions over ideological issues, direction of the movement, power, and social control. Cooptation may occur as stronger forces outside the movement assume increasingly greater control over its institutionalized form. References to "hospice" as a social movement will cease as the term becomes synonymous with a component of the health care industry.

In the 1970s, hospice founders worried keenly about the concept's continued survival. This worry disappeared when institutionalization through Medicare guaranteed hospice programs a position in the American health care system. As hospice matures and responds to the forces of an aging society over the next decade, a new question concerning its future has emerged. Advocates and other interested parties no longer need ask: "Will the hospice concept survive?" The answer clearly is yes, but in what form?

REFERENCES

Abel, E. K. 1986. "The Hospice Movement: Institutionalizing Innovation." *International Journal of Health Services* 16:71–85.

Arlen, M. J. 1978. "The Air." Pp. 63–67 in *Death and Dying: Challenge and Change,* edited by R. Fulton, E. Markusen, G. Owen and J. L. Scheiber. New York: Addison-Wes- ley.

Callahan, D. D. 1987. *Setting Limits: Medical Goals in an Aging Society*. New York: Simon and Schuster.

Charmaz, K. 1980. *The Social Reality of Death*. Reading, MA: Addison-Wesley.

Corless, I. B. 1985. "Implications of the New Hospice Legislation and the Accompanying Regulations." *Nursing Clinics of North America* 20:281–298.

Corr, C. A. and D. M. Corr. 1985. *Hospice Approaches to Pediatric Care*. New York: Springer.

Crane, D. 1975. *The Sanctity of Social Life: Physicians' Treatment of Critically Ill Patients*. Park Avenue, NY: Russell Sage Foundation.

Dahrendorf, R. 1958. "Toward a Theory of Social Conflict." *The Journal of Social Conflict* 11:170–183.

DiMaggio, P. J. and W. Powell. 1983. "The Iron Cage Revisited: Institutional Isomorphism and Collective Rationalization in Organizational Fields." *American Sociological Review* 48:147–160.

Dorang, E. S. 1982. "A Record-Keeping Method for Hospice-Related Volunteers." *Rehabilitation Nursing* (Sept–Oct):17–19

Feifel, H. 1959. *The Meaning of Death*. New York: McGraw Hill.

Fraser, I. 1985. "Medicare Reimbursement for Hospice Care: Ethical and Policy Implications of Cost-Containment Strategies." *Journal of Health Politics, Policy and Law* 10:565–578.

Fraser, I., T. Koontz and W. C. Moran. 1986. "Medicare Reimbursement for Hospice Care: An Approach for Analyzing Cost Consequences." *Inquiry* 23:141–153.

Garner, R. A. 1972. *Social Movements in America*. Chicago: Rand McNally.

Gibson, D. E. 1984. "Hospice: Morality and Economics." *The Gerontologist* 24:4–8.

Glaser, B. G. and A. L. Strauss. 1965. *Awareness of Dying*. Chicago: Aldine.

Greer, D. S. and V. Mor. 1985. "How Medicare is Altering the Hospice Movement." *Hastings Center Report* (October):5–9.

Greer, D. S., V. Mor, J. N. Morris, S. Sherwood, D. Kidder and H. Birnbaum. 1986. "An Alternative in Terminal Care: Results of the National Hospice Study." *Journal of Chronic Disease* 39:9–26.

Gubrium, J. F. and R. J. Lynott. 1985. "Alzheimer's Disease as Biographical Work." Pp. 349–367 in *Social Bonds in Later Life: Aging and Interdependence*, edited by W. A. Peterson and J. Quadagno. Beverly Hills, CA: Sage.

Hagestad, G. O. 1986. "The Aging Society as a Context for Family Life." *Daedalus* 115:119–139.

Ingles, T. 1980. "St. Christopher's Hospice." Pp. 47–63 in *A Hospice Handbook*, edited by M. Hamilton and H. Reid. Grand Rapids, MI: William B. Erdmanns.

Kastenbaum, R. 1979. "Healthy Dying: A Paradoxical Quest Continues." *Journal of Social Issues* 35:185–206.

Koff, T. H. 1980. *Hospice: A Caring Community*. Cambridge, MA: Winthrop.

Kubler-Ross, E. 1968. *On Death and Dying*. New York: Macmillan.

Lazarus, K. H. 1985. "Developing a Pediatric Hospice: Organizational Dynamics." Pp. 147–171 in *Hospice Handbook: A Guide for Managers and Planners*, edited by L. F. Paradis. Rockville, MD: Aspen Systems Corp.

Levy, J. A. 1982a. *The Hospice Movement: Creating New Social Worlds for the Dying*. Unpublished Ph.D. dissertation, Northwestern University.

Levy, J. A. 1982b. "The Staging of Negotiations Between Hospice and Medical Institutions." *Urban Life* 11:293–312.

Levy, J. A. 1986. "Mistakes at Work: Building on the Insights of Everett C. Hughes." Paper presented at the annual meeting of the Society for the Study of Social Problems, New York, New York.

Levy, J. A. 1987. "A Life Course Perspective on Hospice and the Family." *Marriage and Family Review* 11:39–64.

Levy, J. A. and A. Gordon. 1987. "Stress and Burn-Out in the Social World of Hospice." *The Hospice Journal* 3:29–51.

Lofland, L. 1978. *The Craft of Dying*. Beverly Hills, CA: Sage.

Longino, C. F. Jr. 1989. "A Population Profile of Very Old Men and Women in the United States." *The Sociological Quarterly* 29: 559–564.

Lynn, J. 1985. "Ethics in Hospice Care." Pp. 303–324 in *Hospice Handbook: A Guide for Managers and Planners*, edited by L. F. Paradis. Rockville, MD: Aspen Systems Corp.

Lynn, J. and M. Osterweis. 1985. "Ethical Issues Arising in Hospice Care." Pp. 199–219 in *Hospice Programs and Public Policy*, edited by P. R. Torrens. Chicago: American Hospital Publishing, Inc.

Marshall, V. W. 1980. *Last Chapters: A Sociology of Death and Dying*. Belmont, CA: Wadsworth.

Mauss, A. L. 1975. *Social Problems as Social Movements*. Philadelphia: J. B. Lippincott.

McCann, B. A. 1985. *Hospice Project Report*. Chicago: Joint Commission on Accreditation of Hospitals.

McKinlay, J. B. and S. M. McKinlay. 1977. "The Questionable Contribution of Medical Measures to the Decline of Mortality in the United States in the Twentieth Century." *Milbank Memorial Fund Quarterly/Health and Society* Summer:405–428.

Mills, C. W. 1959. *The Sociological Imagination*. New York: Oxford University Press.

Palmer, J. L. and S. G. Gould. 1986. "The Economic Consequences of an Aging Society." *Daedalus* 115:295–323.

Paradis, L. F. and S. B. Cummings. 1986. "The Evolution in Hospice in America Toward Organizational Homogeneity." *Journal of Health and Social Behavior* 27:370–386.

Pifer, A. and L. Bronte. 1986. "Introduction: Squaring the Pyramid." *Daedalus* 115:1–11.

Pitorak, E. F. 1985. "Establishing a Medicare-Certified Inpatient Unit." *Nursing Clinics of North America* 20:311–326.

Pollatsek, J. 1987. "Hospice for AIDS Patients— Break Down Barriers and Accept AIDS Patients." *The American Journal of Hospice Care* 4:9–10.

Riley, M. W. 1985. "Women, Men, and the Lengthening Life Course." Pp. 333–347 in *Gender and the Life Course*, edited by A. S. Rossi. New York: Aldine.

Riley, J. W. Jr., 1983. "Dying and the Meaning of Death: Sociological Inquiries." Pp. 191–216 in *Annual Review of Sociology, Vol. IX*. Palo Alto, CA: Annual Reviews Inc.

Sudnow, D. 1967. *Passing On: The Social Organization of Dying*. Englewood Cliffs, NJ: Prentice Hall.

Tames, S. 1987. "Medicare, Medicaid Coverage." In *Perspectives* (a supplement to Medicine and Health). Washington: McGraw Hill.

Tehan, C. 1985. "Has Success Spoiled Hospice?" *Hastings Center Report* 15:10–13.

Torrens, P. R. 1985. "Development of Special Care Programs for the Dying: A Brief History." Pp. 3–29 in *Hospice Programs and Public Policy*, edited by P. R. Torrens. Chicago: American Hospital Publishing, Inc.

Zimmerman, J. M. 1986. *Hospice: Complete Care for the Terminally Ill*. Baltimore-Munich: Urban & Schwarzenberg.

Grief in Old Age:
A Review of the Literature

CHRISTOPHER NIGEL FASEY

INTRODUCTION

Grief and mourning are the human responses to major loss. The usual cause is bereavement of a close relative or friend but a similar response has been described as a reaction to loss of limb or breast, loss of status and loss of fortune (Parkes, 1972). Most societies have evolved formalized rituals and ceremonies to support grieving individuals which recognize the need to deal with the immediate emotions consequent on individual or collective grief (Penny, 1981). In the past 30 years, the physiological and mental processes of grief have been scrutinized closely. We have become interested in the form of normal grief and its duration in order to understand better how and why the healing process of grief can fail. Bereavement and loss have long been recognized as forerunners of mental disorder, especially depression. An analysis of the processes of grief could perhaps help us understand better what can go wrong.

There is, however, surprisingly little work on grief in old age; most studies have looked at grief in young adult populations. Is grief different for older people? How does it manifest itself? How does grief present to doctors? It is possible that grief is overlooked in older people or misdiagnosed as a physical disorder.

Psychiatric textbooks usually discuss grief in old age in the context of studies in younger populations or as part of the general consideration of depressive disorders (Blazer, 1982). Freud's treatise *Mourning and Melacholia* provided a theoretical framework (Freud, 1917) but research studies of grief did not begin until Lindemann's 1944 study of the relatives of the Coconut Grove fire disaster victims (Lindemann, 1944). The question of whether grief is a 'disease' worthy of medical attention was still being debated by Engel in 1961, and the problem of whether affective and physiological changes which accompany grief should be recognized as 'affective disorder' has bedevilled much epidemiological work on depression (Craig and Brown, 1984). That issue will not be addressed in this review, which concentrates on what is known and unknown about the process of grief in elderly people.

NORMAL GRIEF IN ELDERLY PEOPLE

Lindemann (1944) provided useful description of the symptoms experienced by griev-

Source: International Journal of Geriatric Psychiatry, 5, 67–75. Reproduced by permission of John Wiley and Sons Limited, Chichester, England. Copyright 1990.

ing relatives but no details of the prevalence of specific symptoms or their duration. Lindemann's work was important in providing the impetus for future research and established the topic as one for serious psychological investigation.

It is important to consider whether grief changes with increasing age. Work in this field is limited and of variable quality. The first longitudinal study of conjugal bereavement in the elderly was carried out as recently as 1983 by Gallagher and his colleagues. Symptom patterns have been investigated comparing bereaved with non-bereaved groups (Breckenridge et al., 1986). Subjects for these studies have come from a number of sources, for example relatives of people dying in hospital (Clayton et al., 1968) or from all notified deaths in one area, or from bereaved persons already in longitudinal study of an elderly population (Heyman and Gianturco, 1973). Other studies have incorporated older people in a study of bereavement in the general adult population and included an age comparison as part of their results (Clayton et al., 1968; Parkes, 1964a), though in these latter studies the elderly group has unfortunately been small. Different authors have defined old age as being at different ages, being variously over 55, over 60 and over 65.

The main focus of these studies has been the profile of symptoms, particularly depressed mood, but the use of drugs and service provision have also been looked at. The type of periodicity of symptoms have been reported as similar to those of younger age groups (Breckenridge et al., 1986; Gallagher et al., 1983). The old pass through the same three phases of grief as described in many studies (eg Clayton, 1982; Clayton et al., 1968; Parkes, 1970, 1972):

1. Numbness. This is the period immediately after the loss, characterized by an unwillingness to accept the reality of the loss, a feeling of emotional dullness interspersed with episodes of distress and autonomic arousal.

2. Numbness is followed by the 'depressed phase'. This is when full emotional expression of the loss occurs. Crying, low mood, sleep disturbance and anorexia are all common. Feelings of yearning and preoccupation with the deceased may lead to a feeling of awareness of the presence of the deceased. A sentiment of resentment and protest is also common. Anger and guilt are often self-directed, but quite often directed at the dead person. Commonly relatives or professional carers who looked after the deceased during the terminal illness bear the brunt of angry feelings.

3. Resolution is the final stage, when acceptance of the death occurs and the individual returns to normal levels of function and affect. For many years, however, it is normal for the yearning and sadness of grief to recur usually milder and short lived, as significant dates, for example birthdays, Christmas and anniversaries of the death, or just out of the blue when memories are triggered by some other thought or event.

It is difficult to know whether these symptoms are more or less prevalent with advancing age. Clayton et al. (1968) found no significant differences between symptom levels in the over and under 60s, except that the older group found concentration more difficult. She postulated this was a function of age rather than a reaction to loss. Parkes (1964a) found a lower level of use of sedative drug and less frequent medical consultations in the over 65s, but acknowledged that this could reflect differences in expectations rather than decreasing suffering. Breckenridge et al. (1986) compared their results with those of Clayton et al's (1968) whole sample (20–80 yr) and found a decreased prevalence of depressive symptoms in their over 55 year old age group. However, data-gathering methods were very different between the two studies, and there were confounding sociodemographic differences which were not considered. A study in New Zealand showed a high level of distress in the elderly, over half having significantly lowered mood, tearfulness, and sleep disturbance six months after bereavement (Richards and McCallum, 1979).

Bereavement does not bring about the loss of a loved one. Often bereavement brings with it changes in social position and in the immediate social environment. The death of a spouse may mean losing a confidante, sexual partner, companion in activities, and all the other aspects of cohabitation. There is also frequently loss of income, or occasionally an increase, necessitating a sudden change in lifestyle and a disruption of the current social network. Older people are more vulnerable to depression when their social networks are disrupted or restricted (Murphy, 1985; Kay et al., 1964).

The time course of grief is uncertain in all age groups. Early researchers described the length of normal grief as varying between four and eight weeks up to years. It is clear that usually there remains considerable distress at 13 months in the people over 55. One study showed that an elderly bereaved group interviewed 21 months after bereavement had the same distress levels as the non-bereaved comparison group of the same age, suggesting that grief normally ends before this time (Heyman and Gianturco, 1973).

CONSEQUENCES OF GRIEF

Grief is a process accompanied by symptoms recognized by most as abnormal. In that sense it can be considered a pathological process. In its uncomplicated form, however, it follows a self-limiting course. But the outcome of any pathological process can be affected by complication (Engel, 1961). These can be subdivided into three major groups:

1. Atypical or complex grief reactions and other psychiatric morbidity. The psychiatric

illness may apparently have little to do with the loss (Parkes, 1965a). Alcohol and drug abuse should probably be included here (Merry, 1976).

2. Physical morbidity, which is in turn reflected by an increase in:

3. Mortality within the first year of bereavement.

The groups overlap in that physical and psychiatric morbidity frequently coexist and one may mimic the other.

Atypical grief reactions and psychiatric morbidity

Atypical grief reactions are well recognized by clinicians working with elderly people (Blazer, 1982) but there is little known about their incidence in an older population. It might be expected that the prevalence of atypical grief would be similar to that displayed by younger adults but there is no hard evidence either way.

Parkes (1965b) divides the sequelae of grief into two types:

(a) the stress-specific grief response and its variants, which include typical and atypical grief reactions;
(b) non-specific responses, which include psychiatric morbidity and increased mortality.

Depressive disorders are hard to place in any such schema since the natural response to loss involves low mood. In one study of the bereaved elderly a diagnosis of depression could be made in 29% at six months (Richards and McCallum, 1979).

Grief, when not following its natural course, can be said to be chronic, inhibited or delayed.

Chronic grief is a reaction persisting beyond the expected duration at a severity similar to that of the acute form, ie resolution is not achieved within the predicted time. The major problem with this definition is the lack of consensus as to the length of normal grief.

Inhibited grief is characterized by a reduced expression of distress, so that many symptoms are permanently absent and there appears little reaction to the death. It has been suggested that the loss is expressed in an alternative form, such as hypochondriasis, or later recurrent depressions not identified by the individual as related to the death. In the elderly it may take the form of an increase in somatic illness, though the evidence for this is not conclusive (Parkes, 1965b).

Delayed grief is when the initial response of numbness never occurs and a period of apparent normality ensued to be followed by grief only many weeks or months later. This may occur in those who need to cope with complex family changes and support others to the exclusion of their own feelings. Unusually, the delay may be prolonged and the individual experiences apparently unrelated affective symptoms many months or years later (Brown and Stoudemire, 1983; Parkes, 1965b).

Other psychiatric problems can present following bereavement. Not unexpectedly, there will be an increase in depressive illness in predisposed individuals (Bornstein *et al.*, 1973; Clayton *et al.*, 1972; Parkes and Brown, 1972). There may also be an increase in benzodiazepine and alcohol use (Clayton, 1982; Clayton *et al.*, 1968; Mor *et al.*, 1986) related to the lowered mood and anxiety of grief. Bereavement is like any other seriously adverse life event in acting as a trigger for other psychiatric disorders. Both hypomania (Parkes, 1975) and schizophreniform illness (Lindemann, 1944; Parkes, 1975) have been described.

Psychiatric morbidity and grief has also been investigated from another perspective, among patients referred to psychiatrists following bereavement (Parkes, 1964b, 1965b). The largest group were the affective disorders, comprising 65% of recently bereaved admissions as against 47% of non-bereaved admissions. Parkes noted that there was also an increase in admissions for organic disorders, such as dementia, almost certainly related to loss of the supporting, caring relative. Admission rates following loss of a spouse were six times greater than expected. This increase was particularly noticeable in women over 65 years old. Murphy (1982) also found an increase in the number of severe life events (separation from or death of a spouse or child) preceding admission for depression in old age.

A variety of mechanisms have been suggested as instrumental in causing this excess psychiatric morbidity. Ambivalence towards the deceased seems to be the most widely cited, starting with Freud (1917). It is surprising how often this is trotted out as received wisdom, yet there is no research evidence to support it. Other factors mentioned included perceived lack of support (Maddison and Walker, 1967), the circumstances of the death, previous personality and the current mental health of the bereaved.

Elderly people who perceive themselves to be poorly or unreliably supported by family and friends are most likely to become depressed—54% of this group as against 29% of the total bereaved (Richards and McCallum, 1979). Reliable and regular family support may be a protective factor. Elderly people who are not close to other family members are more likely to have a poor response (Bornstein *et al.*, 1973). Outcome is predicted by the perception of individuals' lack of support, rather than by an objective assessment of their actual social network (Maddison and Walker, 1967). Social networks are frequently impoverished in elderly people compared with when the individuals were younger and this can in itself increase psychiatric morbidity (Kay *et al.*, 1964), with decreasing social contact playing a prominent role in functional illness (Murphy, 1982). Further evidence for the importance of social networks comes from the success of interventions which augment them (Cameron and Parkes, 1983).

The circumstances of the death itself may lead to a poor response, particularly uncertainty about whether the death has really occurred, for example the absence of a body following a plane crash or uncertainty about the events surrounding the death. A socially unacceptable death such as a distressing murder or suicide is particularly difficult to come to terms with. Sudden and unexpected death has been implicated as a risk factor but this has been disputed. Several authors have described an increased morbidity following sudden death (Lundin, 1984; Parkes, 1975; Parkes and Weiss, 1983) but others have not replicated this (Clayton et al., 1973). Two studies have demonstrated that morbidity in the elderly is in fact higher if the loss is expected rather than unexpected (Gerber et al., 1975; Richards and McCallum, 1979). This was thought to be due to the long-standing burden of care, the loss of social contacts during the final illness and a neglect of personal health and wellbeing while caring for a sick spouse.

Previous personality is difficult to investigate retrospectively but one may suppose that those who are most vulnerable before the loss are the worst affected after it (Brown and Stoudemire, 1983; Parkes, 1985a). Those with the worst outcome have been described as 'grief-prone personality', an unhelpful description of those who experience intense clinging and pining, who are usually intensely insecure and anxious personalities, often with a previous history of mental illness. Those accustomed to abusing alcohol are liable to drink more at this time and are more likely to commit suicide (Clayton, 1982). Lindemann felt that obsessional personalities were more prone to do badly, but there is no hard evidence to support this.

There are other risk factors relating to the individual at the time of loss—the most obvious being that the worse the initial reaction of excessive anger or self-reproach, the greater the probability of problems later (Vachon et al., 1982b). Parkes has suggested

that previously unresolved losses worsen prognosis (Parkes, 1985a).

Community surveys of psychiatric morbidity in the elderly have not always shown widowhood to be a risk factor. Kay et al. (1964) looked at those bereaved within the previous two years and found no significant difference in morbidity between the widowed and non-widowed. It may be that the difference between Kay's findings and others is that at two years, many bereaved will be expected to have recovered.

Physical morbidity and grief

As with psychological morbidity, there are difficulties in assessing the amount of physical morbidity attributable to bereavement; the more important are listed below.

1. Physical symptoms can be secondary to depressed mood (eg weakness, anorexia, and weight loss) or to increased use of alcohol.

2. Physical symptoms can be produced by autonomic arousal, an expected part of acute grief, but not necessarily recognized as connected to the grief by patient.

3. There may be a tendency to rationalize after the event; physical illness is causally related in the subject's mind to the loss in an effort to explain the meaning of an illness. Early descriptive studies show a higher morbidity rate than controlled studies for that reason (Clayton, 1982).

4. Consultation rates are not a reliable indicator of morbidity. An increase in consultations (Mor et al., 1986; Parkes, 1964a) may relate instead to the bereaved needing support and counselling. This can be openly stated but often physical symptoms are used as a 'ticket of entry' to the doctor's time. The lack of a partner to give reassurance could lead to minor illnesses presenting which would otherwise not have come to medical attention. Alternatively, the actuality of the loss can reduce tolerance to physical discomfort.

5. Abnormal 'illness behaviour' or hypochondriasis can be a manifestation of grief (Devaul and Zisook, 1975).

6. Physical complaints sometimes resemble those of the deceased, where the patient closely identifies with the deceased. While relatively uncommon, this has been well recorded and is a psychological rather than physical complication (Parkes, 1970).

A large minority of bereaved feel generally unwell following the loss. Loss of sleep and appetite, fatigue, a succession of minor ailments and feeling 'run down' and 'below par' are the norm.

There is good evidence that the greater use of health services follows bereavement. In the main this means an increased use of primary care physicians. Indeed, there may be a decrease in the rate of hospital admission (Mor et al., 1986; Raphael, 1977). Studies have not usually reported the focus of the increased consultation rate but Parkes reported an increase in muscular and articular complaints (Parkes, 1964a). These results are not universally agreed and other studies have demonstrated no difference in consultation rate (Clayton, 1975); one has shown a tendency to an increase in admission (Parkes and Brown, 1972) and also an increase in days off sick.

The effect of age on physical morbidity has been little studied and few direct comparisons made. As with the younger population, there is an increase in subjective feelings of poor health—32% at six months after the loss (Richards and McCallum, 1979)—and in consultations and other illness episodes (Windholz et al., 1985).

It has been suggested that elderly people have fewer affective and more physical symptoms in response to loss (Stern et al., 1951), but this latter was an uncontrolled study and it is expected that the elderly as a group will have more physical complaints than younger adults. Later studies do not support these conclusions. Parkes (1964a) reported that younger widows were more likely to have psychiatric consultations and the older to have musculoskeletal complaints, for example osteoarthritis. Later studies show no difference between age groups (Clayton et al., 1968) or more ill health and physical symptoms in younger adults (Clayton, 1975; Maddison and Walker, 1967). The difficulty with many studies is that authors have mistakenly taken consultations or episodes of reported illness as an indicator of physical morbidity. Once the confounding effects of consultation have been taken account of, there is little hard evidence for a true increased morbidity except in one area, that of cardiovascular disease.

Grief is predominantly an affective response to a severe life event. The evidence of psychological disturbance being increased as a result of grief contrast with the conflicting evidence for an increased physical morbidity. The increase in consultations following bereavement is probably largely due to the increased psychological distress rather than to specific physical disorder.

Mortality and grief

It is popular wisdom that bereavement can lead to death from a 'broken heart'. Since 1859 studies of mortality rates have added credence to this, showing greater than expected deaths in the widowed population (Stroebe et al., 1981–82). This has been particularly so in younger age groups and in males, mortality rates being up to seven to eight times those of married people matched for age. These results were taken from cross-sectional studies and cannot be accepted uncritically. There are several possible explanations of these results other than a true rise in death rates. These include:

(a) Health is not an independent variable from marital status in that unhealthy widows and widowers are less likely to remarry and the figures only refer to marital status at time of death.

(b) Unhealthy people tend to marry each other.

(c) Spouses share a joint environment so that the effects of poor diet, smoking and local environmental pollutants impact on both partners.

(d) Both partners may die of a common illness, infection or accident. A person is recorded as being widowed if predeceased by the spouse even when dying from the same direct cause.

(e) Mortality statistics are collected in 10-year probands and within these the widowed are on average one year older than the non-widowed (Parkes *et al.*, 1969; Young *et al.*, 1963). The widowed are often under-represented in censuses and over-represented in mortality statistics.

Longitudinal studies were used to follow up the previous studies in an attempt to establish the true role of bereavement as a cause of death. These have mostly shown an increased mortality, particularly in the six months immediately after death (Rees and Lutkins, 1967). Helsing *et al.*'s (1982) longitudinal study showed an increased mortality across all causes of death in the age group 55–64 and 65–74 years. The most convincing results remain those of Young *et al.* (1963), with the follow-up study nine years later by Parkes *et al.* (1969) on the same sample. They restricted the study to widowers over the age of 55 years at the time of bereavement and showed a significant rise in mortality in the first six months of widowhood but which was followed by a return to normal rates within two years of the bereavement. The excess mortality was entirely accounted for by *males* dying of an excess rate of vascular disease. Despite the evidence that bereavement hastens death, one review has cast serious doubts on the usefulness of most of these studies (Stroebe and Gergen, 1981–82). Stroebe and Gergen criticized the inconsis-

tent results and methodological shortcomings, and pointed out that further studies produced non-significant or negative results (Clayton, 1974). They concluded that the only convincing increase was in the study of widowers mentioned above. The authors felt, however, that there was sufficient indirect evidence to support the contention of death by 'broken heart' and to warrant further research. There is at present only suggestive evidence that women suffer from increased mortality as a result of bereavement.

MANAGEMENT OF GRIEF

The description of the symptoms of grief and its variants can only be useful if it identifies those who are likely to benefit from our help. It is further necessary to establish effective interventions. Most bereaved people neither want nor require professional help and, through individual coping mechanisms and social networks, deal with the loss and may even be strengthened by it. Even in those studies showing a high morbidity, the majority of the sample are well at the end of one year (Bornstein *et al.*, 1973; Gallagher *et al.*, 1983; Richards and McCallum, 1979).

Some understanding of the processes of grief is necessary to guide intervention. In simple terms, this involves accepting the loss and adapting to it, such that normal life can be reestablished, albeit, perhaps, different from that before the loss.

Many types of treatment have been successfully used, both group and individual, depending on the inclination of the therapist. These include analytic psychotherapy (Horowitz *et al.*, 1984), behavioural approach (Mawson *et al.*, 1981), ego psychology (Raphael, 1977) and more eclectic approaches to working through issues and giving space and time to grieve (Clayton, 1982). The common factor in all these approaches is positive encouragement to discuss the deceased rather than avoidance, such that the bereaved become accustomed to their loss and able to contemplate it without undue distress.

A major problem with the research is that, to an even greater extent than in the descriptive papers, it is largely restricted to younger adults. Thus Raphael's (1977) study, which successfully identifies risk factors for poor prognosis and shows the benefits of treating the at-risk group, gives no indication whether the findings can be applied to old people. There is evidence, as described earlier, that the risk factors do hold true, ie:

1. High level of perceived non-supportivenes (Maddison and Walker, 1967)

2. Moderate non-supportiveness with traumatic cause of death

3. Highly ambivalent marital relationship, traumatic death and unmet needs

4. Concurrent life crisis

There are several papers describing the management of grief in the elderly, largely based on clinical experience and work in younger groups. These describe non-specific factors which are important irrespective of treatment model. They include opportunity and permission to discuss the loss, assessment of other needs (eg relating to loss of income) and support and reassurance (Blazer, 1982; Gerber *et al.*, 1975; Parkes, 1985b). Indeed, one descriptive study demonstrated positive benefit from the initial assessment interview, during which no treatment was intended (Richards and McCallum, 1979).

The commonest type of help given is from friends and family, but a few choose to use self-help groups (eg CRUSE) or 'bereavement counselling', offered by a multitude of voluntary and statutory agencies now; however, who uses these and whether they have any impact on the overall outcome of grief is unknown. Talking through distressing feelings to a supportive and receptive listener may ease the burden for those without sufficient support at home.

More specialized help is rarely offered except to the select few, and its efficiency is unknown. Psychoanalytic theory has long held the concept of loss to be important (Freud, 1917, 1924; Pedder, 1982) and, not surprisingly, 'dynamic' approaches have been widely advocated for coping with grief (Blazer, 1982). A research approach has been sadly lacking and even when interventions have been scrutinized more closely, the selected samples have been highly motivated individuals who have sought out this special kind of help.

One study specifically investigated intervention in the elderly bereaved (of whom 70% were over 60) (Gerber *et al.*, 1975). An unselected bereaved group was randomly assigned to treatment or non-treatment. Treatment largely involved counselling and support from social workers or psychiatric nurses and much of it by phone. The results showed a decrease in service use and medication in the treatment group but little overall effect on psychiatric morbidity. Use of psychotropic medication resumed after treatment ceased. It was suggested that selection of those at risk for treatment would show greater benefit.

There is general agreement that in cases where loss precipitates a psychiatric illness it should be treated in the same way as if the condition has arisen *de novo* (Blazer, 1982; Clayton, 1982; Lindemann, 1944; Parkes, 1985a).

Bereavement involves many social changes and these need to be adapted to before a return to normal social functioning is possible. Money may be short because of loss of earning potential, or be more available (due to insurance policies, etc.). The widowed frequently find themselves financially straitened and guidance on entitlement to benefits is often helpful. Following conjugal bereavement social events become more difficult as so many are designed for couples, although the sheer number of elderly widowed women means that many social events are now tailored to their needs, such as bingo, whist drives, bridge clubs, and so on. All this is fine so long as the individual remains physically active, but social isolation increases dramatically as widowhood is compounded by loss of mobility due to physical illness. As age increases, it becomes more likely that one partner will be responsible for the care of the other and if the carer dies alternative care may need to be found. This last may explain the apparent presentation of worsening of dementia after bereavement (Parkes, 1964b). Thus efforts may need to be made to give practical advice, increase social outlets and provide care, domiciliary or institutional. It must again be stressed that many do not require help, and probably for most who do that is provided by family or friends.

The management of grief has been discussed here in terms of problems following the loss. Doctors are also in the position of caring for terminally ill patients, whose relatives are soon to be bereaved. It seems reasonable to suppose that assistance to the relatives at this time would alleviate future suffering. Indeed, studies in specialist care units tend to this (Cameron and Parkes, 1983).

Hospital and primary care staff may have an important preventive role in reducing the morbidity of grief.

There is also the question as to who is best equipped to help the bereaved who need help. This should surely be the first person the bereaved are likely to encounter when seeking out sources of a helping hand. Many agencies therefore deal with grief, including the medical and allied professions, social services, religious organizations and voluntary agencies (eg CRUSE, Age Concern).

The role of the doctor is to be receptive to the bereaved person's need for support and counselling, be on the watch for a prolonged affective response and treat it if necessary, be responsive to the increased demand for appointments for what may seem trivial complaints and alert to what local voluntary organizations and social services had to offer. It is the complaint of many bereavement counselling organizations that the very people who could benefit are never sent to them by the people who are most likely to be aware of the bereavement—their family doctors.

CONCLUSION

There are large gaps in our knowledge of grief in old age, as most studies have excluded subjects above a certain age and those looking at this age group have not been directly comparable with the younger groups and have differing definitions of old age. Most of the evidence included has had to be anecdotal, based on people's clinical experience or extrapolated from younger adults.

With the above in mind, some qualified conclusions can be drawn. The studies largely support the idea that grief follows the same course in all age groups. They further suggest that grief is of the same or lesser severity in the elderly. There seems to be a refutation of the belief that the elderly get more physical symptoms: it is young widows who show the greatest morbidity relative to non-bereaved controls. However, older widowers do seem to suffer increased mortality from vascular disease in the immediate postbereavement period.

In terms of treatment, given that grief is similar in all adult age groups, it may be reasonable to suppose that similar therapies would be effective. There are, however, other factors to consider such as changes in social circumstances with age and differing values between generations.

Failure to recognize bereavement as a cause of morbidity in the old can also lead to inappropriate medical treatment, for example anxiety symptoms may be treated with benzodiazepines which may inhibit grieving, perhaps by interfering with new learning. Polypharmacy is a problem in the over 65s (Malcolm, 1984) and any reduction in unnecessary medication is to be welcomed.

It is the old who experience most close bereavement. There is good evidence that bereavement can precipitate depression and there is also evidence that depression in old age has a poor prognosis (Murphy, 1983; Post, 1972), which leads in turn to an increase in mortality (Avery and Winokur, 1976; Murphy *et al.*, 1988). It also seems that much old age depression remains untreated (Mac-

Donald, 1986). More research into the prognosis, risk factors and management of grief seems to be indicated.

Bereavement is a major stress at all ages and deserving of appropriate attention. It is the cause of much distress, morbidity and mortality. It needs to be recognized and managed appropriately.

REFERENCES

Avery, D. and Winokur, G. (1976) Mortality in depressed patients treated with electroconvulsive therapy and antidepressants. *Arch. Gen. Psychiat. 33*, 1029–1037.

Blazer, D. (1982) Late life bereavement and depressive neurosis. In *Depression in Late Life* (D. Blazer). Mosby (C.V.) Co.

Bornstein, P., Clayton, P. J., Halikas, J. A., Maurice, W. L. and Robins, E. (1973) Depression of widowhood after thirteen months. *Brit. J. Psychiat. 122*, 561–566.

Breckenridge, J. N., Gallagher, D., Thompson, L. W. and Peterson, J. A. (1986) Characteristic depressive symptoms of bereaved elders. *J. Gerontol. 41*, 163–168.

Brown, J. T. and Stoudemire, G. A. (1983) Normal and pathological grief. *J. Am Med. Assoc. 250*, 378–382.

Cameron, J. and Parkes, C. M. (1983) Terminal care: evaluation of effects on surviving family and care before and after bereavement. *Postgrad. Med. J. 59*, 73–78.

Clayton, P. J. (1974) Mortality and morbidity in the first year of bereavement. *Arch. Gen. Psychiat. 30*, 747–750.

Clayton, P. J. (1975) The effects of living alone on bereavement symptoms. *Am. J. Psychiat. 132*, 133–137.

Clayton, P. J. (1982) Bereavement. In *Handbook of Affective Disorders.* (E. S. Paykel Ed.). Churchill Livingstone, London, pp. 403–415.

Clayton, P. J., Desmarais, L. and Winokur, G. (1968) A study of normal bereavement. *Am. J. Psychiat. 125*, 168–178.

Clayton, P. J., Halikas, J. A. and Maurice, W. L. (1972) The depression of widowhood. *British J. Psychiat. 120*, 71–78.

Clayton, P. J., Halikas, J. A. and Maurice, W. L. (1973) Anticipatory grief and widowhood. *British J. Psychiat. 122*, 47–51.

Craig, T. K. J. and Brown, G. W. (1984) Life events, meaning and physical illness. A review. In *Health Care and Human Behaviour.* Academic Press, London.

Creed, F. (1985) Life events and physical illness. *J. Psychosom. Res. 29*(2), 113–123.

Devaul, R. A. and Zisook, S. (1975) Unresolved grief. Clinical considerations. *Postgrad. Med. 59*, 267–271.

Engel, G. (1961) Is grief a disease? A challenge for medical research. *Psychosom. Med. 23*, 18–22.

Freud, S. (1917) *Mourning and Melancholia. On Metapsychology.* Pelican Freud Library, Vol. 11.

Freud, S. (1924) *Ego and the Id. On Metapsychology.* Pelican Freud Library, Vol. 11.

Gallagher, D. E., Breckenridge, J. N., Thompson, L. W. and Peterson, J. A. (1983) Effects of bereavement on indicators of mental health in elderly widows and widowers. *J. Gerontol. 38*, 565–571.

Gerber, I., Rusalem, R., Hannon, N., Battin, D. and Arkin, A. (1975) Anticipatory grief and aged widows and widowers. *J. Gerontol. 30*, 225–229.

Helsing, K. J., Comstock, G. W. and Szklo, M. (1982) Causes of death in a widowed population. *Am. J. Epidemiol. 116*, 524–532.

Heyman, D. K. and Gianturco, D. T. (1973) Long term adaptation by the elderly to bereavement. *J. Gerontol. 28*, 359–362.

Horowitz, M. J., Marmar, C., Weiss, D. S., DeWitt, K. N. and Rosebaum, R. (1984) Brief psychotherapy of bereavement reactions. *Arch. Gen. Psychiat. 41*, 438–448.

Kay, D. W. K., Beamish, P. and Roth, M. (1964) Old age mental disorders in Newcastle upon Tyne. Part II A study of possible social and medical causes. *Brit. J. Psychiat. 110,* 146–158.

Lindemann, E. (1944). Symptomatology and management of acute grief. *Am. J. Psychiat. 101,* 141–149.

Lundin, T. (1984) Morbidity following sudden and unexpected bereavement. *Brit. J. Psychiat. 144,* 84–88.

MacDonald, A. J. D. (1986) Do general practitioners 'miss' depression in elderly patients. *Brit. Med. J. 292,* 1365–1367.

Maddison, D. and Walker, W. L. (1967) Factors affecting the outcome of conjugal bereavement. *Brit. J. Psychiat. 113,* 1057–1067.

Malcolm, M. T. (1984). Alcohol and drug use in the elderly visited at home. *Int. J. Addictions, 19,* 411–418.

Mawson, D., Marks, I. M., Ramm, L. and Stern, R. S. (1981) Guided mourning for morbid grief: A controlled study. *Brit. J. Psychiat. 138,* 185–193.

Merry, J. (1976) Alcoholism in the aged. *Brit. J. Alcohol Alcoholism 15,* 56–57.

Mor, V., McHorney, C. and Sherwood, S. (1986) Secondary morbidity among the recently bereaved. *Am. J. Psychiat. 143,* 158–163.

Murphy, E. (1982) Social origins of depression in old age. *Brit. J. Psychiat. 141,* 135–142.

Murphy, E. (1983) The prognosis of depression in old age. *Brit. J. Psychiat. 142,* 111–119.

Murphy, E. (1985) The impact of depression in old age on close social relationships. *Am. J. Psychiat. 142,* 323–327.

Murphy, E. and Brown, G. W. (1980) Life events, psychiatric disturbance and physical illness. *Brit. J. Psychiat. 136,* 326–338.

Murphy, E., Smith, R., Lindesay, J. and Slattery, J. (1988) Increased mortality rates in late life depression. *Brit. J. Psychiat. 152,* 340–346.

Parkes, C. M. (1964a) The effects of bereavement on physical and mental health: a study of the case records of widows. *Brit. Med. J. 2,* 274–279.

Parkes, C. M. (1964b) Recent bereavement as a cause of mental illness. *Brit. J. Psychiat. 110,* 198–204.

Parkes, C. M. (1965a) Bereavement and mental illness. Part 1: A clinical study of the grief of bereaved psychiatric patients. *Brit. J. Med. Psychol. 38,* 1–12.

Parkes, C. M. (1965b) Bereavement and mental illness. Part 2: A classification of bereavement reactions. *Brit. J. Med. Psychol. 38,* 13–26.

Parkes, C. M. (1970) The first year of bereavement. A longitudinal study of the reaction of London widows to the deaths of their husbands. *Psychiatry 33,* 442–467.

Parkes, C. M. (1972) *Bereavement. Studies of Grief in Adult Life.* Pelican, London.

Parkes, C. M. (1975) Determinants of outcome following bereavement. *Omega 6,* 303–309.

Parkes, C. M. (1980) Bereavement counselling: Does it work? *Brit. Med. J. 281,* 3–6.

Parkes, C. M. (1985a) Bereavement. *Brit. J. Psychiat. 6,* 11–17.

Parkes, C. M. (1985b) Bereavement in the elderly. *Geriat. Med. Today 4,* 55–59.

Parkes, C. M., Benjamin, B. and Fitzgerald, R. G. (1969) Broken heart: A statistical study of increased mortality among widowers. *Brit. Med. J. 1,* 740–743.

Parkes, C. M. and Brown, R. (1972) Health after bereavement. A controlled study of young Boston widows and widowers. *Psychosom. Med. 34,* 449–461.

Parkes, C. M. and Weiss, R. S. (1983) *Recovery from Bereavement.* Basic Books, New York.

Peddler, J. R. (1982) Failure to mourn and melancholia. *Brit. J. Psychiat. 141,* 329–337.

Penny, N. (1981) *Mourning. The Arts and Living.* HMSO, London.

Post, F. (1972) The management and nature of depressive illness in later life: A follow-through study. *Brit. J. Psychiat. 121,* 393–404.

Raphael, D. (1977) Preventive intervention with the recently bereaved. *Arch. Gen. Psychiat. 34,* 1460–1464.

Rees, D. W. and Lutkins, S. G. (1967) Mortality of bereavement. *Brit. Med. J. 4,* 13–16.

Richards, J. G. and McCallum, J. (1979) Bereavement in the elderly. *NZ Med. J. 89,* 201–204.

Stern, K. Williams, G. M. and Prados, M. (1951) Grief reactions in later life. *Am. J. Psychiat. 108,* 289–294.

Stroebe, M. S. and W. and Gergen, K. J. and M. (1981–82) The broken heart: reality or myth. *Omega 12,* 87–106.

Vachon, M. L. S., Rogers, J., Lyall, A., Lancee, W. J., Sheldon, A. R. and Freeman, S. J. J. (1982a) Predictors and correlates of adaption to conjugal bereavement. *Am. J. Psychiat. 139,* 998–1002.

Vachon, M. L. S., Rogers, J., Lyall, A., Lancee, W. J., Sheldon, A. R. and Freeman, S. J. J. Correlates of enduring distress patterns following bereavement: Social network, life situation and personality. *Psychol. Med. 12,* 783–788.

Windholz, M. J., Marmar, C. R. and Horowitz, M. J. (1985) A review of the research on conjugal bereavement: Impact on health and efficacy of intervention. *Comp. Psychiat. 26,* 433–447.

Young, M., Benjamin, B. and Wallis, C. (1963) The mortality of widowers. *Lancet 2,* 454–456.

Discussion Questions for Chapter Twelve

1. Meucci draws parallels between the Nazi eugenics movement and the right to die movement. To what extent are these two movements similar? Where do advanced directives for health care and durable powers of attorney for health care fit into Meucci's argument? Would people who do not want life-sustaining technology used also be part of this "death-making" philosophy?

2. How does the hospice movement's philosophy of "death with dignity" differ from that of advocates for legalized active euthanasia, physician-assisted suicide, and suicide manuals? If widely accepted, would the notion of "death with dignity" undermine these other positions, or do these other positions attempt to solve problems not addressed by the hospice movement?

3. Fasey describes one of the atypical grief reactions as *chronic grief* in which an acute reaction persists beyond the expected duration. This concept, he explains, is troubled by the lack of consensus about the length of *normal grief.* Even though professionals cannot agree on how long is normal to grieve, does our culture have expectations about how long a person ought to suspend involvement in the routines of life following the death of a loved one?

CHAPTER THIRTEEN

Health Care and
Health-Care Policy

THE AMERICAN HEALTH CARE SYSTEM

The American system of health care provides the highest quality of medical care in the world. Nevertheless, the system is fraught with problems including rising costs and lack of access for many. The United States spends more for health care than any nation in the world. More than 13% of our nation's gross domestic product (GDP) goes into health care. In recent years the costs of health care and medical insurance have risen at a rate far exceeding the general rate of inflation. Many reasons have been offered to explain the increase, including high administrative overhead, technological innovation, malpractice litigation and insurance, the practice of defensive medicine, and the shifting of costs for treating the uninsured and inadequately insured to those with the ability to pay. Despite its high cost and high quality, the system serves best only those who can afford to pay. The United States and South Africa are the only nations in the industrialized world that do not guarantee their citizens affordable health care. An estimated 37 million people in this country are without coverage, and many others are underinsured. Still others, including members of the middle class, find themselves cast into poverty as a result of a major illness.

It is widely accepted that the health-care financing and delivery system in the United States is in disarray. In the first selection in this chapter, "An End to Patchwork Reform of Health Care," Robert L. Dickman and colleagues argue that the existing "nonsystem" is not one of design but is a result of a series of patchwork policies that have created new problems.

Support for overhauling the American system of health care is now widespread. Many approaches for change have been proposed. Although quite diverse, they can be placed into four general categories. The first proposed solution is to expand Medicare (the government sponsored health-care program for the elderly, described below) to cover all Americans under a single public plan. Private insurers would have two roles to play, just as they do under the current Medicare system: They would be involved in administering the program and they could offer supplemental insurance policies to cover expenses not covered by Medicare.

The second solution is employer-based health care. Under this plan, employers would be required to provide health-care coverage to employees and their dependents. Hawaii has used a plan similar to this for several years. A variant of employer-based health care, known as "pay or play," allows employers the option of contributing to a public program covering all uninsured Americans, including the unemployed.

The third approach would provide comprehensive benefits to all Americans. It would be financed by payroll or new income taxes. The government would pay medical care expenses from an annual budget in the same way it makes other expenditures. This approach would diminish significantly the role of private insurers.

A fourth category of proposals would rely on tax incentives. Former President George Bush's proposal is an example of this type of approach. Under Bush's plan, the government would allow tax credits and tax deductions to low- and middle-income families to help them pay for private medical insurance.

Although not yet finalized or made public at the time of this writing, the Clinton administration's proposal for health-care reform is an employer-based plan. All Americans would be guaranteed a minimum package of health-care benefits without exclusions for pre-existing conditions. Employers would be responsible for providing this basic package of health insurance to their employees and their families, though employees may be required to make contributions. Groups of health-care providers, such as hospitals, clinics, doctors, and insurance companies, would form "Accountable Health Plans" (AHPs) to develop packages of health-care coverage. The various AHPs would then compete with each other for clients. Health-care purchasing cooperatives (called Health Alliances) would also be formed. They would recruit groups of individuals and businesses in order to purchase health insurance at group rates from AHPs. The underlying principle is "managed competition," which aims to assure health-care coverage to everyone and to control costs through market forces (i.e., the competition among the AHPs). Although no alterations to Medicare have been announced, Medicaid could be folded into the new system by allowing the government to join Health Alliances to purchase health-care coverage for low-income people. The Clinton proposal would also encourage states to take additional steps in developing their own innovative proposals for health-care reform.

HEALTH CARE FOR OLDER AMERICANS

Within the American system of health care are the government-sponsored programs of Medicare and Medicaid. Medicare is a federally funded health-insurance program for the elderly, blind, and disabled who qualify to receive Social Security. Medicaid is a federally and state funded program of medical assistance for low-income people regardless of age.

Although most Americans over 65 are served by Medicare, many still face serious problems paying for health care. Medicare does not cover prescription drugs (unless the patient is hospitalized), eye glasses, dental care, hearing aids, or medical checkups. Beneficiaries must pay deductibles (the first portion of expenses incurred), and if they desire optional insurance for physicians' and other services (called Medicare Part B), they must pay premiums and co-payments (the 20 percent of approved charges not covered by Medicare). In addition, patients are responsible for paying any difference between the Medicare approved rate and the amount actually charged by the physician. Some Medicare beneficiaries purchase "medigap" insurance policies to cover these expenses, but the premiums are expensive, and not all Medicare beneficiaries can afford them. Overall, only about half of the health-care costs of older Americans are covered by Medicare.

In recent decades, Medicare costs have risen at an alarming rate: 16 times as fast as the rate of inflation since the late 1960s (Crystal, 1990). This has led to cost-containment efforts on the part of the federal government for medical services provided under Medicare. The first major step in this direction has been a shift from a retrospective to a prospective system of reimbursement for hospital expenses. Under the retrospective system, hospitals provided services to Medicare beneficiaries and then billed Medicare. In 1983, this system was replaced with a prospective payment system (PPS) in which the amount hospitals providing services could be reimbursed is set before services are provided. Under PPS, illnesses treatable in hospitals are classified into approximately 500 Diagnostic-Related Groups (DRGs), which are used to set the reimbursable amount *before* treatment is provided in order to motivate health-care providers to contain costs. The impact of DRGs on the quality of care is a hotly debated topic as described by articles in this section by Estes ("Aging, Health, and Social Policy: Crisis and Crossroads") and Grau ("Illness-Engendered Poverty Among the Elderly").

A second major step to contain costs in the Medicare program is fee reform. Since early 1992, a new system, known as the Resource-Based Relative Value Scale (RBRVS), has been used to set physicians' fees. The new fee schedule is based on the intensity of the service and the overhead costs incurred by the physician. In the past, surgeons and other performing interventionist procedures were paid higher fees than physicians who provided primary care (*e.g.,* family doctors). In addition to reducing Medicare costs, the new system decreases fees paid to interventionists but increases fees paid to primary care providers.

The new federal law also limits the amount physicians may charge Medicare patients in excess of the Medicare-approved rate. As in the past, physicians who accept "assignment" agree to the Medicare-scheduled fee as full payment. (Since Medicare pays only 80 percent of the scheduled amount, the patient is still responsible for the remaining 20 percent.) Physicians who do not accept assignment charge fees higher than the Medicare schedule, a practice known as balance billing. The new law limits the amount physicians may "balance bill" Medicare patients. As of 1993 physicians are allowed to charge no more than 15 percent over the Medicare-approved rate, and Medicare patients who are poor cannot be charged more than Medicare-scheduled fees.

Rising costs have stimulated debates about rationing health care. One of the most dramatic episodes in this controversy involves the state of Oregon's request for permission from the federal Department of Health and Human Services to disregard certain requirements of the federal Medicaid law in order to implement a proposal to ration health care to low-income people on Medicaid. The Oregon plan ranked all medical services according to their costs and benefits. A list of 709 services was devised; under the proposal, Oregon would refuse to pay for medical treatments that rank below 587 on the list. The size of the Medicaid fund would determine how far down the list coverage would be allowed in the future. The cost savings resulting from this plan would be used to extend Medicaid coverage to all state residents below the poverty level. The Congressional Office of Technology Assessment sharply criticized the plan because it lacked a guaranteed set of benefits. Under the Bush administration, the proposal failed to receive federal approval because of potential violations of the Americans with Disability Act (ADA). More recently, the Clinton administration has given tentative approval to the plan, contingent on the removal of conflicts with ADA.

In "Rationing Health Care: Should It be Done?," Kathleen Perrin describes five positions on the issue of rationing health care: the utilitarian, natural lifespan, intergenerational equity, prudent reasoner arguments, and the position taken by the Advisory Panel to the Office of Technology Assessment. Although each of these positions is unique, all of them begin with the assumption that health care is a scarce commodity and that difficult decisions must be made about who has access to it and who does not.

Other writers, such as Estes ("Aging, Health, and Social Policy: Crisis and Crossroads"), take a wider perspective toward health care, arguing that health care should not be regarded as a commodity but as an individual right. The focus of attention should not be on deciding who should be denied medical care, but on ways of creating a health-care system that serves everyone. From this perspective, rationing is already taking place because the health-care system restricts the access of low-income people. The articles in this chapter by Estes and Dickman and his colleagues view the way health care is organized in the United States as the source of the problem. They have doubts that a market economy in health care as used in the American system can provide affordable health care to everyone. In their view, the political and economic institutions of American society have created an expensive system that fails to serve its citizens. This position argues that scarcity is not the problem and rationing is not the answer. Instead, for-profit health care is the problem and universal access is the answer.

In "Aging, Health, and Social Policy: Crisis and Crossroads," Estes places U.S. health-care policy in historical perspective by describing seven major turning points in aging policy. The future will provide both a challenge and an opportunity as the population ages and the incidence of chronic illness increases. Nevertheless, Estes believes that demographics only form the context in which future social policy will be made; they do not, in themselves, determine the conditions of life for older people. Politics and social policy are more important than demographics in determining the quality of life for the elderly.

LONG-TERM CARE

One of the most pressing questions with regard to older people's health is long-term care. As people reach advanced age, the probability of being unable to live independently increases dramatically. Most long-term care is provided informally by families, friends, and neighbors, and only a small percentage of older people are in nursing homes at any given time (5 percent of those over age 65). Nevertheless, nursing home care is expensive. Annual costs range from $25,000 to $35,000, and in some instances, they are higher (Hooyman and Kiyak, 1993). Medicare does not cover nursing home care except for rehabilitation periods in skilled nursing facilities. Nor do many Americans have long-term care insurance. Government support for long-term care comes mainly in the form of Medicaid, the state and federally funded medical insurance program for the poor. Over 40 percent of nursing home revenues are paid by Medicaid (Hooyman and Kiyak, 1993). Since most middle-income people are unable to afford long-term care, they must "spend down" their assets until they are impoverished before they are eligible for Medicaid. Recent changes in Medicaid laws, however, allow spouses to keep larger amounts of the couple's assets and income if one of them enters a nursing home. The article by Grau ("Illness-Engendered Poverty Among the Elderly") illustrates how those needing long-term care can be driven into poverty.

There is widespread agreement that the current system of paying for long-term care is inadequate. Although long-term care is a risk that all of us face in growing old, our nation has not planned for it. The problem is expected to grow larger as increased numbers of people reach very old age when the risk of needing long-term care is the greatest. The selection by Wiener and Hanley describes the problem of financing long-term care, and points to some possible steps toward addressing it.

REFERENCES

Crystal, Stephen. (1990). Health economics, old-age politics, and the catastrophic Medicare debate. *The Journal of Gerontological Social Work, 15*(3/4), 21–31.
Hooyman, Nancy R. & Kiyak, H. Asuman. (1993). *Social Gerontology* (3rd ed.). Boston: Allyn and Bacon.

An End to Patchwork Reform
of Health Care

ROBERT L. DICKMAN
AMASA B. FORD
JEROME LIEBMAN
SHARON MILLIGAN
ALVIN L. SCHORR

Our system of health care may be said to be one of the longest-lived, most expensive demonstration projects in history—a test of the efficacy of "free-market" health care. The time has come to step back and evaluate the project. We conclude that although superb care has been delivered to some persons in some places, the free-market system has never delivered good health care to everyone at a reasonable cost. Although the Hill-Burton Act, Medicare, Medicaid, health maintenance organizations (HMOs), and other partial measures have improved access to health care, the system during the past few years has shown signs of destabilization.[1] We think a unitary system—that is, a national health service—ought now to be seriously considered.

From the perspective of practicing physicians and social scientists, we offer three general reasons that the country ought now to move to some sort of unitary system.

First, if one reviews the long development of health services in this country,[2] it is impossible to avoid the conclusion that a central error has been the absence of a vision of a whole health care system supported by a public determination to achieve it. No interested party—not organized medicine, providers, the government, or consumer groups—sought the system of health care that we now have. Instead, it consists of a patchwork of separate responses to various problems, with each reform creating a new distortion.

The early struggle for a free-market system, between 1920 and 1950, was won by organized medicine, the insurance industry, and employers. In time, however, unions bargained aggressively for improved health plans, which led to higher costs and provided the impetus for prepaid group practice. Commercial insurance companies, taking heart from the success of the Blues, skimmed off low-risk, low-cost enrollees. As a result of the ensuing price competition, the Blues became increasingly incapable of providing protection to such high-risk groups as the aged.[2] Major population groups were failing to benefit equitably from the improved capacities of health service provid-

Source: New England Journal of Medicine, 317(17), 1086–1089. Reprinted with permission from The New England Journal of Medicine, Waltham, MA. Copyright 1987.

ers. Early political and economic successes of organized medicine and its allies had set the stage for a major entry by government into health care.

In the wake of World War II, that entry took the shape of government-financed expansion in four major health care areas: hospital construction, costing $13 billion in 15 years; medical research, particularly within teaching hospitals (a preoccupation of medical schools since the Flexner report); the Veterans Administration system; and mental health programs. Although these developments met readily apparent needs, their combined effect on health care delivery as a system was mainly accidental. The Hill-Burton Construction Act tended to correct an inequitable distribution of hospitals among states but favored middle-income communities within states. In time, it contributed to the excess of hospital beds within large cities, which in turn contributed to uncontrolled health care costs. Devotion to medical research on the part of teaching hospitals, although valuable in its own right, tended to produce a withdrawal from primary care to the community[3]—an effect not sharply evident until later, when medical schools were subjected to the financial pressures of the 1980s. Meanwhile, reform in terms of equity of care and access for the disadvantaged was long delayed.

Thus, the ground was prepared for the demands for health care reform in the 1960s. Lewis et al.[4] assessed 11 reform efforts initiated during that period, ranging from the attempt to renew and encourage family practice as a specialty to the multibillion-dollar Medicare and Medicaid programs. These reforms represented efforts to overcome existing barriers to access, such as maldistribution of physicians and lack of economic resources. There is little doubt that the aged and the poor gained from these reforms. The overall assessment of the effect on the system, however, was that "most of the programs focused on one barrier [to access] have

either failed to demonstrate the desired impact or else have created secondary, almost intolerable side effects. The multi-barrier approaches have demonstrated impact but have proved politically and economically unfeasible."[4] The reason is that we have long had a market economy in health care; lately, the government has become a powerful player, but it is only one player. Practitioners, hospitals, insurance companies, the pharmaceutical industry, and corporate medicine (the newest entrant) are other players. Patchwork reforms have been undertaken, only to be allowed to wither away (as has happened to the National Health Service Corps and neighborhood health centers). Or, as in the encouragement of family medicine, reforms may be allowed limited growth without improving health services in general. Substantial innovations, such as HMOs, have been transformed and caught up in market processes—that is, they have themselves become bargaining chips in the free market rather than correctives of the system, as was originally intended.[5] Moreover, the innovations that the market absorbs, such as Medicaid, tend to become essential to it, so that attempts to alter them, when their problems are identified, encounter political obstacles equivalent to those faced in attempting to alter sectors of the defense industry.

A further lesson from history is that the first response of the public and government to failed expectations (particularly if the failures are costly) is tougher regulation. That has been the experience with HMOs, Medicare, and Medicaid. Regulation, although it is expensive and may interfere with prompt and appropriate health care, tends itself to be caught up in market forces. The innovation may be allowed to languish (as peer review of hospital practices did) or be turned to the advantage of one competitive player or another. For example, many predict that diagnosis-related groups will lead hospitals to discourage the admission of certain kinds of patients and compete vigorously for others, thus profiting from what was meant to be a cost-containment measure. Paradoxically, dissatisfaction with regulation produces a prescription for more regulation. The long-term trend toward steadily increasing regulation, incorporating financial penalties, is clear.

In short, our experience with a free-market health care system in which improvement or reform is approached piecemeal is that correcting one serious problem leads to another, sometimes more serious; addressing one health care objective (quality, access, equity, or reasonable cost) leads to slighting others.

Now the nation is preoccupied with the issue of cost in health care. We spend at least three times as much per person on health care as other Western countries, without producing demonstrably better health.[6] Furthermore, when mortality is used as an indicator, the United States consistently exhibits one of the highest degrees of inequality in health among 32 industrialized nations.[7] According to Ginzberg, "The answer to why costs continue to rise lies in our open system of health care payments in the United States, which depends on the decisions of federal and state legislatures, large and medium-sized corporations, and consumers."[8] That is, the reason lies in our free-market system. Evidently, a cost-effective health care system cannot be pasted together like a collage.

Our second general reason for considering a unitary, national health care system has to do with the continuing erosion of physicians' autonomy and patients' choices. A health care system largely driven by the market has led to problems that encroach on the intimacy of the doctor-patient relationship. It is clear that physicians in the United States are much more besieged with paperwork and have more people looking over their shoulders than do their Canadian or British counterparts. It is not fitting that in caring for our patients we should be engaged in constant negotiation with them about what their insurance will or will not cover, or that we should have to make medical decisions for them that are based on positive or negative incentives, depending on their particular insurance programs. No one wants to think that physicians make choices for these reasons, but evidence abounds and common sense suggests that the free-market system has a strong influence on the decisions that physicians make.

The proportion of physicians in private practice has slowly been declining for a long time—from 86 percent in 1931 to 68 percent in 1959 and 58 percent in 1980.[9,10] Younger doctors are now almost three times as likely to receive salaries as older doctors[11]—a reflection of the growth of group and corporate medicine and surely also of young physicians' unwillingness to face the growing pressures and restraints of free-market medicine. It is ironic that physicians seem better able to exercise their own professional judgment within the framework of a national health system than under the many disorganized masters that a nonsystem imposes. Still, conversations with Canadian and British colleagues suggest that it is so.

Our third general argument is that, although it has for a long time been conventional wisdom that structural reform of health care delivery is not politically feasible, the politics of the matter are shifting. Although the American public consistently reports general satisfaction with its personal health care arrangements, almost one quarter agree with the statement, "Our health care system has so much wrong with it today that we need completely to rebuild it." Three quarters subscribe to an evidently more moderate statement, that the health care system "requires fundamental change."[12] The views of practicing physicians are very influential, perhaps more so than the views of any other leadership group, yet they are becoming less influential year by year. Two thirds of the public say they are "beginning to lose faith in doctors."[12] These opinions indicate a sense of crisis about health care and suggest that organized medicine's influence on policy development may be declining.

These are merely attitudes; material changes are taking place as well. As we have indicated, American medicine is finding the very principles that it thought a free market would ensure—professional autonomy and free choice by patients—to be increasingly compromised. Physicians have been well prepared to resist government pressures, but they are less prepared to resist corporate and bureaucratic pressures. As Relman observed, in corporate arrangements "economic imperatives may weaken what should be a strong fiduciary relationship between doctor and patient."[13] Physicians are increasingly becoming members of bureaucracies, anyway; the reasons that they opposed structural reorganization for so long no longer apply—certainly not with the same force.

As for the patients and the public, it is well understood that increasing numbers of the poor and nearly poor cannot afford health care. More to the point of political power, of the 29 million Americans under 65 years of age in 1979 who lacked private health insurance, three fourths were not below the official poverty line. The next four years added 6 million people to the preretirement group without coverage, partly because employers had started to restrict health insurance.[14,15] These 35 million or so who are not poor, most of whom are employed persons and their dependents,[16] are more likely than the poor to be voters and members of influential interest groups. Moreover, those who are covered find their ties to their personal physicians weaker for the same reasons that physicians find themselves increasingly interfered with—that is, because medical corporations and the insurance industry have joined the government in imposing controls. Many patients feel harassed by, among other things, an indecipherable paper flow related to insurance coverage and payments. They are sent to un-

familiar physicians and inconvenient hospitals. They face a barrage of advertising for supplementary insurance that, in turn, consumer groups warn against.

Thus, the free-market system in its current form is alienating a substantial part of the tacit alliance—middle-class patients and voters, physicians themselves, and the advocates of the disadvantaged who believed they could make progress incrementally— that for so long prevented the adoption of a national health insurance program. We think that those who look objectively at the political possibilities now will see a novel opportunity to create a national health care system.

The only reasonable solution to current problems (never mind the problems of the future, such as the projected spending of 11.6 percent of the gross national product—a new high—for health care by 1990[8]) is a unitary, national system. Judging by Canadian and British experience, it would permit us to bring the cost of medical care under control. If nothing else (and there is much else), saved administrative costs alone might amount to 8 to 10 percent of current total cost.[17] A national system could help us deal with such neglected issues as the maldistribution of medical resources, the declining quality of care to the urban poor, and the cost of medical education. As hospitals take steps to regulate their costs, one of the first casualties will certainly be medical education, whose previously hidden cost has in the past largely been added to the bill for patient care. Explicit funding of clinical education will then become necessary. Other obvious advantages to a unitary, national system would be improved access for those now uninsured or only partially insured. The elderly, Medicare notwithstanding, are included among the underinsured, as recent controversy about extended coverage for them has made clear.

It is important to make wisely informed choices about the exact nature of the national health care system. Impatience runs high, and proposals are being called novel that merely have the merit of being old enough to have been forgotten.

We cannot continue this patchwork approach to health policy. If we have learned anything at all from history, it is that tinkering—especially multi-billion-dollar tinkering—inevitably creates new problems. Current talk about reform often involves ambiguous terms such as "national system" and "national plan." It is time to address the major unitary alternatives—national health insurance and a national health service—and to debate their relative merits.

We believe that those of us who cherish our relationship with patients should look honestly at what has happened to our profession over the past decade. Are we prepared in the name of the market system to work for corporate masters, to face ever-increasing costs and medical indigency, and to be deluged with regulations and complex reimbursement programs? If we are not, then we should at least examine the possibility of starting over and making medicine the humanitarian profession it once was.

REFERENCES

1. Ginzberg E. The destabilization of health care. N Engl J Med 1986; 315:757–61.
2. Starr P. The social transformation of American medicine. New York: Basic Books, 1982.
3. Lewis IJ, Sheps CG. The sick citadel: the American academic medical center and the public interest. Cambridge, Mass.: Oelgeschlager, Gunn, & Hain, 1983.
4. Lewis CE, Fein R, Mechanic D. A right to health: the problem of access to primary medical care. New York: John Wiley, 1976.
5. Schorr AL. Common decency: domestic policies after Reagan: the public's health. New Haven, Conn.: Yale University Press, 1986:161–71.
6. Macrae N. Health care international. The Economist. April 28, 1984:17–33.
7. LeGrand J. An international comparison of inequalities in health. London: London School of Economics, 1987.
8. Ginzberg E. A hard look at cost containment. N Engl J Med 1987; 316:1151–4.
9. Lerner M. Health progress in the United States 1900–1960: a report of the Health Information Foundation. Chicago: University of Chicago Press, 1963:224.
10. Department of Health and Human Services. Health, United States, 1982. Washington, D.C.: Government Printing Office, 1983. (DHHS publication no. (PHS) 83–1232.)
11. Report of the AMA Council on long-range planning and development. New trend is seen in medical work: study foresees more doctors seeking salaried positions. The New York Times. December 27, 1986:46.
12. Blendon RE, Altman DE. Public attitudes about health-care costs: a lesson in national schizophrenia. N Engl J Med 1984; 311:613–6.
13. Relman AS. Practicing medicine in the new business climate. N Engl J Med 1987; 316:1150–1.
14. Swartz K. Who has been without health insurance? Policy Research Report, Vol. 14. Washington, D.C.: Urban Institute, 1984.
15. Pear R. Fifteen percent of Americans lacking insurance. The New York Times. February 18, 1985:13.
16. Fuchs VR. The counterrevolution in health care financing. N Engl J Med 1987; 316:1154–6.
17. Himmelstein DU, Woolhandler S. Cost without benefit: administrative waste in U.S. health care. N Engl J Med 1986; 314:441–5.

Rationing Health Care: Should It Be Done?

KATHLEEN PERRIN

Dramatic changes have occurred in the health-care system in the United States resulting in a moderate shortage of health-care resources. According to such authorities as former Colorado Governor Richard Lamm and Hastings Center Director Daniel Callahan, when a moderate shortage of health-care resources exists, rationing of the resources is necessary.

Historically, when severe shortages of health-care resources occurred, professionals accepted the need for triage to dispense the resources. Lamm and Callahan are now asserting that even in times of moderate scarcity, health care should be provided only to those who will benefit most, and rationed from groups who will benefit less, such as the elderly.

When authorities describe the shortage of health-care resources, they emphasize that the cost of health care has escalated dramatically from 1980 when it consumed 9% of the gross national product to 1988 when it consumed 11.5%. Critics charge that despite these enormous cost increases, the health care provided is inadequate and unjustly distributed. They emphasize that such increases in cost cannot continue.

Attempts to limit health-care costs have had a variety of effects on the health-care system: prospective payment systems are preventing cost shifting by hospitals to cover the expense of caring for the indigent; hospitals are expanding their profitable services (such as outpatient services) and discontinuing unprofitable services (eg, trauma); and some hospitals are diverting ambulances with critically ill indigent clients when federal or state funds for reimbursing indigent care are exhausted. The results are that a pool of about 35 million Americans lack health insurance and access to health care.

Changes in the service population are occurring that increase the demand for health care. Patients in hospitals are sicker, older (half are over the age of 75), and receive technologically more advanced care. The AIDS population, which is doubling every 9 to 12 months, is beginning to place a burden on health-care services. By 1991, AIDS care will cost about $10 billion per year.

With the increasing number of patients requiring care, there has been a 30% increase in the number of nurses employed since 1977. Despite this record number of employed nurses, a nursing shortage exists. En-

Source: Journal of Gerontological Nursing, 15(9), 10–14. Reprinted with permission from Slack, Inc., Thorofare, NJ. Copyright 1989.

rollment in nursing programs has declined over the past several years and, as the demand for nursing care continues to increase, the nursing shortage is expected to worsen.

If one accepts the proposition that there is a moderate scarcity of health-care resources, then one must ask the following questions: Who will pay for the health care for the elderly and the indigent? How much care will be provided? Will health care be primarily preventive, supportive, or curative? Should age or medical diagnoses be criteria in limiting the amount of health care that an individual may receive? As a matter of public policy, should certain groups receive a limited share of health-care resources?

These questions have been answered in various ways depending on the position of the politician, ethicist, or philosopher responding. For the purposes of this article, the responses justifying the rationing of health care will be described as utilitarian, natural life-span, intergenerational equity, and prudent reasoner arguments. A slightly different position advocating rationing on an individual basis advanced by the Advisory Panel to the Office of Technology Assessment (OTA) will also be presented.

UTILITARIAN ARGUMENTS

Utilitarians tend to look at health care as one of many human needs. They advocate methods that allocate goods to meet the needs of the greatest number of people. Lamm typifies this argument when he states "We are treating our illnesses at the expense of our livelihoods. We spend more than a billion dollars a day for health care while our bridges fall down, our teachers are underpaid, and our industrial plants rust. This cannot continue."[1] Despite our enormous health-care bills, our mortality rates are identical to nations that spend dramatically less.

Lamm insists that rationing of health care already occurs but it is unplanned and unjust rationing. He claims that rationing is done chronologically, economically, geographically, politically, scientifically, and by disease and employment. He argues that rationing by age would be more just. "Most elderly," he states, "don't fear death as much as they fear the pain and suffering, the degradation and loss of autonomy that our Faustian technologies promote."[1] He also argues that we need less technology, fewer hospitals, and fewer physicians, but more nurse practitioners and an emphasis on preventative medicine.

Many utilitarians will engage in a cost benefit analysis to determine the reasonability of an approach. In cost benefit analysis, the goal is to develop a single measure of net worth (usually monetary) in light of which a comparative assessment of technological options can be made. Critics of such an analysis point out that elders are discriminated against because most cost benefit analyses are based on a person's future contributions to society, not past performances. Other critics point out the futility of attempting to calculate the value in dollars, rankings, or scales of intangibles such as life, liberty, and the pursuit of happiness. Calculations made of such intangibles reflect only the preferences of the calculator. There is only one published study that details the attitudes of the elderly toward life-sustaining technologies; this is hardly enough information for a utilitarian calculus reflecting the values of the elderly.

NATURAL LIFESPAN ARGUMENT

Callahan proposes that a natural lifespan is one ending with a natural death. According to Callahan, natural death occurs when:

1. One's life has been accomplished.

2. One's moral obligations to those for whom one has responsibility have been discharged.

3. The death will not seem to others an offense to sense or sensibility, or tempt others to despair and rage at human existence.

4. The process of dying is not marked by unbearable and degrading pain.[2]

He argues that at the end of a natural lifespan (most often between 78 and 82 years), natural death should be accepted and no life-extending technologies should be instituted. He notes that with the rapid increase in the population over 85 and the increase in chronic disease, the gap between expanding health-care needs and limited economic resources will widen.

Recognizing that there are other wasteful sources of spending, such as military expenses, cosmetics, and advertisements, does not constitute an acceptable argument against rationing, according to Callahan. He cautions that such arguments pit one special interest group against another and do not promise any just allocation of resources. They also do not address what he considers to be the fundamental needs of people: technologies that assist individuals to live until the end of their natural lifespan and die gracefully.

Callahan notes that without using the natural lifespan as a guide, it may be unclear when, in the continuum of life beset by medical crises, a person is dying. He offers the following principles:

1. After a person has lived out a normal lifespan, medical care should no longer be oriented to resisting death.
2. Provision of medical care for those who live out a normal lifespan will be limited to the relief of suffering.
3. The existence of medical technologies capable of extending the lives of the elderly who have lived out a natural lifespan creates no assumption whatever that the technologies must be used for that purpose.[2]

One major criticism of Callahan's argument concerns his concept of the "natural lifespan," which he derives from Reynolds. Callahan presumes that individuals will live comfortably and relatively healthily until the end of their natural lifespans, which are in the late 70s or early 80s. He then expects that they will die quickly and quietly. There is little scientific evidence to support the age of 70 or 80 as the end of the natural lifespan, nor any indication that people will simply wear down and die at that age.

Callahan is inconsistent and imprecise about how he would ration technologies for older individuals. For example, people who begin insulin therapy before the predetermined age would be allowed to continue the therapy until they die; however, patients requiring it after that age would not be eligible for insulin. When treating patients, there is not always a clear distinction between medications that are therapeutic and life-prolonging and medications that alleviate suffering. This is especially true of medications for chest pain. It is unclear if Callahan would ration such medications from the elderly.

Callahan has not cited specific technologies as inappropriate for the elderly. He states that the older adult's body is continually wearing down, and with each sequential illness more expensive care and more assistance for living are needed. He wishes to stop the process of gradual loss of function and increasing medical costs by not treating medically treatable illnesses in the elderly. Yet, the OTA has established that age is not a factor in determining the success of a patient's response to such technology.[3] Callahan plans to save the money generated from care of the elderly for other health-care expenses. However, there is no reason to trust that money "saved" from such rationing of care from the elderly would be wisely spent on other health or social needs.

INTERGENERATIONAL EQUITY ARGUMENTS

Preston sparked the debate over intergenerational equity with a controversial analysis of the fairness of public taxing and spending policies for programs serving children and the elderly.[4] He contended that the status of children had been declining in contrast to trends in well-being of the elderly. Others favoring intergenerational arguments add that "federal expenditures for children are only one sixth the outlays for the elderly even though children in poverty outnumber elders in poverty."[5] For many in the intergenerational equity movement, spending on children has the character of prevention and investment, whereas spending on the aged has the aura of maintenance and consumption.

The National Commission to Prevent Infant Mortality points out that for every $1 invested in prenatal care, $3 to $10 are saved.[6] They state that an inappropriate emphasis exists on high technology acute care rather than preventative care. "The nation spends about $2 billion a year on hospital care to keep low birth weight infants alive. For a quarter of the cost, prenatal care could be provided to all pregnant women who now go without."[6]

Those favoring intergenerational arguments would say that a basic tier of health care should be established with women and children receiving priority for preventative health care. Some favor spending equal amounts on children and elderly. Others proclaim that our children are our future, and since they have no political voice, they deserve priority funding.

Critics argue the intergenerational debate is based on a false premise, that the elderly and the young need to compete for the same money. They state that although we owe a debt to our elderly for what they have accomplished and deeded to us, we also have a responsibility to provide for our young, our future. To deny either of these is unthinkable, therefore we must allow for care of both of them. Canadian economists have determined that they can provide comprehensive health and social care for their nation's elderly through the year 2030 if 9% of their gross national product is devoted to health care. This would represent an increase of 2%. Critics charge that Americans waste enormous amounts of money on defense spending, advertising, and cosmetics. This money could be used to provide care for both the old and the young.

PRUDENT REASONER ARGUMENT

Daniels reasons from the perspective of a prudent man who is under the veil of ignorance, which means he has no knowledge of his personal condition. Therefore, he is presumed to reason to assure the fairest of opportunities for all conditions. Daniels' arguments are based on Rawl's theory of justice as fairness.

Daniels states that a "prudent deliberator would prefer a health-care scheme which gives an enhanced chance for everyone to reason the normal lifespan over a scheme which increases chances for some to live longer than normal."[7] The prudent deliberator would favor maximizing the opportunity for individuals to live within the "normal range" for their age group according to Daniels. Health-care service would be rationed to allow a full range of opportunities throughout the lifespan. "However, in later years the services provided might be ones which assist with the activities of daily living rather than ones which prolong life."[7]

Daniels emphasizes that rationing of health-care services by age can only be morally justified when it is part of a comprehensive plan that distributes resources evenly over the lifespan of the individuals it affects. Rationing cannot be a convenient way to justify piecemeal use of age criterion in individual or group decisions. Justice and prudence demand that services to the elderly be tailored to help them enjoy their normal range of opportunity rather than to extend their lifespan. Thus, Daniels would encourage additional supportive services and provision of medical services, but would bar life-extending technologies such as cardiopulmonary resuscitation for the elderly.

A health scheme can be viewed as a savings scheme with contingent claims on health-care services transferred from one's youth to one's old age. Of course, such savings are not vested assets, as is money in the bank; rather, they involve deferring resources from one point in life to another . . . Thus it is rational and prudent to take from one stage of life to another in order to make life better as a whole. But it is morally problematic just when society can take from one person to give to another in order to maximize total happiness.[7]

ADVISORY PANEL

In *Life-Sustaining Technology and the Elderly: Ethical Issues,* the Advisory Panel of the OTA emphasized that chronological age is a poor predictor of the efficacy of a number of life-sustaining technologies.[3] These technologies included cardiopulmonary resuscitation, mechanical ventilation, and dialysis. The Advisory Panel indicated strong convergence of opinion regarding many of the fundamental issues concerning the use of life-sustaining technologies for the elderly. These issues included:

An adult patient who is capable of making decisions has the right to decline any form of medical intervention. However, an individual does not necessarily have a right to unlimited medical treatment or intervention.

Decisions regarding the use of life-sustaining treatments must be made on an individual basis and should never be based on chronological age alone. Chronological age, per se, is a poor criterion on which to base individual medical decisions; however, age may be a legitimate modifier regarding appropriate utilization of life-sustaining medical technologies.

There is a specific need for improved clinical information that would predict the probability of critically or seriously ill patient's survival, functional status, and subsequent quality of life.[3]

The Advisory Panel indicated that rationing of life-sustaining technology is justified on an individual basis by prognosis and quality of life issues. However, there is a lack of good prognostic skills and no consensus on what constitutes an acceptable quality of life. Currently, patients are presumed to want life-sustaining technology unless they, their physicians, and their families waive the use of such technology. Reaching consensus and waiving the use of technology can be a difficult, time consuming, and expensive proposition.

Hearings on the allocation of health-care resources are anticipated in the US Senate. Authorities such as Henry Aaron, a health-care economist with the Brookings Institute, and Senate Majority Leader George Mitchell concur that the government is "about to do something . . . about being in the next couple of years." How our legislators will decide, what values, which theorists, and what emotions will influence them in their decision remains uncertain.

Daniels, suggesting that there is a social obligation to ration health care justly during periods of moderate scarcity, describes two principles that should underlie all rationing decisions:

First, weighing the opportunity cost of one class of treatments or technologies against another must take place in a closed system. When beneficial care is denied, it must be because the resources will be better used elsewhere in the system. Second, principles of justice must govern the decisions about priorities within this closed system—and thus define what counts as better uses of services.[8]

Legislators will soon be making decisions concerning the allocation of health care. It will be important for them to determine if a scarcity of health-care resources actually exists. If a scarcity exists, then Congress will have to decide which principles to use when distributing resources.

REFERENCES

1. Lamm RD. Rationing of health care: The inevitable meets the unthinkable. *Nurse Pract.* 1986; 11(5):581–583.

2. Callahan D. *Setting Limits: Medical Goals in an Aging Society.* New York, NY: Simon and Schuster; 1987.

3. US Congress Office of Technology Assessment, Biological Applications Program. *Life-sustaining Technologies and the Elderly.* Washington, DC: Office of Technology Assessment; 1987.

4. Preston SH. Children and the Elderly in the US. *Sci. Am.* 1984; 12:44–49.

5. Lawlor EF. Intergenerational equity issue. *The Public Policy and Aging Report.* 1987: 1(2), 1–10.

6. Huey F. How nurses would change US health care. *Am. J. Nurs.* 1988; 88(11):1482–1493.

7. Daniels N. Is rationing by age ever morally acceptable? *Business and Health,* 1984; (April):29–32.

8. Daniels N. The ideal advocate and limited resources. *Theor. Med.* 1987; 8:69–80.

Aging, Health, and Social Policy: Crisis and Crossroads

CARROLL L. ESTES

The declining mortality and increasing life expectancy of the elderly during this century is unprecedented in all of previous history. In the United States and in a growing number of countries throughout the world, an aging society is emerging. Bleak images of the future of an aging world mask the fact that the extension of life expectancy associated with improved social, economic, and environmental conditions and improved access to health care reflects a triumph of society. This triumph of aging has put the entire society to the test, as Simone de Beauvoir has observed, "the meaning . . . that old age takes on in any given society . . . reveals the meaning, or lack of meaning of the entirety of life" (de Beauvoir, 1972, p. 10).

The problems of aging were acknowledged in U.S. public policy more than 50 years ago. Since then, a social and policy framework for the next century has been evolving.

HISTORICAL TURNING POINTS IN AGING POLICY

There have been seven major turning points in the evolution of aging policy in the United States.

The first occurred as a result of the Great Depression, which led to a series of legislative initiatives and remedies that dramatically altered the role of the federal government. Widespread bankruptcies and high unemployment created by economic and social forces beyond the control of individuals, employers, states and localities, and private charities could no longer be remedied by the actions of these individuals or entities, despite sometimes valiant efforts, especially by the states. By 1934, 28 states had enacted income provisions for the destitute elderly (ACIR, 1980; Benjamin & Lee, 1983), but more help was needed. With the passage of the Social Security Act in 1935, the principle of federal aid to the states for welfare assistance (initially provided in the Federal Emergency Relief Act of 1933) was firmly established. The Social Security Act also set up a structure for old age insurance, unemployment insurance, and grants for public health and social services. Despite small payments, limited coverage of employee groups, and (by European standards) regressive financing, the Act still held out the long-term goal of providing universal coverage (Benjamin & Lee, 1983). Its passage meant that a floor of income protection for

Source: Journal of Aging & Social Policy, 1 (1/2), 17–31. Reprinted with permission from Haworth Press, Inc., Binghamton, NY. Copyright 1989.

the retired aged had become a basic element of domestic social policy (Achenbaum, 1986). D. H. Fischer (1978, p. 184) describes its significance as follows: "With its enactment the American Republic collectively acknowledged that survival was a basic human right, and that the supply of the minimal means of subsistence to every needy individual was a social obligation." At the same time, the Social Security Act allowed broad discretion to the states in providing for the elderly poor, including the right "to pay woefully inadequate amounts to the needy" (Benjamin & Lee, 1983, p. 66)—as low as $3.93 per month in 1936 for the average Mississippian. In contrast, benefits averaged $31.36 in California (Achenbaum, 1986, p. 27). Nevertheless, the availability of federal funds put pressure on the states by requiring them to establish relief programs in order to qualify for federal assistance. As late as 1937, seven states were denied federal assistance because they had no such program. The federal government was now a major partner in public assistance for the aged poor; and rudimentary nationwide standards were established including statewide benefits, a requirement of money payments to relief recipients, and the right to a hearing for individuals denied eligibility (Altmeyer, 1962).

The second turning point occurred during President Lyndon Johnson's term of office in the form of the Great Society, which by 1965 had addressed the growing problem of access to health care for the elderly and the poor through the enactment of Medicare and Medicaid. These programs significantly enlarged the public role in health financing. Medicare, created as a federally administered insurance program for persons 65 and older, was administered as part of Social Security, mainly to provide mandatory insurance coverage for hospital care (Part A) and voluntary insurance for physician services (Part B). The means-tested welfare program of Medicaid involved a federal-state partnership, and for a limited number of elderly it has been a particularly important source of financing for nursing home care. Medicaid has consistently represented the largest public source of that financing. The year 1965 also saw passage of the Older Americans Act and the initial identification of a set of national goals for the elderly under Title I of that act. These goals included: "an adequate income in retirement; the best possible physical and mental health; full restorative services for those who need institutional care; employment without age discrimination; retirement in . . . dignity; participation; [and] efficient community services . . . readily available when needed. . . . " Although a number of these goals remain frustratingly distant, they are a hallmark of the progress which aging policy must continue to seek.

The third turning point was the federalization of the states' old age assistance programs in 1972, through a new federal-state partnership called the Supplemental Security Income program (SSI) for the blind, disabled, and elderly poor. Implemented in 1974, this program guarantees a minimum income (albeit below poverty level) which is adjusted for cost of living increases; it permits states to provide supplementary payments to eligible individuals above the basic federal SSI level. Eligibility for SSI requires extreme poverty and almost no assets. (Most elderly recipients of SSI are very poor and very old women.)

Fourth was the enactment of the nation's first comprehensive social services program in 1974, Title XX of the Social Security Act, which granted broad discretion to states to provide services for AFDC, SSI, and Medicaid recipients. This is a program which was subsequently "capped" at the federal level and block-granted to the states in 1981. As a consequence, there has been limited growth in social service funding, and the disparity between funds for social service and for medical care continues to grow.

Fifth, and probably most important in the 1970s, were the improvements in Social

Security retirement payments, especially the cost-of-living indexing that has contributed significantly to the dramatic decline in poverty of the elderly during the past 30 years. Social Security income in retirement has been of increasing importance in protecting the elderly from the adverse consequences of periodic swings in the economy that have resulted in four recessions in the past 15 years.

Sixth was President Reagan's New Federalism, the policy revolution of the 1980s. This policy of reinvigorated decentralization coincided with what was dubbed a "fiscal crisis" and "taxpayer revolt" at the state and local levels, starting with California's Proposition 13 in 1978. The 1981 Omnibus Budget Reconciliation Act (OBRA) and the 1982 Tax Equity and Fiscal Responsibility Act (TEFRA) halted the growth of state and local revenues as a share of federal spending, and led most states to adopt austerity policies of their own. Block grants, federal funding reductions, and increased state responsibility were introduced for Medicaid, social services, maternal and child health, and alcohol, drug abuse, and mental health programs, among others.

A seventh turning point was the imposition of medical cost containment policies that have slowed the rate of increase in hospital costs (Feder, Hadley & Zuckerman, 1987). The adoption of hospital prospective payment under Medicare in 1983 has been described as the biggest health policy revolution since Medicare. Simultaneously, the concept of the "no care zone" emerged to describe the fact that many elderly who need home- and community-based services have no way to pay for them and thus do without (Estes, 1987).

This last turning point in public policy—hospital prospective payment according to diagnosis-related group (DRG)—has exacerbated the problem of high out-of-pocket medical costs for the elderly. These costs have risen well above Social Security cost-of-living increases (U.S. House Select Committee on Aging, 1985). The introduction of prospective payment and reductions in the length of hospital stays for the elderly occurred at the very time that cost containment measures were applied to home health benefits under Medicare. At the same time, federal social service funding was block-granted and curtailed; states and localities were still reeling from the fiscal crisis of 1978 followed by federal cuts imposed in 1981; and the elderly population, including the old old, continued to increase in numbers. Medicare policies, through their basic insensitivity to the needs of the elderly for chronic illness care, for home and community care, and for long-term care, have placed enormous pressures and burdens on the states. Research conducted at the Institute for Health & Aging had documented the strain on beleaguered community service providers that are now swamped by the oldest, sickest elders—who are being discharged from hospitals earlier than ever before (Estes, 1986; Estes & Wood, 1986; Wood & Estes, 1988). The elderly and their caregivers, primarily women, have been asked since 1983 to absorb most of the burden of an additional 21 million days of care a year since 1984, a result of Medicare's new DRG-based hospital reimbursement policies (Stark, 1987). This situation has underscored the inadequacy of U.S. long-term care policy, as millions of elders have been dumped out of hospitals "sicker and quicker."

In the 1990s, we cannot fail to be sobered by two troubling phenomena overshadowing health care in the United States. First, an increasing number of Americans are uninsured and underinsured for health care—estimated, respectively, at 17% and 20% of those under age 65 years of age, bringing the total with "inadequate coverage" to 36.7%, i.e., 50 million people under 65 (Darling, 1986; Farley, 1985; Sulvetta & Swartz, 1986). Significantly, at least half of these are employed; they are the working poor. Second, there has been a dramatic rise in out-of-pocket health care costs being borne directly by the elderly—costs that exceed 16% of their annual incomes and are most onerous for elders with middle and lower incomes, for older minorities and for women (Estes & Binney, 1988; U.S. House Select Committee on Aging, 1985). The Part A Medicare deductible for hospital care, for example, has increased 155% in just the past six years (from $204 to $520)—an increase five times as great as the overall rate of inflation (Villers Foundation, 1987). Medicare's annual premium for Part B (physician services) increased 86.5% between 1981 and 1987, and in 1988 the administration successfully imposed an additional 38.5% increase in this premium. This increase raised the cost of the premium by $83, bringing the total annual cost to $298, and it used up fully one third of the 4.2% Social Security cost-of-living increase that the average older person received in 1988 (Shulman, 1987). A major result of the rising cost of health care is that Medicare now covers only 49% of these costs for the elderly.

An important question concerns whether the turning points in the 1980s have been turning points for the states as well. From recent research on state expenditures, we know that 1981 was truly a watershed (Holohan & Cohen, 1986). For example:

- Between 1981 and 1984, Medicaid expenditure growth rates were virtually halted.[1] As J. Holohan J. W. Cohen have documented, "Before 1981, real growth in Medicaid spending averaged more than 5% a year. After 1981, real Medicaid spending remained essentially constant" (1986, p. 98).
- Variation among state Medicaid programs has increased, and inequities between the states have been magnified in terms of the ratio of federal to state dollars: the wealthier states enjoy a higher ratio than poorer states and those states with large poverty populations. A concern here is that the high levels of Medi-

caid spending in a limited number of states may reflect transfers of funds from poorer to richer states—i.e., a redistribution of resources among the states, resulting in taxpayer inequities.[2]

- Access of the poor to medical services has declined.
- Finally, within the Medicaid program, there has been a subtle shift characterized by a *decline* in the proportion of acute care expenditures (declining from 54% to 51%) and an *increase* in the proportion of long-term care expenditures (rising from 46% to 49%) of Medicaid between 1978 and 1984 (Holohan & Cohen, 1986, p. 10).

Medicaid's investment in long-term care is primarily for nursing home care, which benefits approximately 5% of the elderly. Nevertheless, a substantial proportion of Medicaid expenditures are required. This can be contrasted with the mere 1% of Medicare expenditures allocated to nursing home care and approximately 2% for home care. Because of the emphasis on institutionalization and its "spend down" provisions, Medicaid has been described as a program that promotes both the impoverishment and the dependency of older persons. Only about one in three (36%) of the noninstitionalized elderly poor have Medicaid protection even though this program is intended to cover most of their health costs not covered by Medicare (Villers Foundation, 1987). Because of this situation, the Commission on Elderly People Living Alone (1987), sponsored by the Commonwealth Fund, has recommended that all poor elderly be covered by Medicaid. The Commission also recommended that all near-poor (approximately six million elderly) have the option of purchasing Medicaid coverage on a contributory basis.

SOCIO-DEMOGRAPHIC REALITIES

Just as historic trends and developments provide the foundation for the future, demographic realities provide a context for future policies. Four such socio-demographic realities command attention:

First, the aging society is a phenomenon so sweeping in its import and impact that it will exceed the capacity of any state or community to individually and adequately address the issues that population demographics generate. The variability in age distribution, demands, and resources in the different states and geographic regions (Rice & Wick, 1985) precludes sufficient state-level financing either for long-term care or for acute care. Some form of significant federal participation in policy solutions will be absolutely essential. Federal economic and social policies differentially affect the economies and the populations of the different states. Residents of the different states should not be held hostage to global and national economic policies and problems that have significant consequences for the economies and industries of the different states.

Second, declining mortality rates and increased life expectancy do not automatically equal improved health; that is, longer life does not inevitably mean healthier life. While there is debate in the scientific community, an impressive line of researchers would essentially agree with Dorothy Rice's assessment that two phenomena will be occurring simultaneously: There will be an increasing number of old people in quite good health and an increasing number with prolonged severe limitations (1986, p. 165). The overall picture is one of increasing disability as well as increasing life expectancy. Some researchers (Brody, Brock & Williams, 1987) estimate that for each good, active functional year gained, about 3.5 compromised years will be added to the life span.

As research has well established, the extension of life expectancy has also created a number of new problems (e.g., chronic illness and the thinning of social supports) that are not particularly amenable to solution by the current medical model of acute and high-tech care. This means that states have much

work to do in designing and demonstrating models of care that differ fundamentally from the model of medical care incorporated in Medicare—models of care that address a broad range of social supportive assistance, housing, and income.

Third, in addressing the phenomenon of societal aging, it must be remembered that decades of research have consistently demonstrated a strong and persistent relationship between health and socio-economic status, as measured by longevity, disability, and chronic illness (Dutton, 1986; Luft, 1978). Given that these relations hold across the age span, the elderly with low incomes are more likely to evince poor health than others. Elders with low incomes, as well as minorities and women, bear a higher share of disability and activity limitation (Butler & Newacheck, 1981; Rice & La Plante, 1988). At most ages, women not only have a higher prevalence of disability, but are also more likely to be institutionalized than men (Soldo & Manton, 1985). Because of the relation between income and health, Social Security—as the primary source of postretirement income for the majority of the elderly with moderate to low incomes[3]—is, in one sense, the most important health policy that the nation provides its elders. Health care costs are also inversely related to income; those with lower incomes tend to have higher health costs, yet they also are more likely to have lower rates of insurance coverage (thus, higher out-of-pocket costs). Research also shows that access to medical care is more limited for those who are uninsured than for those who are insured. Unfortunately, the uninsured tend to be both lower-income and more at risk for illness.

The health of those with relatively limited access to medical care may be further jeopardized (Hadley, 1982). As evidence of the contribution of medical care to decreased mortality and morbidity, Hadley cites a 14% decline between 1970 and 1978 in the mortality rate for the entire population, coinciding with significant increases in medical care use through Medicare and Medicaid. A major implication is that the assurance of access to health care is a vital element in efforts to improve the nation's health for young and old alike.

Although poverty among the elderly has significantly declined, deep and persistent pockets of poverty remain, particularly among older minorities and women. Minorities experience two to three times the poverty rate of whites, with 71% of all aged blacks being poor and economically vulnerable, i.e., within 200% of the poverty line (Villers Foundation, 1987, p. 25). For blacks, infant mortality is almost double the rate of whites; and life expectancy, particularly for black males, is much shorter than for whites. Striking also is the repeated finding of the importance of social networks and social support, as well as socio-economic factors, in predicting physical and mental health, indeed, life expectancy (Berkman & Syme, 1983). Those most at risk to falling through the gaps in public and private health insurance are minority elderly, those 85 years and older, and the elderly who live alone (Commission on Elderly People Living Alone, 1987).

Finally, health status early in life is also likely to be predictive of health status in old age. Thus, interventions need to apply early in the life span to improve health outcomes later in the life span. Policy interventions need to be aimed at a number of behavioral and environmental levels, including broad-scale efforts to reduce poverty and to assure access to health care in order to create an environment conducive to health. It is essential to acknowledge that in general, in spite of the import of lifestyle in health, individuals are not responsible for their illness. As the President's Commission for the Study of Ethical Problems in Medicine and Biomedical and Behavioral Research (1983) observed, "Although lifestyle and the environment can affect health status, differences in the need for health care are for the most part unde-

served and not within the individual's control."

For those who are presently old, state-level policies that supplement income through SSI and that assure the availability of cost-of-living increases will continue to be important, as will solutions to the growing housing problems of millions of elders. For those who will become old, policy needs to reflect the empirically based understanding of health in a life-course perspective: that one's health chances cannot be divorced from the social, behavioral, and environmental factors that shape one's entire life-course. Access to health care, especially primary and preventive care, is important very early and throughout the life-course.

Fourth and finally, is the socio-demographic fact that aging is largely a woman's issue (Zones, Estes & Binney, 1987). It is women who live longest and who will outnumber men by three to one among the oldest old; it is women who are the major providers of the nation's long-term care (rendering 80% of that care); and it is women who are likely to live alone, have low incomes, and bear high out-of-pocket health costs in old age (Arendell & Estes, 1987). Present predictions are for a collision course between the demographics of increased longevity, the nation's consistent and continuing policy of long-term care based primarily on women's work in the family, and a severe shortage of caregivers (Soldo & Manton, 1985).

CONCLUSION: A HISTORIC OPPORTUNITY

It has been observed that politics, not demography, determine how old age is defined in our society and the material conditions of the elderly's existence therein (Myles, 1984). The politics of austerity have been the most important political factor shaping virtually every facet of the contemporary policy landscape at the state level.

Socio-demographics signal both a challenge and an opportunity for the public and private sectors. For the public sector, both the federal government and the states have a vital role to play. In considering the options, policymakers need to pay close attention to the views of the public. Those views, like every other aspect of life in modern America, are shaped by the aging of the population. The results of a 1986 national poll on long-term care conducted for the American Association of Retired Persons and the Villers Foundation (R L Associates, 1987a) illustrate the point. This telephone survey poll with a national random sample of registered voters reveals that:

1. Long-term care is a problem that affects the majority; it has "universal impact." More than 60% of those interviewed reported having had some experience, either in their own families or through close friends, with the need for long-term care; more than half of the remainder expected to face a long-term care problem in their families within the next five years.

2. Long-term care is a major financial concern for families, illustrated by the fact that 90% agreed that having a family member who needs long-term care would be financially devastating for most working and middle-income families. By more than a 4-to-1 ratio, voters felt that nursing home costs would be either "impossible to pay" or "a major sacrifice."

3. According to more than six of every seven respondents, government should get involved in long-term care. Interestingly, this view held for 82% of registered Republicans and 92% of Democrats. As important, this support for some government program was overwhelming in all age groups and income levels.

4. Americans are willing, by a 5-to-2 margin, to pay increased taxes for a government long-term care program that would cover all elderly.

5. Finally, long-term care advocacy carries a positive image of "leadership and vision." By a 3-to-1 margin, respondents rejected the idea that favoring long-term care brands a politician as a "big spender."

While these poll results may appear surprising to some, the evidence indicates that they do not appear to be aberrant. A similar poll conducted in New Hampshire concluded with almost identical results (R L Associates, 1987b). The support for public involvement in solutions to the problem of long-term care is significant. Other poll data corroborates the substantial support that the American public has shown for making changes in the U.S. health care system. More than half (51%) of Americans polled in 1984 indicated that "fundamental changes are needed to make the health care system work better," and 31% in another poll reported that "the American health care system has so much wrong with it that we need to completely rebuild it" (see Harris & Associates, 1985; Navarro, 1987; Schneider, 1985; Taylor, 1986).

The recent victory of the Massachusetts Campaign for Health Care for All through the passage of state legislation to assure universal access to health care for all residents of the state is another sign of the current direction of public sentiment. At this historical moment, the public appears to be ahead of the policymakers in grasping the most significant domestic issue facing U.S. society in the 1990s.

The current policy "solutions" offered in health care, including the 1988 catastrophic health insurance bill, will still leave an unacceptably high and growing number of Americans excluded from access to what we proudly hail as the finest health care system in the world. Neither cost shifting, deregulation, competition, nor for-profit health care will bring us any closer to universal access to health care, including long-term care, in the United States.

Above all, a recommitment to the public interest and to public solutions is needed. Health care must be an inalienable right, not a commodity. Access, affordability, and cost containment require abandoning our current maze of pluralistic financing mechanisms and the adoption of a universal, rational, public financing mechanism. The health of the population is in the national interest.

NOTES

1. Expenditures rose rapidly in the 1970s (15.6% a year between 1973 and 1979). Between 1978 and 1981, Medicaid's growth rate in expenditures averaged 16.1% annually; between 1981 and 1984, it was 7.5% in nominal dollars; in constant dollars it was 5% in the first period and unchanged in the second. Thus, real spending increases stopped after 1981. (See Holohan & Cohen, 1986, chapter 2.)

2. The majority of Medicaid spending occurs in a relatively few states. Twenty percent is in New York and 10% is in California, alone. These two states and five others (Pennsylvania, Illinois, Michigan, Ohio, and Texas) were responsible for one half of total Medicaid 1984 spending. Per capita state spending ranged from $382 in New York to $52 in Wyoming; the national average was $148. Per recipient spending also varied more than threefold in some states. These variations are reflected in long-term care and acute care. Variations in population coverage rates across the states showed about a sixfold difference between the lowest and highest states. States in the Northeast and the Upper Midwest, along with Washington, D.C., tend to be higher in spending, while states in the South and West spend less. (See Holohan & Cohen, 1986, chapter 3, especially pp. 17–20.)

3. Of the total income for persons aged 65 and over in the United States in 1980, 43% was obtained from Social Security, 18% from other retirement pensions, 15% from interest on savings, and 16% from earnings (U.S. Senate, 1983). However, for the elderly with incomes below $10,000, Social Security actually provides over half of their income.

REFERENCES

Achenbaum, W. A. (1986). *Social Security: Visions and revisions.* Cambridge: Cambridge University Press.

ACIR [Advisory Commission on Intergovernmental Relations]. (1980). *The federal role in a federal system: The dynamics of growth. Public assistance—The growth of a federal function.* Washington, DC: ACIR.

Altmeyer, A. J. (1962). *The formative years of Social Security.* Madison: University of Wisconsin Press.

Arendell, T., & Estes, C. L. (1987). Unsettled future: Older women, economics and health. *Feminist Studies, 7*(1), 3–25.

Benjamin, A. E., & Lee, P. R. (1983). Intergovernmental relations: Historical and contemporary perspectives. In C. L. Estes & R. J. Newcomer et al., *Fiscal austerity and aging* (pp. 59–82). Beverly Hills, CA: Sage.

Berkman, L., & Syme, L. (1983). Social networks, host resistance, and mortality: A nine year follow-up study of Alameda County residents. *American Journal of Epidemiology, 109,* 186–204.

Brody, J., Brock, D. B., & Williams, T. F. (1987). Trends in the health of the elderly population. In L. Breslow, J. E. Fielding, & L. B. Lave (Eds.), *Annual Review of Public Health,* No. 8 (pp. 211–234). Palo Alto, CA: Annual Reviews, Inc.

Butler, L., & Newacheck, P. (1981). Health and social factors affecting long term care policy. In J. Meltzer, F. Farrow, & H. Richman (Eds.), *Policy options in long term care* (pp. 38–77). Chicago: University of Chicago Press.

Commonwealth Fund Commission on Elderly People Living Alone. (1987). *Old, alone and poor: A plan for reducing poverty among elderly people living alone.* New York: Commonwealth Fund.

Darling, H. (1986). The role of the federal government in assuring access to health care. *Inquiry, 23,* 286.

de Beauvoir, S. (1972). *The coming of age.* New York: Putnam.

Dutton, D. (1986). Social class, health and illness. In L. Aiken & D. Mechanic (Eds.), *Applications of social science to clinical medicine and health policy* (pp. 31–62). New Brunswick, NJ: Rutgers University Press.

Estes, C. L. (1986). The politics of ageing in America. *Ageing and Society, 6*(2), 121–134.

Estes, C. L. (1987, February 26). *Hearing: Medicare hospital DRG margins.* Subcommittee on Health, Committee on Ways and Means, U.S. House of Representatives.

Estes, C. L., & Binney, E. A. (1988). Toward a transformation of health and aging policy. *International Journal of Health Services, 18*(1), 69–82.

Estes, C. L., & Wood, J. W. (1986). The nonprofit sector and community-based care for the elderly in the U.S.: A disappearing resource? *Social Science and Medicine, 23,* 1261–1266.

Farley, P. (1985). *Selectivity in the demand for health insurance and health care.* Hyattsville, MD: U.S. Center for Health Services Research.

Feder, J., Hadley, J., & Zuckerman, S. (1987). How did Medicare's prospective payment system affect hospitals? *New England Journal of Medicine, 317,* 867–873.

Fischer, D. H. (1978). *Growing old in America.* Oxford: Oxford University Press.

Hadley, J. (1982). *More medical care, better health?* Washington, DC: Urban Institute.

Harris, L. & Associates. (1985). *Equitable health care survey.* Washington, DC: EQUICOR.

Holohan, J., & Cohen, J. W. (1986). *Medicaid: The trade-off between cost containment and access.* Washington, DC: Urban Institute Press.

Luft, H. (1978). *Poverty and health: Economic causes and consequences of health problems.* Cambridge, MA: Ballinger.

Myles, J. (1984). *Political economy of public pensions.* Boston: Little, Brown.

Navarro, V. (1987). Federal health policy in the U.S.: An alternative explanation. *Milbank Memorial Fund Quarterly, 65*(1), 81–111.

R L Associates for the American Association of Retired Persons (AARP) and the Villers Foundation. (1987a). *The American public views their long term care.* Princeton, NJ: R L Associates.

R L Associates. (1987b). *New Hampshire likely primary voters view long term care.* Princeton, NJ: R L Associates.

Rice, D. (1986). Living longer in the U.S.: Social and economic implications. *Journal of Medical Practice Management, 1*(3), 162–169.

Rice, D., & LaPlante, M. (1988). Chronic illness, disability and increased longevity. In S. Sul-

livan & M. Ein Lewin (Eds.), *The economics and ethics of long term care and disability* (pp. 9–55). Washington, DC: American Enterprise Institute for Public Policy.

Rice, D., & Wick, A. L. K. (1985). *Impact of an aging population: State projections.* Final Report to U.S. Administration on Aging. San Francisco: Institute for Health and Aging, University of California.

Schneider, W. (1985). Public ready for real change in health care. *National Journal, 3,* 664–665.

Shulman, E. (1987, December 7). *Senior citizens news.* National Council of Senior Citizens, No. 316.

Soldo, B., & Manton, K. (1985). Health status and service needs of the oldest old: Current patterns and future trends. *Milbank Memorial Fund Quarterly, 63,* 286–319.

Stark, F. (1987, February 26). Introduction. Hearings on Medicare Hospital Margins, Subcommittee on Health, Committee on Ways and means, U.S. House of Representatives.

Sulvetta, M. B., & Swartz, K. (1986). *The uninsured and uncompensated care: A chartbook.* Washington, DC: National Health Policy Forum.

Taylor, H. (1986, April 8). Testimony before the U.S. House Select Committee on Aging, Washington, DC.

U.S. House of Representatives. (1985). *Health care cost containment: Are America's aged protected?* (Hearing, Select Committee on Aging). Washington, DC: U.S. Government Printing Office.

U.S. President's Commission for the Study of Ethical Problems in Medicine and Biomedical and Behavioral Research. (1983). *Securing access to health care: A report on the ethical implications of differences in the availability of health services: 1.* Washington, DC: U.S. Government Printing Office.

U.S. Senate, Special Committee on Aging. (1983). *Developments in aging.* Washington, DC: U.S. Government Printing Office.

Villers Foundation. (1987). *On the other side of easy street.* Washington, DC: Villers Foundation.

Wood, J. B., & Estes, C. L. (1988). "Medicalization" of community services for the elderly. *Health and Social Work, 13*(1), 35–42.

Zones, J. S., Estes, C. L., & Binney, E. A. (1987). Gender, public policy and the oldest old. *Ageing and Society, 7,* 175–302.

Illness-Engendered Poverty Among the Elderly

LOIS GRAU

The decade of the 1960s was characterized by a societal sensitivity to the plight of the disadvantaged—minority groups, women, and the aged. Aged Americans were portrayed as disenfranchised citizens, abandoned by their families and vulnerable to the ravages of illness and poverty. Social concern for their plight was reflected in the development of special interest and advocacy groups for the elderly, and legislative actions such as Medicare, Medicaid, and the Older American's Act—programs designed to enhance the quality of life of aged Americans.

The situation changed in the 1980s. Rather than asking what society can do for the aged, policymakers are questioning whether, in fact, we have not done too much for older Americans (Kutza, 1981). Current interest revolves around issues of intergenerational transfers and responsibilities, family care of elderly members, and categorical entitlements to costly old age programs. This conservative shift in perspective can be explained, at least in part, by two sets of factors: the reorientation of political interest from the "war against poverty" to issues of national defense and the federal budget deficit; and data that indicate that today's elderly are far better off economi-

cally than their counterparts of twenty years ago.

Today's elderly *are* economically better off than their predecessors. For the first time in recent history, the proportion of older people as a whole who fall below the poverty line, 13 percent, is smaller than that for the population as a whole (Uhlenberg & Salmon, 1986). This statistic, however, fails to capture the economic diversity of the elderly population where a significant minority of persons enter old age with incomes near the poverty line and become impoverished during the course of aging. Traditional economic measures do not reflect the dynamics of poverty, particularly the interplay between poverty and illness among older Americans. Those who enter old age in poverty are more likely to suffer poorer health than their more affluent counterparts, and chronic illness among the more affluent can lead to impoverishment as a result of public policies that require individuals to "spend down" to poverty levels in order to qualify for publicly supported health and social programs.

In addition, while it has been suggested that the elderly poor are better off than those with higher incomes because of their entitlement to publicly supported health and social

Source: Women & Health, 12(3/4), 103–118. Reprinted with permission from Haworth Press, Inc., Binghamton, NY. Copyright 1987.

service programs, the poor still receive significantly less care relative to the rest of the population, despite their dramatic increase in health service utilization since the advent of Medicaid (Davis, Gold & Makuc, 1981). As will be described later, Medicaid-financed services are often inadequate to meet the multiple health and social needs of the elderly who wish to remain in the community during the last years of their lives. This problem is particularly acute for those who live alone, the vast majority of whom are women.

WHO ARE THE ELDERLY POOR?

Today, the majority of older Americans are doing comparatively well. Their relative health has improved consistently and substantially over the past two decades (Palmore, 1986) as has their economic well-being. Also, earlier myths which portrayed the aged as socially isolated and abandoned by their children have been disproven. Most older persons remain in regular and frequent contact with their children. Family and friends provide what Cantor (1983) terms a "social care system" in which continuous or intermittent ties and interchanges of assistance help older persons to maintain their psychological, social and physical integrity over time. Only when this system breaks down, or the need for care and assistance exceeds available resources, do elderly persons turn to formal health and social services and face the question of how to pay for needed care.

But what is true for most is not true for all. Currently 13 percent of the elderly live below the poverty line. A significant number of others, while not poor in terms of national poverty income standards, find it difficult or impossible to meet high living costs or purchase needed medical, health or social services. Those most vulnerable are the "near poor," with incomes that fall just above the poverty line. Currently, more elderly fall into

this category than any other age group (Lehrman, 1980).

Moreover, poverty among the elderly is not a random event—its mostly likely victims are women. Although older women are economically better off in absolute terms than their counterparts of earlier decades, one out of five lives in poverty today. Women comprise 60 percent of the elderly but make up 72 percent of the aged poor. Older women as a whole have lower average incomes than older men. In 1985 the average monthly Social Security benefit for women was $399 as compared to $521 for men (U.S. Department of Health and Human Services, 1985).

Women are also at a disadvantage because of their minimal participation in job-related pension plans. Only 20 percent of aged women receive pension benefits as compared to 43 percent of aged men. Women who do qualify for benefits receive only one-half the pension income of men. Nor have women been as able as men to upgrade their economic status through participation in the labor force after retirement. In 1984, only 7 percent of women as compared with 17 percent of men over the age of 65 were employed (Congressional Clearinghouse on the Future, 1985).

Unmarried women are the most likely to be poor. Twenty-two percent of all widows are poor, a poverty rate one and one-half times that of the aged population as a whole (U.S. Bureau of the Census, 1985). Older women are three times as likely as older men to be unmarried and thus rely on a single income. This is the result of men's propensity to marry younger women and the greater longevity of women. Also, single women generally receive lower Social Security payments because of lower preretirement incomes and their tendency to engage in work not recognized by the Social Security system, such as child care and the care of aged family members.

Minority membership increases the risk of poverty in old age. Blacks and Hispanics represent the poorest groups of aged Americans. Thirty-six percent of aged Blacks and 38 percent of aged Hispanics lived in extreme poverty in 1982 (U.S. Congress, 1983). In 1981, minority women fared even worse, with 80 percent of aged Black women (Women's Equity Action League, 1985) and 50 percent of older Hispanic women in poverty (Berger, 1983) compared to 20 percent of all aged women.

POVERTY AND ILLNESS

Those who are poor and old are also more likely to suffer from ill health. Women and minorities with low incomes and low educational levels have a higher incidence of disease than their economically more affluent counterparts (Butler & Newacheck, 1981). Disease affects an individual's ability to carry out the routine activities of daily living, behaviors that are most important in terms of physical, social, and psychological well-being. Again, such functional-impairment rates are disproportionately high among the poor, the majority of whom are women and who are most vulnerable, with rates twice as high as those of the nonpoor aged (U.S. Department of Health, Education, and Welfare, 1983).

Older women live longer than older men, and they are more likely than men to experience multiple, chronic, and increasingly debilitating diseases prior to death. Men are more likely to die of shorter-term fatal illnesses. Thus, many poor older women must contend with their own health deficits and those of their spouses. The burden of caretaking, the personal losses of widowhood, and often their own ill health are usually accompanied by few resources beyond those available from family, friends and public programs.

ILLNESS AND POVERTY

Cross-sectional economic data on poverty among the elderly fail to capture the dynamics of the process of impoverishment over time. The importance of this problem is highlighted by recent work underscoring the fluidity of poverty throughout the life span, where many persons, including the elderly, move in and out of poverty as a result of situational factors that elevate or deplete expendable income (Holden, Burkhauser & Myers, 1986).

Age-related situational factors increase the risk of impoverishment. Widowhood is possibly the most economically devastating event of this kind. In addition, both older men and women also typically experience a reduction in income after retirement. This relative impoverishment may be balanced for some persons by age-related economic advantages—lower living expenses, such as less need for clothing and transportation due to the exit from the work force, no responsibility for minor-age children, age-related tax advantages, and programs such as Medicare and Medicaid. However, aging is associated with certain economic disadvantages and deficits such as fixed incomes in an inflationary economy, age-related job discrimination for those who wish to work, and the high cost of health care not covered by Medicare. The interplay of the assets and deficits for aged persons is largely dependent on personal expectations, total economic assets, health status, and ability to rely on support from family members.

Of particular interest here is illness-engendered poverty, which occurs when health-care costs exceed an individual's ability to pay. Those most likely to fall on the deficit side of the old-age economic equation as a result of illness are persons whom Smeeding (1986) refers to as the "'tweeners," individuals in the lower-middle income range who are without benefit of Medigap supplemental health insurance and in-kind housing subsidies and who rely on Social Security as their primary source of cash income. When faced with illness, 'tweeners are likely to have no choice but to spend down to penury in order to qualify for means-tested cash and in-kind transfers in the form of Medicaid and Supplemental Security Income. Among middle-income elderly, three in five meet two of the three conservative inclusion criteria for 'tweeners. As might be expected, single elderly women are particularly vulnerable. Two-thirds of middle-income, single women aged 65 to 74 who live alone are 'tweeners. This statistic increases to 76 percent for middle-income women aged 75 years or older.

Medicare and Medicaid

Medicare and Medicaid are the two major programs that pay for care for the elderly. Medicare is a health insurance program covering a substantial portion of the costs of hospital and physician services for individuals aged 65 and over, for certain disabled persons under age 65, and for persons with end-stage renal disease. It was designed to assist the elderly to obtain acute medical care services rather than long-term homecare or institutional care.

Much care and assistance that the elderly are most likely to require—dentures, hearing aids, and community or institutional long-term care—are not covered by the program. Medicare does not cover health prevention and promotion interventions for diseases most likely to afflict older women such as breast cancer, osteoporosis, and diabetes. These failures of the program necessitate high out-of-pocket expenditures and, for some, eventual reliance on welfare. In 1984, Medicare expended 63 billion dollars on hospital services and one-quarter billion dollars on physician services. In that same year, less than 1 percent of total Medicare expenditures was devoted to home care and only 3.1 percent to nursing-home care (U.S. Congress, 1985). The costs of long-term care are not covered by private insurance either, which covers less than 1 percent of the nation's nursing-home bill (U.S. Department of

Health and Human Services, 1984), and even less of the total costs of long-term home health care.

Medicare expenditures, although escalating rapidly, still pay only 45 percent of the total cost of health care services for the nation's elderly. Elderly persons with incomes below $10,000 (in 1984 dollars) spend roughly 16.5 percent of their income on direct health care costs or health insurance, while those with incomes under $5,000 expend 21 percent of their total income for these purposes. In 1961, prior to the implementation of Medicare, this figure was only 11 percent, even at poverty-line incomes (Smeeding, 1986). The poor, the majority of whom are women, bear a disproportionate share of this cost-sharing burden (Davis, 1986).

The majority of the poor and near-poor are not covered by supplemental "Medigap" insurance and thus face possible destitution should they experience a catastrophic illness. Supposedly, the Medicaid program covers persons unable to pay for needed health care not reimbursed by Medicare. Medicaid is a federal welfare program designed to provide medical care to the poor of all ages. Although participating states are required under federal guidelines to provide a minimal set of services, states have wide discretionary power over eligibility criteria, access, and utilization of funded services, leading to wide variation in expenditures among states (Harrington, Estes, Lee & Newcomer, 1986).

In most states, Medicaid eligibility is determined by complex formulas sufficiently strict that almost one-half of the nation's poor do not qualify for the program. Often Medicaid eligibility is tied to eligibility for other welfare benefits such as, in the case of the elderly, to Supplemental Security Income (Joe, Meltzer & Yu, 1985). As a result, individuals who thus qualify for Medicaid-supported services may have welfare incomes inadequate to support their continued residence in the community. This means that these individuals may have no choice but to accept nursing-home placement because of inadequate expendable income and limited Medicaid-supported community-based care. There are exceptions to these circumstances. A New York State long-term health care program is providing needed care in the home as long as costs do not exceed 75 percent of the Medicaid nursing-home reimbursement rate. However, the majority of states have yet to implement such important programs.

A related and serious problem are the economic consequences of "spending down" on spouses, which disproportionately affect women. Medicaid policies require that spouses be economically responsible for each other. In New York State, for example, a woman whose husband qualifies for Medicaid can retain no more than $8,900 of their joint life savings, and her monthly income cannot exceed Medicaid monthly income standards (Nickman, 1986). This impoverishment requirement virtually assures the wife's eventual inclusion on the Medicaid rolls should she become ill.*

Medicaid currently pays roughly 48 percent of the nation's nursing-home bill. However, approximately 65 percent of the nation's nursing-home residents are on the Medicaid rolls. The difference between the two figures reflects the proportionally higher costs paid by private-pay residents, an unknown number of whom are at any one point in time in the process of spending down themselves. And for every married Medicaid nursing-home resident there is, somewhere, an impoverished spouse. (The exception is families who have divested assets.)

---

*Since Medicaid is a state and federally funded program, states have discretion in setting the amounts (within a range set by the federal government) of assets and monthly income spouses of institutionalized Medicaid patients can retain. In 1992, spouses were allowed to keep a minimum of $13,700 or half of the couple's assets up to a maximum of $68,700. In addition to assets, states could allow spouses to keep from $1,218 to $1,718 in monthly income. Cost of living adjustments can alter these amounts annually.—ED.

SPENDING DOWN: THREE CASE EXAMPLES

The process of spending down to Medicaid eligibility levels is, in and of itself, relatively simple—a matter of depleting economic assets on health care until eligibility levels are reached. Persons at lowest risk of spending down into illness-engendered poverty are typically those who are in good health or whose illness requires only periodic, short-term acute medical care; have Medigap insurance or the economic resources to cover Medicare co-payments; and have family on whom they can rely for personal care and household assistance; or, lastly, are able and willing to spend $2,400 to $5,000 per month on homecare or nursing-home care. Persons at greatest risk of illness-engendered poverty are those who have more or less the opposite characteristics—persons who suffer from chronic debilitating illness, who are of moderate income, and who lack needed informal support from family members.

The following cases demonstrate the complexities of "spending down" and the critical role that knowledge of the system plays in predicting spend-down outcomes. State-to-state variation in eligibility criteria and confusion about the economic consequences of spending down on family members (even among professionals who administer the system) are barriers to the education of the at-risk public.

The first case demonstrates the dilemma of a daughter who is economically dependent upon her ailing mother.

Case 1—The Decision Not to Spend Down

Belle, and her only daughter Marilyn, aged 72, shared the expenses of a modest apartment. By pooling their incomes they were just able to make ends meet.

Belle died last spring at age 97. The real problems began seven months prior to her death when she sustained a fall and was hospitalized. Although no bones were broken, Belle became incontinent, bedridden, and confused in the hospital. Despite Belle's deterioration, Marilyn was informed that Belle would be discharged after seven days because hospitalization was no longer deemed medically necessary. Marilyn was given the choice of taking Belle home or placing her in the one local nursing home that would accept residents who would shortly qualify for Medicaid.

Marilyn faced a dilemma. She knew she could not adequately cope with Belle's personal care needs because she, herself, suffered from an eye disease and was physically weak as a result of a recently healed broken ankle. On the other hand, Marilyn found the nursing home to be a smelly and unpleasant place with staff who seemed to care little about Belle's problems. Moreover, should she institutionalize Belle, Marilyn would lose Belle's income, which she needed to help pay the rent. As a result, Marilyn felt she had no choice but to take Belle home.

Marilyn's life was thus reduced to caring for Belle and attempting to cope with Belle's confusion and constant demands. Medicare paid for an occasional visit from a Visiting Nurse and for a nurse's aide four hours a week, which helped, but did not relieve the sleepless nights or Marilyn's growing frustration and depression. One afternoon, after Belle had yelled the same set of questions and insults at Marilyn for hours, Marilyn escaped outside and sat in the car for a few moments of peace and quiet. Soon, however, Belle somehow managed to unlock the back door and find Marilyn. Marilyn's frustration was such that she simply drove away, leaving Belle leaning on her walker in the driveway.

Belle died at home four months later. Today, Marilyn looks back with guilt at her occasional failures to cope with Belle's demands and to provide the constant love and care she believed her mother deserved. However, the interest on Belle's small estate of $18,000 has enabled Marilyn to continue, albeit just barely, to make ends meet.

The second case exemplifies the growing phenomenon of divestment of personal assets to reduce the state's "take" during the spend-down process, while the third case demonstrates the ignorance many Americans have about the eventual consequences of spending down.

Case 2—"Gaming the System"

Peter did his homework. When his mother began to evidence frailty at age 80 he consulted legal experts in order to develop a strategy to protect at least some of her assets should she eventually require nursing-home care. He learned that if he divested her money two or more years prior to Medicaid application, these monies could not be recovered by the state.

Peter transferred all but $30,000 of his mother's assets to his name. $30,000 was retained in order to "buy in" to a high-quality nursing home should this become necessary, as local nursing homes of high repute gave admission preference to persons who could afford to pay out-of-pocket, i.e., spend down, for at least one year prior to conversion to Medicaid. Persons without economic resources were generally limited to less desirable places or to homes with long waiting lists.

Three years later, Peter's mother's condition deteriorated to the point that she required round-the-clock homecare by a nursing aide, which quickly depleted her reserves. This fact, and questions about the quality of care she was receiving, led Peter to apply to eight homes that he thought to be adequate facilities. Peter soon discovered, however, that because of a shortage of beds in the region, his mother's application was in competition with others who had greater economic assets. Three months later, as his mother's assets are approaching zero, he hopefully awaits word of acceptance. He has reached the point where he has become willing to guarantee one year of payment from his (formerly her) assets to increase his mother's chances of admission to a decent nursing home.

Case 3—The Consequences of Innocence

Mary, a 50-year-old widow is, much to her surprise and dismay, homeless. For the past ten years, she and her teenage daughter shared a duplex with Mary's parents. Mary's income as a store clerk, coupled with her father's pension, had provided the family a relatively comfortable, but not extravagant life.

Three years ago, Mary's father suffered a stroke of sufficient severity that he required nursing-home care. His few savings were soon depleted and he went on Medicaid. Seven months later he died. Shortly thereafter Mary's mother became increasingly frail and confused. Eventually she too was placed in a nursing home under Medicaid. Last year, she died.

Sometime after the funeral, Mary was informed that the duplex, which she believed to be her own through inheritance, was to be confiscated by the state and sold at auction to defray the costs incurred by her parents' nursing home stays. Although Mary tried to get enough money together to buy the house, she was unsuccessful. To date she has had no luck finding an apartment of adequate size in a decent neighborhood that she can afford.

These three encounters with the Medicaid system suggest the diverse ways it influences the lives of the elderly and their families. Marilyn could not understand why Medicare, a health insurance program for the elderly, did not cover homecare and nursing-home care, services that are most likely to be needed by the aged. Nor could she understand the hospital's eagerness to discharge her mother without an acceptable discharge plan in that to her knowledge, Medicare did cover hospital care. She was overwhelmed by her limited choices of placing her mother in an apparently poor nursing home at the cost of her own economic independence, or of providing round-the-clock home care that was beyond her physical strength.

Peter, on the other hand, wonders how people without the economic assets to "buy in" to a decent nursing home manage to get their mothers into an acceptable facility. He also is concerned with the potential economic abuse children can impose on their parents as a result of a divestment. And, although Peter believes he had no choice but to circumvent the law, he does feel somewhat guilty knowing that he has violated the spirit, if not the letter, of Medicaid regulations. However, the relatively small amount of monies he controls as a result of divestment will be used according to his mother's wishes, to assist his own children financially.

Mary is bewildered and angry. She had no idea that spending down would result in the loss of what she always thought of as her home. She is particularly distressed because after her parents' retirement, she contributed substantial amounts of money to home maintenance and taxes in addition to paying off the remaining mortgage. Had she known, Mary would have had no qualms about changing legal ownership in order to protect the only major asset her parents ever had.

Cost Containment

The situations described above are in large measure the result of the recent radical shift in health care policy from expansion of entitlements and services to restrictions on service use. Since 1983, the federal government has been shifting a larger portion of health costs to Medicare beneficiaries and their families through greater use of services with co-insurance, use of services not covered by Medicare, and larger deductibles (for hospital care it was $400 per hospital stay in 1985 and $492 in 1986). Homecare is also facing increasingly rigid eligibility guidelines. For example, although Medicare recipients must require "skilled" care, care only can be "intermittent" in kind, resulting in fewer visits per client.

Possibly the most radical cost-containment measure is the Medicare Prospective Payment System (PPS) that was implemented in 1983. PPS pays hospitals prospectively on the basis of a patient's classification in one of 468 Diagnostic-Related Groups (DRGs). The intent is for hospitals to increase revenues by decreasing patients' length of stay and use of hospital resources. But, as a result, older persons are being discharged earlier and with higher acuity levels than in the past, leading to an increased need for formal community homecare or for family care. The need for out-of-hospital care is of particular importance for women as they are less likely to have a spouse to provide informal homecare following hospital discharge. As a result, they must often rely on informal family care from children or turn to formal community homecare services that may not be affordable due to the limitations of Medicare coverage.

Prospective payment systems have also been implemented for Medicaid reimbursement of nursing-home care, as in the New York State Resource Utilization Group system. It is likely that other states will soon follow suit. One concern is that reimbursement categories adequately reflect service needs so that certain groups of elderly—for example, those with chronic mental disorders—are not discriminated against in admission policies because they bring in fewer dollars than others. Prospective payment systems for homecare are currently being tested and it is likely that they too will be implemented in the near future, decreasing access to homecare even further.

While cost-containment measures may be laudable attempts to assure that persons receive appropriate care from appropriate providers in a cost-effective manner, the difficulty is that such efforts reduce flexibility within the system. Thus if a particular service or type of care is not available or adequate at the time that it is needed, the system may not permit compensation for the use of other sources of care or assistance, even if only temporarily. Cost-containment measures do not recognize gaps in services such as inadequate Medicare coverage of nonprofessional homecare, day care, and respite services. Tightening access to existing services will underscore these deficiencies. As

current cost-benefit formulas do not measure the health and social consequences of non-utilization of needed services, these consequences may not be evident in the statistics.

SUMMARY AND DISCUSSION

Poverty in old age is not simply an economic matter. It is too often associated with simultaneous "poverty" of health and "poverty" of freedom to make fundamental choices about the conditions under which one chooses to live during the last years of life. Women, especially women who are poor or who become poor as a result of age-related events such as widowhood and chronic illness, are at particular risk for such all-encompassing poverty. Currently, the social responses to this problem include Medicare, an insurance program, and Medicaid, a welfare program. While these programs are certainly better than having no insurance and welfare programs at all, gaps in Medicare coverage and the wide variation in Medicaid entitlements across states make old age a time of uncertainty for most Americans.

Current health-care policy for the elderly rests on the assumption that impoverishment is a precondition for receipt of publicly supported care, the same assumption that applies to those in younger age groups who receive public assistance. There is, however, a critical difference between the two groups. The young are poor because of their inability to engender income, for whatever reasons. They may qualify for a variety of social programs and strategies that hold potential for economic self-determination. The majority of elderly, on the other hand, are poor because of the age-related events of widowhood and illness, facts of life beyond the individual's and society's control. Older people inevitably face illness at some point in time between the onset of old age and death and the likelihood that the illness will be chronic and economically debilitating is greatest for women. The fact that women are most likely to experience illness-engendered poverty is a consequence of the privilege of long life, a privilege tempered by life-long economic inequality and old-age-related chronic illness.

The question that must be asked is whether chronic illness should precipitate impoverishment for large numbers of older people as a result of their own illnesses or those of their spouses. Another issue is divestment. Divestment laws have been implemented in most states to prevent older persons from turning over their assets to others when it is clear that they need costly nursing-home care. Most laws require that assets must be diverted two or more years prior to Medicaid eligibility. These laws may serve only to delay the eventual divestment process and to bias evasion techniques in favor of those with access to legal information and counsel, that is, the well-off and those with the most to gain from "gaming" the system.

The difficult questions posed by illness-engendered poverty and by divestment arise in part from the absence of an equitable system of financing long-term care that would spread economic risk so that individuals are not impoverished as a result of old-age illness nor are motivated to "game" the system to prevent impoverishment. Welfare programs such as Medicaid that impoverish the working class while at the same time enable the wealthy to receive free life-long care from the state are fraught with problems.

The United States and the Republic of South Africa are the only two developed countries of the world that fail to provide a system of long-term care for their elderly citizens. One solution is a national health care system. Other "experiments" could include various types of long-term care insurance, reorientation of incentives from costly hospital and nursing-home care to comprehensive and articulated community-based services, and expansion of Medicare benefits. This is not to suggest that individuals not bear any responsibility for financing at least some of their own health care. For too many, however, health financing policies serve as an antecedent to poverty and poverty is far too often an antecedent to death.

REFERENCES

Berger, P. (1983). The economic well-being of elderly Hispanics. *Journal of Minority Aging*, 36–46.

Butler, R. N. & Newacheck, P. W. (1981). Health and social factors affecting long-term care policy. In J. Meltzer, F. Farrow & H. Richman *Policy Options in Long-term Care*. Chicago: University of Chicago Press.

Cantor, M. (1983). *Social care for the aged in the United States: Issues and challenges*. Reprint. New York: The Haworth Press, Inc.

Congressional Clearinghouse on the Future (1985). Tomorrow's elderly: *Issues for Congress*. Prepared for the House Select Committee on Aging: Congressional Institute for the Future.

Davis, K. (1986). What about the poor? *Generations, 9*, 13–15.

Davis, K., Gold, M. & Makuc, D. (1981). Access to health care for the poor: Does the gap remain? *Annual Review of Public Health, 2*, 159–182.

Harrington, C., Estes, C., Lee, P. & Newcomer, R. (1986). Effects of state Medicaid policies on the aged. *The Gerontologist, 26*, 437–443.

Holden, K. C., Burkhauser, R. V. & Myers, D. A. (1986). Income transitions at older stages of life: The dynamics of poverty. *The Gerontologist, 26*, 292–297.

Joe, T. C., Meltzer, J. & Yu, P. (1985). Arbitrary access to care: The case for reforming Medicaid. *Health Affairs, 4*, 59–74.

Kutza, E. (1981). *The benefits of old age*. Chicago: The University of Chicago Press.

Lehrman, R. (1980). Poverty statistics serve as nagging reminder. *Generations: Journal of the Western Gerontological Society, 4*, 17.

Nickman, J. R. (1986). Helping New York elders pay for long-term care: Opportunities for public-private cooperation. Prepared for *New York Affairs.* In press.

Palmore, E. B. (1986). Trends in the health of the aged. *The Gerontologist, 26,* 298–302.

Smeeding, T. M. (1986). Nonmoney income and the elderly: The case of the 'tweeners. *Journal of Policy Analysis and Management, 5,* 707–724.

Uhlenberg, P. & Salmon, M. P. (1986). Change in relative income of older women, 1960–1980. *The Gerontologist, 26,* 164–170.

U.S. Bureau of the Census (1985). Characteristics of the population below the poverty level: 1983. *Current Population Reports,* Series P-60, No. 147. Washington, DC: U.S. Government Printing Office.

U.S. Congress, Senate Special Committee on Aging (1983). *Developments in aging, 1983.* Washington, DC: Government Printing Office.

U.S. Congress, Senate Special Committee on Aging (1985). *Developments in aging, 1985.* Washington, DC: Government Printing Office.

U.S. Department of Health, Education, and Welfare (1983). *Income and resources of the aged.* Washington, DC: Government Printing Office.

U.S. Department of Health and Human Services (1984). *Long-term care financing and delivery systems: Exploring some alternatives.* (HCFA Publication No. 03174). Washington, DC: Government Printing Office.

U.S. Department of Health and Human Services (1985). *Monthly benefit statistics program data: Old-age survivors, disability, and health insurance.* Washington, DC: Government Printing Office.

Women's Equity Action League (WEAL) (1985). *Facts on Social Security.* Washington, DC: WEAL.

The Bumpy Road
To Long-Term
Care Reform

JOSHUA M. WIENER
RAYMOND J. HANLEY

The United States does not have, either in the private or the public sectors, satisfactory mechanisms for helping people anticipate and pay for long-term care. The disabled elderly and their families find, often to their surprise, that neither private insurance nor Medicare covers the costs of long-term care to any significant extent. The disabled elderly must rely on their own resources or, when these have been exhausted, turn to welfare in the form of Medicaid. Despite the strong desires of the elderly for home care, public funding is overwhelmingly for nursing home care.

The aging of the baby boom generation, combined with rapidly falling mortality rates for the elderly, will lead to sharply increased demand for long-term care that will require substantially greater public and private spending far into the next century. Thus, the challenge is to reform long-term care financing and delivery so that we do not just end up with a much larger version of the current inadequate system.

HOW DO WE PAY FOR
LONG-TERM CARE NOW?

Most elderly people are not disabled. Of the 28.6 million Americans aged 65 and over in 1985, less than a quarter (6.3 million) were disabled (Rivlin and Wiener 1988). But the prevalence of disability is high for the very elderly. Only about 13% of people aged 65–74 were disabled in 1985, but that proportion rises to 58% for people aged 85 and over. Mortality rates at advanced ages have come down dramatically in recent years, bringing increases in the number of disabled elderly.

Most disabled elderly are cared for at home, which is where they greatly prefer to be. Caregivers are usually relatives—generally spouses, daughters, or daughters-in-law—and occasionally friends (Stone et al, 1987). This unpaid care frequently puts great strain on families. Among the disabled elderly in 1985, about 20% received some paid home care, and about 21% were in nursing homes.

Source: Caring, 9(3), 12–16. Reproduced by permission of the National Association for Home Care, from CARING Magazine, Vol. 9, No. 3, 1990.

Most families who seek long-term care find it beyond their financial reach. The cost of a year in a nursing home averages about $25,000 and can be much higher. Although families are the predominant provider of long-term care in the United States, nursing homes dominate long-term care financing. Total nursing home and home care expenditures for the elderly were estimated to be $39 billion in 1988 (Brookings-ICF Long-Term Care Financing Model, unpublished estimates). Relatively little spending goes for home care, accounting for only about 16% of the total.

The striking fact about long-term care financing is that such a trivial portion of the bill is paid by Medicare or private insurance. Only 3% of the elderly have any private long-term care insurance (Van Gelder 1989); about 1% of total nursing home expenditures for the elderly are paid by private insurance (Letsch et al. 1988). Medicare does provide a limited amount of skilled nursing facility and home health care, but coverage is limited to skilled care. Medicare accounted for 35% of total home care expenditures for the elderly in 1988. Most long-term care patients, who need unskilled care, are not eligible for services. Medicaid is the primary source of public funding for long-term care, accounting for 78% of all government funding.

Although the United States has a highly developed private insurance industry and broad social insurance coverage, especially for the elderly, little attention has been paid to ways of financing long-term care. The development of insurance approaches has been inhibited by uncertainty, arising out of two characteristics of long-term care:

• Because long-term care is needed primarily by the very elderly, a long time is likely to elapse between the initial purchase of an insurance policy (eg, age 65) and its use (eg, age 85). Possible changes in mortality rates, inflation, use of serv-

ices, and the risk of disability over this period create major uncertainties both for buyers and sellers of long-term care financing mechanisms.

• Long-term care is currently provided primarily by relatives. Thus, there is considerable risk of "induced demand" (greater use of paid care once financing is available), especially for home care.

Whatever the reasons, the United States so far has relied for long-term care financing on a patchwork of private out-of-pocket spending and a means-tested welfare program. Pressure on this patchwork system will continue to mount as the population of disabled elderly increases.

INCREASING STRAINS ON THE SYSTEM

Over the next several decades, the bill for long-term care is certain to rise rapidly. Using an updated version of the Brookings-ICF Long-Term Care Financing Model, we have made detailed projections of the elderly population to the year 2018 (assuming that the current long-term care financing system does not change), together with their income, resources, and likely use of long-term care.

First, the number of older people will grow rapidly, and the number of very elderly will rise even faster. Because they will be older, more of the population over age 65 will be disabled. The increase in disabled elderly will mean more users of long-term care. While the number of people over age 65 is projected to increase 62% over the period, the nursing home population will increase 91% and the number of home care users will increase by 83%.

Second, older people will be significantly better off financially by 2018, but the income and assets of the age 85 and older population will continue to lag substantially behind younger elderly. Real incomes of all elderly will increase by more than 50% over the next three decades due to more and higher pensions, increases in Social Security benefits, and income from assets. Moreover, since the cost of nursing home and home care is likely to increase at roughly the same rate, long-term care services are unlikely to become more affordable.

Third, long-term care spending will increase rapidly. If nursing home and home care costs rise 5.5% per year (compared with a 4% increase assumed for the general price level), total long-term expenditures for the elderly will increase from $39 billion to $120 billion in 2018 (in constant 1989 dollars), an increase of 208%. Home care spending for the elderly will increase by 217%, rising from $6 billion in 1988 to $19 billion by 2018.

OPTIONS FOR THE FUTURE: THE PRIVATE SECTOR

There are a wide variety of alternative ways that long-term care might be financed in the future. Several widely discussed private-sector initiatives are listed below.

- pooling the risk of high long-term care expenses through private long-term care insurance;
- increasing incentives for private saving by creating individual medical accounts (IMA), savings accounts earmarked for long-term care that would receive favorable tax treatment by the federal government;
- increasing the ability of older people to use the equity accumulated in their home (normally their principal asset) to pay for long-term care through home equity conversions (HEC);
- establishment of continuing care retirement communities (CCRC) or residential complexes with independent living units for older people and a guaranteed availability of care (from occasional

home care to full nursing home care if needed) for the lifetime of residents;
- formation of social/health maintenance organizations (S/HMO), an extension of the health maintenance organization concept of prepaid health care financing to include long-term care services.

In projecting the potential market for private sector initiatives for the next three decades, we made optimistic assumptions about the number of people who would participate in private sector financing and the willingness of insurers and others to offer products. Our purpose was to determine the most that can reasonably be expected from the private sector with respect to participation, proportion of long-term care expenses financed, and reduction in the use of Medicaid.

Our projections indicate substantial potential for growth of private sector financing mechanisms for long-term care. A potential multibillion dollar market is almost entirely untapped. People purchasing these products will have better financial protection.

Even under optimistic assumptions about who would participate, however, private sector financing cannot be relied on to do the whole job. Private sector approaches are unlikely to be affordable by a majority of elderly, to finance more than a modest proportion of total nursing home and home care expenditures, or to have more than a small impact on Medicaid expenditures and the number of people who spend down to Medicaid financial eligibility levels. For example, we estimate that by 2018, private long-term care insurance sold to those aged 65 and older may be affordable by 25–54% of the elderly, to account for 7–17% of total nursing home expenditures and 1% of home care expenditures, and to reduce Medicaid nursing home expenditures and the number of Medicaid patients by 1–16%.

Although options other than insurance may provide a bit more home care, those general conclusions also apply to individual medical accounts, continuing care retirement communities, and social/health maintenance organizations. Home equity conversions and private insurance sold to people under age 65 are the only options in which a substantial majority of the elderly might participate. However, home equity conversions have limited potential for paying large long-term care bills directly, and thirty years from now, private insurance sold to people under age 65 might pay for only 17% of nursing home expenditures.

Private sector options have a limited impact because they are so expensive that most elderly cannot afford them (Friedland 1990; Zedlewski et al. 1989; and Families USA 1990). According to the Health Insurance Association of America, long-term care insurance policies introduced in 1988 cost an average of $920 if purchased at age 65, rising to $3,010 per person if purchased at age 79 (Gelder and Johnson 1989). Thus, married couples must pay annual premiums of between $1,800 and $6,000 a year, a considerable amount by any measure.

Although private long-term care insurance policies are rapidly evolving, policies now available are also limited in the amount of financial protection that they offer. There has been a real improvement over the last few years in the quality of nursing home benefits, but home care benefits remain either nonexistent or fraught with restrictions. Policies often require prior nursing home use, limit length of home care use to some fraction of nursing home use or another relatively short period, pay only for care when patients "would otherwise be institutionalized," or cover strictly skilled in-home services. In general, existing private long-term care insurance policies provide coverage that is only slightly broader than Medicare's home health benefit.

There is no inherent reason why insurers could not eliminate these restrictions and provide better financial protection. The problem is that improved coverage and affordability are tradeoffs within the elderly population. That is, coverage improvements are likely to make products more expensive, thus reducing affordability. This is likely to be especially important for home care, where the possibility of increased use under insurance is large because so few disabled elderly in the community currently receive formal services.

OPTIONS FOR THE FUTURE: THE PUBLIC SECTOR

While it is desirable for the private sector to play a much greater role in financing care, our projections indicate that it is not reasonable to count on private initiatives to play more than a modest role. The question then becomes: should the nation stick with a means-tested public welfare program as its major program for financing long-term care or should it enact a new program of social insurance?

The principal argument for staying with a means-tested approach is that Medicaid, despite its many deficiencies, does meet the most urgent needs of the low-income disabled elderly population at minimal cost to the taxpayer. For example, the entitlement character of Medicaid means that expenditures tend to rise with need and are not arbitrarily limited by the appropriation process. Although Medicaid is targeted to the poor, it also provides a safety net for the middle class. The spend-down requirements mean that Medicaid finances only the care that the income and the assets of the elderly cannot, thus keeping public expenditures down. The institutional bias ensures that persons receiving publicly financed care are predominantly the severely disabled. And, finally, home care services, although not as widespread as many would like, are moderately available to program participants.

Making the Medicaid means test less onerous, reimbursement rates more adequate, and expanded home care more available would make life better for the disabled elderly, but still retain the fundamental welfare character of the program. Although incremental improvements in Medicaid are attractive, public charity always carries a stigma, and efforts to reduce taxpayer costs are likely to perpetuate a two-class system with inferior care and status for Medicaid patients. Moreover, it is an odd welfare program whose eligibility requirements are met by a majority of the people using services. In other US welfare programs. such as Aid to Families with Dependent Children and the Supplemental Security Income program, only a small minority of the population is expected to be financially eligible.

The other broad approach is social insurance coverage of long-term care, most likely through expansion of the Medicare program. Under this approach, everyone would pay into the social insurance program and earn the right to benefits without having to prove impoverishment.

The advantages of this approach are near-universal coverage, as with Social Security and Medicare, and the ability to spread the cost over the largest possible number of people. In addition, public insurance can be financed in such a way that upper-income people pay more than lower-income people. For example, under Part A of the Medicare program, the $50,000 worker pays five times in taxes what the $10,000 worker pays for exactly the same set of benefits. Thus, an important drawback for private insurance is that it is the most regressive way to finance benefits.

Public costs to pay for a public insurance program would be substantial, but not unmanageable. We estimate that the incremental public costs of a fully implemented public insurance program in 1993 would vary from $19 billion to $44 billion (in 1989 dollars) depending on program design. A full-scale home care-only program could cost $15 billion in 1993.

By almost any standard, these expenditures are large. It should be recalled, however, that most of the costs associated with a public insurance program will be incurred by society with or without the program. This is especially true if private insurance expands greatly. Society will not be able to escape those costs. The real issue is whether these costs will be borne largely by the relative few who need extensive nursing home or home care or whether the costs will be spread more broadly over society as a whole, and what should be the balance between public and private approaches.

Moreover, although recent public opinion poll results are somewhat more ambiguous in their findings, several surveys have found that people want and are willing to pay for a public long-term care insurance program. In a national survey of voters sponsored by the American Association of Retired Persons and the Families USA Foundation, 68% of respondents were willing to pay additional taxes ranging from $10 to $60 a month depending on income (RL Associates 1988). In a survey of people aged 45 and older, a solid majority supported additional taxes to pay for a public long-term care program and responses varied only slightly (Hamilton, Frederick and Schneiders 1988).

CONCLUSION

Long-term care financing reform has moved up dramatically on the nation's political agenda and is now widely recognized as one of the country's most pressing social policy issues. In 1988, almost all of the major health players in Congress—including Senators Mitchell, Kennedy, and Durenberger and Representatives Stark, Waxman, and Gradison—introduced long-term care financing reform bills. In addition, long-term care financing reform is partly the subject of two congressionally mandated commissions—the US Bipartisan Commission on Comprehensive Health Care (also known as the Pepper Commission) and the Advisory Council on Social Security. It is also part of the White House policy review of health care being led by Department of Health and Human Services Secretary Louis Sullivan.

Without question, the political debacle over the repeal of the Medicare Catastrophic Coverage Act of 1988, with its strong overtones of generational conflict, has cooled the ardor of Congress to tackle long-term care reform with large new public programs. Indeed, for the short run, the prospects for expanded public funding for long-term care are poorer now than they were just one year ago, but still much greater than they were five years ago.

Over the long run, however, neither the president nor the Congress will be able to duck the issue indefinitely. During the 1990s, virtually all of the parents of the baby boom generation will become elderly. Both these parents and their baby boom children will have to face long-term care, not as an abstract concept but as a real life, intensely personal issue. As a result, they are likely to put intense pressure on their elected representatives to "do something" to help them pay for nursing home and home care.

Major new initiatives are needed both in the private sector and in the public sector to improve the financing of long-term care. Americans need to recognize that long-term care is a normal risk of growing old and one that requires anticipation and planning. A large and virtually untapped market awaits private long-term care insurance and other private initiatives. Continued development of that market by the private sector, with encouragement from the government, could make long-term care much more affordable for a substantial fraction of the population. However, even with maximum likely development of private options, public spending for long-term care, mostly under Medicaid, will continue to increase rapidly for the foreseeable future. Since continued reliance on a welfare program to finance long-term care is undesirable, ways should be found to substantially broaden Medicare coverage to include more long-term care.

FURTHER READING

Brookings-ICF Long-Term Care Financing Model. Unpublished estimates.

Families USA Foundation, in collaboration with J. P. Firman and S. Polniasek. *The Unaffordability of Nursing Home Insurance.* Washington, DC: Families USA Foundation, 1990.

Friedland, R. B. *Facing the Costs of Long-Term Care.* Washington, DC: Employee Benefit Research Institute, 1990.

Hamilton, Frederick, and Schneiders. *AARP 10th Annual Survey.* Washington, DC: American Association of Retired Persons, 1988.

Health Insurance Association of America. "Long-Term Care Market Continues to Grow: Group Market Triples in Size." Washington, DC: Health Insurance Association of America News Release, 1989.

Letsch, S. W., K. R. Levit, and D. R. Waldo. "National Health Expenditures, 1987." *Health Care Financing Review* 10 (Winter 1988): 109–122.

RL Associates. *The American Public Views Long-Term Care.* Washington, DC: American Association of Retired Persons and The Villers Foundation, 1987.

Rivlin, A. M., and J. M. Wiener, with R. J. Hanley and D. A. Spence. *Caring for the Disabled Elderly: Who Will Pay?* Washington, DC: The Brookings Institution, 1988.

Stone, R., G. L. Cafferatta, and J. Sangl. "Caregivers of the Frail Elderly: A National Profile." *Gerontologist* 27 (1987): 616–26.

Van Gelder, S., Health Insurance Association of America. Personal communication with author, 1989.

Van Gelder, S., and D. Johnson. *Long-Term Care Insurance: Market Trends*. Washington, DC:

Health Insurance Associates of America, 1989.

Zedlewski, S. R., R. O. Barnes, M. K. Burt, T. D. McBride, and J. A. Meyer. *The Needs of the Elderly in the 21st Century*. Washington, DC: The Urban Institute, 1989.

Discussion Questions for Chapter Thirteen

1. The proposals for health-care reform described in the introduction to this chapter differ in the level of free-market involvement, which Dickman and his colleagues view as one of the major sources of difficulty in our system. Which approach is the most viable solution to our nation's health-care problems, and which is the most politically feasible? Are the proposals that exclude the free-market system better than those that include it?

2. The proposals for rationing health care described by Perrin are based on the assumption that health-care resources are scarce, and that tough decisions must be made about who has access to them. Is it true that health-care resources must be limited, or is it possible for everyone to have access to high quality health care?

3. Estes argues that health care must be viewed as an inalienable right, not a commodity. What changes would have to be made in our health-care system and our society as a whole in order to make health

care a right of citizenship? Who, if anyone, would oppose these changes?

4. Some would argue that those who "game" the system by divesting themselves of assets in order to qualify for Medicaid are unethical. Others would say that this is a rational approach to dealing with the possibility of illness-engendered poverty described by Grau. Is divestment rational or unethical? Are solutions to this dilemma possible on an individual level or is change in social policy necessary?

5. Wiener and Hanley refer to long-term care as a normal risk of growing old, yet our society depends on a welfare system to pay for it. In many other areas of normal risk, we have private insurance (*e.g.*, fire insurance, auto insurance) and public insurance (*e.g.*, unemployment insurance, Social Security Disability Insurance, Medicare) to protect ourselves. Why do we not similarly protect ourselves against the need for long-term care? Why is this issue so difficult for us to solve?

CHAPTER FOURTEEN

Aging and Social Policy

Social policy shapes the conditions of life for older people. As shown in the previous chapter, government policy on health care has a major impact on the well-being of elderly people. The selections in this chapter address pressing policy issues with respect to generational equity, social security, and gender equality.

In the recent past, a great deal of concern has arisen regarding fair treatment of different generations. Building on the new public perception of older people as economically better off than younger people (see Chapter 10), advocates for "intergenerational equity" take aim at government programs for the elderly as the cause of deteriorating conditions faced by the young. A major target in this debate is the Social Security system. Fueled by huge federal budget deficits and demographic projections indicating unfavorable ratios of workers to retirees in the future, fear has been incited among the young that their tax dollars are being used to pay benefits to well-off older people through a Social Security system that will be unable to provide for them in their old age.

Although Social Security is often blamed for the budget deficit, in the short term, it actually helps reduce it. This is because the Social Security retirement trust fund is accumulating huge surpluses which, by law, must be placed in the U.S. Treasury and counted as government revenues. These large sums are then lent to the federal government and used to pay for current expenditures.

Defenders of Social Security point out that the viability of the system to pay benefits in the future is not simply a function of demographics of aging (*i.e.*, the ratio of workers to retirees), but also the productivity of the labor force. If future workers are highly productive, the system will be able to generate enough tax dollars to pay benefits without burdening workers (Bernstein, 1989). In fact, even though the worker-to-beneficiary ratio is less favorable now than when Social Security benefits were first paid out, the system is able to generate sufficient revenues in large part because workers are more productive now than they were in the past.

Critics of Social Security often overlook that the system benefits the young as well as the old. By providing financial support for the elderly, Social Security helps relieve the young from the responsibility of supporting their parents. Social Security is also a portable pension system that covers young workers on every job they will have. The system also benefits the young through disability insurance, which pays benefits to minor dependents in cases of disability or death of a covered parent (Kingson, 1989).

In response to critics who complain that poverty rates among the elderly are lower than among other segments of the population, defenders of Social Security proclaim this as evidence of a highly successful social program, pointing out that if it were not for Social Security, nearly one-half of the elderly population would be below the poverty line.

In "Generational Equity: Pitting Young Against Old," Lenard W. Kaye describes the argument made by generational equity advocates and then challenges it on the basis of its "misunderstandings and misleading generalizations about an aging society."

In "Mother, Apple Pie, and Social Security—It's Not Time to Change," James H. Schulz defends Social Security against its attackers by arguing that the reasons for Social Security today are the same as they were at its inception. Schulz places Social Security in the context of the modern welfare state, showing its reasons for existence in a capitalist economy and pointing out shortcomings of alternative approaches for providing economic security in old age.

Gerontologists have noted that problems of aging are largely problems of women. Although public programs for the elderly provide the same services and benefits to elderly persons regardless of gender, elderly men and women differ in many respects including life expectancy, economic status, living arrangements, marital status, and health-care needs. Since men and women have different needs and resources, the impact of public programs on the sexes differs. In "Public Policies: Are They Gender-Neutral?" Marilyn Moon demonstrates the way in which apparently gender-neutral policies place older women at a disadvantage.

REFERENCES

Bernstein, Merton C. (1989). The viability of Social Security and Medicare in an aging society. *Houston Law Review, 26,* 799–812.

Kingson, Eric R. (1989). Misconceptions distort Social Security policy discussions. *Social Work, 34,* 357–362.

Generational Equity:
Pitting Young Against Old

LENARD W. KAYE

In the past several years there has emerged a political perspective which has taken aim at the relative status of the elderly versus the young in this country. It is strongly reflected in a group called Americans for Generational Equity (AGE). AGE, a Washington, D.C., based organization has, it seems, attracted a growing number of politicians, intellectuals, and members of the media who influence the development and ultimate enactment of domestic policy. Advocates of generational equity, including Senator David F. Durenberger, a Republican from Minnesota; Representative James R. Jones, a Democrat from Oklahoma; Representative Jim Moody, a Democrat from Wisconsin; and former Governor Richard Lamm of Colorado, now at Dartmouth College; appear convinced that the elderly have become a major cause of this country's budget deficit.

These advocates argue that (1) programs for the elderly represent a major cause of the current budget deficit and economic problems; (2) demographic trends will bring on an intolerable burden of care placed on the shoulders of younger workers; (3) the elderly receive too large a portion of current public social welfare expenditures to the detriment of young people and other groups;

and (4) younger people will not receive their fair share of returns for investments made in Social Security and Medicare.[1] Consider what appear to be some of the consequences, both direct and indirect, of this increasingly popular political philosophy:

- The Gramm-Rudman-Hollings budget-cutting bill, passed in December 1985, proposes to achieve a balanced budget in 1991 by setting projected annual deficit amounts. It represents a broad-based change in philosophy in terms of government's responsibility for its older citizens and for all people, for that matter. It makes the Older Americans Act, housing programs, block grants, energy assistance programs, Medicare and Social Security administrative costs all subject to automatic cuts.

- The theme of generational equity is receiving growing attention from the media with the picture of "the burdensome older population" an increasingly popular topic of news stories.

- Programs and policies are already reflecting a changing view of the older population and what should be the government's rightful share in the responsi-

Source: New England Journal of Human Services, 8(1), 8–11. Reprinted with permission from the New England Journal of Human Services, Grand Rapids, MI 49503. Copyright 1988.

bility for their welfare. A few examples are in order:

a) Diagnosis related groups (DRGs) have created hard and fast definitions of hospital reimbursement rates for the treatment of specific categories of diseases resulting in what many believe is the growing tendency for the elderly to be released "quicker and sicker" from this nation's hospitals. The economic incentive to limit the length of hospital stay of Medicare patients, in particular, portends, according to many, negative consequences for the elderly. Others go so far as to say that DRGs threaten to restrict access by the aged to health care, to compromise its quality and to impede the development of new medical technologies.

b) Even HMOs, which were seen as a panacea for the treatment of the elderly, may be backfiring. Limited Medicare reimbursement rates for the HMOs combined with high service utilization rates among elderly subscribers have caused HMOs specializing in serving older consumers to consider charging premiums for older subscribers or refusing to accept Medicare subscribers altogether.

c) Public officials are interpreting Medicare home care regulations more restrictively. This policy trend has resulted in a large number of seemingly eligible elderly home care recipients being put on waiting lists or rejected outright for service coverage.

d) Recent Medicare provisions determining the allowable fees doctors may charge for Medicare patients are another example of a new policy that may make access to health care more difficult for the elderly. Already, the American Medical Association has challenged the new law, claiming that such provisions would create a two-tiered system treating Medicare beneficiaries differently from all others. While at first glance this policy may be perceived as beneficial to the elderly by holding down fees charged by Medicare-participating physicians, greater

numbers of these same physicians are threatening to withdraw from participation each day. This would force the elderly to either seek new physicians or remain with their former physicians and potentially suffer an increasingly burdensome medical care bill.

e) Pending federal policy also seems to be taking direct aim at undercutting the welfare of the elderly. President Reagan proposed cuts of $4.7 billion in the Medicare budget for fiscal 1988, followed by cuts totaling $50 billion over the next five years. He proposed nearly doubling the premiums for new enrollees in Medicare Part B, delaying by one month a person's eligibility for Medicare, and cutting funds for Section 202 housing for the elderly and handicapped along with meal programs and other support services for participants in this federal housing program.

f) Proposed Medicare coverage of catastrophic illness also reflects a clear bias against the elderly. The plan, endorsed by the Secretary of Health and Human Services and the President, addresses only acute catastrophic illness resulting in hospital stays in excess of sixty days and not coverage of long-term care, the primary concern of the older population.

The generational equity approach is a public policy framework which, in the final analysis, is based on a series of misunderstandings and misleading generalizations about the aging society. What are these flaws?

First, it frames policy issues in terms of competition and conflict between young and old and between the working population and those who are not employed. Already, more than ninety national organizations representing over thirty million Americans of all ages have banded together to fight the notion of generational equity. Representative of national youth and aging organizations alike, Generations United, as it is called, was founded by the National Council on the Aging and the Child Welfare League of America. This coalition is committed to building the bonds of understanding and cooperation among people of all generations. It is rapidly coming to represent a united front on such issues as access to health care, welfare reform, child and elder abuse, and day care for children and dependent older adults. The sense of brotherhood reflected in Generations United confirms that the generations have common interdependent interests. In fact, Generations United represents an organized voice for the children and young families whose needs have been largely ignored, a voice to which the policymakers will be compelled to listen, just as they have increasingly come to listen to advocates of and for the elderly.

Second, the generational equity argument fails in that it sets spending for the aged against spending for children and young families rather than looking at alternative sources for revenue such as Pentagon expenditures or, according to more than a few economists, anticipated increases in our nation's productivity in the years ahead. As Kingson has argued,[2] generational equity advocates assume a sort of zero-sum game: that the American pie is finite in size and will not grow and that spending priorities cannot be reordered. It assumes further that recovered expenditures from aging-related budgets will be redirected for the benefit of children and other nonaged populations. Analysts agree that there can be no presumed link between the recent rise in the poverty rate among children and the decreasing rate of poverty among the elderly. Nor can one presume that cuts in expenditures for one type of federal program will result in increased expenditures in another.

Third, the generational equity argument also fails in not taking into account the interdependence of the generations and the various ways that the elderly return that financial reward which may have been real-ized through the successes of recent policy changes. Reciprocity on the part of the elderly through the transfer of assets to their descendants by means of inheritance, and support for children through their childhood, adolescence and young adulthood are somehow not included in the calculus of intergenerational transfer.[3] Nor is the impact that Social Security and other old age benefits have had on reducing the financial burden formerly carried by families for their elderly relatives. Additionally, the extent to which the elderly have increasingly entered the marketplace and expended their discretionary income (thereby strengthening the economy) has often not been considered.

Fourth, the argument in behalf of generational equity presumes that Social Security has become a poor investment for young workers who will realize an inadequate return when they reach retirement. It is argued that Social Security is a drain on the economy and unstable. Contrary to popular belief, Social Security is quite secure. For example, the overall dependency ratio of workers to nonworkers (a measure of the number of persons sixty-five and over and those under eighteen for every one hundred persons of working age eighteen to sixty-four years) is projected to remain relatively stable for the next forty to fifty years.[4] Furthermore, Social Security is now starting to build up huge reserves and may be contributing to reducing the federal deficit brought on by increased defense expenditures and the recently enacted tax cuts.[5]

Of course, one should not be lulled into believing that Social Security has come to represent simply an additional source of unneeded income for this nation's older population. Without Social Security, almost one in two older adults would be living in poverty (47.6 percent) or approximately 13 million individuals. The elder poverty rolls would quadruple, and the burden carried by private organizations, public welfare programs, and families would rise accordingly.[6]

It is noteworthy as well, that Social Security continues to represent a sacred national social contract which provides the greatest future benefits, relatively speaking, to those at the lower end of the economic scale—low-income workers and limited-income married couples.

And, remember, any criticism lodged against the Social Security system ultimately represents criticism lodged against the 3.4 million young people aged eighteen and under living in families supported by Social Security. Yes, young people in significant numbers benefit from Social Security as well, a fact seldom cited by advocates of generational equity.

Finally, it is worth noting that the generational equity argument does not take into consideration the great diversity found among the aged. While the elderly may have been successful in the past twenty years in moving out of poverty (cutting their rate of poverty by half) as defined by the federal government, a large proportion are now finding themselves to be of marginal status residing in a state of near poverty. Thus, while only approximately 13 percent or 3.5 million elderly were poor in 1985, according to federal definitions, an additional 8 percent or 2.3 million elders were "near poor" (lying between the poverty level and 125 percent of that level); and this refers to the noninstitutionalized aged population only.[7] An additional 5 percent or some 1.5 million older adults reside in nursing homes, the majority of whom have been stripped of their assets and income.

And the generational equity argument loses sight of special subgroups of the older cohort who are considerably more likely to live in poverty than others. Thus, elderly women are twice as likely to be poor as are males (16 percent, compared to 8 percent); 32 percent of elderly blacks are poor, and one in four elderly Hispanics is poor. And, as astonishing as it may seem, the poverty rate for older black women is 34.8 percent, jumping to 54 percent if they live alone. The generational equity argument, as emphasized by Binstock,[8] thus blinds us to inequities within age groups, the inherent weakness of examining problems in generational terms.

Given the rather discouraging development in aging policy in recent times, much of which seems linked to a philosophy increasingly influenced by the propositions of generational equity, what is the role of those who advocate for older Americans? It is no longer enough to train students for careers in the field of aging nor simply to take responsibility for the delivery of services to older people. Rather, we must also become engaged in interpreting the idea of interdependence between the generations. This entails presenting a life span approach in explaining the transfer of resources among the generations. We must understand the greater significance that Social Security and other old age expenditures have in terms of reducing responsibility carried by the family, in insuring the flow of inheritance to younger generations, and in abiding by a promise which has been made to all working Americans since 1935 that they will realize a rightful return on their investment as they enter their much deserved years of retirement. And it is time to forge new coalitions between the young and the old, between working and retired populations, fighting together for generic, broad-based welfare reform in a climate of limited budgetary resources.

Finally, the time is ripe to remind others, and perhaps ourselves as well, that a short-sighted view of gerontological policy makes little sense. In the long run, all of us can expect to live into extended old age, barring an unexpected fatal illness or accident. To do injustice to our current generation of elders, by means of policy change, can only come back to haunt us as each and every one of us—children, young families, and working people—move toward the latter stages of the life course.

NOTES

1. See Eric R. Kingson, Barbara A. Hirshorn, and John M. Cornman, *Ties That Bind: The Interdependence of Generations* (Washington, D.C.: Seven Locks Press, 1986).

2. See Elliot Carlson, "The Phony War: Exploding the Myth of the Generational Conflict Between Young and Old," *Modern Maturity*, February-March (1987): 34–46.

3. See Edward A. Wynne, "Will the Young Support the Old?" in *Our Aging Society: Paradox and Promise,* eds. Alan Pifer and Lydia Bronte (New York: W. W. Norton & Co., 1986).

4. U.S. Bureau of the Census, "Projections of the Population of the United States, by Age, Sex, and Race: 1983–2080," *Current Population Reports,* P-25, No. 952 (Washington, D.C.: U.S. Government Printing Office, 1986).

5. See Villars Foundation, *On the Other Side of Easy Street: Myths and Facts About the Economics of Old Age* (Washington, D.C.: The Villars Foundation, 1987).

6. Ibid.

7. See American Association of Retired Persons, "A Profile of Older Americans: 1986" (Washington, D.C.: American Association of Retired Persons, 1986): 1–9; and U.S. Senate Special Committee on Aging, *Aging America: Trends and Projections, 1985–86 Edition* (Washington, D.C.: U.S. Government Printing Office, 1986).

8. See Carlson, pp. 34–46.

Mother, Apple Pie, and Social Security—It's Not Time to Change

JAMES H. SCHULZ

Current discussions about the economics of aging are dominated by three issues. As they have been provocatively stated:

- Huge federal budget deficits require a major change in federal expenditure policies related to the elderly.
- The rapid aging of the United States population early in the next century requires us to raise the Social Security age of retirement.
- New realities related to the economics of aging require us to move away from Social Security as the principal institution of old-age income maintenance.

In assessing these propositions, it is appropriate to recall how we got to where we are today in the provision of economic security for the aged. What does the past teach us about income maintenance for the elderly in a nation such as ours that relies heavily on a market economy for growth and efficiency? What must such nations do and what (politically) are its citizens willing to do in moderating the human hardship and insecurity that arise by *necessity and with certainty* as a by-product of the constantly fluctuating markets of a free-enterprise system?

Contemporary economic and political commentator James Fallows has expressed it well. He writes (1985, p. 62):

> Capitalism is one of the world's more disruptive forces. It can call every social arrangement into question, make cities and skills and ranks merely temporary. To buy into it is to make a commitment to permanent revolution that few political creeds can match.

Reacting to these destructive, "revolutionary" forces, industrialized countries established modern so-called "welfare states." Programs were created to protect people from the vicissitudes of modern industrial life; they were designed to do this in a dignified and efficient manner (Myles, 1984).

The elderly are the American *success* story in this historical effort. The story of the economic welfare of the aged in the United States today is the story of public and private pensions—about their failures but mostly about their successes. If we look at recent statistics on the income and wealth situation of the elderly we see that:

> ... the elderly in ... [the United States] are beginning to look a lot like the rest of the population: some very rich, lots with ade-

Source: Journal of Aging and Social Policy, 2(1), 69–81. Reprinted with permission from Haworth Press, Inc., Binghamton, NY, 13904. Copyright 1990.

quate income, lots more with very modest incomes (often near poverty), and a significant minority still destitute. This is very different from the past when most [of the elderly] were destitute. (Schulz, 1988, p. 18)

But it is not just the income and wealth situation of the elderly that has changed so dramatically over the years. There is another equally important part of the story. Over the past 50 years a dramatic shift in attitudes and practices toward retirement has taken place. The drop in labor force participation among older male workers in industrialized countries has been nothing short of spectacular. And the trend today toward early retirement continues as strong as ever (Schulz, 1987).

Given this new income and retirement situation:

- Old age in the United States today is no longer a period when the ability to keep one's job determines the ability to age "successfully."
- It is not necessarily a time when declining income inevitably complements declining health, threatening survival.
- And, old age is no longer a period when most people's living options begin to narrow significantly.

Instead, the old ways of aging have given way to a period of meaningful choices between work and leisure, a period of relative income adequacy for many, and for most of the elderly, a period where there are many (often new) living options.

Many people today forget how all this came about. It is not enough to know that the economic status of today's elderly has improved significantly and is getting better every day. To react intelligently to the challenges of huge federal deficits, the "graying" of the population, and contemporary critics of Social Security—we need to understand the origins of the American welfare state. We need to understand yesterday's institution building in terms of today's rising income

and declining employment among the aged. George Santayana said, "Those who cannot remember the past are condemned to repeat it." Are we about to push for changes in aged income policy, an exercise that may cause us to have to rediscover the wheel at some later date?

The modern welfare state is a little over 100 years old. It was in 1881 that Kaiser Wilhelm I of Germany proposed in a message to the Reichstag that German workers be protected by social insurance. This idea of *collective* disability, retirement, and health insurance *sponsored by the government* originated with the Kaiser's Chancellor, Otto von Bismarck. Bismarck saw social security as a way of reducing growing worker discontent and strengthening the position of the central government.

As pointed out by Martin Kohli and Hans-Joachim von Kondratowitz (1987), two major events at the time dramatized the threat to the existing order in Germany (and other countries). First, the Paris Commune of 1871 raised the specter of socialist revolution. In addition, massive economic turmoil occurred in Europe from 1873 to 1879. The economic misery of those years—which was to become a common feature of the depressions and recessions of industrialized nations in the years to come—"was a deep blow to the belief in economic progress and in the self-regulation of the economy by way of unrestricted markets" (Kohli & von Kondratowitz, 1987, p. 134).

Shortly after Bismarck's first innovation, Sweden and Denmark followed the German lead. In the years following, other countries established their own versions of the welfare state. It came to Britain, for example, during the first decade of the 20th century, to the United States in the mid-1930s, and to France and Japan shortly after World War II.

Today, social welfare provision in one way or another absorbs one-fifth to one-third of the gross domestic products of industrial nations (King, 1983). Partly as a result of these costs, and for other reasons, the welfare state is under attack in many countries.

But criticism of the welfare state is not entirely new. It has long been with us. For example, in a well-known 1969 article in *The Public Interest*, Peter Drucker wrote about the "sickness of government." One of the major symptoms of this sickness, he said, was "the fiasco of the welfare state."

> The welfare state turns out to be just another big insurance company, as exciting, as creative, and as inspiring as insurance companies tend to be. . . . The best we get from government in the welfare state is competent mediocrity. More often we do not get even that. . . . And the more we expand the welfare state, the less capable even of routine mediocrity does it seem to become. (1969, p. 7)

Drucker's criticism represents what has been a continuing critique from the right, a resistance or opposition to government-run programs to deal with social problems.

Until recently the criticism has been relatively small, and few people were listening. Today the situation is different. Arguments against the welfare state are numerous, are coming from people across the political spectrum, and are being listened to by many voters. As observed by Rudolf Klein and Michael O'Higgins (1988):

> The apocalyptic right argues that the people have risen against the overreaching state and are re-imposing the primacy of the individual and the economic market. The political center argues that the strains are mostly a consequence of the recent economic disruptions and periodic recessions occurring since the oil price shocks of the mid-Seventies, but can be expected to decline with the resumption of economic growth. And the neo-Marxist left sees the strains as symptomatic of the internal contradictions of capitalism.

What are we to make of the current attacks on Social Security? To suggest abolishing or severely restricting the Social Security programs now in place for older Americans raises a fundamental question. If we cut back on these public programs, where will the shifted responsibility lie? In the absence of the welfare state, who will assume the responsibility? The employer? The individual? The family? Our communities? Voluntary groups?

Let there be no misunderstanding. Someone must assume the responsibility for dealing with the economic insecurity experienced by older citizens in a highly industrialized, market-oriented economy. If one looks closely today at any country in the world, the same conditions of economic insecurity that confronted the Western nations when welfare-state programs were initially established can be found:

- old age with the threat of ill health and disability
- death (and hardship for many of the survivors)
- unemployment and inflation
- economic and industrial disruption on the job, in factories, in communities, and among nations
- unequal distribution of income, accompanied by poverty, malnutrition, and sickness for some people
- potential deprivation if individual saving or pensions fail

What is new today is not these problems; they have not changed. Rather, what is new is the declining confidence many people have in the ability of existing mechanisms to deal with them. And what is also new is the upsurge in calls for "new" approaches to these problems.

Hostile reactions to government are common in periods of major political and economic change and uncertainty. It is clear that the world economy is going through a major restructuring (Piore & Sabels, 1984). And no one is really sure whether the shining sun of American economic leadership and prosperity is temporarily behind a cloud or whether it is about to set for a long, perhaps permanent, night of darkness (Schulz, 1984a).

Calls for change in such periods are common. For example, one of the major critics of Social Security old-age insurance, Peter J. Ferrara (1985) has called for the creation of a "Super-IRA". He argues that American workers should be allowed to contribute up to 20% of their Social Security payroll taxes into a personalized savings account or what is called an individual retirement account (IRA)—receiving a dollar-for-dollar tax credit and reduced Social Security benefits.[1] Ferrara's answer to the welfare-state crisis is to shift from reliance on government-sponsored programs to individual self-reliance, encouraged by tax incentives provided by the federal government. The Super-IRA is one of many proposals that would begin the shift of responsibility from government to either the individual, the family, the community, or the corporation. In the familiar words of former President Reagan, "It's time to get the government off the backs of the people."

In assessing proposals like the Super-IRA, we need to remind ourselves where we have come from. One good way for us today to get a better feeling for what it was like *before* Social Security is to review what it is like *now* for elderly people with regard to long-term care. What kind of a situation do we and our children face if the way we are dealing with long-term care does not change?

Are we prepared to meet the challenge of chronic illness, decreasing mobility, and perhaps loss of mental acuity? If we, as individuals, ultimately must be institutionalized, we'll need, in today's prices, $20,000 to 40,000 a year to pay for nursing home care. Alternately, we may be able to rely on our families, as many now do, and/or "home care," if it is available and we can afford it.

But we have to hope that:

- We don't outlive our families.
- We don't divorce.

- We don't have to confront the issue of elder abuse.
- We don't mind being a "burden" on our families.

And we must hope that:

- We are viewed and treated by our physicians as adults, not as children or as vegetables;
- And that we are *not* viewed as someone better dead than alive by those who care for us.

And we'd better hope, if the time comes for institutionalization:

- That we can find a nursing home that will take us;
- That the nursing home is not one of those institutions with numerous problems (understaffed, given to using excessive medication, or with a dangerous physical environment); and,
- That we have the money to afford it.

But if all else fails, an individual can use up almost all of his or her money (and that of a spouse), and become a pauper and dependent on Medicaid.[2]

No wonder current surveys of older persons find that chronic illness is the biggest fear of older people today. No wonder so many people today are working hard to try to find a mechanism to help people deal with the uncertainties, fears, and financial hardship of long-term care needs.

If we understand the long-term care dilemma today, then we can understand the long-term care dilemma that confronted American society before Social Security: the uncertainty, and hence the fear, in those days about what would happen if *work* were no longer possible was no doubt quite similar to our fears today about long-term care.

In those days before Social Security, most people worked in old age. But a sizeable number were unable to work because of illness or disability. How did these people manage? The uncertainty and disruptions of life were everywhere. Read the history of those times:[3]

- Industrialization and migration were breaking up families.
- The technological revolution and "the business cycle" were wreaking havoc with workers, especially older workers, and the family support structure.
- Most employers fought unions and other attempts to increase wage and job stability.
- Private pensions were designed mostly to benefit employers and were unreliable.
- Banks were unreliable.
- Financial investments like stocks and bonds were unreliable.

Self-reliance was the watchword. But families were more often than not forced to step in and help. And if all else failed, of course, we had those lovely poor houses and county farms to take care of our "dear" old folks. As a last resort, the government was often, but not always, available if one could meet stringent eligibility conditions and were prepared to suffer the degradation and humiliation of below-subsistence benefit levels and the stigma of carefully designed rules and procedures for discouraging the lazy and those un-American types looking for handouts.

The welfare state in the United States and the other countries of the industrialized world was a reaction to the chaos and uncertainty of life in nations with growing populations and rising economic interdependence. Even the rising living standards of the times created problems; there was more to fluctuate and more to protect.

Elsewhere I have discussed in detail why the two basic tenets of Social Security are: security and dignity (Schulz, 1985). As it evolved, Social Security became the cornerstone of the American welfare state; it is a highly certain way of protecting people in a dignified manner from many of the basic economic uncertainties of life. The Social Security program was a reaction to the economic breakdowns of an industrialized society and hence to the *threats* against individuals and families. It was a reaction to "the company town" and business "benevolence." It was a reaction to the personal degradation of family charity and "government welfare." The welfare state sought to provide "a floor of protection" so that individual and industrial initiative could flourish. And they did!

Now, slower growth combined with massive military spending have put financial strains on governments around the world. Our ability to maintain and carry out all the functions of government is currently dependent on our ability to deal with slow economic growth, government deficits, and our sustained military obligations. And so a big part of the crisis of the welfare state is the economic strain brought on by these more general problems.

Financing Social Security today is a major topic about which much could be written: growing OASI reserves (Aaron et al., 1988), cost escalations in Medicare (Altman & Rodwin, 1988), issues of equity for women (Gibson, 1987), and intergenerational equity considerations (Schulz, 1988). As important as these issues are, and given the current strains of government financing, we must not miss the central fact that keeps the welfare state concept as relevant as it was 100 years ago: Industrialized, market-oriented economies generate tremendous insecurity from which their citizens demand some protection. The current crisis of welfare states is the crisis of slow growth and heavy military expenditures—not a budgeting crisis arising out of the growth of so-called "entitlement" programs.

The Social Security old-age pension program is the biggest and perhaps most important part of the American welfare state. As mentioned above, one of the latest ideas for phasing out Social Security is the Super-IRA. With this mechanism we could all invest *our own* funds for the future. We could insure *our own* retirement. We could worry about protecting *our own* money. And, we could deal with inflation in *our own* way.

But before we ask people to take on these challenges, remember a little bit of history. Individual saving and investment for retirement is not such a simple thing.[4] Remember the stockmarket crashes of 1929 and 1987? Remember how the government in the 1940s sold us war bonds and savings bonds at fixed rates—*giving us negative rates of return* during most of the post-World War II period? Remember how our friendly private insurance companies sold us whole-life policies, invested our money, and again gave us negative rates of return? Remember the ceilings on savings account interest rates throughout most of the post-war period, especially during periods of double-digit inflation? Remember the private pension plans that were often unable to deliver promised benefits (until guaranteed in later years by the federal ERISA legislation)? And remember the financial problems of the Pension Benefit Guaranty Corporation—the organization set up to bail out bankrupt private pension plans—an organization that Congress has repeatedly had to bail out by imposing higher premiums on successful businesses with adequately financed plans?

After remembering all these and much more, then make your choice: How much of your discretionary retirement savings would you invest in stocks, corporate bonds, GNMAS, precious metals, pork bellies, real estate, Treasury securities (long, medium, or short), tax-free municipals, junk bonds, or mutual funds (which are now available in almost limitless shapes and forms)?

Sound like fun? Will you need some help in making a decision? There are lots of investment counselors, insurance companies, investment houses, and so forth that will help you for a fee. But beware of the unscrupulous ones, which have already fleeced many investors out of millions of dollars. Even if they are honest, the accomplishments of most financial advisers to date have not been impressive.

Proponents of the Super-IRA are asking us to shift decisionmaking from the public sector to the private, from a collective to an individual approach. But what makes the Chase Manhattan Bank, which has made such bad investments in Mexico and South America, a safer place for your retirement money than the government? And, who did the banks and savings and loan associations turn to for help after they made bad investment decisions (in New York, Illinois, and, most recently, Texas)? The government, of course.

Why is Social Security so popular? First, it can be counted on; Social Security has never once missed mailing out the millions of checks that go out each month to eligible beneficiaries. More important, Social Security and the welfare state are built on a number of fundamental and generally supported propositions. We should remember them:

1. It is both efficient and more secure to build collective mechanisms for old-age support based on the insurance principle—that is, bringing people together to take advantage of the laws of large numbers to keep down costs and raise security.

2. Both parents and children prefer that the major *economic* support for old age be *outside* the family.

3. Families also prefer that support be provided in a way that preserves the dignity of the individual. That is why contributory social security programs replaced the demeaning means-tested programs that preceded them (see Schulz, 1984b).

4. There is a broad consensus that we need to develop mechanisms that take into account both the shortsightedness (the myopia that most people readily admit to) in financial planning and most people's desire to delegate retirement planning to experts—given the complexity of this decisionmaking and the fact that most people would rather do other things with their time.

5. While there is a role for private *collective* action, only governments can ultimately secure the benefits promised in old age—given the economic vicissitudes of regional and industrial shifts, recessions, inflation, and the extraordinary drains of military output and national defense policies.[5]

None of these fundamental propositions has changed significantly over time. They are the underlying basis for political and economic decisionmaking in the area of social policy for old age (and in other areas). And

we must begin any debate on changes in our policies with a recognition of them.[6]

We have come a long way in the search for economic stability and security. When Bismarck and Kaiser Wilhelm acted, they were seeking to promote primarily their own political stability and economic security. Little did they realize the long-term changes their actions would trigger. For today, the "common people" (especially older people) in most industrialized nations enjoy a security that was unthinkable a century ago. We in the United States should be proud of that achievement, as proud as we are of our mothers and apple pie!

NOTES

1. Originally, workers not covered by a retirement plan where they were employed could make tax-deferrable contributions of 15% of earned income up to $1,500 per year to an individual account or annuity. Beginning in 1977, if there was a nonemployed spouse, the maximum was increased to $1,750. Funds in IRAs may be placed in a life insurance company, a bank, a mutual fund, or in certain special government bonds. There are penalties and immediate tax liability if funds are withdrawn prematurely.
2. The Medicare Catastrophic Coverage Act of 1988 seeks to moderate the financial impact on spouses.
3. Many references could be cited. A short historical summary is provided in Schulz (1984b).

See also Lubove (1968), Graebner (1980), and Quadagno (1987).
4. Of course, thorough documentation of this statement would require much more than the suggestive examples given here. For further discussion, see Schulz et al. (1974) and Kotlikoff (1987).
5. For the debate on this point, see Schulz (1988, Chapter 4).
6. This article is not meant to imply that social security programs in the United States and abroad have no problems or that no changes should be made. For a discussion of issues and options, see, for example, Schulz (1988).

REFERENCES

Aaron, H. J., Bosworth, B. P., & Burtless, G. (1988). *Can America afford to grow old?* Washington, DC: The Brookings Institution.

Altman, S. H., & Rodwin, M. A. (1988). Half-way competitive markets and ineffective regulation: The American health care system. *Journal of Health Politics, Policy and Law, 13*, 323–339.

Drucker, P. F. L. (1969). The sickness of government. *Public Interest, 14*, 3–23.

Fallows, J. (1985, March). America's changing economic landscape. *The Atlantic Monthly*, pp. 47–68.

Ferrara, P. J. (1985). Social security reform: Some theoretical observations. In P. J. Ferrara (Ed.), *Social security—Prospects for real reform* (pp. 173–190). Washington, DC: Cato Institute.

Gibson, M. (Ed.). (1987). Income security and long-term care for women in midlife and beyond. Washington, DC: American Association of Retired Persons.

Graebner, W. (1980). *History of retirement.* New Haven, CT: Yale University Press.

King, A. (1983). The political consequences of the welfare state. In S. E. Spiro (Ed.), *Evaluating the welfare state* (pp. 7–25). New York: Academic Press.

Klein, R., & O'Higgins, M. (1988). Defusing the crisis of the welfare state. In T. R. Marmor & J. L. Mashaw (Eds.), *Social security: Beyond the rhetoric of crisis.* Princeton, NJ: Princeton University Press.

Kohli, M., & von Kondratowitz, H. (1987). Retirement in Germany: Towards the construction of the "citizen of the work society." In K. S. Markides & C. L. Cooper (Eds.), *Retirement in industrialized societies* (pp. 131–166). New York: Wiley.

Kotlikoff, L. J. (1987). Justifying public provision of social security. *Journal of Policy Analysis and Management, 6,* 674–689.

Lubove, R. (1968). *The struggle for social security, 1900–1935.* Cambridge, MA: Harvard University Press.

Myles, J. (1984). *Old age in the welfare state.* Boston: Little Brown.

Piore, M. J., & Sabels, C. F. (1984). *The second industrial divide.* New York: Basic Books.

Quadagno, J. (1987). The social security program and the private sector alternative: Lessons from history. *International Journal of Aging and Human Development, 25,* 239–246.

Schulz, J. H. (1984a). The economics of aging: Doomsday or Shangrila? In C. Gaitz (Ed.), *Aging 2000—Our health care destiny, Vol. II* (pp. 305–314). New York: Springer-Verlag.

Schulz, J. H. (1984b). SSI: Origins, experiences, and unresolved issues. In U.S. Senate Special Committee on Aging, *The supplemental security income program: A 10-year overview.* Washington, DC: U.S. Government Printing Office.

Schulz, J. H. (1985). To old folks with love: Aged income maintenance in America. *The Gerontologist, 25,* 464–471

Schulz, J. H. (1987). Issues in aged income maintenance: Population aging and the early retirement "timebomb." In U.S. House Select Committee on Aging and the U.S. Senate Special Committee on Aging, *Legislative agenda for an aging society: 1988 and beyond,* Proceedings of a Congressional Forum, November 1987 (pp. 83–97). Washington, DC: U.S. Government Printing Office.

Schulz, J. H. (1988). *The economics of aging* (4th ed.). Dover, MA: Auburn House.

Schulz, J. H., Carrin, G., Krupp, H., Peschke, M., Sclar, E., & Van Steenberge, J. (1974). *Providing adequate retirement income.* Hanover, NH: Brandeis University Press by the University Press of New England.

Public Policies:
Are They Gender-Neutral?

MARILYN MOON

The development of public policy seldom explicitly considers the impact on gender. And even when public programs are created with the needs of women in mind, their appropriateness may change over time as the roles of men and women in our society also change. The impact of public policy on older women is molded by the socioeconomic status of women and their life histories as well as the formal rules and policies that determine coverage and benefits.

Why should we be concerned about gender and public policy? In assessing the impact of public programs, issues of fairness and appropriateness constitute critical dimensions. And gender is certainly one of the factors against which such fairness can be analyzed. But the test of whether policies are appropriately gender-neutral is not a simple matter of intentions. Nor is it entirely satisfactory to look at impacts of public programs and policies by sex to determine fairness. Some variation in impact may be appropriate if other circumstances differ. For instance, if women are more likely than men to need long-term care, a program that resulted in a proportional distribution of benefits between men and women might be inappropriate although appearing to be gender-neutral.

This article briefly explores how public programs treat men and women differently, what the implications are for fairness, and raises some possibilities for change. Before looking at how public programs are constructed and interact by gender, however, it is instructive to set the stage with a brief look at how older men and women differ by some critical socioeconomic factors.

GENDER DIFFERENCES THAT AFFECT POLICY

Even when public policies make no gender distinctions, they may result in different impacts because older men and women have different resources and needs. The critical factors relate to income and healthcare—because most of the public policies directed at older persons aim to raise the income of elders or protect them against healthcare expenditures—and to living arrangements and life expectancy. Many of these matters are discussed in other articles in this issue and are only briefly mentioned here.

Older women are much more likely than older men to be poor or near-poor; women subsist on substantially lower incomes. For example, in 1988, the most recent year in

Source: Generations, 14(3), 59–63. Reprinted with permission from *Generations,* 833 Market St., Suite 512, San Francisco, CA 94103, and the author. Copyright 1990 by the American Society on Aging.

which data are available, 14.9 percent of all women over the age of 65 were poor, while only 8 percent of all men in this age group had incomes below the poverty threshold. Median income—the income of an average individual—was $12,471 for older men but only $7,103 for older women (U.S. Bureau of the Census, 1989a).

Moreover, a closer look at the poverty status of elderly unrelated individuals—persons classified by the Census Bureau as living apart from relatives—shows an even more dramatic picture (see Table 1). These persons, who generally live alone, are the most vulnerable among the elderly and are predominantly women. More than one in four of such women have incomes below the poverty line, and for black and Hispanic women, the figures show more than 50 percent having incomes below the poverty line.

It is often claimed that older Americans are income-poor but asset-rich. Unfortunately for those with low incomes, however, assets are unlikely to come to the rescue. The high averages for asset holdings among those over the age of 65 tend to result from the concentrations of wealth held by the few and from housing assets that may have risen dramatically with inflation in some areas of the country. If one considers contingency assets (that is, net worth excluding the value of the house and any interest in a family business), older persons of modest means often have few resources that can readily be used to supplement their incomes. For example, a majority of persons with incomes below the poverty line have contingency assets of less than $500 (see Table 2).

Only among those with incomes above twice the poverty line do a majority of individuals have more than $5,000 in contingency assets.

Finally, no picture of the economic status of the elderly is complete without a sense of the demands of health expenditures on resources. Older men and women face often daunting healthcare needs that tend to rise with age. The large numbers of very old women are particularly at risk, especially for the costs of long-term care. Estimates of private spending on healthcare for those aged 65 and above were $2,007 per capita in 1987 (Waldo et al., 1989). While some of that private spending includes contributions from employers for retirees' healthcare, most of it would have to be borne by the individual.

Women are more likely to live into their 90s and to live alone—often surviving for many years after the death of a spouse (U.S. Bureau of the Census, 1989b). Not only are there more women in the age groups in which chronic, long-term-care needs increase dramatically, but these women are less likely to live with a spouse or other family member who can offer them needed help. Thus, such women, who often have been the caregivers to their spouses, must in many cases do without help and are likely to end up in an institution when they become functionally dependent.

The enormous progress made in the living standards of older Americans has still left many behind, vulnerable to large expenses for health- and long-term care.

And those left at the bottom are disproportionately female.

TABLE 1 Rates of Poverty by Sex (1988).

	All Persons 65+	Persons Living Apart from Relatives*		
		All 65+	Blacks	Hispanics
	Percent in Poverty			
Women	14.9	25.5	56.5	53.6
Men	8.0	19.6	35.6	32.9
Total	12.0	24.1	50.0	46.1
	Number of Poor (in thousands)			
Women	2,518	1,854	348	80
Men	965	425	100	28
Total	3,482	2,279	448	108

Source: U.S. Bureau of the Census, 1989a.

*Likely to be living alone

TABLE 2   Distribution of Personal Contingency Assets for Persons 65 & Older (1984).

Contingency Asset Amount	Total	Poverty Ratio					
		Less than 1.0	1.0 to 1.49	1.5 to 1.99	2.0 to 2.99	3.0 to 3.99	4.0 or more
Total	100.0	100.0	100.0	100.0	100.0	100.0	100.0
Less than $500	25.3	62.2	40.6	26.3	17.5	13.6	7.8
None	16.3	44.6	27.3	15.4	9.7	8.0	4.7
$1 to $499	9.0	17.6	13.3	10.9	7.8	5.6	3.1
$500 to $4,999	21.1	21.9	30.3	27.5	22.4	17.9	9.2
$5,000 or more	53.6	16.0	29.1	46.2	60.1	68.5	83.0
$20,000 or more	30.8	2.7	9.8	21.5	29.8	42.1	64.3

Source: Del Bene and Vaughn, 1989.

WOMEN & CURRENT PROGRAMS

Public resources directed at persons age 65 and above are largely dominated by income and health programs. Indeed, Social Security, Supplemental Security Income, Medicare, and Medicaid dwarf other public expenditures on older persons.

Social Security. The largest and most complex government program benefiting elders is Social Security. Widely hailed as both the most effective antipoverty program ever devised and a critical income supplement to those of moderate means, Social Security offers an array of benefits tied to the wage history of either the individual or spouse. Social Security consciously set out to offer several types of women's benefits. For older women, dependent and survivor benefits were designed on the assumption that most women would work in the home and depend upon the husband's eligibility for Social Security.

The rise of the two-earner family has created enormous debate and pressure to adopt changes in the structure of Social Security—usually in the form of some type of earnings-sharing program. As yet, however, this part of Social Security remains virtually unchanged, largely because the options are either very costly or would help some women by hurting others (Congressional Budget Office, 1986). The diversity of labor-force experiences among women makes it difficult to devise changes to recognize the contributions of two-earner families and to protect the benefits to women who never participated in the labor force. Actually, two main questions are often intermingled in discussions of earnings sharing: What is the more equitable approach in translating contributions into benefits, and what changes would protect the most vulnerable (for example, widows over age 80)? The answers may be in conflict, further complicating the issue of how to change Social Security.

Changes in Social Security enacted over the years sometimes help and sometimes discriminate against women. For example, amendments to the Social Security Act that have increased the number of years to be used in calculating contributions into the system have worked to the disadvantage of women who have dropped out of the work force for some time. The lower earnings of women on average as compared to their spouses and years out of the labor force to rear children mean that their own Primary

Insurance Amounts are generally less than one-half those of their husbands (the dependent benefit). Consequently, despite the changing labor-force attachment of women, the majority of them still receive dependent's benefits rather than a Social Security benefit earned through their own labor-force history.

On the other hand, benefits for divorced women have been enhanced to recognize this major demographic shift. Dependent and survivor benefits under the original program helped only women who remained married. Amendments to Social Security have added coverage for women who divorce after more than 10 years of marriage (Social Security Administration, 1988).

An overall assessment of Social Security's fairness is difficult because of the system's complexity and because it reflects the many other factors that influence women's lives. Any discrimination that women face in finding jobs and earning equal pay is translated into lower benefits. But is Social Security unfair as a result? Actually, Social Security is likely to offer some compensation—either through the progressive nature of the benefit structure or through the dependent's benefit upon which so many women rely. It is probably unrealistic to expect Social Security to fully offset the impact of discrimination. On the other hand, policies that extended the number of labor-force years used in the benefit calculation might be viewed as discriminatory. Still, such policies ought to be carefully assessed against other goals as well.

Supplemental Security Income. Perhaps the strongest argument that women are discriminated against in public programs could be drawn for the Supplemental Security Income (SSI) program—not because of gender-specific policy per se, but because older women tend to outlive their spouses and live alone. SSI was enacted to provide a minimum guaranteed income for the most needy

of the elderly and disabled. The simple fact is that the basic federal benefits under SSI are more generous for couples than for singles (as compared to the poverty thresholds). In 1988, the SSI guarantee level was $354 per month—or 75 percent of the federal poverty threshold for a person over the age of 65 living alone—and $532 per month for a couple—90 percent of the relevant poverty threshold (Committee on Ways and Means, 1989). That is, couples' incomes are protected to a level closer to the defined poverty level of income than are the incomes of widows and other older persons living alone, whose incomes are protected to a lower level.

But it is precisely women living alone who are the most vulnerable. In 1987, nearly half (48.1 percent) of elderly persons living in poverty were women living alone (U.S. Bureau of the Census, 1989c). The practical follow-up question is to what extent do such women receive help from Supplemental Security Income. Is it reasonably distributed, in practice, among those in need?

Looking first at all poor women, it appears that receipt of SSI is fairly distributed. Of all poor persons over the age of 65, 71.3 percent were women (in 1987), and women accounted for 72.7 percent of all SSI recipients age 65 and over (U.S. Bureau of the Census, 1989c). But as discussed above, the disparity in SSI benefits stems not from men versus women but rather singles versus couples. Women who are classified by the Census as unrelated individuals represent 52.3 percent of all elderly poor, but only 41.6 percent of all elderly SSI recipients. These findings suggest that the lower guarantee and the potentially difficult task of reaching women who may be isolated and unaware of eligibility for SSI results in disproportionately small benefits for most older women.

In addition, any inequities that arise in SSI have impacts on other program participation as well. Eligibility for food stamps and Medicaid benefits is often tied to receipt of SSI. While it is possible to qualify for Medicaid on other grounds in some states, it is more difficult to do so. Consequently, SSI represents a key to access to other benefits as well.

Medicare. Eligibility for Medicare extends to all persons age 65 and older who qualify for any type of Social Security benefit, as well as younger adults who are disabled. Eligibility and benefits are defined based on the individual, with no distinctions on the basis of living arrangements or other socioeconomic characteristics, and thus some of the complications of programs such as Social Security are avoided.

Differences in benefits received by older persons by sex reflect variation in health status, patterns of use of care, and what health expenditures are covered by Medicare. Consequently, there are substantial variations between men and women in Medicare benefit amounts received each year. A major source for this variation can be found in the hospital payments (Part A of Medicare). Women are less likely to have a hospital stay than are men in any given year. Since hospital costs are very comprehensively covered by Medicare, higher reimbursements are paid on behalf of men (Leader, 1988).

Does this mean that women are not treated fairly in this instance? Here is an example of how difficult a call these types of judgments can be. Most people would say that they are better off if they do not need surgery or a stay in the hospital; thus, few women would be likely to prefer to be more like men in this regard. If the coverage is reasonably defined, differences in receipt of benefits would not be a good test of fairness. However, that is not the only dimension of the question. Medicare is often faulted for providing better coverage of the very acute healthcare needs of the elderly, while neglecting chronic needs. Even aside from long-term care, the chronically ill generally need more drugs and more visits to the physician but fewer hospital stays. Yet Medicare requires large amounts of cost-sharing for physician visits and covers no outpatient prescription drugs. In this case, coverage may be biased against the chronically ill. And women are more likely to have such chronic conditions than are men (National Center for Health Statistics, 1987).

The Medicare Catastrophic Coverage Act, passed in 1988 and rescinded in 1989, would have helped the balance in Medicare by extending coverage to prescription drugs, by creating a cap on physician cost-sharing, and by initiating some important expansions in Medicare's coverage of long-term care. For the foreseeable future, Medicare is likely to represent a less generous program for older women than for older men.

Medicaid. As a healthcare program limited to the poor, Medicaid offers important benefits to women, who are more likely to have low incomes than are men. A large share of the benefits provided to older persons goes for long-term care—primarily in nursing homes. And as was already mentioned, women are more likely to receive care in nursing homes (National Center for Health Statistics, 1987).

The lack of generosity in provision for home- and community-based care, both from Medicaid and other programs such as the Older Americans Act and social service block grants, affects both men and women. Regardless of whether the beneficiary is a man or woman, the spouse is often the caregiver, and home services may be as important to the caregiver as to the disabled person. The same issue is relevant for the spousal impoverishment protections passed with the Medicare Catastrophic Coverage Act, but retained as law when the act was repealed. The institutionalized spouse is technically the beneficiary, but the community-dwelling spouse is the one receiving the protection. Who benefits in this case? It is probably most reasonable to assume that both spouses do.

FUTURE POLICY ISSUES

What directions are likely for public policy in the future, and will public policy be sensitive to women's concerns? At least at present, it is hard to imagine major changes in public policy to expand coverage or increase benefits. Moreover, the unpopularity of the Catastrophic legislation and the resulting political reaction suggest further limits on what programs will be likely for elderly Americans in the near future.

That suggests, for example, that no major earnings-sharing proposal is likely to be considered under Social Security. Moreover, not only are broad-based social programs such as a comprehensive long-term-care program viewed as too expensive, increasingly they are viewed as helping a new category of the undeserving—the wealthy elderly.

More likely areas for improvement in the near term are in SSI and Medicaid. And expansions in both of these programs would most likely be quite beneficial to women. Improving the federal guarantee for singles would ease one major point of inequity in the program, and any easing of other requirements such as asset limits would enable more women to receive help since they are more likely to have limited resources. Continued expansion of Medicaid to enhance home- and community-based benefits or fur-

ther expand the spousal impoverishment provisions would probably help both men and women in an equitable way.

Finally, it is likely that some changes in public policy may come at the expense of the elderly, either in the form of higher taxes or lower benefits. For example, increasing the tax on Social Security is often proposed either for supporting changes in benefit programs for the elderly themselves or for general deficit reduction. Others suggest estate taxes that might affect the surviving spouse. More radical proposals have sometimes called for elimination or severe reduction in the cost of living adjustments (COLAs) made each year under Social Security. The equity of such tax increases and benefit reductions needs to be analyzed. For example, taxation of Social Security would have a much lower impact on women overall than a COLA limitation that would become increasingly severe for the very old. But not all women would fare the same under each proposal. In a political environment that treats public monies as very scarce, with benefits more likely to be cut than expanded, the biggest challenges may well come in deciding how to equitably distribute the pain. Such decisions will be based on a broad range of factors, of which gender is only one.

REFERENCES

Committee on Ways and Means, U.S. House of Representatives, 1989. *Background Material and Data on Programs within the Jurisdiction of the Committee on Ways and Means, 1989 Edition.* Washington, D.C.: U.S. Government Printing Office.

Congressional Budget Office, 1986. *Earnings Sharing Options for the Social Security System.* Washington, D.C.: U.S. Government Printing Office.

Del Bene, L. and Vaughn, D., 1989. "Health Needs and Economic Resources of the Aged." Washington, D.C.: Social Security Administration. Mimeo.

Leader, S., 1988. "The Treatment of Women Under Medicare." In S. Sullivan and M. E. Lewin, eds., *The Economics and Ethics of Long Term Care and Disability.* Washington, D.C.: American Enterprise Institute.

National Center for Health Statistics, 1987. *Health Statistics on Older Persons: United States, 1986.* Washington, D.C.: U.S. Department of Health and Human Services, U.S. Government Printing Office.

Social Security Administration, 1988. *Social Security Bulletin: Annual Statistical Supplement, 1988.* Washington, D.C.: U.S. Department of

Health and Human Services, U.S. Government Printing Office.

U.S. Bureau of the Census, 1989a. *Money Income and Poverty Status in the United States: 1988 (Advance Data)*. Washington, D.C.: U.S. Department of Commerce, Current Population Reports, Series P-60, No. 166, U.S. Government Printing Office.

U.S. Bureau of the Census, 1989b. *Population Profile of the United States, 1989*. Washington, D.C.: U.S. Department of Commerce, Current Population Reports, Series P-23, No. 159, U.S. Government Printing Office.

U.S. Bureau of the Census, 1989c. *Poverty in the United States: 1987*. Washington, D.C.: U.S. Department of Commerce, Current Population Reports, Series P-60, No. 163.

Waldo, D. R. et al., 1989. "Health Expenditures by Age Group, 1977 and 1987." *Health Care Financing Review* 10(4):111–20.

Discussion Questions for Chapter Fourteen

1. Gerontologists and demographers make a distinction between "generations," which are steps in natural descent such as from a parent to a child, and cohorts, which are groups of people who have in common some event such as their year of birth. Given that generations are linkages between family members that share each other's lives in many ways, are their real interests in conflict with each other? Do members of different generations really perceive themselves at odds with one another over social policy issues such as Social Security, as the generational equity argument suggests? Would most nonelderly people want their parents' Social Security and Medicare benefits reduced? Would the nonelderly prefer to assume the responsibility for their parents' needs in order to have a reduction in Social Security Taxes?

2. Some people, concerned about the future viability of Social Security, advocate privatizing retirement preparation through individual investments. On the other hand, James H. Schulz warns of the risks of staking one's economic security in retirement on private investments, claiming that market economies generate a high level of insecurity and that only governments can secure the benefits promised in old age. Who is right? Given that most of us who reach old age will be either unable or unwilling to work to support ourselves at that point, are we better off trusting ourselves privately through the market or trusting ourselves collectively through the government?

3. What are the underlying reasons why public policy affects elderly women differently from elderly men? Are these inequalities due to a disregard for women's concerns, a lack of understanding of the different impact of policy on men and women, or simply happenstance? Would gender-conscious aging policies be an effective way to remedy these inequalities? Could arguments similar to Moon's be made regarding the effect of public policy on members of different cultural and racial groups?

CHAPTER FIFTEEN

Aging in the Future

Much of the interest in the aging of our society has been generated by concern about the future. How will future cohorts of elderly people fare? Will they have prepared adequately for retirement? Will the publicly supported social programs be in place to serve them? Demographic projections indicate that, beginning in the second decade of the next century, the United States will experience a "senior boom" resulting from the aging of the post-World War II baby boom cohorts born between 1946 and 1964. The increase in the number of older people expected in the next century magnifies many of the concerns examined in earlier chapters of this book, including the viability of Social Security, the affordability of medical care, and the provision of long-term care.

Concerns about the future are intensified by certain economic and non-economic characteristics of future cohorts of the elderly, as well as by the viability of political support for programs for older people. This final chapter includes articles on each of these concerns.

ECONOMIC CHARACTERISTICS OF FUTURE COHORTS OF THE ELDERLY

Economic issues are often at the core of concern for aging populations, but certain assumptions about those who will make up future cohorts of the elderly are particularly disturbing. It is widely believed that, because of the large size of their cohorts, baby boomers have faced intense competition for jobs, higher interest rates, inflated housing prices, and lower wages. Consequently they have lower rates of savings. To the extent that they do save for their later years, the large numbers of older people all wishing to sell off their assets at the same time to finance their retirement may diminish their value. Some writers have argued that most baby boomers are not economically well off. Despite media portrayals of baby boomers as yuppies, a tremendous amount of inequality exists within this group. Many more baby boomers are in poverty than in high income brackets (Light, 1988).

Amidst the widespread concern about the economic condition of the baby boom cohorts and their future in old age, Richard A. Easterlin and his colleagues present an optimistic view. In "Retirement Prospects of the Baby Boom Generation: A Different Perspective," they challenge many aspects of the widely shared view of the baby boomers' difficult condition, claiming that in comparison to their predecessors, they are not as bad off as many think, and on average are likely to enter old age in a much better economic position than did previous cohorts. The reason is they have made economic and demographic adjustments in response to their adverse labor market conditions. In brief, they have improved their economic status because they have deferred marriage and had smaller numbers of children (or none at all), and females in these cohorts have increased their participation in the labor force.

NONECONOMIC CHARACTERISTICS OF
FUTURE COHORTS OF THE ELDERLY

Economic concerns are not the only factors that affect the well-being of the elderly. The economic and demographic adjustments made by baby boomers as described by Easterlin and his colleagues are viewed by Frances K. Goldscheider as consequences of the gender revolution. According to her perspective, these changes come at a high cost, albeit in noneconomic terms. In "The Aging of the Gender Revolution: What Do We Know and What Do We Need to Know?" Goldscheider describes how changes in gender roles will affect the lives of future cohorts of elderly people.

Goldscheider argues that younger cohorts who will reach old age in the next century "will have been on the leading edge of the gender revolution." In contrast to the division of sex roles in the marriages of earlier cohorts, more recent cohorts have placed greater emphasis on sharing responsibilities, and this has placed strain on marriages, as shown by increased divorce rates. Women's increased labor force participation has also given them more economic independence, and so weak marriages are less likely to endure. Moreover, remarriage rates after divorce have declined among both men and women. Taken together, Goldscheider believes these changes will have a significant adverse effect on men in old age. She contends that men will lose the benefits they have reaped from marriage in terms of mental and physical health and that divorce will continue to have a significant negative effect on the contact fathers have with their children. Moreover, as the number of old unmarried men grows in the future, the problems they face in terms of social isolation and lack of social support will become more widespread.

POLITICAL AND SOCIAL SUPPORT FOR THE ELDERLY

As Easterlin and his colleagues explain in the selection included in this chapter, low birth rates and women's increasing labor force participation may mean that the *total* dependency ratio, which includes both young and old in relation to the working population, will still be below its historically high levels when the baby boom cohorts retire. Consequently, the burden on the working-age population to support the elderly may not be as great as many people think. Nevertheless, many gerontologists are concerned about the future of political support for the elderly. In "Challenges of Aging in Tomorrow's World: Will Gerontology Grow, Stagnate, or Change?", Robert Morris attributes the relatively good circumstances of today's older population to the recent history of political consensus regarding the elderly. Nevertheless, Morris is apprehensive about the future, fearing an erosion of the consensus. Slow economic growth, declining wages, and an increased emphasis on privatized wealth and privatized solutions to social problems have the potential to undermine the support for the aged. Division has appeared among the elderly themselves, as the well-off segment resists increased taxation to support the less well-off and disabled elderly who are politically much weaker but more favorable toward public programs.

Sociologist Richard Appelbaum (1977) has written, "The future is made, not predicted." The future of aging in America will be, in large measure, what we make it. Those who study and work in the field of gerontology can have an important role to play in shaping the conditions of life for tomorrow's older people. Morris calls for those concerned with the future of aging to become active, to work toward the reintegration of the elderly into social and economic life, and to use the talents of the elderly. He also advocates a reintegration of the interests of the aged with other age groups because, at root, many of the troubles faced by the aged are faced by others as well.

REFERENCES

Appelbaum, Richard. (1977). The future is made, not predicted: Technocratic planners versus public interests. *Society, 14*(4), 49–53.

Light, Paul C. (1988). *Baby boomers.* New York: W. W. Norton.

Retirement Prospects of the Baby Boom Generation: A Different Perspective

RICHARD A. EASTERLIN
CHRISTINE MACDONALD
DIANE J. MACUNOVICH

This paper assesses, on the basis of experience to date, the economic status of the baby boom cohorts as they approach retirement in the next century. Recent improvement in the economic status of the elderly has received much attention since brought to the fore by Preston (1984). At least part of this improvement has been attributed to the greater accumulated assets and pension rights that have been carried into retirement by recent retirement cohorts (Duncan, Hill, & Rodgers, 1986).

These findings, however, refer only to pre-baby boom cohorts. The question remains: What will be the economic prospects of the baby boom cohorts as they enter old age? A common assumption is that the retirement outlook of baby boom cohorts is poor, because of their Social Security benefit prospects. Longman (1985), addressing the possible future insolvency of the Social Security system, suggests that "unless a number of fundamental trends are soon reversed, the Baby Boomers are headed for a disastrous retirement." In addition to prospective Social Security problems, baby boomers are known to have experienced difficulties in the labor market (Welch, 1979; Lillard & Macunovich, 1989), which seemingly forebode a reduction in personal sources of support compared with their predecessors. Levy and Michel (1986) note that a male born in 1935 gained 118% in average real income passing from age 25 to 35, whereas a male baby boomer born in 1948 gained only 16% during the same 10 years of the life cycle.

The present analysis shows that, contrary to popular impression, the baby boom cohorts, on average, are likely to enter old age in an even better economic position than pre-boom cohorts. This is because economic and demographic adjustments that they have made, such as deferred marriage, reduced childbearing, and increased labor force participation of wives, have compensated for their relatively low wage rates.

CONCEPTS, DATA, AND METHODS

The definition of economic status employed here is designed to take account of the demographic adjustments that people make to influence their economic status. For example, if a cohort is experiencing adverse labor mar-

Source: The Gerontologist, 30(6), 776–783. Reprinted with permission from The Gerontological Society of America, Washington, DC 20005. Copyright 1990.

ket conditions, more of its members will opt for single status and some of these will turn up in the Bureau of the Census' sample survey as unrelated individuals, a group completely omitted in most comparisons of economic status. (In 1988 among males aged 20–39, over one in five was classified as an unrelated individual; in 1965 only 6% were so classified.) Also, members of such a cohort who form families are likely to decide to have fewer children. In both cases decisions are being made (to postpone or forgo marriage or to have fewer children) with a view to maintaining or improving economic status. If one were to focus only on the family as the unit of study, disregarding size of family and (by definition) excluding unrelated individuals, the role of these decisions in affecting the economic status of a cohort is lost from view.

In the present analysis, the economic status of an individual is defined as the total money income per adult equivalent (adjusted for price level change over time) in the household in which the individual resides. The definition of income is that of the Bureau of Census' Current Population Survey: pretax, posttransfer money income, including public and private pension income, public assistance, other welfare payments, and alimony and child support payments. Income in kind is excluded. To adjust for price level change over time, the CPI-X1 index is used (for discussion of this index, see U.S. Congressional Budget Office, 1988). The definition of household is also the same as that of the Current Population Survey, except that here, unmarried couple households have been identified whenever possible, and differentiated from other types of households. Unmarried couple households are identified according to the Bureau of Census definition: two unrelated adults 15 years of age or over of the opposite sex living together in a household in which no other adults are present.

Income per adult equivalent (IAE) is computed for each household by dividing the household's total money income by the number of adult equivalents in the household, derived according to Fuchs' scale (1986). The aim of the conversion to a per adult equivalent basis is to obtain a better measure of individual differences in economic status by allowing for variations in household size and adult-child composition, and for economies of scale in consumption. There is evidence that international income comparisons are somewhat sensitive to the equivalence scale adopted (Burkhauser et al., in press). However, we find little effect on inferences about trends based on our adjustment to a per adult equivalent basis compared with the most common alternative, that based on equivalence scales derived from poverty thresholds (Macunovich & Easterlin, 1990, appendix A).

The economic status of an individual is assumed to correspond to the average economic status of the household in which the individual resides. This is similar to the assumption in governmental estimates of the poverty rates of persons, that an individual is in poverty if the family of which one is a member is so classified.

A birth cohort is a group of individuals born in a given year or period. Baby boomers are commonly defined as those born in the period 1946–64. The present analysis includes four 5-year baby boom cohorts, ranging from the leading edge cohort (born 1945–49), to that born at the baby boom peak (1955–59), to the trailing edge cohort (1960–64).

The average economic status of a cohort is measured as the mean value of the IAEs of all of the persons composing that cohort, excluding only those in group quarters. Although this procedure for determining the average status of a cohort may seem obvious, it is not the way that inferences are commonly made about differences by age (or cohort) in the population. This is because age of *head* of household (or family) is typically used as the basis for inferring such variations. It goes almost without saying that an individual of a given age may be living in a household or family headed by a person of a much different age.

The data used here are from the March Current Population Survey (CPS) tapes for quinquennial years 1965 through 1985 plus 1988. Demographic status is measured as of March of the survey year, but income refers to the previous calendar year. The life cycle income profile of a cohort is obtained by linking income averages for appropriate age groups from successive surveys (Table 1). For example, the birth cohort of 1935–39 was 26–30 years old in 1965 (the first survey date), 31–35 years old in 1970, 36–40 years old in 1975, and so on. By linking the income averages for these age groups it is possible to trace the average economic status of the 1935–39 birth cohort as it aged from 26–30 years to 49–53 years in the period of 1965–1988.

The six dates studied here are chosen to span as fully as possible the period for which data are available, and to provide observations at approximately 5-year intervals on each birth cohort. Observations at this frequency should give a representative picture of a cohort's underlying life cycle income trend, with one exception. Fluctuations in the economywide unemployment rate cause deviations from the basic trend. Moreover, these fluctuations, although they affect all age groups, impinge most severely on persons under age 35, the ages for which most of our observations on baby boomers are available. Fortunately, in 4 of the 6 years included here (1964, 1974, 1979, and 1987), the economywide unemployment rate was quite similar, between 5.2% and 6.2%. It was an unusually low 3.5% in 1969 and a relatively high 7.5% in 1984. In the subsequent analysis, we present income profiles both for all six dates and for the four dates with similar unemployment rates. Because we are interested in comparing preretirement income status, the profiles are terminated at ages 55–59.

ECONOMIC STATUS AND PROSPECTS OF THE BABY BOOMERS

Figure 1, based on data for all six dates, presents the life cycle pattern of real mean income per adult equivalent for successive birth cohorts from 1915–19 to 1960–64. For example, the birth cohort of 1935–39 is observed from the point when its average age was 27 and its average income was approximately $10,000 to when it was 50 with an income averaging over $19,000. (All income figures here are expressed in terms of the purchasing power of a dollar in 1987.) Be-

TABLE 1   Mean Income Per Adult Equivalent, in 1987 Dollars, by Birth Cohort, 1964–1987.

			Year			
Cohort	*1964*	*1969*	*1974*	*1979*	*1984*	*1987*
1915–19	11,398 (45–49)	14,773 (50–54)	15,266 (55–59)	—	—	—
1920–24	10,566 (40–44)	13,935 (45–49)	15,584 (50–54)	16,725 (55–59)	—	—
1925–29	10,297 (35–39)	12,756 (40–44)	14,805 (45–49)	17,028 (50–54)	17,673 (55–59)	—
1930–34	10,173 (30–34)	12,303 (35–39)	13,700 (40–44)	15,863 (45–49)	17,768 (50–54)	18,726 (53–57)
1935–39	9,736 (25–29)	12,315 (30–34)	13,123 (35–39)	14,953 (40–44)	16,955 (45–49)	19,248 (48–52)
1940–44	9,443 (20–24)	12,794 (25–29)	13,977 (30–34)	15,134 (35–39)	16,224 (40–44)	18,525 (43–47)
1945–49	8,246 (15–19)	11,914 (20–24)	13,965 (25–29)	15,643 (30–34)	16,462 (35–39)	17,931 (38–42)
1950–54	—	10,145 (15–19)	12,507 (20–24)	15,346 (25–29)	15,686 (30–34)	17,108 (33–37)
1955–59	—	—	10,775 (15–19)	13,682 (20–24)	15,244 (25–29)	16,533 (28–32)
1960–64	—	—	—	11,487 (15–19)	13,170 (20–24)	15,481 (23–27)

Note: Age of birth cohort shown in parentheses.

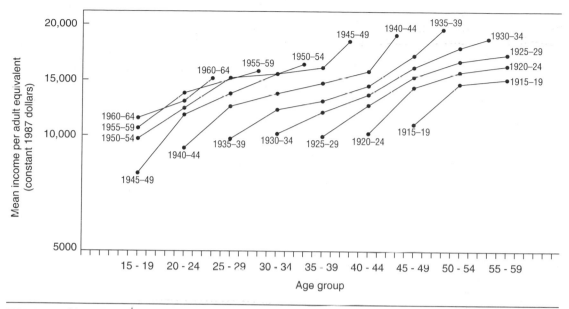

FIGURE 1   Mean income per adult equivalent: Life cycle profiles for 5-year birth cohorts 1915–19 to 1960–64.

cause data are limited, only segments of the experience of each cohort can be observed.

Although the life cycle income trend of each cohort is reasonably apparent in the figure, fluctuations in the economywide unemployment rate, as noted, create fluctuations in the income profiles. These impinge on the various cohorts at different ages, making comparison more difficult.

A clearer picture of the basic income profiles emerges if the 2 years with disparate unemployment rates are omitted (Figure 2). We feel that this figure presents a better representation of each cohort's basic life cycle income trend, and accordingly, base our discussion on it, but the generalizations below would be essentially the same if Figure 1 were used.

The vertical distance between curves can be used to compare the mean income of cohorts at a given age. Thus, vertical comparison of the cohorts at ages 45–49 through 55–59 establishes what is commonly accepted—that those currently retiring, the co-

horts of 1925–29 and 1930–34, are better off than their predecessor cohorts. For example, at ages 45–49, real income per adult equivalent of the birth cohort of 1930–34 averaged 28% higher than that of the birth cohort of 1915–19.

What may come as a surprise to many, however, is that this upward march of economic status continues with the baby boom cohorts. This is shown by the four curves at the left side of the diagram depicting the income profiles of the 1945–49 through 1960–64 birth cohorts. Vertical comparisons of these cohorts with their predecessors reveals that the baby boomers have higher income levels at given ages than pre-boom cohorts. For example, at ages 25–29, the first baby boom cohort (that of 1945–49) averaged an adult equivalent income 44% higher than the pre-boom birth cohort of 1935–39; the peak baby boom cohort, that of 1955–59, averaged 56% higher. A comparison of the magnitude of the upward income shift of the later baby boom cohorts with the earlier ones suggests that

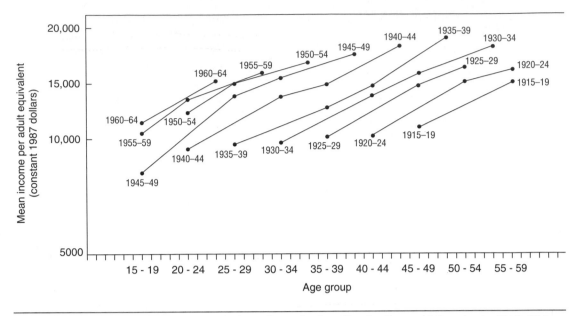

FIGURE 2   Mean income per adult equivalent: Smoothed profiles for 5-year birth cohorts 1915–19 to 1960–64 (excludes observations for 1969, 1984).

that the rate of improvement slowed between the leading and trailing edge of the baby boom, but it is still somewhat early in the observation of the youngest cohorts to be sure of this.

The general pattern is that each younger cohort—including the baby boomers—starts out better off than its predecessor, and that this advantage is maintained throughout the life cycle. Assuming that this pattern holds in the future, the implication is that the baby boomers will approach retirement age with higher income per adult equivalent than any prior cohorts. As noted, the improvement of the trailing edge over the leading edge of the baby boom generation is moderate, but taking all four cohorts together, the baby boomers seem well on their way to higher income levels than their predecessors. It is noteworthy that by 1987 the baby boomers, ranging in age from 23 to 42, had reached income levels of $16,000 to $18,000, about the same as those achieved in their middle and late

fifties by the currently retiring cohorts of 1920–24 through 1930–34 (Table 1).

The present analysis deals only with average economic status, and does not discuss income distribution. It is possible that the baby boom generation might reach retirement with a higher average income than its predecessors, but also greater inequality, and consequently a more severe problem of supporting the elderly poor. We can at present only note this possibility. Although there have been valuable general studies of income distribution (Danziger & Gottschalk, 1987; Levy, 1987) and cross-sectional analyses of age groups (Crystal, 1986; Crystal & Shea, 1990; Radner, 1987; Smeeding, Torrey, & Rein, 1987), the measurement and projection of income inequality as cohorts move through the life cycle is a virtually untouched topic of research. Studies based on panel data come closest to doing this, but these are typically confined to fairly short periods, provide less than comprehensive coverage of the population, and do not use overall measures of income inequality (see Burkhauser et al., 1985; Burkhauser & Duncan, 1988). We hope to say more on this at some future time.

Returning to the subject of average economic status, we cannot be sure, of course, that the better average income status of the baby boomers will translate into a better economic position at retirement. But one indication that this will be so is the substantial private and public employee pension coverage of baby boomers. In 1984 among wage and salary workers, pension coverage of the leading edge of the baby boom generation was virtually the same as that of older cohorts—somewhat over 70%—and coverage of the later baby boom cohorts was only 5–10 percentage points less, despite the comparative recency of their entry into the labor force (Table 2, column 3).

Although vesting rates for the baby boom cohorts were somewhat less than for older cohorts, this was due to their shorter tenure in the labor force and hence their lessened opportunity to satisfy the usual vesting requirement of 10 years with one's current employer (column 4). (Similar differentials by age to those in columns 3 and 4 are shown

in Andrews, 1985, though at slightly lower levels.) It is reasonable to assume that the vesting rates for the baby boomers will rise as they age. Indeed, given the substantially greater labor force participation of females among the baby boom generation, it is quite possible that as the baby boomers approach retirement age, both their coverage and vesting rates will be higher than for those currently approaching retirement. This assumes, of course, that major changes in employer policies regarding provision of pension benefits are not in store. (Predicting such changes and their effects would be a project in itself. Ongoing developments are working in opposing directions—e.g., vesting after 5 rather than 10 years versus the shift from defined benefit to defined contribution plans.) It is also pertinent to note that a recent study (Ferraro, 1990) found an unexpectedly high increase between 1974 and 1981 in retirement preparation activities of the baby boom cohort of 1950–56 compared with pre-baby boom cohorts.

Turning to other assets, it is widely believed that the baby boomers have suffered in terms of home ownership as a result of high interest rates and rising home prices. It is true that home ownership rates fell notice-

TABLE 2 Pension Coverage and Vesting Rate of Wage and Salary Workers Aged 25+ Years, by Age, 1984.

Age	Period of birth	% of workers covered by a pension plan	% of covered workers that are vested
All workers, 25+		67.1	67.3
25–29	1955–59	60.4	47.4
30–34	1950–54	65.9	61.4
35–39	1945–49	70.8	67.2
40–44	1940–44	72.1	72.4
45–49	1935–39	72.0	78.4
50–54	1930–34	70.1	81.7
55–59	1925–29	72.3	81.8
60–64	1920–24	63.4	79.5

Source: U.S. Bureau of the Census (1987).

ably between 1977 and 1983, the period when interest rates soared to new post-World War II highs, although the impact of this was felt by all age groups, both baby boom and pre-boom (Avery, Elliehausen, & Canner, 1984). Even so, the baby boomers' home ownership percentage is not much less than that of their predecessors. The following compares the home ownership rate among persons aged 25–34 in 1986 (the baby boom cohort born 1952–61) with that of the corresponding age group 16 and 21 years earlier (the pre-boom cohorts born 1936–45 and 1931–40):

	Date of observation	Percentage owning own home
Baby boomers	1986	42.9
Pre-boomers	1970	48.0
	1965	47.0

(The figures for the pre-boomers are from Durkin & Elliehausen, 1978; for the baby boomers, the figure was supplied by Nancy McArdle, Harvard University Joint Center for Housing Studies, from the 1986 Federal Reserve data tape.) Moreover, the lower figure for the baby boomers is at least partly due to their different demographic mix. As shown in the next section, there is a markedly smaller proportion of married couples with children among baby boomers, and home ownership rates for this group average about twice as high as for others (Avery, Elliehausen, & Canner, 1984). In the absence of a return to the extremely high interest rates of the early 1980s, it seems reasonable to suppose that given their relatively favorable income per adult equivalent, baby boomers' home ownership rates will in time equal or exceed those of their predecessors.

Our data also provide a hint that baby boomers have, to some extent, accumulated more financial assets than their predecessors. Although we do not have information on the CPS tapes on assets as such, we do have data on the income generated by such assets—interest, dividends, and rents—commonly termed property income. The following compares the percentage reporting more than $1,000 property income (in 1987 prices) among persons aged 30–34 in 1987 (the baby boom cohort born 1953–57) with that of the corresponding age group 18 years earlier (the pre-boom birth cohort of 1935–39):

	Date of observation	Percentage with property income
Baby boomers	1987	7.9
Pre-boomers	1969	3.6

For both cohorts the percentages shown are certainly too low (only about 45% of property income is reported in the CPS), but the higher percentage of baby boomers with property income does not reflect a trend toward better reporting. Estimates of underreporting for 1972 and 1983 yield virtually identical figures (U.S. Bureau of the Census, 1973, 1989a). However, the higher percentage for the baby boomers does partly reflect a higher return on assets (for the baby boomers, long-term interest rates were about 30% higher, although short-term money market rates were moderately lower). If, to adjust for this, we raise (generously) the property income cut-off for the baby boomers from $1,000 to $1,300, the figure for the baby boomers falls from 7.9% to 6.9% still considerably higher than the 3.6% figure of the pre-boom group. This differential is probably a reasonable indication of the greater extent of substantial financial asset ownership among the baby boomers.

Although more needs to be done to clarify the comparative picture of baby boomers versus their predecessors with regard to asset acquisition, the figures above on pensions, home ownership, and property income seem reasonably consistent with the inferences from the income data drawn here.

The prospect is that in comparison with those currently retiring, baby boomers approaching retirement age will have higher incomes and as good or better private and public pension coverage, home ownership rates, and financial asset holdings.

In a recent study of the prospective cost of caring for the disabled elderly, the underlying projections of income and assets, based on an elaborate simulation technique, yield conclusions very similar to ours. Comparing persons 65–74 in 2016–20 (the leading edge of the baby boom) with those 65–74 in 1986–90, median family income and median family assets (adjusted for changing prices) are projected, respectively, to be 115% and 39% higher (Rivlin & Wiener, 1988). The estimates here of IAE put the 10-year birth cohort at the leading edge of the baby boom roughly 85% ahead of their predecessors 30 years ago. (This estimate is obtained from Table 1 by combining the average difference between the baby boom cohort and its predecessor 20 years earlier with the average difference between the latter and its predecessor 10 years earlier.) If this differential were to persist, our figures would thus yield a somewhat more conservative estimate than Rivlin and Wiener's (1988) of the improvement in real income for the baby boomers: 85% versus 115%.

HOW BABY BOOMERS HAVE DONE IT

How have the baby boom cohorts been able to improve their economic position, despite their comparatively adverse labor market conditions? The answer is primarily by a variety of demographic and economic adjustments that have compensated for their adverse wage and unemployment rates.

Although we cannot enter into a detailed analysis here, the contrasts between the baby boomers and pre-boom cohorts can be easily demonstrated (see also Easterlin, 1987). To illustrate, we take for comparison the baby boom cohort of 1950–54 and the pre-boom cohort of 1935–39 at the time when each was 26–30 years old; these two cohorts provide a fairly representative contrast between the baby boomers and their predecessors.

The first point of note is the marked decline in the proportion of baby boomers that are members of married couple, two-parent families, from 73% to 48% (Table 3, columns 1 and 2). Of this 25 percentage point decline, four-fifths is accounted for by a shift to childless living arrangements; the remainder, by a rise of those in single-parent situations.

The implications of this demographic shift for the economic status of the baby boomers is apparent when one considers how income per adult equivalent varies by demographic status (Table 3, columns 3 through 6). In both cohorts, childless persons' income averaged about 55% higher than that of persons in married couple, two-parent families, whereas that of single parents averaged about one-quarter lower (columns 5 and 6). Although the demographic shifts of baby boomers involve movements toward both higher and lower income situations, the shift toward the higher income situation (that of childless persons) has been dominant in affecting the baby boomers' average income. There are two reasons for this. First, the magnitude of the demographic shift to the higher income situation is much greater. Second, the income gap between the higher income and traditional married couple, two-parent situation is greater than that on the lower income side. Thus, the baby boomers have, on balance, improved their economic status by avoiding parenthood, and opting for childless living arrangements. These childless situations embrace a variety of circumstances, all of which have increased in relative importance: forming a single-person household, living with one's parents or with others, or forming a childless marital or nonmarital union.

Two other devices may be noted by which the baby boomers have improved

TABLE 3 Cohorts of 1935–39 and 1950–54 at Ages 26–30: Percentage Distribution and Income Per Adult Equivalent by Presence of Children, Type of Union, and Living Arrangements.

| | % Distribution | | Income per adult equivalent | | | |
| | | | Amount (1987 dollars) | | Index[a] | |
Persons	1935–39 cohort	1950–54 cohort	1935–39 cohort	1950–54 cohort	1935–39 cohort	1950–54 cohort
All persons	100	100	9,736	15,346	110	119
Childless persons	20	40	14,070	19,999	159	155
Not in union						
Single-person household	3	9	14,923	20,205	168	157
Living in parents' household	5	6	11,545	16,776	130	130
Living with others	3	6	13,967	19,292	158	150
In union						
Married	10[b]	16	14,990	21,507	169[b]	167
Unmarried	—[c]	3	—[c]	18,980	—[c]	171
Persons in married couple, two-parent families	73	48	8,862	12,888	100	100
Persons in single-parent families	7	11	6,497	9,343	73	73
Male single parent in own or other household	—[c] ⎫	3	—[c] ⎫	11,484	—[c] ⎫	89
Male or female single parent in unmarried couple	—[c] ⎬ 4	1	—[c] ⎬ 7,883	12,006	—[c] ⎬ 89	93
Female single parent in parents' or other household	—[c] ⎭	2	—[c] ⎭	10,420	—[c] ⎭	81
Female single parent in own household	3	5	4,277	7,246	48	56

Note: Detail may not add to total because of rounding.
[a] Married couple, two-parent families = 100.
[b] Includes a small number of unmarried couples.
[c] Sample size less than 100.

their economic status compared with their predecessors. First, among families with children, the average number of children has been reduced by 0.5 children, from 2.4 to 1.9 (Table 4, columns 1 and 2). This means that there are fewer claimants among whom a given family income needs to be shared. Second, in married couple, two-parent families, there has been a rise in the number of earners per household (Table 4, columns 3 and 4). (In single-parent families, earners per household declined, but a disproportionately large decline in children per household tended to offset this.) Thus, aside from the changes in

Table 3, baby boomers have improved their economic status by reducing household size and, to some extent, by increasing earners per household.

Because demographic factors have played an important role to date in the economic advance of the baby boom generation, it is important to consider their likely impact in the future. Although baby boomers have had unusually low fertility before age 30, childbearing rates for women over 30 have been rising in recent years. If this catching up were to push the baby boomers to an average completed family size as great as that of their

TABLE 4   Cohorts of 1935–39 and 1950–54 at Ages 26–30: Mean Number of Children under 18 Years Old Per Household and Mean Number of Earners Per Household by Presence of Children and Type of Union.

Persons	Children per household		Earners per household	
	1935–39 cohort	1950–54 cohort	1935–39 cohort	1950–54 cohort
All persons	1.94	1.14	1.54	1.74
Childless persons	0.00	0.00	1.82	1.82
Persons in married couple, two-parent families	2.40	1.90	1.43	1.68
Persons in single-parent families	2.64	1.91	1.90	1.66

predecessors, then the prior advantageous economic effect of their low fertility would, in time, be negated. In fact, however, survey evidence on fertility expectations indicates that the completed fertility of baby boomers will fall far short of their predecessors. For the baby boom cohorts, expectation of completed family size averages in the neighborhood of two children, compared with three for their predecessors (U.S. Bureau of the Census, 1981, 1988). Similarly, a reversal in female labor force participation rates that would adversely affect the economic status of the baby boomers seems unlikely. Projections to the year 2000 foresee rates for the baby boomers above those of their predecessors (U.S. Bureau of the Census, 1989b). The lower fertility expectations of the baby boomers, and hence reduced child care burden, is, of course, consistent with higher female labor force participation.

One demographic change in prospect, however, will work against the baby boomers. The lower fertility of the baby boomers means that as they approach retirement they will receive less of a boost to their personal economic status than their predecessors did as a result of children moving out of the family household. Although in itself this would somewhat flatten the income profiles of baby boomers relative to their predecessors as they move toward retirement ages, it is likely to be countered in part by a com-

paratively favorable effect relative to prior cohorts from the trend in female labor force participation.

DISCUSSION AND CONCLUSIONS

Most analysts, in addressing the retirement prospects of the baby boom generation, focus on the Social Security system and its role in dictating the baby boomers' future economic situation. This perspective, though important and relevant, disregards the potential contribution of the baby boomers' personal income experience to their retirement status. This paper seeks to complement the usual analysis by filling this void.

The present analysis shows that, on the basis of experience to date, the baby boom cohorts, on average, are likely to enter old age in substantially better economic position than pre-boom cohorts. Despite relatively adverse labor market conditions, baby boomers have improved their economic status relative to pre-boom cohorts by economic and demographic adjustments that have more than compensated for labor market difficulties. Relative to pre-boom cohorts, more baby boomers have remained single, they have reduced childbearing, and females in this cohort have higher rates of labor force participation. These developments have substantially outweighed the one adverse demographic change, the relative growth of single-parent families, and had a sizable net beneficial impact on the economic status of the baby boom cohorts as a whole.

Several caveats are in order. First, the demographic adjustments just mentioned—particularly childlessness and low fertility—might be argued to have a potential downside effect. Concerns about the Social Security and health care prospects of the baby boomers derive directly from the fact that their low fertility implies that when they retire there will be a relatively low ratio of the working age to older dependent population. Moreover, fewer children means less opportunity for informal family care of the elderly and hence greater need for formal care.

Our intention is not to dismiss such concerns, but to provide a corrective by pointing to the positive effects of low fertility on the personal economic status of the baby boomers. However, it is worth pointing out that if one credits the present demographic projections, they imply not only greater old age dependency, but also a historic low in youth dependency when the baby boomers retire. If one considers the *total* dependency rate, taking account of both young and old, the prospect is that this rate will be below its historic high when the baby boomers retire. Thus it is possible that the ability of the working age population to shoulder the burden of higher taxes to support programs for older dependents will be greater than is often assumed, because of reduced needs to support younger dependents. A continued uptrend in female labor force participation may also help offset the projected rise in old age dependency (see Easterlin, 1988; United Nations, 1988, for further discussion of these points).

Second, our analysis has focused on the average economic status of baby boomers, poor and nonpoor alike. As mentioned, it is possible that the baby boom generation might reach retirement with higher average income than its predecessors, but also with greater income inequality. Moreover, if those in the lower end of the income distribution were differentially affected by high housing prices and high interest rates, the problem of the elderly poor would be exacerbated by disproportionately low home ownership. Clearly for policy purposes, one needs to attend not only to averages, but to distributional considerations as well.

Finally, the present analysis has addressed only the prospective economic status of the baby boomers. Economic status does not, of course, measure total welfare, though it is one component of welfare. As suggested, family considerations—the formation of a union or having a child—may be sacrificed in the interest of economic status, but such sacrifices certainly affect an individual's sense of total well-being. Moreover, such sacrifices carry over into retirement in that there will be fewer (or no) children to provide companionship and similar types of support for elderly persons. Concern about this is certainly relevant to assessing the overall well-being of baby boomers in retirement. This paper, however, is directed toward the concern foremost in the literature, the economic prospects of the baby boomers, and, on this score, the outlook seems more favorable than is commonly assumed.

REFERENCES

Andrews, E. S. (1985). *The changing profile of pensions in America.* Washington, DC: Employee Benefit Research Institute.

Avery, R. B., Elliehausen, G. E., & Canner, G. B. (1984, September). Survey of consumer finances, 1983. *Federal Reserve Bulletin.*

Burkhauser, R. V., Butler, J. S., & Wilkinson, J. T. (1985). Estimating changes in well-being across life: A realized versus comprehensive income approach. In M. David & T. Smeeding (Eds.), *Horizontal equity, uncertainty, and economic well-being* (pp. 69–87). Chicago: University of Chicago Press.

Burkhauser, R. V., & Duncan, G. J. (1988). Life events, public policy, and the economic vulnerability of children and the elderly. In J. L. Palmer, T. Smeeding, & B. Boyle Torrey (Eds.), *The vulnerable* (pp. 55–88). Washington, DC: Urban Institute Press.

Burkhauser, R. V., Duncan, G. J., Hauser, R., & Berntsen, R. (in press). Economic burdens of marital disruptions: A comparison of the United States and the Federal Republic of Germany. *Review of Income and Wealth*.

Crystal, S. (1986). Measuring income and inequality among the elderly. *The Gerontologist, 26,* 56–59.

Crystal, S., & Shea, D. (1990). Cumulative advantage, cumulative disadvantage, and inequality among elderly people. *The Gerontologist, 30,* 437–443.

Danziger, S., & Gottschalk, P. (1987). Earnings inequality, the spatial concentration of poverty, and the underclass. *American Economic Review, 77,* 211–215.

Duncan, G. J., Hill, M., & Rodgers, W. (1986). The changing fortunes of young and old. *American Demographics,* August, 26–33.

Durkin, T. A., & Elliehausen, G. E. (1978). *1977 Consumer Credit Survey.* Washington, DC: Board of Governors of the Federal Reserve System.

Easterlin, R. A. (1987). *Birth and fortune* (2nd ed.). Chicago: University of Chicago Press.

Easterlin, R. A. (1988, December). Population and the European economy: Making mountains out of molehills? Paper presented at the Symposium on Population and European Society at the European University Institute, Florence, Italy.

Ferraro, K. F. (1990). Cohort analysis of retirement preparation, 1974–1981. *Journal of Gerontology, 45,* 521–531.

Fuchs, V. (1986). Sex differences in economic well-being. *Science, 232,* 459–464.

Kingson, E. R. (1988). Generational equity: An unexpected opportunity to broaden the politics of aging. *The Gerontologist, 28,* 765–772.

Levy, F. S. (1987). *Dollars and dreams: The changing American income distribution.* New York: Russell Sage Foundation.

Levy, F. S., & Michel, R. C. (1986). An economic bust for the baby boom. *Challenge,* March-April, 33–39.

Lillard, L. A., & Macunovich, D. J. (1989). Why the baby bust cohorts haven't boomed yet: A reconsideration of cohort variables in labor market analyses. Paper presented at the annual meeting of the Population Association of America, Baltimore.

Longman, P. (1985). Justice between generations. *The Atlantic Monthly,* June, 73–81.

Macunovich, D. J., & Easterlin, R. A. (1990). How parents have coped: The effect of life cycle demographic decisions on the economic status of preschool age children, 1964–1987. *Population and Development Review, 16*(2), 299–323.

Preston, S. (1984). Children and the elderly: Divergent paths for America's dependents. *Demography, 21*(4), 435–457.

Radner, D. B. (1987). Money incomes of aged and nonaged family units, 1967–84. *Social Security Bulletin, 50*(8), 9–28.

Rivlin, A. M., & Wiener, J. M. (1988). *Caring for the disabled elderly. Who will pay?* Washington, DC: The Brookings Institution.

Smeeding, T., Torrey, B. B., & Rein, M. (1987). Comparative well-being of children and elderly. *Contemporary Policy Issues,* April, 57–72.

United Nations (1988). *Economic and social implications of population aging.* New York: Author.

U.S. Bureau of the Census (1973). *Current population reports,* Series P-60, No. 90, December. Washington, DC: U.S. Government Printing Office.

U.S. Bureau of the Census (1981). *Fertility of American women, June 1981, Current Population Reports,* Series P-20, No. 378. Washington, DC: U.S. Government Printing Office.

U.S. Bureau of the Census (1987). *Pensions: Worker coverage and retirement benefits. Current Population Reports,* Series P-70, No. 12. Washington, DC: U.S. Government Printing Office.

U.S. Bureau of the Census (1988). *Fertility of American women, June 1988. Current Population Reports,* Series P-20, No. 436. Washington, DC: U.S. Government Printing Office.

U.S. Bureau of the Census (1989a). *Current Population Reports,* Series P-60, No. 166, October. Washington, DC: U.S. Government Printing Office.

U.S. Bureau of the Census (1989b). *Statistical Abstract of the United States, 1989.* Washington, DC: U.S. Government Printing Office.

U.S. Congressional Budget Office (1988). *Trends in family income, 1970–1986.* Washington, DC: U.S. Government Printing Office.

Welch, F. (1979). Effects of cohort size on earnings: The baby boom babies' financial bust. *Journal of Political Economy, 87*(5), 565–596.

2

The Aging of the Gender Revolution: What Do We Know and What Do We Need to Know?

FRANCES K. GOLDSCHEIDER

There has been an explosion of research on the elderly and their family relationships over the last decade, research that could best be characterized as glowing. The elderly are described in terms of a warm network of kin ties, focused primarily on the marital bond and, to a lesser extent, on their children. They are increasingly affluent, making intergenerational kin ties of an instrumental nature nearly superfluous until the very end of life. In fact, they are continuing to care for their adult children, who are having difficulties launching their own occupational and marital careers.

In many ways, this literature reads like that focusing on the American family as a whole in the 1950s and 1960s, when, at the height of the baby and marriage boom, the family appeared to be a strong and successful institution, dominating social life in a way that challenged earlier theorists concerned with the eroding centrality of family in modern lives. But the researchers of that time did not know that the 1950s, and its peculiar patterns, would end; nor did they know what would follow. Now, to a much greater extent, we do know and as demographers, we would be irresponsible if we did not try to connect what is happening to younger cohorts with their lives in old age. For those currently entering their elderly years are *the parents of the baby boom*, and they confused analysts when they were young. Their children, the children of the baby boom, are a new cohort, one that has had very different lives; we should not let the older cohorts' experiences in late adulthood mislead us into thinking that the younger ones' will be similar, because the two cohorts' experiences in young adulthood were so very different.

The currently elderly and near elderly have benefited from the demographic and economic transformations of modernity, but did not participate in the family revolutions that followed. They are members of a deviant cohort, at least in family terms, that temporarily reversed trends begun earlier. They married young, had children in solid but prudent numbers, and experienced greater marital continuity than any previous cohort, because of the decline in mortality. Even those few who divorced remarried at an extremely rapid rate.

Source: Research on Aging, 12(4), 531–545. Reprinted by permission of Sage Publications, Inc. Newbury Park, CA 91320. Copyright 1990.

In contrast, the cohorts entering old age in the 21st century will have been on the leading edge of the gender revolution, a revolution that has strained their lives throughout their adulthood during the last third of the 20th century. The rapid growth of labor force participation among women, the tremendous rise in divorce and in childbearing out of marriage, and the overall decline in marriage and remarriage have raised profound questions about the family and its future; these questions have clear bearing on the family relationships of the elderly, both male-female relationships and intergenerational relationships, particularly between fathers and their children. These emergent cohort patterns of family life challenge our understanding of kinship among the elderly and raise important questions that require a new research agenda.

Increasingly, the elderly—men and women—will *not* be married; and if they are, it will not be their first marriage. Their marriages occurred in the early years of the divorce explosion, and their children are the first generation in which substantial proportions have experienced mother-only families and the loss of paternal contact and support, *even though their fathers are alive.* Research has focused on women and children as the "victims" in this context, as they have lost resources based on sharing male incomes. However, in old age, as employment-based resources become less central and as family relationships based on marriage and parenthood grow in importance, it is males who are at risk. These risks can best be understood by linking cohort change to key family changes—in divorce, in female labor force participation, in remarriage, and in intergeneration relationships.

RESEARCH ON THE ELDERLY FAMILY

Current research on the family in later life is still reacting to a theoretical orientation common among family scholars in the 1940s and 1950s: that the American family has been weakening and that its weakest links are to the elderly. A generation of scholars of social change, following Burgess and Locke (1945), had theorized about the family as a critical institution that was losing its "functions"; modern families were contrasted with an image of some past, premodern family where multigenerational family extension was the norm and, presumably, families were closer, warmer, and stronger than the "isolated" nuclear family with its "isolated elderly" of the modern era.

The 1960s saw a strong reaction to this view among family analysts across a wide front. One analytic tradition debunked the presumed decline in family extension. Levy (1965) showed that high fertility and mortality in the past meant that few families could ever have been extended much of the time; and Burch (1967) showed that even in developing societies, most families are relatively small and include few members outside the nuclear core. The general conclusion from those studies was that there was really no change in the family; that it has always been nuclear, and any other view, in the words of William Goode (1970), was simple "nostalgia."

Those whose research focused on the family life of the elderly knew that these analyses were somehow not portraying changes in living arrangements correctly, given the dramatic increase in the proportions living alone underway, but the decline in family extension was seen as a benefit for the family relationships of the elderly, not a loss. Intergenerational coresidence is associated in most people's minds with loss of privacy and with intergenerational conflict, based to a great extent on coresidence's historical linkage with poverty and overcrowding, on one hand, and with the conflicts between an immigrant population and its children over far more than space, on the other. Intergenerational coresidence under conditions of relative affluence and shared values could, of course, be much less stressful, and might even be supportive. Nevertheless, the dramatic increase in residential independence in the later years of the life course has normally been considered by scholars of the elderly family as a benefit, not a loss, to the quality of family relationships among the elderly.

Instead, their reaction to concerns over family decay focused more on other dimensions of intergenerational interaction—on contact and support. Here, the image of "isolated elderly" was thoroughly crushed, so much so that scholars coined the term, "modified extended family" to portray a family with strong intergenerational links, despite low levels of intergenerational coresidence. For example, Shanas (1980) showed that three quarters of the elderly were in some weekly contact with their children, a finding replicated widely. Summing up this research in her presidential address to the annual meeting of the National Council on Family Relations, Joan Aldous (1987) presented evidence on aging middle-class couples showing that "their lifestyle presents that 'attractive image of aging' which Neugarten (1974) hoped a decade ago would 'allay the fears of the young about growing old.' "

But new research on the family challenges that consensus. Current and past research on the elderly family appears to be peculiarly innocent, given what we know about family change among younger cohorts during these years. For it is research that is based on cohorts that have not experienced the revolution in women's roles, which has led to dramatic increases in female labor force participation and economic independence. As a result, this research has barely nodded to the concomitant dramatic rise in divorce and in out-of-wedlock childrearing. It has taken the nuclear family for granted, together with the traditional division of roles between men and women, within and outside the household.

As a result, this research tradition and the cohorts it has focused on have led us to be concerned about the needs of *women* in our consideration of the unmarried elderly, because traditional age differences in age at marriage and traditional family roles greatly exacerbate the gender difference in longevity, with the result that the poor and solitary are very likely to be women. But unless we take into account research on the family changes being experienced by younger cohorts over the last several decades, we are likely to be blind to the problems of the growing numbers of elderly unmarried men that we will be confronting in the early years of the 21st century, as a result of the aging of the gender revolution.

THE GENDER REVOLUTION: WHAT IS IT?

The gender revolution rests on the growing economic independence of women. Given women's strong *preference* to be married, most do; but they do not *have* to remain married; they can support themselves in relative comfort and live in relative privacy, because they do not have to live with their parents, married siblings, or children. Hence weak marriages are now at much greater risk of dissolution, because women can leave them with less fear and men can leave them with less guilt.

An argument has been developed elsewhere that suggests that the decline in marriage does not represent a rejection of marriage, per se, but rather of *traditional* marriage and the traditional gender roles underlying it, as marriage has become increasingly out of step with the rest of our social institutions (Goldscheider and Waite forthcoming). As the gender revolution reaches into the family, young couples are increasingly shaping marriages based on sharing not only the economic responsibilities but also the domestic and parental responsibilities, and, perhaps, even the relationship maintenance responsibilities that are such large parts of the total family enterprise. This change constitutes a tremendous revolution in gender relationships, one which has been resisted by all the forces underlying this most traditional of institutions. But during the revolution, marriage has become very fragile.

And the gender revolution is far from over; its greatest costs may have been those due to the decrease in marriage and remarriage, and the increase in divorce. Divorce has economic costs, but it also has social and emotional costs. And there are costs in terms of intergenerational relationships, a critical area of research on the elderly. We need to assess these costs for the generation that has first experienced them and that will become elderly in the early years of the 21st century.

The Rise in Divorce

The elderly families that have been the focus of so much research over the last quarter of a century came to adulthood, formed their families, and organized their adult lives during the 1950s or earlier. The early years of their marriages passed during a period of relatively low divorce risks, and although they joined the divorce explosion by doubling their own rate of divorce later in their marriages, this increase was on a very low base; less than 15% of males aged 70 to 74 in 1970 had ever divorced and this proportion should rise to little more than 25% for this age group as of 1990, based on their level of 23% in 1980 when they were 10 years younger. But demographers are estimating that current divorce rates imply that between one half and two thirds of all marriages will end in divorce (Martin and Bumpass 1989). Because divorce rates have been at this level for the last 10 years or so, the proportion ever divorced among those entering their postretirement years is likely to exceed 50% by the year 2010, doubling in 20 years.

This increase has been barely noticed in studies of the family in later life. Aldous (1987) noted the increase in divorce, but pre-

sented data on current marital status that show that there was no increase between 1950 and 1980 in the proportion divorced among males over the age of 65 and an increase of only 2% to 6% among males aged 55 to 64 over the same period. However, measures of current marital status erase evidence of the experience of divorce, because the remarried are included with those still in intact first marriages and some of the consequences of divorce linger on after remarriage, as we will see. And it seems quite possible that the remarriage market may decline rapidly in the near future, because the lives of older women in the cohorts soon to be elderly have shifted increasingly away from family centeredness and toward productivity in the marketplace, unlike those among the currently elderly.

The Rise in Female Economic Activity

The increase in female employment is another dimension of the gender revolution that has barely touched the current generation of elderly families. The traditional family, with its powerfully gender-differentiated roles, was their experience. They may have been battered by the high male unemployment rates of the economic depression of the 1930s and women may have worked many hours during the separations forced by World War II; however, for most, their marriages returned to the "normalcy" of the 1950s, which strongly rejected such aberrations as "unnatural."

Women who reached age 60 in 1960 had spent on average only 11 of the 40 or so years of their adult lives participating in the labor force, and this had increased relatively little among those currently entering old age, to 16 years among those aged 60 in 1990 (calculated from Smith and Ward 1984). But this increase will accelerate rapidly in the very near future. By the year 2000, women then aged 60 will have been working for 20 years, an increase in a decade nearly as great as that for the previous 3 decades; and another decade will show an even bigger increase, to 26 years by 2010. More sophisticated projections would show that this increase will continue to accelerate through the early decades of the 21st century, reaching near parity with men.

What is the significance of this shift in female roles among the elderly? Hasn't Social Security provided older women as much or more economic independence based on their husband's lifetime earnings (Sorensen and McLanahan 1987)? It is likely that this change will affect the family lives of the elderly even when these working women retire, affecting not only their marriages, which will experience the same egalitarian pressures that the marriages of younger people have felt, but also their remarriages. It will reinforce the trend that is making marriage, particularly traditional marriage, less central in women's lives. And when the rate of remarriage falls for women, it can also fall for men. So we need to study the impact of past economic activities of women and of divorce on the aging cohorts of the 21st century.

The Decline in Remarriage

Accompanying these two changes is a third, the decline in marriage and particularly in *remarriage*. Recent evidence suggests that most of the decline in *first* marriages simply reflects the increases in age at marriage, as more young adults are not marrying directly out of school, but prolonging both schooling and early work experience before marriage. The proportion of men and women who never marry is not expected to rise above the levels common in this century (Schoen, Urton, Woodrow, and Baj 1985). Most are expected to marry eventually.

It is not so easy to dismiss the decline in remarriage, which has occurred both for women and for men, although nearly all the analyses currently available focus on women. Table 1 shows that although remarriage rates after divorce continue to be higher for men than for women, male rates are falling just as rapidly. Divorced men aged 45 to 64 are remarrying only 73% as fast in 1980 as they were in 1970; among males under 45, the remarriage rate has dropped by nearly half, to 58% of its 1970 level.

The decline in the male remarriage rate has typically been overlooked, because the rate is so much higher than that for women. The sex differences in mortality and in age at marriage have so far guaranteed that the few older men who survived their wives had a large and varied market of widowed women eager to marry them. In the currently elderly population, family care has been the only productive role most women have ever had. So although social security means that they do not *need* to remarry after widowhood, their own experiences have limited their sense of adulthood outside of the family, with the result that they are likely to compete strongly for the opportunity to remarry,

TABLE 1   Remarriage Rates (per 1,000 persons) of Divorced Men and Women, 1970 and 1980.

Age	Men			Women		
	1970	*1980*	*1980/1970*	*1970*	*1980*	*1980/1970*
25–44	325	188	58	179	122	68
45–64	108	79	73	42	30	71
65+	23	23	100	6	5	83

Source: National Center for Health Statistics, Vital Statistics of the U.S., vol. 3, Marriage and Divorce, 1970, pp. 1–22; 1980, pp. 1–23. Adapted from Table 5.7 in Sweet and Bumpass (1987).

seeking to reacquire their central adult role. For those who study sex segregation in occupations, there is a parallel with the concept of "crowding," in which too many women compete for the few "female-typed" jobs in the pink-collar ghetto, thereby reducing wages for them all. It is likely that the remarriage market has been operating in the same way, given the few opportunities for adult roles available to women outside of marriage until the very recent past; but in the new cohorts of the elderly, women's eagerness to reenter traditional marriages in later life may decline much as has their eagerness to take jobs only as nurses or secretaries.

If so, the already rapid declines in rates of remarriage are likely to accelerate. Scholars have frequently worried that the increase in female labor force participation would reduce women's willingness and availability to care for their elderly parents. We already know that many working women respond to the burden of child care by choosing not to have so many—or any—children. It seems likely that more women will also respond to the prospect of remarriage and the opportunity to care for a new elderly husband the same way. This will dramatically change the family roles of the cohorts soon to enter old age. And because the reason for entering the remarriage market will increasingly be because of divorce, rather than spousal death, there will still be problems, even for those who do remarry. And these problems will be disproportionately for men. How so?

This may seem an unusual statement, because most of the research on the costs of divorce has focused on children and on women, portraying the emotional and financial disruptions each experience. Women bear the greater financial costs of divorce because of our custody norms and laws and the low levels of child support paid by many fathers (Weitzman 1985). But these custody patterns also mean that the intergenerational tie between mother and child is maintained, but that between the father and the child is

compromised. Let us briefly explore the potential consequences of divorce and of non-marriage—key elements of the gender revolution—for the elderly of the 21st century.

Consequences of Divorce for Child Contact

One of the major contributions of research on the family in later life has been that on intergenerational relationships, relationships that the decline in mortality, and hence increased survivorship, now insure will last for many years. Most of us can expect to be in an adult-adult relationship with our parents and also with our children for more years than we are in adult-minor child relationship with them. This research has shown that such relationships can be very important; children provide a substantial fraction of the instrumental care needed in old age (Soldo, Agree, and Wolf 1988), and they contribute substantially to the emotional well-being of older persons, particularly of the unmarried elderly.

However, nearly all the studies on intergenerational relationships have studied older women or couples. There have been too few older unmarried men to study; thus research on the consequences of divorce for the relationships between parents and their adult offspring is in its infancy. Nevertheless, we have two recent studies of the effect of divorce on father-child relationships in adulthood that suggest that the costs of divorce for men are substantial, far greater than for women.

The first study focused on fathers over 60 with adult children and found strong effects of divorce both on contact with children and on perceiving them as a source of support in time of need (Cooney and Uhlenberg 1990). Although nearly 90% of never-divorced men have weekly contact with their children, this is true for only half of ever-divorced men; and 10% of such men have essentially no contact with their offspring. Similarly, although nearly four out of five never-divorced fathers name children as a source of support, this is the case for less than half the ever-divorced fathers. Their multivariate model suggests that the odds that an ever-divorced father mentions a child for such support are only 32% of those that a never-divorced father would do so (antilog of their coefficient on divorce of –1.15).

This study also shows that remarriage does not mitigate these effects. Their sample of ever-divorced older men was small, but the direction of effects for remarriage suggests that remarriage does not strengthen overall father-child relationships, and for many measures, weakens them further; and divorced men's relationships with stepchildren are similar to the weak ties that they have with their biological children. In this population of currently elderly, ever-divorced fathers, most of whom have remarried, the father-child bond is weak.

The second study used the same data, but took the perspective of the younger generation (Lawton 1990). People were asked about the *quality* of their relationships with their living mothers and fathers and about their history of living with each parent during childhood. These results indicate that divorce, both during and after childhood, disrupts relationship quality, but that the negative effects are greater for divorce that occurs during childhood and are three to four times stronger for relationships with fathers than with mothers.

It is possible that neither of these studies, both of which focus on divorce many years ago, are representative of later generations. Their divorces occurred early in the divorce explosion, before it became part of "normal" experience; children then may have felt greater hostility toward the departing parent than do children experiencing divorce now, when it is something they share with many of their friends. If so, the effects may be decreasing.

However, data on recent father-child interaction in the aftermath of divorce suggest that there is likely to be even less contact in the future. Furstenberg (1988) reviewed evidence from the 1980s on such contact that shows that half of all early adolescent children living in mother-only households had no contact with their fathers in the previous year and that contact declined rapidly with time since divorce. These levels of contact are substantially *lower* than those reported by divorced elderly fathers with their grown children shown in the first study (Cooney and Uhlenberg 1990). The authors of this study interpret these differences to mean that, as we often hear anecdotally, many children reach out to their absent fathers after reaching adulthood. But it could also mean that when divorce was rare and even more rarely involved children (Sweet and Bumpass 1987), fathers worked harder to maintain relationships with their children than many divorcing fathers do in the 1980s. If so, the costs of divorce for men's intergenerational relationships may be increasing.

Gender Differences in Marital Status Consequences

Paradoxically, then, the gender revolution, via divorce, is weakening men's intergenerational family ties and, thereby, increasing the importance of marriage for their family relationships, just as their prospects for remarriage are declining. We are used to having mostly unmarried women in our studies of the well-being of the elderly; what can we expect from the increase in unmarried men? Actually, there is already a research literature that tells us that although the married are better off than the unmarried on a wide range of indicators of well-being, the differences are normally greater for men than for women: "his marriage" is better for him than "her marriage" is for her (Bernard 1972; Gove 1973), at least for those in traditional marriages.

The most dramatic gender differences are in mortality rates, although similar results have been found for mental health and other measures of life satisfaction and well-being. In an earlier study on mortality, this author compared the married with those who were maintaining their own household while living alone. The two groups were selected on the basis of reasonably good health and financial well-being, to avoid the problems of selectivity that plague most studies of marital status differentials in which the unmarried often include disproportionately those too ill or too poor to be married.

Table 2 shows that married men have much lower mortality than those living alone. Although the differences are greatest in middle age, the risk of death is 2.4 times as great for men aged 55 to 64 who are living alone as for those who are married and still 30% higher even among those aged 65 to 74. These differences are much less for women, although they also decline with age. In fact, unlike findings in studies that compare gender differences in mortality by marital status categories, the oldest women who were living alone had *lower* mortality risks than did married women of the same age. This finding needs to be replicated for the 1990s and beyond; it is possible that more men are adapting to living alone and are fashioning a substitute network of relationships as many

women do, although current evidence on gender differences in friendship maintenance and renewal does not suggest that this is the case (Fischer and Oliker 1983).

DISCUSSION

Many of these facts are not new; occasional papers in the past have focused on widowers and portrayed all the extremes of isolation that current analyses of the family relationships of the elderly have overlooked (e.g., Berardo 1970). They portray domestic disorganization, at least in many cases, together with weak and problematic social relationships, depression, and death. But if isolation has always been a social problem for unmarried males, for many generations it has been so demographically unusual that it was rarely seen as such. And it is likely that the field of family research, which has focused almost exclusively on either couples or women and children, has probably helped to blind us to the problems that have existed.

With the aging of the gender revolution, the numbers of old unmarried men will grow dramatically; they will be much more difficult to ignore. The rapid growth in female labor force participation has provided a substantial number of women with substitutes for weak or problematic marriages. Although the cohorts currently entering young

TABLE 2   Death Rates by Age, Sex, and Family Status United States 1966–68.

Gender and Family Status	Age			
	35–44	*45–54*	*55–64*	*65–74*
Males				
Married	3.2	8.1	20.4	44.6
Living alone	14.1	32.0	49.8	57.3
Risk of living alone/marriage	4.4	3.9	2.4	1.3
Females				
Married	2.1	4.6	9.1	23.8
Living alone	5.0	8.1	11.9	20.9
Risk of living alone/marriage	2.3	1.8	1.3	0.9

Source: Computed from data presented in Kobrin and Hendershot (1977).

adulthood may be finding ways to increase the strength and quality of their marriages, by forging new bonds based on working together to create and maintain their family lives, few among those who will be entering their retirement years in the near future have done so; instead, they will have experienced high rates of marital breakdown and decreasing probabilities of remarriage. Even among those who are remarried, high proportions will have problematic or *no* relationships with their biological children, which their stepchildren will not replace.

The family lives of those who are currently elderly may well be strong and supportive, for women and for men. But with the aging of the gender revolution, there will soon be new cohorts entering old age that will be very different, with a history of family ties that are broken, weakened, and confused. How divorce is redefining intergenerational relationships of all kinds—not only between parents and children, but between grandparents and grandchildren and also among siblings—is an important area that requires systematic research. These research challenges are urgent ones, with equally urgent implications for social policies on aging. And we have barely begun to address them.

REFERENCES

Aldous, J. 1987. "New Views on the Family Life of the Elderly and the Near-Elderly." *Journal of Marriage and the Family* 49:227–34.

Berardo, F. 1970. "Survivorship and Social Isolation: The Case of the Aged Widower." *Family Coordinator* 19:11–25.

Bernard, Jessie. 1972. *The Future of Marriage*. New York: World.

Burch, T. 1967. "The Size and Structure of Families: A Comparative Analysis of Census Data." *American Sociological Review* 32:347–63.

Burgess, Ernest and Henry Locke. 1945. *The Family: From Institution to Companionship.* New York: American Book.

Cooney, T. and P. Uhlenberg. 1990. "The Role of Divorce in Men's Relations with Their Adult Children After Mid-Life." *Journal of Marriage and the Family* 52:677–88.

Fischer, C. and S. Oliker. 1983. "A Research Note on Friendship, Gender, and the Life Cycle." *Social Forces* 62:124–32.

Furstenberg, F. 1988. "Good Dads—Bad Dads: Two Faces of Fatherhood." Pp. 193–218 in *The Changing American Family and Public Policy* edited by Andrew Chetlin. Washington, DC: Urban Institute.

Goldscheider, F. and I. Waite. Forthcoming. *No Families, New Families: The Transformation of the American Home*. Berkeley, CA: University of California Press.

Goode, William. 1970. *World Revolution in Family Patterns*. New York: Free Press.

Gove, Walter R. 1973. "Sex, Marital Status, and Mortality." *American Journal of Sociology* 79:45–67.

Kobrin, F. and G. Hendershot. 1977. "Do Family Ties Reduce Mortality? Evidence From the United States, 1966–1968." *Journal of Marriage and the Family* 39:737–45.

Lawton, Leora. 1990. "The Quality of Parent and Adult-Child Relationships and Family Structure." Paper presented at the annual meeting of the Population Association of America, Toronto, May.

Levy, M., Jr. 1965. "Aspects of the Analysis of Family Structure." Pp. 1–63 in *Aspects of the Analysis of Family Structure*, edited by A. Coale, L. Sellers, M. Levy, D. Schneider, and S. Tomkins. Princeton, NJ: Princeton University Press.

Martin, Theresa Castro and Larry L Bumpass. 1989. "Recent Trends in Marital Disruption." *Demography* 26:37–51.

Neugarten, B. 1974. "Age Groups in American Society and the Rise of the Young-Old." *Annals of the Journal of Political and Social Sciences* 415:187–89.

Schoen, Robert, William Urton, Karen Woodrow, and John Baj. 1985. "Marriage and Divorce in Twentieth Century American Cohorts." *Demography* 22:101–14.

Shanas, E. 1980. "Older People and their Families: The New Pioneers." *Journal of Marriage and the Family* 42:9–15.

Smith, J. and M. Ward. 1984. *Women's Wages and Work in the 20th Century.* Santa Monica, CA: RAND.

Soldo, B., E. Agree, and D. Wolf. 1988. "The Balance Between Formal and Informal Care." Pp. 193–216 in *Aging and Health Care: Social Science and Policy Perspectives,* edited by M. Ory and K. Bond. New York: Routledge.

Sorensen, A. and S. McLanahan. 1987. "Married Women's Economic Dependency, 1940–1980." *American Journal of Sociology* 93:659–87.

Sweet, J. and L. Bumpass. 1987. *American Families and Households.* New York: Russell Sage.

Weitzman, Lenore J. 1985. *The Divorce Revolution.* New York: Free Press.

Challenges of Aging in Tomorrow's World: Will Gerontology Grow, Stagnate, or Change?

ROBERT MORRIS

The end of every millennium, and of every century (this one is only 11 years away) have traditionally been times of either optimism or anxiety, time for great change or for affirming old faiths. If the idea of millennial or centenary change seems fanciful, recall that the end of the 19th century saw the beginning of the progressive era in the United States, and the end of the 18th saw the American and French revolutions. The 1988 meeting of the Gerontological Society may be a modest anticipation of that tradition for the organizations and professional persons occupationally concerned about the elderly.

Although neither historian nor philosopher, I shall review certain trends that are likely to transform the present system of activities by agencies and scholars that is based on a past consensus about the conditions of being old and about how the nation can improve these conditions. What may be altered are priorities of agencies serving the elderly, the research interests of scholars, and the approaches of professional staffs. Those trends include: the erosion of consensus about public responsibility, the changed profile of the older population, the adverse consequences of continuous proliferation in programs, manpower shortages, and limits of professionalization. Depending on whether one is a pessimist or optimist, one can anticipate a struggle to justify the present pattern or can welcome the opportunity to create a new one. The opportunity I foresee is a new commitment to the well-being of people of all ages, in which the elderly play a leading, not only a beneficiary role, and in which those who study the conditions of the aged play a proactive role.

A HUNDRED YEARS OF IMPROVEMENT

First consider what activism by and for the aged has achieved in the past 100 years. Before the Civil War, the elderly usually shared the life risks of all citizens of any age, but were often rather privileged in an agricultural society where they were likely to control wealth and were respected in a strong religious tradition (Achenbaum, 1978). This situation changed under the pressure of

Source: The Gerontologist, 29(4), 494–501. Reprinted with permission from The Gerontological Society of America, Washington, DC 20005. Copyright 1989.

rapid industrialization, large scale immigration, and a change in the economic structure during the last half of the 19th century. More and more, the urban elderly came to be viewed as a group likely to be sick, decrepit, and unable to fit into the new industrial age. The Veterans Bureau began to shelter dependent old veterans. Some revivalist and reform ministers began to question the wisdom and virtue of the aged; one prominent speaker said, "These traditions of the elderly are grand sources of most of the data errors of the present day" (Cole, 1986). In the first third of the 20th century, there was only one state pension system (in Alaska, before 1923), and only five more survived constitutional hurdles by 1929. This movement toward old-age pensions grew more slowly than did the more popular effort to relieve widows and children through mothers aid.

By the depression of the 1930s, the present perception of the aged began to take shape, resulting in enactment of the Social Security Act. Economic conditions, the growing numbers of aged, and high unemployment supported treating the aged as a separate population, relatively homogeneous, poor, likely to be sick or feeble, and deserving of support. The elderly moved out of the mainstream of economic life, and began to organize themselves as a special interest group (e.g., the Townsend Movement in the 1930s), which conformed well to the American political system in which special groups contend with each other for their shares of public attention.

Today attention to the elderly by government and private groups is due in part to the perceived (it is not clear how real) political power wielded by the elderly and their advocating organizations, and partly to a cultural and religious tradition of shared intergenerational obligation. In several ways the aged, as a *group,* are as privileged in public policy as are others, even though several subgroups remain in deep distress.

THE PRESENT CONDITIONS OF THE ELDERLY

The end results of national policies during this century in the lives of the elderly are significant. More and more the socioeconomic profile of the aged population approximates that of all ages. With Medicare they have access to health services equal to that of other groups (no matter how flawed that system is); Social Security plus occupational pensions brings their income curve to approximately that of all ages. Older individuals are less likely to live in poverty than the rest of the population (12.4% vs. 13.6%), although black elderly are more likely to be in poverty, and fewer white elderly are poor (10.7%). Compared with the total population, a higher proportion of the aged have incomes below $20,000 and a small proportion have incomes over $20,000. But if we look at net worth, which covers assets as well as income, a higher proportion of older people than the national average have total assets over $45,000 (for example 25% of aged versus 19% of all individuals have assets between $50,000 and $100,000).

Mortality and morbidity rates have improved. If we used today the standards used when the Social Security Act was adopted in 1935 (the expected years of life after retirement), the retirement age could be at 73 or 75, not 65 years (Chen, 1988). Legislation for the aged constitutes the foundation of our welfare system for all ages. True, while most elderly people are more like all Americans, others lack their advantages—incomes of the very sick, old, widows, and minorities are still grossly inadequate—they make up the poverty group among the aged. But most elders, as a *group,* are better educated and healthier, and have more income and freedom to live where they wish than did their forbears.

Such achievements add up to a major success story, although public discourse still talks about *the* problem of the aged, not about the unfinished aspects of success.

INTIMATIONS OF CHANGE

The foundation for the present arrangements has been a broad consensus among political parties. This consensus seems to be eroding along two fault lines. Several trends have also begun to emerge that intimate not only where the impulse for change comes from, but the direction it may take: the complexity and frustration of continuous organizational proliferation and segmentation; personnel shortages; the destabilizing tempo of scientific and technological rapid change; renewal by the elderly of a search for reengagement with society, including the evolution of new roles; economic and demographic change; and diverging interests of the elderly population.

One symptom of *coming* change is the steady decline in confidence in or anxiety about the Social Security system. In 1975, between 50 and 60% of those aged 25 to 44 were confident in it; by 1986, that percentage had dropped by half. Among those over age 65, confidence dropped only by 15%, from 82% of respondents to 70% (Chen, 1989). Opinion polls are mixed, but the code words of tax resistance and intergenerational conflict (or competition) are so widely used in public and private discussion that the change in outlook cannot be ignored.

What follows is an exploration of the matrix of forces associated with this drop in consensus and some proposals for dealing with them.

Eroding Consensus: Economic and Demographic Change

Economic change and population growth are among the basic influences underlying national and political destinies. For this analysis, these forces seem to be moving in opposite directions and creating the rifts in consensus referred to. The relationship between the two needs attention.

The economic dimension. —*One fault line* is the tension between a changing age profile of the population and a changing economy, which disturbs the ways in which the nation allocates its resources. An aging population requires no elaboration here. What is significant is that more older people live longer and their retirement and health costs increase with these added years. This strains arrangements based on earlier data on life expectancy.

At the same time, our, and the world's, economy has changed. Our growth rate has slowed down and the real boom years of the post-World War II years (not the debt-financed boomlet of the 1980s) are past. There is a slower growing social surplus to finance faster growing needs. So a slowing economy collides with growing expectations. Competition among many interests increases for shares of slowly growing national income.

But our national expectations about the good life have also increased. Middle-adult parents and workers want to have a good life, put their children through college, and enjoy the personal use of their earned incomes for their private wants. But even two-earner families find it hard to keep up with these enlarged private expectations.

And finally, the postwar years brought large numbers of workers into a quasi-middle-class income position. This expanded, perhaps dominant, middle class has increased private expectations of more people for more private goods than ever before. From 1950 to 1975 most groups were on a rising escalator of better income, as national wealth increased. Wage as well as salaried workers shared in the confidence that conditions could only get better. By 1975, the escalator began to turn down. Today, real average weekly wages are down; for most in the middle they are less than in 1975, a loss concealed by two-worker family incomes and massive borrowing (Silk, 1988). Most predictions are that this decline in living standards for the middle will continue. Half of new jobs are at or below the poverty level (Chisman, 1987).

In this context it is becoming doubtful whether reductions in military spending, a priority of the past 10 years, will be adequate, by itself, to reconcile these conflicting pressures, even if it becomes politically feasible. We have been led to think that we can resolve the tensions of change by reducing the scope of government and by cutting taxes to give each of us a little more private disposable income. In reality, we are discouraged from seeing that the strains being felt call for political judgments about how to share and allocate the resources. We have been led away from concepts of collective or cooperative efforts to manage the well-being of all, leaving no one out, toward a private, marketplace solution in which divisiveness and difference among groups is accentuated.

However we view the situation, dissensus is clear and tangible. The perception grows that aged people have had their turn and it is time to look at other needs. To modify a Lovelace sonnet, "It's not that we love the elderly less, but we love ourselves more."

Changed conditions and diverging interests of the elderly. —*The second fault line* opening up is the growing division among the elderly themselves. Others have long noted (Binstock & Hudson, 1976) that the aged are not the homogeneous voting-and-influence bloc that politics often assumes. However, those whose total assets and incomes are above the median or in the upper two quintiles of income distribution, and who are still relatively healthy and quite active (perhaps as many as 70% to age 80), have different priorities than do those who are poorer or more disabled (perhaps 20% of the group). The first are still likely to enjoy life, to be more engaged in life of the community, and to resist additional taxation, including taxes

on their pension benefits (although one large advocacy group did support the catastrophic health bill, with its very high tax on the aged). They use the market for independent living arrangements, and are not happy when too many very sick elderly live next door—they are likely to push for nursing home care to "protect" such individuals. The latter, by contrast seek more public expenditure for income, housing, and primary health care, but are less active politically.

The second group of elderly is augmented by the 50-to-60-year-old people who lost jobs and cannot find new employers willing to hire them. They have lost their place in society, are suddenly poor, and anticipate a major drop in retirement income due to reduced terminal earnings. They too are without any health protection.

All three groups may agree on defending Social Security, but differ about priorities: more or less taxes, low-cost housing or life-care condos, more primary care, or job protection. It is hard to see a central rallying cry for these elder groups.

These diverse interests of the elderly have come to approximate the interests of other age groups: affordable housing, income or work security, health care insurance, day care for children as well as aged people, education for all. All such *common human* needs are met organizationally by age-based criteria for entitlement. But we are as yet unclear about how to handle the commonalities that bridge the ages. Each group of any age resists taxation unless it can see a direct benefit for itself.

The fault lines are accentuated by a drift away from belief in risk sharing across the widest possible population groups, a drift that has entered the private as well as the public insurance markets. For example, private health maintenance organizations (HMOs) still cannot incorporate the elderly for protection without tax subsidy—costs for the aged are not spread over all insured enrollees because this would raise premium rates for younger enrollees. In like vein, the recent catastrophic health insurance legislation taxes only the elderly to cover benefits at the rate of several hundred income-tax dollars a year (for some), rather than spreading the costs over the working population of all ages. Segmented insurance, with less risk sharing, subtly widens the gap between generations just when common human needs begin to close it.

The weaker consensus among all groups, and among the elderly, tilts opinion toward policies that separate at-risk populations from those not yet facing difficulty; away from joint effort to meet common human needs in favor of tightly segmented approaches and personal self-insurance by those who have the means.

We could, of course, meet this situation by accepting the tradition that special interest groups do better when they organize separately and compete with each other. Up to now, the aged have had a competitive edge in that process. But I suggest that the edge has been, or is rapidly being, lost.

Institutional and Program Proliferation

The improvements in the conditions of the elderly have been carried out by the creation, between 1933 and 1988, of a remarkable and complex structure of organizations, agencies, and professions that have, on the positive side, produced more specialist care, more variety, and also more jobs for younger workers. In the aggregate they make up a large infrastructure and superstructure for the field of gerontology. The Gerontological Society has grown as a research and scientific body both in numbers and in public recognition. There are at least 259 gerontology education programs in higher education, a growing number of geriatric specializations in medical schools, and a dozen social research centers or institutes. National and regional associations of gerontology flourish.

There are numerous national, regional, and local citizen advocacy groups, all active even when their influence is unclear.

This educational and advocacy superstructure rests on an even more extensive and complicated organizational and bureaucratic infrastructure of thousands of national and local agencies that employ over two million professional and support workers (no one knows how many), who have major interests in aging, although their interests are often conflicting. Their number constitute a major element in the 20th-century service economy.

But, there are serious side effects that are likely to force change in the way we organize our basic approach to the problems of aging. Here are some of the problems:

(a) Specialization and fragmentation is confusing to both provider agencies and consumer, for each specialty is hemmed in by its own eligibility rules, its own professional self-concepts of what is appropriate, and its separate financing. The segmenting of services does not match the unity of a client's life. Not only is it frustrating for clients or patients to make their way through the maze of rules, but professionals themselves hardly know who does what.

(b) In order to make the cumbersome system work, additional layers of organization have been introduced—information, referral, and case management systems—both to control utilization and to help users and providers make their way through the maze. Not surprisingly, this new guidance system takes on the proliferating characteristic of the basic provider structure. In Boston, about 200 independent information agencies already are in place, designed to help the aged population negotiate this maze. In addition, most payers (including insurance companies) and many service agencies employ their own case managers and information specialists to help control costs as well as to guide their patients or clients.

The function of this new layer is itself unclear; not knowing whether the purpose is to meet a client's needs or to save an agency money confuses both clients and staff. Frustration with obfuscation increases.

(c) The system is costly. Each specialty maintains its own administration, fundraising, eligibility rules, promotion and advertising and accounting. The forms and paperwork are different for each, although each requires similar basic information. Each is forced to compete for available and limited funds, often against others rather than in any unified effort to develop a rationalized long-term structure or to overcome public indifference. In health care financing, the complexity adds to the cost of care. Canada, with a private delivery system much like that of the United States, spends 6% of its GNP on health care to cover everyone, whereas the U.S. system costs over 9.5% for only partial coverage (Kane & Kane, 1985).

(d) The sheer complexity of the provider system may, paradoxically, increase the volume of unmet need as much as it increases the variety of services. Each specialty survives by its own excluding rules to fit applicant to specialty. We know little about how many consumers fall between the cracks as they try to fit themselves into more and more specialties.

(e) The confusion has also impeded the acceptance of any overarching concept of long-term care and dependency in modern society. A great deal of organizational energy is devoted to creating specialties to restore independence, certainly a humane and valued economic aim. But insufficient professional energy is left to craft basic systems to care for inevitable dependencies in ways that respect both human life and our desire for economy.

Results such as these are bringing users and payers to the conviction that some fundamental change is necessary in how we design service systems. Some major employers already question our present structure of health services and are showing new interest in national health insurance to replace the employer/private insurance approach we now use. Some form of national health insurance for all is again in the offing, but will it be for acute hospital care only? For drugs? For long-term care as well? If it comes, it will surely alter Medicare. Are gerontologists prepared to advance basic alternatives without being defensive? It may even require advocating more public investment, more private savings, more constraints on uses, or even all three.

In a more basic sense, the proliferation that specialization brings on lacks a comparable mechanism for deciding how the general well-being of society is to be secured. Even more, specialization makes it almost impossible to treat the client/patient as a whole person. Amid all our technology the client/patient remains the major protector of his or her unity and integrity, but confronts a confusing impersonal system whose extensive staff is limited by organization rules and fragmentation.

Personnel and Labor Shortages: Low Technology Functions in the 1990s

The current low unemployment rate highlights a deeper personnel problem, especially for long-term care, that will persist if unemployment increases. It is most evident in the area of low-skill work, which I prefer to call low-technology work (as being less demeaning). Most of our professional attention is directed at ourselves; much less attention is given to the much larger numbers of low-tech workers with self-learned skills on whom the very foundations of professional practice depend. (Think of nursing homes without aides at all or mental hospitals with only psychiatrists or psychologists.) This personnel is low paid, demeaned, neglected. We have assumed we can always replace those who leave in high turnover.

The facts are disturbing. Personnel projections indicate that over the next few decades the proportion of all workers between ages 20 and 65 will decline in relation to those over 65 and under 18 years (Chen, 1988; Rappaport & Plumley, 1988). Young workers, who make up about one-third of the nursing home work force, are projected to decline by 30% in the next eight years (Labor Department).

At the same time the proportion of aged, of sick, of handicapped youth will increase as a result of the demographic curve of a maturing baby boom generation and of our capacity to keep severely disabled children and youth alive for longer periods of time (Morris, 1976).

Ever since the Commission on Chronic Illness in the 1950s, it has been known that policy on aging must combine medical with social care, with social care equal to or much greater than the medical in personnel terms. But our actions have moved in the opposite direction. We value professionalization over hands-on daily care. Small clues abound. Acute hospitals in America, between 1980 and 1986, hired 38,000 additional RNs but used 33,000 fewer LPNs (AHA). In nursing homes, nurses give an average of 7 to 12 minutes time a day to each patient; the balance of the 24-hour day is entrusted to low-tech staff who receive little attention in personnel policy but who give most of the prescribed care (Institute of Medicine, 1983).

These trends and shortages in recruiting low-tech workers have already reduced the volume of long-term care for which policy and money entitle fully eligible patients. In Massachusetts, some nursing homes have closed intake or closed down. Approved home care was denied to over 2,000 home-care, homebound aged (Wilner, 1987). Utilization rates for authorized care ranges from 50% to an average of 80% (Massachusetts Rate Setting, 1987).

Eldercare is not like other service industries; it is labor intensive (at least when clients are helpless). Specialized therapeutic staff and machine technology are no substitutes for the hands-on care required.

Such tendencies will force gerontologists in service agencies and in research to recast and revalue the low-tech worker in the future and his or her place in our hierarchy. Their jobs may have to be redesigned to capitalize on whatever workers are available—today the major underused workers are the able active elderly and minority youth, augmented sporadically and temporarily by immigrants or guest workers. This potential labor supply is now inaccessible for several reasons. Minority youth are not interested in what they see as dead-end jobs, as well as by discrimination, poor education, prejudice, and cultural differences between patients and staff. Some of the able elderly see no opportunity to use their abilities in ways acceptable to them, or because of prejudice against older workers, or because they accept early retirement as inevitable.

Our enterprise will have to revalue the low-tech function as having a recognized career function of its own, with new respect, responsibilities, and probably higher pay. It cannot forever serve only as an escalator to enter another profession.

The current solution to this is higher pay. But higher pay without a change in how the service system uses the low-tech worker will lead only to higher and higher costs, resistance to those costs, the closing of some agencies, with no improvement in care. An analytic start in this direction has been taken in a few university research centers (Brannon et al., 1988).

Loss and Recovery of Role

A powerful impulse for change in the way the public and professionals view the aged comes from the gift of a longer healthy life for more elderly. The economic boom [of the

1980s gave] new impetus to the old question, "What is old age about—withdrawal from society or continued engagement with it?" The present position of the elderly is socially determined in part, not only a natural product of a longer life. Much of our gerontological activity has concentrated on how to enjoy the fruits of health and leisure, how the elderly will create their own segregated world of aging, or how the elderly adapt to the socially constructed world available to them (Guillemard, 1983; Kleemeier, 1983).

I believe that several forces will push us to alter the place many of the aged will fill in a mature society. *First,* the personnel difficulties just mentioned will lead to a need for more active engagement by elders in the economic and social life of the nation—not necessarily compulsory for all, but available to all. Some sectors of the economy are already feeling the pinch of labor shortages, only some of which is due to the unexpectedly robust growth of the past few years. As a result, a number of industries are now expanding their efforts to retrain or to attract older workers—banks, financial services, merchandising (Rothstein, 1988).

The behavior of retiring workers also reinforces this reengagement hypothesis. It also suggests a widespread desire by many workers to continue some useful activity either because they prefer to keep active or because they need more income. Small-scale studies document that as many as one-half of retired workers continue to work, for pay, either part time or in new occupations (Sheppard, 1988; Mutschler, 1984; Newfield, 1970). This development has been overshadowed by the more extensive research attention given to the uses of leisure. These worker behaviors in retirement, not yet fully documented, warrant much more attention: especially the differing aspirations of blue-collar, professional, white-collar and service populations.

Of equal importance will be the need to reexamine the many *unfinished tasks in the modern world* that are not satisfactorily dealt with by current definitions of the marketplace and that will give new impetus to nonprofit as much as to government action. We are not very successful in handling the fallout that constant and rapid technical change imposes on our economic and educational structures, on our family and social relationships, on our environment, and even on our political and electoral processes. The underused active elderly are a resource for meeting the social consequences of these changes, consequences for which economic formulas are not sufficient. The aged population may even insist on new roles. Some university programs are already training older people to conduct policy-relevant research and to engage in significant public policy activities—on behalf of the environment, housing, or feeding the hungry—or to improve services for the mentally or physically ill (Bass, 1988).

The hypothesis of reengagement rather than disengagement is still controversial, and it is true that some elderly want nothing more than to retire, especially those who have worked all their lives in dull and routine tasks. But they are only part of the new elderly. I doubt that an active and educated older population will always accept withdrawal from engagement for a third of adult life (say for the 15 years between ages 65 and 80, or 60 and 75), especially when so much needs attention in an aging and maturing society (Chen, 1988; Pifer & Bronte, 1986; Bass, 1988). If people are an economic as well as a social resource, then 20 million elderly, perhaps 10 million active elderly, are a major unused resource. The scale of unmet social needs suggests that the aged are made redundant not by production technology, but by a combination of social organization of resources and of changeable personal preferences. Even if the current boom is short-lived, there will be enough to do to make neglect of this major human resource unwise—unwise not only because active older people will seek useful roles as they do now, but because our national well-being will have need of their capacities and numbers to produce goods and services for all and to improve the quality of local and national civic life.

If gerontologists are to play a part in this shift, they will give more attention to mainstream economic and social organization rather than concentrating exclusively on the separate arrangements for the elderly outside that mainstream. My predecessors, such as Randall, Tibbets, Oriol, and Binstock, have made similar pleas, but action is slow.

The Changing Character of Science, Professions, and Research Priorities

In order to deal with the problems that the size and complexity of the gerontological system create, gerontologists, whether in research, teaching or service delivery, have to come to terms with the rapid scientific and technological change that has become a force transforming their field daily. On the research side, the public is enthusiastic about a vision of the future that implies (when it does not directly promise) that disability can be conquered and death delayed, even conquered. This has led to such rapid application of technologies flowing from the laboratory that the health care system is substantially destabilized. Professional practice changes daily; the demand for more and more support staff goes on; costs increase at three times the rate of growth in national resource; and cost-control measures proliferate so much that much professional service is now often governed by accountants and clerks far removed from the patient. The changes that these bring to medical care flow out into rapid new demands for community care by agencies less equipped than medicine to respond. Meantime, a fragmented and most incomplete data system limits capacity to trace and understand the changes going on (Neu & Harrison, 1988).

Dissatisfactions with the instability introduced into the service system by rapid technological change increase. Payers and service providers struggle to keep up with escalating costs and with the unpredictability of rapid changes in efforts to control costs. Professionals are on the run to keep up with both new knowledge and increasing regulations of practice. The latter find cost control by mechanical accounting procedures give as much authority over what is done to clerks using paper protocols as to physicians. It is increasingly said that patients are whatever the numerous forms filled out about them say they are, rather than being flesh-and-blood individuals.

Reimbursement for services given has become increasingly arbitrary, with unpredicted delays or retroactive denials, while the paperwork and nonpatient staff time increases exponentially.

At the same time troubling ethical questions increase—ethical matters that concern newborn infants, aged, and youth alike. Should we buy and sell, "farm," or "harvest" genes or organs of the newly dead infants for organ transplant? Who will care for the neurologically damaged newborn infant? What are the limits of heroic efforts to sustain vegetative life, especially when the quality of longer life for so many disabled is hard to bear? How to balance the disparate wants and costs of some to grasp a few more months of life through heroic and still experimental interventions with the wants of many more disabled who need to live tolerably today and for many years? Has the health system any responsibility for the social requirements of living with great disability that are produced (as a kind of failure of success) by frontier science and technology?

Destabilizing speed of change, new constraints on the professions, and troubling ethical questions, all begin to raise doubts about how much and how fast our service systems can take. The evidence for keeping up the headlong pace or for slowing it down is absent, but the tension and distress are real. This could lead to proposals for realigning scientific priorities as between the social sciences (quality of life today) and the physical sciences (evermore cure or prevention in the future). A new balance will be tested between postponing death tomorrow and improving life or relieving distress today.

It is interesting that it is the newer AIDS epidemic, not the older epidemic of aging with disability, that is beginning to produce responsive medical attitudes such as the following: "The leitmotif of this work is that caring is more important than curing. We have been led ... by exquisite technology which took away from the more personal parts of medicine. Now we are learning to do other things that will benefit everybody" (Friedland, 1988). If this attitude does emerge, it will show up in more allocations for social research and attention to results comparable to that given the basic sciences. Perhaps social science will grow to become basic, too.

SPECULATION ABOUT CHANGE IN GERONTOLOGY'S MISSION

Reactive or Proactive Roles

Those who are actively concerned about the aged scholars, research scientists, and service staffs—can play active or passive roles: reacting to changes or acting early to anticipate and shape the nature of change. At the *minimum* they can:

1. Devote more attention in agency operations and in research to the positive side of aging to balance (not replace) the past emphasis on dependency, helplessness, deprivation, and cure of disease;

2. Encourage research and demonstration about the place of low technology in the human services for aging, and perhaps in the larger economic society as well, to test the idea that present organizational and professional patterns are inevitably the best we can have;

3. Broaden inquiry into future roles for those active retired, who are interested, including both entrepreneurial and unpaid cooperative action; and

4. Critically reexamine the imbalance between prevention and cure, and the dealing with death versus improving daily life for those with severe handicaps and minimal support systems.

A Proactive Role

If they choose to be more active, as I would prefer, they could start now to develop an alternative vision, or visions, about what an older society could look like in *practical terms* in the 21st century.

If we could take the millennium seriously, I would urge two focuses:

1. Reverse the past tendency to move the elderly out of the mainstream institutions of social and economic life and begin reintegrating. That may include thinking about the many aspects of modern life that are badly attended to and that trouble us, which may be uncomfortable, for it entails a belief that not all troubles need be excused forever because resources never match wants. It would involve a first look at how human resources at all ages can be engaged in socially significant tasks. What is different now, compared with the past, is that for the first time, we have a large labor resource whose talents are unused due to social policy, not by nature or individual preference *alone.*

2. Second, I would like to reintegrate the interests of the aged (and of their large infrastructure) with those of other age groups. Would it be committing an oxymoron to call for a *nonageist policy on aging?* By that, I mean to view the elderly as the spearhead or vanguard of renewed efforts to meet *common human needs* (a phrase once coined for the 1930s by Charlotte Towle and since forgotten) rather than concentrating on the specialty needs of the aged. The opportunities

are many, since so many of the major deficiencies that trouble the aged trouble others equally: Serious disability in childhood, youth, old age, and the victims of AIDS; housing for the elderly, the homeless, and the working poor; health insurance protection for all; day care for children and for the aged; and so on and on. This would be a modern reply to the ancient questions: Who am I if I am not myself? And what am I if for myself alone? The hard-nosed international journal *The Economist* recently wrote: "The enterprise culture can keep the economy humming. But the community (e.g. social) culture will keep (or make) society sweet."

It may be utopian to expect all gerontologists to lead in revitalizing national efforts to deal with such common problems. But in this task, the Gerontological Society can have a major role without violating its traditions. Its members can use its forums and structure to encourage open and continuing discussion about the broad outlines and the details of the future they would like to see for all age groups and how to move to meet it. Its networks and structure can encourage more research into the basic foundations and the details on which a broad vision must rest. Above all, its structures can help reduce the want of ideas by encouraging discussion of alternative visions about what the future holds for the aging, and not the aging alone, especially those which include evidence, about social organization as well as about individuals. In other words, aspirations, grounded in reality, to try to meet the future rather than waiting for it to happen.

REFERENCES

Achenbaum, W. A. (1978). *Old age in the new land: American experience since 1970.* Baltimore: Johns Hopkins University Press.

American Hospital Association (AHA). (1987). Quoted in *The Economist,* May 14, 1988, p. 30.

Bass, S. (1988). The role of higher education in creating economic roles. In R. Morris & S. Bass (Eds.), *Retirement reconsidered.* New York: Springer.

Binstock, R., & Hudson, R. (1976). Political systems and aging. In R. Binstock & E. Shanas (Eds.), *Handbook of aging and the social sciences.* New York: Van Nostrand Reinhold.

Brannon, D., & others. (1988). A diagnostic survey of nursing home caregivers. *The Gerontologist, 28,* 246–252.

Chen, Y. P. (1989). Low confidence in Social Security is not warranted. *Journal of Aging and Social Policy, 1.*

Chen, Y. P. (1988). Making assets out of tomorrow's elders. In R. Morris & S. Bass (Eds.), *Retirement reconsidered.* New York: Springer.

Chisman, F., & Pifer, A. (1987). *Government for the people,* p. 183. New York: W. W. Norton.

Cole, T. R. (1986). The "enlightened" view of aging: Victorian morality in a new key. In T. Cole & S. Gadow (Eds.), *What does it mean to grow old?* Durham, NC: Duke University Press.

Friedland, G. (1988, Aug. 22). Mission of an AIDS unit—Not to cure but to care. *New York Times,* p. B1.

Guillemard, A. M. (1983). *Old age and the welfare state.* London and Beverly Hills: Sage Publishing.

Institute of Medicine. (1983). *Nursing and nursing education.* Washington, DC: National Academy of Science.

Kane, R., & Kane, R. (1985). *A will and a way.* New York: Columbia University Press.

Kleemeier, R. (Ed.). (1961). *Aging and leisure.* New York: Oxford Press.

Massachusetts Rate Setting Commission. (1987). *The home bound: who cares?* Boston: MRSC.

Morris, R. (1976). Alternative forms of care for the disabled. In D. Bergsma & A. Pulver (Eds.), *Developmental disabilities.* New York: Alan Liss.

Mutschler, P. (1984). What price retirement: Inducing older workers to retire early. Final research report to the Andrus Foundation. Washington, DC: American Association of Older Persons.

Neu, C. R., & Harrison, S. C. (1988). *Post hospital care before and after prospective payment system.* Santa Monica, CA: Rand Corporation.

Newfield, K. (1970). Orientation to later maturity: The wishes and expectations of employed men for post-65 years. Unpublished dissertation. Waltham, MA: Brandeis University.

Pifer, A., & Bronte, L. (1986). *Our aging society*. New York: W. W. Norton.

Rappaport, A., & Plumley, P. (1988). Changing demographic profiles in maturing societies. In R. Morris & S. Bass (Eds.), *Retirement reconsidered*. New York: Springer.

Rothstein, F. R. (1988). Older worker opportunities in the private sector. In R. Morris & S. Bass (Eds.), *Retirement reconsidered*. New York: Springer.

Sheppard, H. (1988). Work continuation vs. retirement: Reasons for continuing work. In R. Morris & S. Bass (Eds.), *Retirement reconsidered*. New York: Springer.

Silk, L. (1988, Sept. 2). How well off are workers? *New York Times*, p. D2.

United States Statistical Abstract. (1984). Washington, DC: Government Printing Office.

United States Statistical Abstract. (1986). Washington, DC: Government Printing Office.

United States Statistical Abstract. (1989). Washington, DC: Government Printing Office.

Wilner, M. A. (1987). Nursing home manpower study. Boston, MA: Federation of Nursing Homes.

Discussion Questions for Chapter Fifteen

1. The research conducted by Easterlin and his colleagues uses calculations of average economic status and does not address the distribution of income among members of baby boom cohorts. If inequality is as great among baby boomers as some have claimed, what significance might this hold for baby boomers in old age? What implications might this inequality have for public programs for the elderly in the future?

2. Goldscheider's description of the consequences of the gender revolution for future cohorts of elderly men is not optimistic. What kinds of social arrangements or support services might be devised to improve the quality of life for old men in the future? What impact might divorced men have on the demand for long-term care? Might divorced elderly men find companionship among the large pool of unmarried elderly women?

3. In his conclusion, Morris calls for alternative visions about what an older society could look like in the 21st century. He urges us to focus on reintegrating the elderly into the mainstream of social and economic life and to reintegrate the interests of the aged with those of other age groups. What are some ways to bring this about? What are your visions for an older society in the next century?

TOPICS GUIDE

This topics guide is intended to help readers locate articles that devote significant attention to a particular subject. The topic areas do not constitute an exhaustive list of subjects in social gerontology, nor do the articles listed under a topic heading form a complete list of those that touch on the subject.

TOPIC		ARTICLE
Abuse	Chapter 7	Korbin et al., "Elder Abuse and Child Abuse: A Consideration of Similarities and Differences in Intergenerational Family Violence"
Age norms	Chapter 1	Butler, "Dispelling Ageism: The Cross-Cutting Intervention"
	Chapter 1	Minkler, "Aging and Disability: Behind and Beyond the Stereotypes"
Baby boom	Chapter 15	Easterlin et al., "Retirement Prospects of the Baby Boom Generation: A Different Perspective"
Caregiving	Chapter 6	Boyd and Treas, "Family Care of the Frail Elderly: A New Look at 'Women in the Middle' "
Cohort, aging, and period effects	Chapter 1	Kovach and Knapp, "Age, Cohort, and Time-Period Confounds in Aging Research"
	Chapter 8	Sparrow, "Job Performance Among Older Workers"
	Chapter 15	Easterlin et al., "Retirement Prospects of the Baby Boom Generation: A Different Perspective"
Compression of morbidity	Chapter 1	Minkler, "Aging and Disability: Behind and Beyond the Stereotypes"
Dementia	Chapter 4	Lyman, "Bringing the Social Back in: A Critique of the Biomedicalization of Dementia"
Disability	Chapter 1	Minkler, "Aging and Disability: Behind and Beyond the Stereotypes"